T0351169

Handbook of Research on Software Engineering and Productivity Technologies:
Implications of Globalization

Muthu Ramachandran
Leeds Metropolitian University, UK

Rogério Atem de Carvalho
Instituto Federal Fluminense, Brazil

ENGINEERING SCIENCE REFERENCE

Hershey · New York

Director of Editorial Content:	Kristin Klinger
Senior Managing Editor:	Jamie Snavely
Managing Editor:	Jeff Ash
Assistant Managing Editor:	Michael Brehm
Publishing Assistant:	Sean Woznicki
Typesetter:	Jeff Ash
Cover Design:	Lisa Tosheff
Printed at:	Yurchak Printing Inc.

Published in the United States of America by
Engineering Science Reference (an imprint of IGI Global)
701 E. Chocolate Avenue
Hershey PA 17033
Tel: 717-533-8845
Fax: 717-533-8661
E-mail: cust@igi-global.com
Web site: http://www.igi-global.com/reference

Library of Congress Cataloging-in-Publication Data

Handbook of research on software engineering and productivity technologies : implications of globalization / Muthu Ramachandran and Rogirio Atem de Carvalho, editors.
    p. cm.

Includes bibliographical references and index.
Summary: "This book provides integrated chapters on software engineering and enterprise systems focusing on parts integrating requirements engineering, software engineering, process and frameworks, productivity technologies, and enterprise systems"--Provided by publisher.

ISBN 978-1-60566-731-7 (hardcover) -- ISBN 978-1-60566-732-4 (ebook) 1. Software engineering. 2. Software productivity. 3. Globalization. I. Ramachandran, Muthu. II. Carvalho, Rogirio Atem de.

QA76.758.H357 2009
005.1--dc22
                           2009001059

British Cataloguing in Publication Data
A Cataloguing in Publication record for this book is available from the British Library.

All work contributed to this book is new, previously-unpublished material. The views expressed in this book are those of the authors, but not necessarily of the publisher.

List of Contributors

Table of Contents

Section 1
Integrated Requirements Engineering and Software Engineering:
Process and Frameworks

Section 2
Productivity Technologies

Section 3
Enterprise Systems and Globalisation

Detailed Table of Contents

Section 1
Integrated Requirements Engineering and Software Engineering:
Process and Frameworks

Chapter 1
    Chetankumar Patel, Leeds Metropolitan University, UK
    Muthu Ramachandran, Leeds Metropolitan University, UK

Developing software that meets the customers or stakeholders' needs and expectation is the ultimate goal of the software development methodology. To meet their need we have to perform requirement engineering which helps to identify and structure requirements. In traditional software development methods end users or stakeholders predefined their requirements and sent to the development team to analysis and negotiation to produce requirement specification. In many cases it is risky or very difficult and not economical to produce a complete, verifiable set of requirements. Traditional software development has a problem to deal with requirement change after careful analysis and negotiation. This problem is well tackled by the Agile Practices as it's recommends an on-site customer to represents their requirements through user stories on story cards. Generally customers have rarely a general picture of the requirements or system in their mind which leads problems related to requirements like requirements conflicts, missing requirements, and ambiguous requirements etc, and does not address non-functional requirements from exploration phase. This chapter introduces best knowledge based guidelines for agile requirements engineering to enhance the quality of requirements (story cards).

Chapter 2
    Jean-Louis Boulanger, CERTIFER, France

This chapter resumes the requirements engineering in a model-based methodology for embedded automotive software. The methodology relies on two standard languages: EAST-ADL for automotive architecture description and SysML for systems modeling. The requirements engineering in the methodology describes phases of elicitation, modeling, traceability, verification and validation. It is illustrated by applying on a case study -- the knock controller -- a part of the engine management system.

This chapter aims to reveal agile techniques that have been applied to software development and have resulted in meaningful improvements in software productivity. Available literature generally state some claims on the gains associated with the use of particular agile methodologies in software development. What lacks however, is a comprehensive analysis of how the application of agile techniques as a family will lead to improvement in software productivity. This chapter therefore provides such details. Software productivity techniques provide ways of measuring three things in order to determine the productivity of software; software products, software production processes and structures, and software production setting. Agile methodologies improve software productivity by focusing on the software production process and structures. The fundamental concern of this chapter is to show that agile methodologies measure the production process activities in a different but effective way from the more traditional approaches. For example, time-to-market is reduced by use of an iterative incremental development approach.

Chapter 4

This chapter describes the evolution of approaches to empirical software engineering from goal and data-driven to the latest purchaser-centered approach. The new Japanese Software Traceability and Accountability for Global software Engineering (STAGE) project is developing this approach to ensure the transparency of software development processes and products for software purchasers by "tagging" software with empirical software development data. Global software development raises unprecedented difficulties for developers, including the international and intercorporate coordination of development and distribution, the change to composition as the primary development approach, the shift to software everywhere talking to everything, and continuing upgrades and interaction with released software. To work effectively in this environment, empirical data collection, analysis, and feedback must extend throughout the software lifecycle including both production and usage data.

While successful at increasing code churn rates, global software development and evolution suffers from several quality assurance challenges. First, sub-groups within developer communities often work on loosely coupled parts of the application code. Each developer (sub-group) typically modifies a local "copy" of the code and frequently checks-in changes (and downloads other developers' changes). Consequently, after making a change, a developer may not immediately realize that the local change has inadvertently broken other parts of the overall software code. This situation is compounded as there is little direct inter-developer communication -- almost all communication is done via web-based tools such as code commit log messages, bug reports, change-requests, and comments. This chapter outlines the challenges that global software development adds to the already-complex quality assurance process. Two case studies of real software projects implemented in a disturbed manner demonstrate the importance of continuous integration testing and the positive consequences of increasing the diversity of quality assurance techniques/tools. Finally, it concludes with an outline of how software integration testing needs to be enhanced to meet the new challenges of globalization.

Chapter 6

This chapter describes an ongoing process to define a suitable process improvement model for story cards based requirement engineering process and practices at agile software development environments. Key features of the SMM (Story card Maturity Model) process are: solves the problems related to the story cards like requirements conflicts, missing requirements, ambiguous requirements, define standard structure of story cards, to address non-functional requirements from exploration phase, and the use of a simplified and tailored assessment method for story cards based requirements engineering practices based on the CMM, which is poorly addressed at CMM. CMM does not cover how the quality of the requirements engineering process should be secured or what activities should be present for the requirements engineering process to achieve a certain maturity level. It is difficult to know what is not addressed or what could be done to improve the process. The authors also presents how can be the identified areas of improvement from assessment can be mapped with best knowledge based story cards practices for agile software development environments.

With the continuous development and rapid progress of information techniques, complexity and scale of information systems are expanding increasingly, which consequently brings our research focus on how to ensure the effective exchange of information and efficient interconnection between each part of a information system. However, different modeling paradigm, languages and platforms cause grammatical and semantic diversity to the existing information resources, a challenging approach to information resources management is needed to promote deep sharing of those information resources and implement rapid integration based on them. To realize semantic interoperation between diverse information systems and resources, the authors combine meta-modeling methodology in software engineering and ontology from philosophy to exploit a novel methodology named Theory of Ontology & Meta-modeling. Based on the methodology, the authors contributed to an international standard project ISO/IEC 19763-3: Metamodel for ontology registration since 2003, which was officially published as an international standard in Dec, 2007. Furthermore, we developed a Management and Service platform for Semantic Interoperability on Manufacturing Informationalization Software Component Repository (SCR). It can support ontology-based software component attributes classification, registration and management using ISO/IEC 19763-3 standard, and implement semantic (ontology) based software component query and retrieval. Based on above mentioned techniques, this platform can facilitate the management of semantic interoperability, which provides the reliable infrastructure for the reusing and sharing of heterogeneous software component resources.

Elias Canhadas Genvigir, Federal University of Technology – Paraná – UTFPR , Brasil
Nandamudi Lankalapalli Vijaykumar, National Institute for Space Research – INPE, Brasil

This chapter presents a research about the Software Requirements Traceability. The main elements of traceability, definitions, problems and prospects are presented. The chapter is organized by topics and its beginning is a review about requirements engineering, its categories (Elicitation, Analysis and Negotiation, Documentation, Validation, and Management) and its role in software development. Afterwards, the requirements management and its elements (Identification, Change Management and Traceability) are described. Traceability is discussed; its aspects and problems are exploited as well as its classifications, techniques, links, metrics and models. Finally the Conclusion presents the main points that can be explored in future researches.

Sathya Ganeshan, Leeds Metropolitan University, UK
Muthu Ramachandran, Leeds Metropolitan University, UK

Software Product Lines have been in the scene of software development since the 1970s. Throughout this time, it has changed from a hot topic that was discussed in universities and seminar halls as future goal of companies, to an everyday reality. There are many crucial aspects that decide the success of a software product line. One among them is the identification, development and maintenance of core assets. This chapter aims at providing a brief introduction to this area of software product lines and ways to improve productivity through efficient core asset management.

T.R.Gopalakrishnan Nair, Dayananda Sagar Institutions, Bangalore, India

R. Selvarani, Dayananda Sagar Institutions, Bangalore, India

Muthu Ramachandran, Leeds Metropolitan University, UK

This chapter discusses a comprehensive analysis model of the concurrent software industry which is a collection of different sub-models interacting and communicating objectively with a cause-effect relationship. This model is not merely process centric but it also deals with the resources, skills and methods with an entity model which forms an important factor of the comprehensive approach. Process is considered as an activity performed over the resources with a particular level of skill set transforming the input. In this comprehensive model, the factors associated with various sub models like process, technology, business, risk and multi domain are considered and integrated through communication links, threading all the models in transforming the system specification into the product within the cycle time with an active cost. The final model will be able to accept a spectrum of input from the industry, ranging from finances, human resources, business practices, technology and software production process and come out with metrics correlated to the observables of that particular company or group.

R. Selvarani, Dayananda Sagar Institutions, Bangalore, India

T.R.Gopalakrishnan Nair, Dayananda Sagar Institutions, Bangalore, India

Muthu Ramachandran, Leeds Metropolitan University, UK

Kamakshi Prasad, JNTU, Hyderabad, India

The complexity of modern software, the commercial constraints and the expectation for high quality product demands the accurate fault prediction based on OO design metrics in the class level in the early stages of software development. The object oriented class metrics are used as quality predictors in the entire OO software development life cycle even when a highly iterative, incremental model or agile software process is employed. Recent research has shown some of the OO design metrics are useful for predicting fault-proneness of classes. In this chapter the empirical validation of a set of metrics proposed by Chidamber and Kemerer is performed to assess their ability in predicting the software quality in terms of fault proneness and degradation. The authors have also proposed the design complexity of object-oriented software with Weighted Methods per Class metric (WMC-CK metric) expressed in terms of Shannon entropy, and error proneness.

Section 2
Productivity Technologies

Susan Entwisle, Monash University, Australia

Sita Ramakrishnan, Monash University, Australia

Elizabeth Kendall, Melbourne Institute of Technology, Australia

Programming languages provide exception handling mechanisms to structure fault tolerant activities within software systems. However, the use of exceptions at this low level of abstraction can be error-prone and complex, potentially leading to new programming errors. To address this the author have developed a model-driven exception management framework (DOVE). This approach is a key enabler to support global distributed solution delivery teams. The focus of this chapter is the evaluation of the feasibility of this approach through a case study, known as Project Tracker. The case study is used to demonstrate the feasibility and to perform an assessment based on quality and productivity metrics and testing of the DOVE framework. The results of the case study are presented to demonstrate the feasibility of our approach.

Chapter 13

In this chapter, the development and evolution of mobile applications is viewed from an engineering perspective. A methodology for deploying patterns as means for improving the pragmatic quality of mobile applications is proposed. In doing so, relevant quality attributes and corresponding stakeholder types for mobile applications are identified, the role of the development process is emphasized, and the challenges in making optimal use of patterns are presented. The underling feasibility issues involved at each step are analyzed. The activities of selection and application of patterns are explored. The use of patterns during macro- and micro-architecture design of mobile applications is illustrated. The implications of the use of patterns in a Mobile Social Web context are briefly highlighted.

Software systems today are complex and have many possible configurations. Products released with inadequate testing can cause bodily harm, result in large economic losses or security breaches, and affect the quality of day-to-day life. Software testers have limited time and budgets, frequently making it impossible to exhaustively test software. Testers often intuitively test for defects that they anticipate while less foreseen defects are overlooked. Combinatorial testing can complement their tests by systematically covering t-way interactions. Research in combinatorial testing includes two major areas (1) algorithms that generate combinatorial test suites and (2) applications of combinatorial testing. The authors review these two topics in this chapter.

In last years, software development activity tends to be decentralized, thus expanding greater development efforts towards more attractive zones for organizations. The type of development in which the team members are distributed in remote sites is called Distributed Software Development (DSD). The main advantage of this practice is mainly that of having a greater availability of human resources in decentralized zones with less cost. On the other hand, organizations must face some disadvantages due to the distance that separates the development teams related to project organization, project control and product quality. Coordination becomes more difficult as the software components are sourced from different places, and new processes and tools are needed. This work presents a systematic review of the literature related to the problems of DSD with the purpose of obtaining a vision about the solutions proposed up to the present day.

Chapter 16

Software testing has gained immense importance in the present competitive world of developing software more quickly, more efficiently and more accurately. Testing activity is carried out throughout the lifecycle of software development and not only towards the end of development. Time and effort required to correct errors, detected later is much more compared to those, which are detected earlier. This has direct impact on costs and has led to a splurge of research activities in this domain. Model-based testing has recently gained attention with the popularization of modeling itself. It refers to testing and test case generation based on a model that describes the behavior of the system. The OMG initiative MDA has revolutionized the way models would be used for software development. There are a number of modeling techniques in use today- some have formal syntax like Z, VDM while some are semi-formal like UML. The authors have made a comprehensive summary of a considerable number of research works on Model Based testing. First, the issues, challenges and problems of model based testing have been discussed. Then the different methods developed for testing or test case generation based on the models are summarized. Finally a list of model based testing tools used for testing has been collectively presented.

Traditional Model Driven Development (MDD) frameworks have three critical issues: (1) abstraction gap between modeling and programming layers, (2) a lack of traceability between models and programs, and (3) a lack of customizability to support various combinations of modeling technologies and implementation/deployment technologies. In order to address these issues, this chapter proposes a new MDD framework, called Matilda, which is a framework to build execution runtime engines (or virtual machines) for software models. It directly executes models defined with certain modeling technologies such as UML and BPMN by automatically transforming them to executable code. Matilda is designed based on the Pipes and Filters architectural pattern, which allows for configuring its structure and behavior flexibly by replacing one plugin with another one or changing the order of plugins. Also, plugins can be deployed on multiple network hosts and seamlessly connect them to form a pipeline. This facilitates distributed software development in which developers collaboratively work at physically dispersed places. This chapter overviews Matilda's architectural design, describes the implementations of Matilda-based virtual machines, and evaluates their performance.

Chapter 18

The efficiency and effectiveness of Quality of Service QoS performance methods in a Distributed Database Management System DDBMS environment are measured by their successfully simulation on the real world applications. To achieve the goals of the simulation modules and to analyze the behaviour of the distributed database network system and the QoS performance methods of fragmentation, clustering and allocation, an integrated software tool for a DDBMS supported by the OPNET is designed and presented. It is developed to wisely distribute the data among several sites on a database network system, effectively enhance the QoS performance at lower cost, successfully provide reliability to the DDBMS in case of site failure, and efficiently increase the data availability where multiple copies of the same data are allocated to different sites. The integrated software tool supply the database administrators with a software that is friendly use, easy to navigate, comprehensive, and expandable that simulate the techniques of database fragmentation, clustering network sites, and fragment allocation and replication in a DDBMS. The tool performs the database transactions operations efficiently and effectively through reliable forms that allow the database administrators to control over their operations and follow up the system improvements and QoS enhancements. The performance evaluation and simulation results indicate that the proposed methods significantly improves the QoS performance in the DDBMS even with manageable extra information, network sites, communication and processing cost functions.

Chapter 19

This chapter presents an approach for certified design of railway critical systems. This approach, which realizes the software development cycle, relies on metamodeling architecture and model-transformations. It combines semi-formal UML models and formal models in order to check, proof and generate code by refinement; we use the process algebra FSP to check the dynamic behavior and B to generate proved code. Initially, we select an UML subset, which could be uses to model the key aspects of critical systems. Then, from this subset, we perform projections to obtain B and FSP models which are exploited by tools for checking, refinement and proof.

Chapter 20

The success of initiating a software product line based approach on an organization depends on a few critical factors. Among them is a thoroughly performed commonality analysis process. This can be imagined as a collecting the supplies and road map required to reach a particular destination. This chapter analyses this critical process and presents our own views and methods of conducting commonality analysis.

Chapter 21

The aim of this chapter is to introduce a reader to the world of software product lines, how it is used and what the future of this field might be. The authors present some of the success stories of organizations who have employed this approach, the benefits they have derived as opposed to conventional approaches. They also present their own views and innovations in touch with cutting edge developments in this field.

Chapter 22

Component-based software engineering (CBSE) has rapidly gained currency over recent years. Software developed as components and as assemblies of components has realised the reuse slogan originally associated with object-oriented design. In this chapter the authors define what software components are along with their different characteristics and classifications. They also cover the widely debated definitions of software components to emphasise the fact that components possess different properties that can mean different things to different people. They discuss the impact of using components on the software development lifecycle and review a number of different approaches developed to procure and integrate components in software systems. Finally, the risks associated with using software components are discussed in detail with along with a trust model. Trends in CBSE research are discussed towards the end to explore some potential areas of future research.

Chapter 23

Natural disasters are increasingly frequent in recent years taking peoples lives and destructions to our economy, for example, Hurricane Katrina (US 2006), Tsunami (Asia 2004), and other IT related failures. The major aims of this study were to outline the disaster management steps, actions and procedures in the computer environment. The study focused on the role of Information Technology manager (IT) in case of any disaster events. IT manager job to perform a pre-disaster preparedness, mitigation and prevention necessary steps to protect the organisation Information Technology manager resources. Than proposes a model for Disaster Recovery management. This model will support contingencies and will provide a continuous planning management and monitor its activities along with a clear description of the hierarchical roles and activities. Also proposes a model for contingency and continuity planning management and it's activities. This model consists of hierarchical roles and activities.

Section 3
Enterprise Systems and Globalisation

Chapter 24

After the implementation peak of ERPs that occurred during the pre- and post-Y2K periods, the high-end ERP market started to saturate and major ERP vendors started to seek for new business opportunities, in special towards Small and Medium-sized Enterprises (SMEs). On the buyer side, demands for becoming more competitive in a globalized market, have been pushing SMEs to adopt ERP too. Additionally, influenced by the free/open source movement, new types of ERP licensing appeared by the beginning of the decade, creating a classification according to the basic licensing model: free/open source ERP (FOS-ERP) and proprietary ERP (P-ERP). Therefore, this chapter aims at exploring the merge between SMEs, P-ERP, and FOS-ERP, by analyzing the differences between the two proposals and offering guidance for prospective adopters.

Chapter 25

Enterprise Resource Planning (ERP) covers the techniques and concepts employed for the integrated management of businesses as a whole, from the viewpoint of the effective use of management resources, to improve the efficiency of an enterprise. One way of looking at ERP is as a combination of business processes and information technology. The objective of this chapter is to highlight the research challenges in ERP projects from the viewpoint of software engineering and draw round the solutions in hand. This chapter on the directed basic research in ERP systems gives us two outputs: (1) A comprehensive framework presenting the current research problems in the ERP systems from the viewpoint of software engineering and (2) The channel to solve these problems. The outcome is a high quality, reliable and complete ERP software solution.

Chapter 26

Database technology has been a significant field to work in for developing real life applications in network information systems. An enterprise's reliance on its network and database applications in Distributed Database Management systems (DDBMS) environment is likely to continue growing exponentially. In such a system the estimation and prediction of Quality of Service (QoS) performance improvements are crucial since it increases understanding the issues that affect the distributed database networking system behaviour; like database fragmentation, clustering database network sites, and data allocation and replication that would reduce the amount of irrelevant data and speed up the transactions response time. This chapter introduces the trends of database management systems DBMS and presents an integrated method for designing Distributed Relational networking Database Management System DRDBMS that efficiently and effectively achieves the objectives of database fragmentation, clustering database network sites, and fragments allocation and replication. It is based on high speed partitioning, clustering, and data allocation techniques that minimize the data fragments accessed and data transferred through the network sites, maximize the overall system throughput by increasing the degree of concurrent transactions processing of multiple fragments located in different sites, and result in better QoS design and decision support.

The design and implementation of an ERP system involves capturing the information necessary for implementing a system that supports enterprise management. This process should go down through different abstraction layers, starting on enterprise modeling and finishing at coding. For the case of Free/Open Source ERP, the lack of proper modeling methods and tools jeopardizes the advantages of source code availability. Moreover, the distributed, decentralized decision-making, and source-code driven development culture of open source communities, generally does not rely on methods for modeling the higher abstraction levels necessary for an ERP solution. The aim of this chapter is to present a development process and supportive tools for the open source enterprise system ERP5, which covers the different abstraction levels involved, taking into account well established standards and practices, as well as new approaches, by supplying Enterprise, Requirements, Analysis, Design, and Implementation workflows and tools to support them.

From a project management perspective, it is imperative that project managers be able to deal with such geographically separated diverse groups in an effective manner. This implies that they need to address two critical issues: (i) Resource planning / forecasting based upon the need for software maintenance, which is influenced by the number of bugs occurring in the various software components, and (ii) understanding the interaction patterns among the various software developers. This chapter concentrates on these two specific issues, both relating to issues of staffing / resource allocation, that impact cost and influence effective project management, using data produced from open-source software (OSS) repositories.

Emergency needs occurs anywhere anytime by naturally, manually and accidentally in addition to worldwide death by hunger and poverty. As such, the need of response system should be there to tackle this emergency. Natural disasters are increasingly frequent in recent years taking peoples lives and destructions, for example, Hurricane Katrina US 2006 and Tsunami Asia 2004. This study proposes a model for Classification of Natural Disasters and Catastrophic Failures activity model. This model consists of hierarchical roles and activities. It is critical that organization must support and provide infrastructure for managing and preventing disasters and its aftermath to a full recovery. Furthermore, this chapter also proposes a triangular model for global emergency response systems, which can be used as a preventive measure, as well as post-recovery management system for managing and tackling emergencies. This model also proposes the use of emerging technologies such as ubiquitous computing and wireless communications systems. Nowadays, people use these wireless technologies to communicate in case of a disaster. Lastly, the study proposes another two models namely the Disaster Risks categorization model, which help identify and to assess the threat levels.

Foreword

The service industry has emerged as the prominent industry, and the software industry is at the heart of this transformation. The service-based view of the firm describes the new way of conceptualizating organizations and has led to an increasingly Web-based service industry. It is reasonable to envision a world in which services will become the main way of specifying, developing and providing functionality.

The software engineering community will play a central role in this paradigmatic shift and contributions like this book are essential to inform the professional and academic software engineering community about the current and future challenges, trends and solutions.

The term software industrialization indicates that there is no intention to start from scratch in the process of designing software engineering processes and practices. Rather, established manufacturing practices form a widely appreciated point of reference. This includes especially the desire for standardization in the form of patterns, software reuse, modularity and advanced software configuration capabilities.

The discipline of developing, deploying and managing software is well-researched and a plethora of methodologies, frameworks, reference models, tools and techniques supports nowadays the software engineer. However, despite this matured supportive environment, a range of challenges demands substantial shifts in the current practices of software engineering.

First, software engineering demonstrates like hardly any other sector the full utilization of a flat world. Globally distributed development processes have become the established way to build software in large projects. This leads to new challenges in terms of project management and the overall coordination of globally distributed contributions, standards and quality assurance to name just a few. Globalization does not only comprise developing in a flat world but also for a flat world meaning that internationalized software has to cater for the requirements of different regional languages, legislations and user expectations among others.

Second, agility has become a main obligation for software engineering. Agile development ensures early interactions with the user base and leads to a fluent transition from requirements engineering to software engineering. The iterative nature of agile development and the demand to provide early demonstrators demand reconsiderations of classical, often sequential software development processes. Among others, it requires ongoing interactions with various stakeholders along the software engineering process facilitated by intuitive but expressive powerful conceptual models.

Third, software engineering is now in many cases an open process. Open source models have led to entire new levels of transparency and accessibility in this process. Open innovation and a long tail of software engineers are examples for how the wisdom of the crowds can increase the development capacity. It also demonstrates, however, the limitations of current software lifecycle and governance models.

Fourth, the center of attention of software engineering keeps on changing. The classical concentration on data, functions and processes is increasingly complemented with a focus on services. While the technical benefits of service-oriented software engineering are well accepted, a similar level of appreciation is still missing in the specification of business requirements.

Fifth and finally, engineering off-the-shelf-solutions has become a mainstream activity. Enterprise Resource Planning is the most prominent form of this type of software. In this type of software the actual finalization of the engineering process is done in the form of configuration and customization. However, the high demand for this type of software stands in sharp contrast to the still modest development of dedicated frameworks and processes for such software.

Globalized, agile, open, service-oriented and configurable are just a few of the attributes of the current software engineering practice. A list of challenges that is by no means complete.

This well choreographed book approaches these interrelated challenges in three sections.

Section 1 proposes processes and frameworks for integrating requirements and software engineering. It is not a surprise that agile development plays a central role in the related chapters.

Section 2 is concerned with the productivity of software engineering. Model-based engineering, advanced software testing and componentization are a few of the selected issues that are discussed here.

Section 3 is dedicated to the development of Enterprise Systems in a global context. The special requirements of small and medium-sized organizations and open source development are two of the challenges that are covered in this part.

In light of the significant and fast emerging challenges that software engineers face today, the editors of this book have done an outstanding job in selecting the contents of this book. I am confident that this book will provide an appreciated contribution to the software engineering community. It has the potential to become one of the main reference points for the years to come.

Michael Rosemann
Brisbane, December 2008

Michael Rosemann *is a Professor for Information Systems and Co-Leader of the Business Process Management Group at Queensland University of Technology, Brisbane, Australia. Michael has experiences as the Chief Investigator of a number of research projects funded by competitive European and Australian schemas. He has been a member of the prestigious Australian Research Council College of Experts in 2006/07. He is the author/editor of six books, more than 140 refereed papers and Editorial Board member of eight international journals incl. the Business Process Management Journal. His papers have been published in journals such as MIS Quarterly, IEEE Transactions on Knowledge and Data Engineering, Information Systems, European Journal of Information Systems and Decision Support Systems. He also presented his work at all global major IS conferences. His papers won the best paper award at CAiSE (1999), PACIS (2004) and ACIS (2005) and two of his PhD students won national PhD awards. Michael is the co-inventor of seven US patent proposals and co-editor of the book 'Process Management' that is also available in German, Russian and Chinese. Michael has been the General Chair of the 5th International Business Process Management Conference in 2007 and was the invited keynote at BPM 2008. Dr Rosemann chairs the Australian BPM Community of Practice (http://bpm-collaboration.com) and established QUT as a main vendor of BPM training (www.bpm-training.com). Michael has intensive consulting experiences and provided advice to organisations from various industries including telecommunications, banking, retail, insurance, utility, logistics, public sector and film industry. He has been a speaker at events of organisations such as SAP, Oracle and Infosys.*

Preface

INTRODUCTION

Software Engineering (SE) is a disciplined and engineering approach to software development and management of software projects and complexity. Currently, software exists in each and every product from toys, powered tooth brushes, electric shavers (have 10,000 lines of embedded software code), TV and entertainment systems, mobile, computers, portable devices, medical systems, and home appliances, and to large scale software such as aircraft, communication systems, weather forecasts, grid computing, and many more. Today, the software business is a global economy which has contributed to a better life style across the world. Therefore a book of this nature can bring industry and academia together to address the need for the growing applications and to support a global software development.

Global Software development and productivity related technologies are the key to today's globalisation which would not have occurred without this productivity. New technologies and concepts are being developed, prompting researchers to find continuously new ways of utilizing both old and new technologies. In such an ever-evolving environment, teachers, researchers and professionals of the discipline need access to the most current information about the concepts, issues, trends and technologies in this emerging field.

Global Software Development Challenges

Global software development (GSD) is the new business paradigm that organisations are adopting to meet their business challenges and derive competitive advantage. Global software development efforts have increased in recent years, and such developments seem to become a business requirement for various reasons, including cost, availability of resources, and the need to locate developments closer to customers, speeding time-to-market, obtaining extra knowledge, and increasing operational efficiency. Increased globalisation of software development creates software engineering challenges due to the impact of time zones, diversity of culture, communication, or distance. However, there is still much to know about global software development before the discipline becomes mature. Some of the challenges are identified in our framework as shown in Figure 1. Existing studies (Dedrick and Kraemer 2006, and Herbsleb 2007) have proposed several solutions that can make GSD more effectively. It is not just the time and distance which are the major issues in managing GSD challenges, but also software tools and best practices. This handbook is concerned about current enterprise software development practices including productivity technologies impacted on a global software industries. Most important of all, lessons are learned from successful experiences and drawbacks.

Figure 1. Global software development challenges

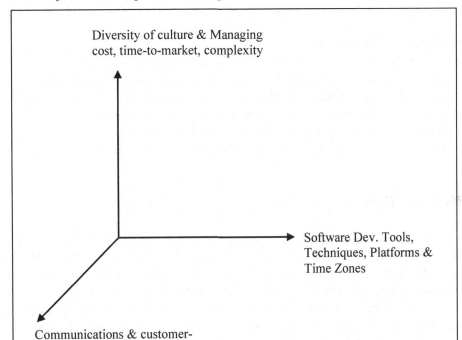

The diversity of culture has significant effects in terms of project delivery due to education and experience levels, cultural events, festivals, and government regulations.

Research Issues

Interplay between Software Engineering and Enterprise Information Systems will dominate the current and further research in the areas such as Software Services, Productivity, and Globalisation. Some of the specific areas of research are:

- Empirical evaluations of effectiveness of global software projects
- SE methodologies and processes for global software development
- Infrastructure required for global software development
- Effectiveness of agile methods in global software development
- Methods and tools for global software development: requirements engineering, architecture, design, coding, verification, testing and maintenance
- Quality, process and configuration management for global software development
- Management of risks such as organisational and cultural differences
- Methods and practices for effective project performance in a distributed environment
- Task allocation in global software development
- Organisational and business views

- Strategic issues in distributed development
- Knowledge transfer, knowledge management strategies and informal sharing in global software development
- Cognitive issues in global software development
- Communication and collaboration in globally distributed teams
- Impact of cultural and geographical differences on global software development
- Collaboration technologies such as multimedia, presence awareness, and web technologies
- Socialisation process required to manage global software development
- Managing offshore collaboration and global software outsourcing
- Global emergency response systems and natural disaster management

BOOK ORGANISATION

Software productivity and related technologies are the key to today's globalisation which would not have occurred without this productivity. New technologies and concepts are being developed, prompting researchers to find continuously new ways of utilizing both older and new technologies. In such an ever-evolving environment, teachers, researchers and professionals of the discipline need access to the most current information about the concepts, issues, trends and technologies in this emerging field. The *Handbook of Software Engineering and Productivity Technologies: Implications of Globalization* will be most helpful as it provides comprehensive coverage and definitions of the most important issues, concepts, trends and technologies in Software Engineering and Software Technology. This important new publication will be distributed worldwide among academic and professional institutions and will be instrumental in providing researchers, scholars, students and professionals access to the latest knowledge related to information science and technology. Contributions to this important publication will be made by scholars throughout the world with notable research portfolios and expertise. This handbook is aimed to provide five parts:

Section 1: Integrated Requirements Engineering and Software Engineering: Process and Frameworks. This part provides chapters on Agile Software Engineering, Requirements Engineering, Software Metrics, Testing, and Productivity.

Section 2: Productivity Technologies. This part consists of chapters on software tools and methods that support productivity. Chapters include model-driven systems, combinatorial testing, distributed software development, QoS for distributed database applications, software components, software product line engineering, and global disaster recovery management systems.

Section 3: Enterprise Systems and Globalisation. This part consists of chapters on ERP systems, QoS, Open source software development, and Emergency Response Systems.

.

REFERENCES

Dedrick, J., and Kraemer, L. K (2006) Is production pulling knowledge work to China? A study of the notebook PC industry, Computer, Special issue on Globalization, July 2006, Vol. 39/N.7

Konana, P (2006) Can Indian software firms compete with global giants, Computer, Special issue on Globalization, July 2006, Vol. 39/N.7

Robson, R (2006) Globalization and the future of standardization, Special issue on Globalization, July 2006, Vol. 39/N.7

Herbsleb, D. J (2007) Global Software Engineering: The Future of Socio-technical Coordination, Proc of IEEE Computer Society, Future of Software Engineering (FOSE'07)

Acknowledgment

This handbook would not have been possible without the cooperation and assistance of many people. The editors would like to thank Joel Gamon at IGI Global and Rebecca Beistline for their expertise in organizing and guiding this project. We thank all the authors who contributed to this book, without their willingness to share their knowledge, this project would not have been possible. Many of them also served as reviewers of other chapters, therefore we doubly thank their contribution. We would like to thank the book's Advisory Board for their suggestions and help reviewing the chapters. We also acknowledge our respective institutions for supporting us for this project. Finally, the editors wish to acknowledge their families for their understanding.

Muthu Ramachandran
Leeds Metropolitian University, USA

Rogério Atem de Carvalho
Instituto Federal Fluminense, Brazil

Section 1
Integrated Requirements Engineering and Software Engineering:
Process and Frameworks

Chapter 1
Best Practices Guidelines for Agile Requirements Engineering Practices

Chetankumar Patel
Leeds Metropolitan University, UK

Muthu Ramachandran
Leeds Metropolitan University, UK

ABSTRACT

Developing software that meets the customers or stakeholders' needs and expectation is the ultimate goal of the software development methodology. To meet their need we have to perform requirement engineering which helps to identify and structure requirements. In traditional software development methods end users or stakeholders predefined their requirements and sent to the development team to analysis and negotiation to produce requirement specification. In many cases it is risky or very difficult and not economical to produce a complete, verifiable set of requirements. Traditional software development has a problem to deal with requirement change after careful analysis and negotiation. This problem is well tackled by the Agile Practices as it's recommends an on-site customer to represents their requirements through user stories on story cards. Generally customers have rarely a general picture of the requirements or system in their mind which leads problems related to requirements like requirements conflicts, missing requirements, and ambiguous requirements etc, and does not address non-functional requirements from exploration phase. This chapter introduces best knowledge based guidelines for agile requirements engineering to enhance the quality of requirements (story cards).

1. INTRODUCTION

Developing software that meets the customers or stakeholders' needs and expectation is the ultimate goal of the software development methodology. To meet their need we have to perform a requirement engineering step, which is one of the crucial steps in to software development methodology. Overall project success and failures of the project is depending on the user requirements. Requirements elicitation process is one of the challenging processes in the software development methods. In traditional software development methods end users or stakeholders predefined their requirements and sent to

DOI: 10.4018/978-1-60566-731-7.ch001

the development team to analysis and negotiation to produce requirement specification. Traditional software development has a problem to deal with requirement change after careful analysis and negotiation. This problem is well tackled by the XP, which is one of the agile software development methodologies.

Extreme (XP) programming is a conceptual framework of practices and principles to develop software faster, incrementally and to produce satisfied customer. It is a set of twelve practices and four principles, which makes XP successful and well known among all the agile software development methods. The goal of XP is to produce the software faster, incrementally and to produce satisfied customer (Beck 2000). According to Boehm the cost of change grows exponentially as the project progresses through it lifecycle (Boehm 1981). The relative repair cost is 200 times greater in the maintenance phase than if it is caught in the requirement phase (Faluk 1996). XP maintain the cost of change through iterative software development methods and Refactoring.

In XP, Development starts with planning game where customer writes user stories on story cards. Those cards are estimated by the developer, based on those estimation customer priories them depends on their needs to establish a timebox of an iteration. Developers develop those story cards through pair programming and test driven development. At last customer provides acceptance test to accept the developed functionality. In between they consider all of the XP practices in mind to improve the quality of the software.

Story cards are one of the important aspects of the XP. They are playing vital role in XP. It describes functionality of system or software to be build that will be valuable to either purchaser or user of software. User stories are composed of three aspects (Cohen 2004):

- A written description of the story used for planning and as a reminder

- Conversation about the story that serves to flush out the details of the story
- Tests that convey and document details and that can be used to determine when a story is complete

Story cards are written by the customer in XP to articulate their business needs. According to Cohn story cards must be testable, estimatable, valuable to the customer, small and independent (Cohn 2003). These story cards must be written by the customer because they know their business need very well compared to developer.

XP strongly recommend an onsite customer to write their business need. Business is well understood by the customer. But generally customers have rarely a general picture of the requirements or system in their mind (Kotyana and Somerville 1997). Traditional XP story card framework or template is not well defined for the requirements elicitation. It supports to write requirements or user needs in two to three sentences and it not discover any information rather than user functionality. Different stakeholders have different needs. End user has rarely a picture of a clear of system to write down the user stories. This will lead to problems related to requirements like requirements conflicts, missing requirements, and ambiguous requirements etc, and not address non-functional requirements from exploration phase. Due to this reason they hardly make a decision or predict wrong priority of the requirements or story cards. Two third of the projects are failed because of ambiguous and incomplete user requirements, and poor quality of the requirements. For small to medium organizations, proper requirements prioritization and selection can mean the difference in not only project success or failure but also overall company survivability (Azar, J. et. al. 2007). Different users have different perspective of system in same organization. Different background can make problems to priories the requirements in XP. Different stakeholders have different needs and different requirements and different prioritization

Figure 1. Traditional Story Card (Back 2000)

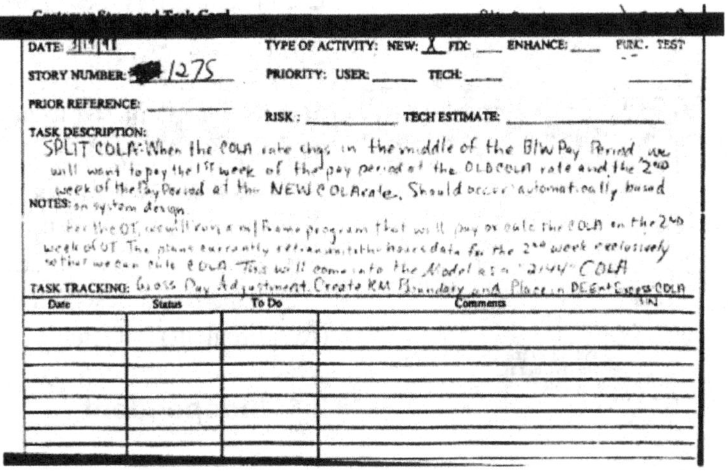

values so requirements conflicts there. A critical aspect of the requirements process is the selection of the an appropriate requirements set from the multitude of competing and conflicting expectation elicited from the various project stakeholders or from an onsite customers (Wiegers, K. 1997). The CHOAS report published in 1995 shows that almost half of the cancelled projects failed due to a lack of requirements engineering effort and that a similar percentage ascribes good requirements engineering as the main reason for project success ([Chaos 95]

XP methodology highly relies on the onsite-customer interaction with the developer to identify or to tell which features to implement in a next release. XP builds software systems based on customer's domain knowledge and his/her expertise. In traditional XP or agile software development methodology story cards are written by the customers perhaps with the help of developer. Therefore each user story or story card must be split into unique and independent requirement.

Traditionally user story is written on the 2" X 3" Cards. Usually any size is acceptable to write user story on story cards. Following Figure 1 shows an example of the story card used in the real project as proposed in (Beck 2000) which

provides a traditional structure of story card.

According to general template of story card, it is really difficult to well tackle the user requirements expressed on the cards. Traditionally developed story cards are not providing enough information of user functionality. They express user functionality in single to couple of sentences, which is really difficult to do analysis, and they lead problem related to under or over estimate, and based on that estimation there is a possibility of wrong story cards prioritization as well. We apply this traditional story card method to the real project user story Figure 2 shows the story cards written through a traditional way, which is just a short and vague statement of user requirement. This story card does not provide any information related to acceptance testing as well.

This is a story card for an online e-commerce store. In this story cards user trying to express their requirement as

'Each and Every online purchaser needs to register with unique username and password before purchasing anything from the online store'

As a result of this investigation we propose a new prototype to improve requirement elicitation

Figure 2. An example of traditional story card

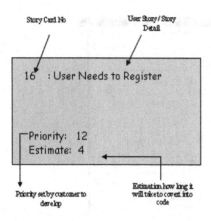

process in XP. This will help to customer and developer to improve the quality of the user stories or story cards, and to address functional and non-functional requirements on story cards based on the story cards and requirements engineering guidelines. We also propose an 'INSERT' model or methodology to perform requirements engineering in XP. This article compares, traditional requirement engineering and traditional XP requirements engineering approach with our new improved 'INSERT' technique to capture user requirements for agile software development environments. We also analyze commonalities and differences of both approaches and determine possible ways how agile software development team and customers can benefit from our improved requirements elicitation methods. In this chapter we discuss about extreme programming and requirement elicitation process through story cards first and then after the challenges and problems on XP software development methodology. This is followed by discussion of related research regarding to an 'INSERT' requirement elicitation method of the story cards for XP based projects.

2. AN 'INSERT' PROCESS IN EXTREME PROGRAMMING (XP)

As a result of this investigation we propose a new 'INSERT' model to improve the quality of user story and to address customer requirements properly and on verifiable way the acronyms INSERT is as:I: IndependentN: NegotiableS: Small enough to fit into iterationE: Estimatable or easy to EstimateR: Representation of user functionality (Requirement)T: Testable

2.1. Independent

Story cards must be independent or we have to take care as much as possible to avoid dependencies between story cards. Dependencies between story cards lead a problem related to estimation and prioritization. For example customer selected a high priority of story cards which is depend on low priority story cards, this situation make estimation harder than it suppose to be. In our insert model we do take care of dependencies between story cards. We take care as much as possible to flush out the dependencies between story cards. This type of story cards mostly captures atomic requirements which are directly transferable to a single use case and a design class.

2.2. Negotiable

Stories on Story card also are negotiable. Story cards are short description of the user requirements they are not working as a contract. User story is a reminder to have a conversation between developer and customer. If it is negotiable than only than it gives better chance to developer to understand customer needs, their business need and their domain knowledge as well. This type of story cards mostly captures complex requirements which relates to more than one used cases and scenarios.

2.3. Small

Stories on the story cards need to be small enough to fit into iteration. Too big story or too small story is not going to fit into the timebox of iteration. To solve this problem we suggest to write an acceptance test with the story it self. There is a direct co-relation between story and acceptance tests. If story many acceptance tests that means it is big to fit into iteration and needs to be split into two story cards based on the acceptance tests. If story is small on the story card then combine them with another small story to fit them into the same iteration. This type of story cards captures a part of a independent and negotiable requirements and may also represent a non-functional requirements.

2.4. Estimatable

Estimation is a crucial value of the story card. Based on the developer's estimation customer decide which functionality is going to be first and which one is next. On traditional XP cards estimation is complex. There are several reasons for that like developers do not have domain knowledge, or they are technically not sound, or story cards are too big. Our proposed model considers these all problems and tries to solve this problem by acceptance tests, which will help to bring domain knowledge and technical knowledge to customers and developers.

2.5. Representation of System Functionality

This is an import and crucial part of the story cards. There isn't any tool or documentation that proves that the user story expressed on the story cards is valuable to the user or not. Stories on the story cards are written by the customer, so XP assume that requirement is correct, which leads problem related to requirement change and rework. To solve this problem we again focused on acceptance tests

and strongly recommended to write them with the story cards. This acceptance test will help to write user stories on the verifiable ways.

2.6. Testable

Story cards must be testable. If it is difficult to test the story then that means story card is expressing non-functional requirements instead of user functionality. It is easy to write functional test or acceptance test for the functionality (functional requirements) in our model if you are able to write functional test or acceptance test that means the story is testable. Successfully passed all acceptance test means story card is fully developed.

This insert process is also based on the best knowledge based requirements engineering guidelines which are described in the section 3

Consider the following Figure 3 which shows our new improved requirements elicitation process to capture user story on story cards based on the INSERT values.

In our approach we recommended a customer or stake holder who is on site has comprehensive application domain and business knowledge to put a developer into the picture.

Application domain knowledge and customer business knowledge from customer will help developer to focus on stockholder's business needs and requirements and help them to cover any missing functionality. Customer business knowledge helps developers to understand how the system will affect and interact with the different part of the business, and help to identify and understand different stakeholders, who are directly or indirectly affected by the system.

At the end of this successful discussion, customer starts story elicitation process and write the draft statement of requirements on story cards. These story cards are further analyzed, which assist to customer and developer to identify any problems and missing functionality. Missing functionalities become defect in working software. This scenario will help developers

Figure 3. INSERT method for requirements elicitation process in XP

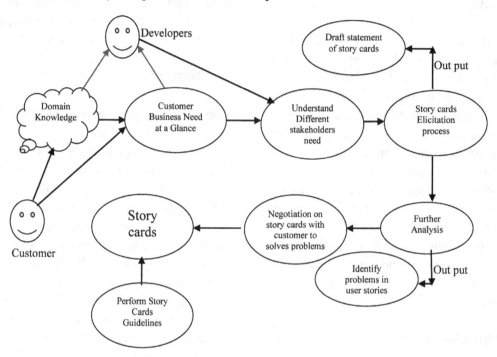

to focus on non-functional requirements. Also helps to keep in mind what they have to do to improve all the aspects of the business through structured system. Identified problems are being negotiated between developers and customer to acquire story cards. Following Figure 4 shows an example of story cards captured through the new improved requirement elicitation process based on the INSERT model.

Figure 3 INSERT method for requirements elicitation processes in XP, addresses the requirements capturing in XP with on-site customer. INSERT is based on a set of best practice guideline that helps both developers and customers to refine, clarify, and re-solve requirements conflicts with mutual discussion. The key benefits to apply the best practice guidelines are as

- Higher quality, lower cost requirements documents (Story cards).
- More understandable story cards compared to traditional story cards.

- Avoids misunderstandings among user requirements captured on story cards
- To reduce cost of changing the requirements at any stage of project life cycle
- To reveal technology we are using for a project is realistic
- Discovery of all likely sources of story cards
- Requirements are focused on core business needs
- Domain constraints often leads to critical requirements identification
- User finds easy to understand scenarios and to describe associated requirements.
- Easy to prioritize requirements
- Reveals ambiguities and inconsistency in the requirements
- Acceptance testing allows more stakeholders to participate in requirements validation.
- To support non-functional requirements

Figure 4. Story cards captured through the new improved requirement elicitation process based on the INSERT model

STORY CARD NO: 16	Project Name E-Commerce	Estimation: 4 Hours
Story Name: User Registration		Date: 16/08/2007 1:30 PM

STORY:	Acceptance Test:
User needs to register with unique username and password before purchasing anything from the online store	1. User Id must be unique 2. Try to register with duplicate user id and Password 3. Try to register user name only 4. Try to register with password only 5. Forget Password Link
Note: User Can View or Visit store as a Visitor but needs to register before purchasing anything	Risk: Low

Points to be Consider: There isn't any non-functional requirement at this stage

We also provide automated support tool to direct the processes of story card driven requirements capturing.

Traditional method of story cards is still valuable and some of the guidelines are really crucial and unique. Onsite customer and simplicity of story cards are among them. In our proposal we also strongly recommended an onsite customer which is traditional story cards practice or guideline. In this section we tried to identify the improvement area of the story cards the following table will shows the commonality and variability between the story cards through traditional and INSERT model. This is just a prototype we still working on the story cards guidelines to extend them up to research level.

3. BEST PRACTICES GUIDELINES

3.1. Story Cards must be Small and Complete

As we discussed into the section 2.1 Stories on the story cards need to be small enough to fit into iteration. Too big story or too small story is not going to fit into the timebox of iteration. This is a crucial guideline for the story cards based agile software development. the benefits to apply this guidelines are as 1) gives an ease in iteration planning 2) it is easy to understand.

3.2. Define a Standard Story Card Structure

Story card should have a common structure which should contain information regarding to on-site customer, developer, related story cards, risk, user story (requirements), time, non-functional constraint, domain name, and acceptance tests. A standard structure for story cards means that anyone can use their knowledge of previous story cards when reading a new story cards. They can find information more easily and understand the relationship between parts of the story cards. The standard structure of the story cards works as a checklist for developers and customer and reduces the chances of them accidentally omitting information. Ideally story cards should express the purpose of the user story or story cards, scope of story cards, product or function perspective, user characteristic, and assumptions and dependencies if exist. Standards make story card easier to read. Standards make story cards (Requirements) easier to collect, and standards make story cards easier to write as well.

3.3. Write Requirement on the Story Card in the Format of the Summary or Abstract in Two to Three Sentences Long

You should always write requirement on the story card in the format of the summary or abstract in two to three sentences long, which summarise the purpose and principle of the story cards. It is much easier for developer and customer to figure out user story if they have abroad picture of what they are trying to understand. Summarising the requirements allows story cards to make forward reference to other requirements.

3.4. Dependencies of Story Cards

As we discussed into the section 2.1 the Story cards must be independent or we have to take care as much as possible to avoid dependencies between story cards. Dependencies between story cards lead a problem related to estimation and prioritization.

3.5. Define an Unambiguous Story Cards

Story card is unambiguous, if and only if, story card statement has only one interpretation. At a minimum, defined terms must describe functionality of the software.

3.6. Define Simplicity on Story Cards (Story Cards must be Simple)

Simplicity is the core value of the Agile software development or extreme programming. All Busi-

ness terminology also needs to be predefined to make story cards as simple as possible. Simplicity helps or solves problems related to requirement change and priority.

3.7. Story Cards must be Consistent

Consistent statement of story card does not include contradictory, incoherent and conflicting statements, so which will not lead to wrong discussions.

3.8. Story Card Must Present Business Requirements

The story card should always express or explain why the functionality captured on story card is required and how it will contribute to the overall business objectives of the iteration. It is important to consider because when proposal or user story changes are made, we can use business case for the system to assess where or not the proposed changes are sensible.

3.9. Story Cards must be Estimatable

The description of the user requirement to be developed as given in the story cards is a realistic basis for estimating story cards cost and development time. Estimation is a crucial value of the story card. Based on the developer's estimation customer decide which functionality is going to be first and which one is next. On traditional XP cards estimation is complex. There are several reasons for that like developers do not have domain knowledge, or they are technically not sound, or story cards are too big. We consider these all problems and try to solve this problem by acceptance tests, which will help to bring domain knowledge and technical knowledge to customers and developers.

3.10. Define Specialised Terms used in the Story Cards

Specialised terms used in the story cards must be predefined during the domain analysis. This will define the terms which are specific to application domain. For example the system is concerned with mobile application, it would include terms such as Bluetooth, GPRS, and WAP etc.

3.11. Story Card should Easy to Change or Modify

It is always a good and handy to change story cards whenever necessary. The key benefit is it will reduce the cost of changing requirements. Producing or writing new story cards always expensive and time consuming. If story cards are not changeable then it is difficult to accommodate change during the test driven development and pair programming.

3.12. investigation of System Feasibility

It is beneficial to carry out feasibility study, before investigating efforts and allocating expenses on requirement engineering for story cards work shop. This will tell us the suitability of the implemented given existing technology and effectively integrated with our current way of working.

3.13. Identify and Consider the System Stakeholders from the Onsite Customer

Each system has a multiple stakeholders who are going to get benefit in a direct and indirect way from the system which is being developed. Different system has different stakeholders. As a part of the story card workshop or user story elicitation process, we should consider all kind of the stakeholders and consult them to discover their specific needs for story cards. If we do not

consider all the stakeholders who are going to affected by the introduction of the story cards, we are likely to miss important requirements. The system may have to rework to include these requirements on the later date. Identifying stakeholders and discussing the system with them makes people fell that they are the part of the requirement elicitation process

3.14. Valuable to the Customer

Each story card is valued by the customer. It is really difficult to find out the story card is valuable to customer or not. The best way to ensure that each story is valuable to the customer or user is to have the customer to write the stories.

3.15. Define System Boundaries during the Domain Analysis for Story Cards

Domain analysis is a good practice to follow the successful requirement engineering process. During the requirement engineering process, we should identify which story cards are system requirement story cards, which are presenting the operational process associated with system, and which story cards are outside the scope of the system onsite customer often unclear about what should and what should not be in the system. They may suggest inappropriate requirements sometime. So it is a good practice to eliminate the requirements or story cards which are outside of the scope.

3.16. Story Card must be Negotiable

Stories on Story card also are negotiable. Story cards are short description of the user requirements they are not working as a contract. User story is a reminder to have a conversation between developer and customer. If it is negotiable than only than it gives better chance to developer to understand customer needs, their business need and their domain knowledge as well. This type of story cards mostly captures complex requirements which relates to more than one used cases and scenarios.

3.17. Prioritise Story Cards Based on the Different Factors

This is one of the challenging issues for the extreme programming. Story cards are prioritized, if each requirement has an identifier to indicate, for example, its importance or volatility. In terms of importance, we can classify story cards into essential, conditional, and optional. The iteration or software needs to fulfil essential requirements in an agreed manner to be acceptable. While conditional requirements enhance the software, their absence does not make it unacceptable.

3.18. Use Language Simply, Consistently and Concisely

It is recommended, customer expresses a story card in natural language, write their requirement using simple, consistently, and concise language. Try to avoid complex sentences, long sentences, paragraphs and ambiguous terminology. When user story is written using simple language it is easier to read and understand. More people can understand story cards that are written in a simple way. It takes less time to explain the user story to developers.

3.19. Check the Story Cards meet the XP Principle and Values

Before putting forward story cards into development stage, one of the developers should carry out a quick standards check to ensure that the story cards meet the XP principle and values.

3.20. Uniquely Identify each Story Cards and User Stories on Story Cards

Each story card should be assigned a unique identifier or story card no. unique identifier may helps to make a reference to related requirements for tractability. If we store story cards on a database system the story card identifier works as a unique columns to identify story card on database

3.21. User Story Writing Technique

The best user story writing technique is face to face interview with pair wise story writing technique. (Business expert and developer)

3.22. On-Site Customer

This is the crucial practice of extreme programming to have a proper online customer. On-site customer helps to drive the story cards towards the business direction.

3.23. Consideration of Domain Analysis

Domain constraint is the system requirements which is retrieve from the domain analysis of the system. We should study the domain and do domain analysis and understand constraint as a part of the story card elicitation process. Domain analysis generates system story cards and place limitation on other requirements. If we take domain considerations into account, there may be insuperable legal, organisational or physical obstacles to implementing the proposed story cards.

3.24. Write Story Cards from Multiple Viewpoints (Collect Requirements from Multiple Viewpoints)

There are many influences on the story card for a XP based projects. These includes the stakeholders, end-user of the system, whor are involved in the process. These stakeholders are potential source of system requirement or story cards and they have their own viewpoint on the service that the system. If you collect requirements from the single point of the view, we unlikely to meet the needs of other stakeholders in the system. Collecting story cards or requirements from their multiple viewpoint is a useful way of prioritising requirements.

3.25. Specify Non-Functional Requirements also on Story Cards

It is a good practice; we should specify quantitative values to the story cards. This is most applicable to the non-functional requirements. Non-functional requirements are the requirements which are concerned with attribute of the system.

3.26. To Link between Story Card Requirements and Stakeholder

We should always note the relationship between story cards and stakeholders related to that story cards. It will increase the traceability of the system.

3.27. Propose or Define Validation Plan for Story Cards (Write Acceptance Tests)

This is an import and crucial part of the story cards. There isn't any tool or documentation that proves that the user story expressed on the story cards is valuable to the user or not. Stories on the story cards are written by the customer, so XP assume that requirement is correct, which leads problem related to requirement change and rework. To solve this problem we again recommended and focused on acceptance tests and strongly recommended to write them with the story cards. This acceptance test will help to write user stories on the verifiable ways. For each story card propose one or more

acceptance tests to check if the system meete that requirement. Proposing possible tests is an effective way of revealing requirements problems such as incompleteness and ambiguity. If it is difficult to write acceptance test, then there is some kind of requirements problems there.

A story card is correct, if and only if, the iteration or software has to meet all the customer's requirements. Or a correct story card must accurately and precisely identify conditions and limitation encountered by the software. According to IEEE requirements standard there is no tool can automatically ensure correctness. But in the case of extreme programming it is easy to check correctness of story cards through acceptance testing from beginning.

3.28. Use a Database System to Store Story Cards Compared to Write them on the Card and Destroy

Rather than maintaining requirements on cards, establish a story cards database and store the individual story cards in the database. Managing story cards in a database make easier to maintain the link between the story cards

3.29. Assess Story Cards Risk

For each story cards, carry out a risk analysis in which we suggest possible problems which may arise in the implementation of that story cards. Explicit risk assessment means identifying story cards which are likely to cause particular difficulties to the system developers. If these can be identified at this stage, it may be possible to modify the story cards to reduce the risks to the development process. Assessing risk to story cards often reveals that insufficient information about the requirement is available and that further details should be discovered from requirement stakeholders.

Table 1. Story card guidelines supported by the different approaches

Story cards feature and guidelines	Mike Cohn	INSERT (SoBA)	Kent Beck	3C Approach
Story cards must be small and complete	√	√	√	√
Define a standard story card structure.		√		
Include the summary or abstract in two to three sentences of the requirements	√	√		
Dependencies of story cards	√	√		
Define an unambiguous story cards. (unambiguous)		√	√	
Define simplicity on story cards. (Simple)	√	√	√	√
Story cards must be consistent		√		
Story card must represent business requirements	√	√	√	
Define specialised terms used in the story cards		√		
Make the story cards easy to change		√		
Investigation of system feasibility		√		
Identify and consult the system stakeholders from the onsite customer		√		
Valuable to the customer.	√	√	√	√
Define system boundaries during the domain analysis for Story cards		√		
Story card must be negotiable		√	√	
Prioritise story cards based on different factors	Limited	√	Limited	Limited
Use language simply, consistently and concisely		√		
Check the story cards meet the XP Principle and values		√		
Uniquely identify each story cards and user stories on story cards		√		
User story writing technique.	√	√	Limited	
On-site customer	√	√	√	√
Domain analysis		√		
Write story cards from multiple viewpoints		√		
Specify non-functional requirements also on story card.		√		
Try to links between story card requirements and stakeholder		√		
Propose or Define validation checklist for story cards (Write acceptance tests)		√		
Use a database system to store story cards compared to write them on the card and destroy		√		
Assess story cards risk.		√		
Prioritize requirements based on the story card's value and XP values		√		
Reduced development Efforts.		√		
defined or representation of requirements by the developer and customer		√		√

3.30. Reduced Development Efforts

The preparation of the story cards forces the various concerned group in the customer organisation. To consider rigorously all of the requirements before design begins and reduce later redesign, recording and retesting. Careful review of the story cards can reveal omissions, misunderstanding, and inconsistency early in the development cycle when these problems are easier to correct.

3.31. Defined or Representation of Requirements by the Developers and Customer

Establish the basis for agreement between developers and suppliers on what the system has to do. The enough and complete description of the functionality on the story cards to be performed by the software specified in the story card will assist the potential users to determine if the software specified meets their needs or how the software must be modified to meet their needs. Customer (Domain Expert, Business Analyst) knows very well their system or business. While developer will easily find out the risk involved into the requirements.

Table 1 shows the guideline supported by the different approaches. Where SoBA is an automated tool for story cards based agile software development based on the 'INSERT' Methodology and best practices guidelines for story card.

4. CASE STUDY

We apply INSERT technique based on the best knowledge based guidelines to the few functional and unique requirements of the same project called e-commerce online store. Table 2 and Figure 5 show a result, this shows that the INSERT model increased quality of the user story on story cards

Table 2. Comparison of traditional methods and INSERT method on key story cards

Story Card No	User Story Title	No Of Passed Guidelines		Quality Percentage of user Story	
		Traditional story cards	**INSERT Story Cards**	**Traditional Story Card**	**(Improved) Quality by INSERT Story Cards**
1	Admin Login	12	30	35	85
2	User Registration	14	32	40	91
3	Payment Method	13	29	38	83
4	Shipping Products	10	27	29	77

Figure 5. Comparison graph of traditional methods and INSERT method on key story cards

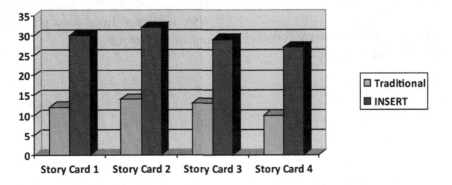

compared to the traditional methods. We apply this INSERT model to the key requirements or key story cards of the project to set up a prototype of this model.

5. CONCLUSION

The use of story cards for user stories in many Extreme Programming software development projects has been widespread. Several popular traditional methods for story cards (eg, Cohen M, Kent B) have been used in successful fashion at some extent, but all lack of the powerful features for story cards guidelines, right sort of information on story cards and quality of user stories on story cards. They also do not involve anybody apart from customer on story writing workshop. This chapter has described the INSERT model, new proposed frame work of story cards, and a new improved requirements elicitation process in XP. The experience with INSERT model and new framework of story cards indicates that it is feasible to contemplate improving user stories and story cards in Extreme programming.

6. REFERENCES

Beck, K. (2000). *Extreme programming Explained Embraced Change*. Reading, MA: Addison-Wesley.

Beck, K., & Fowler, M. (2000). *Planning Extreme Programming*. Reading MA: Addison-Wesley Press.

Boehm, B. (1981). *Software Engineering Economics*. Englewood Cliffs, NJ: Prentice Hall.

Cohn, M. (2003). *User stories applied for Agile Software Development*. Reading, MA: Addison-Wesley.

Faulk, S. (1996). Software Requirements: A Tutorial. In M. Dorfman & R. H. Thayer (Eds.) *Software Engineering*, (pp. 82-103). Washington, DC: IEEE Computer Society Press.

Karlsson, J. (1996). Software Requirements Prioritizing. *IEEE Proceeding of ICRE '96*.

Karlsson, J., & Ryan, K. (1997). A cost-Value Approach for Prioritizing Requirements. *IEEE Software*.

Kotyana, G., & Sommerville, I. (1997). *Requirements Engineering Processes and Techniques*. Hoboken, NJ: John Wiley and Sons Ltd.

Niu, N., Easterbrook, S. (2007). So You Think you know other's goal? A Repertory Grid Study. *IEEE Software, March/April*.

Paetsch, F., Eberlein, A., & Maure, F. (2003). Requirements Engineering and Agile Software Development. In *Proceedings of the Twelfth IEEE International Workshops on Enabling Technologies: Infrastructure for Collaborative Enterprises 2003 (WETICE'03)*.

Ramachandran, M. (2005). *A Process Improvement Framework for XP based SMEs*. Paper presented at 6th International Conference on Extreme Programming and Agile Processes in Software Engineering, Sheffield, UK, June 2005.

Wiegers, K. (1999, September). First Things First: Prioritizing requirements. *Software Development*, 7(9). Retrieved from www.processimpact.com/pubs.shtml#requirements

Chapter 2
Requirements Engineering in a Model–Based Methodology for Embedded Automotive Software

Jean-Louis Boulanger
CERTIFER, France

ABSTRACT

This chapter resumes the requirements engineering in a model-based methodology for embedded automotive software. The methodology relies on two standard languages: EAST-ADL for automotive architecture description and SysML for systems modeling. The requirements engineering in the methodology describes phases of elicitation, modeling, traceability, verification and validation. It is illustrated by applying on a case study -- the knock controller -- a part of the engine management system.

INTRODUCTION

Modern car is now equipped with more and more functionalities dependent on embedded electronics, ranging from powertrain and chassis control to body comfort and infotainment. These functionalities are distributed over a networked Electronic Control Units (ECU). The size and complexity of software for these embedded electronics increase rapidly with its cost raising from 10% of the overall cost in 1970 to 40% in 2010. Actually, 90% of innovations in the automotive industry concerns embedded electronics and 80% among them are software see Bortolazzi, J. (2004).

A big challenge in developing automotive software concerns the quality. Automotive systems are safety-critical systems where failures may cause severe damages or loss, so software errors led directly to car recalls. According to the report Gumbrich, S. (2004), one-third of the recalls in recent year is caused by software errors. More efforts are needed on software's verification and testing.

Another challenge concerns the reduction the time of development. The automotive market is shared by manufacturers, suppliers and tool vendors, and all needs shorten processes which favor the exchangeability among them and the reuse of software in different product lines. They also need to follow requirements along the development, from the specification to design and code, to anticipate

DOI: 10.4018/978-1-60566-731-2.ch002

and communicate its changes throughout teams.

New paradigm in software development is born in this context to face these challenges. In Europe, automotive actors tried to cooperate on a common base for software development. The result of this corporation is EAST-ADL (2004), a recently defined standard. EAST-ADL is an architecture description language dedicated to automotive software. It provides a mean to describe the functionality of a vehicle, from high level requirement to implementation details. It focuses on structural aspect, leaving behavioral aspect for existing tools. EAST-ADL is based on Unified Modeling Language 2 (UML (2007)) but has automotive-specific constructs and semantics in order to make system models unambiguous, consistent and exchangeable.

Model-based development (MBD) is a preferred approach for automotive software because it improves the specification, design, and implementation phases. Model-based development benefits from the Systems Modeling Language (SysML (2006)), another recently defined by Object Management Group (OMG). SysML (2006) gives a means to early represent into models the requirements and physical parametric of automotive systems. SysML (2006) has also the capacities of facilitate the design and verification.

The research project MeMVaTEx (2008) addresses a model-based methodology that emphasizes the requirements validation and traceability. The methodology invests two languages: EAST-ADL (2004) for automotive architecture description and SysML (2006) for system modeling. The methodology describes step-by-step process with appropriate tools supporting each step. It aims to give a \textit{seamless} solution for industrial use. An automotive case study -- the engine knock controller -- a part of the Engine Management System (EMS) is used to illustrated the methodology.

This paper shows the requirements engineering in the methodology. It describes phases of elicitation, modeling and traceability, verification and validation, and accompanied tools. The methodology concerns other aspects like safety, real-time, variability, or model transformation that will not be addressed here. Our related works A. Albinet, J-L. Boulanger, H. Dubois and al. (2007), C. André, F. Malet, and M.-A. Peraldi-Frati (2007), J-L. Boulanger and Q-D. Van (2007), A. Albinet, S. Begoc, J-L. Boulanger and al. (2008), J-L. Boulanger and Q-D. Van (2008)can be found on the Web site MeMVaTEx (2008).

EAST-ADL OVERVIEWS

EAST-ADL (2004) stands for Electronic Architecture and Software Tools-Architecture Description Language. The language is defined in the Embedded Electronic Architecture (EEA) project, one of many project from Information Technology for European Advancement (ITEA)[1]. Important car manufacturers, suppliers, tool vendors, and research institutes in Europe take part in this project to give birth EAST-ADL. This language is intended to support the development of automotive embedded software, by capturing all the related engineering information, including software, hardware, and its environment.

The language EAST-ADL reflects different views and details of the architecture and is structured in five abstraction layers as illustrated in figure 1.

These layers are:

- Vehicle level (VL) describes electronic features in driver's point of view.
- Analysis level (AL) gives abstract functional definition of features in system context.
- Design level gives (DL) detailed functional definition of software including elementary decomposition.
- Implementation level (IL) describes reusable code and system configuration for hardware deployment.

Figure 1. EAST-ADL abstraction layers

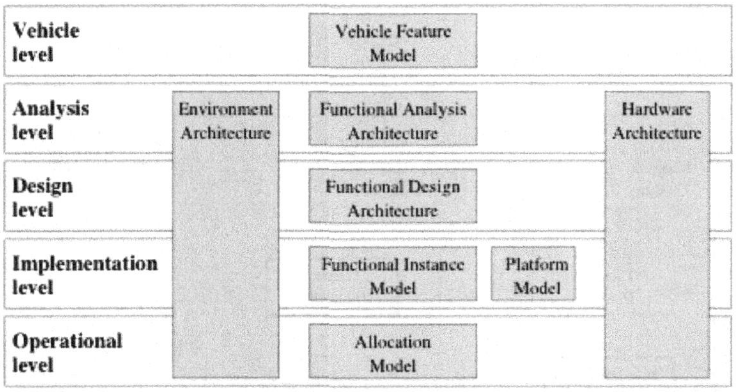

- Operational level (OL) supports final binary software deployment.

EAST-ADL (2004) has just revised in the project ATESST (2008). Version 2 of EAST-ADL now links directly to AUTomotive Open System Architecture (AUTOSAR)[2], another initiative from automotive industry which standardizes software architecture and interfaces for ECUs. Essentially, AUTOSAR's scope concerns the last two Implementation and Operational levels of the EAST-ADL. The project ATESST[3] tries to the harmonize EAST-ADL 2 and AUTOSAR with summaries can be found in P. Cuenot, D. Chen, S. Gérard and al. (2007).

SYSTEM MODELING LANGUAGE

Since its adoption in 1997 by Object Management Group (OMG) to the last version UML2 in 2007, UML is successfully used by software engineers for modeling their software. Web applications and banking transactions benefits particularly from UML. However, UML lacks important elements to be used by system engineers to modeling their systems, e.g., no means exists for modeling requirements, physical constraints among components, or internal transactions between subsystems. Many specific profiles were invented, giving partly

solutions for some problems.

System Modeling Language (SysML) is an OMG standard, developed with objective to fill the semantic gap between systems, software, and other engineering disciplines. By definition, OMG SysML (2006) enables system engineers in different domains to analyze, specify, design, and verify their complex systems, enhancing systems quality.

Technically, SysML (2006) reuses a subset of UML2, adding new diagrams and modifying others. It includes diagrams that can be used to specify system requirements, behavior, structure, and parametric relationships, known as the four pillars of SysML (2006). Of the four pillars, only requirements and parametric diagrams are entirely new. Figure 2 gives the complete SysML diagrams. More descriptions and applications of SysML diagrams can be found in L. Balmelli (2006).

The project MeMVaTEx (2008) pays particular attention on the requirement diagram. This diagram represent text requirement in the model. A requirement may have links to other requirements or to modeling actefacts via a set of four new stereotyped dependencies (see figure 3).

- <<derive>> indicates the derivation of requirement from other requirements.
- <<refine>> indicates that an element is a refinement of a textual requirement.

Figure 2. The SysML diagram taxonomy

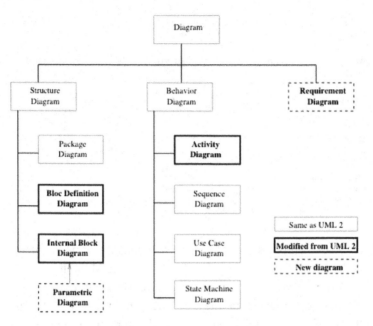

- <<satisfy>> shows the satisfaction of requirement by design.
- <<verify>> shows the link from a test case to the requirement it verifies.

With these new stereotypes, engineers can follow forward and backward any requirement from the the phase of specification, how it is broken into sub-requirements, which design blocks satisfy requirement or which parts of code are concerned. With thousands of requirements may change during the development of an ordinary automotive project see Gumbrich, S. (2004), the new capacity of SysML (2006) helps keeping the requirements traceability.

New SysML stereotype introduces the link requirement-test case that is crucial for the requirements verification and validation because strict regulations in the automotive domain like IEC 61508 (2000) or the future ISO~26262 (see Siemens (2006)) now impose that each requirement must be tested by test case. In SysML (2006), a test case is intended to be used as a general mechanism to represent any of the standard verification

Figure 3. New SysML stereotypes for requirement

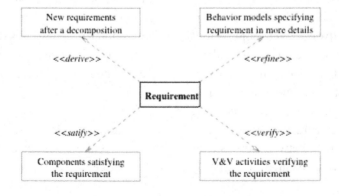

Figure 4. Illustration of the desired combustion (left) and knock phenomenon (right) in a 4-cycle gasoline engine.

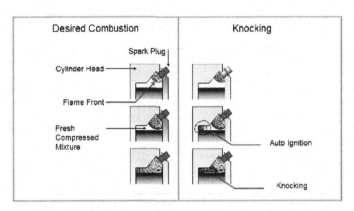

methods for inspection, analysis, demonstration, or test. SysML (2006) has the capability for representing test cases and attaching them to their related requirements or use cases. A test case can be an operation or a behavioral model (Interaction, State Machine, Sequence or Activity Diagram).

These new capacities of SysML (2006) will be detailed through the case study in the next section.

THE CASE STUDY: ENGINE KNOCK CONTROLLER

In a four-stroke gasoline engine, air and vaporized fuel are drawn in the first stroke (intake). In the second stroke, fuel vapor and air are compressed and ignited (compression). Fuel combusts and piston is pushed downwards in the third stroke (combustion) and exhaust is driven out in the last stroke (exhaust). The cycle can be seen in the left of the figure 4.

In practice, ignition usually occurs before the end of the second stroke in order to maximizing power and fuel economy and minimize exhaust emission. Under some circumstances, when the temperature and pressure of the unburned air/fuel mixture exceeds a critical level, a second auto-ignition occurs as shown in the right of the

figure 4. The two-flame crossing produces a shock wave with rapid increase in cylinder pressure. The impulse caused by the shock wave excites a resonance in the cylinder at a characteristic frequency. Damages to piston, ring, and exhaust valves can result if sustained heavy knock occurs.

An appropriate anti-knock control, represented in figure 5, is applied to each cylinder at every engine cycle from low engine speed up to the highest engine speed. A knock control system consists of one or several noise sensors, and a controller which acquire the noise through the sensors, and computes the correction during the combustion phases of the cylinders. The controller can detect knocks using spectral analysis techniques M. Zadnik, F. Vincent, R. Vingerhoeds and al. (2007). The controller decided to advance or retard the ignition to correct.

REQUIREMENTS ENGINEERING IN THE CASE STUDY

The V-Model

We use the V-model in the figure 6 to illustrate the requirements engineering phase by phase. It begins with the requirement elicitation from the specification document. Then requirement are

Figure 5. Knock controller description

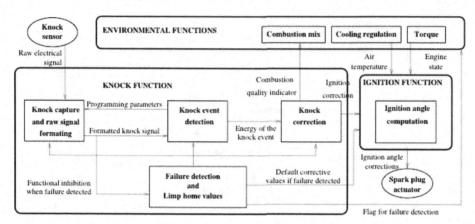

represented in models from architecture level to design level down to the code. Verification and validation (V&V) are present along the requirement engineering, showing V\&V activities in each phase and for each requirement.

Requirement Elicitation

This phase consists of a list of requirements that can be exploited during the next phases. System engineers, safety experts, and time are needed to build a complete and consistent list of requirement. Most of project's failure is due to insufficient attentions in this phase, as reported in I.F. Alexander and R. Stevens (2002).

In MeMVaTEx project, requirements are classified by EAST-ADL levels. At each level, requirements are numbered and structured in functional (F) and non-functional (NF). Non-functional requirement are classified by categories such as performance (P), safety (S) and availability (A). Note that the respects of regulation in automotive domain introduce safety requirements at each level, resulting more complexity in the design and test. It also led us to extent the SysML Requirement stereotype to a particular MeMVaTEx Requirement stereotype

Table 1 gives some examples of requirements of the knock controller. Requirements are actually stored in tabular applications like Word or Excel.

MeMVaTEx Stereotype

The SysML Requirement stereotype as defined by the standard contains a description "Text", an

Figure 6. Verification and Validation activities in V-model development

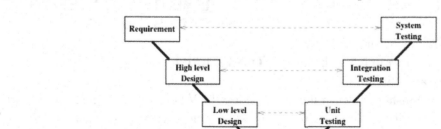

Table 1. Requirements in the case study

ID	Requirement
VL-F-2	Motor Unit shall produce torque upon feature request.
VL-F-9	Engine Control shall manage knock phenomenon.
VL-NF-A-1	Engine Control shall report diagnosis results in order to identify failures.
AL-F-10	Knock control function shall know the piston position in order to measure and correct the knock on the right cylinder.
AL-F-12	Knock correction sub-function shall be triggered each time the knock value is greater than a threshold.
AL-NF-S-1	Knock function shall not generate a knock noise stronger than the previous one.
DL-F-1	The capture must end when the Knock Acquisition Window Duration (expressed in cranksaft angular degree) has elapsed.
DL-NF-P-3	The sub-function Filtering must be performed in X ms

identifier ("Id") and links to other requirements, design element, and test case for each requirement (see figure 7, left). When taking into accounts other aspects of analysis, verification, and validation, this definition is not detailed enough. In order to better support the requirements engineering, we have interest in extending this SysML Requirement stereotype by adding new fields. These fields are described in details in A. Albinet, S. Begoc, J-L. Boulanger and al. (2008). We call the new stereotype called MeMVaTEx Requirement (see figure 7, right).

Modeling and Traceability

This phase consists of selecting requirements from an upper level and links it to one or many requirements from the lower levels using one of four stereotypes defined above. Doing that correctly guarantees the bidirectional traceability from requirement to design and code. We show an example of requirement modeling from the Vehicle level to design level in figure 8. Requirements are classified by EAST-ADL~2 levels. In the diagram, the requirements traceability from Vehicle Level to Design Level is shown: AL-F-12

Figure 7. The SysML Requirement stereotype (left) and MeMVaTEx Requirement stereotype (right)

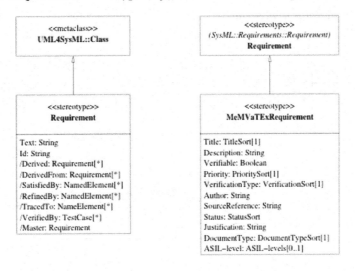

Figure 8. Requirement modeling in reference to EAST-ADL levels -- screenshot from ARTiSAN Studio

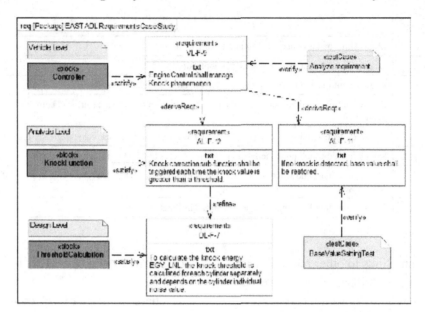

is a functional requirement at the Analysis Level. It is derived from the requirement VL-F-9 at Vehicle Level, and then refined to DL-F-7 at Design Level. The three requirements are respectively satisfied by KnockCorrection, EngineControl, and ThresholdCalculation blocks.

The basic design of KnockFunction block is sketched in a Block Definition Diagram in the figure 9. It show blocks involved and its item flows. Each block in the KnockFunction can be detailed by using Internal Diagram Block (IBD).

Verification and Validation

The V&V is an important phase in software development. V&V activities concern two aspects:

- Verification of the realization, i.e. did we build the product right? It is the analysis of the works that have been done, generally

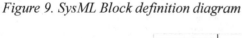

Figure 9. SysML Block definition diagram

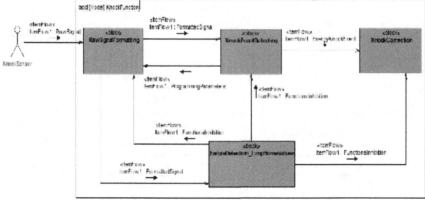

document analysis, code inspection and review, unit and integration testing.

- Validation of the application, i.e. did we build the right product? This is a test phase whose objective is to show that intended services are fulfilled. This test phase is realized on the product.

In MeMVaTEx project, it is needed that V&V activities must link to and test each requirement as requested by safety regulations. We show a test case, represented by an activity diagram in the figure 10, planned for the requirement like DL-NF-1 ``The capture must end when the Knock Acquisition Window Duration has elapsed ''. In this case, the internal structure of the capturing block and how it works may be known by the tester. This kind of test is called white-box testing.

There are also functional requirements such as AL-F-10 ``Knock control function shall know the piston position in order to measure and correct the knock on the right cylinder.'' In this case, tester may have no knowledge of the internal structure

of the knock control block. This kind of test is known as black-box testing. Input data is sent to the structure and the output is compared to expected output, giving the verdict. This test can be resumed in the figure 11.

Framework Tools

Tools are listed in refer to the V-model (cf. figure 12). On the left branch, requirement management (RM) tools like DOORS, RequisitePro, or TNI Reqtify are used in projects with large number of requirement. They have the capacities of managing and tracing requirement and support team's corporation.

Major modeling tools such as Telelogic Rhapsody Rhapsody, IBM Rational, or ARTiSAN Studio support UML/SysML and have the capacities to import specific profiles. It can also export models into an interchangeable format.

Simulink is a prime tool at the implementation level. Simulink gives the most details descriptions of a functional block. Simulink and its tool suite

Figure 10. A test case realized with an activity diagram

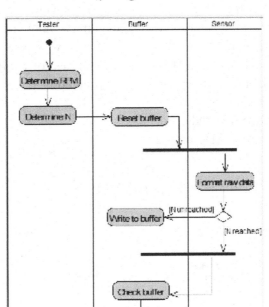

Figure 11. A test case realized with a sequence diagram

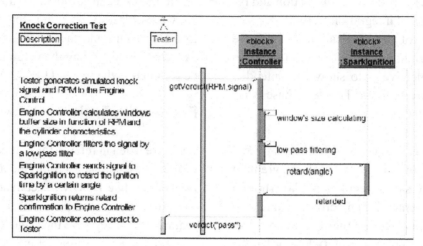

can generate code and test cases, and verify the design by simulation.

On the right branch, the validation can be reinforced by running software on simulator (software-in-the-loop, SIL) or by injecting code on dedicated hardware then running simulation (hardware-in-the-loop, HIL) see for example dSPACE (2007). Finally, a prototype testing validates the product. The validation is enterprise and proprietary solution.

In the MeMVaTEx project, there are about many hundreds requirements for the knock controller. It can be managed using only Office applications like Word and Excel. The use of RM like Reqtify or DOORS is planned for future use when the number of requirements is big enough.

Modeling is done using ARTiSAN Studio. For particular purpose, we need EAST-ADL profile and MARTE (2007), another UML profile for real-time modeling. These profiles are imported into ARTiSAN Studio. ARTiSAN can connect to RM tools to import requirements from or export traceability or requirement tables as seen in Table 2.

At implementation level, ARTiSAN introduces an integration with Simulink models that will give systems engineers the ability to define and simulate function block diagrams in Simulink and export them into a SysML model in ARTiSAN for ongoing development and maintenance.

For now, test cases are generated manually and the use of many validation tools is under consideration.

Figure 12. Tools accompanying the methodology represented in V-model

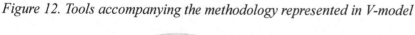

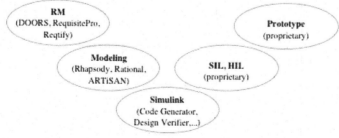

Table 2. The requirement table corresponding to the model in the figure 7

Name	Txt	Derived	Derived From	Refines	Refined By	Satisfied By	Verified By
VL-F-9	Engine Control shall manage Knock phenomenon.		«requirement» AL-F-12 (Requirements::AL) «requirement» AL-F-11 (Requirements::AL)			«block» Controller (Requirements)	«Use Case» Analyze requirement (Requirements)
AL-F-11	If no knock is detected, base value shall be restored.	«requirement» VL-F-9 (Requirements::VL)					«Activity Diagram» BaseValueSettingTest (Requirements) «Operation» BaseValueSetting (Testing::BaseValueSetting)
AL-F-12	Knock correction subfunction shall be triggered each time the knock value is greater than a threshold.	«requirement» VL-F-9 (Requirements::VL)		«requirement» DL-F-7 (Requirements::DL)		«block» KnockFunction (Requirements)	
DL-F-7	To calculate the knock energy EGY_LNL, the knock threshold is calculated for each cylinder separately and depends on the cylinder individual noise value.				«requirement» AL-F-12 (Requirements::AL)	«block» ThresholdCalculation (Requirements)	

CONCLUSION

Actual context in developing software for embedded electronics raises challenges of managing the complexity of software while still guaranteeing the quality and productivity. Automotive industry introduces many standards as a base from which automotive actors will compete on implementing software using proper process and methodology. This paper presents requirements engineering in a model-based methodology proposed by the project MeMVaTEx. in order facilitate the requirements validation and traceability. The methodology is structured by EAST-ADL abstraction levels and benefits from the systems modeling SysML. By a case study, we show the engineering of requirement through different phases and suggest tools for each phase.

Software using these standards is planned to be implemented in real car from 2010 see J. Sandberg (2006). Processes and tools for software may change or emerge by then. MeMVaTEx methodology is not definitive but open for changes and evolution before a seamless solution is reached.

REFERENCES

Albinet, A., Begoc, S., Boulanger, J.-L., et al. (2008). The MeMVaTEx methodology: from requirements to models in automotive application design. In *Proc. Embedded Real-Time Software*, January 2008.

Albinet, A., Boulanger, J.-L., Dubois, H., et al. (2007). Model-based methodology for requirements traceability in embedded systems. In *Proc. ECMDA*, June 2007.

Alexander, I. F., & Stevens, R. (2002). *Writing Better Requirements*. Reading, MA: Addison-Wesley.

André, C., Malet, F., & Peraldi-Frati, M.-A. (2007). A multiform time approach to real-time system modeling: Application to an automotive system. In *Proc. IEEE Industrial Embedded Systems, July 2007*.

ATESST. (2008). *Advancing traffic efficiency and safety through software technology*. European Commission [Online]. Retrieved from www.atesst.org

Balmelli, L. (2006). *An overview of the systems modeling language for products and systems development*. Tech. Rep., IBM, February 2006.

Bortolazzi, J. (2004). *Challenges in automotive software engineering*. Presented at International ICSE workshop on Software Engineering for Automotive Systems.

Boulanger, J.-L., & Van, Q.-D. (2007). A requirement-based methodology for automotive software development. In *Proc. MCSE,* July 2007.

Boulanger, J.-L., & Van, Q.-D. (2008). Experiences from a model-based methodology for developing embedded electronic software in automobile. In *Proc. ICTTA, April 2008*.

Cuenot, P., Chen, D., Gérard, S., et al. (2007). *Towards Improving Dependability of Automotive System by Using the EAST-ADL Architecture Description Language* (LNCS, vol. 4615, no. 200). Berlin: Springer.

dSPACE (2007). *ECU testing with hardware-in-the-loop simulation*.

EAST-ADL (2004). Electronic Architecture and Software Tools - Architecture Description Language. *Embedded Electronic Architecture Std. 1.02*, June.

Gumbrich, S. (2004). Embedded systems overhaul: It's time to tune up for the future of the automotive industry. *IBM Business Consulting Services,* (December).

IEC 61508 (2000). Functional safety of electrical/electronic/programmable electronic safety-related systems. *International Electrotechnical Commission Std. 61508.*

Marte (2007). Modeling and Analysis of Real-time and Embedded systems. *OMG Std. Final Adopted Specification, August.*

MeMVaTEx. (2008). Méthode de modélisation pour la validation et la traçabilité des exigences. *Continental AG and ANR.* [Online]. Retrieved from www.memvatex.org.

Sandberg, J. (2006). *AUTOSAR today: A roadmap to an autosar implementation.* Master's thesis, Chalmers University of Technology, Sweden.

Siemens (2006). *Introduction to future ISO 26262.* Siemens VDO internal presentation.

SysML (2006). The Systems Modeling Language}. *OMG Std. Final Adopted Specification, May.*

UML (2007). Unified Modeling Language. *OMG Std. Final Adopted Specification, February.*

Zadnik, M., Vincent, F., Vingerhoeds, R., et al. (2007). SI engine knock detection method robust to resonance frequency changes. In *International Conference on Engines for Automobiles*, September 2007.

ENDNOTES

[1]   http://www.itea-office.org
[2]   http://www.autosar.org
[3]   http://www.atesst.org

Chapter 3
Agile Software Engineering

Ernest Mnkandla
University of Johannesburg, South Africa

ABSTRACT

This chapter aims to reveal agile techniques that have been applied to software development and have resulted in meaningful improvements in software productivity. Available literature generally state some claims on the gains associated with the use of particular agile methodologies in software development. What lacks however, is a comprehensive analysis of how the application of agile techniques as a family will lead to improvement in software productivity. This chapter therefore provides such details. Software productivity techniques provide ways of measuring three things in order to determine the productivity of software; software products, software production processes and structures, and software production setting. Agile methodologies improve software productivity by focusing on the software production process and structures. The fundamental concern of this chapter is to show that agile methodologies measure the production process activities in a different but effective way from the more traditional approaches. For example, time-to-market is reduced by use of an iterative incremental development approach.

INTRODUCTION

It may seem a little mischievous to use the term `agile software engineering` in this context or any other context for that matter, but it has been used in this chapter simply to emphasize the values that an agile perspective to software development and software engineering has added to the entire discipline of software engineering. Agile software engineering can be defined as the streamlined production of software systems with a focus on a quality end product, relevant customer requirements, and following a minimalist approach to the process density.

There is still a high level of skepticism about the benefits of agile software development methodologies especially in organizations or individuals that have not applied these methods or seen

DOI: 10.4018/978-1-60566-731-7.ch003

them in use. However, it should be made clear that there is published evidence of the benefits of developing software the agile way in sources such as (Abrahamsson et al, 2002; Beck, 1999; Beck and Andres, 2004; Boehm and Turner, 2004; Cockburn, 2000; Lindvall et al, 2002; Collins-Cope, 2002; Fowler, 2000; Highsmith, (2001); Highsmith, 2002b; Highsmith, 2004; Turk et al, 2002). Nevertheless it is important that we continue to publish empirical evidence of the successful application of agile methodologies. In general there is a constant growth in scholarly publications such as books, journals, conference proceedings, white papers and other experience reports that continue to validate the relevance of agile development.

This chapter provides a detailed analysis of how software productivity is achieved through the use of different agile processes.

Software productivity like other agile development concepts and practices such as software quality assurance, iterative incremental development, inclusion of the customer in the development team, pair programming (from Extreme Programming -XP) et cetera is clouded with controversy as to how it is measured in agile processes and whether the metrics used in such efforts prove agile to be productive. In business, people always talk about the bottom line i.e. ROI, it is almost synonymous to what is stated in the 'good old book', after 'the Wiseman' has advised on almost all issues of life and humanity he gives 'the conclusion of the whole matter' which in essence summarises the purpose of all humanity. The conclusion of the whole matter in software development is that 'our investment should yield working code and a return on our investment' else we labour in vain.

Agile development is about doing software development rather than talking about it, and those who have applied agile methods in their software development projects have gained margins that are hard to ignore in the areas of product relevance (a result of embracing requirements instability) and quick delivery (a result of

iterative incremental development) (Mnkandla, and Dwolatzky, 2007). There is also evidence of unequalled financial savings on project costs (Highsmith, 2002b). Those who have not yet joined this new fun way to develop software probably due to a lack of understanding of the fundamental concepts underlying agile methodologies, or mere unwillingness to face the winds of change have been left out of the frenzy (Mnkandla and Dwolatzky, 2004a). Hence this chapter intends to give the necessary understanding by defining agile methodologies and revealing how the use of agile methodologies leads to improvement in software productivity. The metrics and techniques used to measure software productivity in agile development will also be reviewed.

Chapter Objectives

The objective of this chapter is to introduce you to the fundamentals of measuring software productivity in agile software development methodologies in order to unravel the real benefits of agile development. After reading this chapter you will have better understanding of:

- What agile development means in terms of software productivity
- The major difference between agile development and the other approaches
- The agile techniques that will improve software productivity
- The empirical evidence of improved software productivity in agile development

BACKGROUND

This section will start by defining agile methodologies based on the existing definitions and practices on agile methodologies. Software productivity will also be briefly defined. The theory of agile development will also be explained in order to reveal the underlying philosophy that is in fact based on improving software productivity.

What is Agile Development?

The most precise definition of agile software development methodologies can be obtained by summarising the detailed and comprehensive definition given by Mnkandla (2006), and Mnkandla and Dwolatzky (2007) where agile methodologies are defined theoretically, functionally, and contextually. Agile methodologies can thus be defined as:

The development of a system in parts as inspired by the customer and the continuous integration of these parts following planned repeated modifications while the development team and techniques emerge into a formidable winning system through the use of simple concepts such as flexibility, simplicity, trust, and choosing a minimal-overhead route that will lead to working code.

Success in agile development depends on several issues, but the most important ones are:

- The developer organization's willingness to adopt agile development and remain agile with the blessings of top management, it could be called 'the agile barometer'.
- Working with a team leader who values agile development and is able to inspire the team to observe and respect agile values and principles.
- Forming a development team of individuals who are willing to: follow the agile approach, passionately develop applications, respect each other, learn new things, and work hard to deliver according to their commitment.
- Accountability, trustworthiness, and effective communication.
- Giving the customer's requirements precedence over developer aesthetics.

What is Software Productivity?

Software productivity can be considered to be the law of software development. You see, the law is like a mirror, the law does not decide a way of life for anyone, neither does it correct anyone's wrong actions, the law simply shows you what you have done wrong and spells out the penalty thereof. More like what a mirror does, it will not clean your muddy face nor tell you to go and wash your face, it simply shows clearly how dirty your face is. Now think of software development without concern for software productivity; that would be similar living without concern for the laws of nature. It means we would develop software and use it without any concern of its effective use, its efficient use, and its return on our investments. So then software productivity is a law that governs the efficiency of the output of our software development efforts.

Scacchi (1995) believes that how much productivity you see in software is determined by what you measure and how you measure it. There are two categories of factors that affect the variance in software productivity; product related factors, and process related factors, and they contribute a large percentage (Scacchi, 1995). Therefore if we are to improve software productivity meaningfully we need to focus on these two. To improve on both the process and the product related factors focus should be on improving each of the phases of the software production process commonly known as the software development life cycle. Brynjolfsson (1993) advocates the improvement of software productivity through the reduction of the product costs and indirect costs. This means streamlining the processes and increasing revenue to add more value to the product. In agile development this is called eliminating the waste (Poppendeick and Poppendeick, 2003). In this case waste means anything that does not add value to the final product.

Agile Development and Software Productivity

The philosophy of agile development is ingrained in a desire to develop quality working software without incurring much overhead. Therefore all the values, principles, and practices that define agility are focussed on improving software productivity by ensuring that only the necessary work is done (efficiency), only the relevant product is delivered (quality), all the changes in customer requirements are welcomed, and the development team uses the process not the other way round. So at the heart of these specialised techniques for developing software is the desire not only to improve productivity but to also improve quality of both the development process and the product. In agile development the process is not that thing that the organization has somewhere in its archives and that nobody is using, but it is the actual, current, and practical way of developing software at any given time in the organization.

The rest of the sections will go into the details of how agile development meets the requirements of software productivity.

HOW AGILE DEVELOPMENT IMPROVES SOFTWARE PRODUCTIVITY

This section discusses in detail how agile values, principles and practices lead to software process improvement.

In the Agile Manifesto (Agile Alliance, 2001) the members of the Agile Alliance say their aim is to develop better software (in other words productive software) while helping other to do likewise. The manifesto then goes on to list the four values of agility as follows (Agile Alliance, 2001):"Individuals and interactions **over processes and tools**Working software** over comprehensive documentation**Customer collaboration** over contract negotiation**Responding to change** over

following a planThat is, while there is value in the items on the right, we value the items on the left more"

These values and principles were derived from what these experienced practitioners found to be their practice which differed from what their documented methodologies were stipulating. Agile methodologies were therefore born out of best practice and not from unfounded theoretical imaginations. The agile values are implemented or represented through a set of the following agile principles (Agile Alliance, 2001):"

1. Our highest priority is to satisfy the customer through early and continuous delivery of valuable software.

2. Welcome changing requirements, even late in development. Agile processes harness change for the customer's competitive advantage.

3. Deliver working software frequently, from a couple of weeks to a couple of months, with a preference to the shorter timescale.

4. Business people and developers must work together daily throughout the project.

5. Build projects around motivated individuals. Give them the environment and support they need, and trust them to get the job done.

6. The most efficient and effective method of conveying information to and within a development team is face-to-face conversation.

7. Working software is the primary measure of progress.

8. Agile processes promote sustainable development. The sponsors, developers, and users should be able to maintain a constant pace indefinitely.

9. Continuous attention to technical excellence and good design enhances agility.

10. Simplicity--the art of maximizing the amount of work not done--is essential.

11. The best architectures, requirements, and designs emerge from self-organizing teams.

12. At regular intervals, the team reflects on how to become more effective, then tunes and adjusts its behaviour accordingly"

Then each of the many and ever growing number of agile methodologies such as Extreme Programming, Scrum, Lean development, Crystal, Agile Modeling, Catalyst to name but a few, observe certain agile practices that are an implementation of these generic guidelines or principles and the four values.

Improving Productivity through Valuing Individuals and Interactions

Giving hints on how to improve software productivity Scacchi (1995) lists a number of possible actions that include "getting the best out of well-managed people". That is more of a soft skills issue than a technical one. We all wish we could get the best out of everyone that we live with, work with, or even from those we socialize with. In agile development soft skills are very important. The IT industry has learnt over the relatively few years of its existence that the technical issues do not usually lead to project failure but the failure to handle people issues usually leads to project failure. Therefore, in agile development the individuals who constitute the development team are valued more than the processes that guide their work. Anything that affects the wellbeing of any team member has to be solved with urgency in order to get the best from the people.

Looking at the agile principles listed above we find that the fifth principle "Build projects around motivated individuals. Give them the environment and support they need, and trust them to get the job done" provides basic guidelines on what a project manager (or facilitator as they are often called in agile development) should do in order to have an effective team. The project manager should devise ways of motivating the team members around the values and priorities of the project. The project manager should also

create a good (conducive to innovation) environment for the team. In agile development there are different techniques and practices for ensuring a good environment such as stand-up meetings in XP and daily scrum in Scrum which are used to provide opportunity for feedback, accountability, face-to-face communication, innovation, and identification of problems that may negatively affect the flow of project activities.

The twelfth principle "At regular intervals, the team reflects on how to become more effective, then tunes and adjusts its behaviour accordingly" focuses on the need for the team members to improve software productivity by identifying and concentrating on effective team behaviour. Sometimes team members can behave in an unbecoming manner despite having signed a team contract, hence in agile development there is more value in conducting regular meetings to tune and adjust the team's behaviour rather than depending solely on a team contract. In fact in agile development it is best for teams to be allowed to organize themselves the best way they find feasible as this will lead to the emergence of a good architecture and design, and also effective team work. Principle number eleven also emphasises this point.

Improving Productivity through Valuing Working Software

Software development is known for its piles and piles of documents from the planning documents to requirements and specification documents, to functional manuals and user manuals et cetera, and programmers hate preparing such documents. As software development techniques and tools improved over the years the need for some of these documents decreased and they simply ended up on organization shelves gathering dust. The cost of preparing these documents is considered to be part of the cost of a software development project. One of the possible actions listed by Scacchi (1995) for improving software productivity is "to make development steps more efficient and more effective". In agile development the practitioners found that software productivity could be improved greatly by reducing the effort put on documentation or even eliminating the unnecessary ones and replacing them with working code, which is in fact the real reason for a software development project. We may have wonderful documentation but if we have no working code then the productivity rate is zero. Agile development does not say that documentation is unnecessary but just that it is less valuable than working code and therefore developers should focus on the most valuable part.

Agile principle number one and principle number three emphasize the value of working software. Agile development values the delivery of working software to the customer in accordance with the scheduled iterations. What it means is that the customer can start using the software before the final product is delivered. This certainly improves software productivity.

Improving Productivity through Valuing Customer Collaboration

Customer collaboration is one of the most controversial values of agile development. In any software development project the customer will always be included in one way or the other. It is an agreed fact that the customer calls the shots in any successful business. The unique thing about agile customer collaboration is the way it is done. In agile development the customer does not only provide the problem or requirements; the customer becomes part of the development team and literally sits with the people doing the work to provide all the necessary information about the set of stories being developed during each iteration. Some people feel that since the customer has left his/her normal duties in the organization to work with developers it becomes a cost to the organization. If the project is properly planned for, the resources that are required for the project would be clearly documented and considering that

the inclusion of the customer in the development team adds value and quality to the product, it is a necessary move, an investment not an expense. At the heart of agile development is satisfying the customer. In the more traditional methodologies that are heavy on documentation the customer is satisfied mainly by the documents and less by the product since the product would not effectively include the changing requirements. In agile development the customer becomes part of the development team in order to ensure that the product's relevance is constantly guided towards what the customer requires.

Agile principle number four emphasizes the importance of collaboration between the business people and the developers. This perspective to software development ensures that the developers continue to work towards a product that remains relevant to the customer until the day it is delivered and the project closed. Quality is the delivery of a product that meets the customer's requirements, hence agile development delivers quality software. This is a great improvement in software productivity especially considering that software development organizations have a tendency to deliver very 'good' products that have long been overtaken by fast changing business requirements, which results in unsatisfied customers and unproductive software.

Improving Productivity through Valuing Response to Change

Allowing the changing requirements to continuously feed into the work can lead to scope creep. That is the main excuse that most developers give for fixing requirements and delivering an irrelevant product. In agile development the rationale is to add value to the changing requirements and give the customer a lead over competition by delivering the most relevant product in the market at that point. Controlling scope creep in such an environment becomes a skill that the project manager must have. Agile developers deal with this problem through the use of simplicity; choosing the simplest things that can be done that lead to a relevant product, and selecting and committing to what is possible for each iteration. In essence agile developers manage scope creep by time-boxing a selection of user stories that can be completed in a given iteration. Agile principle number two emphasizes the idea of giving the customer competitive advantage by allowing changes in the requirements up to the last moments of development. Most opponents to agile development would not like the idea of allowing changes in such a manner because it is hard work. But who said developing a relevant quality product was easy? It is a discipline that requires discipleship about your profession. If you find it too much then you are probably in the wrong profession. It is like a structural engineer working through pages and pages of formulas in order to design a robust bridge. To a historian who analyses political situations and presents forecasts on the next political ill of the world, the engineer's formulas would really be for the 'crazy'.

To conclude this section, agile development in all its underlying philosophies, values, principles and practices is grounded on the deep need to develop better quality software, faster, efficiently, effectively and to the satisfaction of the customer. If this is not an improvement in software productivity then nothing is.

THE FUTURE TRENDS IN AGILE DEVELOPMENT

The techniques that agile development utilises are not necessarily peculiar to agile methodologies but have been used and are still being used by others under different names and themes. What makes agile different is:

- The combination of the techniques.
- The courage to take these techniques to extremes but with discipline.

This makes agile development an aggressive approach, which can only be adopted by those who are driven by innovation and are keen to change their past and lead the future.

The future of agile development from the perspective of software productivity is moving more towards the adoption of agile development in:

- Outsourced environments.
- ERP development.
- Distributed teams.
- Large software development houses that traditionally used heavier processes.

Traditional PMI type of projects where people are realising bit by bit that agile methodologies are a group of methodologies that can work well with the more general project management framework.

The future of agile development as given by Mnkandla and Dwolatzky (2007) still remains interesting as more evidence on agile adoption and consideration permeates the IT world in professional groups such PMI.

"Agile methodologies are certainly moving towards higher levels of maturity due to a number of things. The first contribution to agile maturity is the availability of comprehensive sources of simple descriptive and analytical information about agile methodologies. The second contribution to agile maturity is the growth in academic research interest in agility which has resulted in a lot of empirical data being collected and scientifically analyzed to prove and disprove anecdotal data about agile processes. The third contribution to agile maturity is a result of the massive exchange of practical experiences amongst the different practitioners involved in agile software development" (Mnkandla and Dwolatzky, 2007).

CONCLUSION

This chapter revealed agile techniques that have been applied to software development and have resulted in meaningful improvements in software productivity. The chapter explained in detail the philosophy behind agile development and covered the agile values and principles in order to reveal the fundamental concepts of software productivity improvement that form the root of agile development. As the adoption of agile methodologies continues to rise it has become clear that some select a few of what they consider good principles and practices of agility. While that may result in certain levels of improvement in software productivity, the real benefits of agility come from the unique combination of agile practices that are enjoyed by those applying agility in its entirety.

REFERENCES

Abrahamsson, P., Salo, O., Ronkainen, J., & Warsta, J. (2002). Agile Software Development Methods: Review and Analysis. *VVT Publications, 478*, 7–94.

Agile Alliance. (2001). *Manifesto for Agile Software Development.* Retrieved May 02 2008 from http://www.agilemanifesto.org.

Beck, K. (1999). *Extreme Programming Explained: Embrace Change* (pp. 10-70). Reading MA: Addison-Wesley.

Beck, K., & Andres, C. (2004). *Extreme Programming Explained: Embrace Change.* Reading, MA: Addison-Wesley Professional.

Boehm, B., & Turner, R. (2004). *Balancing Agility and Discipline: A guide for the perplexed* (1st ed. pp. 165-194). Reading, MA: Addison-Wesley.

Brandt, I. (1983). A Comparative Study of Information Systems Development Methodologies: Proceedings of the IFIP WG8.1 Working Conference on Feature Analysis of Information Systems Design Methodologies. In T.W. Olle, H.G. Sol, & C.J. Tully, (eds.) *Information Systems Design Methodologies: A Feature Analysis* (pp. 9-36). Amsterdam: Elsevier.

Brynjolfsson, E. (1993). The Productivity Paradox of Information Technology. *Communications of the ACM, 36*(12), 66–77. doi:10.1145/163298.163309

Cockburn, A. (2000). Selecting a Project's Methodology. In *IEEE Software*, (pp. 64-71).

Collins-Cope, M. (2002). *Planning to be Agile? A discussion of how to plan agile, iterative and incremental developments* [white paper]. Ratio Technical Library. Retrieved July 20, 2008 from http://www.ratio.co.uk/whitepaper_12.pdf

Fowler, M. (2000). Put Your Process on a Diet. *Software Development, 8*(12), 32–36.

Fowler, M. (2002). The Agile Manifesto: where it came from and where it may go. *Martin Fowler articles.* Retrieved May 26 2008 from http://martinfowler.com/articles/agileStory.html.

Highsmith, J. (2001). The Great Methodologies Debate: Part 1: Today, a new debate rages: agile software development versus rigorous software development. *Cutter IT Journal, 14*(12), 2–4.

Highsmith, J. (2002a). Agile Software Development: why it is hot! *Cutter Consortium white paper, Information Architects, Inc,* (pp. 1-22).

Highsmith, J. (2002b). *Agile Software Development Ecosystems* (pp. 1-50). Reading, MA: Addison-Wesley.

Highsmith, J. (2004). *Agile Project Management.* Reading, MA: Addison-Wesley.

Lindvall, M., Basili, V. R., Boehm, B., Costa, P., Dangle, K., Shull, F., et al. (2002). Empirical Findings in agile Methods. *Proceedings of Extreme Programming and agile Methods - XP/agile Universe*, (pp. 197-207).

Mnkandla, E. (2008). *A Selection Framework for Agile Methodology Practices: A Family of Methodologies Approach.* Doctoral Thesis, University of the Witwatersrand, Johannesburg, South Africa.

Mnkandla, E., & Dwolatzky, B. (2004a). Balancing the Human and the Engineering Factors in Software Development. *Proceedings of the IEEE AFRICON 2004 Conference*, (pp. 1207-1210).

Mnkandla, E., & Dwolatzky, B. (2004b). A Survey of agile Methodologies. *Transactions of the South Africa Institute of Electrical Engineers, 95*(4), 236–247.

Mnkandla, E., & Dwolatzky, B. (2007). Agile Software Methods: State-Of-The-Art. In I. Stamelos, and P. Sfetsos, (Ed.) *Agile Software Development Quality Assurance* (pp. 1-22). Hershey, PA: Information Science Publishing.

Poppendeick, M., & Poppendeick, T. (2003). *Lean Software Development: An Agile Toolkit for Software Development Managers* (pp. xxi–xxviii). Reading MA: Addison Wesley.

Pressman, R. S. (2001). *Software Engineering a Practitioner's Approach.* New York: Mcgraw-Hill.

Scacchi, W. (1995). Understanding and Improving Software Productivity. In D. Hurley (ed.), *Advances in Software Engineering and Knowledge Engineering*, (Vol. 4, pp. 37-70).

Schuh, P. (2004). *Integrating Agile Development in the Real World,* (pp. 1-6). Boston: Charles River Media.

Schwaber, K. (2004). *Agile project management with Scrum.* Redmond, CA: Microsoft Press.

Schwaber, K., & Beedle, M. (2002). *Agile Software Development with SCRUM* (pp. 23-30). Upper Saddle River, NJ: Prentice-Hall.

Turk, D., France, R., & Rumpe, B. (2002). Limitations of Agile Software Processes. In *Proceedings of the Third International Conference on eXtreme Programming and Agile Processes in Software Engineering*, (pp. 43-46).

KEY TERMS AND DEFINITIONS

Agile Methodologies: The development of a system in parts as inspired by the customer and the continuous integration of these parts following planned repeated modifications while the development team and techniques emerge into a formidable winning system through the use of simple concepts such as flexibility, simplicity, trust, and choosing a minimal-overhead route that will lead to working code.

Agile Values: The four fundamental concepts (preferred by agile developers) underlying the development of software and the process to be followed.

Agile Principles: The twelve generic guidelines that provide the course of action in the life of agile practitioners.

Agile Practices: The more specific activities that are provide practical implementation of the agile principles.

Agile Software Engineering: The streamlined production of software systems with a focus on: a quality end product, relevant customer requirements, and following a minimalist approach to the process density.

Software Productivity: Software productivity is a law that governs the efficiency of the output of the software development effort.

Software Quality: ISO 9000 defines quality as the totality of characteristics of an entity that bear on its ability to satisfy stated or implied needs. Where 'stated needs' means those needs that are specified as requirements by the customer in a contract, and 'implied needs' are those needs that are identified and defined by the company providing the product.

Chapter 4
Putting a TAG on Software
Purchaser–Centered Software Engineering

Mike Barker
Nara Institute of Science and Technology, Japan

Kenichi Matsumoto
Nara Institute of Science and Technology, Japan

Katsuro Inoue
Osaka University, Japan

ABSTRACT

This chapter describes the evolution of approaches to empirical software engineering from goal and data-driven to the latest purchaser-centered approach. The new Japanese Software Traceability and Accountability for Global software Engineering (StagE) project is developing this approach to ensure the transparency of software development processes and products for software purchasers by "tagging" software with empirical software development data. Global software development raises unprecedented difficulties for developers, including the international and intercorporate coordination of development and distribution, the change to composition as the primary development approach, the shift to software everywhere talking to everything, and continuing upgrades and interaction with released software. To work effectively in this environment, empirical data collection, analysis, and feedback must extend throughout the software lifecycle including both production and usage data.

INTRODUCTION

What would you think if you bought a car, and when there was a problem with it, the mechanics said they didn't know how it was put together, so they couldn't fix it? You'd tell them to get the manual, wouldn't you? And wonder just what kind of mechanics they are.

But when software doesn't work right, all too often the development information is long gone. The developers are on other projects, and the development documents are not available. No one knows exactly how it was configured, or what the usage environment has been. So crashes are shrugged off or ignored, because there's no way to look back. Or is there?

DOI: 10.4018/978-1-60566-731-7.ch004

This is the problem that the StagE project addresses. How can we collect data during the software lifecycle and then keep track of it so that we can trace root causes of errors?

This chapter discusses the issues that lead to the StagE project, which is currently investigating the use of software tags as a way to collect data, especially during development, which provides transparency, and then maintain the connection between the software products and the data during the software lifecycle, creating traceability. The chapter gives a brief background on empirical software engineering, then describes the purchaser-centered approach that software tagging supports. It then looks at how widespread use of such software tags might affect the software development process, especially in the global context. This chapter is a report on a work in progress, so while it outlines problems and the proposed approach of using software tags to provide purchasers with additional visibility into development processes and traceability across lifecycle and development boundaries, it does not report on the success of such use. You, the readers, will be the developers and purchasers who determine whether software tags are used, and how successful they are.

BACKGROUND

Top-Down, Bottom-Up, or Sideways: Getting the Data Right or Getting the Right Data?

One of the key questions in empirical software engineering is exactly what data do you want to collect. Empirical software engineering has used two basic approaches to decide what data to collect. The first, goal-driven metrics, typically starts with high-level goals or business directions and works down to specific data and metrics. One difficulty with this is that the data collection often is very specific to the environment and projects. The second approach has been to start

with automated data collection and work upward to develop abstractions and analyses. Perhaps the leading example of this is the Hackystat project, which provides a wide array of data collection tools and a platform to tie them together. (Johnson, 2008) One of the difficulties with this approach has been linking the low-level data to business goals and abstractions.

Goal-driven metrics and data-driven approaches have shown the abilities of empirical software engineering to improve the software process. However, the managers and developers often have different interests from the purchasers of the software, suggesting that changing the stakeholders driving the selection and use of the data can provide a more effective process for selection and application of empirical measurements. But before we look at that new approach, let's take a brief look at the older approaches.

The Conventional Approach to Empirical Software Engineering: Goal-Driven Metrics

Today, there are several national projects on empirical software engineering in Japan (EASE Project, 2007; SEC, 2008), Australia (NICTA, 2008), Germany (IESE, 2008), and the USA (Ce-BASE, 2004). We can find many research papers concerning empirical topics in major conferences in software engineering.

In most conventional projects and papers, only software developers use empirical data about software development to improve software quality and productivity. However, developers' needs for software quality and productivity are often too abstract to relate to the data collected in software projects. Models and techniques that derive the "data to be collected and analyzed" from the "goal to be achieved" play an important role. The GQM (Goal/Question/Metric) approach proposed by Prof. Basili, and Measurement Information Model defined in ISO/IEC 15939 may be helpful. In addition, real-time data collection, analysis, and feedback are also important. Postmortem analysis and feedback are not powerful enough to achieve various kinds of goals in software quality and productivity.

The EASE Project: A Data-Driven Approach

The EASE (Empirical Approach to Software Engineering) project is an example of such projects. The EASE project was started in April 2003 as part of the "e-Society" initiative, one of the leading projects of the Ministry of Education, Culture, Sports, Science and Technology, Japan. The project aimed to establish Empirical Software Engineering, a development approach based on scientific evidence, in the field of software development where there are many issues regarding reliability and productivity.

EASE has released EPM (Empirical Project Monitor) as open source software. EPM provides software project managers and developers with tool-based real-time data collection with negligible workload. In cooperation with Prof. Basili, the project has also applied the GQM approach to software projects of two cooperating enterprises. These activities can be considered as a Goal Driven Approach. To encourage a Data Driven Approach in empirical software engineering, EASE has also devised several data analysis techniques; "ranking engine of the components based on Component Rank method," "code clone analysis," and "data estimation with collaborative filtering."

MAIN FOCUS

The StagE Project: A Purchaser-Centered Approach

However, in the conventional approach, purchasers cannot see the empirical data to ensure the quality and productivity of software they ordered. Of course, most developers consider the productivity and quality of software they develop from the viewpoint of their purchaser and utilize empirical data to meet purchaser requirements and give satisfaction to him/her. However, there are limitations to such a vendor-centered approach in empirical software engineering; for example:

- If serious failure happens in software in use, the purchaser will not have objective data and evidence enough to investigate errors and faults of the failure and fix them and to develop a plan to prevent them in the future.
- In global outsourcing and offshore development of software, most software vendors purchase some parts of the software instead of developing it. Vendors cannot grasp or validate whether an appropriate procedure was used to develop such software parts.

In August 2007, NAIST and Osaka University started the StagE (Software Traceability and Accountability for Global software Engineering) project (StagE, 2008) as a collaborative project funded by the Ministry of Education, Culture, Sports, Science and Technology, Japan. Figure 1 shows an overview of StagE project, describing the relation among five research subthemes, products, and groups. This project aims to develop the following techniques:

- collecting empirical data from multi-vendor software development project,
- analyzing the empirical data, and
- attaching the analysis results as a "Software Tag" to the released software.

The software tag is an essential technology to promote software traceability and to establish a secure and safe IT society. By checking the tag, purchasers can grasp and validate that vendors used appropriate procedures to develop the software. Purchasers can refuse to use software if

Figure 1. An overview of the StagE project

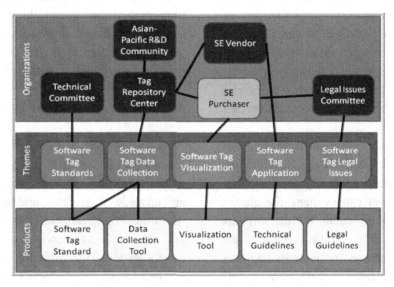

the tag shows vendors did not use an appropriate procedure to develop the software.

Figure 2 shows an overview of the concept of software tag. A software tag is a collection of empirical data and their abstracted data. It is mainly composed of "open tag" and "secret tag". The open tag contains the data directly presented to the software purchaser. The software purchaser can evaluate the data, and know the quality of the process and product. The secret tag mainly contains raw empirical data that is proprietary to the software developers. It may contain development secrets and/or know-how; therefore, the data is encrypted to maintain secrecy. The decryption key would be kept at the developer side until a controversy arises between the software purchaser and developer. The current standard proposes that the vendor and purchaser negotiate decisions about what data belongs in which part during the initial project discussions.

Figure 2. An overview of the software tag scheme

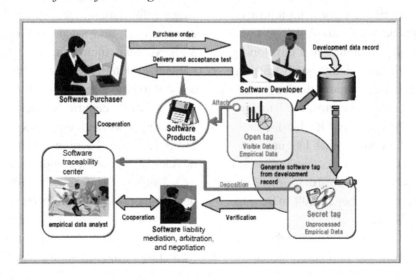

The software tag is a key vehicle to improve "visibility" and "transparency" of software project. This is very useful for both the software purchaser and the software developer, since it reassures the purchaser that they can "see" what happens during development (transparency) and trace the origins of problems back into the development process (traceability).

By using a software tag, the software purchaser can identify and understand the development process that currently is mostly a developers' secret. The purchaser can evaluate the quality of the processes and products. For the software developer, a software tag can prove their proper activities in the software project. In addition, software tags can identify and trace the quality of the activities of sub-contractors. This becomes especially important as software parts are developed through global subcontracting.

Standardizing software tags will help to improve trade custom of software development contract. Evaluation of the software products and project based on subjective empirical data in the software tag will lead the society more healthy way. The scheme is very useful for offshore and global development in the sense that the traceability and transparency of software development are established with fairly low overhead of the developers.

The StagE project is now defining the use cases and formats for the software tag and empirical data in more detail and rigor, with industrial participation from both software developers and purchasers. It is also designing and developing empirical data collection, analysis, abstraction, and repository tools to support this approach. The StagE project released a Japanese language standard for the software tag on October 14, 2008, with discussion of a draft English language version at the 2nd Workshop on Accountability and Traceability in Global Software Engineering (ATGSE2008) held December 2, 2008, in Beijing, China. (ATGSE, 2008)

The Purchaser-Centered approach in the StagE project will give software purchasers peace-of-mind by providing a practical way to select safe, high-quality software products based on a new standard for transparent software development. This high standard will increase the competitive power of participating software developers.

A Scenario or Two of Use

Although it is early in the StagE project, we envision scenarios such as these, concerning purchase of software systems, combination of components and upgrades to systems, and handling faults.

In the first scenario of purchase, a software purchaser orders a software system that includes a software tag. This tag is a unique identifier for information in a repository. The software developer can store empirical data during development in the repository, perhaps using company encryption to ensure the safety of proprietary information, and identifying some information as public, perhaps with public key signatures as evidence of who placed this information in the repository. The public information will include a standard format to make it easier for users to analyze this quality evidence. When the purchaser receives a software system, they can use the tag to check on the public information in the repository to verify that the desired development process and quality has been provided. If the purchaser accepts the product, they can also use the repository to store usage information, such as configuration data, error reports, and usage measurements. Figure 3 shows what such a tag and repository might contain, although the exact contents and formats are still to be determined.

A second scenario concerns combinations of components and upgrades to systems. For example, it has become common for software developers to obtain components from offshore or subsidiary vendors, who often protect their development data as proprietary. Using the tag and repository approach, the software developer purchasing components examines the public information in the repository just as in the simple

Figure 3. A tag and repository data

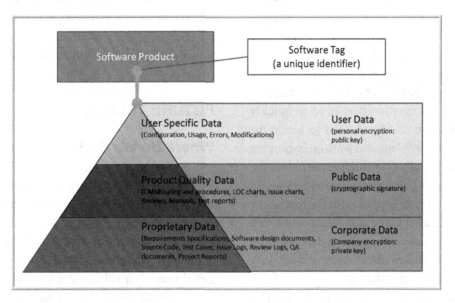

scenario already described. When they accept components and use them in their systems, the tags and information about the components becomes part of the system, so that a single product might have several tags and information chunks in the repository. Similarly, software products in real use often have upgrades and patches of various kinds, which would also have information kept in the repository. Figure 4 illustrates this aggregation of tags concept, although again the details of how this tracing will be performed is under development.

Essentially, it should be possible at any time for a user or other interested party to identify clearly the exact combination of components, upgrades, and so forth that a specific user system contains, allowing rapid and effective responses to problems and faults.

Third, in fact, is the scenario for dealing with faults. One of the most obvious problems when a fault occurs is simply finding the right documents and other information - which is exactly what the tag and repository provide. Right now, more

Figure 4. Software components and upgrades to a product

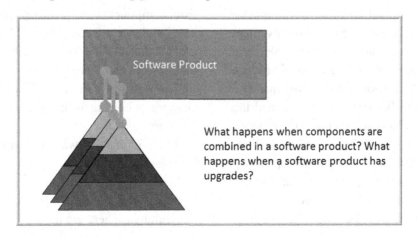

systems are being designed to report errors and receive updates online, which can be combined with the tag and repository system to provide a continuing "black box" for software systems. So with the software tag and repository, when a fault occurs, the company or even an independent expert has the information they need to quickly locate the problem and fix it - and to locate the root causes of the problem, and work on improving the process and products to eliminate or reduce the problem for others before they even experience it. Further, corporate analysis can use the repository to examine classes of faults and the processes that led to them, since the standardized data provides the ability to look across products and identify common trends and problems.

Although they are sketchy at this point, these kinds of scenarios indicate the impact that the StagE project expects a tag and repository system to have on purchasing and maintenance of software systems, a part of the lifecycle that is often estimated at 80% of the software cost. Making sure that purchasers have a reliable method of evaluating the quality of software products, and that there is good support for dealing with faults, provides the core of a purchaser-centered approach to empirical software engineering.

What about CMMI?

The Capability Maturity Model ® Integration (CMMI) often is seen as a major measure of quality especially in global software development. However, CMMI focuses on process improvement across the 22 process areas. It is possible for a company to have a good rating and still produce end products that are not of the desired quality.

StagE explicitly links the end products with the work products and measurements of the process. In fact, while the CMMI rating and procedures may be a part of the information in the repository, StagE focuses on how this product was developed. Rather than a measure of the general corporate capabilities, this is a measure of how the processes

were applied and a specific product developed. In a sense, CMMI tells you how well a company should be able to do their work. StagE tells you how well they did the work on a specific product.

FUTURE TRENDS

Where Do We Go From Here?

The era of global software development demands that we deal with many differences to develop effective, efficient software processes. This chapter points to several major ones such as the boundary-crossing nature of modern global software development, a shift to composition as a major development method, the change to ubiquitous networked software, and shifting models of deployment and support. In response to this tsunami of change, software engineering needs to support empirical data collection, analysis, and feedback throughout the software life cycle.

Barry Boehm lists 10 key trends that systems and software engineering face in the near future. Global software development must respond to the first eight trends. Interweaving software with systems engineering is commonplace, with software a consumer commodity focusing on end-user value. As a commodity in daily use, dependability is necessary, despite the growing rate of change. The new environment for software engineering consists of interoperable systems of systems built from components and pieces glued together with an abundance of computational resources and global connectivity. (Boehm, 2006) As the era of global software development sweeps us into the future, we must carefully consider some of the changes occurring in the perpetual whitewater that surrounds us.

First, global software development crosses boundaries. For example, global software development typically involves multiple companies with varying relationships, multiple nations, and cultures. There are multiple legal, financial, and development environments involved. A key problem for global software development is that social mechanisms that coordinate work in a co-located setting do not work effectively in a distributed project. Communications breakdowns, lack of awareness, and incompatibilities result in a number of problems. (Herbsleb, 2007)

Second, modern software development is more a matter of selection and composition than greenfield or "from the ground up" development. The widespread use of development environments with a range of libraries, clones, patterns, COTS applications and services, and public domain software means that the software products are composed of a mixture of elements from various sources. We are just starting to learn how to develop such software and what approaches work in this field.

Third, this is the era of ubiquitous, networked software. Games, televisions, DVD players and recorders, refrigerators, washing machines, cell phones - most consumer items now have computers with large amounts of software in them. Car manufacturers often only have black-box specifications of subsystems, and find it difficult or impossible to find errors or modify the subsystems. (Pretschner, Broy, Kruger, and Stauner, 2007) With bluetooth and similar protocols becoming widespread, all of these different systems will be talking to each other.

Fourth, the models of release, deployment, and upgrades are shifting. The shift toward relatively continuous online updating moves us towards upgrades as part of the support and maintenance service instead of as discrete products. We are also starting to see use of the network connectivity to provide information back to the company about errors. (Clause and Orso, 2007)

Within this environment of the global software development, then, we look at the problem of error detection, treatment, and traceability. With software designed for multithreaded, fail soft and recovery operation, how do we even detect, log, and report errors? Approaches such as Clause and

Orso describe begin to provide the technical means for identifying and collecting data at the point of the field failure (Clause and Orso, 2007), but given the composite nature of the software, how do we relate that to the empirical data from the development process? One of the key recommendations for application lifecycle management is retaining design and project information. (Dearle, 2007)

Empirical software engineering research often has focused on data collection, analysis, and feedback during the development of software. (Sjoberg, Dyba, and Jorgensen, 2007) However, three of the six risks in Global Software Development relate to client use, including failures of COTS elements and unresponsive vendors, loss of system architecture and business process history, and high service expectations by users. (Bhuta, Sudeep, and Subrahmanya, 2007). With half of the enterprise software development risks related to issues after development, can we continue to separate development from use and ignore the later arena?

The software engineering community has talked about experience factories to capture important information about the development processes and feed that back to new projects as a continuing improvement strategy (Basili, Bomarius, and Feldmann, 2007). We have developed tools to collect, analyze, and display information about the development processes and databases that allow us to develop statistics and estimations based on similar projects. (Mitani, Matsumura, Barker, Tsuruho, Inoue, and Matsumoto, 2007)

However, the life cycle of software has always been longer, with support and maintenance asserted to use up to 80% of the lifecycle costs. And with development now crossing boundaries, that lifecycle becomes even more complicated. Even if data was available during production, it is normally discarded or lost as project teams are reorganized after release and as the components cross corporate and national boundaries.

Figure 5. A schematic of a tag system

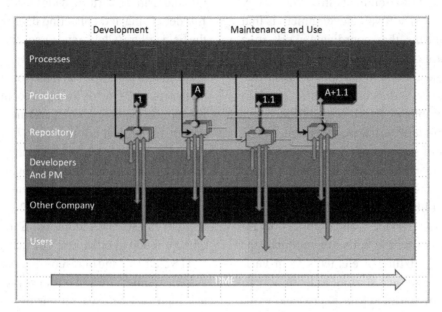

The Challenge

Figure 5 illustrates how a software tag and repository system might operate. The repository collects and holds empirical data taken from the software processes, while software products are "tagged" to allow easy access to the data in the repository. The information is available to developers, project managers, other companies, and end-users, although their access may differ, with developers having access to private information and other companies and end-users have access to the public information.

The challenge, then, is how to collect and use empirical software engineering data across the lifecycle of global software development. And the StagE project provides us with a "black box" for storing the data about software processes and products so that a software crash doesn't mean we have to re-engineer everything - we can just go back and look at the record.

CONCLUSION

This chapter has introduced some of the challenges and concepts behind the use of software tags to support the purchaser-centered approach to empirical software engineering. Global software engineering development, with parts developed in various countries and industries, the growing use of composition, and the spreading use of ubiquitous software that talks with everything, demands that data collection, analysis, and feedback be an integrated part of the entire lifecycle. Software tagging provides a way to connect and trace the information from the earliest steps of development through the final use of the software.

The question is not whether such an approach is possible, or even helpful. The experience of numerous projects shows that making such information available provides developers, maintainers, purchasers, and anyone associated with the software lifecycle with useful, even vital information. Industrial and government agencies concerned about the quality of software that they purchase have already enthusiastically endorsed the early standard for the software tag approach. So the only question is whether you are going to allow your software vendor to continue to hide information from you, or whether you will demand that they use software tags to let everyone see the quality of their software? After all, you wouldn't buy a piece of meat in the grocery store without a quality label -- why would you buy software in a plain brown bag?

ACKNOWLEDGMENT

This work is being conducted as a part of the Stage Project, the Development of Next Generation IT Infrastructure, supported by the Japanese Ministry of Education, Culture, Sports, Science and Technology. This work is the result of discussions with Koji Torii, Hajimu Iida, Shinji Kusumoto, Shuji Morisaki, and many other project members. EASE URL: http://www.empirical.jp/e_index. html (http://www.empirical.jp/e_index.html) (http://www.empirical.jp/e_index.html) (http:// www.empirical.jp/e_index.html)). Stage URL: http://www.stage-project.jp/en_index.php (http:// www.stage-project.jp/en_index.php) (http://www. stage-project.jp/en_index.php) (http://www.stage-project.jp/en_index.php))

REFERENCES

ATGSE. (2008). Workshop on Accountability and Traceability in Global Software Engineering (ATGSE2008). Technical Report ISCAS-SKLCS-08-07, State Key Laboratory of Computer Science, Institute of Software, Chinese Academy of Science.

Basili, V. R., Bomarius, F., & Feldmann, R. L. (2007). Get Your Experience Factory Ready for the Next Decade -- Ten Years After "How to Build and Run One". *29th International Conference on Software Engineering, 2007, ICSE 2007 Companion,* 167-168.

Bhuta, J., Sudeep, M., & Subrahmanya, S. V. (2007). A Survey of Enterprise Software Development Risks In a Flat World. *First International Symposium on Empirical Software Engineering and Measurement, 2007, ESEM 2007,* 476-478.

Boehm, B. (2006). Some future trends and implications for systems and software engineering processes. *Systems Engineering, 9*(1), 1–19. doi:10.1002/sys.20044

Clause, J., & Orso, A. (2007). A Technique for Enabling and Supporting Debugging of Field Failures. *29th International Conference on Software Engineering, 2007, ICSE 2007.* 261-270.

Dearle, A. (2007). Software Deployment, Past, Present And Future. *Future of Software Engineering, 2007 . FOSE, 07,* 269–284.

EASE Project. (2007) Retrieved September 11, 2008, from http://www.empirical.jp/e_index. html

Herbsleb, J. (2007). Global Software Engineering: The Future of Socio-technical Coordination. *Future of Software Engineering, 2007 . FOSE, 07,* 188–198.

Institute for Experimental Software Engineering (IESE). (2008) Retrieved December 1, 2008, from http://www.iese.fhg.de/

Johnson, P. (2008). Retrieved December 5, 2008, from http://code.google.com/p/hackystat/

Mitani, Y., Matsumura, T., Barker, M., Tsuruho, S., Inoue, K., & Matsumoto, K. (2007). Proposal of a Complete Life Cycle In-Process Measurement Model Based on Evaluation Of an In-Process Measurement Experiment Using a Standardized Requirement Definition Process. *First International Symposium on Empirical Software Engineering and Measurement, 2007, ESEM 2007,* 11-20.

National Information and Communication Technology Australia (NICTA). (2008). Retrieved November 25, 2008, from http://nicta.com.au/

NSF Center for Empirically Based Software Engineering (CeBASE). (2004). Retrieved December 4, 2008, from http://www.cebase.org/.

Pretschner, A., Broy, M., Kruger, I. H., & Stauner, T. (2007). Software Engineering for Automotive Systems: A Roadmap. *Future of Software Engineering, 2007 . FOSE, 07*, 55–71.

SEC. (2008) Retrieved December 5, 2008, from http://www.ipa.go.jp/english/sec/index.html.

Sjoberg, D. I. K., Dyba, T., & Jorgensen, M. (2007). The Future of Empirical Methods in Software Engineering Research. *Future of Software Engineering, 2007 . FOSE, 07*, 358–378.

StagE Project. (2008) Retrieved December 8, 2008, from http://www.stage-project.jp/.

KEY TERMS AND DEFINITIONS

Composition: Software construction using components or parts.

Empirical Software Engineering: Software engineering based on empirical data.

Goal-Driven Metrics: Data collection and analysis based on business goals.

Purchaser-Centered: Driving the development methods and decisions based on purchaser lifecycle benefits, rather than developer-centered ease.

StagE: Software Traceability and Accountability for Global Software Engineering Project.

Transparency: Providing visibility into the development process for purchasers.

Traceability: providing information to allow tracing the origin of problems into the development process by purchasers.

Software tag: A collection of empirical data and abstracted information from the development process associated with a software product.

Ubiquitous, Networked Software: Software in almost all consumer products, with data networking connecting it all.

Chapter 5
Enhancing Testing Technologies for Globalization of Software Engineering and Productivity

Amir H. Khan
University of Maryland, USA

Atif M. Memon
University of Maryland, USA

ABSTRACT

While successful at increasing code churn rates, global software development and evolution suffers from several quality assurance challenges. First, sub-groups within developer communities often work on loosely coupled parts of the application code. Each developer (sub-group) typically modifies a local "copy" of the code and frequently checks-in changes (and downloads other developers' changes). Consequently, after making a change, a developer may not immediately realize that the local change has inadvertently broken other parts of the overall software code. This situation is compounded as there is little direct inter-developer communication -- almost all communication is done via web-based tools such as code commit log messages, bug reports, change-requests, and comments. This chapter outlines the challenges that global software development adds to the already-complex quality assurance process. Two case studies of real software projects implemented in a disturbed manner demonstrate the importance of continuous integration testing and the positive consequences of increasing the diversity of quality assurance techniques/tools. Finally, it concludes with an outline of how software integration testing needs to be enhanced to meet the new challenges of globalization.

1. INTRODUCTION

As software becomes increasingly complex, pervasive, and important for the general consumer across the world, there is an unprecedented demand for new software. It is no longer practical to develop software in one part of the world and "export" it to other parts. Moreover, as new economies emerge and strengthen across the world with improved educational infrastructure, software development expertise is also becoming distributed. Together with improved global telecommunication networks, it is not surprising that the answer to today's software needs is sought in globalization of development.

DOI: 10.4018/978-1-60566-731-7.ch005

Globalization of software development has several advantages. First, it has led to unprecedented code churn rates; developers work in shifts around the world, leveraging the world's time zones to evolve commercial and open-source software around-the-clock. Second, it has enabled the development of large and complex software – software experts from around the world collaborate, sharing their experiences to solve difficult coding and design problems. Third, it has accelerated the improvement of software architectures – there has been an increased interest in component-based software applications – developers work on different loosely-coupled components simultaneously to build the software. Finally, it has led to new agile processes that advocate collaborative development.

Distributed and global development has also created new challenges, especially for quality assurance. Because sub-groups within developer communities work on loosely coupled parts of the application code, each developer (sub-group) typically modifies a local "copy" of the code and frequently checks-in changes (and downloads other developers' changes). Consequently, after making a change, a developer may not immediately realize that the local change has inadvertently broken other parts of the overall software code. This becomes worse because there is little direct inter-developer communication as almost all communication is done via web-based tools such as code commit log messages, bug reports, change-requests, and comments. Because of these challenges, a large number of multi-site software projects have suffered from significant quality issues (Porter, A., Yilmaz, C., Memon, A.M., Schmidt, D.C. & Natarajan, B., 2007).

The next section presents an overview of some techniques used to test evolving software. Sections 3 and 4 present case studies of two medium-sized multi-site software projects. These case studies describe the software testing related challenges encountered in those projects. They also help to further understand the various types of testing related challenges that future projects are likely to encounter as global software development becomes more complex. Finally, Section 5 outlines current directions in software testing research and practice that are helping to address the software testing challenges in a global development scenario.

2. TESTING TECHNIQUES FOR EVOLVING SOFTWARE

The ongoing quest of the software industry to keep software of all sizes integrated throughout the course of its development, has led to the mainstream adoption of many enabling practices. Nightly/daily builds and smoke tests (Karlsson, Andersson, & Leion, 2000), (McConnell, 1996a), (Olsson, 1999) have become widespread (Robbins, 2000), (Halloran, Scherlis, 2002). During nightly builds, a development version of the software is checked out from the source code repository tree, compiled, linked, and "smoke tested" ("smoke tests" are also called "sniff tests" or "build verification suites" (Marick, 1998)). Typically, unit tests (Robbins, 2000) and sometimes acceptance tests (Crispin, House, Wade, 2001) are executed during smoke testing. Such tests are run to (re)validate the basic functionality of the system (Marick, 1998). Smoke tests exercise the entire system; they do not have to be an exhaustive test suite but they should be capable of raising a "something is wrong here" alarm. A build that passes the smoke test is considered to be "a good build." As is the case with all testing techniques (Schach, 1996), it is quite possible that problems are found in a good build during more comprehensive testing later or after the software has been fielded.

Daily building and smoke testing have been used for a number of large-scale commercial and open-source projects. For example, Microsoft used daily builds extensively for the development of its Windows NT operating system (McConnell, 1996). By the time it was released, Windows

NT 3.0 consisted of 5.6 million lines of code spread across 40,000 source files. The NT team attributed much of the project's success to their daily build process. The GNU project continues to use daily builds for most of its projects. For example, during the development of the Ghostscript software, daily builds were used widely. The steps for daily builds involved compiling the source, executing smoke tests, and updating the CVS repository. Similarly, WINE (WINE Daily Builds, 2003), Mozilla (Mozilla, 2003), AceDB [14], and openwebmail (Open WebMail, 2003) use nightly/daily builds.

There are several tools that may be used to setup and perform smoke testing of software applications. Popular examples include CruiseControl (Cruise Control, 2003), IncrediBuild (FAST C++ Compilation—IcrediBuild by Xoreax Software, 2003), Daily Build (Positive-g-Daily Build Product Information—Mozilla, 2003), ANT *(Apache Ant, 2008)*, and Visual Build (Kinook Software—Automate Software Builds with Visual Build Pro, 2003). Most of these tools provide more or less identical functionality. CruiseControl, Daily Build, and Visual Build are frameworks for setting up and running continuous build processes. They include plug-ins for tools, e.g., for e-mail notification and source control. Web interfaces provide views to details of the current and previous builds. IncrediBuild speeds up daily building and smoke testing by performing distributed compilation of source; it distributes the compilation task across several available machines in an organizational network. It has been found to be effective for nightly/daily builds of Microsoft Visual C++ (6.0, 7.0, and 7.1) applications.

3. FIRST CASE STUDY: MISSION RECONSTRUCTION SYSTEM (MRS)

Logical Overview of the System: This first case study discusses a software-intensive system called the *Mission Reconstruction System* (MRS) developed for the training of emergency-response teams (e.g., police, fire fighters, park rangers) in remote National Parks. MRS provides authentic digital reconstruction of different types of rescue missions. Emergency response personnel at rescue sites are equipped with devices that record their exact time-stamped locations and transmit them back in real time to a central base station. Personnel at this station can examine/visualize the incoming information to make mission strategy changes. Personnel employ the MRS for real-time reconstruction of their missions as well as for post-mission analysis. The system is considered to be one of the core training aids in the emergency response application domain that it serves. And a large and growing number of personnel use this training-aid on a day-to-day basis.

Technologies Used to Implement the System: MRS is a medium-size system with around 300 KLOC (Java, C, and C++); it relies heavily on 2D and 3D graphics libraries to produce accurate visualizations of missions in real-time as well as reconstruction for post-mission analysis. The nature of the domain requires that many of the modules of MRS perform according to certain Quality-of-Service (QoS) guarantees – these modules were implemented in C and C++. The visualizations were implemented in Java. MRS runs on PC-based machines on top of the Windows operating system.

Logistics Issues of the Developer/Client: The client was at a National Park location without reliable electronic communication. It was very expensive to host the development team at the client site. The nearest National Park was around a thousand miles away from the software development center.

Project Timeline: The MRS needed to be operational within a year with a small predetermined set of hardware devices. The complete development work would continue for an additional three years. The hardware devices used to communicate with the MRS would continue to evolve as new agencies were added. Each agency had its own set of hardware devices.

Overview of the Study: Certain requirements (e.g., visualizations) were fairly stable in some respects; some others (e.g., the nature of hardware devices) were very volatile; the latter had the potential to destabilize the overall software. To minimize overall risk, the development was distributed – a small team was stationed at the client site; the majority of developers were stationed at the developers site (called the *development center*). Communication between these two teams was via a CD mailed using a courier service.

More specifically, the development activities are described in chronological order.**YEAR 1:** During the initial phase of the project the primary focus of the client-site team was to discover end-user requirements and build the overall structure of the system and its modules. Different types of throw-away prototypes were developed in order to understand the user requirements. Side by side, various high-level design alternatives were being evaluated. This preliminary analysis led to the definition of the following modules:

Data Processing Modules: These were a growing set of software applications used for processing data coming primarily from various hardware devices. This data had to undergo a number of processing steps in order to be brought into the MRS' mission format. It is also important to note that each hardware device, in addition to generating valid data, also output a number of error codes as well as anomalous data. The error codes provided various types of hardware error status indications, whereas the anomalous data usually resulted from failures in certain types of hardware. The data processing applications were required to process valid data as well as deal with the error codes and the anomalous data.

MRS Missions' Storage: The MRS missions were stored in a system-level database, XML documents, and binary and text files.

Services Library: Real-time as well as post-mission access to MRS Missions was facilitated through a Services Library. This library provided commonly needed services for accessing MRS Missions as well as for making certain updates to the MRS Missions.

User Applications: These were the applications with which the users interacted. They primarily comprised of 2D/3D graphics-based mission visualization applications. All these applications used the Services Library to access MRS Missions both in real-time as well as after the mission.

Meanwhile the developer-site team was evaluating and comparing various tools and technologies in order to make the right choices for the project.

Once the above four modules were defined, the client-site team was trimmed to save overall cost – the members moved back to the developer-site. All developers worked on the four modules. In the absence of a cost-effective and secure means of electronically exchanging software, documents, and data between the two facilities, the team chose to use an overnight courier delivery service for speedy delivery of all product artifacts[1]. The overnight delivery service turned out to be a cost-effective and fairly reliable means of communication between the two sites. Through this experience the team also learned not to underestimate the low-cost and high-bandwidth capacity of overnight courier delivery service.

During the first year of the project the team deliberately avoided the use of an automated *configuration management* (CM) system, since the structure and interfaces of the MRS software were gradually unfolding. Using the CM system at that stage would have added to the overhead without adding significant value.**YEARS 2, 3, and 4:** By the beginning of the second year of the project the team transitioned to a CM system, which was maintained at the software development center. By now more than half of the team was working at the software development center. The two teams continued to use the overnight courier delivery service for sending each other updates of the software and other work products. And the CM server was kept up-to-date on a regular basis.

By now the team had found that one of their most critical challenges was to deal with the continuously-unfolding nature of the hardware interface details. As described earlier, the MRS received data from a number of simple to fairly sophisticated hardware devices. In the absence of some of the interface documentation, the team had to discover part of the hardware data format information through trail-and-error methods. This process of gradual interface-discovery lasted throughout much of the course of the project.

To be sure, the team was able to successfully insulate the software from these ongoing interface discoveries. However, as is the case in most real projects, many of these interface discoveries were disruptive enough to necessitate changes in the structure and interfaces of many of the MRS modules. And one of the major challenges for the team was to incrementally develop and deliver a quality product in the face of these ongoing interface discoveries. In fact, one of the reasons to use an incremental and somewhat iterative development approach was precisely to mitigate these kinds of risks.

A typical case of discovery of new format details or just the arrival of some garbage data would trigger changes in at least some of the data processing modules. Usually, corresponding changes would also be needed in the MRS Missions' Storage structure to cater for these new changes. These two changes would usually lead to changes or enhancements in the Services Library. And finally, all the User Applications that used the impacted portions of the Services Library would have to modify their code to reflect the changes.

It is also important to note that many of these changes had the potential of disrupting the system operations at the end-user site. Since the system had been in heavy use at the end of the second year of development, any data format discovery had the potential of disrupting these operations. Every time the system could not handle a new data format issue, the affected missions could not be reconstructed thus requiring immediate modifications and/or enhancements in the MRS software. Obviously, this period of disrupted system operations had to be kept to an absolute minimum.

Many of these format changes were occurring almost on a weekly basis. And if left unchecked even for a few days, they had the potential of creating immediate and massive integration, quality, and delivery challenges for the team. And since the team was geographically distributed and using slow and somewhat primitive means of communication, these changes had the potential of jeopardizing the whole project.

Some upstream planning diligence had helped the team select a risk-mitigated incremental, and somewhat iterative development approach. A modular system design with a clear separation-of-concerns helped the team localize the effect of a large number of changes. And finally, a small surgical-style team (Brooks, 1995) working in an environment that fostered collaboration and open communication, helped the team to rapidly respond to changing interfaces and other technical challenges.

The team used frequent high-level design walkthroughs to maintain design quality. In addition to that, portions of code were occasionally re-written or informally refactored to maintain the quality of the code. Finally, a notable emphasis on testing was used to maintain quality of a growing product.

From the testing perspective the entire project offered a number of tough challenges. The testing team was essentially dealing with a moving target as the interfaces and the structure of the system evolved throughout the course of the project. One of the main responsibilities of the testing team was to pull the system from the CM server on a regular basis – sometimes daily, and perform various Smoke Tests (McConnell, 1996a). And approximately every week, the testing team did system integration testing. This regular integration of the system ensured that the team maintained fairly constant progress and risks of big-bang integration were kept under check.

It is important to note that the MRS team's temptation to not integrate frequently in favor of adding new features was initially fairly high. This was especially so because the team was geographically separated. Close to the end of the first year of the project, as the team decided to deploy an initial version of the product at the end-user site, they faced significant integration challenges. In fact, the integration effort took the form of a mini-project during which all other development progress came to a halt. However, several weeks of software reconciliation effort made the team to commit itself to frequent product integration throughout the rest of the project.

Lessons Learned from Study 1: Ultimately the team was able to deliver a good quality system that quickly became popular within its end-user community. Clearly, one of the keys to the success of the team was its decision to integrate the system on a regular basis. A number of engineering practices adopted during the MRS project enabled the team to keep the software in a deployable condition throughout the project. The lesson learned was that frequent building and smoke testing helps to stabilize the software and address interfacing issues.

Today, many teams around the world are able to integrate and deploy the software much more frequently than what the MRS team was able to achieve (although weekly integration was considered a significant achievement during the days of MRS development) (Fowler, 2006).

4. SECOND CASE STUDY: PROJECT 'HARMONY'

Logical Overview of the System: This second case study is about software for a portable heart-rate monitoring device. The software project is aptly named as *Harmony* – inline with the com-

pany's vision to promote good health through aerobic workouts. This device is fairly popular among health-aware individuals as well as among endurance athletes. The device is worn like a wristwatch and provides instantaneous heat-rate updates. A belt is wrapped around the chest of the user which senses the heartbeats and transmits them to the device.

The company produces a wide range of different types of heart-rate monitors targeting different market segments. This particular heart-rate monitor is considered a feature-rich premium product of the company. A wide range of competing heart-rate monitors are also available in the market. However, this particular monitor is popular because of its accuracy, reliability, ease-of-use, and price-performance.

Harmony is the core of this device – it is the embedded software that controls the device's functionality. This software performs in real-time while residing in a resource-constrained hardware environment.

Similar to the first case study discussed above, this project was also done by two geographically distributed teams. Many of the challenges arising out of the distributed nature of the project were handled in a manner similar to that of the first case study. In this case study we will focus on the quality challenges faced by the team and how the team handled those challenges. Readers will be able to understand some useful distinctions as to how the various testing techniques employed by the team contributed towards meeting the quality goals of the project.

Technologies Used to Implement the System: *Harmony* is an embedded software with around 85 KLOC. An extensive use of COTS and opportunistic code refactoring helped the team keep the number of lines-of-code to be developed within a reasonable range. The software is developed using the C# technology. The bulk of the software deals with the real-time processing of data and the control of various components inside the device.

Project Timeline: The product manager had a one-year deadline from initial concept development to final product role-out. Everyone in the team understood, and bought into, this narrow and critical window of marketing opportunity.

Software Quality Expectations: The heart-rate monitoring device company is renowned for its high quality products. This new premium product will help the company establish itself in the highly profitable premium product niche. Therefore this product has to not only maintain but enhance the company's brand identity. At the technical level this meant that the software team had to produce an essentially defect-free product full of new features that worked in real-time and resided in a resource-constrained hardware environment.

Clearly, the nature of the project was critical and its success, as well as failure, had long-term implications for the company. In order to meet the aggressive quality and schedule goals of this project, the team decided to increase the intensity of some of their existing engineering practices as well as bring about some new improvements. These changes/improvements in the engineering approach are the focus of the rest of the study.

Overview of the Study: Before signing off for the project the team did a brief study of the scope of work and came up with initial time, effort, and schedule estimates. The team found that an effective and extensive use of *commercial off-the-shelf* (COTS) components (Egyed, Muller, Perry, 2005) and automated software testing tools would be critical to meeting the tough time-to-market and quality goals. Additionally, it was also decided that a one-to-one developer-tester ratio would be maintained in order to do rigorous software and system testing.

Throughout the project the software team made extensive use of a lab environment comprising of various hardware and software based simulators/emulators. Through this lab environment the software team was able to do initial integration testing of software for hardware components that were still under development. At pre-defined stages the hardware and software teams would integrate the various software and hardware components in lab environment as well as perform multiple System-Level Testing (SLT) cycles.

Following is a description of various development activities given in chronological order:

Inception Phase: The Inception Phase of the project lasted for about two months. During this period the systems engineering team and part of the software team worked together to prepare the Software Requirements Specifications (SRS); they used an informal process model that was originally inspired by IBM Rational Unified Process (RUP) (IBM Rational Unified Process, 2008). The rest of the software team was focused on identifying, evaluating, comparing, and finally selecting the various COTS and automated software testing tools.

The chosen tools included profilers, static code analyzers, and high-level design and code quality & complexity metrics generators. Additionally, a COTS product was also identified to provide leverage to the developers.

The choice of these COTS and automated tools had implications not only for this project but for other future undertakings by this company. Other software teams were expected to follow suite after the successful adoption of these newly selected technologies by the *Harmony* team.

Initially there was some resistance towards these COTS and automated tools. Some team members interpreted the absence of the act of coding at that stage as a sign of absence of progress. However, ultimately everyone was convinced that the use of COTS and automated testing tools played a pivotal role in the success of the project.

Elaboration Phase: The goal of the Elaboration Phase was primarily to come up with an executable product architecture. This phase turned out to be relatively short since most of the architectural structure came with the COTS itself. This phase was also opportunistically used to build hands-on skills over the tools and COTS.

Much of the resistance towards COTS and automated tools was addressed through coaching and mentoring by the senior team members (Eckes, 2003). For instance, a couple of informal sessions on the use of code and high-level design quality metrics sparked the interest of the developers in using them. Likewise team members who became more conversant with the use of profiler and static code analyzer tools shared the knowledge with other team members.

Initially, despite the presence of a feature-rich and robust COTS library that matched developers' requirements, some of the developers were still building many of the features from scratch. However, as some of the team members showed promising progress using COTS, there was enough 'social proof' for the rest of the team to fully commit itself to COTS usage.

The high-level design quality metrics tool was especially helpful during the Elaboration Phase as it pointed towards some critical high-level design complexities and issues. One of the reasons that encouraged regular use of the metrics tool was the minimal cost of using and interpreting the results from it. For the developers this tool was a low-cost no-excuse reason to significantly improve the quality of their high-level design.

The other tools – namely the profiler and the static code analyzer, mostly captured the attention of the test engineers during this stage. These tools required relatively more effort to learn. Feedback provided by these tools usually needed to be interpreted/analyzed by the engineers in order to become meaningful. As a result more effort was needed to extract value out of these tools.

During the Elaboration Phase the focus of the developers was on building the high-level design of the product, therefore they were not able to pay much attention to the profiler and static code analyzer. Management purposely chose not to push the developers to learn these tools at that stage. They realized that the successful use of these tools by the test engineers would ultimately encourage the developers to adopt them as well.

Working with these tools the test engineers found that these tools could help them find a variety of defects at an earlier stage of development. Early defect detection clearly meant reduced development time and improved product quality (Boehm & Basili, 2001) (McConnell, 1996b). With these benefits it was clear that these tools would play a critical role during the Construction Phase.

Construction Phase: The Construction Phase was divided into several small iterations. Each iteration was planned to be two weeks long. It took a couple of iterations for the team to become comfortable with the newly adopted automated tools and COTS. Specifically, some of the experiences of working with COTS are described below:

Increased Productivity: One of the most obvious benefits of using COTS was a significant increase in developers' productivity. The features available in the COTS simplified and accelerated the development of a number of product features. Although significant amount of upfront time & effort was invested in learning the COTS, it was more than offset by the productivity gains during the rest of the development.

Improved Quality: Because of the high quality of COTS the delivered features had relatively less defects (compared to past projects' defects trends of similar features build from scratch.) As a result the usual re-work effort also reduced significantly. The team felt that their upfront efforts of comparing and choosing the right COTS finally paid off.

Added Features: The final heart-rate monitor product had more software features than originally planned. Although the team did not want to engage in gold-plating of the product, there were a number of highly-desirable 'goodies' that were left out of the Product Specifications. These features were initially kept out of the specifications as they were estimated to be very costly in terms of development time and effort. However, as their familiarity with the COTS grew, the team found that many of these features could be added cost-effectively into the product.

Similarly, some of the experiences of working with automated testing tools are described below:

Early Defect Detection: The test engineers, as well as the developers, saw a sharp increase in their ability to find a variety of defects at an early stage. These included many tricky defects such as the presence of memory leaks in software despite the automatic garbage collection feature provided by the underlying technology. Early detection of defects meant relatively less cost to fix defects ultimately leading to better product quality.

Performance Improvement: Another side benefit of these tools was that developers became more aware of their commonly made mistakes and made fewer similar errors in future iterations.

Transition Phase: During the Transition Phase the software was to be embedded inside the heart-rate monitor device. This integration phase turned out to be much smoother as compared to prior product integration experiences. The number of high-severity defects was also significantly low as compared to previous projects.

Lessons Learned from Study 2

Project Harmony was considered a major success. The team was able to deliver high-quality software within a very tight schedule. The use of COTS and automated tools helped inculcate quality throughout the development lifecycle. The product integration of *Harmony* was especially in glaring contrast with other projects of the company. The swift integration of the product was a welcome relief as intense pressure during product integrations was a norm in this company.

To be sure, there were other factors as well that contributed towards the success of this project. For example, the team increased the intensity as well as the discipline with which they used to review their engineering artifacts. In this project all the engineering artifacts; such as product specifications, high-level designs, and code; were reviewed much more regularly and methodically. These process improvements, in addition to the use of COTS and automated tools, also played a pivotal role in the success of the project.

With so many improvement initiatives within this project it is a bit difficult to objectively quantify the contribution of each improvement towards quality and schedule. However, anecdotal evidence suggests that the combined effect of both COTS and automated tools had a significant impact on the project schedule and the overall quality of the software.

Through their experience of using the automated tools the team was also developing a sense of usage-frequency for each tool. The developers tended to use some of the tools every time they compiled the software, whereas other tools tended to get used at the time of nightly builds or on some critical occasion. Still there were other tools that were used just a few times during an entire iteration.

As a general rule, tools whose execution time was less and whose results were subject to less or no user interpretation/analysis tended to be used more frequently. Whereas tools that required more user-input, such as configuring the various parameters prior to running, or required user interpretation/analysis to understand tool results, were used relatively less frequently. In other words, cost-benefit was driving the frequency of tools usage.

Finally, while in this case the team was successful in the swift adoption of COTS and automated tools, we must caution the reader over potential challenges/risks associated with adopting COTS and other tools. While there is enough published industry evidence to support the use of COTS and automated tools, care needs to be taken while making the choices. In addition to meeting immediate project requirements, the medium to long-term suitability of the tools should also be evaluated. While the right choices of COTS and tools could potentially become strategic advantage for a company, incorrect choices might lead to development nightmares ranging from basic incompatibilities to total architectural mismatches in case of COTS (Brooks, F.P., 1987).

5. CONCLUSIONS AND THE CONCENTRIC CONTINUOUS INTEGRATION TESTING

This chapter outlined the challenges that global software development adds to the already-complex quality assurance process. Two case studies of real software projects implemented in a disturbed manner demonstrated the importance of continuous integration testing. Moreover, Study 2 showed the importance of increasing the diversity of techniques and tools used for quality assurance. The lessons learned from these two case studies show that the distributed nature of global software development requires the enhancement of testing techniques that are themselves *global* in that they quickly test each local increment of the software during development. They should be *disciplined* in that each developer has a specific role in the overall testing process. There is a need for processes with diverse supporting techniques/tools for continuous integration testing of globally developed applications; this process should connect modern model-based testing techniques with the needs of global software development. The key idea of this process is to create concentric testing loops, each with specific software testing goals, requirements, tools/techniques, and resource usage.

For example, one can envision an instance of this process with three such loops. The tightest loop, called the crash testing loop, operates on each code check-in (e.g., using CVS) of the software. It is executed very frequently and hence is designed to be very inexpensive. The goal is to perform a quick-and-dirty, fully automatic integration test of the software. Software crashes are reported back to the developer within minutes of the check-in. The second loop is called the smoke testing loop which operates on each day's software build. It is executed nightly/daily and hence is designed to complete within 8-10 hours. The goal of this loop is to do functional "reference testing" of the newly integrated version of the software. Differences between the outputs of the previous (yesterday's) build and the new build are reported to developers.

The third, and outermost loop is called the "comprehensive testing" loop. It is executed after a major version of the software is available. The goal of this loop is to conduct comprehensive integration testing, and hence is the most expensive. Major problems in the software are reported. An overview of this process is shown in Figure 1. The small octagons represent frequent CVS code check-ins. The encompassing rectangles with rounded corners represent daily increments of the software. The large rectangle represents the major version. The three loops discussed earlier are shown operating on these software artifacts.

It is important to note that the need to keep the software product integrated and tested at all times grows with the size and complexity of the software as well as with the geographical distribution of the team. This means that the occasions when the temptation to delay the integration of the software is the most, are exactly the times when integration is most needed. Not surprisingly, the entire software industry is heading towards an engineering paradigm where more and more emphasis is placed on continuous integration of the software.

It is reassuring to know that today a number of enabling engineering practices, new innovations in software process, and a number of modern tools and technologies are making continuous integration a reality both for collocated and geographically distributed teams.

ACKNOWLEDGMENT

This work was partially supported by the US National Science Foundation under NSF grant

Figure 1. Different loops of continuous integration testing

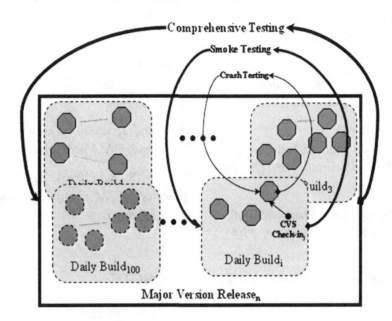

CCF-0447864 and the Office of Naval Research grant N00014-05-1-0421.

REFERENCES

Apache Ant (2008). Retrieved from http://ant.apache.org

Boehm, B., & Basili, V. (2001). *Software Defect Reduction Top 10 List.*

Brooks, F. P. (1987). No Silver Bullet: Essence and Accidents of Software Engineering. *Computer, 20*(4), 10–19. doi:10.1109/MC.1987.1663532

Brooks, F. P. (1995). *The Mythical Man-Month.* Reading, MA: Addison Wesley Longman Inc.

Crispin, L. House, T. & Wade, C. (2001). The Need for Speed: Automating Acceptance Testing in an Extreme Programming Environment. In *Proc. Second Int'l Conf. eXtreme Programming and Flexible Processes in Software Eng.,* (pp. 96-104).

Cruise Control (2003). Retrieved from http://cruisecontrol.sourceforge.net/.

WINE Daily Builds, (2003). Retrieved from http://wine.dataparty.no/

Eckes, G. (2003). *Six Sigma for Everyone.* New York: John Wiley & Sons Inc.

Egyed, A., Muller, H. A., & Perry, D. E. (2005, July-August). Guest Editors' Introduction: Integrating COTS into the Development Process. *Software IEEE, 22*(4), 16–18. doi:10.1109/MS.2005.93

FAST C++ Compilation—IcrediBuild by Xoreax Software, (2003). Retrieved from http://www.xoreax.com/main.htm.

Fowler, M. (2006). *Continuous Integration.* Retrieved from http://www.martinfowler.com/.

Halloran, T. J., & Scherlis, W. L. (2002). High Quality and Open Source Software Practices. In *Meeting Challenges and Surviving Success: Second Workshop Open Source Software Eng., May.*

Karlsson, E.-A. Andersson, L.-G. & Leion, P. (2000). Daily Build and Feature Development in Large Distributed Projects. In *Proc. 22nd Int'l Conf. Software Eng.,* (pp. 649-658).

Kinook Software—Automate Software Builds with Visual Build Pro, (2003). Retrieved from http://www.visualbuild.com/.

Marick, B. (1998). When Should a Test Be Automated? *Proc. 11th Int'l Software/Internet Quality Week,* May.

McConnell, S. (1996a). Best Practices: Daily Build and Smoke Test. *IEEE Software, 13*(4), 143–144.

McConnell, S. (1996b). Software Quality at Top Speed. *Software Development, August.*

Mozilla, (2003). Retrieved from http://ftp.mozilla.org/

Olsson, K. (1999). *Daily Build—The Best of Both Worlds: Rapid Development and Control.* Tech. Rep., Swedish Eng. Industries.

Open WebMail (2003). Retrieved from http://openwebmail.org/.

Porter, A., Yilmaz, C., Memon, A. M., Schmidt, D. C., & Natarajan, B. (2007). Skoll: A Process and Infrastructure for Distributed Continuous Quality Assurance. *IEEE Transactions on Software Engineering, 33*(8), 510–525. doi:10.1109/TSE.2007.70719

Positive-g-Daily Build Product Information—Mozilla, (2003). Retrieved from http://positive-g.com/dailybuild/.

Rational Unified Process, I. B. M. (2008). Retrieved from http://www-306.ibm.com/software/awdtools/rup/

Robbins, J. (2000). *Debugging Applications.* Redmond, CA: Microsoft Press

Schach, S. R., (1996). Testing: principles and practice. *ACM Computing Surveys (CSUR) March, 28* (1).

ENDNOTE

[1] It is important to note here that while software development projects are increasingly done as globally distributed undertakings, not all the places are equipped with state-of-the-art communication and other infrastructure facilities. Many software organizations, especially the ones in the developing countries, at times face lack of choice propositions when it comes to communication and other infrastructure facilities.

Chapter 6
Story Card Process Improvement Framework for Agile Requirements

Chetankumar Patel
Leeds Metropolitan University, UK

Muthu Ramachandran
Leeds Metropolitan University, UK

ABSTRACT

This chapter describes an ongoing process to define a suitable process improvement model for story cards based requirement engineering process and practices at agile software development environments. Key features of the SMM (Story card Maturity Model) process are: solves the problems related to the story cards like requirements conflicts, missing requirements, ambiguous requirements, define standard structure of story cards, to address non-functional requirements from exploration phase, and the use of a simplified and tailored assessment method for story cards based requirements engineering practices based on the CMM, which is poorly addressed at CMM. CMM does not cover how the quality of the requirements engineering process should be secured or what activities should be present for the requirements engineering process to achieve a certain maturity level. It is difficult to know what is not addressed or what could be done to improve the process. The authors also presents how can be the identified areas of improvement from assessment can be mapped with best knowledge based story cards practices for agile software development environments.

1 INTRODUCTION

Requirements elicitation process is one of the challenging processes in the software development methods. In traditional software development methods end users or stakeholders predefined their requirements and sent to the development team to do analysis and negotiation to produce requirement specification. Traditional software development has a problem to deal with requirement change after careful analysis and negotiation. This problem is well tackled by the XP, which is one of the agile software development methodologies.

Extreme (XP) programming is a conceptual framework of practices and principles to develop software faster, incrementally and to produce satis-

DOI: 10.4018/978-1-60566-731-7.ch006

fied customer. It is a set of twelve practices and four principles, which makes XP successful and well known among all the agile software development methods. The goal of XP is to produce the software faster, incrementally and to produce satisfied customer (Beck, 2000). According to Bohem (1998) the cost of change grows exponentially as the project progresses through it lifecycle (Bohem 1981). The relative repair cost is 200 times greater in the maintenance phase than if it is caught in the requirement phase (Faluk, 1996). XP maintain the cost of change through iterative software development methods and Refactoring.

While CMM and CMMI or software process improvement has gained a lot of attention during the last decade. Due to the increasing competition in the software market faster delivery, high quality products and customer satisfaction are the major concerns for software organisations. A quality process can have a positive impact on services, cost, on-time delivery, development technology, quality people and quality of products (Zahran, 1998).

Getting requirements on story cards right continues to be a universal problems same as the requirements problems in the traditional methodology. Story cards errors can be costly in terms of low time, lost revenue, loss of reputation and even survival (Beecham, *et al.*, 2005). A critical aspect of the requirements process is the selection of the an appropriate requirements set from the multitude of competing and conflicting expectation elicited from the various project stakeholders or from an onsite customers (Wiegers, 1997).

Looking at methods of CMM for process quality, measurement and improvement they tend to cover the area of requirements engineering poorly. It covers the area of requirements engineering inadequately. CMM does not cover how the quality of the requirements engineering process should be secured or what activities should be present for the requirements engineering process to achieve a certain maturity level. Some time it is really difficult to assess the maturity of a requirements

engineering process for a certain projects, and it is difficult to know what is not addressed or what could be done to improve the process.

As agile software development methodology is the iterative software development methodology based on the story cards, for small to medium organisation and main objectives are lower cost, high productivity and customer. The CMM tends not to focus the software process on an organisation's business objectives in their software process improvement programme (Paulk, 1998). The main thing is that CMM and ISO 9000 do not say much about requirements engineering and subsequently little about how the quality of the requirements engineering process should be maintained and ensured (Gorschek and Tejle, 2002). Herbsleb and Goldenson (1996) reported the use of the CMM in several software organisations. The study consistently showed significant organisational performance improvements that were directly associated with process maturity. The study also mentioned that the CMM improvement path is not always smooth, the efforts generally took longer and cost more than expected. While story card is agile software developments practice. Agile software development methodology is targeted to lower cost. Some of the KPAs have been found difficult to apply in small projects (Brodman and Johnson, 1997). This may be because CMM was originally structured for big enterprises (Lyard and Orci, 2000). CMM addresses practices such as document policies and procedure that large organisations need because of their size and management structure ((Brodman and Johnson, 1997).

Normally story cards for agile software development do not support the heavy documentation at all and people communicate verbally on on-going basis. Unlike CMM, CMMI does not just focus on software process management; it also considers other department such as marketing, finance and purchasing (Ahern, *et al.*, 2003). So it could be seen unnecessarily complex, when it is applied to agile software development practices like Extreme programming, Scrum and lean development.

CMM can be described a common sense application of the process management and quality improvement concept to software development and maintenance but it focuses on software development and does not cover the requirements engineering process (Somerville, *et al.*, 2000; Kotoyana, *et al.*, 1998). Without the standard for ensuring the quality of requirements engineering process, it is hard to ensure the result of the requirements engineering process. A consequence of this can be that requirements do not reflects the real needs of the customer of the system, requirements are inconsistent, incomplete requirements and requirements are not specified in a standardised and adequate manner (Gorschek and Tejle, 2002).

When businesses adapt the CMMI they should be familiar with the CMM practices (Menezes, 2002). CMMI Based upon the software CMM and has most of the same process areas. It may also inherit some of the same problems as CMM, such as the problem in reaching higher capability levels (Boehm, 2003). This is not acceptable against the agile software developments principle and motivation.

There is a need for a requirements process improvement model to suit story cards based requirements engineering process. Therefore the purpose of this chapter is to propose and evaluate a requirements process improvement model for story cards based requirements engineering process and enhance the adaptability of story cards based requirements engineering process. We propose a model for assessing the story cards based requirements engineering process within software engineering projects. This model should cover the area of story cards based requirements engineering process and practices for agile software development. The model can be used to evaluate the story cards based requirements engineering process maturity for certain projects.

The Story card Maturity Model (SMM), requirements improvement framework offers many advantages. The SMM includes an assessment method that guides the user to understand current story cards based requirements engineering process. The rationale for building the SMM is as:

- To define a generic process model for Story cards based requirements engineering process improvement that is suitable for RE at agile software development environments.
- To design and implement an automated tool that support to apply the proposed model in order to help facilitate process improvement.
- Identify and define story cards based requirements engineering practices
- Recognise story cards based requirement engineering practices problems
- Access and agree story cards based RE practices improvement priorities
- Relate story cards based RE practices problem to RE practices improvement goals
- Contains guidelines for many story cards related requirements engineering activities
- Is designed to be tailored to focus on specific process areas
- Goal focused
- Maturity structure to help with process prioritisation.

This chapter propose an approach for simplified and tailored assessment method for story cards based requirements engineering process using CMM(I), and present how assessments can be performed on story cards based RE process. In this chapter we explain the main stage involved in developing a model that guides practitioners to understand their story cards based requirements engineering process. We aim to support the practitioners by providing guidelines for story cards process improvement within the familiar framework. This study focuses on the story cards based requirement engineering process and not the individual feature or behaviour of the system. In this section we discussed about the research challenges, CMM, CMMI and agile software development. This section is followed by the process improvement framework for story cards.

1.1 Capability Maturity Model (CMM)

Capability maturity model was produced by the software engineering institute at Carnegie Melon University during the 1980s. Many companies throughout the world use the software CMM as their software process improvement model. Result of using this method is generally positive with improved process leading to higher quality software (Beecham, S. et al., 2003). According to Humphrey (Humphrey, W. S. 1993)

"When faced with a problem software people generally find their own solutions, even when the problem has been solved many times before. The fact that it is so hard to build on other people's work is the single most important reason why software has made so little progress in the last 50 years".

The CMM is a conceptual framework based on industry best practices to assess the process maturity, capability, and performance of a software development organisation; it covers practices for planning, engineering, and managing software development and maintenance (Herbsleb and Goldenson 1996). CMM has been widely accepted as a reference model for process assessment and improvement. It has become the de facto standard for software process assessment and improvement (Persse, 2001, Paulk et al., 1995, Raynus, 1999, Li, Chen and Lee 2002). CMM consists of five levels of maturity as Initial, Repeatable, Defined, Managed and optimizing (Paulk, C. et al., 1993). The following figure 1 show and summarize the five capability levels (Paulk, C. et al., 1993, Paulk, C. et al., 1995).

Figure 1. The key process area by maturity level (adapted from Paulk et al., 1995)

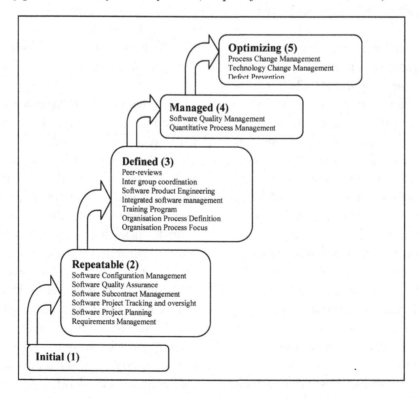

Initial: At this level the software process is characterised as ad hoc, and occasionally even chaotic. At this level few processes are defined and success depends on individual efforts and heroics.

- *Repeatable:* The basic project management processes or plans are established to track cost, schedule, and functionality. The necessary process discipline is in place to repeat earlier successes on projects with similar applications.

- *Defined:* The software process for both management and engineering activities is documented, standardised, and integrated into a standard software process for the organisation. All the projects use an approved, tailored version of the organization's standard software process for developing and maintaining software.

- *Managed:* Detailed measures of the software process and product quality are collected. Both the software process and products are quantitatively understood and controlled.

- *Optimizing:* continuous process improvement is enabled by quantitative feedback from the process and from piloting innovative ideas and technologies.

As can be seen in the figure 1 each maturity level comprise of Key Process Area (KPA). The goals of KPA summerise the states that must exist for that key process area to be implemented in an effective and permanent way. The extent to which the goals have been accomplished is an indicator of how much capability the organisation has established at the maturity level. The Goals signify the scope, boundaries, and intent of each KPA (Paulk et al., 1995). The Key process areas at maturity level one focus on Heroes and massive efforts, at level two focus on project management and commitment processes next maturity level, defined level focus on defined engineering process while level four and five,

managed and optimizing focus on product and process quality, and continuous process improvement respectively(Zaharan 1998). The process rating maturity level rating of an organisation is measured as, the extent to which KPAs are implemented and institutionalised at each level. The extent of implementation for specific KPA is evaluated by assessing the common features as (Paulk et al., 1995).

- Commitment to perform policies and leadership
- Ability to perform
- Activities performed
- Measurement and Analysis
- Verification of implementation

1.2 CMMI (Capability Maturity Model Integration)

CMMI was developed by the SEI recently. The CMM is the original version of the CMMI, and as CMM was originally funded by the US Department of Defence (DoD) to help qualify DoD's Software vendors' capabilities (Chrissis, Konrad and Shrum 2003) CMMI integrates all CMM versions mainly to reduce implementation cost (Ahern, Clouse and Turner, 2003) by

- Eliminating Inconsistency
- Reducing duplication
- Maintaining common component rules
- Increasing clarity and understanding
- Providing common terminology
- Assuring consistency with ISO/IEC 15504

The CMMI model is for improving and assessing the performance of development organisations (Chrissis et al., 2003). CMMI is a powerful tool to guide process improvement initiatives, not only for software development but for many related field such as System engineering, product acquisition, and team management (Boehm et al., 2002). CMMI is a powerful tool to guide process

Figure 2. CMMI staged approach (Ahern et al., 2003)

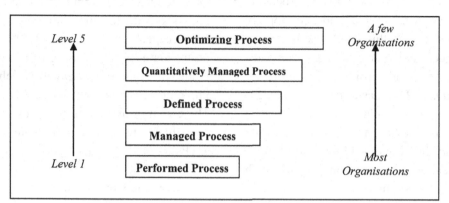

improvement initiatives, not only for software development but for many related fields such as system engineering, product acquisition, team management (Boehm et al., 2002). It has been shown to reduce the risks associated with development projects, increase efficiency and improve the overall quality of products and deliverables (Ahern, Clouse and Turner, 2003). The CMMI has two separate model representations staged and continuous (Ahern, clouse and Turner 2003)

As can be seen in the figure 2 illiterates the five levels of CMMI which are similar to the CMM models, and Process areas are illustrated in table 1 and 2.

1.3 Agile Software Development (ASD) Methodology

Agile software development methodology is a framework to develop the software. In the late 1990's several methodologies began to get increasing public attention. Each had a different combination of old ideas, new ideas, and transmuted old ideas. But they all emphasized close collaboration between the programmer team and business experts; face-to-face communication (as more efficient than written documentation); frequent delivery of new deployable business value; tight, self-organizing teams; and ways to craft the code and the team such

that the inevitable requirements churn was not a crisis (Agile alliance). According to Ambler (2005), an author of Agile modelling 'Agile is an iterative and incremental (evolutionary) approach to software development which is performed in a highly collaborative manner by self-organizing teams with "just enough" ceremony that produces high quality software in a cost effective and timely manner which meets the changing needs of its stakeholders.' This methodology gives priority to incremental software development methods, which is called iteration in agile software development method. Pay attention on face to face communication over documents. A recent set of development techniques that apply a human-centred approach aims to deliver high-quality products faster, and to satisfy customer (Ceschi 2005) and more people oriented rather than process oriented.

1.3.1 The Agile Manifesto

In the Agile Manifesto (Agile Alliance, 2001) the members of the alliance say their aim is to develop better software (in other words productive software) while helping other to do likewise. The manifesto then goes on to least the four values of agility as follows (Agile Alliance, 2001):"

Table 1. the Process Areas for Each Maturity Level (Ahern et al., 2003)

Maturity Level	Process Area
Maturity Level 1	No Process Area Associated with the maturity level 1
Maturity Level 2	Requirements Management Project Planning Project Monitoring and Control Supplier Agreement Management Measurement and Analysis Process and Product Quality Assurance Configuration Management
Maturity Level 3	Requirements Development Technical Solution Product Integration Verification Validation Organisation Process Focus Organisation Process Definition Organisation Training Integrated Project Management Risk Management Integrated Teaming Integrated supplier Management Decision analysis and resolution Organisational Environmental for integration
Maturity Level 4	Organisational Process Performance Quantitative Project Management
Maturity Level 5	Organisational Innovation and deployment Casual Analysis and Resolution

1. **Individuals and interactions** over processes and tools
2. **Working software** over comprehensive documentation
3. **Customer collaboration** over contract negotiation
4. **Responding to change** over following a plan

That is, while there is value in the items on the right, we value the items on the left more" The agile values are implemented or represented through a set of the following agile software principles (Agile Alliance, 2001):"

- Highest priority is to satisfy the customer through early and continuous delivery of valuable software.
- Welcome changing requirements, even late in development. Agile processes harness change for the customer's competitive advantage.
- Deliver working software frequently, from a couple of weeks to a couple of months. With a preference to the shorter timescale.
- Business people and developers must work together daily throughout the project.
- Build projects around motivated individuals. Give them the environment and support they need, and trust them to get the job done.
- The most effective and efficient method of conveying information to and within a development team is face-to-face communication
- Working software is the primary measure of progress.
- Agile processes promote sustainable

Table 2. The process areas in the continuous representation (Ahern et al., 2003)

Category	Process Area
Project Management	Project Planning Project Monitoring and control Supplier agreement management Integrated project management Integrated training Risk management Quantitative project management
Process Management	Organisational process focus Organisational process definition Organisational training Organisational process performance Organisational innovation and deployment
Support	Configuration management Process and product quality assurance Measurement and analysis Casual analysis and resolution Decision analysis and resolution Organisational environment for integration
Engineering	Requirements management Requirements management Technical solution Product integration Verification Validation

development. The sponsors, developers, and users should be able to maintain a constant pace indefinitely

- Continuous attention to technical excellence and good design enhances agility
- Simplicity the art of maximizing the amount of work not done is essential.
- The best architectures, requirements, and designs emerge from self organizing teams.
- At regular intervals, the team reflects on how to become more effective, then tunes and adjusts its behaviour accordingly.

There are several agile software development methods as:

- Extreme Programming (XP) (Kent Beck 1999)

- Scrum (Jim HighSmith)
- Adaptive Software Development (Jim Highsmith)
- Future Driven Development
- The Rational unified Process
- Crystal Family of Methodology (Alistair Cockburn)
- Open Source Software Development

Among these all agile software development methodology, Extreme Programming (XP) is one of the most popular agile methods. This is lightweight Agile Software Development Method (Beck K. 2000) and address to where customer requirements are vague and change over time. (Beck K. 2000). This method is suitable for small to medium enterprise.

2. PROCESS IMPROVEMENT FRAMEWORK FOR STORY CARDS

2.1 Story Cards Based Requirements Engineering Maturity Model (SMM)

According to Christie (1999), defining processes is recognised as critical elements in the software process improvement (Christie, 1999) yet to be useful model must be clear simplification of the complex world it is modelling (David, 2000). To keep the representation clear, understandable and usable the SMM links the Story Cards based requirements engineering practices to maturity levels, but it is not an exhaustive representation of agile software development practices. The SMM model is based on the agile requirements engineering values, practices and principles.

The SMM model is designed to improve and enhance the agile software development methodology and boost up the agile requirements principles and objectives like the lower cost, customer satisfaction, requirements quality, etc. Figure 3 introduces the SMM (Story card Maturity Model for agile software development requirements engineering). We divided our SMM model into four maturity level compared to the CMM five level maturity model This high level view of the model shows how story cards based requirements engineering practices mature from an initial or ad-hoc level to continuously improving level based on the agile principles and practices. In this model each level has a pre defined goal to help practitioner or organisation focus on their improvement activities. The ultimate goal of the SMM (Story cards maturity model) is as:

- Customer satisfaction
- Maintain story cards (requirements) change
- Solution to Vague requirements
- Obtain an understanding of the user story on the story card

- Obtain commitment to the user story (user Requirements)
- Maintain bidirectional traceability of requirements
- Identify inconsistency between project work and user story
- Identify and involve stakeholders instead of single on-site customer
- Manage Requirements Stories, on-site customer, daily meeting,
- Establish Estimates of story cards and define acceptance tests with story cards
- Develop a project plan based on the story cards

2.1.1 Level 1: Initial Level (Not accommodating at all)

There is no process improvement goals defined at this unstructured level.

The story cards practices or story card based requirement engineering process is very slim at this level and not necessarily repeatable. Organisations typically do not provide a stable environment for story cards based requirements engineering practices. Level 1 company do not have defined story cards practices. Here at this level RE problems were found to be common. The main problems at this level relate to overtimes, schedule slips, communication, requirements quality and vague requirements. These companies operate in their own unique way and depend on particular people rather than whole team. Paulk et al (1995) describe for traditional software process, success at this level is depends on 'the competence and heroics of the people in the organisation and cannot be repeated unless the same individuals are assigned to the next project'.

2.1.2 Level 2: Explored

Level 2 denotes a more structured and complete software development practices than level 1. Organisation with level 2 capability experienced

Figure 3. The SMM model

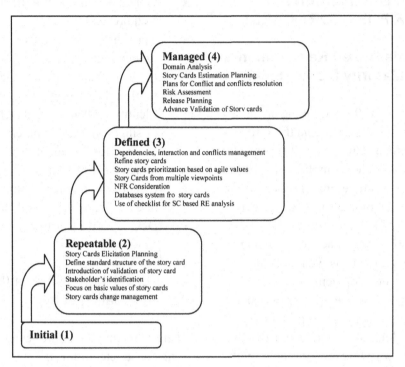

fewer problems with their software development process than their level 1 counterparts.

Problems with communication, complex requirements management and undefined RE process along with staff retention. Technically difficulty for level 2 companies centred on communication (mutual interaction), and to handle complex requirements.

An organisation at this level has focused on the cost, schedule and functionality and story cards elicitation process, the story cards elicitation practice is used to elicit user goals, elicit the functional requirements, An organisation at this level has introduced policies that ensure that story cards (Requirements) are specified and used the standard structure of the story cards and story cards are written by the on-site customer. Level 2 in general denotes that an organisation has devoted resources to the identification of story cards (requirements engineering) practices as a whole.

In general companies at this level 2 process capability have established the scope of the story

cards, story cards based requirements elicitation and identification of stakeholders to track schedules, requirements (Story cards), cost and functionality.

The SMM at level 2 maturity aims to help developers and customers to identify and improve problems related to requirements elicitation and identification of stakeholders by learning from previous project success and failures. This is achieved by an assessment of current process and to identify where weakness lie will help development team gain a general overview and allow them to address any planning or requirements issues associated with individual projects. The Appendix 1 summaries goals, key process areas and assessment questionnaires for SMM maturity level 2.

2.1.3 Level 3: Defined Level

Level 3 denotes a more focus on practices related to customer relationship management, consideration of dependencies, interaction, conflicts between story cards, acceptance testing on early stage of story cards, prioritization of story cards based on the agile values for iteration planning and stakeholders are consulted to improve the quality of the story cards.

The customer relationship is maintained very well at this level. At this level companies ensure a deeper understanding of acceptance testing for the requirements testing, and subsequently stakeholders are consulted to elicit the requirement from the multiple viewpoints.

At this level companies stored the story cards on the database or the computer system for story cards reuse compared to use and throw concept of the traditional story cards. Story cards analysis can be done through the checklist based on the story cards and agile requirements value and principles.

Level 3 companies had increased their control over their technical practices like requirements testing practices and furthermore the practices related to dependencies of story cards and requirements conflicts are focused, but saw little improvement on the support of the RE process. They improved user understanding of story cards or requirements, internal and external communication but continued to report problem on analysis of domain where the system is going to be implemented and estimation of story cards. At this level no structured risk assessment is performed. Furthermore no consideration is taken towards non-functional requirements.

The SMM at level 3 maturity aims to help developers identify and improve problems related to customer relationship; story cards early testing (Acceptance Testing), dependencies and conflicts management of story cards. This is achieved by an assessment of current process and to identify where weakness lie. The goals, key process areas and assessment questionnaires for SMM maturity level 3 is summarised in the Appendix 1.

2.1.4 Level 4: Improved (People Orientation and Project Management Practices)

Companies at this maturity level are in a position to collect detailed measure of the story cards based requirements engineering process or practices and product quality, both the story cards based requirements engineering practices and products are quantitatively understood and controlled using detailed measurements (Paulk et al. 1995)

At this level the system's environment is studied in greater detail, not only the technical aspect but also the demands coming from the application domain, as well as the business process where the system should support. The improved level of the SMM model is also focused on the estimation of story cards, risk assessment, release planning and testing for non functional requirements. At this level the development team also focus on the advance validation of the story cards and identifies the unit tests from the story cards for the development stage. This is an internal attribute of the team which is not directly visible to the customer. Level 4 denotes a more active and mandatory examination of risk.

The SMM at level 4 maturity aims to help developers or managers to identify the non-functional requirements to improve the quality and to improve the estimation and release planning. This is achieved by an assessment of current process and to identify where weakness lie. The Appendix 1 summaries goals, key process areas and assessment questionnaires for SMM maturity level 4.

3. SOFTWARE PROCESS IMPROVEMENT ROADMAP FOR SMM

The SMM model is summarised in figure 4. The key features of the process are as:

- Adaptability and suitability assessment is carried out by the agile team members which are any like developers, coach, testers with collaboration of on-site customer. This is found to be a useful process during the SMM implementation. The purpose of involving this process is to ensure or to identify that the organisation follows the story cards based requirements engineering practices and process or not. If not then this adaptability and suitability recommends what they needs to do to follows the story cards based agile software development.

- Early in the SMM programme the business objectives or business goal are defined by the agile team. The goals drive much of the subsequent activity, especially the selection of KPAs or maturity level and prioritisation of the area for improvements.

- A tailored version of the SMM assessment (similar like CMMI model but the key process areas and goals are entirely different than CMMI) is carried out by the agile team, to identify area for improvement. This is also indicating the maturity level of the software process.

- The plan for the improvement is identified based on the inputs provided to the assessment questionnaires for each maturity level key process areas. In this plan, practices should be identified to support the implementation of the prioritised area for improvements.

- After the identification of the KPAs for each maturity level, a guide based approach was designed to capture the best practices in order to improve the prioritised area for improvement.

4. THE ADAPTABILITY AND SUITABILITY ASSESSMENT

Adaptability framework is based on the questionnaires, like the determining the main problems in the existing requirements engineering process or requirements engineering practices used or intend to use during the next project, existing knowledge on traditional requirements engineering practices and story cards based requirements engineering practices and process, customer relationship with development team, customer availability during the project, developers attitude or characteristic towards the process and by assessing their knowledge on agile requirements process.

An adaptability questionnaire is actually divided in the following four sections.

- Requirements engineering process used or intends to use.
- Problem identification during the story cards based requirements engineering process and Solution adopted or trying to adopt to solve problems
- Customer availability and relationship
- Developers and Managers knowledge on Agile requirements engineering

Our adaptability assessment brings three result based on the answers supplied on the adaptability Model. Those results are as following

1. Recommended to adopt story cards based requirements engineering methodology on you pilot project.
2. Ready to adopt a story cards based requirements engineering methodology but needs an improvement or needs to pay attention or focus on the recommended area.
3. Pilot project is not suitable for story cards based requirement engineering methodology, but they can still apply agility after adopting agile software development knowledge

Figure 4. The SMM process

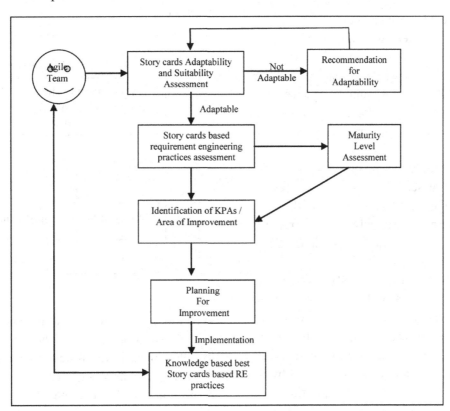

The story cards based requirements engineering process adaptability assessment requires an extensive knowledge of story cards practices and requirements engineering process. This adaptability just not cover one aspect of the requirements engineering based on the story cards, it covers all aspect of the story cards based requirements engineering process and it puts people in the centre of the assessment instead of process itself.

5. STORY CARDS BASED REQUIREMENTS ENGINEERING PROCESS ASSESSMENT METHOD AND IDENTIFICATION OF KPAS FOR IMPROVEMENT

The purpose of the assessment method is to assess the current story cards based requirements engi-

neering process. Process assessment consists of the knowledge on story cards based requirements practices and business case workshop, which focus on process improvement and provides a roadmap for process improvement. The SMM assessment model is based on a story cards based requirements engineering practices and process. It is a modified and customisable version of the SW-CMM assessment questionnaires. Emphasis placed on story cards based requirements practices, developers and on-site customers. This process is expected to enhance the communication and understanding; in particular it is expected to clarify the actual issues of the people involved in the process improvement actions. SMM recommended having a shared vision of the process improvement and any one can control process improvement activities at any stage. The following figure 5 shows to identify the areas for process improvement.

SW-CMM provides a guideline for good management and engineering practices, with a strong emphasis on management, communication, and co-ordination for development and maintenance of the software process. But as can be seen earlier SW-CMM does not suitable or acceptable for the agile software development practices and requirements engineering practices are poorly addressed.

The SMM model's main objective is to tailor the story cards based requirements practices and process for the agile environments; therefore identifying the maturity level of the agile requirements practices is a crucial activity in the SMM model.

The main objective from the SW-CMM assessment is to assess the capability of an organisation and identify the key process area as opportunities for process improvement. The main objective of the SMM assessment is to identify the areas for improvement. This approach is achieved by the SMM trough its own assessment questionnaires based on the story cards based requirements engineering practices, principles and values. See Appendix 1 for SMM assessment questionnaires. In SMM the KPA identifies the issues that must be addressed to achieve a maturity level in SMM maturity model. Each KPA identifies the cluster of goals considered important for enhancing process capability. These related activities are called the key practices. An automated tool has been built to facilitate the work of the SMM method.

The SMM assessment in this project is tailored to suit story cards based agile software development environments, their needs and objectives such as eliminating the practices which are not necessary for them and adding new practices which directly related to story cards based requirements engineering practices. Thus the SMM assessment method is flexible and does not involves any unnecessary KPAs or questionnaires.

Self assessment is the most common way of performing software process assessment (Dutta et al., 1999). The popularity for self assessment lies

Figure 5. Areas for improvement assessment framework

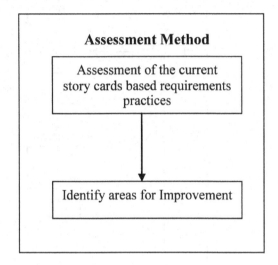

in its low cost, good accessibility and ownership of the result (Dutta et al., 1999). We are going to follow the self assessment for the story cards based requirements engineering process assessment. Automated assessment also considered for this approach.

SMM assessment questionnaires responses are: Yes, Partially, No, Not Applicable (N/A). This assessment response are very similar to SW-CMM response Yes, No, N/A and Don't Know. In our approach response partially permits the assumption that part of the process or work may have been performed or if performed then not fully addressed. N/A is selected when the practice is not possible to implement. If the answer is Yes than the practice is fully implemented and well addressed in the project. If No then it's not addressed at all.

In SMM assessment area of improvement is identified if the answer of the questionnaires is as Partially, No or N/A. Using these criteria the percentage for each KPAs can be calculated as follows:

$$\frac{\sum(Y_n) + \frac{1}{2}\sum(P_n) * 100}{\sum(T_n) - \sum(NA_n)}$$

Table 3. General idea of analysing the questionnaires

Answers	No of Answers	Total Questions	Total of Answers Expect N/A	KPA rating
Yes	3	7	6	83.33%
Partially	2			
No	1			
N/A	1			

Where Yn = Number of Yes answersPn = Number of Partially answersTn = Total Number of the questionsNAn = Number of N/A answers.

The following table 3 shows the general idea of analysing the questionnaires.

From table, 83.33% in the KPA rating is representing the capability level of the assessed KPA. The interpretation of this as following

- *Fully Achieved:* 86% to 100% there is evidence of a complete and systematic approach to and full achievement of the defined key practices in the assessed KPA. No significant weaknesses exist across the defined organisation unit.
- *Largely Achieved:* 51% to 85% there is evidence of sound systematic approach to and significant achievement of the defined key practices in the assessed KPA. Performance of the key practices may vary in some areas.
- *Partially Achieved:* 16% to 50% there is evidence of sound systematic approach to and achievement of the defined key practices in the assessed KPA. Some aspect of achievement may be unpredictable.
- *Not Achieved:* 51% to 85% there is little or no evidence of achievement of the defined key practices in the assessed KPA.

6. MAPPING THE AREA OF IMPROVEMENT WITH KNOWLEDGE BASED BEST AGILE PRACTICES

Current software process improvement models or CMM models are not compatible or difficult to identify the area of improvement for the agile software development practices and as we discussed earlier they are not well addressed to mature the requirements engineering practices. Therefore we suggested using the knowledge of the best story cards based requirements engineering practices that have proven successful in solving problems. Consider the following figure 6, which shows how the identified are of improvements are mapped with the knowledge based best story cards based requirements engineering practices.

The figure 6 is the conceptual framework and it is mainly concerned with capturing and enhancing the knowledge of story cards based RE practices. The primary concern of the framework is how the process improvement knowledge is captured or identified, how this knowledge is being stored, and how this knowledge of existing story cards based RE practices maps to the identified area of improvement. This guide is mainly concerned with the solving particular problems covered during the story cards based RE practices assessment, and enhances those related story cards based RE practices.

In table 4, example cells shaded in grey means the corresponds practices in the header of the highlighted cell is mapped to the identified area of improvement within the row of the highlighted

Figure 6. Capturing and mapping are of improvement with story cards based best RE practices

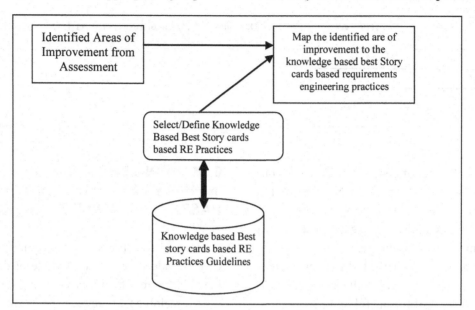

cell. That means the identified area of improvement takes the shaded correspondent practices as suggested by the agile team to be suitable to improve the identified area of improvement

We have developed a tool, story cards maturity model for measuring the success of story cards based RE process and also its impact on software process improvement models like CMM (Capability Maturity Model). The purpose of this form is to enable people with little or even no knowledge of story cards based RE practices, to estimate quickly easily whether story cards based RE methodology will fulfil their needs and requirements. The program consists of a form containing a handful of simple questions. The answers from these questions will provide immediate feedback on whether agile requirements practices are appropriate for the person who answered the question.

The form will ask questions about the critical areas surrounding agile requirements engineering practices; particularly story cards based requirements engineering practices. We need to identify with as few questions as possible whether story cards practices are, or are not appropriate. The

following aspects have been identified as critical for story cards based requirements practices:

- team size
- client on site
- team location

In order to provide a somewhat more subtle analysis, the following (less critical) aspects have also been selected:

- requirements volatility
- facilities strategy

Figure 7 is the illustration of our tool support which provides a web interface and online assessment forms to assess suitability for introducing story cards based RE practices into any organisation. The interface has been made simple thus allowing a first time user to fill in the form right away and getting a result within a few minutes. The results will be colour coded to help result interpretation and a summarised result will also be available. We have developed a web based

Table 4. Example of mapping process improvement best agile RE practices to area of improvement

KPA	Areas for Improvements	User stories	Acceptance Testing	Release Planning	Planning Game	Product Backlog	Information Radiator	Daily Meeting	On-site Customer	Self organising team	Task & Effort estimation	Task on info. radiator	Reflection Workshop	Interviews for elicitation	Observation of story cards
2.6 Story Cards change management	2.6.1 Story card is going to divide into task cards														
	2.6.2 Story card is testable														
3.2 Refine Story cards	3.2.1 Story cards must come with acceptance tests														
	3.2.2 Story cards must represent the business requirements														
4.2 Story cards estimation planning	4.2.1 Story cards are easy to estimate														
	4.2.2 Provide a basis for estimation, cost and schedule														
	4.2.3 Use the past story cards estimation from the similar project area														

Figure 7. Automated tool support

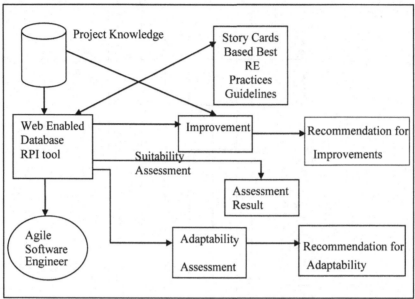

tool which provides an assessment and analysis for migrating to agile requirements.

7. RESULTS

We discussed our approach with three different organisations. The following table 5 summarize the participating companies.

We are still at an early stage of this project, so conclusions are necessarily tentative, and based on informal observation and discussion. All of the technical managers were very supportive of the idea of Agile requirements process improvement framework for agile software development means Story card Maturity Model (SMM) were

found in all the companies. Business managers tended to be somewhat more sceptical, and will require evidence of payback before becoming fully convinced of the usefulness of this approach. There was general acceptance and enthusiasm for a more quantitative approach. Company A is now well into the implementation phase of their SMM programme, and already report improvements in project planning and Agile requirements engineering process. However more analysis will be needed to determine if this is in fact a direct result of the improvements initiated as part of the SMM programme. It is important that improvements are applied in key process areas that will provide visible payback within a fairly short period. Certainly there should be measurable benefits

Table 5. Participating companies

	Type of company	Business Area	Total number of employees	Number of software developers
Company A	Independent	Flyer Design	28	11
Company B	Independent	Software House	23	9
Company C	Independent	Web development and hosting	19	12

visible with about a year from the outset, or else confidence and support for the SMM programme will be eroded. In all companies baseline measurements are being put in place that will allow us to measure the return on investment, and this will be the principal means by which we will evaluate the effectiveness of our approach.

8. CONCLUSION

The capability maturity models for software and process improvement were applicable to the agile methods (agile RE Process as well) or not, this is a still challenging issue in the field of the software engineering. In this chapter we describe why and how we have adapted the Agile requirements engineering process improvement framework and story card maturity model to focus on agile RE practices of agile software development methodology. We demonstrate an improvement methodology through a series of models that focus on the adaptability, suitability and improvement process of agile RE practices. Here we demonstrate how organisation can switch into agile organisation. In this chapter we also developed questionnaires for each level which will identify the key process area for improvement and which best knowledge based agile RE practice need to be considered to improve that KPAs by mapping the Area of Improvement with knowledge based Best Agile RE Practices. This chapter will provide a foundation for future development in the area of Agile RE process improvement for agile software development.

9. FUTURE WORK

A validation study of our SMM model is going to carry out with a group of experts in both research and industry. Future work includes creating a more flexible and an automated tool for an assessment to identify the KPAs or area of improvement for agile RE practices. Verification and evaluation is still required, and future work includes testing the model in an industrial setting.

REFERENCES

Agile Manifesto. (2006). *Manifesto for Agile Software Development.* Retrieved March 1, 2006 from http://agilemanifesto.org

Ahern, D. M., Clouse, A., & Turner, R. (2003). *CMMI Distilled: A Practical Introduction to integrated Process Improvement* (2nd ed.). London: Addison Wesley.

Beck, K. (2000). *Extreme Programming Explained: Embrace Change.* Reading, MA: Addison- Wesley Press.

Beecham, S., Hall, T., & Rainer, A. (2003, September). Defining a Requirements Process Improvement Model. *Software Quality Journal, 13*(13), 247–279.

Boehm, B. (2003). Value-Based Software Engineering. *ACM SIGSOFT Software Engineering Notes, 28*(2), 3–15. doi:10.1145/638750.638775

Boehm, B., Port, D., Jain, A., & Basili, V. (2002). Achieving CMMI Level 5 Improvements with MBASE and the CeBASE Method. *Cross Talk Journal.* Retrieved October 11, 2007 from http://www.stsc.hill.af.mil/CrossTalk/2002/may/boehm.asp

Bohem, B. (1981). *Software Engineering Economics.* Englewood Cliffs, NJ: Prentice Hall.

Brodman, J., & Johnson, D. (1997, May 19th). A Software Process Improvement Approach for small organisation and small projects. In *Proceedings of the 19th International Conference in Software Engineering,* Boston (pp. 661-662). New York: ACM Press.

Casey, V., & Richardson, I. (2002). *A Practical Application of Ideal Model*. Product Focused Software Process Improvement, 4th International Conference (PROFES), December 9-11, Rovaniemi – Finland (pp.172-184). Berlin: Springer.

Chrissis, M. B., Konrad, M., & Shrun, S. (2003). *CMMI: Guidelines for Process Integration and Product Improvement*. London: Addison Wesley.

Chrissis, M. B., Wemyss, G., Goldenson, D., Konrad, M., Smith, K., & Svolou, A. (2003). CMMI Interpretive Guidance Project: Preliminary Report [Internet]. Software Engineering Institute. Retrieved June 6th, 2004 from http://www.sei.cmu.edu/pub/documents/03.reports/pdf/03sr007-body-revised.pdf

Christie, A. M. (1999). Simulation in support of CMM-based process improvement. *Journal of Systems and Software*, *46*, 107–112. doi:10.1016/S0164-1212(99)00004-7

Cockburn, A. (2004). *Crystal Clear A Human-Powered Methodology for Small Teams, and it*. Reading, MA: Addison- Wesley Press.

Dangle, K., Larsen, P., & Shaw, M. (2005). Software process improvement in small organisation: A case study. *IEEE Software*, *22*(6), 68–75. doi:10.1109/MS.2005.162

Dutta, S., Lee, M., & Wassenhove, L. K. (1999). Software Engineering in Europe: A study of best practices. *IEEE Software*, *16*(3). doi:10.1109/52.765792

Dyba, T. (2003). Factoes of Software Process Improvement Success in Small and Large Organizations: An Empirical Study in the Scandinavian Context. In *Proceedings of the 9th European Software Engineering Conference held jointly with 10th ACM ACM SIGSOFT International symposium on foundations of software Engineering*, September 2003, Helsinki – Finland (pp.148-157). New York: ACM Press.

Faulk, S. (1996). Software Requirements: A Tutorial. In M. Dorfman & R. H. Thayer (Eds.) *Software Engineering* (pp 82-103).

Glib, T. (2003). Software Project Management Adding Stakeholder Metrics to Agile Projects. *The European Journal for the Informatics Professional*, *IV*(4), 5–9.

Gorschek, T., & Tejle, K. (2002). *A Method For Assessing Requirements Engineering Process Maturity in Software Projects*. Master Thesis, Blekinge Institute of Technology.

Herbsleb, J. D., & Goldenson, D. R. (1996). A Systematic Survey of CMM experience and results. In *Proceedings of the 18th international conference on Software Engineering*, May 1996, Berlin, Germany(pp.323-330). Washington, DC: IEEE Computer Society.

Highsmith, J. (2004). *Agile Project Management, Creating innovative products*. Reading, MA: Addison-Wesley.

Ihme, T., & Abrahamsson, P. (2005). The Use of Architechural Patterns in the Agile Software Development of Mobile Applications. *International Journal of Agile Manufacturing*, *8*(2), 97–112.

Johnson, J., Boucher, K. D., Connors, K., & Robinson, J. (2001). Collaborating on Project Success. *Software Magazine*. Retrieved January 20th 2008, from http://www.softwaremag.com/l.cfm?Doc=archive/2001feb/collaborativeMgt.html

Kotonya, G., & Somerville, I. (1998). *Requirements Engineering – Processes and Techniques*. Chichester, UK: John Wiley & Sons.

Li, E., Chen, H., & Lee, T. (2002). Software Process Improvement of Top Companies in Taiwan: a comparative study. *Total Quality Management*, *13*(5), 701–703. doi:10.1080/0954412022000002081

Lyard, A., & Orci, T. (2000). Dynamic CMM for Small organisations. *Proceedings ASSE 2000, the first Argentine Symposium on Software Engineering*, September 2000, Tandil- Argentina, (pp.133-149).

Nawrocki, J., Walter, B., & Wojciechowski, A. (2001). Towards the maturity model for extreme programming. *27th Euromicro Proceedings,* September 4-6, (pp.233-239).

Paulk, M., Curtis, M., & Weber, C. (1993). *Software Process Maturity Questionnaire: Capability Model version 1.1.* Carnegie Mellon-Software Engineering Institute. Retrieved January 1, 2007 from http://www.sei.cmu.edu/publications/documents/93.reports/93.tr.024.html

Paulk, M., Weber, C., & Curtis, M. (1999). The Capability Maturity Model for Software. In K. Emam & N. Madhavji (Eds.), *Elements of software process Assessment and Improvement* (pp. 3-22). Washington, DC: IEEE Computer Society Press.

Paulk, M. C. (1998). Using the Software CMM in Small Organisations. *The Joint 1998 Proceedings of the Pacific Northwest Software Quality Conference and the Eighth International Conference on Software Quality*, 13-14 October 1998, Portland, OR, Software Engineering Institute, (pp.350-361).

Paulk, M. C. (2001). Extreme Programming from a CMM Perspective. *IEEE Software*, *18*(6), 19–26. doi:10.1109/52.965798

Paulk, M. C., Weber, C. V., Curtis, B., & Chrissis, M. B. (1995). *The Capability Maturity Model for Software: Guidelines for Improving the Software Process (SEI)*. Reading, MA: Addison Wesley.

Persse, J. R. (2001). *Implementing the Capability Maturity Model*. Hoboken, NJ: John Wiley & Sons Inc.

Pikkarainen, M., & Mantyniemi, A. (2006). *An Approach for Using CMMI in Agile Software Development Assessments: Experiences from Three Case Studies, SPICE 2006 conference*, Luxemburg.

Raynus, J. (1999). *Software process improvement with CMM.* London: Artech House.

Schwaber, S., & Beedle, M. (2002). *Agile Software Development With Scrum*. Englewood Cliffs NJ: Prentice Hall.

Somerville, I., & Sawyer, P. (2000). *Requirements Engineering – A Good Practice Guide*. Chichester, UK: John Wiley & Sons.

Tim, K. (2004). *Practical insight into the CMMI*. New York: Artech house.

Turner, R., & Jain, A. (2002). *Agile meets CMMI: Culture clash or common cause XP/Agile universe 2002*. (LNCS Vol. 2418 pp. 60-69). Berlin: Springer.

Wiegers, K. (1999). First Things First: Prioritizing requirements. *Software Development, 7*(9) September. Retrieved from http://www.processimpact.com/pubs.shtml#requirements

Zaharan, S. (1998). *Software Process Improvement: Practical Guidelines for Business Success,* (1st Ed.). Reading, MA: Addision-Wesley.

APPENDIX: 1

Table A1.

Maturity Level	KPAs	Areas for Improvements
Level 1: Initial Level	No KPAs defined at this level	no process improvement goals defined at this unstructured level
Level 2	2.1 Story cards Elicitation Planning	2.1.1 Elicit Goal
		2.1.2 Elicit Functional requirements
		2.1.3 Define the scope of the story cards
		2.1.4 Identify non-functional requirements
	2.2 Defines standard structure of the story cards.	2.2.1 identification of structure fro the story cards
		2.2.2 Story cards Description section
		2.2.3 Story card is two to three sentences long, which include the summary or abstract of the user requirements requirement
		2.2.4 Story cards unique number
		2.2.5 Date of capturing
		2.2.6 Small and complete
		2.2.7 Other factors being considered
	2.3 Introduction of the validation of story cards	2.3.1 Requirement is traceable (Requirements traceability is ensured)
		2.3.2 Presented by the customer
		2.3.3 Specified acceptance tests criteria
	2.4 Stockholder's identification	2.4..1 conducted your own research to identify the stake holders of the story cards or requirements presented on the story cards
		2.4.2 On site customer is a domain expert
		2.4.3 Consider the stakeholders
		2.4.4 Identified where the system is going to be used
		2.4.5 There is a on-site customer to make and present the requirements
	2.5 Focus on the basic value of the story cards	2.5.1 Story card is simple
		2.5.2 Story card is testable
		2.5.3 Story card (Requirements presented on story card) is negotiable.
		2.5.4 Story card is valuable to customer
		2.5.5 Story card is easy to estimate
	2.6 Story Cards change management	2.6.1 Story card is going to divide into task cards
		2.6.2 Story card is testable
		2.6.3 It is easy to change story cards
		2.6.4 Story cards are negotiable
		2.6.5 Define modifiable story cards

Maturity Level	KPAs	Areas for Improvements
Level 3	3.1 Dependencies, Interaction and Conflict management	3.1.1 Story cards are independent
		3.1.2 Define an unambiguous story cards
		3.1.3 Story card is consistent
		3.1.4 Use language simply, consistently and concisely
		3.1.5 considered the influencing factors from the human domain are when writing story card
	3.2 Refine Story cards	3.2.1 Story cards must come with acceptance tests
		3.2.2 Story cards must represent the business requirements
	3.3 Story cards prioritisation based on agile software development values	3.3.1 Have you got the plan or tool for story cards prioritisation
		3.3.2 Are you prioritise story cards based on the XP principles and values
		3.3.3 Are you able to prioritise story cards at any stage
		3.3.4 Are you reprioritise story cards when new story cards are arrived
		3.3.5 Do you re-prioritize story cards when any kind of changes occurs?
	3.4 Stakeholders are consulted through on site customer OR Story cards from multiple viewpoints.	3.4.1 Try to link story card requirements and stakeholders
		3.4.2 On-site customer is there until the date of delivery
		3.4.3 Write story cards from multiple view point (Collect requirements from multiple viewpoints)
	3.5 Non functional requirements consideration	3.5.1 Specify quantitative requirements also on the story cards
		3.5.2 Peer-reviews for NFR
	3.6 Database system for story cards	3.6.1 Use a database system to store story cards compared to write them and throw to destroy
		3.6.2 Do you use the story cards from other project developed in the same area
	3.7 Use of checklist for story cards based RE analysis	3.7.1 Use checklist to do requirements or story cards analysis
		3.7.2 Check the story cards meet the Agile/XP Principles and values

Maturity Level	KPAs	Areas for Improvements
Level 4	4.1 Domain analysis	4.1.1 Look for domain analysis
		4.1.2 Define specialised terms used in the story cards
		4.1.3 Define the system boundaries during the domain analysis
	4.2 Story cards estimation planning	4.2.1 Story cards are easy to estimate
		4.2.2 Provide a basis for estimation, cost and schedule
		4.2.3 Use the past story cards estimation from the similar project area
	4.3 Plan for conflicts and conflicts resolutions	4.3.1 Uniquely identified each story cards and user stories on story cards
		4.3.2 Do you have any unique identifier plan or tool or technique for each story cards
		4.3.3 User stories are written by customer and programmer after the mutual understanding of them
		4.3.4 Reduce the development efforts
	4.4 Risk Assessment	4.4.1 Problem understanding
		4.4.2 Assess the story cards risk
		4.4.3 Do you apply the risk assessment to the story cards
	4.5 Release Planning	4.5.1 Have you classified story cards for the iteration planning
		4.5.2 Release planning is set by customers depends on the story cards
		4.5.3 Are you re-prioritise story cards with regularity
	4.6 Advance validation of story cards.	4.6.1 Define or propose validation checklist for story cards
		4.6.2 Assess the story cards correctness
		4.6.3 Provides the baseline for the validation and verification
		4.6.4 Do you conduct the story cards review with on site customer and development team?
		4.6.5 Do you plan to write acceptance tests same time on as capturing story cards?
		4.6.6 Do you apply the technique for story cards inspections?
		4.6.7 are you considering non-functional requirements on story cards
		2.6.8 Do you quantify the non-functional requirements

Chapter 7
Theory of Ontology and Meta-Modeling and the Standard
An Enabler for Semantic Interoperability

Keqing He
Wuhan University, China

Chong Wang
Wuhan University, China

Yangfan He
Wuhan University, China

Yutao Ma
Wuhan University, China

Peng Liang
Wuhan University, China

ABSTRACT

With the continuous development and rapid progress of information techniques, complexity and scale of information systems are expanding increasingly, which consequently brings our research focus on how to ensure the effective exchange of information and efficient interconnection between each part of a information system. However, different modeling paradigm, languages and platforms cause grammatical and semantic diversity to the existing information resources, a challenging approach to information resources management is needed to promote deep sharing of those information resources and implement rapid integration based on them. To realize semantic interoperation between diverse information systems and resources, the authors combine meta-modeling methodology in software engineering and ontology from philosophy to exploit a novel methodology named Theory of Ontology & Meta-modeling. Based on the methodology, the authors contributed to an international standard project ISO/IEC 19763-3: Metamodel for ontology registration since 2003, which was officially published as an international standard in Dec, 2007. Furthermore, we developed a Management and Service platform for Semantic Interoperability on Manufacturing Informationalization Software Component Repository (SCR). It can support ontology-based software component attributes classification, registration and management using

DOI: 10.4018/978-1-60566-731-7.ch007

ISO/IEC 19763-3 standard, and implement semantic (ontology) based software component query and retrieval. Based on above mentioned techniques, this platform can facilitate the management of semantic interoperability, which provides the reliable infrastructure for the reusing and sharing of heterogeneous software component resources.

1. CHALLENGE IN SOFTWARE ENGINEERING: SEMANTIC INTEROPERABILITY

With the continuous development of information techniques, information systems are now merging into our life and even becoming an essential and indispensable part in the social infrastructure. From general computing system to complex database management system and Enterprise Resource Planning (ERP) system, various kinds of information systems are scattered in different application domains and areas so that they can be typically deemed as distributed systems. Meanwhile, rapid progress of information techniques drives the evolution of software development paradigm. More specifically, with the shifting from object-oriented techniques to component based development method, not only the granularity of software modular grows bigger, but also the middle-ware technologies and component-based development become the main and popular techniques for software development. Furthermore, the raising of web services (Curbera, 2001; Newcomer E., 2002), service-oriented architecture(SOA) (Thomas, 2004; Newcomer, 2005), and semantic web (Berners-Lee, 2001; Daconta, 2003) cause great changes in both ingredient and development method of web-based information systems. On one hand, web services and semantic web services with greater granularity and more complicated structure are now regarded as the unit of current information systems; on the other hand, it is recommended to create information systems by dynamically linking and integrating existing information resources and service resources on the web. This situation leads to the fact that complexity and scale of information systems are expanding increasingly, which

consequently brings our research focus on how to ensure efficient interconnection, intercommunication and interoperation between each part of a common information system.

In the realm of software engineering, when the studied objects take radical changes in the scale, the essential problem of our research will change correspondingly. Considering a single information system, the primary task is to achieve the given functionality of it. Otherwise, if the whole functionality of a system will be realized through several information resources or other systems, this kind of system will be created by linking and integrating specified resources. Here, the key issue of developing current information system is how to organize and manage varied information resources systemically, enhance accessible rate of them, and finally promote knowledge sharing and interchange between them. However, different development methods and platforms make information resources differ in syntax and semantics, which might hamper the understanding and interacting between them. Therefore, effective solutions should be taken as a bridge to connect information resources and implement interoperation between them.

Generally speaking, interoperability is the ability to communicate and share data across programming languages and platforms(ISO, 1993). On information domain, interoperability will be defined as "the ability of two or more systems or components to exchange information and to use the information that has been exchanged (IEEE, 1990)" or "the ability of a collection of communicating entities to (a) share specified information and (b) operate on that information according to an agreed operational semantics(Lisa, 2004)". While we talk about interoperation between information

Figure 1. Information description languages and interoperation

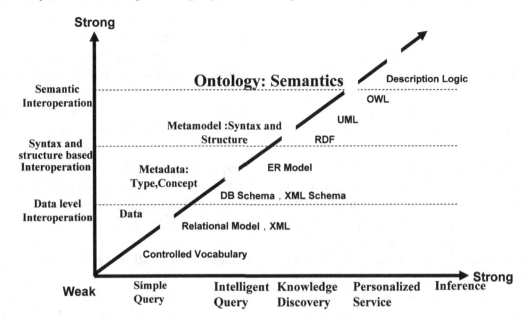

systems, we should pay more attention to their behavior of interaction with each other. So in terms of the previous definitions on interoperability, interoperation between information systems can be defined as: the capability that the message sent by one information system can be received, understood and processed by the other information system so that they can cooperate with each other to perform a specific task.

Since different information systems adopt different description languages and have different service capability, interoperation between them can be implemented at different levels, as Fig. 1 shows. Actually, people expect information systems can provide stronger service capability: from simple search to intelligent query and even to knowledge discovery, software is expected to provide appropriate services so that they can meet personalized requirements from various kinds of users. For this purpose, information description languages progress rapidly and their capability for representing semantics is strengthened accordingly, which can be used to support interoperation on different levels.

- Data dictionary, Entity-Relationship (ER) model and XML can help data level interoperation.
- Metadata abstract datatype and data element as the meta information of data, which can facilitate syntax and structure based interoperation between information resources.
- Meta-model is used to describe the structure of complex information, which is more complicated than metadata. Meta-model abstracts syntax and structure of various models so that it can also support syntax-based interoperation between information systems. For example, UML (Unified Modeling Language) meta-model defines modeling structure and principles of UML models, which can realize syntax interoperation between them.
- Ontology conceptualizes concepts and the relationship between them within a universe of domain. It expresses explicit meaning of exchanged information and the inherent relation between them.

Consequently, ontology is the basis of semantic interoperation.

Suppose that there are two information systems named A and B respectively. If information models they adopted are the same, then the interoperation between them can be conducted in an easy way. That is, the same data descriptive and modeling language can make the system A completely understand the messages sent by system B and then realize the data-level interoperation between A and B. On the other hand, if information models used in two systems are different, it is necessary to create the ontology mapping between them. Generally speaking, the process of modeling information model should obey specified modeling rules and adopt the corresponding modeling languages. Therefore, it is feasible to ensure the syntax interoperation between them based on the common meta-model and mapping rules between these two modeling languages. Furthermore, if the exchanged messages are meaningful, interconnection between these two information systems can be treated as semantic interoperation. Especially, Fig. 1 implies that efficient semantic interoperation will considerably enhance the service capability of systems. So undoubtedly, semantic interoperation is one of the active topics in current research and ontology is the key technique to realize semantic interoperation.

2. THEORY OF ONTOLOGY AND META-MODELING

To realize semantic interoperation between diverse information systems and resources, meta-modeling methodology in software engineering and ontology originating from philosophy are merged in this paper as a novel methodology, Theory of Ontology & Meta-modeling (He, 2005a; He, 2005c). First of all, it treats ontology as the classification mechanism of information resources to register and manage them in an orderly manner. Second, meta-modeling technology enables syntax-level interoperation on the abstract meta-level. The most important is that by means of semantic annotation, ontology can provide a comprehensive description, merging structural, syntax and semantic information, for models and meta-models in the meta-modeling architecture. Hence, theory of ontology & meta-modeling can guide effectively the sharing and exchanging of complex information resources on the web, consequently it is also the basis of semantic interoperation between heterogeneous information resources.

2.1 What is Ontology

The concept "Ontology" comes from philosophy, in which it is the study of the kinds of things that exist and can be used to describe the characteristic of "beings". In 20th century, ontology was formally introduced into computer science domain, involving knowledge engineering, natural language processing, knowledge representation, etc., because ontology explicitly expresses the implication of concepts in a specific domain. Especially, those concepts with specified implication can unify the common understanding of the universe of domain and then establish the foundation for communications between people.

Well, what is ontology? In information domain, the most popular and widely acceptable definition of ontology is, ontology is an explicit specification of a conceptualization(Gruber, 1993). In this definition, term "conceptualization" means that ontology can be treated as an abstract model of a phenomenon in the given world, and "explicit" implies that ontology specifies the precision of concepts, types of concept and their relations. Furthermore, Borst extended the previous definition as "An ontology is a formal specification of a shared conceptualization (Borst, 1997)". In his opinion, the term "sharing" illustrates an agreement between ontology users so that different people can get consensus on the same thing and communicate with each other, and "formal" hints that the accurate and precise mathematical description that ontology adopts can be understood and processed by machines to realize human-machine interaction.

Actually, ontologies are content theories about the sorts of objects, properties of objects and relations between objects that are possible in a specified domain of knowledge (Chandrasekaran, 1999). Currently, information resources are now augmenting increasingly and become more and more complicated, so we can use ontology to capture the semantics of information from various sources, give them a concise, uniform and declarative description (Fensel, 2001), which later can be treated as the semantic foundation of knowledge sharing and exchanging between people, people and machine as well as machines.

Due to the strong support that ontology provides to semantic interoperation between information systems, deep researches have been initiated on developing ontology modeling and descriptive languages, creating standard ontology for specific domains, or ontology inference, etc. What's more, most of them got some progresses in practice. Meanwhile, although issues on ontology registration, ontology evolution management, ontology mapping and ontology-based semantic annotation are very complex, relevant researches have been underway all around the world. More specifically, Karlsruhe University of Germany analyzed the process of ontology evolving and then proposed a base model for ontology life-cycle management(Baclawski, 2002; Stojanovic, 2004; Haase, 2004); State Key Lab. of Software Engineering(SKSLE), Wuhan University, China leaded the project on international standard, ISO/IEC 19763-3(1st Edition), to register administrative information of ontologies(ISO/IEC 19763-3, 2007) (He, 2005b; Wang, 2006). Especially, the developing standard named ISO/IEC 19763-3(2nd Edition) concentrated on evolution information of ontologies that are registered based on the first version(ISO, 2006) (He, 2007b; He, 2006).

Therefore, these two versions can collaborate with each other to form a comprehensive solution for ontology management (He, 2007a).

2.2 Meta-Modeling Technique and Meta-Model

Meta-modeling is a kind of meta computing method for abstract construction and aggregation of complex information structure. It can be used to manage information resources in a normative way and realize deep sharing of resources in Internet. So both academia and industry treat meta-modeling as the key technique to ensure semantic interoperation between information resources.

If meta-modeling technique is applied to objects in a specific research domain, we can abstract their characteristics, use modeling notations to represent them as models and finally get the corresponding meta-models. And accordingly, the features of meta-models are listed as follows:

(1) **Generality:** the meta-model can define the common characteristics in structure and behavior of multiple base objects;

(2) **Reversibility:** the meta-model can be extracted from the instance model; and instantiation of meta-model is the corresponding normative model.

(3) **Extensibility:** pre-defined extension mechanism, and the meta-model can be extended due to the practical requirements without modifying original structures and constraints;

(4) **Transformability and mapping ability:** mutual transformation between the models based on same meta-model using transformation and mapping rules.

Obviously, the meta-model plays important roles in two aspects: on one hand, it greatly promotes the standardization and unification of models; on the other hand, it supplies with the guarantee for sharing information and interop-

Figure 2. The four-layer meta-modeling architecture (OMG, 2006)

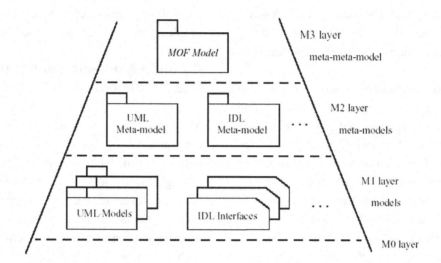

erability among models, according to the common features among models constructed from the same meta-model. The MOF (Meta Object Facility)(OMG, 2006) is the classic meta-model specification recommended by OMG (Object Manage Group). It is a well-extensible data management framework and defines a well-known four-layer meta-modeling architecture (as shown in Fig.2).

- **M0 Layer:** it is the instance layer in MOF, and is composed of abundant desired instances including model instances (for instance, the computer in real world) and application data instances (for example, Tom). Although objects may be greatly different from each other in their states, values etc, their structures and value ranges may have some similarities. Based on these, the model can be gotten by abstraction.
- **M1 Layer:** it is the model layer, the abstraction of object instances, to describe the common features of the instances of M0 layer, for instance, UML model. Modeling structures may be of analogous, although modeling objects and languages are probably distinct. Thus, the meta-model can be

attained by constraining the model structures and concepts.
- **M2 Layer:** it is meta-model layer, which is extracted the common modeling elements and constraints among elements of various models from M1 layer. For instance, the UML meta-model, CWM meta-model etc.
- **M3 Layer:** it is metameta-model layer depicting the common features of structures and semantics among meta-models of different modeling languages on the M2 Layer. Consequently, the MOF model, defined by the language based on the meta-language, would be on the layer of M3.

2.3 Details of Ontology and Meta-Modeling Theory

Ontology theory is a meta theory in nature, and it is constructed based on description logic. Ontology is an explicit specification of a conceptualization. The advantage of ontology can be summarized in two points: on one hand, ontology concept is similar to the thinking of human beings, and easy to understand; on the other hand, ontology theory is based on description logic, which is the formalization basis for the deduction. Thereby,

Figure 3. An Ontology Definition Meta-model of OWL within the MOF Framework (Brockmans, 2006)

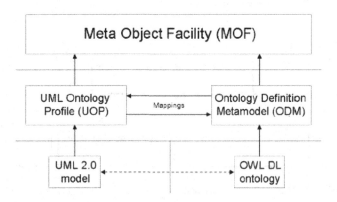

the combination of ontology theory and meta-modeling method in software engineering, which forms the theoretical basis of the meta-modeling, will strengthen the modeling and representation capability of meta-models, and facilitate considerably the semantic sharing of information resources (Cao, 2002). Especially, UML technique and MOF meta-modeling mechanism have already been applied widely in the software engineering community, while ODM (Ontology Definition Meta-model) makes UML Profile as one of feasible techniques to support the ontology development and maintenance, which is the basis for the relevant integration of ontology modeling and meta-modeling theories. Taking Ref. (Brockmans, 2006) as example, it illustrates how to guide the construction of ontology model based on MOF meta-model and UML Profile. The detailed steps are illustrated in Fig.3: (1) defining ODM and UOP based on MOF; (2) defining the visual symbolic notations for OWL DL ontologies through UML Profile, thereby bidirectional mapping can be created between ODM and UOP; (3) getting the two sorts of instances of OWL ontology model and UML model respectively by instantiation, and implementing the transformation between them based on the above defined mapping. Therefore, one of the effective ways to achieve the theory of Ontology & Meta-modeling is that, provid-

ing the appropriate mechanism for introducing ontology on the basis of existing meta-modeling theory and technique, and then making use of the rich semantics of ontology model to help us. Two ontology introducing mechanisms are presented as follows:

(1) Construction method (heavy-weighted method): during the meta-modeling process, a descriptive ontology concept is introduced as a classifier. The meta-model defined in this method is related with ontology model directly, and the meta-model can be affected by the evolution of ontology model. This method is generally used in the situation in which the meta classes in meta-model are defined by top level ontology for its stability. For instance, OWL-s(Chris, 2006) is a kind of meta-model of Web service, and describes for Web service the related concepts and relationships among them by using OWL concepts, e.g., Class, ObjectProperty, DataProperty, subClass etc. In the OWL-s meta-model, Output and Parameter are the classes, and Output is the subclass of Parameter.

(2) Annotation method (light-weighted method): in the meta-modeling process, the property set of classifier in this meta-model is defined by descriptive ontology introduced

Figure 4. Registry information instances of registry items based on RIM (OASIS, 2002)

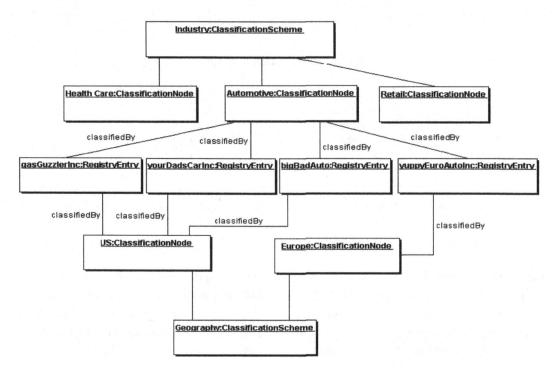

by annotation method. The relationship between the ontology model and meta-model defined by this method is a loose-coupled relationship. The properties of classifier in the meta-model are generally annotated by domain ontology and application ontology. For instance, Registry Information Model (RIM) is the meta-model of ebXML(OASIS, 2002), and defines the relations among the core concepts in the electronic business area. For the on-registry object, the relationship between the object and ontology can be built through the three classifiers of Classification, ClassificationScheme, and ClassificationNode. Fig. 4 shows the registry information instances of registry items extended based on RIM, where gasGuzzler-Inc is a registry item. Based on ontologies of Geography and Industry, their properties, US and Automotive, can be extended respectively.

3. META-MODEL FRAMEWORK FOR INTEROPERABILITY (MFI): INTERNATIONAL STANDARD ISO/IEC 19763

3.1 Overview of MFI

Due to the spread of E-Business and E-Commerce over the Internet, the effective exchange of business transactions and other related information across countries and cultures has been a great concern for people both inside and outside the IT industry. To follow these trends, many standardization activities have focused on the common facilities or generic modeling methods, such as e-business exchange format (e.g. XMI(OMG, 2000), SOAP(W3C, 2003)), description facility of information resources (e.g. RDF(W3C, 2004), XML(W3C, 2006)), Business process integration facilities (e.g. BPEL or BPMN), Registry facilities (e.g. MDR(ISO, 2004), ebXML R&R(OASIS, 2002)), etc. Obviously, these specifications enable the wide business cooperation between different organizations.

For this purpose, the contents described with these standards should be stored in the registries. Currently, many registries and repositories have been developed by defining suitable meta-models, which can be used to unify the format of registered objects and the relations between them. In general, meta-model is the model describing a series of models. That is, meta-model abstracts and standardizes the common syntax, semantic and structural features of models, modeling tools and modeling rules. Moreover, metaclasses and meta-relationships designated in a meta-model can be generalized as models in different ways; and vice verse, models generated from the same meta-model have inherent relations, and can realize the interoperation to some degree. In recent years, a great number of registries and repositories have been created to meet requirements of various organizations. However, structural and semantic differences in their meta-models hamper effective collaboration among communities. Therefore, a novel facility is needed to promote interoperation between existing heterogeneous registries, especially the interoperation between meta-models

they adopt, and generate a harmonized registry federation. To satisfy these requirements, this Meta Model Framework for Interoperability(MFI) family provides the facilities for describing various types of registries or meta-models as a consolidated set of meta-model frameworks and facilitates semantic interoperation between those meta-models.

More specifically, MFI proposes a series of mechanisms to describe, register and manage different types of meta-models and registries, including registration and description facility for various kinds of reusable modeling constructs, description and registration mechanisms for rules of model mapping and transformation to enable the harmonization of registry contents, etc. Fig.5 illustrates the overview of MFI.

MFI-2(Core model)(ISO, 2007a) is not only the essential part of MFI family but the foundation for defining other parts of MFI. Core Model designates a set of normative modeling elements and rules in the basic registration mechanism for models, so the rest of MFI family have to inherit some concepts and modeling elements from Core model. MFI-3(Meta-model for ontology registration, MOR)(ISO, 2007b) describes a meta-model

Figure 5. Overview of MFI

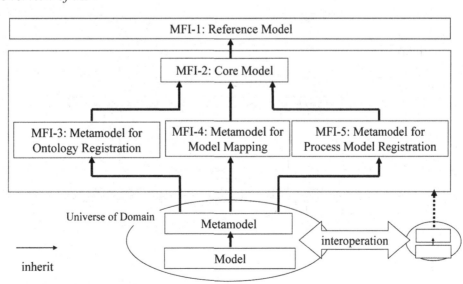

that provides a facility to register administrative information of ontologies. MFI-4(Meta-model for model mapping)(ISO, 2007c) can be used to register any sort of mapping rules between objects, such as meta-models, model elements or data elements, so that it can help model and data transformation at different levels. MFI-5(Meta-model for process model registration)(ISO, 2007d; Wang, 2007; Wang, 2008) provides a meta-model to register administrative, structural and semantic information of heterogeneous process models.

3.2 Meta-Model for Ontology Registration

Meta-model for ontology registration (ISO/IEC 19763-3)(ISO, 2007) is part 3 in MFI family, and its main objective is to register and manage administrative information with respect to structure and semantics of ontologies. MFI-3 provides a generic mechanism for ontology to promote semantic interoperation between ontologies, especially ontology-based interoperation between

information systems (He, 2005c; Wang, 2005). In 2003, ISO/IEC JTC1 SC32 approved that the work on the project ISO/IEC 19763-3 was to be taken on Prof. He Keqing's research group of SKLSE, Wuhan University, China, and Prof. He Keqing was requested as the editor of this project. In Dec, 2007, it was officially published as an international standard.

3.2.1 Overall Structure of ISO/IEC 19763-3

The differences in ontology descriptive languages and ontology development techniques make it difficult to fulfill semantic interoperation between ontologies. Fortunately, overall structure of ISO/IEC 19763-3 illustrates a comprehensive solution, as Fig. 6 illustrates.

With the vertical view of Fig. 6, ISO/IEC 19763-3 defines a three-layer structure "Ontology_Whole- Ontology_Component-Ontology_Atomic_Construct" to register common information of ontologies. It implies that ontology consists

Figure 6. Overall structure of ISO/IEC 19763-3

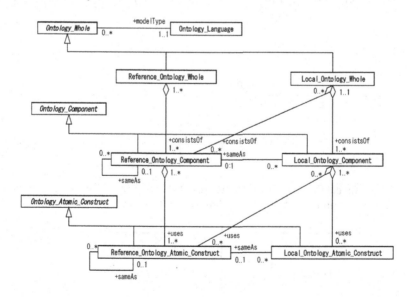

of ontology components and ontology component is composed of ontology atomic construct, which is treated as the smallest ingredient of ontology. Here, the three-layer structure emphasizes only on the language-independent information of ontologies and ignore their differences caused by representations. So for any ontology to be registered, ontology component and ontology atomic construct will respectively correspond to sentences and non-logical symbols (such as concepts, instances) of the ontology.

With the horizontal view of Fig. 6, ISO/IEC 19763-3 also specifies two kinds of ontology, Reference_Ontology_Whole(RO) and Local_Ontology_Whole(LO) to distinguish different roles that ontology plays in different cases. RO is used to represent common ontology in some domains, which is created and maintained by authorities and/or relevant domain experts to make it stable. Different from RO, LO is often used by particular information systems, which reuses some elements of ROs and makes some changes to meet different needs. As a result, if two LOs are derived from the same RO, there must be some inherent semantic relations between them. Then the information systems respectively adopting these two LOs can interoperate with each other on the basis of the common RO.

In addition, LO can also reuse some parts of RO, modify the reused part as well as add new elements in ISO/IEC 19763-3. So in Fig.6, it can be found that Reference_Ontology_Component (ROC) forms RO but LO is composed of two kinds of ontology component: one is ROC that is borrowed from RO directly; the other is Local_Ontology_Component(LOC) that is special for LO and generated by modifying or adding. Similarly, ROC consists of Reference_Ontology_Atomic_Construct(ROAC), while LOC is composed of both ROAC and Local_Ontology_Atomic_Construct(LOAC).

3.2.2 Examples

In this section, a case study in (Wang, 2006) will be demonstrated to show how to realize semantic interoperation between two information systems based on the same RO. In this case, RO M is the ontology that is released by some standardized organization and expressed with RDFs. Ontology M says that "Credit card is used to pay purchases." and "Customer uses credit card". Then OWL-based ontology A and ontology B will be adopted by two specified information systems as the corresponding LOs. More specifically, Ontology A reuses "Credit Card" in M and changes "customer" to "buyer". Here we will take LO A as an example to show that it is feasible not only to use ISO/IEC 19763-3 for registration of ontology, ontology component and ontology atomic construct, but to record the reusing relation between LO and RO.

Table 1 lists the registration information of Ontology A, which means that the name of the registered ontology is "A" and it is described with OWL. Ontology A consists of two LO, i.e ROC01 from ontology M and LOC01 defined by A itself.

Table 2 shows the registration information of LOC01. It means that the name of the registered ontology component is LOC01, which contains three ontology atomic constructs, i.e. one concept "buyer" from LO A, two concepts "Credit_Card" and "uses" from RO M.

Table 1. Registration information of Ontology A

Attribute/Reference	Literal/Instance
Administration_record	*Administraton_Record03*
URI	*uri_A*
ontologyName	*A*
modelType	*OWL*
consistsOf	*OID of uri_M#ROC01*
	OID of uri_A#LOC01

Table 2. Registration information of Ontology_Component LOC01

Attribute/Reference	Literal/Instance
Administration_record	*Administraton_Record04*
namespace	*uri_A#*
sentenceIdentifier	*LOC01*
consistsOf	*OID of uri_A#buyer*
	OID of uri_M#Credit_Card
	OID of uri_M#uses

Table 3. Registration information of Ontology_Atomic_Construct "Credit_Card"

Attribute/Reference	Literal/Instance
Administration_record	*Administraton_Record02*
namespace	*uri_M#*
nonLogicalSymbol	*Credit_Card*

Table 3 implies the registration information of ontology atomic construct named "Credit_Card". It is a non-logical symbol from ontology M.

4. APPLICATION OF MFI-3 IN THE MANUFACTURING INFORMATIONALIZATION

Informationalization is the trend in the global economic and social development, and the software industry is fundamental and strategic industry in this trend. In the last few years, the environment and policies for the software industry in China are ameliorated gradually, and the growth rate is increased rapidly. The impact of the software industry on the economic development is strengthened. Meantime, it is also a key age for the transformation of software development methods and the adjustment of the software industrial structure and division. The component-based software development (CBSD) is becoming the main stream in the software development methods. The CBSD method provides the technical support for the production of software in industrial way, and has a great impact to the transformation of software development methods and the adjustment of the software industrial structure and division. The CBSD method is also regarded as one of the key factors for advancing the software industry. With the maturation of related technologies, the software component resources are becoming pervasive over the Internet environment; on the contrary, the research on the software component resource management gets limited achievement. The existing methods and techniques for the software component classification, registration (e.g. ComponentSource, ebxmlrr, UDDI(Accenture, Ariba, Inc., 2000)), repository, and interoperability management are not capable to meet the requirements posed by the complex information structure (attribute, interface) of software component resources (e.g. composition, circulation, management, and reuse), which consequently hinders the development of software enterprises in China.

To this end, it is necessary to investigate the key methods and techniques for software component development and management, to make standards in the international, national and industrial level for the standardization of the production, testing, circulation, and sharing of software components; to establish the infrastructure for software component development for the purpose of application of CBSD methods and techniques. For this purpose, we developed the "Management and Service platform for Semantic Interoperability on Manufacturing Informationalization Software Component Repository(SCR)" based on the ISO standard ISO/IEC 19763-3. This platform can support the encapsulation, classification, registration, repository management of software components. This platform is based on the Client/Server architecture, and provides the programmable interface based on web services, which can be extended flexibly with SOA (Service-Oriented Architecture).

The major difference between this platform and other existing software component repositories (e.g. Shanghai software component repository, Peking University JadeBird software component repository) is the ontology-based software component attributes classification, registration and management using ISO/IEC 19763-3 standard, and implementation of semantic (ontology) based software component query and retrieval. Based on above mentioned techniques, this platform is quite open to other platforms, and facilitates the management of semantic interoperability, which provides the reliable infrastructure for the reusing and sharing of heterogeneous software component resources. The detailed architecture of this platform is shown in Fig.7.

The detailed architecture of software component repository platform is shown in Fig. 8. First, we specify the domain model in the manufacturing informationalization using ontology technique, and use the ontology as the logical mechanism in the repository storage, which makes the software component repository as a knowledge repository on software component. The semantic-based query and deduction can be executed on this knowledge repository, which implements the query and management of software components, and ensure the synchronized evolution between domain knowledge and information model of software component repository. The other advantage of ontology-based classification and registration is the user-friendly services for users, which realizes the simple declarative language or query interface in natural language. Second, we employ the UML as the uniform notation for the design, development, publication, registration and application process of software component, and tailor the latest UML 2.0 specification to accommodate the characteristics of software component in the domain of KAIMU manufacturing, which integrates the component diagram, state chart diagram, class diagram and use case diagram effectively to represent the interface and behavior of software component. Third, we design the service interface based on web service, which makes the platform independent from operating system and programming languages. This is fundamental for the heterogeneous system integration and third

Figure 7. Overview of software component repository

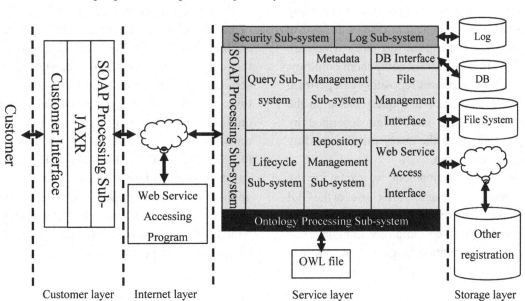

Figure 8. Detailed Architecture of software component repository platform

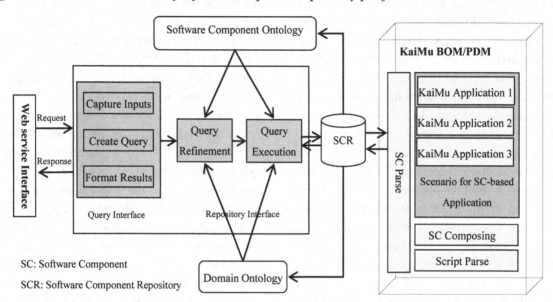

party software component trading. This platform can implement easily the query in natural language due to the employment of ontology technique, which is a great benefit for common user. For example, user queries the software component repository using web service interface, and gets the query result. In this query process, the predefined component ontology and domain ontology can monitor the query optimization and execute the query, i.e. the query can be optimized according to the software component attributes defined in ontology, and filter out the attributes which are not defined in the software component ontology. The software component repository can perform the ontology deduction and query based on the software component knowledge described by ontology, and return the query result according to the query condition.

In the system development, we use Java as the implementation language, and Eclipse for the GUI development of software component repository. We adopt OWL (Web Ontology Language) as the ontology description language, and Protégé as the ontology editor tool for the development of manufacturing domain ontology and software component ontology. Jena is employed for the ontology model operation and ontology model database. The ontology defined in OWL is parsed into ontology model, and stored in the database. This platform can also support the IBM DB2 database by the extension of the database connection classes (database types, connected users and password, etc) in Jena.

This project is theoretically based on the theory of ontology & meta-modeling, which is a concrete application of the ISO/IEC 19763-3 standard in the semantic interoperability management and service (ontology-based classification, registration, repository management, model mapping, ontology query, etc) for complex information resources integration. As latest information till Oct, 2007, the BOM (Bill of Material) products constructed by software components have been applied in mechanics, electronics, light industry, and textile industry, etc, including 239 enterprises, which advances considerably the technical level of manufacturing enterprises.

ACKNOWLEDGMENT

This research project was supported by the National Basic Research Program of China (973) under Grant 2007CB310801.

REFERENCES

Accenture, A. Inc., Commerce One, Inc., Fujitsu Limited, et al. (2000). UDDI Technical White Paper.

Baclawski, K., Kokar, M. M., & Waldinger, R. J. (2002). *Consistency Checking of Semantic Web Ontologies. the First International Semantic Web Conference on the Semantic Web* (pp. 454-459). London: Springer-Verlag.

Berners-Lee, T., Hendler, J., & Lassila, O. (2001). The Semantic Web. *Scientific American, 5*, 29–37.

Borst, W. N. (1997). *Construction of Engineering Ontologies for Knowledge Sharing and Reuse.* PhD thesis, University of Twente, Enschede.

Brockmans, S., & Haase, P. (2006). *A Metamodel and UML Profile for Rule-extended OWL DL Ontologies -A Complete Reference.* Tech. Rep. University Karlsruhe (TH), Karlsruhe, Germany.

Cao, Y., Zhao, J., Han, Y., & Dai, G. (2002). A Paradigm of Software development for Mass Customization. *Journal of Computer Research and Development, 39*(5), 593–598.

Chandrasekaran, B., Josephson, J. R., & Benjamins, V. R. (1999). What are ontologies, and why do we need them? *IEEE Intelligent Systems, 14*(1), 20–26. doi:10.1109/5254.747902

Chris M., & Lewis, G. A. (2006). *Model Problems in Technologies for Interoperability: OWL Web Ontology Language for Services (OWL-s).* CMU/SEI Technical Notes (CMU/SEI-2006-TN-018).

Curbera, F., Nagy, W. A., & Weerawarana, S. (2001). *Web Services: Why and How.* Workshop on object oriented web services, OOPSLA, Florida.

Daconta, M. C., Obrst, L. J., & Smith, K. T. (2003). *The Semantic Web: A Guide to the Future of XML, Web Services, and Knowledge Management.* Indianapolis, IN: Wiley Publishing.

Fensel, D. (2001). *Ontologies: Silver Bullet for Knowledge Management and Electronic Commerce.* Berlin: Springer.

Gruber, T. (1993). A Translation Approach to Portable Ontology Specifications. *Knowledge Acquisition, 5*, 199–220. doi:10.1006/knac.1993.1008

Haase, P., Sure, Y., & Vrandecic, D. (2004). *Ontology Management and Evolution - Survey, Methods and Prototypes.* Technical Report.

He, K., He, F., & Li, B. (2005a). Research on Service-Oriented Ontology &Meta-Modeling Theory and Methodology. *Chinese Journal of Computers, 28*(4), 524–533.

He, Y. (2007a). *Research on ontology management metamodels for semantic interoperability.* Ph.D Thesis, Wuhan University, China.

He, Y., & He, K. (2007b). Ontology Evolution Management Framework for Reliable Semantic Interoperation. *Computer Engineering, 33*(18), 26-27, 30.

He, Y., He, K., & Wang, C. (2005b). Metamodel Framework for Ontology Registration (MMF4Ontology Registration) for Semantic Interoperation. *1st International Conference on Semantics, Knowledge and Grid (SKG 2005),* (p. 84). Beijing: IEEE Press.

He, Y., He, K., & Wang, C. (2005c). Research on Semantic Web Service-Oriented MMFI for Complex Information Registration. *IEEE International Workshop on Service-Oriented System Engineering (SOSE 2005),* (pp. 237-243). Beijing: IEEE Press.

He, Y., He, K., & Wang, C. (2006). Ontology Registration Based Approach for Trustable Semantic Interoperation. *Computer Engineering and Applications, 34*(pp. 8-9, 25).

Institute of Electrical and Electronics Engineers (IEEE). (1990). *IEEE Standard Computer Dictionary: A Compilation of IEEE Standard Computer Glossaries.* New York, IEEE Press.

International Organization for Standardization (ISO) (2004). *ISO/IEC 11179: Information technology – Metadata Registries.*

International Organization for Standardization (ISO) (2006). *ISO/IEC 19763-3: Information technology – Framework for metamodel interoperability –Part 3(2nd Edition): Metamodel for ontology evolution.* Working Draft.

International Organization for Standardization (ISO) (2007b). *ISO/IEC 19763-3: Information technology – Framework for metamodel interoperability –Part 3: Metamodel for ontology registration.*

International Organization for Standardization (ISO). (2007c). *ISO/IEC 19763-4: Information technology – Framework for metamodel interoperability –Part 4: Metamodel for Model Mapping.* Committee Draft.

International Organization for Standardization (ISO). (2007d). *ISO/IEC 19763-5: Information technology – Framework for metamodel interoperability –Part 5: Metamodel for Process Model Registration.* Working Draft.

International Organization for Standardization (ISO) (1993). *ISO/IEC 2382: Information Technology-Vocabulary.*

International Organization for Standardization (ISO). (2007a). *ISO/IEC 19763-2: Information technology – Framework for metamodel interoperability –Part 2: Core Model.* Final Committee Draft.

Lisa, L. Brownsword, D. J. Carney, D. Fisher, et al (2004). *Current perspectives on interoperability.* Pittsburgh, PA: Software Engineering Institute, Carnegie Mellon University, CMU/SEI-2004-TR-009.

Newcomer, E. (2002). *Understanding Web Services.* Boston: Addison-Wesley.

Newcomer, E., & Lomow, G. (2005). *Understanding SOA with web services.* Boston: Addison-Wesley.

OASIS/ebXML Registry Technical Committee. (2002). *OASIS/ebXML Registry Information Model.*

Object Manage Group(OMG). (2006). *Meta Object Facility (MOF) Core Specification.* Retrieved from http://www.omg.org/docs/formal/06-01-01.pdf

Object Management Group(OMG). (2000). *OMG XML Metadata Interchange (XMI) Specification.*

Stojanovic, L. (2004). *Methods and Tools for Ontology Evolution.* Ph.D Thesis, University of Karlsruhe, Karlsruhe, Germany.

Thomas, E. (2004). *Service-oriented architecture: A Field Guide to Integrating XML and Web Services.* Upper Saddle River, NJ: Prentice Hall.

Wang, C. (2005). *Research on Framework of Meta-Model Interoperability for Ontology Registration.* Master Thesis, Wuhan University, China.

Wang, C. (2008). *Research on Process Model Management Framework for Mass Customization.* Ph.D Thesis, Wuhan University, China.

Wang, C., & He, K. (2007). Extending Metamodel Framework for Interoperability (MFI) to Register Networked Process Models. *Dynamics of Continuous Discrete and Impulsive Systems- Series B- Applications & Algorithms, 14*(S6), 72–78.

Wang, C., He, K., & He, Y. (2006). MFI4Onto: Towards Ontology Registration on the Semantic Web. *6th International Conference on Computer and Information Technology (CIT 2006)* (p. 40). Seoul: IEEE Press.

World Wide Web Consortium. (W3C). (2003). *Simple Object Access Protocol (SOAP) Specification*. Retrieved from http://www.w3.org/TR/soap12/

World Wide Web Consortium. (W3C). (2004). *Resource Description Framework (RDF)*. Retrieved from http://www.w3.org/RDF/

World Wide Web Consortium. (W3C) (2006). *Extensible Markup Language (XML)* 1.0 (Fourth Edition). Retrieved from http://www.w3.org/TR/REC-xml/

KEY TERMS AND DEFINITIONS

Local Ontology: ontology that is specialized for defined applications and based on at least one reference ontology.

Metamodel Framework for Interoperability (MFI): framework for registering artifacts that are based on meta-model and model.

Semantic Interoperability: the ability to exchange and use information between two or more entities.

Meta-Modeling: a methodology of how to extract common information from models and create a meta-model.

Universe of Domain: all those things of interest that are concrete or abstract and that have been, are, or ever might be.

Ontology: description of a universe of domain in a language that a computer can process.

Reference Ontology: ontology that is usable and sharable by a community of interest.

Chapter 8
Requirements Traceability

Elias Canhadas Genvigir
Federal University of Technology – Paraná – UTFPR, Brazil

Nandamudi Lankalapalli Vijaykumar
National Institute for Space Research – INPE, Brazil

ABSTRACT

This chapter presents a research about the Software Requirements Traceability. The main elements of traceability, definitions, problems and prospects are presented. The chapter is organized by topics and its beginning is a review about requirements engineering, its categories (Elicitation, Analysis and Negotiation, Documentation, Validation, and Management) and its role in software development. Afterwards, the requirements management and its elements (Identification, Change Management and Traceability) are described. Traceability is discussed; its aspects and problems are exploited as well as its classifications, techniques, links, metrics and models. Finally the Conclusion presents the main points that can be explored in future researches.

1 INTRODUCTION

Software production activity, also known as software development process, has been improving due to the demands in quality increase of those products.

The demand for more quality, cost decrease added to introduction of new technologies naturally forces to process improvement. Those facts are not new and this occurs in several other production areas that employ different techniques to increase their development processes. In particular for software the research area involved with the process improvement is the Software Engineering (Bauer, 1969; IEEE, 1990; IEEE, 2004).

The very first model ever employed in the software development process, that proposed work segmentation, is the waterfall model. It was able to allow a structured overview about the software development and its structure was the foundation stone to propose new processes as new necessities were required.

There are other development models such as prototyping, incremental, evolutionary, and spiral.

DOI: 10.4018/978-1-60566-731-7.ch008

It is interesting to observe a common point in all these models: all of them start with Requirements Engineering. Generally speaking, Requirements Engineering is the process to identify stakeholders and their needs, and documenting these in such a way that makes analysis, communication, and subsequent implementation feasible and at the same time leading to a product of quality and reliability (Nuseibeh & Easterbrook, 2000).

The fact that Requirements Engineering being the first activity within the software production process can be better explored by analyzing the following statements:

"The main goal of Requirements Engineering is to define the purpose of the system proposed and to define its external behavior" (Antoniou et al., 2000).

"The primary measure of success of a software system is the degree to which it meets the purpose for which it was intended" (Nuseibeh & Easterbrook, 2000).

The first statement refers to the definition of purpose, which is an inherent characteristic during the initial activities both in projects and research methodologies (Basili et al., 1994; Solingen & Berghout, 1999).

The second refers to meet the intended purpose. If a software development's basis is to come up with a solution to a given problem, then it is of a fundamental importance the knowledge of the exact dimension of the problem to be solved. Requirements are initially discovered in projects and to understand them is a basic condition for the next phases.

Thus, one can get an idea of the importance with respect to requirements and why the Requirements Engineering occurs in the initial phases within the development process.

Requirements engineering activities can be divided into five categories: Elicitation, Analysis and Negotiation, Documentation, Validation, and Management. These definitions alternate among different authors (Jarke & Pohl, 1994; Sawyer et al., 1998; Graham, 1997; Kotonya & Sommerville, 2000; Sommerville, 1995) but the concepts are similar:

- Elicitation – It is the activity that involves the discovery of the requirements of the system. In this activity the system developers work together with customers and users to define the problem to be solved, the services that the system should provide, the system performance requirements, the characteristics of hardware and other resources inherent in the system. There are three levels of requirements elicitation: business, user, and functional.
- Analysis and Negotiation – The customers and users needs must be in compliance with the definitions of software requirements. This activity is used to analyze in detail the requirements and resolve possible conflicts between those involved with the system.
- Documentation – Requirements need to be documented to serve as a basis for the remainder of the development process. This documentation must be made in a consistent way and must follow some standards to demonstrate, in several levels of detail, the requirements specification.
- Validation – This activity ensures that the software requirements specification is in compliance with the system requirements. This means that the requirements will be checked to assess whether they have acceptable representation and description beyond the analysis of properties as correctness, completeness, consistency and feasibility.
- Management – The Requirements management activity should assist the requirements evolution maintenance through the process development covering all

Figure 1. Requirements engineering process (Based on: NASA, 1990; Kotonya & Sommerville, 2000)

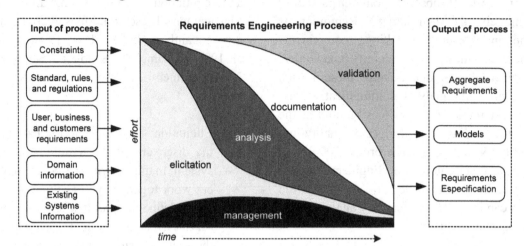

processes involved in changes in the system requirements

2 REQUIREMENTS MANAGEMENT

One of the major difficulties for the requirements engineering is the control and the aggregation of new system requirements. This occurs due to the impact of proposed changes, the process inflexibility and the difficulty in providing support to apply these changes.

Requirements Engineering aims to solve such problems. Its main concerns are managing changes to agreed requirements, managing the relationships between related requirements, and managing dependencies between the requirement document and other documents produced during other software engineering processes Sommerville & Sawyer, 1998).

Leffngwell and Widrig (2000) define the requirements management as a systematic approach to elicitation, organization, and documentation of a process that establishes and maintains agreement between the customer and the project team on the changing requirements of the system. Though a difficult task, the requirements change is seen as something normal and inevitable, an inherent fact of software.

So, requirements management can be seen as a parallel process to support other requirements engineering activities (Sommerville & Sawyer, 1998; Kotonya & Sommerville, 2000) taking place even after the specification phase. Requirements engineering process and the requirements management activity, occurring during the process, can be seen in Figure 1.

Requirements management can be divided into three specific areas:

a. Identification – Activities related to identification and storage requirements. Identification practices focus on the assignment of a unique identifier for each requirement and basically there are 4 techniques for its implementation: Natural identification scheme for hierarchical requirements, that identifies offspring requirements following parent requirement's identification (Leffingwell & Widrig, 2000); Dynamic renumbering, which allows automatic interdocument renumbering of paragraphs when inserting information using word processing systems and cross references (Kotonya & Sommerville, 2000); Database record identification, in which each requirement added into a database is considered as an entity so that it can be uniquely identified, versioned, referenced and managed (Kotonya & Sommerville, 2000); Symbolic identification, requirements are identified using symbolic names related to the contents of the requirement for example, EFF–1, EFF–2.

b. Change management – Activities related to requirements changes as impact analysis, communication, stability measurement and incorporation of elements in the system. System requirements are changeable during the entire life cycle and system developers must continuously and carefully manage the changes of system requirements to provide a useful and satisfying system for their customers at a reasonable cost and time (Kobayashi & Maekawa, 2001). Leffingwell and Widrig (2000) introduce five guidelines to manage changes: 1)Recognize that changes are inevitable, and plan for their implementation, 2)Baseline the requirements, 3)Establish a single channel to control changes, 4) Use a change control system to capture changes, 5) Manage changes hierarchically. In addition to general guidelines there are several authors that define methods to managing changes in requirements as Crnkovic et al. (1999) proposing support to changes management during the product life cycle; Lindsay et al. (1997) emphasize the fine granularity; Lam et al. (1999) introduce metrics for use in support, in this case the main management activity is the measurement; and Kobayashi and Maekawa (2001) who created the model NRM (Need–based Requirements Management) that consisted of objects concerned with specifying system requirements, e.g., needs, goals, actions, stakeholders, systems, behaviors, etc., and relationships among them analyzing these feature based on the following four aspects (Where, Who, Why, What).

c. Traceability – Traceability activities as definition of links between requirements and other artifacts produced in the development process. Traceability is the main goal of this work and it will be thoroughly explored below.

3 TRACEABILITY

Requirements traceability begins at elicitation advancing through the system development until the maintenance and it is the main activity of the requirements engineering (Nuseibeh & Easterbrook, 2000).

Traceability is intimately associated with producing software artifacts related to requirements, and relationships among these requirements. In fact, requirements traceability ensures a continuous agreement between the stakeholders and the artifacts produced during the development process of the software (Letelier, 2002). Besides, it enables a clear understanding of the relationships among software requirements, design and implementation. Software designer can be guided to identify which elements satisfy the requirements and those that do not satisfy (Palmer, 2000).

Traceability can also aid in identifying variations in schedules as well as project costs (Palmer, 2000; Davis, 1993; Dömges & Pohl, 1998; Pinheiro, 2003). It is also very useful to project managers to verify whether requirements were observed within the software components, resolving conflicts among requirements, verify requirements in the test process and other issues (Sayão & Leite, 2004).

Depending on its semantics, traceability may be used to: (a) assist in verifying requirements; (b) establish the effect of changes in the requirement specification by means of artifacts or documentation (e.g. design, test and implementation); (c) understand the evolution of an artifact; and (d) understand the aspects of design and support of Rationales (Tang et al., 2007). Thus, creating and maintaining such relationships may provide an efficient basis to guarantee software quality, dealing with changes and software maintenance (Spanoudakis et al., 2004).

3.1 Classifications of Traceability

The capacity to trace a requirement from its origin up to all its refinements is defined as Forward Tracing, and the capacity to trace refinements from requirements is defined as Backward Tracing (Davis, 1993). These two capacities should be inserted in every type of traceability, and it is a basic property to conduct a complete traceability. A traceability process is considered as a failure if it does not execute both capacities. Traceability can be: a) horizontal and vertical; and b) pre and post–traceability.

Horizontal traceability is a traceability between versions and variants of a requirement, or other artifacts, within a particular phase of its life. Vertical traceability illustrates traceability between requirements and artifacts produced during the process development throughout the project life cycle (Belford et al., 1976; Ramesh & Edwards, 1993; Gotel, 1995). A simplified distinction between horizontal, vertical, forward, and backward traceability is shown in Figure 2.

Kotonya and Sommerville (2000) emphasize the direction of traceability and further extend vertical traceability with '*to*' and '*from*' attributes as well as with traceability between requirements and other artifacts. This classification describes bi–directional nature of traceability (extended by (Kotonya & Sommerville, 2000) base on (Davis, 1993)):

- Forward–to traceability: traceability of sources (customer requirements, system

Figure 2. Horizontal and vertical traceability (Adapted from: Gotel, 1995)

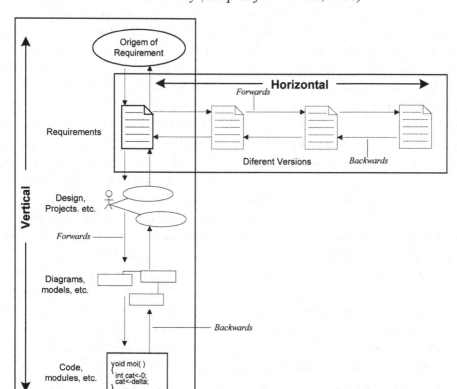

level requirements, etc) to requirements.
- Forward–from traceability: traceability of requirements to design specifications.
- Backward–to traceability: traceability of design specifications to requirements.
- Backward–from traceability: traceability of requirements to their sources (customer requirements, system level requirements, etc)

The second type of traceability deals with pre–traceability, which is concentrated in the life cycle of requirements before they are included in the requirements specification, and post–traceability, concentrates in the life cycle of requirements after being included in the requirements specification (Gotel & Finkelstein, 1994).

Figure 3 shows the pre and post–traceability, it is possible to observe that requirements knowledge is distributed and merged in successive representations.

Gotel and Finkelstein (1994) distinguish Pre and Post–Traceability. Although both these types of traceability are needed it is crucial to understand their subtle differences, as each type imposes its own distinct requirements on potential support.

The main differences, between Pre and Post–Traceability, involve the information they deal with and the problems they can assist.

Post–traceability depends on the ability to trace requirements from, and back to, a baseline (requirements specification) (Figure 3), through a succession of artifacts in which they are distributed. Changes to the baseline need to be re–propagated through this chain (Gotel & Finkelstein, 1994).

Pre–Traceability depends on the ability to trace requirements from, and back to, their originating statement(s), through the process of requirements production and refinement, in which statements from diverse sources are eventually integrated into a single requirement in the requirements specification. Changes in the process need to be re–worked into the requirements specification. Changes to the requirements specification need to be carried out with reference to this process, so they can be instigated and propagated from their source. This requires visibility of the subtle interrelationships that exist between initial requirements (Gotel & Finkelstein, 1994).

3.2 Techniques of Traceability

The establishing, the maintenance and the relationships representation, that are present in different traceability types, are conducted through some traceability technique. The use and development of these techniques originated in the early 70s

Figure 3. Pre and post–traceability (Adapted from Gotel, 1995)

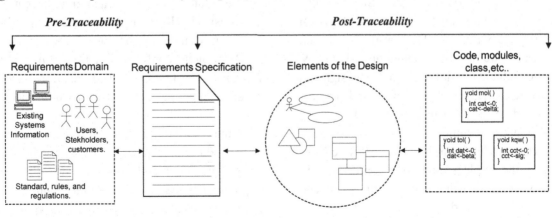

(Aizenbud–Reshef et al., 2006), and the first method used to express and maintain traceability was cross–referencing (Evans, 1989).

Other techniques can be used both to represent and to establish relationships including standard approaches such as matrices (Davis, 1993; West, 1991); keyphrase based scheme (Jackson, 1991); document integration (Lefering, 1991); hypertext links (Alexander, 2002; Glinz, 2000; Kaindle, 1993); graphs (Pinheiro & Goguen, 1996); formal methods (Cleland–Huang & Christensen, 2003; Antoniol et al., 2000; Tryggeseth & Nytrø, 1997); dynamic schemes (Cleland–Huang & Christensen, 2003; Antoniol et al., 2000; Tryggeseth & Nytrø, 1997); assumption based truth maintenance system (Tang, 1997; Smithers et al., 1991); and constraint networks (Bowen et al., 1990).

Automated or semi–automated traceability techniques had also been developed, such as the detection of existence of links using machine learning (Faisal, 2005); automatic analysis of consistency in low–degree polynomial time (Chechik & Gannon, 2001); techniques for Information Retrieval (Jung, 2006; Lancaster, 1968; van Rijsbergen, 1979) as the Latent Semantic Indexing – LSI (De Lucia et al., 2004; Deerwester et al., 1990) that may be used to recover relationship links by means of formalizing semantics (Deng et al., 2005).

Recent research show that techniques based on Information Retrieval can be used to dynamically discover links (Antoniol et al., 2000; Hayes et al., 2003; Marcus & Maletic, 2003; Spanoudakis, 2002), besides allowing the relationship between several types of artifacts (Deng et al., 2005) such as source code and documentation (Marcus & Maletic, 2003; Antoniol et al., 2002), design and requirements (Hayes et al., 2003), and requirements and artifacts (Zisman et al., 2003).

A popular technique, known as Software Reflexion Model (Murphy et al., 2001) checks whether the implemented code conforms with the project model using mapping rules between the project model and the source model extracted from the implemented code. Another research in

this same line belongs to Richardson and Green (2004) that uses an automated synthesis to infer links.

Besides traceability between artifacts, some other techniques such as Event–based traceability – EBT (Cleland–Huang & Christensen, 2003) can be used to associate performance requirements (Cleland–Huang & Christensen, 2003; Cleland–Huang et al., 2002; Cleland–Huang et al., 2003), as well as to trace the quality of requirements based on well known design patterns (Gross & Yu, 2001), that can be related and linked using their invariants (Cleland–Huang & Schmelzer, 2003).

3.3 Traceability Links

The main resource used to maintain and represent the traceability relationships is the link.

Several proposals have been made for traceability links as well as for models that provide support: (i) to some standardization focusing on maintenance process and (ii) to represent such links.

Basically, links are associated towards some methodological information of the development process. In that aspect, links were created for object–oriented (Spanoudakis et al., 2004), aspect–oriented (Egyed, 2004), viewpoints–based development (Sabetzadeh & Easterbrook, 2005), or model–driven development (Aizenbud–Reshef et al., 2006; Almeida et al., 2006). Besides of links can be created for environmental and organizational aspects (Ramesh & Jarke, 2001); on the type of information to be traced (Toranzo et al., 2002); or on the configuration integrating textual specifications (Letelier, 2002). The drawback in these is that links are created and used for specific purposes only.

In the case of Requirements Engineering, links were used in the following activities: validation, analysis, evolution, and cross–referencing between requirements and artifacts (Palmer, 2000). Also the following processes make use of this resource: project management (to assist the prediction of

Figure 4. Basic elements of a link

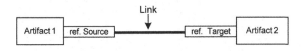

cost, restrictions or impacts); maintenance; test (generation of test cases based on scenarios or models); and quality assurance process (software validation) (Cleland–Huang & Christensen, 2003; Pinheiro & Goguen, 1996; Palmer, 2000; Gotel & Finkelstein, 1994; Jarke, 1998; Papadopoulou, 2002; Riebisch & Hubner, 2005).

Links can be formalized as follows: $A=\{a_1,a_2,a_3,...,a_n\}$ represents all the artifacts produced and identified by the development process; $E=\{e_1,e_2,e_3,...,e_n\}\subset A$ represents links; and $R=\{r_1,r_2,r_3,...,r_n\}\subset A$ represents requirements.

A link establishes an explicit relationship between two artifacts $a1$ and a_2. $a_1 \rightarrow a_2$ are considered as directly linked while an indirect link uses an intermediate artifact such as in $a_1 \rightarrow a_2 \rightarrow a_3$ (Cleland–Huang et al., 2003).

Information about source and target artifacts is enough to support backward and forward traceability, Figure 4, but other requirements engineering activities such as schedules and conflict resolution may require other attributes for their execution (Dick, 2002; Dick, 2005).

Several categories of links may be determined by means of attributes and properties or even through application of these links within the development process. Literature has already suggested some types of links to be used in traceability.

Ramesh and Jarke (2001) define four types of links: Satisfies, Depends–on, Envolves–to and Rationales. Satisfies and Depends–on are a group called product related, this set describe properties and relationships of design objects independent of how they were created, whole Envolves–to and Rationales are a group called process related because it can be captured only by looking at the history of actions taken in the

process itself and cannot be recovered from the product relationships alone.

Toranzo et al. (2002) consider six type of links: Satisfaction – it indicates that the origin element has dependence on satisfaction with a target class; Resource – the origin class has dependence on the resource with the target class; Responsibility – it determines participation, responsibility or action of participants on generated elements; Representation – it registers the representation or modeling of requirements in other languages; Allocation – it represents the relationship between the origin and target class, being this last class a subsystem; and Aggregation – it represents the composition between elements.

Pohl (1996), in his dependence model, defines eighteen different links of dependence (Dahlstedt & Persson, 2003) they are categorized in five classes: Condition; Content, Documents, Evolutionary and Abstraction.

De Lucia et al. (2005) present three types of links: Dependence – a directed link between a master and a slave artifact, the slave artifact depends on or is impacted by changes to the master artifact, Undirected – artifacts impact on each other, and Composition – the master artifact is part of the slave artifact.

Spanoudakis et al. (2004) based on studies of the software systems documentation, identified four types of relations between standards of requirements, use cases and object–oriented analysis models: Overlap relations – it denotes that the connected elements refer to a common feature of the underlying system or its domain. Thus, a relation of this type expresses the potential of a dependency between these elements; Requires_Execution_Of – it denotes that the sequence of terms requires the execution of the operation to which it is related; Requires_Feature_In – it denotes that the relevant part of the use case cannot be conducted without the existence of the structural or functional feature required by the requirement statement or the relation denotes that one of the requirement statements refers to the existence of a feature of a system that is required by the other; Can_Partially_Realize relations – The meaning of the relation is that the execution of the use case can execute part of the requirement statement.

Aizenbud–Reshef et al. (2006) define four types of relationships: Imposed – is a relationship between artifacts that exists due to a violation of the relationship creator; Inferred – is a relationship that exists because the artifacts satisfy a rule that describes the relationship; Manual – is a relationship that is created and maintained by a human user, this relationship can be either imposed or inferred; and Computed relationship – is created and maintained automatically by a computer. There are two basic types of computed relationships: Derivation – this relationship denotes that, given the content of an artifact, it is possible to compute valid content for the related artifact; and Analysis – it is a type of inferred relationship created by analysis programs that examine code or models against a set of rules.

A summary of the link types is presented in Table 1.

3.4 Traceability Metrics

Software metrics can provide objective information necessary for technical and managerial insight into, control, and improvement of the development effort (Costello & Liu, 1995). They should provide quantitative information to support those tasks (Norman & Martin, 2000) and they can be used to improve the productivity and the quality of both product and process (SEI, 1988).

According to (Roche, 1994) software metrics are inserted in the software measurement context and they cover topics such as:

- Performance evaluation and models
- Algorithmic/computational complexity
- Reliability models
- Cost and effort estimation
- Quality models and measures
- Structural and complexity measures

- Design measures
- Productivity measures and models

Metrics for traceability use data on links and other techniques of representation to show how an organization maintains the measurement on the requirement relationships. The information obtained can determine whether all the relationships required by a dependency are met, setting specifications incomplete or too complex for the system, and can also be used to prevent incorrect interpretations of other metrics. Moreover, they can expose requirements leakage that is, the appearance of lower level requirements with no valid origin at the system level (Costello & Liu, 1995).

Costello and Liu (1995) define five types of traceability metrics: next–level coverage (COV) metrics, full depth and height coverage (DHCOV) metrics, linkage statistics, inconsistent traceability metrics (ITM), and undefined traceability metrics (UTM).

COV metrics include the number of requirements that trace consistently to the next level up (COVup), the number of requirements that trace consistently to the next level down (COVdown), and the number of requirements that trace consistently to the next level in both directions (COV). DHCOV metrics involve a similar analysis, but evaluate traceability to the highest (HCOV) and lowest (DCOV) levels of specification. Note that for systems with three or fewer levels of specification, COV and DHCOV metrics are identical. Linkage statistics measure the complexity of traceability data by providing amounts of the number of higher/lower level requirements to which each requirement in a specification is traced. ITM include numbers of requirements in a specification that have at least one inconsistent traceability link upward (ITMup) and downward (TIMdown). Finally, UTM include the number of requirements in a specification with no traceability links upward (UTMup) and downward (UTMdown) (Costello & Liu, 1995).

Table 1. Examples of links described in the literature, they are classified by author and link groups

Author	Groups	Link type
Ramesh and Jarke (2001)	Product Related	Satisfies
		Depends–on
	Process Related	Envolves–to
		Rationales
Toranzo et al. (2002)		Satisfaction
		Resource
		Responsibility
		Representation
Pohl (1996)	Condition	Constraints
		Precondition
	Documents	Example_for
		Purpose
		Test_Case_for
		Comments
		Background
	Abstraction	Refines
		Generalizes
	Evolutionary	Elaborates
		Formalizes
		Based_on
		Satisfies
		Replaces
	Content	Similar
		Compares
		Contradicts
		Conflicts
De Lucia et al. (2005)		Dependence
		Undirected
		Composition
Spanoudakis et al. (2004)		Overlap
		Requires_Execution_Of
		Requires_Feature_In
		Can Partially Realise
Aizenbud–Reshef et al. (2006)		Imposed
		Inferred
		Manual
	Computed	Derivation
		Analysis

Hull et al. (2002) also propose a discussion about traceability metrics. Based on the satisfaction relationship type, and moving down through the requirements, the authors define three dimensions and two other elements for the measurement of traceability.

To determine which aspects of these dimensions are useful in terms of measuring the requirements engineering process, it is necessary to distinguish between two types of indicators: i) Layer metrics: measurements relating to a single stage of development, e.g. just to the systems requirements layer; ii) Global metrics: measurements spanning several stages of development (Hull et al., 2002).

The three dimensions and the other two elements are presented below:

- Dimensions:
  a. Breadth – It relates to coverage, and as such it is a layer metric. The coverage can be used to measure progress of process that creates traceability at a single layer. It measures the extent to which requirements are covered by the adjacent layer above or below.
  b. Depth – It looks at the number of layers that traceability extends upwards or downwards from a given layer, making it a global metric.
  c. Growth – It is related to potential change impact. How many requirements at lower levels are related to a single requirement at the top level?
- Other elements:
  a. Balance – Its idea is to look at the distribution of Growth factors for individual requirements between two given layers, and examine those that lie in the outer quartiles of the distribution. The goal is to identify requirements that have an abnormal high or low Growth factor, and subject them to special scrutiny.
  b. Latent Change – A single change request, may suddenly introduce a chain of potential latent change into the system. In such circumstances, it would be highly desirable to track progress and estimate the consequential work.

Traceability metrics presented aims to facilitate the improvement of the quality of the traced requirements, which is very appropriate. But a more critical eye on the metrics in place, can point to lack of concern about the quality of links, which may be useful for other activities of the requirements engineering.

All proposals of traceability metrics gather information to determine the requirements quality, while the traceability quality itself is not evaluated.

The standards for software quality follow a pattern of refinement where the higher level elements of the development process are refined into smaller elements. An example of this can be seen in the standards ISO/IEC – 12207 (ISO/IEC, 1995), which is about the life cycle of the development process, in IEEE – 830 (IEEE, 1998), dealing with specification of requirements of software, and the IEEE – 1233 (IEEE, 1998b), addressing the development of the specification of requirements for systems.

The same pattern of refinement does not occur with the traceability, i.e., link which is the main element of maintenance and representation of relationships, used in the lowest level of the process of requirements management, is not explored in quality factor but only used as a tool to assess the quality of elements in higher levels.

Despite being used by several software engineering processes there is still a lack for clear standards for the traceability quality. That characteristic may be observed in the standards CMMI–DEV (SEI, 2006) that points to a specific practice: 1.4 Maintain Bidirectional Traceability of Requirements, or ISO/IEC 15504–2 (ISO/IEC, 2003) which issues basic practices: ENG.3.4 – Establish traceability and PRO.4.5 – Maintain traceability. As stated by Angelina et al. (2006) the standards and norms do not include traceability metric to ensure the consistency, completeness, reliability, usability and efficiency of the implementation of traceability.

3.5 Models for Traceability

Another important research area for the traceability are models. According to Mellor et al. (2003) a model is a coherent set of formal elements describing something built for some purpose that is subject to a particular form of analysis. It may be expressed by a language (either textual or graphical) in which a certain degree of abstraction can be achieved.

In the case of traceability, models are developed based on information with respect to traceability domain (users, practices, methodologies, norms, etc.).

Several authors use models to represent concepts related to traceability such as the definition of different types of links.

Ramesh and Jarke (2001) proposed a metamodel for traceability using as a basis extensive empirical research about the consequences of different uses, perspectives and information needs of those involved in the development process.

They found three categories of information associated with traceability: stakeholders; sources (standards, norms, rules, etc.); and objects (conceptual objects, models, or artifacts), which were used to establish the metamodel.

Besides these three categories the research enabled the authors to classify users of traceability. The users were classified with respect to their practices, in two separate groups: high–end and low–end users. Based on this classification two models were created to represent their traceability processes.

In addition to creating a conceptually simple but very broad metamodel in terms of elements and links, research by Ramesh and Jarke (2001) presents a very interesting classification on users of traceability, assigning a significant figure to the practices employed by the users within their organizations. But, this model also pre–establishes the types of links to be used, even when these pre–established types of links can be divided and used as reference. Another problem found in the model, proposed by Ramesh and Jarke (2001), is that it does not have a description of attributes that can be added to enhance the semantics of the link, despite the existence of the important type of link Rationale.

Model proposed by Toranzo et al. (2002) uses graphical representation based on UML. This model classifies information to be traced into four classes: Environmental, Organizational, Managerial, and Development. Based on this classification, the authors developed the following: a meta–model; an intermediate model; and a process to apply requirements traceability strategies. The Toranzo et al. (2002) model addresses management issues such as the link that belongs to the category of responsibility. This is noted by the influence of the defined classification context (Environmental, Organizational, Managerial and Development). However, the types of links are also pre–defined and addressed in the context used in the model. Other management and traceability standards, as addressed to the vision may not be completely addressed to express their links.

A discussion on the problem of pre–specification of links in the traceability models is found in (Aizenbud–Reshef et al., 2006). The authors propose a solution to this problem, using the concept of Model–Driven Architecture MDA. This proposal considers that creation of models for systems must include requirements metamodel, and the resulting models, which include a requirements explicit model, can provide traceability between requirements and other artifacts. The existence of these models does not provide mechanisms to produce, automatically, the links between requirements and its dependencies, i.e., due to the fact of possessing semantics to produce significant links does not guarantee an effective strategy for traceability. Thus the links need to be constructed and maintained manually.

According to Aizenbud–Reshef et al. (2006) the idea would generate the artifacts, and its basic structures, and produce the links between them, and if necessary the links would be detailed. In this case MDA could be an alternative to accomplish these tasks.

Despite the observation about the traceability models which have pre–defined types of links Aizenbud–Reshef et al. (2006) proposed an architecture–based solution, which may turn into a problem for developing processes based on other concepts. However this proposal can be very relevant to those involved with the MDA.

An alternative to the problem of pre–definition of the types of links can be a model based on the generalization of all kinds of artifacts that may be part of the process of traceability, focusing on the representation of information. This feature allows both the creation of new types of bonds and other artifacts, as the need of those involved in traceability. This model is represented in Figure 5.

The idea is to include all types of artifacts into the traceability process focusing mostly on representing information. This feature promotes creation of both new types of links and artifacts according to the necessity of the involved elements of traceability. Two particular cases justify this generalization. The first one is with respect to aggregation of new fields to be incorporated into a certain type of link or artifact. The second enables insertion of new types of artifacts.

For the first case, the links, for most of the existing applications, are just a connection between

two artifacts where information is not aggregated to this connection. Therefore, it is essential to enable the association of information of the process (quality, rationale) to the link. These information should be represented in the model.

The second case consists in the necessity of including new types of links or other artifacts during an ongoing project or for a new project. Definition of types of links right in the beginning of a project does not reflect the reality in which a project might face changes or adjustments during its development.

4 CONCLUSION

The correct traceability use can help a lot of activities within the development process. It can improve the quality of the product as well, as the software process.

In spite of the traceability importance some of its aspects can be explored in future research.

With respect to traceability models, presented in this work, it is possible to see that they provide pre–defined standards of groups of links and those groups can be supported by their models. Research does extensive observations about the traceability practices, but their models are limited as the types of links are fixed. Then, the models are defined to cover a specific approach for solving their problem domain (Aizenbud–Reshef et al., 2006).

There is a perspective of a better understanding of the explicit relationships between models, modelers and what is modeled will be the basis for further work in the context of current requirements engineering research and practice. This concept will be able to lead to a proper understanding of how traceability properties may be identified and integrated (Morris & Gotel, 2007).

The link description can be better exploited. The link types, in most cases, only represent the connection between two elements of the development process. These models do not enable inclusion of entities that define properties of the links,

Figure 5. Model for link generalization (Adapted Genvigir and Vijaykumar, 2008)

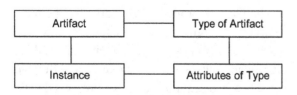

called attributes, or yet of the richer semantics. This means that essential information to establish analysis, impact evaluation, derivation or coverage about the traceability are not at all supported or even represented by such models (Dick, 2002; Dick, 2005; Hull et al., 2002).

Finally, it is essential to improve the existing standards and to develop new metrics for the traceability. These elements can contribute to ensuring consistency, completeness, reliability, usability and efficiency for the traceability. These topics remain open and deserve a better discussion and demonstration of feasibility.

5 REFERENCES

Aizenbud–Reshef, N., Nolan, B. T., Rubin, J., & Shaham–Gafni, Y. (2006). Model traceability. *IBM Systems Journal, 45*(3), 515–526.

Alexander, I. (2002). Toward automatic traceability in industrial practice. In *International Workshop on Traceability in Emerging Forms of Software Engineering* (pp. 26–31), Edinburgh, UK.

Almeida, J. P., Eck, P. V., & Iacob, M. (2006). Requirements traceability and transformation conformance in model–driven development. In *International Enterprise Distributed Object Computing Conference* (pp. 355–366). Washington, DC: IEEE Computer Society Press.

Angelina, E., Alarc'on, P. P., & Garbajosa, J. (2006). Analyzing and systematizing current traceability schemas. In *Annual IEEE/NASA Software Engineering Workshop* (pp. 21–32). Los Alamitos, CA: IEEE Computer Society Press.

Antoniol, G., Canfora, G., Casazza, G., De Lucia, A., & Merlo, E. (2002). Recovering traceability links between code and documentation. *IEEE Transactions on Software Engineering, 28*(10), 970–983. doi:10.1109/TSE.2002.1041053

Antoniol, G., Casazza, G., & Cimitile, A. (2000). Traceability recovery by modeling programmer behavior. In *Working Conference Reverse Engineering* (pp. 240–247). Washington, DC: IEEE Computer Society Press.

Antoniou, G., Macnish, C., & Foo, N. Y. (2000). A note on the refinement of nonmonotonic knowledge bases. *Knowledge and Information Systems, 2*, 479–486. doi:10.1007/PL00011653

Basili, V. R., Caldiera, G., & Rombach, H. D. (1994). The goal question metric approach. *Encyclopedia of Software Engineering, 1*(4), 528–532.

Bauer, F. (1969, January). *Software Engineering: Report on a conference sponsored by the NATO Science committee,* (p. 231). Garmisch, Germany .

Belford, P. C., Bond, A. F., Henderson, D. G., & Sellers, L. S. (1976). Specifications a key to effective software development. In *International Conference on Software Engineering* (pp. 71–79). Los Alamitos, CA: IEEE Computer Society Press.

Bowen, J., O'grady, P., & Smith, L. (1990). A constraint programming language for life–cycle engineering. *Artificial Intelligence in Engineering, 5*(4), 206–220. doi:10.1016/0954-1810(90)90022-V

Chechik, M., & Gannon, J. (2001). Automatic analysis of consistency between requirements and designs. *IEEE Transactions on Software Engineering, 27*(7), 651–672. doi:10.1109/32.935856

Cleland–Huang, J., Chang, C. K., Hu, H., Javvaji, K., Sethi, G., & Xia, J. (2002). Automating speculative queries through event–based requirements traceability. In *IEEE Joint Conference on Requirements Engineering* (pp. 289–296). Los Alamitos, CA: IEEE Computer Society.

Cleland–Huang, J., & Christensen, C. (2003). Event–based traceability for managing evolutionary change. *IEEE Transactions on Software Engineering, 29*(9), 796–810. doi:10.1109/TSE.2003.1232285

Cleland–Huang, J., & Schmelzer, D. (2003). Dynamically tracing non–functional requirements through design pattern invariants. In *Workshop on Traceability in Emerging Forms of Software Engineering,* Montreal, Canada.

Cleland–Huang, J., Settimi, R., Lukasik, W., & Chen, Y. (2003). Dynamic retrieval of impacted software artifacts. In *Midwest Software Engineering Conference.*

Costello, R., & Liu, D. (1995). Metrics for requirements engineering. *Journal of Systems and Software, 29*(1), 39–63. doi:10.1016/0164-1212(94)00127-9

Crnkovic, I., Funk, P., & Larsson, M. (1999). Processing requirements by software configuration management. In *25th Euromicro Conference* (pp. 260–265).

Dahlstedt, Å. G., & Persson, A. (2003). Requirements interdependencies – moulding the state of research into a research agenda. In *International Workshop on Requirements Engineering: Foundation for Software Quality* (pp. 71–80).

Davis, A. M. (1993). *Software requirements: objects, functions and states*. Upper Saddle River, NJ: Prentice–Hall.

De Lucia, A., Fasano, F., Oliveto, R., & Tortora, G. (2004). Enhancing an artifact management system with traceability recovery features. In *International Conference on Software Maintenance* (pp. 306–315).

De Lucia, A., Fasano, F., Oliveto, R., & Tortora, G. (2005). ADAMS re–trace: a traceability recovery tool. In *European Conference on Software Maintenance and Reengineering* (pp. 32–41).

Deerwester, S., Dumais, S. T., & Furnas, G. W., K., T., & Harshman, R. (1990). Indexing by latent semantic analysis. *Journal of the American Society for Information Science American Society for Information Science, 41*(6), 391–407. doi:10.1002/(SICI)1097-4571(199009)41:6<391::AID-ASI1>3.0.CO;2-9

Deng, M., Stirewalt, R. E., & Cheng, B. H. (2005). Retrieval by construction: A traceability technique to support verification and validation of UML formalizations. *Journal of Software Engineering and Knowledge Engineering –IJSEKE, 15* (5), 837–872.

Dick, J. (2002). Rich traceability. In *International Workshop on Traceability In Emerging Forms of Software Engineering* (pp. 35–46).

Dick, J. (2005). Design traceability. *IEEE Software, 22*(6), 14–16. doi:10.1109/MS.2005.150

Dömges, R., & Pohl, K. (1998). Adapting traceability environments to project–specific needs. *Communications of the ACM, 41*(12), 54–62. doi:10.1145/290133.290149

Egyed, A. (2004). Resolving uncertainties during trace analysis. In *Symposium on Foundations of Software Engineering* (pp. 3–12).

Evans, M. W. (1989). *The Software Factory: A Fourth Generation Software Engineering Environment*. New York: Wiley–Interscience.

Faisal, M. H. (2005). *Toward automating the discovery of traceability links*. Doctoral Thesis. University of Colorado.

Genvigir, E. C., & Vijaykumar, N. L. (2008). A Modeling Proposed for Generalization of Traceability Links. [in Portuguese]. *Revista de Informática Teórica e Aplicada, XV*(2), 181–202.

Glinz, M. (2000). A lightweight approach to consistency of scenarios and class models. In *International Conference on Requirements Engineering* (pp. 49–58). Washington, DC: IEEE Computer Society.

Gotel, O. C. Z. (1995). *Contribution Structures for Requirements Traceability*. Thesis (Doctor of Philosophy) Faculty of Engineering of the University of London, London.

Gotel, O. C. Z., & Finkelstein, A. (1994). An analysis of the requirements traceability problem. In *First International Conference Requirements Engineering* (pp. 94–101). Washington, DC: IEEE Computer Society Press.

Graham, I. (1997*). Requirements engineering and rapid development: an object oriented approach*. Reading, MA: Addison Wesley Professional.

Gross, D., & Yu, E. (2001). From non–functional requirements to design through patterns. *Requirements Engineering Journal, 6*(1), 18–36. doi:10.1007/s007660170013

Hayes, J. H., Dekhtyar, A., & Osborne, E. (2003). Improving requirements tracing via information retrieval. In *IEEE Requirements Engineering Conference,* (pp. 138–150).

Hull, E., Jakson, K., & Dick, J. (2002). *Requirements Engineering*. London: Spring Verlag.

IEEE Computer Society Press (2004). *Guide to the software engineering body of knowledge – SWEBOK: trial version (version 1.00).*

Institute of Electrical and Electronics Engineers. (1990). *IEEE Standard Glossary of Software Engineering Terminology: IEEE Std – 610.12–1990*. New York: EUA.

Institute of Electrical and Electronics Engineers. (1990). *Standard Glossary of Software Engineering Terminology: IEEE Std 610.12*. New York: EUA.

Institute of Electrical and Electronics Engineers. (1998). *IEEE Guide for developing system requirements specifications: IEEE Std – 1233*. New York: EUA.

Institute of Electrical and Electronics Engineers. (1998). *Recommended practice for software requirements specifications: IEEE Std 830–1998*. New York: EUA.

International Organization for Standardization (1995). *ISO/IEC 12207:1995 Information technology - Software life cycle processes.*

International Organization for Standardization (2003). *ISO/IEC 15504–2:2003/Cor.1:2004(E): Information technology – process assessment – part 2: Performing an assessment.*

Jackson, J. A. (1991). Keyphrase based traceability scheme. In *Colloquium by the Institution of Electrical Engineers Professional Group C1 (Software Engineering) – Tools and Techniques for Maintaining - Traceability During Design* (pp. 2/1–2/4). London: IEE – The Institution of Electrical Engineers.

Jarke, M. (1998). Requirements traceability. *Communications of the ACM, 41*(12), 32–36. doi:10.1145/290133.290145

Jarke, M., & Pohl, K. (1994). Requirements engineering in 2001: managing a changing reality. *Software Engineering Journal, 9*(6), 257–266.

Jung, J. J. (2006). Ontological framework based on contextual mediation for collaborative information retrieval. *Information Retrieval, 10*(1), 85–109. doi:10.1007/s10791-006-9013-5

Kaindle, K. (1993). The missing link in requirements engineering. *ACM SIGSOFT Software Engineering Notes, 18*(2), 30–39. doi:10.1145/159420.155836

Kobayashi, A., & Maekawa, M. (2001). Need–based requirements change management. In *Conference on the Future of Software Engineering* (pp. 171–178). Washington, DC: IEEE.

Kotonya, G., & Sommerville, I. (2000). *Requirements engineering: process and techniques*. Chichester, UK: John Wiley & Sons.

Lam, W., Loomes, M., & Shankararaman, V. (1999). Managing requirements change using metrics and action planning. In *European Conference on Software Maintenance and Reengineering* (pp. 122–128).

Lancaster, F. W. (1968). *Information Retrieval Systems: Characteristics, Testing and Evaluation.* New York: Wiley.

Lefering, M. (1993). An incremental integration tool between requirements engineering and programming in the large. In *IEEE International Symposium on Requirements Engineering* (pp. 82–89).

Leffingwell, D., & Widrig, D. (2000). *Managing Software Requirements: A unified approach.* Los Angeles, CA: Addison Wesley Longman.

Letelier, P. (2002). A framework for requirements traceability in UML–based projects. In *International Workshop on Traceability In Emerging Forms of Software Engineering* (pp. 30–41), New York.

Lindsay, P., Yaowei, L., & Traynor, O. (1997). A generic model for fine grained configuration management including version control and traceability. In *Australian Software Engineering Conference* (pp. 27–36).

Marcus, A., & Maletic, J. (2003). Recovering documentation–to–source–code traceability links using latent semantic indexing. In *IEEE International Conference on Software Engineering* (pp.125–132). Washington, DC: IEEE Computer Society Press.

Mellor, S. J., Clark, A. N., & Futagami, T. (2003). Model–driven development. *IEEE Software, 20*(5), 14–18. doi:10.1109/MS.2003.1231145

Morris, S. J. & GoteL, O. C. Z. (2007). Model or mould? A challenge for better traceability. In *International Workshop on Modeling in Software Engineering.* Los Alamitos, CA: IEEE Computer Society Press.

Murphy, G. C., Notkin, D., & Sullivan, K. J. (2001). Software reflexion models: Bridging the gap between design and implementation. *IEEE Transactions on Software Engineering, 27*(4), 364–380. doi:10.1109/32.917525

National Aeronautics and Space Administration. (1990). *Manager's Handbook for Software Development: Software engineering laboratory series* –SEL–84–101 – revision 1. Greenbelt, MD: EUA.

Norman, E. F., & Martin, N. (2000). Software metrics: roadmap. In *Conference on the Future of Software Engineering* (pp. 357–370). New York: ACM Press.

Nuseibeh, B., & Easterbrook, S. (2000). Requirements engineering: a roadmap. In *International Conference on Software Engineering* (pp. 35–46). New York: ACM.

Palmer, J. D. (2000). Traceability. In R.H. Thayer, & M. Dorfman, (Ed.), *Software Requirements Engineering* (pp. 412–422). Los Alamitos, CA: IEEE Computer Society Press.

Papadopoulou, P. (2002). *Evaluation of a Requirements Traceability System.* MSc Thesis, Department of Computing, City University.

Pinheiro, F. (2003). *Requirements Traceability.* In J. C. S. P. Leite & J. H. Doorn (Eds.), *Perspectives on software requirements* (pp. 91–115). Norwell, MA: Kluwer Academic Publishers.

Pinheiro, F., & Goguen, J. (1996). An object–oriented tool for tracing requirements. *IEEE Software, 13*(2), 796–810. doi:10.1109/52.506462

Pohl, K. (1996). PRO–ART: Enabling requirements pre–traceability. In *International Conference on Requirement Engineering* (pp. 76–84).

Ramesh, B., & Edwards, M. (1993). Issues in the development of a requirements traceability model. In *International Symposium on Requirements Engineering* (pp. 256–259).

Ramesh, B., & Jarke, M. (2001). Toward reference models for requirements traceability. *IEEE Transactions on Software Engineering*, *27*(1), 58–93. doi:10.1109/32.895989

Richardson, J., & Green, J. (2004). Automating traceability for generated software artifacts. In IEEE *International Conference on Automated Software Engineering* (pp. 24–33). Washington, DC: IEEE Computer Society.

Riebisch, M., & Hubner, M. (2005). Traceability–driven model refinement for test case generation. In *IEEE International Conference and Workshops on the Engineering of Computer–Based Systems* (pp. 113–120). Washington, DC: IEEE Computer Society.

Roche, J. M. (1994). Software metrics and measurement principles. *ACM SIGSOFT Software Engineering Notes*, *19*(1), 77–85. doi:10.1145/181610.181625

Sabetzadeh, M., & Easterbrook, S. (2005). Traceability in viewpoint merging: A model management perspective. In *International Workshop on Traceability in Emerging Forms of Software Engineering* (pp. 44–49). New York: ACM.

Sawyer, P., Sommerville, I., & Viller, S. (1998). *Requirements process improvement through the phased introduction of good practice, Software Process – Improvement and Practice: Requirements engineering adaptation and improvement for safety and dependability – REAIMS* (Esprit Project 8649), (pp. 19–34).

Sayão, M., & Leite, R. J. (2004). Rastreabilidade de Requisitos. [*in Portuguese*]. *Revista de Informática Teórica e Aplicada.*, *13*(1), 57–86.

Smithers, T., Tang, M. X., & Tomes, N. (1991). The maintenance of design history in AI–based design. In *Colloquium by The Institution of Electrical Engineers Professional Group C1 - Tools and Techniques for Maintaining Traceability During Design* (pp 8/1). London: IEE – The Institution of Electrical Engineers.

Software Engineering Institute – SEI – Carnegie Mellon University. (1988, December). *Software Metrics: SEI curriculum module SEI–CM–12–1.1.* Pittsburgh, PA: EUA.

Software Engineering Institute – SEI – Carnegie Mellon University. (2006). *CMMI for Development: Technical report (CMMI–DEV) CMU/SEI–2006–TR–008 Version 1.2.* Pittsburgh, PA: Author.

Solingen, R. V., & Berghout, E. (1999). *The Goal/Question/Metric Method: A practical guide for quality improvement of software development.* Maidenhead, UK: McGraw–Hill.

Sommerville, I. (1995). *Software engineering.* Harlow, UK: Addison Wesley.

Sommerville, I., & Sawyer, P. (1998). *Requirements engineering: a good practice guide.* Lancaster, UK: John Wiley & Sons.

Spanoudakis, G. (2002). Plausible and adaptive requirements traceability structures. In *ACM International Conference on Software Engineering and Knowledge Engineering* (pp. 135–142). New York: ACM.

Spanoudakis, G., Zisman, A., & Péres, E. & M., Krause, P. (2004). Rule–based generation of requirements traceability relations. *Journal of Systems and Software*, (2): 105–127. doi:10.1016/S0164-1212(03)00242-5

Tang, A., Yan, J., & Jun, H. (2007). A rationale–base architecture model for design traceability. *Journal of Systems and Software*, *80*(6), 918–934. doi:10.1016/j.jss.2006.08.040

Tang, M. X. (1997). A knowledge–based architecture for intelligent design support. *The Knowledge Engineering Review*, *12*(4), 387–406. doi:10.1017/S0269888997004025

Toranzo, M., Castro, J., & Mello, E. (2002). An approach to improve requirements traceability. In *Workshop of Requirements Engineering, (in Portuguese)* (pp. 194–209).

Tryggeseth, E., & Nytrø, O. (1997). Dynamic traceability links supported by a system architecture description. In *International Conference on Software Maintenance* (pp. 180–187). Washington, DC: IEEE.

van Rijsbergen, C. J. (1979). *Information Retrieval*. London: University of Glasgow.

West, M. (1991).Quality function deployment in software development. In *Colloquium by The Institution of Electrical Engineers Professional Group C1 (Software Engineering) – Tools and Techniques for Maintaining Traceability During Design* (pp. 5/1–5/7). London: IEE – The Institution of Electrical Engineers.

Zisman, A., Spanoudakis, G., Péres, E. M., & Krause, P. (2003). Tracing software engineering artifacts. In *International Conference on Software Engineering Research and Practice* (pp. 448–455).

KEY TERMS AND DEFINITIONS

Requirements Engineering: The process of identification, analysis, documentation and management of requirements so that they are useful for implementation, consistent with the needs of stakeholders and to provide the software product quality.

Requirements Management: A parallel process to support other requirements engineering activities such as identification, change management and requirements traceability throughout the development process.

Requirements Traceability: The ability to define traces between requirements and other artifacts throughout the development process; and to follow those traces in any direction.

Traceability Links: The main resource used to maintain and represent the traceability relationships. A link establishes an explicit relationship between two artifacts.

Models: A set of elements describing something built for some purpose that is subject to a particular form of analysis.

Techniques: Technical and managerial procedures that aid in the evaluation and improvement of the software development process.

Stakeholders: Individuals or organizations involved or affected by the system and who have an influence on the requirements. They could be end-users, managers, suppliers and customers.

Chapter 9
Software Product Lines to Faster Achieving Productivity

Sathya Ganeshan
Leeds Metropolitan University, UK

Muthu Ramachandran
Leeds Metropolitan University, UK

ABSTRACT

Software Product Lines have been in the scene of software development since the 1970s. Throughout this time, it has changed from a hot topic that was discussed in universities and seminar halls as future goal of companies, to an everyday reality. There are many crucial aspects that decide the success of a software product line. One among them is the identification, development and maintenance of core assets. This chapter aims at providing a brief introduction to this area of software product lines and ways to improve productivity through efficient core asset management.

INTRODUCTION

Throughout the years Software Product Line based development of applications have received wide interest. They are now represented in some shape or form in most of the development world, ranging from a simple reuse of code to the most structured and ambitious projects. Among the many factors that decide the success of a product family is a well defined role for core assets. Core assets have been researched and talked about since the dawn of product lines themselves. Most notably core assets were studied by Software Engineering Institute or

SEI. According to them the goal of core assets is to develop a production facility to create a family of products (Clements & Northrop, 2004). The importance given by SEI to core assets can be understood from figure 1.

Figure 1 gives the most condensed view of SEI's software product line's essential activities. The figure shows three intertwining activities of core asset development, product development and management in a never ending cycle. The three cycles are dependent on each other and cannot function alone in the absence of the other activities. Among the two engineering divisions primarily agreed

DOI: 10.4018/978-1-60566-731-7.ch009

Figure 1. SEI's essential product line activities SEI (2004) http://www.sei.cmu.edu/productlines/frame_report/config.man.htm)

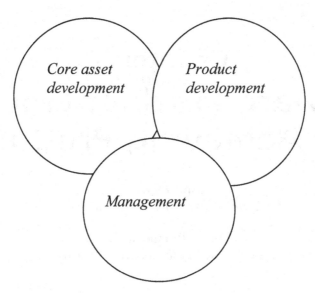

upon within a software product lines, the creation, development and maintenance of core assets falls within the domain engineering disciple. In spite of the wide interest core assets have received over the years, it is surprising to learn that not many works are available about them (Sun Her et al, 2007), their role in a product line. In fact there is a lack of clear definition of what constitutes a core asset as varying think tanks suggest different ways of identifying them.

This chapter tries to explore the basic concepts associated with core assets and also provides our own method for managing them.

STARTING WITH CORE ASSETS

Core assets are those entities that form the building blocks of creating a new product. They could be anything ranging from code, architecture to components, test cases etc. In short these are the entities that are to be reused. It should also be understood that since they are designed for reuse to the maximum, they are automatically the commonalties that are most treasured upon in the initial commonality analysis stage. Here after in this chapter, we shall denote software product lines as SPL and commonality analysis as CA.

To put it simply, core assets can be considered as the small plastic Lego blocks that are used to build any kind of toy structure. Figure 2 explains this concept.

Figure 2 might be a little simplified, but serves its purpose. These colorful building blocks of Lego can be considered as assets of varying characteristics. Provided with the right architecture, these blocks could be put in the right place to create a meaningful structure. The product development process, in diagram 2 shamelessly over simplifies the task. In the SPL world, this would include tools, architecture and product development process put together. Now that we had a simple idea of what a core asset is, let us look at what constitutes a core asset.

True to our definition, core assets could be anything that could be used to build a product with reusability in mind. So the following can be termed as core assets, but the reader should beware that the definition of what constitutes a core asset might vary depending on organization and the domain.

Figure 2. Core assets: Building blocks of product family

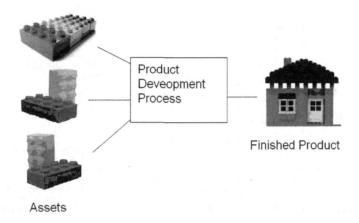

- Architecture
- Test cases, data
- Code segments
- Requirements
- Best Practices
- Use cases
- Charts and diagrams
- Records of commonly faced problems and their solutions
- Components

The reader might be aware at this point that anything can be a core asset. All those entities that contribute to developing a product or a family of products can rightfully be called as a core asset. At this point, the crucial question would be, where does software reusability come into the picture? The answer would be that all those assets that can contribute to the development of the majority of the envisaged products could be safely considered as a core asset.

Figure 3 attempts to provide a more detailed view of the working of core assets.

In figure3, core assets are fed through a development process which includes a common accepted architecture which can align the different assets into their respective positions. Domain knowledge is also a key factor which decides what the product should be. These collections of processes that involve creation of assets and those facilities that use those assets to generate a family of products are commonly called domain engineering. The actual process of creating the products is called application engineering.

The commonality analysis process is used to decide what the members of a family should be (Clements & Northrop, 2004). Each product is unique as differentiated by its variation. One might ask, how would the variations be defined within these core assets? The answer would be that there would be predefined variation points within the architecture. Core assets that are to serve as variability would be installed appropriately at these variation junctions. This task falls into the application engineering phase. We have so far seen how core assets are being used within development. Let's now see their origins and the criteria under which they are created.

CREATING, MINING AND MANAGING CORE ASSETS

Core assets are obtained normally through one of the following ways:

- Developed
- Mined

Figure 3. Core assets and product family development

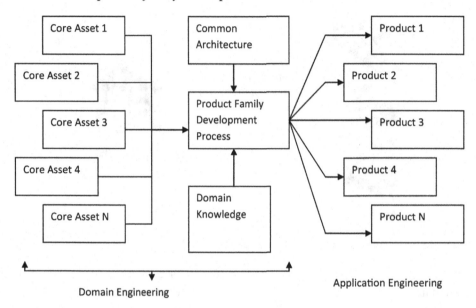

- Bought as COTS (Commercial Off The Shelf products)
- Using existing assets

Developed

This is when a particular asset of a prescribed characteristic is developed for usage within the organization. This is a plain old method of developing assets for a set of requirements. The requirements could marketing, functional or policy based.

Mined

This is more efficient and time saving where an asset is mined from an existing product..

Bought as COTS

This is one more way of dealing with time constraints. Assets are bought from commercial manufacturers whose services include providing components for specific purposes. While saving time, the generally accepted drawback of this approach is that since the functioning of these components is hidden, problems that occur while using these might be hard to handle.

Using Existing Assets

Assets can also be created or mined from existing assets. The mined asset normally is more efficient or includes new requirements as a result creating a more advanced version of an already existing asset that is in touch with the change in market and demands.

As we observed from the above, there are many sources for obtaining a core asset. Once the assets have been identified, the next phase would be to use tools, techniques and the common architecture to generate the products that were planned initially. This part could be made easier if the previous tasks were conducted extensively. There have been a few attempts to automate this part of the process (Gi Min, 2006). Gi Min et al (2006) introduce a method of Model Driven Architecture where core assets are used to generate products automatically. We on the other hand would be more supportive towards a system in which tools are designed to use the core assets and align them with the architecture for rapid generation of products. This tool selection or creation process again falls into the category commonality analysis phase.

SCOPING CORE ASSETS

Another important aspect that is to be noted while discussing about core assets is the scope of the assets that are to be manufactured, obtained or mined. Scoping in general gives a boundary within which the assets reside. If the scope is too small, we shall have a constricted product family which finds hard to breathe or respond to market needs rapidly. On the other hand, if the scope is too large, we have a situation where there is too many different products and the product line collapses back into the one-off production owing to the large about of variations permitted into the system by the scope. The trick is to find a middle ground and decide a scope that satisfies all stake holders and in the mean while allowing space for future growth and success. Considering the above complications, the job of scoping could sure prove to be a discouraging one. But domain engineers with a wealth of experience in that particular domain and who understand what the products need to be and what is expected from the organizational goals, it is an interesting task that usually provides a high pay off.

The following are some of the Rules that are to be adhered while selecting a scope for a product family

- Provide clear cut scope with fixed boundaries.
- Scope should mirror organizational goals.
- Always allow space for new technologies.
- Design scope that is not too skeptical and conservative nor too ambitious.
- Scope should fall within the range of the technical expertise of the human resource available at hand.

- Scope should not rely too much on outward technologies.
- Whenever the scope is increased to allow change, care is taken that all stakeholders of the project agree to the change in a positive manner.

Having mentioned the above criteria, care is taken that the core assets selected for the product lines are agreeable of what is generally expected of them. According to Clements & Northrop (2004), each core asset is encapsulated with an associated process that describes how it shall be used in development of the family of products. This could be helpful in two ways

- General help on how to use an asset, what products it could be used on and the list of requirements that this particular asset addresses.
- Distinguishing a particular asset from other. In organizing the asset within the asset repository.

We have so far seen how scoping of assets is achieved. Let's now look into organizing these assets.

CORE ASSET REPOSITORY

When a product line matures, so does the number of assets. It becomes necessary at this point to employ some kind of a structured method that manages all these assets. This might prove highly helpful for the team of domain analysts who use these assets and the associated information in the future. Before venturing further into the subject, it must be duly noted that, the repository's scope would be limited only to that organization or product line from which it was built. In other words, it is specific to that particular domain and cannot be used or contracted as COTS.

We propose the construction of a Library or a repository of Assets in which each asset that enters the library has to be appropriately tagged and catalogued. Assets that undergo change have to be recorded and documented. We considered the similarity between design patterns and assets. Sommerville (2004) has suggested the method of pattern name, description of problem area, solution description and statement of consequence and trade-offs for distinguishing each asset. Despite the fact that the concept of design pattern is completely different, overall it specifies how to manage a large number of assets which might be used in managing assets with some minor modifications.

Apart from numbering the asset and cataloging it, certain additional information for each asset be added for quick reference.

- The approximate time frame of when the asset was created.
- Asset name.
- If it is currently used by any family member and the description of the member.
- Any test results or test data available to test that asset (in case of high level language code).

- When this asset was last modified.
- Any tradeoffs that might have to be considered while using this asset.
- Any specific requirements that should be fulfilled in order to use the particular asset.
- Which requirements and use cases are linked to the asset.

Along with the asset specific information, the above questionnaire could also be used to gather standard details about that asset which might be resourceful in the future.

The figure 4 shows a model for maintenance of assets.

Each asset undergoes the process of encapsulation, where information about each asset accumulated. This package might include asset specific, standard information and an indexing system to identify a specific asset. Care is taken that these information are brief and clear. These capsules of core assets are then added to the Repository or library of assets. The process of building a library is an evolving process and each and every new item that enters the library are tagged and any change made to old items is recorded. This could also be another subject area.

Figure 4. A view of asset management for product line development

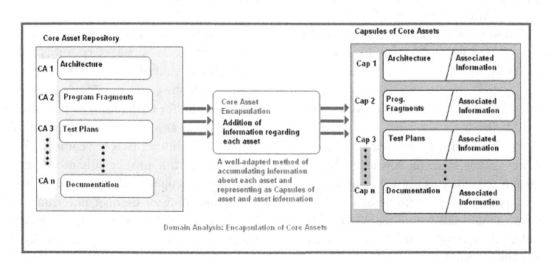

Core Assets that have undergone change needs to be managed in the same way as version management in products.

EVOLUTION OF CORE ASSETS AND TRENDS OF THE FUTURE

With the increase in software product line or family oriented software production in the rise, the role of assets and how they are managed have also changed. In the future we envision asset management to be more robust and customized. With the current trend of family oriented development, we expect the following surges in this area

- Assets are more organized
- Assets are designed so as to accommodate predicted additions that are expected from the future requirements. This needs a committed participation of domain experts during asset development.
- Informed decisions are made by domain experts to identify a new asset and also discard/alter assets who have passed their prime.
- Assets are always developed in view to be fixed within architecture and not the other way around.
- Assets are more robust and care is taken that the functions of the cots products acquired are well streamlined with the architecture. Care is also taken that the third party responsible for developing these products provide long term commitment incase alterations are required from the cots.

CONCLUSION

We see the role of assets within product family world increase over the next few years. Many aspects that we have studied about assets suggest that it is worthwhile investing time and cost developing assets. The overhead spent here reflects in itself in other areas of the product development in the form of considerable savings in time and increased quality. To conclude we highly recommend that a structure SPL approach should include a well developed asset mining and maintenance schemes within its models.

REFERENCES

Clements, P., & Northrop, L. (2004). *Software Product Lines: Practices and Patterns. SEI series in Software Engineering.* Reading, MA: Addison-Wesley Publications.

Gi, H., & Dong, S. (2006). *A Technique to Represent Product Line Core Assets in MDA/PIM for Automation* (LNCS). Berlin: Springer.

http://www.sei.cmu.edu/productlines/frame_report/config.man.htm (n.d.). Pittsburgh, PA: Software Engineering Institute, Carnegie Mellon University.

Sommerville (2004). *Software Engineering, (7th, Ed.).* Reading, MA: Addison Wesley.

Sun, J., Hyeok, K., Ji, H., Oh, S., Yul, S., & Dong, S. (2007). *A framework for evaluating reusability of core asset in product line engineering.* Information and Software Technology archive.

Weiss, D. (2004). *Defining Families: Commonality analysis.* Murray Hill, NJ: Lucent Technology, Bell Laboratories.

Chapter 10
Comprehensive Software Industry Analysis Model (CSIAM)

T.R. Gopalakrishnan Nair
Dayananda Sagar Institutions, Bangalore, India

R. Selvarani
Dayananda Sagar Institutions, Bangalore, India

Muthu Ramachandran
Leeds Metropolitan University, UK

ABSTRACT

This chapter discusses a comprehensive analysis model of the concurrent software industry which is a collection of different sub-models interacting and communicating objectively with a cause-effect relationship. This model is not merely process centric but it also deals with the resources, skills and methods with an entity model which forms an important factor of the comprehensive approach. Process is considered as an activity performed over the resources with a particular level of skill set transforming the input. In this comprehensive model, the factors associated with various sub models like process, technology, business, risk and multi domain are considered and integrated through communication links, threading all the models in transforming the system specification into the product within the cycle time with an active cost. The final model will be able to accept a spectrum of input from the industry, ranging from finances, human resources, business practices, technology and software production process and come out with metrics correlated to the observables of that particular company or group.

I. INTRODUCTION

The software industry has witnessed massive growth since its transformation from a pristine sector catering only to scientific research. This exponential growth has posed a lot of challenges related to standards and process models. The available models today, though partially useful, have been deemed inappropriate for the present growth scenario. The need of the hour is a comprehensive model that takes into account the aspects that implicitly or explicitly facilitate the industry. The present standards or models are process centric (http://www.sei.cmu.edu/cmmi, Carod, Martin & Aranda, 2004). The idea of

DOI: 10.4018/978-1-60566-731-7.ch010

software development revolves only around the process neglecting other important aspects such as business aspects, risk aspects, technological aspects, and aspects of multi domain analysis. This paper intends to develop individual models for each of the aspects mentioned above and finally integrate them to arrive on a comprehensive model which can facilitate and identify the key factors of success in the software industry.

This comprehensive analysis model is making use of the rationality of the software engineering as a structured collection of practices carried out through suitable resources. It will be treated as an entity to interact with the various other limbs of the software industry contributing to the success of a software business operation. The existing models and ideas supporting this aspect will form an integral part of the process unit of this model. This model will develop a metric system which indicates a set of performance indices of the companies in response to the variation of best practices prevailing in those companies. These metrics on the software companies will distinguish one company from the other though all of them have achieved a stamping of high maturity in the process view in conventional methods and exhibiting behaviors contrasting one to another leading to puzzles and ambiguities for a commercial deal. Comprehensive Software Industry Analysis Model (CSIAM) presumes that a comprehensive metric system of industry like this can address the failure rate of software projects existing in the field (Menkhaus & Andrich 2005).

II. PROCESS TRANSFORMATION TO A SUPER RESOURCE SCENARIO

In fact software technology has moved quite a long way for the last 20 years from where process centric thoughts blossomed (http://www.sei.cmu.edu/cmmi, & Morgan) and implemented improvements in process that could bring geometric response in the generation of software products.

Nevertheless, the technology has changed and the resources have grown quantitatively and qualitatively in significant size. It continuously demands process changes to suit the growth and sometimes even consuming a part of the process into the intelligence of the active resource. This transformation is inevitable and will be on a growing path along with the crowding of the new processors and intelligence power, taking place in computing systems. So the productivity of the software generation system is not purely dependent on old process centric factors (Menkhaus, Frei & Wuthrich, 2006) which are evident from the data that equally process certified production units performing with different productivity and quality. This calls for an open and liberal view to the software engineering of today without historical binding of thoughts prevailing in software generation by process refinement.

Modern software generation is not entirely depended up on process. Even if unbelievable improvements are brought into process, there will be only marginal differences in the form, fit and function (FFF) of product and the quality of product because today's process based production can not account the resources and skills aptly. In reality, these days the process itself is getting integrated with software generation intelligence which is concurrently getting transferred to machines (Menkhaus, Frei & Wuthrich 2006) which is remaining unnoticed. Every successful product requires a minimum standard of logically correct process. The active resources play a significant role currently and will play an entire role in the production of software, when increasingly autonomic systems are introduced in software industry. The present scenario needs a shift from process centric software generation to process and resource centric software generation models. It resolves many issues in the current software industry (Zhong, Madhavji & El Emam, 2000) including the differential performance of the software companies having the same process standards (Rauterberg & Aeppli 1996).

Figure 1. Networked architecture of software generation

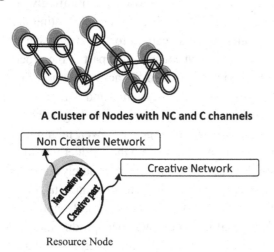

A Cluster of Nodes with NC and C channels

Non Creative Network

Creative Network

Resource Node

In an era of 1970s and 1980s, when the capabilities of active resources like the processors and software systems were at a lower order, highly structured and powerful process were required to bring out the successful software products (Rauterberg & Aeppli, 1996). The troubles of software generation were many in the early stages. If the processes were not well defined for the activities to be performed on meek resources or the sequence of the activities were not optimized for development, the generated products used to deviate from the requirements considerably. If there were no measurement of the activities and there were no definition of the human contribution (Zhong, Madhavji & El Emam 2000), the scenario would have produced lumps of software, which could not have met the objectives (Rauterberg & Aeppli 1996). The software generation carried out today need to be viewed as an action performed over a cluster of nodes where each node has two parts such as creative and non creative segment Figure 1. As the technology evolved, autonomic/creative and non-autonomic part of the software generation underwent complete transformation, which enabled the production of the objective software with intelligent platforms and modified tools, which reflected the accumulation of hitherto

generated skills. The work is carried out now using these systems much more smoothly than the older products that could do the work only with rigorous and accurate process (Zhong, Madhavji & El Emam 2000). In addition to this, the exponential growth witnessed by software industry due to the advantages of all out growth in processors, software technology and communication paradigms has generated a lot of challenges related to standards and process models (Rauterberg & Aeppli, 1996).

The available models of today, though partially useful, have been felt inappropriate for the present growth scenario. The software engineering model should undergo a transformation to increase the efficiency (Hofmann, Yedlin, Mishler & Kushner, 2007) of the process taking into consideration the capabilities of autonomic and non-autonomic domains (Figure 1) of the super resource scenario. Every node in a software generation network contains a creative part and a non-creative part over which a process is imposed. Autonomic systems like human elements are creative and generate approaches and algorithms, while non-autonomic part is not creative. It does repetitive transformation of creative output to computer software modules with its processing power and intelligence level, which is on a rapid growth (Ahern, Clouse & Turner 2008).

A. The Growth Model

The growth of autonomic and non-autonomic entities involved in software production is depicted in Figure 2 and it clearly shows the process of process-improvement becoming continuously insufficient to contain the transformations happening in IT and software generation modes. The primitive zone indicates the prominence of human thoughts (Zhong, Madhavji & El Emam 2000) for process for better efficiency of software production with available meek resources at that scenario (Ahern, Clouse & Turner 2008;Boehm, 2000). In the present scenario (1998-2008) the

Figure 2. Super resource scenario

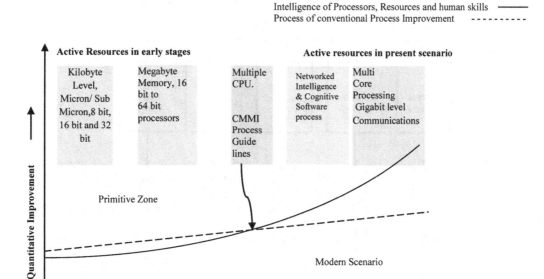

old non-autonomic/non-creative resources experienced tremendous growth through complex and intelligent application development paradigm, multi-fold improvements in languages intelligence capabilities, possibilities of multiprocessing, terabytes storage capacity, high speed devices, and high bandwidth communication with intelligent network. There is a revolutionized scenario of Information Technology when compared to 10 years back in software factories (Boehm, 2000), which is characterized by more cognitive elements in environment, better performing human intelligence (creative component) influenced by the evolution of software technology and higher grade hardware and software (Zhong, Madhavji & El Emam 2000) (the non creative component).

Hence the enveloping process of process improvement on software production is becoming mute with its inborn framework of low profile dependency on resources and human skills. There is a visible lacuna in achieving higher efficiency in extracting the potential of active resources, which are absorbing more intelligence into them.

Many more sophisticated-approaches and development paradigms are going to arrive in future in software technology that will continuously induct human earned capability in to them. The present scenario -with 'process alone is the back bone' approach- may not be suitable for the analysis of success and failure of software production and the performance of the industry. Hence a comprehensive software industry analysis model including various active resources as shown in Figure 1 comprising creative and non creative components needs to be considered.

A Software production unit is a network that consists of nodes having creative and non-creative parts and clusters of nodes. At the level of a node, the process is borne by the creative part constituting the main autonomic (human) system and that is interacting with the non creative system. When compared to the past autonomic and non-creative resources have improved to a greater level. For example, the primitive machines of early 90s have changed to highly intelligent software generating platforms currently. They are going

131

Figure 3. Multi window visualization of software industry

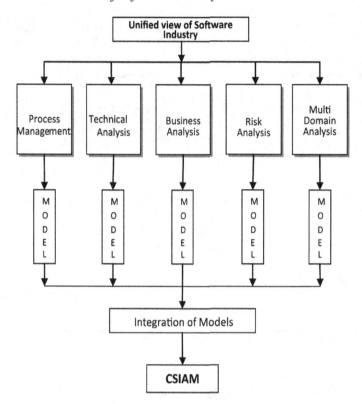

to get transformed to be highly cognitive if we review the systems and approaches evolving in various laboratories around the world. The efficiency of software generation depends on the dual manifestation of each node of the cluster containing creative entity with cognitive translation capability and the production interaction of the non-creative entity.

III. COMPREHENSIVE ANALYSIS MODEL DESCRIPTION

This comprehensive analysis model Figure 3 will identify the various parameters (Wang, 2006;Robillard & Detienne, 1998; Rauterberg; Rauterberg, Schluep & Fjuld, 1997) that affect the aforesaid properties and exploit them to develop a conclusive model. It will thus bring out the influence of these aspects of software industry through

modeling techniques. The core aspects of this analysis model are Process management, business aspects, risk aspects, technological aspects and cross domain aspects. A brief description of these aspects is as follows.

The present Capability Maturity Model (CMMI) (http://www.sei.cmu.edu/cmmi) for the software industry is mainly capable of handling *Process management,* but the problem persists in their fusion with the models of other aspects. Therefore, an exhaustive rework on the available model is required to make it comply with the other individual models (Hofmann, Yedlin, Mishler & Kushner 2007; Garcia & Turner, 2006 ; Siviy, Penn & Robert 2007; Chrissis, Konrad, Shrum, CMMI(R); Ebert, Christ of Akins & Anthony, 2007) The financial and management properties of any industry play a vital role in its success and software industry (Menkhaus & Andrich, 2005) is not an exception. Other aspects under consideration are invariably dependent on these properties. The consideration and integration (Boehm, 2000) of this *Business aspect* will not only broaden the spectrum of analysis but lead to more intricate analysis of the industry as a whole. *Risk aspects* that are not modeled and included in the analysis of industry leads to the uncertainty that prevails in this sector (Cardoso, 2006).

A mathematical model will provide a finely detailed assessment of the risks associated with the sub-factors such as defect management, maintainability, reliability and reusability and thus enhancing the quality and cost effectiveness of the product. The model adhering to this aspect will also cover the risks associated with the business process. It will help foresee constraints and legal hurdles and help us tackle them effectively. *Technological aspects* of the software industry primarily identify itself with technological advancements. It is thus inevitable for the industry to depend on advancing technology as it not only increases productivity but also determines the quality of the output (Cardoso 2006). Technological upgrades are sustained by monetary inputs therefore a model which can strike a faultless balance between the two is required. Many other domains, which were considered of trivial importance till now, have to be exhaustively analyzed (*Multi domain Analysis*). Reflection of work ideas of the human resources (Tomaszewski Farias, Mungas & Reed, 2008) and the creative properties of the company has to be taken into account (Boehm 2000; Bandinelli, Fuggetta & Ghezzi 1993). The sub-factors (such as time, satisfaction and work environment), which are conducive (Boy 2007) to improve the productivity and help increasing competency levels, have to be assessed in order to obtain an individual model. This integrated approach will also discuss the Client-Vendor Communication Model.

IV. PROGRESS BEYOND THE STATE-OF-THE-ART

The state-of-the-art in software process modeling today is the CMMI (Capability Maturity Model Integration) and to some extent the Six Sigma model (6 σ). The CMMI is a process centered (Hofmann, Yedlin, Mishler & Kushner 2007; Garcia & Turner 2006; Siviy, Lynn Penn & Robert 2007; Chrissis, Konrad, Shrum, CMMI(R)) model and it is a process of conventional process and it does not suitable for the intelligence, resources and human skills that are prevailing in the present scenario. The shortfalls of CMMI and the need for Comprehensive analysis model are discussed in the following section.

V. THE NEED OF A COMPREHENSIVE MODEL

The brief description of CMMI in the previous section asserts that this model is exceedingly process centric (Hubert F. Hofmann, DeborahK. Yedlin, John W.Mishler & SusanKushner (2007) ; Suzanne Garcia & Richard Turner (2006) ; Jeannine M. Siviy, M. Lynn Penn & Robert W (2007) ; Mary Beth Chrissis, Mike Konrad, Sandy Shrum, CMMI(R)) and does not necessarily account for other important aspects. As any other reference model or methodology for software process, the CMMI is not void of problems and drawbacks (Hubert F. Hofmann, DeborahK.Yedlin, John W.Mishler & SusanKushner (2007) ; Suzanne Garcia & Richard Turner (2006) ; Jeannine M. Siviy, M. Lynn Penn & Robert W (2007) ; Mary Beth Chrissis, Mike Konrad, Sandy Shrum, CMMI(R); Ebert, Christ of Akins & Anthony (2007)). A few of the notable constraints and drawbacks are enlisted here.

A. Inclination towards Larger Organization

CMMI has evolved from the CMMs (Capability Maturity Models) which were developed for large organizations (**Hofmann, Yedlin, Mishler & Kushner 2007; Garcia & Turner 2006; Siviy, Penn & Robert, 2007; Chrissis, Konrad, Shrum, CMMI(R)**; Spinellis, Diomidis, Mariam, Naseem, Pepa & Caroline 2007). The Structuring of CMM was sponsored by the U.S Governmental organizations that are known for being large, bureaucratic bodies, promoting more form over substance. Even Judy Bamberger, one of the key authors of the CMM, agrees that the CMM reflects the large, aerospace, contract-software development environment it was originally intended to address (Morgan; Siviy, Penn & Robert, 2007). Thus CMMI needs less interpretation for a multinational corporation than a small software developing enterprises when process part is concerned.

B. Software Process over Business Process

It concentrates mainly on the process as a factor in software development (Siviy, Penn & Robert 2007; Chrissis, Konrad, Shrum) sparing out people and technology. It is sometimes criticized that CMMI promotes the process over all other issues (even over some core issues like coding software) and that implementing CMMI is thus no guarantee that a software project will succeed (Sommerville, Sawyer & Viller 1999). CMMI deliberately focuses on the process and omits people and technology. The implementation of CMMI can significantly raise the probability of success in a software process (Siviy, Penn & Robert, 2007; Carod, Martin & Aranda, 2004; Menkhaus & Andrich, 2005) by virtue of its lengthy rigor.

C. Process Management Using Metrics

The suggestions of scientifically managing the software process with metrics only occur beyond the Fourth level (Morgan; Wallace & Kuhn, 1999). There is less validation of cost savings of the processes to business, other than vague references to empirical evidence (Wallace & Kuhn, 1999). It is expected that a large body of evidence would show that adding all the business overhead demanded by CMMI somehow increases IT headcount, business cost, and time to market without sacrificing client needs (Carod, Martin & Aranda, 2004; Menkhaus & Andrich 2005).

D. Lack of a Reliable Index

Two organizations, which comply or follow the same CMMI level exhibit a lot of difference (Sommerville, Sawyer & Viller 1999). The exclusion of important dimensions from the software process can simply be held responsible for the same (Ebert, Christof Akins & Anthony 2007; Crnkovic 2008). All these drawbacks can be eliminated if and only if we have a comprehensive reference model that incorporates each domain associated with the software industry.

VI. OVERVIEW OF DESIGN AND IMPLEMENTATION

From the perspective of software industry the comprehensive analysis model has a key impact on product quality and complexity control. A sound variable design prevents or minimizes the occurrence of faults. The design of Comprehensive analysis model is as shown in Figure 4.

Prototype design and implementation begins with the *Knowledge Induction* through domain analysis and product line experiences from various experts globally. During this process, they

Figure 4. Prototype design and implementation

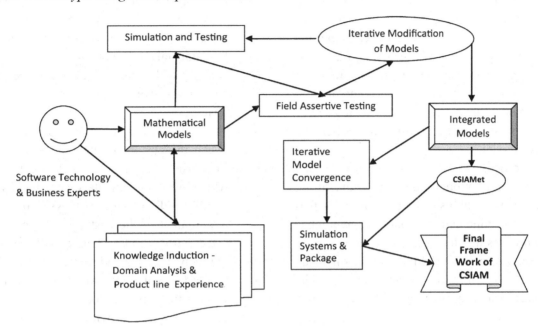

continuously interact with selected industry. This knowledge is used for arriving at the preliminary mathematical model using formal translation methods, Bond Graph Theoretical Methods, cost effective ER diagram satisfying graph theoretical approaches. The *Discrete Simulation Technique* is used in certain occasions to find out statistical response of the models where metrics moves to undefinable range. *Simulation and testing* process is one of the backbone approaches (Menkhaus & Andrich, 2005) which are given to create a reliable and provable body of CSIAM which could be used for both client and vendor segment resulting in a comprehensive view of the industrial process of software production.

Field assertive testing process can be carried out in realistic locations selected from software industries across the world. The model will be applied across high profile, moderate and lower order industry and their operations. In Iterative modifications process of models, the framed mathematical model with the help of expertise knowledge is tested with real world data and calibrated for optimum suitability (Sommerville, Sawyer &

Viller, 1999). Integration of various Models are the *integration* of the domain models will be done by establishing effective communication among the components of the different models and the models themselves. Multiple test run will be carried out to match with the industry pattern and data available in the experimental modeling to successfully reach the final goals of CSIAM.

The model will be checked for balancing indicators in the realization of the software product (Sommerville, Sawyer & Viller, 1999) across the domain of process, technology, business risk and other multi domain aspects. The integrated model thrives for establishing an appropriate, saturated, stable, cognitive communication between the models to realise a cohesive CSIAM capable of producing industry metrics. The models are formed such a way that it can undergo transformation as the technology mutation takes place in annual cycles.

At this juncture, a set of industry analysis metrics known as Comprehensive Software Industry Analysis Metrics (CSIAMet) can be arrived for the measurement and calibration of performance of software industry parameters in different domains of their activity, which will further lead to indexing the best practices in generating the software. Repetitive model estimation and correction, gap analysis and corrective operation or work individual sub system models and integration of models are carried out in order to achieve maximum suitability of this comprehensive analysis model.

The process of continuous evaluation and optimisation of models for best results fitting into the current industry levels is a major part of iterative refinement of models. Convergence is the process in which the model output gives exact metrics of different industries, which can be used for calibration of the industries. The feedback system of arriving at the best results is also incorporated in this model. Properly pruned and molded Comprehensive Software Industry Analysis Model (CSIAM) emerges at this stage.

VII. FUTURE WORK

This analysis model is implemented through a powerful application system to arrive at a Management Metric Estimation Tool (M^{2}ET) for the industries to improve their operation pertaining to each and every domain and consequently improve the quality of their product in congruence with their clients positioning (Hinkle, 2007). This model based paradigm will dynamically rate the industries using comprehensive industry metrics and thus provide valuable input to a client for selecting a vendor.

VIII. FINAL MODEL CRITERIA TO BE SATISFIED

• CSIAM will implement a set of rational metrics on active resources and process operating over that.

• CSIAM will also facilitate discussions among different stakeholders in the business, allowing them to agree on the key fundamentals and work towards common goals. It will thus facilitate enhanced interaction between various modules of a business.

• This will ensure more transparency between the customers and the companies. The business metrics and software metrics which are complementary constituents of CSIAM will enable the analysis from the requirement of the customer to the terms and conditions of the contract will be quantitatively analysed and framed.

• CSIAM will integrate and derive Standardized metrics for the business process in conjunction with the software development process.

IX. CONCLUSION

The Comprehensive Industry Analysis Model enables wide areas for research. The preliminary transformations from old concepts that process alone can improve the software production (http://www.sei.cmu.edu/cmmi) and that is the primary index for software engineering model promoting more cognitive software generation environment as defined in CSIAM can enable a sweeping change in a highly manpower dependent industry morphing it in to a machine dependent industry having better metrics to measure it in a comprehensive and unified manner. The ethics and practices of CSIAM can be institutionalised through a consortium of Business Moderators, Industry Organizations, professional bodies and governmental arms for trade practices.

X. REFERENCES

Aaen, I. (2003). Software process improvement: Blueprints versus recipes. *IEEE Software, 20*(5), 86–93. doi:10.1109/MS.2003.1231159

Ahern, D., Clouse, A., & Turner, R. (2008). *A Practical Introduction to Integrated Process Improvement,* (3rd Edition). Reading, MA: Addison-Wesley Professional.

Bandinelli, S. C., Fuggetta, A., & Ghezzi, C. (1993). Software process model evolution in the SPADE Environment. *IEEE Transactions on Software Engineering, 19*(12), 1128–1144. doi:10.1109/32.249659

Boehm, B. (2000). Unifying software engineering and systems engineering. *Computer, 33*(3), 114–116. doi:10.1109/2.825714

Bosse, T., Sharpanskykh, A., & Treur, J. (n.d.). *On the Complexity Monotonocity.* Thesis for Dept. of Artificial Intelligence, De Boelelaan 1081a, 1081 HV, the Netherlands.

Boy, G. A. (2007). Perceived complexity and Cognitive Stability in Human-Centered Design. *Proceedings of the HCI International Conference, Beijing, China.*

Cardoso, J. (2006). *Approaches to Compute Workflow Complexity.* "Dagstuhl Seminar," The Role of Business Process in Service Oriented Architectures, Dagstuhl, Germany.

Chrissis, M. B., Konrad, M., & Shrum, S. (2003). CMMI(R): Guidelines for Process. Integration and Product Improvement (2nd Ed.). Reading, MA: Addison-Wesley.

Crnkovic, I. (2008). *Component Based Software Engineering–New challenges in Software Development.* Malardalen University, Department of computer engineering, Sweden.

Ebert, Christ of Akins & Anthony, (2007). Bookshelf. *Software 24*(3), 110-112.

Garcia, S., & Turner, R. (2006). *CMMI (R) Survival Guide: Just Enough Process Improvement.* Reading, MA: Addison-Wesley Professional.

Hinkle, M. M. (2007). Software Quality, Metrics, Process Improvement, and CMMI: An Interview with Dick Fairley. *IT Professional, 9*(3), 47–51. doi:10.1109/MITP.2007.57

Hofmann, H. F., Yedlin, D. K., Mishler, J. W., & Kushner, S. (2007). *CMMI for Outsourcing Guidelines for software, systems, and IT Acquisition.* Reading, MA: Addison Wesley Professional.

Jones, C. (1996). The economics of software process improvement. *Computer, 29*(1), 95–97. doi:10.1109/2.481498

Kan, S. H. (2002). *Metrics and Models in Software Quality Engineering.* Boston: Addison –Wesley Longman Publishing Co., Inc.

Martinez Carod, N., Martin, A., & Aranda, G. N. (2004). *A Cognitive Approach to Improve Software Engineering Processes.* International Conference on Cognitive Informatics, ICCI'4 Canada.

Menkhaus, G., & Andrich, B. (2005). Metric Suite for Directing the Failure mode Analysis of Embedded Software Systems. *In Proc. of the 7th International Conference on Enterprise Information Systems (ICEIS'05).*

Menkhaus, G., Frei, U., & Wuthrich, J. (2006). *Analysis and Verification of the Interaction Model in Software Design.* Retrieved from http://www.sei.cmu.edu/cmmi

Morgan, P., (n.d.). *Process Improvement-Is it a lottery?* Marting and Associates-Software Process Improvement Resources and Assessments Results.

Persse, J. (2007). *Project Management Success with CMMI: Seven CMMI Process Areas.* Upper Saddle River, NJ: Prentice Hall PTR.

Rauterberg, M. (1996). *How to measure Cognitive Complexity in Human – Computer Interaction.* ED-MEDIA 96, Charlottesville, NC, AACE.

Rauterberg, M., & Aeppli, R. (1996). *How to measure the behavioural and Cognitive Complexity of learning process in Man-Machine Systems,* (pp.581- 586). Educational Multimedia and Hypermedia-ED- MEDIA'96, Charlottesville, NC, AACE.

Rauterberg, M., Schluep, S., & Fjuld, M. (1997). *How to model behavioural and cognitive complexity in Human -computer interaction with Petri nets.* IEEE Workshop on Robot and human communication.

Robillard, P. N., & Detienne, F. (1998). *Measuring cognitive Activities in Software Engineering.* ICSE98, 20th International conference on Software Engineering, Kyoto, Japan.

Siviy, J. M., Penn, M. L., & Robert, W. (2007). *Standard CMMI (R) and Six Sigma: Partners in Process Improvement.* Reading MA: Addison Wesley Professional.

Sommerville, I. Sawyer & P. Viller (1999). Managing process inconsistency using viewpoints. *IEEE Transactions on Software Engineering, 25(*6), 784 – 799.

Spinellis, Diomidis, Mariam, Naseem, Pepa & Caroline, (2007). Bookshelf - Software engineering for the rest of us. *Software IEEE, 24*(4), 107-109.

Tomaszewski Farias, S., Mungas, D., & Reed, B. R. (2008). The measurement of Everyday Cognition (ECog) Scale Development and Psychometric Properties. *Neuropsychology, 22*(45), 31–544.

Von Wangenheim, C.G., Anacleto & Alviano, A. (2006). Helping small companies assess software Processes. *Software, 23*(1), 91–98. doi:10.1109/MS.2006.13

Wallace, D. R., & Kuhn, D. R. (1999). Failure Modes in Medical Device Software. An Analysis of 15 Years of Recall Data. *Journal, Information Technology Laboratory, NIST Gaithersburg . MD,* 20899.

Wang, Y. (2006). *Cognitive Complexity of Software and its Measurement.* 5th IEEE International on Cognitive Informatics (ICCI'06).

Zhong, X., Madhavji, N. H., & El Emam, K. (2000). Critical factors affecting personal software Processes. *Software, 17*(6), 76–83. doi:10.1109/52.895172

Chapter 11
Software Metrics Evaluation Based on Entropy

R. Selvarani
Dayananda Sagar Institutions, Bangalore, India

T.R. Gopalakrishnan Nair
Dayananda Sagar Institutions, India

Muthu Ramachandran
Leeds Metropolitan University, UK

Kamakshi Prasad
JNTU, Hyderabad, India

ABSTRACT

The complexity of modern software, the commercial constraints and the expectation for high quality product demands the accurate fault prediction based on OO design metrics in the class level in the early stages of software development. The object oriented class metrics are used as quality predictors in the entire OO software development life cycle even when a highly iterative, incremental model or agile software process is employed. Recent research has shown some of the OO design metrics are useful for predicting fault-proneness of classes. In this chapter the empirical validation of a set of metrics proposed by Chidamber and Kemerer is performed to assess their ability in predicting the software quality in terms of fault proneness and degradation. The authors have also proposed the design complexity of object-oriented software with Weighted Methods per Class metric (WMC-CK metric) expressed in terms of Shannon entropy, and error proneness.

I. INTRODUCTION

Object-oriented design and development are popular concepts in today's software development environment, object-oriented (OO) development has proved its value for systems that must be maintained and modified. OO software development requires a different approach from more traditional functional decomposition and data flow development methods,

DOI: 10.4018/978-1-60566-731-7.ch011

including the metrics used to evaluate OO software. The concepts of software metrics are well established, and many metrics relating to product design quality have been developed and used. One approach to controlling software maintenance costs is the utilization of software metrics during the development phase, to help identify potential problem areas in the design.

Software design complexity is a highly important factor affecting the cost of software development and maintenance. If we can determine the impact of complexity factors on maintenance effort, we can develop guidelines which will help reduce the costs of maintenance by recognizing troublesome situations early in the development phase. In response to these situations the managers may take appropriate decision to reduce the design complexity of the system, to develop tools that support maintenance of complex modules, to write documentation that helps the developer to manage the complexity better, to allocate the resources to reflect the situation.

This paper presents the empirical evaluation of CK metrics (Chidamber, Shyam & Kemerer 1994) for object oriented design based on measurement theory and ontology. These measures applied in software system could be used to aid management in estimating the cost and schedule of future projects, evaluating the productivity impacts of new tools and techniques, establishing productivity trends over time, improving software quality, forecasting future staffing needs, and anticipating and reducing future maintenance requirements.

A method based on information theory has also been proposed for examining software design complexity using one of the widely accepted OO complexity design metrics in the context of empirical complexity threshold criteria to assess system-wide software degradation. We have considered five C++ projects done by different group of students. The analysis showed that components with high design complexities were associated with more maintenance activities than those components with lower class complexities.

II. METRIC EVALUATION CRITERIA

Metrics are defined by Fenton and Pfleeger in (Fenton & Pfleeger, 1996) as output of measurements, where measurement is defined as the process by which values are assigned to attribute of entities in the real world in such a way as to describe them according to clearly defined rules. Software metrics are the measures of attributes of a software system (Weyuker, 1988). Traditional functional decomposition metrics and data analysis design metrics measure the design structure independently. OO metrics treats function and data as a combined, integrated object (Chidamber, Shyam & Kemerer, 1994). To evaluate a metric's usefulness as a quantitative measure of software quality, it must be based on the measurement of a software quality attribute. The metrics evaluate the OO concepts such as methods, classes, cohesion, coupling, and inheritance. The metrics focus on internal object structure, external measures of the interactions among entities, measures of the efficiency of an algorithm and the use of machine resources, and the psychological measures that affect a programmer's ability to create, comprehend, modify, and maintain software.

III. EMPIRICAL LITERATURE ON CK METRICS

There are a number of empirical studies on CK metrics (Chidamber, Shyam & Kemerer 1994; Booch, & Grady, 1994; Bansiya, Davis, & Etzkon, 1999). The existing empirical studies have been compared and the analysis of their results has been reported by Subramanyam and Krishana (Bansiya, Davis, & Etzkon, 1999). To improve the effectiveness of developer interactions in the study, we have adopted a ground theory (can be defined as a systematic qualitative approach to research methodology where research hypothesis and theories can be formulated based on the data collected, (Subramanyam, & Krishnan, 2003) dialogue and structured questionnaire to study the effectiveness of the empirical evaluation. Current empirical studies, most notably by Booch (Booch, & Grady 1994) and Subramanyam and Krishnan (Bansiya, Davis, & Etzkon, 1999) who outline four major steps involved in the object oriented design process.

- Identification of Classes (and objects): The key abstractions in the problem space are identified and labeled as potential classes and objects.
- Identification of semantics of Classes (and objects): The meaning of classes and objects identified in the previous step is established, this includes the definition of the life cycles of each object from creation to destruction.
- Identify the relationship between Classes (and objects): Classes and objects interactions, such as patterns of inheritance among and patterns of visibility among objects and classes are identified.
- Implementation of Classes (and objects): Detailed internal views are constructed, including definitions of methods and their various behaviours. In the existing several design methodologies, the design of class is consistently declared to be the central to the OO paradigm. Since the class deals with the functional requirements of the system, it must occur before system design (mapping object to processors and processes) and program design (reconciling of functionality using the target languages, tools etc.). Given the importance of class design the metrics outlined in this paper specifically are designed to measure the complexity of the design of classes. Weyuker has developed a formal list of properties for software metrics and has evaluated a number of existing metrics using these properties (Weyuker, 1988). Of

nine properties proposed by Weyuker, the following six properties are widely accepted by the researchers.

Property 1: Non-coarseness
Given a class P and a metric μ another class Q can always be found such that: $\mu(P) \_ \mu(Q)$. This implies that not every class can have the same value for a metric; otherwise it has lost its value as a measurement.

Property 2: Non-uniqueness (notion of equivalence)
There can exist distinct classes P and Q, $\mu(P) = \mu(Q)$. This implies that two classes can have the same metric value, i, e., the two classes are equally complex.

Property 3: Design details are important
Given two class designs, P and Q, which provide the same functionality, does not imply that $\mu(P) = \mu(Q)$. The specifics of the class must influence the metric value. The intuition behind the property 3 is that even though two class designs perform the same function, the details of the design matter in determining the metric for the class.

Property 4: Monotonicity
For all classes P and Q, the following must hold: $\mu(P) \overset{2}{} \mu(P+Q)$ and $\mu(Q) \overset{2}{} \mu(P+Q)$ Where P+Q implies combination of P and Q[10] . This implies that the metrics for the combination of two classes can never be less than the metric for either of the component classes.

Property 5: Non equivalence of interaction
$\exists P, \exists Q, \exists R$, such that: $\mu(P) = \mu(Q)$ does not imply that and $\mu(Q+R)$. This suggests that the interaction between Q and R can be different than interaction between Q and resulting in different complexity values for P+Q and Q+R.

Property 6: Interaction increases complexity
$\exists P, \exists Q$ such that: $\mu(P)\,\mu(Q) < \mu(P+Q)$. The principle behind this property is that when two classes are combined, the interaction between classes can increase the complexity metric value.

A. OO-Specific Metrics

The OO design metrics are primarily applied to the concepts of classes, coupling, and inheritance.

Predicting design defects can save cost enormously. CK suite of metrics has been successfully applied in identifying design defects early during the design process. The summary of CK design metrics are described as follow:

1) **Weighted Methods per Class (WMC):** It is a class level metric. A class is a template from which objects can be created. This set of objects shares a common structure and a common behaviour manifested by the set of methods. The WMC is a count of the methods implemented within a class or the sum of the complexities of the methods (method complexity is measured by cyclomatic complexity). The number of methods and the complexity of the methods involved is a predictor of how much time and effort is required to develop and maintain the class. The larger the number of methods in a class, the greater the potential impact on children, since children inherit all of the methods defined in a class. Classes with large numbers of methods are likely to be more application specific, limiting the possibility of reuse. This metric measures understandability, reusability, and maintainability (Chidamber, Shyam & Chris Kemerer, 1994; Rosenberg; Fenton & Pfleeger, 1996; Hudli, Hoskins & Hudli 1994; Lorenz, & Kidd, 1994). WMC is a good indicator for implementation and test effort.

2) **Response for a Class (RFC):** RFC, looks at methods and messages within a class. A message is a request that an object makes of another object to perform an operation. The operation executed as a result of receiving a message is called a method The RFC is the set of all methods (internal, external) that can be invoked in response to a message sent to an object of the class or by some method in the class. This metric uses a number of methods to review a combination of a class's complexity and the amount of communication with other classes. If a large number of methods can be invoked in response to a message, testing and debugging the class requires a greater understanding on the part of the tester. A worst-case value for possible responses assists in the appropriate allocation of testing time. This metric evaluates the system design as well as the usability and testability.

As RFC is directly related to complexity, the ability to test, debug and maintain a class increase with an increase in RFC. In the calculation of RFC, inherited methods count, but overridden methods do not. This makes sense, as only one method of a particular signature is available to an object of the class. Also, only one level of depth is counted for remote method invocations.

3) **Lack of Cohesion of Methods (LCOM):** Cohesion is the extension of information hiding. (Fenton, & Pfleeger, 1996) Degree to which methods within a class are related to one another and work together to provide well-bounded behaviour. Effective OO designs maximize cohesion because they promote encapsulation. LCOM uses data input variables or attributes to measure the degree of similarity between methods. Any measure of method separateness helps identify flaws in the design of classes. There are two ways to measure cohesion 1. (Rosenberg) The percentage of methods that use each data field in a class can be calculated and the average of the percentages can be subtracted from

100 which indicate the level of cohesion. If the percentage low, the cohesion will be more and if it is high then there will be low cohesion 2. The count of disjoint sets at from the intersection of the sets of attributes used by the methods also will indicate the level of cohesion. For a good cohesion and less complexity, the class subdivision must be well defined. Classes with low cohesion could probably be subdivided into two or more subclasses with increased cohesion. Any measure of disparateness of methods helps identify flaws in the design of classes. It is a direct indicator of design complexity and reusability.

4) **Coupling Between Object Classes (CBO):** Coupling is a measure of the strength of association established by a connection from one entity to another (Rosenberg). Classes (objects) are said to be coupled when a message is passed between objects, when methods declared in one class use methods or attributes from the other classes. Tight coupling between super classes and their subclasses is introduced by inheritance. For a good OO design balance between coupling and inheritance is required.

CBO is a count of the number of other classes to which a class is coupled (Linda H. Rosenberg). It is measured by counting the number of distinct non inheritance-related class hierarchies on which a class depends. Excessive coupling is detrimental to modular design and prevents reuse. In order to improve modularity and promote encapsulation, inter-object class couples should be kept to a minimum. The larger the number of couples, the higher the sensitivity to changes in other parts of the design; maintenance is therefore more difficult. The higher the inter-object class coupling, the complexity will be increased and more rigorous testing is needed. Complexity can be reduced by designing systems with the weakest possible coupling between modules. This improves modularity and promotes encapsulation (Rosenberg). CBO evaluates efficiency and reusability (Chidamber, Shyam & Kemerer, 1994; Booch, 1994; Weyuker, 1988; Rosenberg; Fenton, & Pfleeger, 1996; Hudli, Hoskins, & Hudli 1994; Lorenz, & Kidd, 1994).

5) **Depth of Inheritance Tree (DIT):** Inheritance is a type of relationship among classes that enables programmers to reuse previously defined objects, including variables and operators (Fenton, & Pfleeger, 1996). Deep inheritance hierarchies can lead to code fragility with increased complexity and behavioral unpredictability. The depth of inheritance hierarchy is the number of classes (nodes) connected to the main class (root of the tree). The deeper a class within the hierarchy, the greater the number of methods it is likely to inherit, making it more complex to predict its behavior. Deeper trees constitute greater design complexity, since more methods and classes are involved, but the greater the potential for reuse of inherited methods. A support metric for DIT is the number of methods inherited. This metric primarily evaluates efficiency and reuse but also relates to understandability and testability (Chidamber, Shyam & Kemerer 1994; Booch, 1994; Rosenberg; Fenton, & Pfleeger, 1996; Hudli, Hoskins & Hudli, 1994; Lorenz, & Kidd, 1994).

6) **Number of Children (NOC):** For a given class, the number of classes that inherit from it is referred to by the metric Number of Children (number of child classes) (Fenton, & Pfleeger, 1996). The greater the number of children, the greater the reuse and likelihood of improper parent abstraction, and it may be an indication of sub classing misuse. If a class has a large number of children, it may require more testing of the methods of that class, thus increase the testing time.

This metric evaluates efficiency, reusability, and testability of the design of the system. It is an indicator of the potential influence a class can have on the design and on the system (Chidamber, & Kemerer 1994; Rosenberg)

IV. SOFTWARE METRICS AND ENTROPY CONCEPT

The distinction between reversible and irreversible process was first introduced in thermodynamics through the concept of 'entropy' (apd-El-Hafiz, 2001). In the modern context, the formulation of entropy is fundamental for understanding thermodynamic aspects of self organization evolution of order and life that we see in Nature. When a system is isolated, energy increase will be zero. In this case the entropy of the system will continue to increase due to irreversible processes and reach the maximum possible value. This is the state of the thermodynamic equilibrium .In the state of equilibrium, all irreversible process cease. When a system begins to exchange entropy with the exterior then, in general it is driven away from the equilibrium, and the entropy producing the irreversible process begins to operate. This 'state of disorder' is characterized by the amount of disordered energy and its temperature level. Here we have to highlight the following facts as a summary of entropy.

- The entropy of a system is a measure of the amount of molecular disorder within the system
- A system can only generate but not destroy the entropy.
- The entropy of the system can be increased or decreased by energy transports across the boundary

The energy sources in the universe were rated on entropy /usefulness scale from zero entropy. The low entropy energy is useful.

The use of entropy as a measure of information content of software systems that has led to its use in measuring the code complexity of functionally developed software products. The metric is computed using information available in class definitions. The correlation study used the final versions of class definition. The high degree of positive relationship between entropy based class definition measure and the design complexity measure of class implementation complexity verify that the new entropy measure computed from class definitions can be used as a predictive measure for class implementation complexities provided the class definitions do not change significantly during the implementation.

Current studies on entropy (Lavenda, & Dunning-Davies, 2003) have been applied mainly to measure the code complexity measures. Our aim in this research is to apply the concept entropy measures for analysis and predict design defects based on grounded empirical analysis which is a structured and interactive approach to user dialogue for collective data based on sociological study. This involves observing how software engineers develop their software and their work environment in which the actual software has been developed. We believe this will have a direct impact on the quality of the software that has been produced.

The class complexity related to number of methods in a class is one of the fundamental measure of the 'goodness' of a software design. The most accepted widely studied WMC metric from CK metric suites plays as an important measure for system understandability, testability, and maintainability. This design metrics is a good predictor of time and effort requirement to develop and maintain the class, but when it is associated with entropy metric, it gives an insight about the design degradation or disorder of the system and recommends for redesigning of the system in the early stage itself which in turn reduce the cost of the system.

Table 1. CK-WMC Threshold- NASA-SATC data

System Category	CK-W MC Threshold (x)	Risk Interpretation
1	$1 \leq x \leq 20$	Good values of class complexity.
2	$20 \leq x \leq 100$	Moderate high values of complexity.
3	$x > 100$	High class complexity, cause for investigation

V. ENTROPY (INFORMATION THEORY) BASED OBJECT ORIENTED SOFTWARE SYSTEM COMPLEXITY MEASUREMENT

In object-oriented programming, the class complexity measures information flows in a class based on the information passing relationship among member data and member functions. The inter-object complexity for a program measures information flows between objects. Total program complexity is measured by class complexity and inter-object complexity. The term 'software entropy' has been defined to mean that software declines in quality, maintainability and understandability through its lifetime. Here Shannon's entropy equation is used to establish a measure of OO software degradation that is easy to use and interpret. WMC (weighted method per class), a well-established CK metrics is used to asses this criteria. WMC thresholds are the basis for our metric measurement. We have used the threshold criteria for WMC published by Rosenberg, et al. Software Assurance Technology Center (SATC), NASA Goddard Space Flight Center, in 1998 (Kastro, 2004). These thresholds were based on their experiences at NASA with OO projects. It is shown in Table 1, and will be used without modification in this application. Table 1, gives the threshold criteria and interpretation of risk. The use of these thresholds in industry allows software managers to make judgments about the class complexity of their software in terms of effort required for testing the system and the level of confidence required in software deployment.

A. Properties of Shannon's Entropy

The Shannon entropy, *Hn*, is defined as:

$$H_n(P) = -\sum_{k=1}^{n} p_k = 1 (n \geq 1) \tag{1}$$

$$P_k \geq 0 \ (k = 1, 2, \ldots, n) \text{ and } \sum_{k=1}^{n} p_k = 1 \ (n \geq 1) \tag{2}$$

Where, H System = System Complexity Entropy. k = Integer value 1, 2, ... j, representing each of the categories considered. P_k = Total number of classes that are in category PN = Total number of system cases (equal to the sum of all the P_k s).

Because a logarithm to the base 2 is used, the resulting unit of information is called the bit (a contraction of binary unit). The Shannon entropy satisfies many desirable properties. The following properties of the selected mathematical approach are more suitable for this application. (Aczél, & Daróczy).

1. **Non negativity:** Information about an experiment makes no one more ignorant than he was before. [28,29] $Hn(P) \geq 0$
2. **Symmetry:** The amount of information is invariant under a change in the order of events.
   $Hn(P) = Hn(p_{k(1)}, p_{k(2)}, \ldots, p_{k(n)})$,
   where k is an arbitrary permutation on {1, 2, ..., n}.
3. **Normality:** A "simple alternative", which in this case is an experiment with two outcomes

of equal probability 0.5, promises one unit of information.

$$H_2(0.5, 0.5) = 1$$

4. **Expansibility:** Additional outcomes with zero probability do not change the uncertainty of the outcome of an experiment.

$$H_n(P) = H_{n+1}(p_1, p_2, ..., p_n, 0)$$

5. **Decisivity:** There is no uncertainty in an experiment with two outcomes, one of Nonnegativity them of probability 1, the other of probability 0.

$$H_2(1, 0) = 0$$

6. **Additivity:** The information, expected from two independent experiments, is the sum of the information expected from the individual experiments.

$$H_{nm}(P*Q) = H_n(P) + H_m(Q)$$

7. **Subadditivity:** The information, expected from two experiments, is not greater than the sum of the information expected from the individual experiments.

$$H_{nm}(P*Q) \leq H_n(P) + H_m(Q)$$

8. **Maximality:** The entropy is greatest when all admissible outcomes have equal probabilities.

$$H_n(P) \leq H_n(1/n, 1/n, 1/n ....., 1/n)$$

B. Measures of Information and their Characterizations

The concept of entropy, as a measure of information, is fundamental in information theory. The entropy of an experiment has dual interpretations. It can be considered both as a measure of the uncertainty that prevailed before the experiment was accomplished and as a measure of the information expected from an experiment (Rosenberg, L. H. (1998)). An experiment might be an information source emitting a sequence of symbols (i.e., a message) $M = \{s_1, s_2, s_3, ... s_n\}$, where successive symbols are selected according to some fixed probability law, with which the symbols occur $P = (p_1, p_2, ..., p_n)$ (Abramson, N (1963); Hamming, R (1980)).

In this paper the uncertainty measure that prevailed before the experiment is performed. The maximum entropy is achieved when $Si = Si+1 = Si+2 = Si+3$, or when all the classes are evenly distributed. Shannon's equation "dampens" the effect of a few very highly complex methods to skew the overall complexity of the system. This is because the equation limits the contribution of the entropy score from each category to the overall (system) entropy score.

C. The Shannon's Entropy Relationship (Frakes, Fox, & Nejmeh, 1991)

Shannon's Entropy equation provides a way to estimate the average minimum number of symbols based on the frequency of the symbols. By treating the software system as an information source, the function calls or method invocation in object oriented systems resemble the emission of symbols from an information source. Thus the probabilities required for computing the entropy are obtained using an empirical distribution or function calls or method invocations.

VI. EXPERIMENTAL ANALYSIS

If we treat a software system as an information source then the symbols emitted from the system can be the operators within a program, where operators are a special symbol, a reserved word, or a function call (Hamming, 1980). Another technique can be based on data flow relationships (Harrison, 1992). The technique adopted here considers the function calls in procedural programming as the symbols emitted from a software system (or module). In object oriented programming, we replace function calls with method invocations. The rationale behind this choice is that performing calls to different functions resembles emitting a message of many symbols particular to the considered module. The complexity of the design in object

Table 2. Project metrics

Project Metric	P1	P2	P3	P4	P5
Classes:	37	46	120	139	148
Files:	35	34	56	65	90
Library Units:	209	234	267	168	289
Lines: 211	6734	10342	9758	12439	14116
Lines Blank:	788	675	1253	1569	2378
Lines Code:	3258	8567	8450	11236	12564
Lines Comment:	2759	7498	7456	9696	10997
Lines Inactive	0	0	0	0	0
Executable Statements:	1604	5078	4589	6752	7629
Declarative Statements	791	1126	569	2319	2746
Ratio Comment/Code:	0.85	0.87	0.88	0.89	0.88

oriented system is the weighted method per class. The probabilities are obtained using an empirical distribution of the function calls. The WMC metric measurement by NASA SATC is based on the number of distinct functions or modules in a class and the complexity is the message transfer between the modules in the class. The WMC complexity measurement is done by considering the different summations, in the definitions of entropies, over the number of distinct functions or modules in a class .In this design metric, there is no possibility of 0 modules in any of the classes, hence the WMC metric recommended by NASA-SATC starts from 1. The information will be zero, if there are no functional calls in a module. We have considered the following five different Java projects by different teams of students as examples to demonstrate the application of our technique to understand the disorder of the project. This model is used to predict the disorder associated with the system in the class level. Table 2 depicts the program metrics obtained by analyzing the projects with Understand java. The total number of classes in each project as shown in Figure 1 is divided in to samples according to the NASA SATC metric. The measures calculated are Shannon generalized entropies as given by equations (1) and the results are consistent. As stated by

the designer in the program's documentation: "The only algorithms at all difficult are those for parsing, which are rather ad hoc but apparently correct. (Kim, Shine, & Wu, 1995). This fact is identified by this information measure, which have the highest value for the module of higher design complexity. The next highest value was appropriately given to the module of comparatively lesser design complexity. If we check the rest of the classes, it is clear that the information content asures give meaningful and intuitive results.

The goal of Object oriented Design, is "to design the classes identified during the analysis phase and the user interface". In this design model, the system architecture may have a large number of simple classes, rather than a small number of complex classes for better reusability and maintainability, which in turn displays lesser design complexity. Figure 1 depicts the class distribution among the sample projects of our study. It is observed that the project with larger number of classes is comparatively less prone to degradation because the entropy $\alpha = 0.59$. The entropy of a software system is a class of metrics to assess the degree of disorder in a software system structure. Entropy covers all the components of a software system at different abstraction levels, as well as the traceability and relationships among them.

Figure 1. Project-class distribution

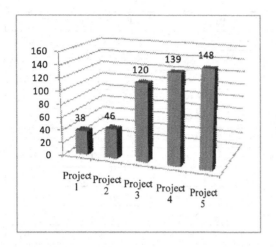

It is a direct measure for design complexity and quality of the system (cf. Figure 2).

Table 3 depicts the result of application of Shannon entropy equation to verify the utility of

complexity metrics for predicting the complexity of initial OO classes. The NASA SATC WMC threshold criteria are used to form the sample set of classes in each project. In this analysis it is observed as the degradation level of project 2 is higher than other projects.

VII. CONCLUSION AND FUTURE WORK

The benefits of object-oriented programming are the resulting simplicity and understandability of the problem through the use of abstraction. However, even OO software is not immune to the effects of brittleness, or degradation. We believe that this entropy degradation metric with OO design metrics thresholds may be useful in evaluating OO software, specifically large Java

Figure 2. Project complexity

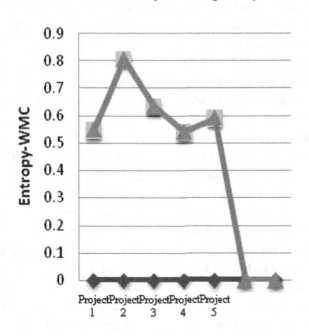

Table 3. Java projects entropy degradation- WMC

Project	Total Classes	S1	S2	S3	WMC Entropy α ≤ 1	N*(WMC Entropy)
P1	38	34	3	1	0.546781	20.777678
P2	46	38	6	2	0.807802	37.158811
P3	120	105	12	3	0.633912	76.0694421
P4	139	126	7	6	0.541312	75.2433682
P5	148	132	11	4	0.591036	87.4733282

and C++ systems. This metric may be of most value in programming environments where legacy code is being reengineered into object- oriented programs. We have developed a model, based on Shannon's entropy equation (eqn-1) with their mathematical properties (non negativity, symmetry, normality, Expansibility, decisivity, and maximality, additivity and subadditivity) to measure the design complexity of the projects with the CK-WMC metric using the variations of the WMC metric and widely accepted threshold values for interpreting the complexity. The measure based on the Chidamber and Kemerer version of WMC, where a complexity score of '1' is assigned to each method in a class showed the most promise at being a good indicator of system degradation. The group of classes with higher entropy scores are more prone for degradation It is extremely difficult in assessing the module independency in a software system. Hence the complexity score, the 'Shannon entropy' is of degree $\alpha \leq 1$. The probability for computing the entropies are obtained using the empirical distribution of the methods in a class. The Shannon entropy is more consistent for different values of WMC metric. As α increase the measure becomes coarse and indicates the high degradation possibilities of the Object oriented software system. The NASA/ Rosenberg threshold risk criteria provided the best correlation to system degradation, because of the grouping of the classes into three categories according to the metric criteria. Software measurement has been a successful approach in evaluating and predicting process capability through personnel performance. Future research includes the assessment of performance of various teams involved in making this software products using various design metrics and algorithms to drive quantifiable results in a software organization for assessing and managing the process. In addition the utility of the developed measures as indicators of some external quality or maintainability attributes needs to be investigated.

VIII. REFERENCES

Abramson, N. (1963). *Information Theory and Coding*. New York: McGraw-Hill.

Aczél, J., & Daróczy, Z. (1963). *On Measures of Information and their Characterization*. New York: Academic Press.

apd-El-Hafiz, S.K (2001). Entropies as measure of software information. *Software maintenance, Proceedings IEEE International conference* (pp. 110 -117).

Banker, R.D., Datar, S.M., Kemerer, C.F. & Zweig, D. (1993). Software Complexity and Software Maintenance Costs. *Comm. ACM, 36*.

Bansiya, J., Davis, C., & Etzkon, L. (1999). An Entropy-Based Complexity Measure for Object-Oriented Designs. *Journal of Theory and Practice for Object Systems*, 5(2).

Basili, V. R., Briand, L. C., & Melo, W. L. (1996). A Validation of Object-Oriented Design Metrics as Quality Indicators. *IEEE Transactions on Software Engineering, 22,* 751–761. doi:10.1109/32.544352

Booch, G. (1994). *Object Oriented Analysis and Design with Applications.* New York: The Benjamin / Cummings Publishing Company, Inc.

Borgatti, S. (2008) *Introduction to Grounded Theory.* Retrieved from http:// www.analytictech. com /mb870 /introtoGT.htm

Cartwright, M., & Shepperd, M. (1996). *An Empirical Investigation of Object-Oriented Software in Industry.* Technical Report TR 96/ 01, Dept. of Computing, Talbot Campus, Bournemouth University.

Chidamber, S., & Kemerer, C. (1994). A Metrics Suite for Object-Oriented Design. *IEEE Transactions on Software Engineering,* 476–492. doi:10.1109/32.295895

Chidamber, S. R., & Kemerer, C. F. (1994). A Metrics Suite for Object-Oriented Design. *IEEE Transactions on Software Engineering, 20,* 476–493. doi:10.1109/32.295895

Frakes, W. B., Fox, C. J., & Nejmeh, B. A. (1991). *Software Engineering in the UNIX/C Environment.* Englewood, Cliffs, NJ: Prentice Hall.

Hamming, R. (1980). *Coding and Information Theory.* Englewood Cliffs, NJ: Prentice-Hall.

Harrison, W. (1992). An entropy based measure of software complexity. *IEEE Transactions on Software Engineering, 18*(11), 1025–1029. doi:10.1109/32.177371

Henry, S., & Li, W. (1992). Metrics for Object-Oriented Systems. *Proc. OOPSLA '92 Workshop: Metrics for Object-Oriented Software Development,* Vancouver, Canada.

Hudli, R., Hoskins, C., & Hudli, A. (1994). *Software Metrics for Object Oriented Designs.* Washington, DC: IEEE.

Jacobson, I. (1993). *Object Oriented Software Engineering: A Use Case Driven Approach.* Reading, MA: Addison-Wesley Publishing Company.

Kastro, Y. (2004). *The Defect Prediction Method for software Versioning.* Bogazici University.

Kim, K., Shine, Y., & Wu, C. (1995). Complexity measures for object oriented programming based on entropy. *Proceedings of the Asian pacific Conference on Software Engineering* (pp. 127-136).

Lavenda, B. H., & Dunning-Davies, J. (2003). Arxiv: physics/0310117v1[physics.class-ph].

Li, W., & Henry, S. (1993). Object-Oriented Metrics that Predict Maintainability. *Journal of Systems and Software, 23,* 111–122. doi:10.1016/0164-1212(93)90077-B

Lorenz, M., & Kidd, J. (1994). *Object Oriented Software Metrics.* Upper Saddle River, NJ: Prentice Hall Publishing.

Nielsen, S. (1996). Personal communication.

Rosenberg, L. H. (n.d.). *Software Quality Metrics for Object-Oriented Environments.* Unisys Government Systems Lawrence E. Hyatt, Software Assurance Technology Center. Fenton, N.E. & Pfleeger, S.L. (1996). Software Metrics: A Rigorous and Practical Approach (2nd Ed.) London: Int'l Thompson Computer press.

Rosenberg, L. H. (1998). *Applying and Interpreting Object Oriented Metrics.*

Schach, S. R. (2007). *Object oriented and classical software engineering,* (6th Ed., pp.64-75). New York: McGraw-Hill.

Sharble, R. C., & Cohen, S. S. (1993). The Object-Oriented Brewery: A Comparison of Two Object-Oriented Development Methods. *Software Eng. Notes, 18,* 60–73. doi:10.1145/159420.155839

Sommerville, I. (1992). *Software Engineering*. Reading, MA: Addison-Wesley Publishing Company.

Subramanyam, R. & Krishnan, M. S. (2003). Empirical analysis of CK metrics for object-oriented design complexity: implications for software defects. *IEEE Trans. on SE, 29*(4).

Van, P. (2003). *Wrekly non local irreversible thermodynamics*. arxiv:condmat / 0112214 v3 [cond-mat.mtrl-sci].

Weyuker, E. (1988). Evaluating Software Complexity Measures. *IEEE Transactions on Software Engineering, 14*(9), 1357–1365. doi:10.1109/32.6178

Section 2
Productivity Technologies

Chapter 12
Model-Driven Exception Management Case Study

Susan Entwisle
Monash University, Australia

Sita Ramakrishnan
Monash University, Australia

Elizabeth Kendall
Melbourne Institute of Technology, Australia

ABSTRACT

Programming languages provide exception handling mechanisms to structure fault tolerant activities within software systems. However, the use of exceptions at this low level of abstraction can be error-prone and complex, potentially leading to new programming errors. To address this we have developed a model-driven exception management framework (DOVE). This approach is a key enabler to support global distributed solution delivery teams. The focus of this paper is the evaluation of the feasibility of this approach through a case study, known as Project Tracker. The case study is used to demonstrate the feasibility and to perform an assessment based on quality and productivity metrics and testing of the DOVE framework. The results of the case study are presented to demonstrate the feasibility of our approach.

INTRODUCTION

Rapid advances in information technology and consumer demand have motivated the development of increasingly rich, complex software systems. Within these software systems, exceptions are inevitable and increasing due to the diverse range of potential points of deviations and errors, including hardware, software, and human error (Garcia, F.Rubira, Romanovsky, & Xu, 2001; Patterson et al., 2002). Modern programming languages, including Java (Arnold, Gosling, & Homes, 2000) and C# (Williams, 2002), provide exception handling mechanisms to systematically handle errors within these software system to meet reliability requirements (Alexander Romanovsky, 2003; Perry, Romanovsky, & Tripathi, 2000). However, while exception handling can improve the design of an

DOI: 10.4018/978-1-60566-731-7.ch012

application, the use of exception handling is labor intensive, error prone, provides limited support for communication, and is inflexible (Howell & Vecellio, 2000; Klein & Dellarocas, 2000; Reimer & Srinivasan, 2003).

Much of the exception handling research to date has concentrated on addressing the objectives of exception handling as a language design issue (Garcia et al., 2001), or providing the software developer with exception usage design patterns and software frameworks (Anderson, Feng, Riddle, & Romanovsky, 2003; Garcia & Rubira, 2000; Reimer & Srinivasan, 2003). However, despite the advantages, experience has shown that progress in understandability and reusability within most problem domains other than limited vertical frameworks and class libraries, (such as user interface, databases, virtual machines, etc), has failed to meet expectation (Eisenecker & Czarnecki, 2000; Greenfield, Short, Cook, & Kent, 2004).

This finding extends beyond just exception handling, to a wider range of software development. (Coplien, 1998; Eisenecker & Czarnecki, 2000; Greenfield et al., 2004; Mellor, Scott, Uhl, & Weise, 2004) argue that significant advances in reuse and the management of complexity can be potentially achieved by transitioning to system families. These families are represented using higher level abstractions of the problem domain, represented as models, in order to meet problem domain requirements. Model transformation facilitates the automatic construction of highly customized intermediate or end applications based on high-level problem domain models. These models are configured to leverage elementary, reusable domain-specific assets rather than programming languages (Eisenecker & Czarnecki, 2000; Greenfield et al., 2004; Mellor et al., 2004). The model-driven approach is a key enabler to support global application delivery teams to design and deliver projects using geographically distributed teams. This approach allows the architect that is co-located with the customer to design the system using high-level models. These models can then be provided to the application development team to automatically construct the application.

This approach aims to promote productivity, maintainability, and expressiveness, and aid in the management of complexity by supporting higher levels of abstraction that systematically reuse domain-specific assets (such as domain-specific languages, common architecture, components, documentation, etc). To achieve this, model-driven development is based on software product-line engineering practices (also known as system-family engineering). This approach seeks to capture commonalities among systems within a given problem domain while managing variations in a systematic manner (Paul Clements & Northrop, 2001; Eisenecker & Czarnecki, 2000; Greenfield et al., 2004; Weiss & Lai, 1999). This family based software development process is divided into two parts: domain engineering that focuses on engineering-for-reuse and application engineering that focuses on engineering-with-reuse.

The limitations of language-based approaches to exception management and the potential benefits of model-driven development have motivated our research into model-driven development for exception management (Entwisle, 2007). Researchers such as Capozucca et al. and Greenfield et al. (Capozucca, Gallina, Guelfi, Pelliccione, & Romanovsky, 2006; Greenfield et al., 2004) have expressed the importance of providing support for non-functional requirements, such as security, exception handling, and so on, within model-driven approaches in order to manage complexity, promote communication amongst stakeholders, and improve software quality. As discussed in Czarnecki et al. and Greenfield et al. (Czarnecki, Eisenecker, Gluck, Vandevoorde, & Veldhuizen, 2000; Greenfield et al., 2004), the model-driven development approach provides the necessary processes and techniques to leverage high quality domain-specific assets, subsequently leading to significant benefits in the development of software systems. To date, the application of model-driven development approaches to provide exception handling capabilities has been primarily restricted to high-level discussions about the potential use of aspect-oriented platforms and frameworks to define constraints and support quality of service (QoS) (Filman, Barrett, Lee, & Linden, 2002; Gray, Bapty, Neema, & Tuck, 2001; Weis, 2004). Preliminary research has commenced in the area of model-driven development and exception handling for distributed software systems focusing on concurrent exceptions based on Object Management Group (OMG) UML QoS and Fault Profile (Object Management Group, 2005). The Correct Project (Capozucca et al., 2006; Guelfi, Razavi, Romanovsky, & Vandenbergh, 2004) investigates the stepwise development of complex fault tolerant distributed systems. The proposed approach is based on model-driven architecture to support the automated generation of applications, based on the Java programming language, from a UML model. Our work rests on the same underpinnings as this research. However, we extend it, as our focus is broader. We investigate the model-driven methods, generative programming techniques, frameworks and toolsets required to architect a generic, extensible exception management framework (Entwisle, 2007). This framework automates the generation of exception management features for an application.

The remainder of this paper is structured as follows: The Model-Driven Exception Management Framework section provides a high level overview of the DOVE framework. The Common Exception Policies section provides outlines the common exception policies that are used in our case study. The Project Tracker Case Study section outlines the requirements, design, and development, and metrics for Project Tracker, respectively. Entwisle et al. (Entwisle, 2007) outline additional case studies to demonstrate modeling workflows and concurrent exception handling. The Related Works section discusses related work in the area of model-driven development for exception management. Finally, the Conclusion and Future

Direction section provides our conclusion and discusses future work.

MODEL-DRIVEN EXCEPTION MANAGEMENT FRAMEWORK

Figure 1 shows the system-family engineering methodology for the model-driven exception management framework, known as the DOVE framework (Entwisle, 2007; Entwisle, Schmidt, Peake, & Kendall, 2006). The primary focus of the framework is to simplify the development of applications by the means of a modeling framework that supports automated generation of exception management features. To enable this the DOVE framework provides the meta-level architecture, domain specific languages, model transformation engine and services upon which reusable domain specific exception management libraries (such as network exceptions, database exceptions, web services exceptions, and so on) can be added. This allows the software architect to model the exception management requirements for an application in architectural models using domain-specific modeling languages, rather than hand crafting the implementation. These models then provide the meta-data required by the model transformation engine to facilitate the automated generation of source code that implements the defined exception management requirements.

Figure 2 illustrates the layered architecture for the DOVE framework (Entwisle, 2007; Entwisle & Kendall, 2007; Entwisle et al., 2006). This extensible meta-level software architecture provides exception-agnostic modeling and management mechanisms to diagnose and resolve exceptions. The DOVE framework is made up of a number of components. The key components include:

- **Platform:** This consists of the runtime environment and modeling tools required to support the reference implementation of the DOVE framework.

Figure 1. System family engineering methodology

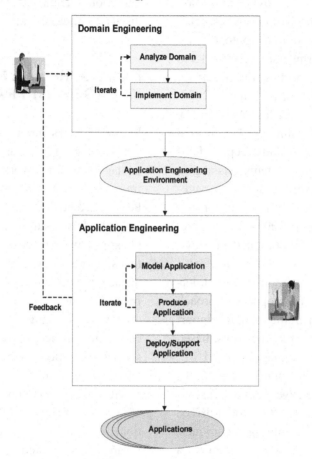

- **Core Middleware:** This offers core services such as coordinated atomic actions, diagnostics, exceptions, monitoring, and so on.
- **User Level Middleware:** This includes the domain specific languages, domain-specific exception management libraries, and the model transformation coupled with custom application development tools that support the specification of an application's exception management requirements.
- **Model-Driven Applications:** Model-driven applications are developed by a software architect using domain specific languages and model transformation engine.

COMMON EXCEPTION POLICIES

The RELIANT domain engineering method (Entwisle, Ramakrishnan, & Kendall, 2008; Entwisle, Ramakrishnan, Peake, & Kendall, 2007) was developed to support the design and development from initial conception to implementation of the common exception policies outlined in this section. The domain definition and scope is to capture a set of common exception handling policies that can be reused across domains. The domain analysis consists of factoring in trends in application development, analysing programming language runtimes and libraries for exception management, and analysing ten existing open source exemplar systems.

Table 1 outlines statistics collected on ten J2EE and .NET open source application patterns

Figure 2. Model-driven exception management framework layered architecture – DOVE framework

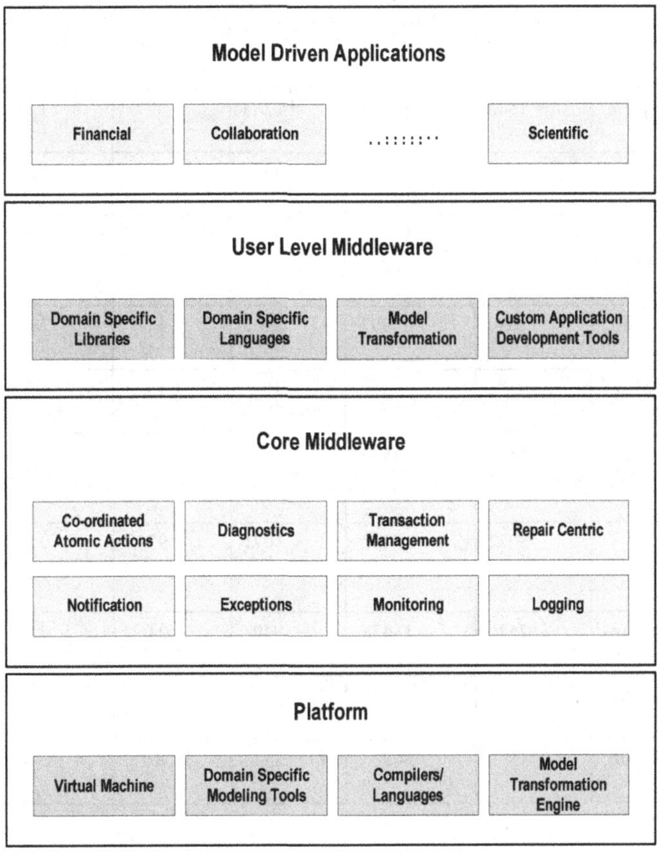

of exception handling. The applications listed A1-A5 are J2EE applications and A6-A10 are .NET applications. The majority of these applications (A1-A4 and A6-A9) have been randomly selected based on size and represent a range of application domains (enterprise resource planning (ERP), customer relationship management (CRM), application frameworks, and application development environments). The Pet Store reference application was also selected because implementations of this application are available for both Java (A5) and .NET (A10). The statistical data was collected using a custom utility that parsed source code files recursively within a specified directory, to extract data on the number of methods, number of handlers and their associated exception handling response within a class.

The analysis of the existing exemplar systems shows that within these applications the most commonly caught exception types are: generic exceptions and SQL exceptions. The miscellaneous exceptions category is comprised of application domain specific exceptions and various exceptions types from the programming languages standard library. The various exception types have been aggregated together because they are not widely used in the exemplar systems that were analysed. The practice of catching generic exceptions has been identified as an anti-pattern for exception management. Thus, the modelling of an exception policy for generic exceptions will not be supported in the RELIANT domain engineering method. The analysis also revealed that despite an increasing need to address security within the

Table 1. Exception handling application statistics

Applica-tion	Application Name	# Classes	# Methods	# Handlers	# Generic Exceptions	# Sql Exceptions	# Security Exceptions	# Misc. Exceptions
A1	Compiere (Compiere, 2006)	1840	31264	2243	477	173	0	152
A2	OpenTaps (OpenTaps, 2006)	999	12776	4250	260	54	3	1113
A3	Tapestry (Apache Ja-karta Project - Tapes-try, 2006)	1247	8567	551	69	8	3	471
A4	Spring (Spring, 2007)	3030	27992	2332	147	28	0	1158
A5	Pet Store (Sun Micro-systems, 2007)	32	379	48	13	0	0	9
A6	MonoDevelop (MonoDevelop Proj-ect, 2007)	1887	14933	457	142	0	0	167
A7	SharpDevelop (SharpDevelop Proj-ect, 2006)	3072	25492	1071	93	0	0	14
A8	SharpForge (Sharp-Forge Project, 2007)	757	13438	940	246	0	11	372
A9	Tustena (Tusena, 2006)	497	3236	269	20	2	1	93
A10	Pet Shop (Microsoft, 2006)	43	362	23	6	0	0	6

application layer (Lanowitz, 2005) the exemplar applications' exception coverage for security errors was limited. Thus, we conclude that a common exception policy for handling application security is required. The analysis of the exemplar applications also showed that system level exceptions are not being managed within an application. Thus, if a runtime error occurred the application would not gracefully terminate. To support appropriate clean up actions (e.g. free resources, notify user, record system information for troubleshooting, etc) being performed, we believe that system level exceptions need to be managed within an application. The overall conclusion of the domain analysis is that the common exception policies that are required and could be reused across domains are: database errors, runtime error, and security error. Table 2 outlines the use cases for these common exception policies.

The domain specific language for the common exception policies are for database, security, and system exception. These common exception policies are used in both the Project Tracker and Online Bank case studies (Entwisle, 2007). The security exception and the system exception policies replace the original exception with an access denied and fatal system exception, respectively, that contain general information on the error. The database exception policy and the associated library support are based on a domain-specific extension to the framework we engineered for database errors. This extension includes support for the following exceptional events: database unavailable, constraint violations, row not in table, invalid constraint exception, and invalid attempts to access and modify nulls and read only fields. If the database error handler is unable to resolve the error the original exception is replaced with a

Table 2. Common exception policies use cases

Use Case	Description
Handle Database Error	A database exception has occurred. A system check must be executed to verify that the database server is running. If the service is not running an attempt to restart the service should be executed. If the database is successfully restarted notify the end user that they must retry the failed transaction. If the database exception is raised due to another error (constraint violations, row not in table, invalid constraint exception, etc) then notify the user that a data error has occurred. In both cases, the exception details should be published to the windows event log.
Handle Unexpected Error	An unexpected failure has occurred. The exception details should be published to the windows event log. The end user should be notified to contact the system administrator of the failure.
Handle Security Error	A security exception has occurred. The exception details should be published to the windows event log. The end user should be notified that access has been denied to perform the requested operation.

data layer exception. The original exception that triggers the execution of the policies is replaced in order to prevent propagating sensitive information on the state of the application or infrastructure to untrusted clients, which may be used to compromise the security of the application.

The SystemException exception policy is associated with the exception type System.SystemException. This exception indicates that a system level error has been detected. These errors occur due to failed runtime checks, such as out of memory, and array out of bounds, and they can occur during the execution of any method. The default post handling action for this policy is set to rethrow. This enables services to notify the client of the exception. The exception propagated to the client is a FatalSystemError.

The DatabaseException exception policy is associated with the exception type System.Data.SqlClient.SqlException. This exception indicates that a failure has occurred when the client attempts to interact with the Microsoft SQL Server (Rankins, Bertucci, Gallelli, & Silverstein, 2007) database. The DatabaseErrorHandler exception handler is responsible for attempting to resolve the error by restarting the potentially failed SQL Server using the DatabaseStoppedException-Handler in the exception management database library. The default post handling action for this policy is set to rethrow. Thus, if the DatabaseErrorHandler does not resolve the error this enables the services to notify the client of

the exception. The exception propagated to the client is a DataLayerError.

The SecurityException exception policy is associated with the exception type System.Security.SecurityException. This exception indicates a security error has been detected. The default post handling action for this policy is set to rethrow. This enables the business services to notify the client of the exception. The exception propagated to the client is an AccessDeniedError.

PROJECT TRACKER CASE STUDY

This section outlines the requirements, design and development of the Project Tracker case study. Project Tracker provides features for a manager to track projects and their associated resources (Lhotka, 2006). This case study focuses on implementing a subset of Project Tracker's functionality to demonstrate how the DOVE framework can be used to model the exception management requirements of a business application. The generated artefacts, such as source code, database scripts and configuration scripts, leverage the elementary, reusable DOVE framework services. Figure 3 shows the use case model for the Project Tracker case study.

Table 3 outlines Project Tracker's functional use cases. The infrastructure use cases related to exception management are outlined in the Common Exception Policies section.

Figure 3. Project Tracker use case model

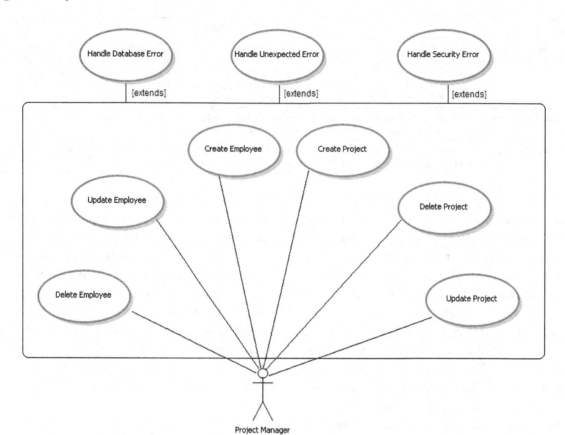

Figure 4 shows the application model for the Project Tracker case study. The application model consists of two services: ProjectService and EmployeeService. These services allow a manager to perform the standard online business transactions to create, update, and delete projects and resources.

The entity model consists of a project that has zero to many associated resources.

Table 4 outlines the business classes in the Project Tracker application model. The business classes all contain create, update, retrieve and delete methods. The business classes have

Table 3. Overview of Project Tracker use cases

Use Case	Description
Create Project	The project manager can create a new project.
Create Employee	The project manager can create a new employee.
Update Project	The project manager can modify the project details and or assigned resources.
Update Employee	The project manager can modify an employee's personal details.
Delete Project	The project manager can delete a project. The resources associated with the project will not be deleted.
Delete Employee	The project manager can delete an employee. The employee will be removed for assigned projects.

Figure 4. Project Tracker application model

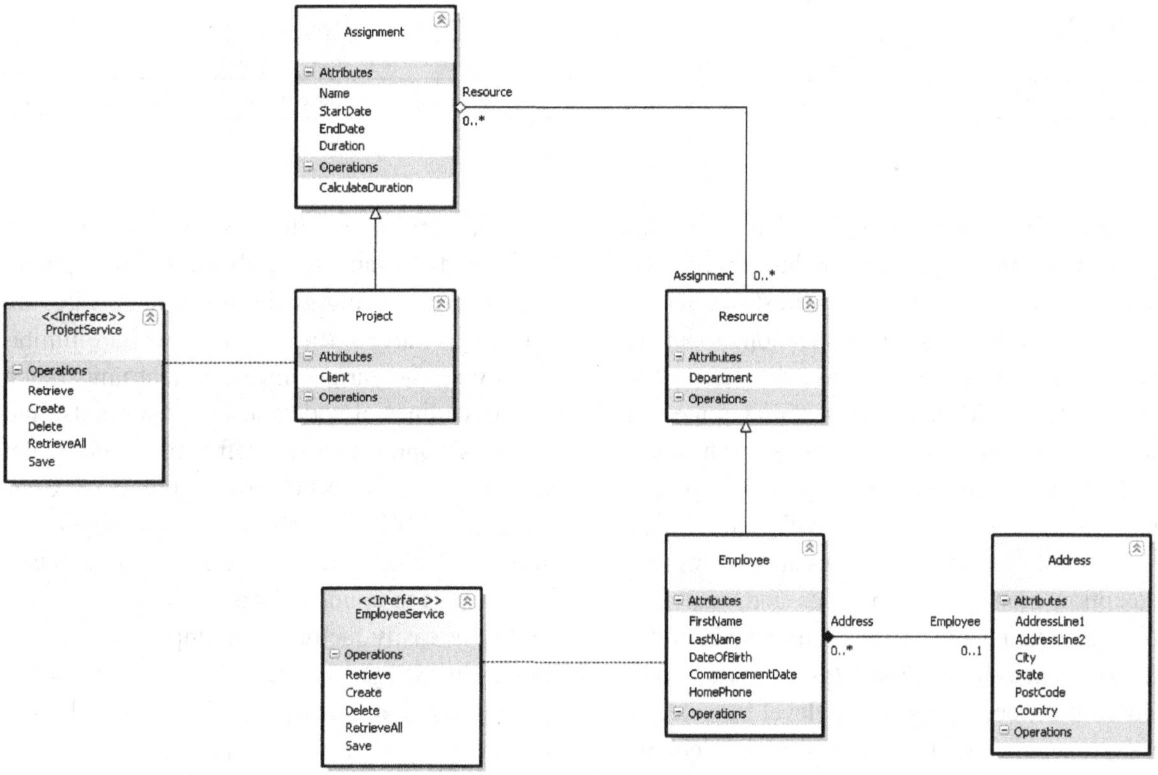

Table 4. Project Tracker business classes

Business Class	Description
Assignment	Represents an assignment. An assignment has a fixed duration and associated resources.
Project	Represents a project. A project is a type of assignment. A project can have multiple resources assigned to it for fixed duration. If the project is deleted the associated resources are not deleted.
Resource	Represents a resource. A resource is assigned to a project.
Employee	Represents an employee who works on an assignment. An employee is a type of resource.
Address	Represent an address. An address is associated with an employee. If the employee is deleted the associated address is deleted.

two exception policies associated to support the infrastructure exception management related use cases. They are: database exception and system exception policies.

Table 5 outlines the business services in the Project Tracker application model. The business services have been designed to support Project Tracker's use cases. The business services have two exception policies associated to support the infrastructure use cases. They are: security exception and system exception policies.

The common exception policies discussed in

Table 5. Project Tracker business services

Business Services	Description
ProjectService	Provides service-oriented interface to create, update, delete and retrieve project details.
EmployeeService	Provides service-oriented interface to create, update, delete and retrieve employee details.

Common Exception Policies section have been associated to the Project Tracker business classes and services to support the infrastructure use cases. The Project Tracker application model has been configured to support cascading exception policies. This allows the application engineer to define exception policies to handle system exceptions at a global level. This policy is inherited by all model elements contained within the Project Tracker application model. This allows common exception management policies and responses (such as logging and notification) to be bound to the model at a single point. This supports a separation of concern at the model level for selected exception policies. The contained model elements have overridden inherited exception policies. The application has been configured with a notification sink for publishing exceptions to the windows event log.

The Project Tracker application is comprised of 11 classes and two configuration files. The 11 classes are packaged into three namespaces. They are: Entities, Services and WindowsApp. The classes within the Entities and Services namespaces and the configuration files were generated using the DOVE framework's model transformation engine. The WindowsApp was developed using standard application development techniques. The line of source code for Project Tracker across the three namespaces is 2352. The configuration files contain 217 lines of source code. This represents a total of 2569 lines of source code.

To evaluate our approach, we use standard application developer productivity and defect rates to extrapolate out the time taken to implement and find errors, correct and test them for our case studies using standard development approaches.

This provides a baseline to assess our approach compared to standard application development approaches. The productivity and defect rates are based on source lines of code. There are limitations with the various measurement units (such as source lines of code and function points) and analysis approaches for software development (Fowler, 2007; B. Kitchenham, Jeffery, & Connaughton, 2007). The limitations associated with source lines of code include a lack of standard approaches to count lines of code and a limited ability to easily factor in the impact of the programming language, architecture and reuse on the measurement. However, while source lines of code are imperfect they do provide a pragmatic and consistent measure of productivity and defects for our evaluation (MacCormack, Kemerer, Cusumano, & Crandall, 2003). Thus, despite their limitation we have selected to use source lines of code as the unit of measure to support our analysis. Further, the IEEE Standard 1045 Software Productivity Measurement ("IEEE Standard for Software Productivity Metrics," 1993) also uses source lines of code as a basis for measuring output and it also outlines a standard for counting source lines of code.

The standard application development productivity rate is 40 lines of code per hour (Humphrey, 1995) and 480 defects per thousand lines of code (J. Rubin, L. Tracy, & J. K. Guevara, 2005). Thus, using standard application development approaches Project Tracker has an estimated effort of 64 hours to implement with potentially 1233 defects. For a modest-size application, such as Project Tracker, five to 10 or more hours would be required to find each defect in the testing phase. The time to correct defects in test ranges from two to 20

Figure 5. Project Tracker source code by category

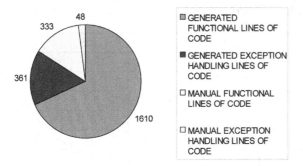

hours (Humphrey, 1995). Hence, if the standard number of defects was realised and not addressed until the testing phase finding errors, correcting them and testing could require between 8632 and 36994 hours. The magnitude of the time and costs associated with defects not found until the testing phase is potentially large. However, this does not usually eventuate as organisations normally use code reviews and other techniques in an attempt to remove defects from the requirements, design and code early in the software development lifecycle rather than testing only at the implementation phase (Humphrey, 1995). Figure 5 shows the ratio of source code that has been automatically generated and manually developed to implement both the functional and exception management features of Project Tracker.

The model transformation engine facilitates the reuse of source code through the automated generation of the application's implementation based on the models. From software reuse you can expect improvements in timeliness, decreased maintenance effort, reliability, efficiency, consistency and investment (Meyer, 2000). By relying on reuse of generated source code there is the guarantee, or at minimum, expectation that the developer of the model transformation templates will have undertaken extensive testing and other quality assurance activities to ensure that the reusable software is of high quality and typically contains less defects compared to applications

that are developed using standard language-based approaches. Tolvanen et al. (Tolvanen, Sprinkle, & Gray, 2006) state that because the source code is generated in model-driven development both syntax and logical errors do not normally occur resulting in significant improvements in quality. Thus, the assumption used to calculate improvements in quality and productivity in our evaluation is that the model transformation templates generated source code does not contain defects. The use of model-based testing techniques and tools could be used to address this issue and significantly aid in improving quality.

Table 6 and Table 7 outline the statistics for the generated classes for the Project Tracker application's functional and exception management requirements, respectively. Table 8 outlines the statistics for the configuration files for Project Tracker. The DOVE framework automated the generation of 1610 lines of source code to support Project Tracker functional requirements and 361 lines of source code to support Project Tracker exception management requirements. Thus, based on standard productivity and defect rates, the DOVE framework's model transformation engine has reduced the effort to implement Project Tracker by 49 hours, and it has eliminated 946 potential defects. The exception management features generated by the DOVE framework needed to be customised to implement appropriate return statements and to display error messages to the end user. This involved manually writing 48 lines of source code. The effort to implement this customisation is 1 hour with potentially 23 defects being introduced in Project Tracker.

Figure 6 shows an extract of the application-specific exception policy configuration file that is generated during model transformation. As shown in this extract the CustomHandler DatabaseErrorHandler will be invoked if a System.Data. SqlClient.SqlException occurs in the Assignment entities CalculateDuration method.

Figure 7 shows the Project Tracker Assignment CalculateDuration method that was generated

Table 6. Project Tracker functional source code statistics

Class	Gend. Functional Loc	Est. Effort	Est. # Defects	Manual Functional Loc	Est. Effort	Est. # Defects
ProjectTracker.Entities.Address	352	9	170	0	0	0
ProjectTracker.Entities.Assignment	376	9	180	0	0	0
ProjectTracker.Entities.DataManager	36	1	17	0	0	0
ProjectTracker.Entities.Employee	76	2	36	0	0	0
ProjectTracker.Entities.Project	48	1	23	0	0	0
ProjectTracker.Entities.Resource	317	8	152	0	0	0
ProjectTracker.Services.EmployeeService	203	5	97	0	0	0
ProjectTracker.Services.ProjectService	202	5	97	0	0	0
ProjectTracker.WindowsApp.EmployeeForm	0	0	0	122	3	59
ProjectTracker.WindowsApp.MainForm	0	0	0	132	3	63
ProjectTracker.WindowsApp.ProjectForm	0	0	0	79	2	38
Totals	**1610**	**40**	**772**	**333**	**8**	**160**

Table 7. Project Tracker exception handling source code statistics

Class	Gend Exception Handling Loc	Est. Effort	Est. # Defects	Exception Handling Loc Modified	Est. Effort	Est. # Defects	Eh Loc Added	Est. Effort	Est. # Defects
ProjectTracker.Entities.Address	0	0	0	0	0	0	0	0	0
ProjectTracker.Entities.Assignment	33	1	16	0	0	0	1	0	0
ProjectTracker.Entities.DataManager	0	0	0	0	0	0	0	0	0
ProjectTracker.Entities.Employee	0	0	0	0	0	0	0	0	0
ProjectTracker.Entities.Project	0	0	0	0	0	0	0	0	0
ProjectTracker.Entities.Resource	0	0	0	0	0	0	0	0	0
ProjectTracker.Services.EmployeeService	164	4	79	0	0	0	3	0	1
ProjectTracker.Services.ProjectService	164	4	79	0	0	0	3	0	1
ProjectTracker.WindowsApp.EmployeeForm	0	0	0	0	0	0	8	0	4
ProjectTracker.WindowsApp.MainForm	0	0	0	0	0	0	24	1	12
ProjectTracker.WindowsApp.ProjectForm	0	0	0	0	0	0	9	0	5
Totals	**361**	**9**	**174**	**0**	**0**	**0**	**48**	**1**	**23**

Table 8. Project Tracker generation statistics – application configuration

Configuration	Gend. Loc	Est. Effort	Est. #
App.config	14	0.5	7
ExceptionPolicy.config	203	5	97
Totals	217	5.5	104

Figure 6.

```
<ExceptionPolicy>
  <ExceptionPolicyEntry>
  <Name>DatabaseException</Name>
  <ExceptionType>System.Data.SqlClient.SqlException</ExceptionType>
  <Assembly>System.Data</Assembly>
    <SourceExceptions>
      <SourceException>
        <Assembly> ProjectTracker.Entities </Assembly>
          <Class>Assignment</Class>
            <Operation>CalculateDuration</Operation>
          </SourceException>
      <SourceException>
        . . .
      </SourceException>
      </SourceExceptions>
  <ExceptionHandlerChain>
    <ExceptionHandler>
      <Type>CustomExceptionHandler</Type>
      <GUID>b599d2cc-f9b2-4ea3-868a-7817d3d5cc66</GUID>
    </ExceptionHandler>
    <ExceptionHandler>
      <Type>WrapExceptionHandler</Type>
      <GUID>3ed71de3-2660-4d42-bcce-242553041e75</GUID>
    </ExceptionHandler>
  </ExceptionHandlerChain>
  <WrapHandlers>
    <WrapHandler>
      <GUID>3ed71de3-2660-4d42-bcce-242553041e75</GUID>
      <Type>DataLayerException</Type>
      <Assembly>EMF.ExceptionManagement</Assembly>
      <Message>Data error has occurred. Please contact your System
Administrator.</Message>
    </WrapHandler>
  </WrapHandlers>
  <ReplaceHandlers>
  </ReplaceHandlers>
  <CustomHandlers>
    <CustomHandler>
      <GUID>b599d2cc-f9b2-4ea3-868a-7817d3d5cc66</GUID>
      <Type>
      </Type>
      <Assembly>EMF.ExceptionManagement.Database</Assembly>
      <Parameters>
      </Parameters>
    </CustomHandler>
  </CustomHandlers>
  <PostHandlingAction>Rethrow</PostHandlingAction>
  </ExceptionPolicyEntry>
</ExceptionPolicy>
```

Figure 7.

```
Private int CalculateDuration(){
   try{
      // TODO: Provide implementation for custom operation
   }catch (SqlException sqlexception){
      PostHandlingAction handler = ExceptionManager.HandleException(
         new ExceptionSource(), sqlexception);
      if (handler.Action == PostHandlingActionEnum.NotifyUser){
         // TODO: Notify user of Application-Specific Error Message
      }else if (handler.Action == PostHandlingActionEnum.Rethrow){
         throw handler.CurrentException;
      }
   }finally{
      // TODO: Release resources
   }
   return 0;
}
```

during model transformation. This method was selected to show the output from the model transformation engine. The method has catch handlers based on the modelled exception policies.

The CalculateDuration method has been tested to verify that it could recover from the database server being offline. To perform this test, the database was manually stopped while the Project-Tracker application was running. A CalculateDuration operation was then invoked when an attempt to retrieve assignment details was performed. This resulted in the DatabaseErrorHandler being invoked by DOVE frameworks exception management services. This handler successfully restarted the database service and returned a post handling action to notify the user of the exception. This post handling action is required when the database is successfully restarted as the user must retry their failed transaction. The message returned to the user is application-specific. Thus, during model transformation a comment is generated in the source code informing the application developer to update the source code. In our case study, this has been updated with an application-specific message to retry the failed transaction.

In this section, we have demonstrated the feasibility of the DOVE framework through the development of the Project Tracker application. The DOVE framework provided the application engineer with the modelling notation and tools required to model the features of the project tracking application. The model transformation engine generated a significant portion of the functional and exception management features based on the model. As outlined in this section, the automated generation of these features results in substantial improvements in quality and productivity. The application engineer is able to extend and refine the generated application to implement custom behaviours that could not be expressed within the model. Similar results have been found by other researchers and companies when investigating the impact of model-driven development on productivity (Staron, 2006). The Middleware Company model-driven development for J2EE using model-driven architecture (MDA) case study concluded that the MDA team developed their application 35% faster than using traditional software development approaches (The Middleware Company, 2003). Computer Associates

(CA) claim that the model-driven development of J2EE development using CA Gen takes just 60% of the time compared with using traditional software development approaches (Computer Associates, 2007).

RELATED WORK

The most closely related work to our research is the Correct Project (Guelfi et al., 2004). The Correct Project aims to investigate the iterative development of complex fault tolerant systems from architectural descriptions. Our research has a number of similarities with this project. For example, the same coordinated atomic actions protocol (Zorzo & Stroud, 1999) is used to manage concurrent exceptions in multiple processes. However, our approach is broader as it investigates how to architect a generic framework for modeling various domain specific exception types. It also includes both sequential and concurrent exceptions.

The evaluation of domain engineering methods and software product line approaches to software development is an important emerging area of research. The ability to evaluate the methods and framework is of significant importance because in a software product line context the lifespan of the reusable domain specific assets is typically longer compared to standard software development, is widely replicated and reused within domain specific applications, and must be adaptable (Etxeberria & Sagardui, 2005). There are limited case studies in the area of model-driven approaches to exception management.

Etxeberria and Sagardui (Etxeberria & Sagardui, 2005) outline a framework for the initial classification of product line requirements, evaluation times, evaluation techniques and evaluation methods. This framework is used to form the criteria for a survey of sixteen evaluation methods and metrics. This survey of methods can be used to assist in selecting the appropriate method dependent on the

time of the evaluation and the quality attributes that must be supported. The majority of the methods surveyed focus on product line quality attributes (commonality, variability, etc) at a product line architecture level (Etxeberria & Sagardui, 2005). Griman et al (Grimán, Pérez, Mendoza, & Losavio, 2006) conduct a feature analysis of three different architectural evaluation methods applied to a single case study. The feature analysis uses the DESMET methodology (B Kitchenham, Linkman, & Law, 1997) to assess the Architecture Tradeoff Analysis Method (ATAM) (P. Clements, Kazman, & Klein, 2002), Architectural Evaluation Method (AEM) (Losavio, Chirinos, Matteo, Levy, & Ramdane-Cherif, 2004) and Design and Use of Software Architectures (Bosch, 2000). The major architecture evaluation methods used to evaluate software product lines are Software Architecture Analysis Method (SAAM) (P. Clements et al., 2002) and ATAM. The SAAM method, developed by Software Engineering Institute (SEI) at Carnegie Mellon University, is a scenario based evaluation method to evaluate the quality attributes of the architecture. ATAM, the successor to SAAM, is a scenario based evaluation method that uses the business drivers and the software architecture elicited from the project decision makers as input into the assessment. These are then refined into scenarios and architectural decisions are made to support the requirements. A qualitative analysis of the scenarios and decisions results in the identification of risks, non-risks, and tradeoffs within the architecture. Both SAAM and ATAM were developed to evaluate single product architectures but they are also able to assess software product line attributes, such as variability, extensibility, etc. The Holistic Product Line Architecture Assessment (HOOPLA) (Olumofin & Mišic, 2007) extends the ATAM method. It is based on a two phased approach to holistically assess the core architecture of the software product line and the product architecture for the individual product requirements.

There are wider evaluation approaches that not only consider the quality attributes but consider other aspects such as the relationship between the business and architecture, context and domain. This includes Product Line Architecture Design Method Evaluation Framework (Matinlassi, 2004), Software Product Family Evaluation Framework (Linden, Bosch, Kamsties, Kansala, & Obbink, 2004), and the BAPO (Business, Architecture, Process, and Organisation) model (van der Linden, 2002). The BAPO model defines an evaluation framework along four dimensions of Business, Architecture, Process and Organisation to the alignment to the organisation, the process, and the product line architecture.

CONCLUSION AND FUTURE WORK

In this chapter, we have demonstrated the feasibility of a model-driven approach to exception management, based on the DOVE framework, through the development and assessment of the Project Tracker application. The DOVE framework provided the application engineer with the modeling notation and tools required to model the features of the project tracking application. The model transformation engine generated a significant portion of the functional and exception management features based on the model. As demonstrated in the Project Tracker Case Study Section, the automated generation of these features results in substantial improvements in quality and productivity. The application engineer is able to extend and refine the generated application to implement custom behaviors that could not be expressed within the model.

The DOVE framework provides a solution for architects to specify the architecture of an application independent of the underlying platform specific concerns. The focus is on service behaviour, domain entities and exception policies, which are described using high level abstractions that promote communication amongst various stakeholders. These user models reflect the functional and behavioural properties of the application. Furthermore, the model transformation engine and core exception management libraries provide a sound architectural foundation for code generation. The model transformation engine and core libraries could be extended to support multiple languages and platforms.

The adoption and use of the model driven framework for exception management does present challenges in terms of flexibility, modification and change management. The domain-specific visual modeling languages for exception management only permit a limited amount of customization at specified variation points. The architect may discover they need a richer set of modeling concepts, relationships and constraints to effectively model the exception management requirements for an application. This iterative development of the exception management framework is to be expected. To address this domain engineering must be performed to extend and refine the modeling language and other domain assets as new and updated requirements for the exception management domain are developed.

Another consideration is that the framework requires familiarity with exception management concepts and the framework itself. Thus, the initial adoption may lead to temporary decreases in productivity. The application development team must also follow change management processes and be proficient in the use of version control and merge tools to support managing changes in the model and in the previously generated assets when regenerating a model.

In the future, we plan to complete additional case studies to provide further data to assess the improvements in productivity and quality, to investigate the mechanism to support domain and application evolution, and also provide input into the refinement and extension of both the RELIANT domain engineering method and the DOVE framework.

REFERENCES

Alexander Romanovsky, J. K. (2003, June). *Action-Oriented Exception Handling in Cooperative and Competitive Concurrent Object-Oriented Systems.* Paper presented at the Advances in Exception Handling Techniques, Darmstadt, Germany.

Anderson, T., Feng, M., Riddle, S., & Romanovsky, A. (2003). Error Recovery for a Boiler System with OTS PID Controller. *Exception Handling in Object-Oriented Systems Workshop at ECOOP 2003.*

Apache Jakarta Project - Tapestry. (2006). *Tapestry.* Retrieved June 2005, from http://tapestry.apache.org/

Arnold, K., Gosling, J., & Homes, D. (2000). *The Java Programming Language* (3rd ed.). Reading, MA: Addison-Wesley.

Bosch, J. (2000). *Design and Use of Software Architectures.* Reading, MA: Addison-Wesley Professional.

Capozucca, A., Gallina, B., Guelfi, N., Pelliccione, P., & Romanovsky, A. (2006). CORRECT Developing Fault-Tolerant Distributed Systems. *European Research Consortium for Informatics and Mathematics, 64.*

Clements, P., Kazman, R., & Klein, M. (2002). *Evaluating Software Architecture. Methods and Case Studies.* Reading, MA: Addison-Wesley Professional.

Clements, P., & Northrop, L. (2001). *Software Product Lines Practices and Patterns* (3rd ed.). Reading, MA: Addison-Wesley Professional.

Compiere. (2006). *Compiere.* Retrieved May 2006, from http://www.compiere.com/

Computer Associates. (2007). *The ROI of Developing Applications With CA Gen* (Tech. Rep.).

Coplien, J. O. (1998). *Multi-Paradigm Design for C++* (1st Ed.). Reading, MA: Addison-Wesley Professional.

Czarnecki, K., Eisenecker, U. W., Gluck, R., Vandevoorde, D., & Veldhuizen, T. L. (2000). Generative Programming and Active Libraries. In *Selected Papers from the International Seminar on Generic Programming* (pp. 25-39). Berlin: Springer-Verlag.

Eisenecker, U., & Czarnecki, K. (2000). *Generative Programming: Methods, Tools, and Applications* (1st Ed.). Reading, MA: Addison-Wesley Professional.

Entwisle, S. (Oct 2007). *Model Driven Exception Management Framework.* PhD Thesis, Monash University, Melbourne, Australia.

Entwisle, S., & Kendall, E. (2007). A Model Driven Exception Management Framework. In P. Pelliccione, H. Muccini, N. Guelfi & A. Romanovsky (Eds.), *Software Engineering of Fault Tolerant Systems* (Vol. 19). Singapore: World Scientific Publishing.

Entwisle, S., Ramakrishnan, S., & Kendall, E. (2008, July 2008). *Domain Analysis of Exception Management.* Paper presented at the IADIS International Conference Informatics 2008, Amsterdam, The Netherlands.

Entwisle, S., Ramakrishnan, S., Peake, I., & Kendall, E. (2007). *RELIANT Domain Engineering Method for Exception Management* (Tech. Rep. No. 2007/218). Melbourne, Australia: Monash University.

Entwisle, S., Schmidt, H., Peake, I., & Kendall, E. (2006, October 2006). *A Model Driven Exception Management Framework for Developing Reliable Software Systems.* Paper presented at the Proceedings of the 10th IEEE International Enterprise Distributed Object Computing Conference (EDOC'06), Hong Kong.

Etxeberria, L., & Sagardui, G. (2005, September). *Product-line Architecture: New Issues for Evaluation.* Paper presented at the in Proceeding of 9th International Conference on Software Product Lines (SPLC2005), Rennes, France.

Filman, R. E., Barrett, S., Lee, D., & Linden, T. (2002). Inserting Ilities by Controlling Communications. *Communications of the ACM, 45*(1), 116–122. doi:10.1145/502269.502274

Fowler, M. (2007). *Cannot Measure Productivity.* Retrieved 1st August 2007, from http://www.martinfowler.com/bliki/CannotMeasureProductivity.html

Garcia, A. F., & Rubira, C. M. F. (2000). An Exception Handling Software Architecture for Developing Robust Software. *Exception Handling in Object-Oriented Systems Workshop at ECOOP 2000.*

Garcia, A. F., & Rubira, F., C. M., Romanovsky, A., & Xu, J. (2001). A Comparative Study of Exception Handling Mechanisms for Building Dependable Object-Oriented Software. *Journal of Systems and Software, 59*(2), 197–222. doi:10.1016/S0164-1212(01)00062-0

Gray, J., Bapty, T., Neema, S., & Tuck, J. (2001). Handling Crosscutting Constraints in Domain-Specific Modeling. *Communications of the ACM, 44*(10), 87–93. doi:10.1145/383845.383864

Greenfield, J., Short, K., Cook, S., & Kent, S. (2004). *Software Factories: Assembling Applications with Patterns, Models, Frameworks, and Tools.* New York: Wiley.

Grimán, A., Pérez, M., Mendoza, L., & Losavio, F. (2006). Feature Analysis for Architectural Evaluation Methods. *Journal of Systems and Software, 79*(6), 871–888. doi:10.1016/j.jss.2005.12.015

Guelfi, N., Razavi, R., Romanovsky, A., & Vandenbergh, S. (2004, October 2004). *DRIP Catalyst: An MDE/MDA Method for Fault-tolerant Distributed Software Families Development.* Paper presented at the 19th Annual ACM Conference on Object-Oriented Programming, Systems, Languages, and Applications, Vancouver, Canada.

Howell, C., & Vecellio, G. (2000). Experiences with Error Handling in Critical Systems. *Advances in Exception Handling Techniques in Object-Oriented Systems Workshop at ECOOP 2000.*

Humphrey, W. S. (1995, September 1995). *A Personal Commitment to Software Quality.* Paper presented at the Proceedings of the 5th European Software Engineering Conference, Lisbon, Portugal.

IEEE Standard for Software Productivity Metrics. (1993). *IEEE Std 1045-1992.*

Kitchenham, B., Jeffery, D. R., & Connaughton, C. (2007). Misleading Metrics and Unsound Analyses. *IEEE Software, 24*(2), 73–78. doi:10.1109/MS.2007.49

Kitchenham, B., Linkman, S., & Law, D. (1997). DESMET: A Method for Evaluating Software Engineering Methods and Tools. *Computing and Control Engineering, 8*(3), 120–126. doi:10.1049/cce:19970304

Klein, M., & Dellarocas, C. (2000). *Domain-Independent Exception Handling Services That Increase Robustness in Open Multi-Agent Systems.* Working Paper CCS-WP-211, Massachusetts Institute of Technology, Cambridge, MA. Retrieved from http://ccs.mit.edu/papers/pdf/wp211.pdf

Lanowitz, T. (2005). *Now Is the Time for Security at the Application Level* (Tech. Rep.). Stamford, CT: Gartner.

Lhotka, R. (2006). *Expert C# 2005 Business Obejcts.* Berkeley, CA: Apress.

Linden, F. d., Bosch, J., Kamsties, E., Kansala, K., & Obbink, H. (2004, August). *Software Product Family Evaluation.* Paper presented at the Proceedings of the 3rd International Conference on Software Product Lines (SPLC '04), Boston, MA, USA.

Losavio, F., Chirinos, L., Matteo, A., Levy, N., & Ramdane-Cherif, A. (2004). ISO Quality Standards for Measuring Architectures. *Journal of Systems and Software, 72*(2), 209–223. doi:10.1016/S0164-1212(03)00114-6

MacCormack, A., Kemerer, C. F., Cusumano, M., & Crandall, B. A. (2003). Trade-Offs between Productivity and Quality in Selecting Software Development Practices. *IEEE Software, 20*(5), 78–85. doi:10.1109/MS.2003.1231158

Matinlassi, M. (2004, May 2004). *Comparison of Software Product Line Architecture Design Methods: COPA, FAST, FORM, KobrA and QADA.* Paper presented at the Proceedings of 26th International Conference on Software Engineering.

Mellor, S. J., Scott, K., Uhl, A., & Weise, D. (2004). *MDA Distilled.* Reading, MA: Addison-Wesley Professional.

Meyer, B. (2000). *Object-Oriented Software Construction* (2nd Ed.). New York: Prentice-Hall.

Microsoft. (2006). *Pet Shop.* Retrieved April 2006, from http://msdn2.microsoft.com/en-us/library/ms978487.aspx

MonoDevelop Project. (2007). *MonoDevelop.* Retrieved June 2007, from http://www.monodevelop.com/

Object Management Group. (2005). *UML Profile for Quality of Service and Fault Tolerance.* Retrieved 3rd August 2005, from http://www.omg.org/docs/ptc/05-05-02.pdf

Olumofin, F. G., & Mišic, V. B. (2007). A Holistic Architecture Assessment Method for Software Product Lines. *Information and Software Technology, 49*(4), 309–323. doi:10.1016/j.infsof.2006.05.003

OpenTaps. (2006). *OpenTaps.* Retrieved May 2006, from http://www.opentaps.org/

Patterson, D. A., Brown, A., Broadwell, P., Candea, G., Chen, M., Cutler, J., et al. (2002). *Recovery-Oriented Computing (ROC): Motivation, Definition, Techniques, and Case Studies.* UC Berkeley Computer Science Technical Report UCB/CSD-02-1175, Berkley, CA.

Perry, D. E., Romanovsky, A., & Tripathi, A. (2000). Current Trends in Exception Handling. *IEEE Transactions on Software Engineering, 26*(10), 921–922. doi:10.1109/TSE.2000.879816

Rankins, R., Bertucci, P., Gallelli, C., & Silverstein, A. T. (2007). *Microsoft SQL Server 2005 Unleashed.* Sams.

Reimer, D., & Srinivasan, H. (2003). Analyzing Exception Usage in Large Java Applications. *Exception Handling in Object-Oriented Systems Workshop at ECOOP 2003.*

Rubin, J., Tracy, L. & Guevara, J. K. (2005). *Worldwide IT Benchmark Report 2006: Volume 4: Current Software Engineering Performance Results: Defect Rates* (Tech. Rep. No. G00133966).

SharpDevelop Project. (2006). *SharpDevelop.* Retrieved May 2006, from http://wiki.sharpdevelop.net/

SharpForge Project. (2007). *SharpForge.* Retrieved June, from http://sharpforge.org/

Spring. (2007). *Spring Framework.* Retrieved January 2007, from http://www.springframework.org/

Staron, M. (2006, October 2006). *Adopting Model Driven Software Development in Industry - A Case Study at Two Companies.* Paper presented at the 9th International Conference Model Driven Engineering Languages and Systems (MODELS 2006), Genova, Italy.

Sun Microsystems. (2007). *Pet Store.* Retrieved January 2007, from https://blueprints.dev.java.net/petstore/

The Middleware Company. (2003). *Model Driven Development for J2EE Utilizing a Model Driven Architecture (MDA) Approach: Productivity Analysis.*

Tolvanen, J.-P., Sprinkle, J., & Gray, J. (2006). *The 6th OOPSLA Workshop on Domain-Specific Modeling.* Paper presented at the Object-Oriented Programming, Systems, Languages, and Applications (OOPSLA).

Tusena. (2006). *Tusena.* Retrieved 2nd December 2006, from http://sourceforge.net/projects/tustena/

van der Linden, F. (2002). Software Product Families in Europe: The ESAPS & CAFE Project. *IEEE Software, 19*(4), 41–49. doi:10.1109/MS.2002.1020286

Weis, T. (2004). *Model Driven Development of QoS-Enabled Distributed Applications.* PhD, Technical University of Berlin, Berlin.

Weiss, D. M., & Lai, C. T. R. (1999). *Software Product-Line Engineering: A Family Based Software Development Process.* Reading, MA: Addison-Wesley Professional.

Williams, M. (2002). *Microsoft Visual C#. NET.* Redmond, CA: MS Press.

Zorzo, A. F., & Stroud, R. J. (1999). A distributed object-oriented framework for dependable multi-party interactions. In *OOPSLA '99: Proceedings of the 14th ACM SIGPLAN conference on Object-oriented programming, systems, languages, and applications* (pp. 435-446). New York: ACM Press.

KEY TERMS AND DEFINITIONS

Domain Engineering: Domain Engineering consists of three core phases: Domain Analysis, Domain Design and Domain Implementation. Domain analysis is the activity of gathering and analysing experiences in building systems or parts of a system within a specific domain in the form of reusable assets. Domain design and domain implementation focus of designing and implementing reusable domain-specific languages, components, and code generators to support model-driven development, respectively. Domain Engineering is also referred to as System Family Engineering.

DOVE Framework: DOVE framework provides the modelling languages, core services and tools that enable an application engineer to model concurrent exceptions and sequential exceptions that aid in the detection, diagnosis, and resolution of software failures. The application engineer specifies the exception management capabilities in feature and software models that guide the automated generation of implementation assets that can be re-configured, as required, to detect, diagnose and resolve software failures.

Exception Management: Exception management features within an application are based on its exception handling strategies, policies and requirements. Exception management features aim to support a consistent approach to managing software failures. Exception management includes the detection, diagnosis and resolution of software failures.

Feature Model: The features of the software system are captured within a feature model. While the specific notation of the feature model varies based on the domain engineering methods, a feature model typically consists of four main elements. They are: feature diagram, feature definitions, composition rules, and the rationale for including the feature.

Feature Modelling: Feature modelling is a domain analysis technique that is used to define the software product-line and system families. Features are used to identify and organise the commonalities and variabilities within a domain, and to model the functional and non-functional properties.

Feature Set: Feature set is the set of features within a specific domain. A feature set defines the features and their attributes (such as type, cardinality, etc), including constraints that must be enforced amongst features.

Model-Driven Development: Model-driven development paradigm is an evolutionary shift in software development. It aims to facilitate the automatic construction of highly customised intermediate or end software products based on high-level problem domain models. These models are configured to leverage elementary, reusable domain-specific assets rather than programming languages.

RELIANT Domain Engineering Method: The RELIANT Domain Engineering Method provides a tailorable framework that guides the domain engineer in the design and development activities from initial conception to implementation and deployment of reusable modules for a range of exception domains. The process consists of guidance, common patterns for exceptions, and other assets to support the design of domain-specific modules for different classes of exceptions.

Chapter 13
Using Patterns for Engineering High–Quality Mobile Applications

Pankaj Kamthan
Concordia University, Canada

ABSTRACT

In this chapter, the development and evolution of mobile applications is viewed from an engineering perspective. A methodology for deploying patterns as means for improving the pragmatic quality of mobile applications is proposed. In doing so, relevant quality attributes and corresponding stakeholder types for mobile applications are identified, the role of the development process is emphasized, and the challenges in making optimal use of patterns are presented. The underling feasibility issues involved at each step are analyzed. The activities of selection and application of patterns are explored. The use of patterns during macro- and micro-architecture design of mobile applications is illustrated. The implications of the use of patterns in a Mobile Social Web context are briefly highlighted.

INTRODUCTION

Since the beginning of this century, there have been major advances towards the goal of being able to access the Web via a wireless device. Indeed, many of the predictions about mobility (Feldman, 2000; Varshney & Vetter, 2002) including the cost, volume, and growth of business; number of users and subscribers; affordability and proliferation of wireless devices such as media players, mobile computers such as Personal Digital Assistants (PDAs), and phones;

availability of a variety of applications such as electronic mail, instant messaging, shopping, ubiquity of real-time information, have largely been realized today. In general, mobile access has accommodated many sectors of society (Mennecke & Strader, 2003; Stanoevska-Slabeva, 2003) including academia and industry, and continues to play an increasingly vital role in our daily activities of communication, information, and entertainment.

However, the successes achieved by mobile applications have come with their share of quality-re-

DOI: 10.4018/978-1-60566-731-7.ch013

lated issues (Ghosh & Swaminatha, 2001; Nguyen, Johnson, & Hackett, 2003). There are a new set of challenges as these applications evolve to become 'social' entities for interaction, collaboration, and participation (Jaokar, 2006). The quality-related challenges faced by mobile applications need to be suitably addressed in order to help preserve the successes that they have achieved, and to sustain and strengthen user confidence in them.

In this chapter, our interest is in a systematic approach of engineering quality-centric mobile applications based on the knowledge garnered from past experience and expertise. For that, we rely on the notion of the problem-solving approach of patterns (Buschmann, Henney, & Schmidt, 2007b). The use of patterns has several advantages over other approaches in terms of quality improvement, including that the approach is preventative rather than curative, is supported by a number of developmental processes, and provides practical solutions (along with their rationale) for problems that have been tackled successfully in the past.

The rest of the chapter is organized as follows. We first outline the background necessary for the discussion that follows, and state our position in that regard. This is followed by the presentation of a *Pattern-Oriented Mobile Web Engineering Methodology (POMWEM)* (Kamthan, 2008b) for systematically addressing the quality of mobile applications. POMWEM includes a model consisting of quality attributes at different tiers and the role of patterns as means for addressing them. Next, challenges and directions for future research are outlined. Finally, concluding remarks are given.

BACKGROUND

In this section, the motivation for a systematic approach to addressing the quality in mobile applications and a synopsis of patterns is presented.

Definitions and Characteristics of Mobile Applications

In this chapter, we will use the term wireless device instead of the commonly-used term mobile device as it is not the device but the user that is mobile. Furthermore, we will use the term mobile application to mean a software application that can be accessed by a device whose owner is mobile unless otherwise stated. In general, a mobile application could be standalone or networked. Also, a mobile application is always a wireless application although the converse is not necessarily true (Stanoevska-Slabeva, 2003).

There are certain defining characteristics that make mobile applications unique compared to other software applications, and lead to special considerations towards their quality.

Human/Social Characteristics and Implications

From a social viewpoint, the demographic of mobile applications continues to get broader as the cost of mobile access becomes increasingly attractive and wireless devices become increasingly affordable. Indeed, the use of wireless devices (and, by reference, the mobile applications installed on them) has become increasingly common among people of all age groups, educational background, and cognitive/physiological ability.

Organizational Characteristics and Implications

From an organizational viewpoint, the engineering and deployment of mobile applications is particularly challenging due to the rise of mobile networks/protocols with varying configurations, (largely vendor-driven) proliferation of wireless devices with broad capabilities, and information description languages and media formats with diverse specifications. The situation is further exacerbated by frequent modifications to them.

These factors can place undue burden on the producers of mobile applications in terms of resource planning and personnel training. For example, knowledge of a specific markup or style sheet language may be rendered obsolete in a short period of time, resulting in added cost for retraining.

Technical Characteristics and Implications

From a technical viewpoint, the engineering and deployment of mobile applications is especially demanding. In particular, the *context of use* is almost always relevant in any interactive software application but even more challenging in a mobile environment (Christopoulou, 2008; Dey & Häkkilä, 2008; Finkelstein & Savigni, 2001; Mauney & Masterton, 2008; Tarasewich, 2003) due to the number of possible variants. For example, it should be possible to use a mobile device both when the user is stationary and is mobile.

There are several factors to consider including *network-specific constraints* of variable (and unacceptably low) bandwidth and potential for degraded connectivity, and *device-induced constraints* of heterogeneity and multiplicity, inhibited power source, small memory, limited processing power, restricted ergonomic possibilities, rather basic user interface capabilities, and variations in input and output modalities (based on sight, sound, or touch).

An Engineering View of Mobile Applications

The past approaches for developing mobile applications have largely been from a managerial viewpoint (Coyle, 2001) and/or from a technological viewpoint (Jones & Marsden, 2006; Hjelm, 2000; Heyes, 2002; Paavilainen, 2002). It is only recently that an engineering viewpoint to devel-

oping mobile applications has been undertaken (Kamthan, 2008b; Mahmoud & Maamar, 2006; Ocampo et al., 2003; Salmre, 2005).

The need for managing increasing size and complexity of Web Applications and the necessity of a planned development has led to the discipline of Web Engineering (Kappel et al., 2006; Mendes & Mosley, 2006; Rossi et al., 2008). In an analogy to Web Engineering, we define *Mobile Web Engineering* to be a discipline concerned with the establishment and use of sound scientific, engineering, and management principles, and disciplined and systematic approaches to the successful development, deployment, and maintenance of 'high-quality' mobile applications. For the sake of this chapter, we will consider mobile applications to be products resulting from a Mobile Web Engineering process.

Understanding and Addressing the Quality of Mobile Applications

The need for mobile applications to exhibit 'high-quality' is critical to all stakeholders involved. If unaddressed, there is a potential for a resource in a mobile application to be, for example, inaccessible by a visually impaired user, abruptly freeze upon interaction by a user, or be prohibitive to perfective maintenance by an engineer.

There have been a few initiatives for addressing the quality of mobile applications, which we now briefly discuss. It is evident that traditional quality models can not be applied as-is to mobile applications. In some cases, the significance and means of improvement of individual quality attributes like accessibility (Harper & Yesilada, 2008; Trewin, 2006; Kamthan, 2007a), credibility (Kamthan, 2007b), and usability (Chan & Fang, 2001; Weiss, 2002; Gorlenko & Merrick, 2003) have been discussed. The relevance of a subset of the quality attributes in the ISO/IEC 9126-1 Standard in the context of mobility has been shown (Spriestersbach & Springer, 2004), however, there is no consideration for certain quality attributes such as findability and reliability, and means of quality improvement are not discussed.

There are guidelines and 'best practices' available for the purpose of development, cognitive walkthrough, and heuristic evaluation of user interfaces of mobile applications (Buchanan et al., 2001; Chan et al., 2002; Gong & Tarasewich, 2004). However, these guidelines do not appear to correspond to any quality model or organized in any known manner; not all guidelines are rationalized; in absence of context, some guidelines can appear unnecessary (such as "use a flat hierarchy"), constraining (such as "provide indication of signal strength and downloading progress on every screen") or ambiguous (such as "do not require users to remember items"); and as a whole, they do not address certain usability issues. Furthermore, guidelines, in general, are known (Vanderdonckt, 1999) to have several limitations such as being 'absolute,' not illustrating relationships to each other, and oriented towards experts rather than novices.

The World Wide Web Consortium (W3C) initiative on the Mobile Web Best Practices suffers from limitations similar to guidelines that it is vague. For example, "take reasonable steps to work around deficient implementations," "keep the URIs of site entry points short," or "use clear and simple language" are not readily verifiable.

Patterns for Mobile Applications

The reliance on past experience and expertise is critical to any development. A pattern is commonly defined as a proven solution to a recurring problem in a given context (Buschmann, Henney, & Schmidt, 2007b). A unique aspect of a pattern is its structure, which we now briefly discuss.

Structure of a Pattern

There are several possible views of a pattern. From a structural viewpoint, a pattern is typically described (Meszaros & Doble, 1998) using an ordered list of elements (highlighted in italics in the rest of the chapter) that are labeled as (pattern) *name*, *author*, *context*, *problem*, *forces*, *solution*, *examples*, and *related patterns*. The labels can vary and, to enrich the description, other (optional) elements, particularly those related to metadata, may be included.

The *name* element of a pattern is often a metaphor reflecting the nature of the *solution*, the *author* element gives the identity of the pattern author(s), the *context* element provides the situation or preconditions within which the *problem* occurs, the *forces* element provides the constraints that are resolved to arrive at a *solution*, the *solution* element provides an abstract solution to the problem and is shown to work in practice via an *examples* element, and the *related patterns* element outlines any other pattern(s) to which a pattern is related to in some way. A pattern is usually referred to by its *name*. In the following, the *name* of a pattern is listed in uppercase in order to distinguish it from the main text.

Patterns and Productivity

There are three characteristics of patterns that make them especially suitable in making teams productive: communicability, practicality, and reusability.

A description of a pattern, when properly documented, aims to communicate (1) a practical *process* of arriving at an abstract, broadly applicable, 'best' possible *solution* specific to a *problem* in a given *context*, (2) the reasoning and trade-offs behind this solution, and (3) proven *examples* that illustrate the reuse of the *solution* in different circumstances. This often makes patterns more practical in their applicability compared to, for instance, guidelines. Also, patterns often do not exist in isolation, and are part of an overall vocabulary (namely, a pattern system or a pattern language) that attempts to solve a larger problem than that possible by an individual pattern. In due course, this vocabulary of related patterns can become the *lingua franca* of project teams, thereby contributing to communicability across teams.

Indeed, patterns have been used for the development of certain mobile applications (Risi & Rossi, 2004; Ihme & Abrahamsson, 2005). However, in these cases, the relation of patterns to any development process or to the improvement of quality is not discussed explicitly.

Development Process Models for Mobile Applications and Support for Quality and Patterns

There have been a few initiatives towards introducing process models specific to the development of mobile applications, which we now discuss chronologically. An essentially linear process model for developing mobile applications has been proposed (Mallick, 2003) but it is inadequate in an uncertain environment where risk factors such as flexibility of schedules or changes to requirements need to be accounted for.

Based on a comprehensive literature survey and two development projects, a process model, which we give an acronym OBMP after its authors, for developing mobile applications incrementally has been described (Ocampo et al., 2003). OBMP considers usability in detail and security to some extent, and but the approach to quality is not based on a quality model and it does not consider other quality attributes such as reliability or maintainability. OBMP supports the use of patterns in the design phase (only) but the details of actual selection and applications of patterns are not given.

The Pattern-Oriented Analysis and Design (POAD) (Yacoub & Ammar, 2003) is a pattern-oriented, model-based iterative and incremental analysis and design methodology for developing software systems. POAD suggests means for identifying and composing design patterns. However, POAD does not consider application-domain specific characteristics, does not provide support for explicitly involving the customer or users in the development process, and does not

present a design quality model (to discuss the relationships between design quality attributes and design patterns).

Mobile-D (Abrahamsson et al., 2004) is a process model specially designed for developing mobile applications, and is based on Extreme Programming (XP) (Beck & Andres, 2005), Crystal Methods, the Rational Unified Process (RUP), and Test-Driven Development (TDD). It explicitly supports the use of patterns in macro-architecture design (only) but the details of actual selection and applications of patterns have not been provided.

Inspired by RUP, a spiral model for developing mobile applications that takes the characteristics of wireless devices and the underlying network into consideration has been presented (Mahmoud & Maamar, 2006). This model recommends the use of patterns in the design phase (only) but the quality-related issues are not considered and the details of actual selection and applications of patterns are not given.

A persona-driven, pattern-oriented approach to user interface design has been suggested (Javahery, 2006). However, the coverage is limited to usability-related concerns, is likely to omit patterns not suggested by persona experiences, and limitations of the approach (such as unavailability of a pattern for an experience derived from a given persona) are not discussed.

The Oregon Software Development Process (OSDP) (Schümmer & Lukosch, 2007) has been applied to the development of groupware. OSDP meets all the criteria for selecting a mobile application development process except that of maturity and broad community support. An investigation into the applicability of OSDP for medium-size mobile application projects could be of interest.

Finally, a methodology for integrating security patterns in software has been proposed (Fernandez et al., 2007). However, apart from security, other quality attributes are not considered and the details of actual selection and applications of patterns are not given.

Figure 1. An abstract model of a pattern-oriented and stakeholder-quality centered approach to the development of a mobile application

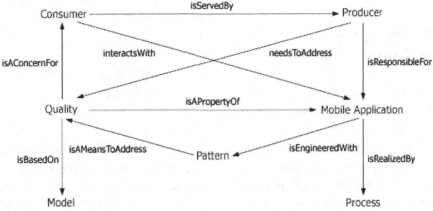

A METHODOLOGY FOR INTEGRATING PATTERNS IN THE DEVELOPMENT OF MOBILE APPLICATIONS

In this section, we introduce POMWEM, a methodology for systematically addressing the quality of mobile applications from a stakeholders' perspective. POMWEM builds on past experience on integrating patterns in Web applications (Kamthan, 2008a; Kamthan, 2008b).

The view of a systematic development methodology for the improvement of quality of mobile applications taken in this chapter rests on the following interrelated hypothesis:

- **Hypothesis 1.** An improvement in the *process* for development can bring about improvement in the quality of the *product*, namely the mobile application itself (Nelson & Monarchi, 2007).
- **Hypothesis 2.** For an understanding of quality of mobile applications from stakeholders' perspective or otherwise, the notion of quality needs to be decomposed into a manageable number of attributes (Fenton & Pfleeger, 1997).
- **Hypothesis 3.** A preventative approach to

addressing quality (attributes) is *at least* as significant as a curative approach (Dromey, 2003).

The set of Hypothesis 1-3 is minimal in the sense that a subset of it is insufficient. Figure 1 (Kamthan, 2008b) illustrates the development environment of mobile applications from a POMWEM viewpoint.

POMWEM consists of the following interrelated and non-linear sequence of non-atomic steps:

1. Selecting the Development Process Model.
2. Identifying and Organizing Quality Concerns from a Semiotic Viewpoint.
3. Acquiring, Selecting, and Applying Suitable Patterns.

The Hypothesis 1-3 stated previously lead to the aforementioned steps 1-3, respectively. It is crucial that the sequence be non-linear so that a step could be revisited for any necessary amendments.

From a practical standpoint, each of the steps 1-3 needs to be feasible. The feasibility study could be a part of the overall planning activity of the mobile application project.

In the following sections, we discuss the work involved in each of these steps, including feasibility issues, in detail.

Step One: Selecting the Development Process Model

A pattern-oriented approach does not mandate the use of a specific development process, however, certain process models can be relatively more enabling than restricting. In light of the unique characteristics of mobility discussed above, it is crucial that a mobile application development process be *flexible*, *human-centered*, and *quality-sensitive*. It is likely that such a process will typically also be non-linear (iterative *and* incremental) to enable piecemeal growth.

We recommend that POMWEM be realized within the framework of an *existing* process environment that already has broad community and tool support in order to keep the cost to a minimum and the learning curve low. To that regard, we recommend the adoption of one of the following process models, each with its own advantages and limitations. XP is a mature and broadly-used agile methodology for software development. XP places 'lightweight' requirements on resources and is suitable for small projects. The Unified Process (UP) (Jacobson, Booch, & Rumbaugh, 1999) is an archetype of model-based and use case-driven process *framework*, of which RUP (proprietary), OpenUP, and OpenUP/Basic (open source) are three notable customizations. RUP and OpenUP rely heavily on modeling and documentation, and are especially suited for large projects. OpenUP/Basic is agile and suited for small-to-medium size projects. Both XP and UP are likely to be familiar to software engineering students as well as professional software engineers. There is provision for the use of patterns during the design phase in both XP and UP, however, patterns can be integrated in other phases as well.

In some cases, the limitations of the aforementioned process models may be ameliorated by appropriate extensions. For example, to improve their human-centeredness, these models could be extended to incorporate user modeling. Further discussion of this issue is beyond the scope of this chapter.

Feasibility of Development Process Model

The selection of a process model for the development of mobile applications will evidently depend on the constraints of the Hypothesis 1-3 and the organizational process maturity. This in turn involves several factors, including budget, availability of qualified personnel, submission time line, and available tool support.

Step Two: Identifying and Organizing Quality Concerns from a Semiotic Viewpoint

From a semiotic (Shanks, 1999) viewpoint, we can view a resource in a mobile application on six interrelated levels: physical, empirical, syntactic, semantic, pragmatic, and social. In this chapter, we shall limit ourselves to the discussion of pragmatic level, which is responsible for the relation of signs to their interpreters. The interpreters in our case are the stakeholders of a mobile application.

Next, we contend that pragmatic quality is a multi-dimensional concept, and decompose it into granular levels that consist of known attributes that can be addressed directly or indirectly. For the definitions of these quality attributes, we resort to the IEEE Standard 1061-1998, the ISO 9241-11:1998 Standard, and the ISO/IEC 9126-1:2001 Standard.

Finally, we assign patterns as means for improving the quality attributes. Table 1 summarizes this construction.

A few remarks regarding Table 1 are in order. It is evident that the priority of quality attributes can vary across mobile applications. For example, accessibility may be at a lower priority in the de-

Table 1. A model for the pragmatic quality of a mobile application

Semiotic Level	Quality Attributes		Means for Quality Assurance
Social Quality Concerns			
Pragmatic	[Tier 3] Maintainability, Usability		Patterns
	[Tier 2] Accessibility, Comprehensibility, Findability, Performance, Reliability		
	[Tier 1] Attractiveness, Availability, Efficiency, Familiarity, Readability		
Physical, Empirical, Syntactic, and Semantic Quality Concerns			

velopment of a mobile application if it is elicited (say, through ethnographic studies) that the target users do not have any known disability issues.

We contend that the quality attributes in Table 1 are necessary, but make no claim of their sufficiency. (For example, we have suppressed functionality as being one of the quality attributes even though it is present explicitly in the ISO/IEC 9126-1:2001 Standard.) The relevance of these quality attributes that justifies their inclusion is discussed in the rest of the chapter.

The quality attributes in Table 1 are not mutually exclusive. Indeed, the quality attributes in Tier 3 depend on that in Tier 2, and those in Tier 2 in turn depend on the quality attributes in Tier 1. For example, if a user cannot read, he/she cannot comprehend the information in a mobile application, and thereby cannot use it or maintain it as desired. Similarly, for a mobile application to be reliable, it must be available. Furthermore, the quality attributes within the same tier in Table 1 are also not necessarily mutually exclusive. For example, the steps taken towards improving reliability (say, fault tolerance) may lead to inclusion of redundant source code or data (that can be unfavorable to maintainability) but enable ease-of-use (that can be favorable to usability).

The Pragmatic Quality: Stakeholder Contract

For the sake of this paper, we view pragmatic quality as a *contract* between a mobile application and a stakeholder.

Based on a systematic approach for identification and refinement of stakeholder classes (Sharp, Galal, & Finkelstein, 1999), we state two broad classes of stakeholders with respect to their *roles* in relationship to a mobile application: a *producer* (provider, manager, engineer, or maintainer) is the one who develops, deploys, or maintains the mobile application, and a *consumer* (novice or expert end-user) is the one who uses the mobile application for some purpose. This classification is based on the *role* of a stakeholder. For example, both the engineer and the user could be the same person, but their roles with respect to the interaction with the mobile application are different.

The relevance of quality attributes in Table 1 varies with respect to stakeholder types.

- **Pragmatic-Tier 1.** The quality attributes of direct concern to an end-user are attractiveness, availability, familiarity, and readability. The quality attributes of direct concern to an engineer are (space and time) efficiency and readability.
- **Pragmatic-Tier 2.** The quality attributes of direct concern to an end-user are accessibility, comprehensibility, findability,

Table 2. The stakeholder types of a mobile application and corresponding quality attributes of concern

Pragmatic Quality Attribute	Producer Concern	Consumer Concern
Accessibility		X
Attractiveness		X
Availability		X
Comprehensibility	X	X
Efficiency	X	
Findability		X
Familiarity		X
Maintainability	X	
Performance		X
Readability	X	X
Reliability		X
Usability		X

performance, and reliability. The quality attributes of direct concern to an engineer is comprehensibility.

- **Pragmatic-Tier 3.** The quality attributes of direct concern to an end-user is usability. The quality attribute of direct concern to an engineer is maintainability. For simplicity, we will consider modifiability, portability, and reusability as special cases of maintainability.

Finally, we note that the significance of quality attributes will vary across different types of mobile applications. For example, the quality needs of a mobile application providing stock quotes will have some similarity with an application providing currency conversion but will substantially differ from that facilitating music download.

Table 2 summarizes the mapping between stakeholder types and quality attributes.

Feasibility of Quality Attributes

The expectations of improving the quality attributes of a mobile application must be feasible in order to be practical. It is evident that not all the pragmatic quality attributes in Table 1 can (at least mathematically) be *completely* satisfied. For example, an a priori guarantee that a mobile application will be usable to *all* users at *all* times in *all* computing environments that the users deploy, is not realistic. Therefore, the quality requirements of a mobile application must reflect the fact that certain attributes can only be *satisficed* (Simon, 1996). Further discussion of this issue is beyond the scope of this chapter.

Step Three: Acquiring, Selecting, and Applying Suitable Patterns

In the last decade, patterns have been discovered in a variety of domains of interest, including those that are applicable to the development of mobile applications (Ahlgren & Markkula, 2005; Ballard, 2007; Mazhelis, Markkula, & Jakobsson, 2005; Noble & Weir, 2001; Risi & Rossi, 2004; Roth, 2001; Roth, 2002; Tidwell, 2006; Van Duyne, Landay, & Hong, 2003). The availability of patterns varies significantly: while some patterns are only available commercially in print form, others are available free-of-cost via repositories on the Web.

In general, the relationship between the set of quality attributes and the set of patterns is many-to-many. This, in turn, necessitates the selection of patterns. The underlying *problem* at hand along with the *context* in which it occurs will play a crucial role in selecting desirable patterns. For example, the RESPONSIVE ENABLING pattern (Tidwell, 2006) may be suitable for Web Applications but not for mobile applications with a relatively smaller user interfaces.

In our case, the selection of a pattern is based on the following factors: (1) its maturity (indicated by an associated confidence rating, if any), (2) extent of its availability as 'open content', (3) its parity to the goal (namely, relation to a quality attribute in Table 1), (4) quality of its description (Meszaros & Doble, 1998), and (5) reputation of author(s).

The main non-mutually exclusive concerns in the application of patterns are the understanding of the pattern description, the order in which patterns are applied, relationships (if any) between patterns, and finally, the result upon the composition of patterns. In particular, if the end result is unsatisfactory, the selection and/or the composition may need to be revisited and revised.

Even though patterns are applicable to any phase of a process, for considerations of space, we will limit ourselves in this chapter to addressing the role of patterns in the design phase of a mobile application. As evident from the discussion that follows, the patterns presented here form a skeleton sequence that traverses through several existing collections of patterns.

Patterns for Macro-Architecture Design of Mobile Applications

The macro-architecture design is the place where high-level design decisions, independent of any implementation paradigm or technology, are made. To that regard, some general considerations are in order.

A mobile application will implicitly or explicitly target some domain such as education, commerce, entertainment, and so on. There are patterns available for certain common genres like EDUCATIONAL FORUMS (for educational institutions) and NONPROFITS AS NETWORKS OF HELP (for non-profit organizations) (Van Duyne, Landay, & Hong, 2003). The application of such genre-specific patterns can increase user familiarity with the mobile application. Furthermore, the organization owning a mobile application may wish to serve (potential) consumers in diverse cultural and/or geopolitical situations (such as, in different countries and using different natural languages). This could be done using the LOCALE HANDLING pattern (Busse, 2002). However, the trade-off in deploying this pattern is that the maintenance responsibilities increase.

Next, the macro-architecture design patterns suggested in the following are based on the fact that mobile applications are a class of distributed request-response-type interactive systems. Specifically, the applicable patterns are (1) an extension of the CLIENT-SERVER pattern (Schmidt et al., 2000) by an intermediary (that includes a transcoder), followed by (2) the APPLICATION SERVER pattern (Manolescu & Kunzle, 2001), which in turn is followed by (3) the MODEL-VIEW-CONTROLLER (MVC) pattern (Buschmann et al., 1996; Buschmann, Henney, & Schmidt, 2007a).

The CLIENT-SERVER pattern supports modifiability and reusability. For example, a server or resources on the server-side could be modified without impacting the client. Also, a single server can support multiple mobile clients simultaneously, or a mobile client could make simultaneous requests for resources residing on multiple servers. For instance, an Extensible Markup Language (XML) document with normative information could be located on one server, which, upon request, would be transformed via an Extensible Stylesheet Language Transformations (XSLT) document located on another server into an Extensible HyperText Markup Language (XHTML) Basic document and presented using

Figure 2. A view of the macro-architecture design patterns in the development of mobile applications

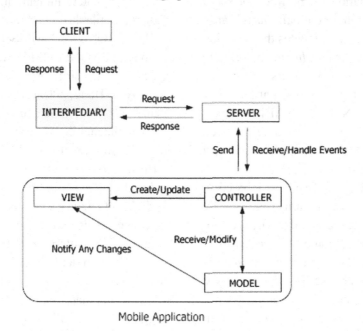

Mobile Application

the Cascading Style Sheet (CSS) Mobile Profile style sheet located on yet another server.

The APPLICATION SERVER pattern also supports maintainability: it isolates the mobile application from other aspects on the server-side such that the communication between the application itself and the server takes place via the SINGLE POINT OF ACCESS (Yoder & Barcalow, 1997) pattern. This separation allows the mobile application to evolve independently.

The MVC pattern advocates the separation of structure from logic or presentation of a document, which leads to three semantically-different components: model, view, and controller. The (at least theoretical) minimization of the coupling between these components improves the modifiability of a mobile application. Since a model is normally not aware of the views and controllers attached to it, the *same* model in a MVC could be used with multiple views and multiple controllers, which in turn improves the reusability of a mobile application. For example, the same information could be adapted (repurposed or transformed) and delivered

to different situations (like different user agent environments or consumer needs). There are several implementations of MVC available in a variety of programming languages such as Java 2 Micro Edition (J2ME)) and PHP Hypertext Preprocessor (PHP), and application frameworks like the Mobile Asynchronous JavaScript and XML (AJAX) or those that accompany Symbian OS.

Figure 2 (Kamthan, 2008b) presents an abstract view of the aforementioned macro-architecture design patterns.

Reliability Design

For addressing reliability (specifically, availability) concerns, the macro-architecture design of server-side components of a mobile application could use a number of patterns (Ahluwalia & Jain, 2006; Manolescu & Kunzle, 2001). For example, the INTRODUCE REDUNDANCY pattern could be used to include extra measures to support the availability of a mobile application. The FAILOVER THROUGH CLUSTERING pattern could be used to introduce redundancy in form of a cluster of multiple servers where if one (primary) server fails, another (secondary) server takes over the responsibility. However, including redundancy comes at the cost of increased maintenance.

If the need arises, a failure message could be relayed directly using the FAILURE NOTIFICATION pattern or indirectly using the HEARTBEAT pattern (where an engineer is informed via periodic broadcasts that a specific server is available; the absence of such a message would then imply its unavailability.)

Patterns for Micro-Architecture Design of Mobile Applications

The micro-architecture design is the place where low-level design decisions that are to be implemented are cast. In the following, the focus is only on the design aspects that impact pragmatic quality. As such, the attention is geared more towards client-side rather than server-side concerns.

Interaction design (Jones & Marsden, 2006) is perhaps the most crucial client-side concern among mobile applications. The goal of interaction design is to make both the content and the user interface useful, easy-to-use, and enjoyable. In this chapter, we consider four of the most critical interaction design aspects of mobile applications, namely information design, navigation design, search design, and presentation design, independent of any specific domain. We note that these aspects of design are not mutually exclusive.

Information Design

The delivery of information could either be static or dynamic. The user interface of a mobile is usually constrained for space and is a major concern during information design. The ONE TRUE WINDOW pattern (Noble & Weir, 2001) suggests invocation of a single window at all times within which the information is rendered.

The information being delivered needs to be organized. This can be systematically realized by the use of the WHOLE-PART pattern (Buschmann

et al., 1996), which enables a hierarchical organization of objects. Since each of these objects can be modified or replaced independently, the WHOLE-PART pattern supports maintainability. Also, since a 'part' can correspond to more than one 'whole,' the WHOLE-PART pattern also supports reusability. However, multiple indirections stemming from client requests and responses for fulfilling them can lead to a loss of performance, particularly when each 'part' itself is structured as WHOLE-PART. The information can be further organized using the CATEGORIES pattern (Noble & Weir, 2001).

The USER CUSTOMIZATION pattern (Noble & Weir, 2001) suggests user-specific personalization of information. The APPLICATION STATE MANAGEMENT pattern (Ballard, 2007) and, specifically, the COOKIES MANAGEMENT pattern (Ballard, 2007) can help locally save state in various situations that involve repetitious tasks (like authentication, supplying e-mail address, and so on) and thereby improve performance. However, support for cookies varies across platforms, which can adversely affect portability of the mobile application. The HIDE AND SEEK pattern (Noble & Weir, 2001) and the RESPONSIVE DISCLOSURE pattern (Tidwell, 2006) are a realization of *progressive disclosure*: they can present information at different levels of abstraction, and thus can improve (space) efficiency. However, client-side implementations of it are not favorable to accessibility and an overuse of menus to implement this pattern can be detrimental to performance. The ALPHABETIC LISTINGS pattern (Ballard, 2007) suggests a well-known way of organizing information, including search results.

There are patterns that can help if there is an interruption in a user task flow. By providing more details, the DIAL 'H' FOR HELP pattern (Noble & Weir, 2001) helps a user get informed about aspects of the mobile application. To err is human, and a mobile application must account for the possibility of exceptional behavior. For example, a user proceeding to search with an empty query string should lead to an error dialog. This can be accomplished by using the ERROR MESSAGES pattern (Ballard, 2007).

Navigation Design

According to the *information foraging theory* (Pirolli, 2007), there is need for information to be structured as well as a systematic means for it to be discovered (or found). For the sake of this chapter, navigation is hypertext-based traversal in information space for some purpose such as casual or targeted browsing for finding information or complementing a reading sequence.

There are various patterns to devise a suitable navigation for mobile applications. The BREAD-CRUMBS pattern (Ballard, 2007) provides a navigation trail that could be used to inform the user of relative location. The PAGE FOOTER pattern (Ballard, 2007) suggests a horizontal navigation on all documents that are presented to a user and consists of entries that remain invariant during transition. The MENU LAYOUT pattern (Ballard, 2007) provides a classic gopher-style hierarchical navigation of resources.

The SCROLLING pattern (Ballard, 2007) takes advantage of user acquaintance with the scrolling functionality (and thus supports user familiarity). However, scrolling large amounts of data can be slow (which hampers performance). An alternate to scrolling is the use of the TABLE BASED LAYOUT pattern (Ballard, 2007).

Search Design

The goal of searching is finding information. The searching patterns, when used appropriately, aid comprehensibility and performance.

The use of STRAIGHTFORWARD SEARCH FORMS pattern (Van Duyne, Landay, & Hong, 2003) with a SIMPLE SEARCH INTERFACE pattern (Lyardet, Rossi, & Schwabe, 1999) requires minimal technical background on part of the user, and will therefore contribute towards comprehensibility. The use of SELECTABLE SEARCH SPACE pattern (Lyardet, Rossi, &

Schwabe, 1999) that can restrict the search to a specific category, the SELECTABLE KEY-WORDS pattern (Lyardet, Rossi, & Schwabe, 1999) that can suggest keywords for improving subsequent search results based on the past experience, and the ORGANIZED SEARCH RESULTS pattern (Van Duyne, Landay, & Hong, 2003) that presents a summary of the most relevant search results, can all improve the effectiveness of the searching activity.

Presentation Design

It has been shown in surveys (Tarasewich, Daniel, & Griffin, 2001) that users highly value the attractiveness of applications on the Web. The elements of presentation apply to all aspects of design discussed earlier.

The CAROUSEL pattern (Ballard, 2007) suggests that the mode of information (say, text or graphics) being served should match the nature of information, thereby supporting comprehensibility. Specifically, A PICTURE IS SMALLER THAN A THOUSAND WORDS pattern (Noble & Weir, 2001) advocates the use of icons for well-known concepts to save space and reading time. However, it is not always possible to map concepts to graphical counterparts and icons are not always transferable across cultures.

The FAÇADE pattern, which is a classic object-oriented design pattern (Gamma et al., 1995), can be used to provide a single interface for the user agents of both mobile and for stationary clients. The weak coupling between subsystems and clients results in improved modifiability of the subsystems.

It is known that, if used appropriately, colors can have a positive impact both cognitively and perceptually, in particular taking into the considerations of the visually impaired. Using patterns like DEEP BACKGROUND, FEW HUES, MANY VALUES, or COLOR-CODED SECTIONS (Tidwell, 2006) a mobile application could be given a unique 'identity.' There are of course other presentation issues that are crucial such choice of

Figure 3. A mosaic of interaction design patterns in the development of a mobile application on a PDA

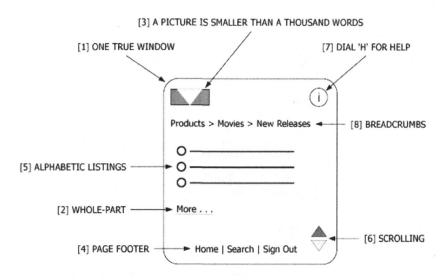

fonts and their properties, layout and positioning of user interface components, use of white space, and so on. These could also be addressed via an appropriate use of patterns.

Figure 3 (Kamthan, 2008b) gives an abstract illustration of some of the interaction design patterns mentioned previously in which the numbers indicate the order of application of patterns.

Table 3 extends Table 1 and provides a mapping between quality attributes and patterns discussed in this chapter. A (+) symbol post-fixed to a pattern *name* reflects a positive impact on the corresponding quality attribute, whereas a (−) symbol reflects a negative impact. The list of patterns is by no means complete and is subject to evolution. The rating scheme can also evolve to become more granular.

Feasibility of Acquiring, Selecting, and Applying Patterns

The adoption and subsequent deployment of patterns in mobile applications needs to be viable, to which there are a number of challenges (Kamthan, 2008a; Kamthan, 2008b) including the following:

- **Availability of Patterns.** For an adoption of a pattern-based approach to the development of mobile applications, it is important that there be design and implementation patterns that can sufficiently 'map' the solution space. However, there is no *a priori* guarantee that for a given quality attribute, there exist suitable patterns (if any).

- **Locatability of Patterns.** Even when it is ascertained that for a given problem a pattern does exist, that pattern needs to be located. There is currently no unique way of classifying or indexing patterns, both of which can pose obstacles in locating desirable patterns. For example, even though there are patterns available that are suitable for mobile applications, they may not be explicitly classified as such. This makes the process of locating desirable patterns somewhat non-systematic.

- **Economics of Patterns.** There is cost in terms of time and effort in learning and adapting any reusable knowledge, including patterns. The cost of using patterns needs to be balanced against the (business and/or pedagogical) value that they provide. It

Table 3. Pragmatic quality attributes of a mobile application and corresponding patterns along with their impact ratings

Pragmatic Quality Attribute	Pattern(s)
Accessibility	CAROUSEL (−) COLOR-CODED SECTIONS (−) FEW HUES, MANY VALUES (−) HIDE AND SEEK (−) USER CUSTOMIZATION (+)
Attractiveness	COLOR-CODED SECTIONS (+) DEEP BACKGROUND (+) FEW HUES, MANY VALUES (+)
Availability	FAIL-OVER THROUGH CLUSTERING (+) FAILURE NOTIFICATION (+) HEARTBEAT (+) INTRODUCE REDUNDANCY (+)
Comprehensibility	ALPHABETIC LISTINGS (+) CAROUSEL (+) CATEGORIES (+) HIDE AND SEEK (+) RESPONSIVE DISCLOSURE (+) SIMPLE SEARCH INTERFACE (+) STRAIGHTFORWARD SEARCH FORMS (+)
Efficiency	A PICTURE IS SMALLER THAN A THOUSAND WORDS (+) HIDE AND SEEK (+) ONE TRUE WINDOW (+) ORGANIZED SEARCH RESULTS (+) TABLE BASED LAYOUT (+)
Familiarity	ALPHABETIC LISTINGS (+) A PICTURE IS SMALLER THAN A THOUSAND WORDS (−) EDUCATIONAL FORUMS (+) NONPROFITS AS NETWORKS OF HELP (+) SCROLLING (+)
Findability	ALPHABETIC LISTINGS (+) BREADCRUMBS (+) HIDE AND SEEK (+) MENU LAYOUT (+) ORGANIZED SEARCH RESULTS (+) PAGE FOOTER (+)SCROLLING (+) SELECTABLE KEYWORDS (+) SELECTABLE SEARCH SPACE (+) SIMPLE SEARCH INTERFACE (+) STRAIGHTFORWARD SEARCH FORMS (+) TABLE BASED LAYOUT (+)
Maintainability	APPLICATION SERVER (+) COOKIES MANAGEMENT (−) CLIENT-SERVER (+) FAÇADE (+) FAIL-OVER THROUGH CLUSTERING (−) INTRODUCE REDUNDANCY (−) MODEL-VIEW-CONTROLLER (+) WHOLE-PART (+)
Performance	APPLICATION STATE MANAGEMENT (+) COOKIES MANAGEMENT (+) HIDE AND SEEK (−) RESPONSIVE DISCLOSURE (+) SCROLLING (−) SELECTABLE KEYWORDS (+) SELECTABLE SEARCH SPACE (+)
Readability	MENU LAYOUT (+) ORGANIZED SEARCH RESULTS (+) TABLE BASED LAYOUT (+)

continued on following page

Table 1. continued

Pragmatic Quality Attribute	Pattern(s)
Reliability	FAILURE NOTIFICATION (+) INTRODUCE REDUNDANCY (+)
Usability	BREADCRUMBS (+) DIAL 'H' FOR HELP (+) ERROR MESSAGES (+) USER CUSTOMIZATION (+)

is not automatic that all available patterns are equally 'mature' and the quality of their descriptions varies. Furthermore, it is rare that a pattern exists in isolation: the cost of *related patterns* need to be factored into the cost of commitment to one pattern.

POMWEM in Perspective

It is evident that POMWEM is neither absolute, nor universally applicable. In this section, we briefly discuss the scope and limitations of POMWEM.

First, the feasibility considerations at each step 1-3 determine the scope of POMWEM. This includes the possibility that for a given *problem*, there may not be any suitable patterns available. Second, the quality model presented in Table 1 could benefit from a more rigorous definition. For example, if expressed in a formal language, the quality model could be instantiated for different mobile application projects with different priorities for quality attributes therein. Third, the process of selecting patterns in our case is informal and largely a manual process. It could be formalized, for example, using multi-criteria decision support (MCDS) techniques such as conjoint analysis.

FUTURE RESEARCH DIRECTIONS

The work presented in this chapter can be extended in a few different directions, which we now briefly discuss.

Extensions of POMWEM

There is provision for evaluation in both XP and UP. However, the steps of POMWEM can be extended to explicitly include formative and summative evaluation of mobile applications, such as inspections and testing, respectively, using approaches that are specific to patterns (Schmettow, 2005).

The Table 1 of POMWEM can be extended in both 'horizontal' and 'vertical' directions. A horizontal extension can be achieved by increasing the granularity of the quality attributes in the pragmatic level. It is also possible to add quality attributes such as *dependability*, *interoperability*, and *safety* to this level.

A vertical extension can be achieved by, for example, considering quality concerns at the social level. Web 2.0 (O'Reilly, 2005) is a pseudonym that is used to describe the apparent 'humanization' and 'socialization' of the Web as it evolves to a medium for participation and collaboration. Furthermore, one of the characteristics of mobile users is that they are 'sociable' (Ballard, 2007). This has evidently inspired the notion of Mobile Social Web, commonly referred to by the pseudonym Mobile Web 2.0 (Jaokar, 2006). The quality attributes of interest at the social level are *credibility*, *legality*, *privacy*, and *security*. The potential benefits of 'collective intelligence' enabled by Mobile Web 2.0 come with their share of negative side-effects (Kamthan, 2007b), and pose various quality-related challenges. Therefore, an extension of POMWEM with respect to quality attributes and the selection of patterns, although of research interest, is not trivial. For example, in its current state, the technological infrastructure of Web 2.0 is not favorable to accessibility (Zajicek, 2007). The flexibility of anybody being able to post information raises the possibility for the distribution of inaccurate medical information from unqualified sources, which is a threat to credibility. The potential for unauthorized sharing of media files in a peer-to-peer mobile environment raises legal issues that need to be addressed. Finally, personalization is crucial for mobile applications but can come at the cost of loss of privacy and security. The aforementioned scenarios can resist the selection of certain patterns such as INTERSTITIAL ADS (Ballard, 2007) (unfavorable to credibility) and USER CUSTOMIZATION (Ballard, 2007) (unfavorable to privacy).

Patterns in Standards

Even though patterns themselves are not standards per se, an explicit support for patterns in international standards is crucial for their broad exposure and acceptance. This is especially the case for standards that cater to the development of information-intensive software systems such as mobile applications.

There is implicit support for patterns in the W3C Mobile Web Best Practices 1.0: Basic Guidelines. There is currently limited explicit support for patterns in standards such as the ISO/IEC 23026:2006 Standard and the ISO 9241-151:2008 Standard. We hope the situation will improve as the use of standards in the development of mobile applications increases and as the ISO 9241 series of standards evolves.

Description, Usage Documentation, and Management of Patterns

For patterns to continue being useful as a source of guidance and knowledge, they must be adequately described, freely available, readily findable, and evolve with the needs of the mobile domain. Also, their use and misuse must be duly documented. To that regard, there is much to be done in the area of offering a suitable description, including representation and presentation of patterns.

It could be useful to have a mobile access to conventional repositories of patterns. Indeed, patterns for mobile applications can themselves be useful in developing such mobile applications, leading to a naturally-occurring synergistical relationship (Kamthan, 2008a).

CONCLUSION

The future of mobility depends on the quality of mobile applications that can be delivered. A disciplined and methodical approach towards the development of a mobile application is necessary for the productivity of engineers, for the longevity of the application, and for its acceptance by the end-users. A systematic and lasting view towards quality, and means for addressing it, are essential to this vision. POMWEM presents a direction to realize that.

It is known that any commitment to quality involves social, technical, and even political trade-offs. POMWEM is no exception. Indeed, as shown in this chapter, an integration of patterns in a mobile application development process is neither free, nor automatic.

In conclusion, the time- and technology-invariance of patterns enables us to duly plan a pattern-oriented approach that can lead to mobile applications with sustainable architecture and design. From a value-based perspective (Biffl et al., 2006) to Mobile Web Engineering, an initial investment in a quality-centric approach to mobile applications using patterns is in interest of all stakeholders where the benefits can outweigh the costs in the long-term.

REFERENCES

Abrahamsson, P., Hanhineva, A., Hulkko, H., Ihme, T., Jäälinoja, J., Korkala, M., et al. (2004, October 24-28). *Mobile-D: An Agile Approach for Mobile Application Development*. ACM SIGPLAN Conference on Object-Oriented Programming, Systems, Languages, and Applications (OOPSLA 2004), Vancouver, Canada, 2004.

Ahlgren, R., & Markkula, J. (2005, June 13-15). *Design Patterns and Organisational Memory in Mobile Application Development*. The Sixth International Conference on Product Focused Software Process Improvement (PROFES 2005), Oulu, Finland, 2005.

Ahluwalia, K. S., & Jain, A. (2006, October 21-23). *High Availability Design Patterns*. The Thirteenth Conference on Pattern Languages of Programs (PLoP 2006), Portland, USA, 2006.

Ballard, B. (2007). *Designing the Mobile User Experience*. Hoboken, NJ: John Wiley and Sons.

Beck, K., & Andres, C. (2005). *Extreme Programming Explained: Embrace Change* (2nd Edition). Reading, MA: Addison-Wesley.

Biffl, S., Aurum, A., Boehm, B., Erdogmus, H., & Grünbacher, P. (2006). *Value-Based Software Engineering*. Berlin: Springer-Verlag.

Buchanan, G., Farrant, S., Jones, M., Thimbleby, H., Marsden, G., & Pazzani, M. (2001). Improving Mobile Internet Usability. *The Tenth International World Wide Web Conference* (WWW10), Hong Kong, China, May 1-5, 2001.

Buschmann, F., Henney, K., & Schmidt, D. C. (2007a). *Pattern-Oriented Software Architecture, Volume 4: A Pattern Language for Distributed Computing*. Hoboken, NJ: John Wiley and Sons.

Buschmann, F., Henney, K., & Schmidt, D. C. (2007b). *Pattern-Oriented Software Architecture, Volume 5: On Patterns and Pattern Languages*. Hoboken, NJ: John Wiley and Sons.

Buschmann, F., Meunier, R., Rohnert, H., Sommerlad, P., & Stal, M. (1996). *Pattern Oriented Software Architecture, Volume 1: A System of Patterns*. Hoboken, NJ: John Wiley and Sons.

Busse, D. (2002, April 21,). *Usable Web Design Patterns for World-Ready E-Commerce Sites*. CHI Workshop on Patterns in Practice: A Workshop for UI Designers, Minneapolis, USA.

Chan, S., & Fang, X. (2001). *Usability Issues in Mobile Commerce*. The Seventh Americas Conference in Information Systems (AMCIS 2001), Boston, USA, August 5-8, 2001.

Chan, S. S., Fang, X., Brzezinski, J., Zhou, Y., Shuang, X., & Lam, J. (2002). Usability for Mobile Commerce across Multiple Form Factors. *Journal of Electronic Commerce Research, 3*(3), 187–199.

Christopoulou, E. (2008). Context as a Necessity in Mobile Applications. In J. Lumsden (Ed.), *Handbook of Research on User Interface Design and Evaluation for Mobile Technology* (Vol. I, pp. 187-204). Hershey, PA: IGI Global.

Coyle, F. (2001). Wireless Web: A Manager's Guide. Reading, MA: Addison-Wesley.

Dey, A. K., & Häkkilä, J. (2008). Context-Awareness and Mobile Devices. In J. Lumsden (Ed.), *Handbook of Research on User Interface Design and Evaluation for Mobile Technology* (Vol. I, pp. 205-217). Hershey, PA: IGI Global.

Dromey, R. G. (2003). Software Quality - Prevention Versus Cure? *Software Quality Journal, 11*(3), 197–210. doi:10.1023/A:1025162610079

Feldman, S. (2000). Mobile Commerce for the Masses. *IEEE Internet Computing, 4*(6), 74–75.

Fenton, N. E., & Pfleeger, S. L. (1997). *Software Metrics: A Rigorous & Practical Approach*. New York: International Thomson Computer Press.

Fernandez, E. B., Larrondo-Petrie, M. M., Sorgente, T., & Vanhilst, M. (2007). A Methodology to Develop Secure Systems Using Patterns. In H. Mouratidis & P. Giorgini (Eds.), *Integrating Security and Software Engineering: Advances and Future Vision,* (pp. 107-126). Hershey, PA: Idea Group.

Finkelstein, A., & Savigni, A. (2001, May 14). *A Framework for Requirements Engineering for Context-Aware Services.* The First International Workshop from Software Requirements to Architectures (STRAW 2001), Toronto, Canada, 2001.

Gamma, E., Helm, R., Johnson, R., & Vlissides, J. (1995). *Design Patterns: Elements of Reusable Object-Oriented Software.* Reading, MA: Addison-Wesley.

Ghosh, A. K., & Swaminatha, T. M. (2001). Software Security and Privacy Risks in Mobile E-Commerce. *Communications of the ACM, 44*(2), 51–57. doi:10.1145/359205.359227

Gong, J., & Tarasewich, P. (2004). *Guidelines for Handheld Mobile Device Interface Design.* The Thirty Fifth Annual Meeting of the Decision Sciences Institute (DSI 2004), Boston, USA, November 20-23, 2004.

Gorlenko, L., & Merrick, R. (2003). No Wires Attached: Usability Challenges in the Connected Mobile World. *IBM Systems Journal, 42*(4), 639–651.

Harper, S., & Yesilada, Y. (2008). Web Accessibility: A Foundation for Research. Berlin: Springer-Verlag.

Heyes, I. S. (2002). *Just Enough Wireless Computing*. Reading, MA: Prentice-Hall.

Hjelm, J. (2000). *Designing Wireless Information Services*. New York: John Wiley and Sons.

Ihme, T., & Abrahamsson, P. (2005). *The Use of Architectural Patterns in the Agile Software Development of Mobile Applications.* The 2005 International Conference on Agility (ICAM 2005), Otaniemi, Finland, July 27-28, 2005.

Jacobson, I., Booch, G., & Rumbaugh, J. (1999). *The Unified Software Development Process.* Reading, MA: Addison-Wesley.

Jaokar, A. (2006). *Mobile Web 2.0: The Innovator's Guide to Developing and Marketing Next Generation Wireless/Mobile Applications*. London: Futuretext.

Javahery, H. (2006). *Pattern-Oriented UI Design based on User Experiences: A Method Supported by Empirical Evidence*. Ph.D. Thesis, Concordia University, Canada.

Jones, M., & Marsden, G. (2006). *Mobile Interaction Design*. Hoboken, NJ: John Wiley and Sons.

Kamthan, P. (2007a). Accessibility of Mobile Applications. In D. Taniar (Ed.), *Encyclopedia of Mobile Computing and Commerce*, (Vol. 2). Hershey, PA: Idea Group Publishing.

Kamthan, P. (2007b). Addressing the Credibility of Mobile Applications. In D. Taniar (Ed.), *Encyclopedia of Mobile Computing and Commerce*, (Vol. 2). Hershey, PA: Idea Group Publishing.

Kamthan, P. (2008a). A Situational Methodology for Addressing the Pragmatic Quality of Web Applications by Integration of Patterns. *Journal of Web Engineering, 7*(1), 70–92.

Kamthan, P. (2008b). Towards High-Quality Mobile Applications by a Systematic Integration of Patterns. *Journal of Mobile Multimedia, 4*(3/4), 165–184.

Kappel, G., Pröll, B., Reich, S., & Retschitzegger, W. (2006). *Web Engineering*. Hoboken, NJ: John Wiley and Sons.

Lyardet, F., Rossi, G., & Schwabe, D. (1999). *Patterns for Adding Search Capabilities to Web Information Systems*. The Fourth European Conference on Pattern Languages of Programming and Computing (EuroPLoP 1999), Irsee, Germany, July 8-10, 1999.

Mahmoud, Q. H., & Maamar, Z. (2006). Engineering Wireless Mobile Applications. *International Journal of Information Technology and Web Engineering, 1*(1), 59–75.

Mallick, M. (2003). *Mobile and Wireless Design Essentials*. Hoboken, NJ: John Wiley and Sons.

Manolescu, D., & Kunzle, A. (2001, September 11-15). *Several Patterns for eBusiness Applications*. The Eighth Conference on Pattern Languages of Programs (PLoP 2001), Monticello, VA.

Mauney, D. W., & Masterton, C. (2008). Small-Screen Interfaces. In P. Kortum (Ed.), *HCI Beyond the GUI Design for Haptic, Speech, Olfactory, and Other Nontraditional Interfaces,* (pp. 307-358). San Francisco: Morgan Kaufmann.

Mazhelis, O., Markkula, J., & Jakobsson, M. (2005, June 13-15). *Specifying Patterns for Mobile Application Domain Using General Architectural Components*. The Sixth International Conference on Product Focused Software Process Improvement (PROFES 2005), Oulu, Finland.

Mendes, E., & Mosley, N. (2006). *Web Engineering*. Berlin: Springer-Verlag.

Mennecke, B. E., & Strader, T. J. (2003). *Mobile Commerce: Technology, Theory, and Applications*. Hershey, PA: Idea Group Publishing.

Meszaros, G., & Doble, J. (1998). A Pattern Language for Pattern Writing. In R. C. Martin, D. Riehle, & F. Buschmann (Eds.), *Pattern Languages of Program Design 3,* (pp. 529-574). Reading, MA: Addison-Wesley.

Morville, P., & Rosenfeld, L. (2006). *Information Architecture for the World Wide Web,* (3rd Ed.). Sebastopol, CA: O'Reilly Media.

Nelson, H. J., & Monarchi, D. E. (2007). Ensuring the Quality of Conceptual Representations. *Software Quality Journal, 15*(2), 213–233. doi:10.1007/s11219-006-9011-2

Nguyen, H. Q., Johnson, R., & Hackett, M. (2003). *Testing Applications on the Web: Test Planning for Mobile and Internet-Based Systems* (2nd Ed.). Hoboken, NJ: John Wiley and Sons.

Noble, J., & Weir, C. (2001). *A Window in Your Pocket: Some Small Patterns for User Interfaces*. The Sixth European Conference on Pattern Languages of Programs (EuroPLoP 2001), Irsee, Germany, July 4-8, 2001.

O'Reilly, T. (2005, September 30). *What Is Web 2.0: Design Patterns and Business Models for the Next Generation of Software*. Sebastopol, CA: O'Reilly Network.

Ocampo, A., Boggio, D., Münch, J., & Palladino, G. (2003). Towards a Reference Process for Developing Wireless Internet Services. *IEEE Transactions on Software Engineering, 29*(12), 1122–1134. doi:10.1109/TSE.2003.1265526

Paavilainen, J. (2002). *Mobile Business Strategies: Understanding the Technologies and Opportunities*. Reading, MA: Addison-Wesley.

Pirolli, P. (2007). *Information Foraging Theory: Adaptive Interaction with Information*. Oxford, UK: Oxford University Press.

Risi, W. A., & Rossi, G. (2004). An Architectural Pattern Catalog for Mobile Web Information Systems. *International Journal of Mobile Communications*, *2*(3), 235–247.

Rossi, G., Pastor, O., Schwabe, D., & Olsina, L. (2008). *Web Engineering: Modelling and Implementing Web Applications*. Berlin: Springer-Verlag.

Roth, J. (2001, September 10). *Patterns of Mobile Interaction*. Third International Workshop on Human Computer Interaction with Mobile Devices (Mobile HCI 2001), Lille, France.

Roth, J. (2002). Patterns of Mobile Interaction. *Personal and Ubiquitous Computing*, *6*(4), 282–289. doi:10.1007/s007790200029

Salmre, I. (2005). *Writing Mobile Code: Essential Software Engineering for Building Mobile Applications*. Reading, MA: Addison-Wesley.

Schmettow, M. (2005, September 13). *Towards a Pattern Based Usability Inspection Method for Industrial Practitioners*. The INTERACT 2005 Workshop on Integrating Software Engineering and Usability Engineering, Rome, Italy.

Schmidt, D. C., Stal, M., Rohnert, H., & Buschmann, F. (2000). *Pattern-Oriented Software Architecture, Volume 2: Patterns for Concurrent and Networked Objects*. Hoboken, NJ: John Wiley and Sons.

Schümmer, T., & Lukosch, S. (2007). *Patterns for Computer-Mediated Interaction*. Chichester, UK: John Wiley and Sons.

Shanks, G. (1999, September 29). *Semiotic Approach to Understanding Representation in Information Systems. Information Systems Foundations Workshop*, Sydney, Australia.

Sharp, H., Galal, G. H., & Finkelstein, A. (1999, August 30-September 3). *Stakeholder Identification in the Requirements Engineering Process*. The Tenth International Conference and Workshop on Database and Expert Systems Applications (DEXA 1999), Florence, Italy.

Simon, H. (1996). *The Sciences of the Artificial* (Third Edition). Cambridge, MA: The MIT Press.

Spriestersbach, A., & Springer, T. (2004). Quality Attributes in Mobile Web Application Development. In F. Bomarius & H. Iida (Eds.) *Product Focused Software Process Improvement* (pp. 120-130). Berlin: Springer-Verlag.

Stanoevska-Slabeva, K. (2003, June 16-21). Towards a Reference Model for M-Commerce Applications. *The Eleventh European Conference on Information Systems (ECIS 2003)*, Naples, Italy.

Tarasewich, P. (2003). Designing Mobile Commerce Applications. *Communications of the ACM*, *46*(12), 57–60. doi:10.1145/953460.953489

Tidwell, J. (2006). *Designing Interfaces: Patterns for Effective Interaction Design*. Sebastopol, CA: O'Reilly Media.

Trewin, S. (2006, May 22). *Physical Usability and the Mobile Web*. The 2006 International Cross-Disciplinary Workshop on Web Accessibility 2006 (W4A 2006), Edinburgh, Scotland.

Van Duyne, D. K., Landay, J., & Hong, J. I. (2003). *The Design of Sites: Patterns, Principles, and Processes for Crafting a Customer-Centered Web Experience*. Reading, MA: Addison-Wesley.

Vanderdonckt, J. (1999). Development Milestones towards a Tool for Working with Guidelines . *Interacting with Computers*, *12*(2), 81–118. doi:10.1016/S0953-5438(99)00019-3

Varshney, U., & Vetter, R. (2002). Mobile Commerce: Framework, Applications and Networking Support. *Mobile Networks and Applications*, 7(3), 185–198. doi:10.1023/A:1014570512129

Weiss, S. (2002). *Handheld Usability*. Chichester, UK: John Wiley and Sons.

Yacoub, S. M., & Ammar, H. H. (2003). Pattern-Oriented Analysis and Design: Composing Patterns to Design Software Systems. Chichester, UK: Addison-Wesley.

Yoder, J., & Barcalow, J. (1997, September 3-5). *Architectural Patterns for Enabling Application Security. The Fourth Conference on Pattern Languages of Programs (PLoP 1997)*, Monticello, VA.

Zajicek, M. (2007, May 7-8). *Web 2.0: Hype or Happiness? The 2007 International Cross-Disciplinary Workshop on Web Accessibility (W4A 2007)*, Banff, Canada.

KEY TERMS AND DEFINITIONS

Delivery Context: A set of attributes that characterizes the capabilities of the access mechanism, the preferences of the user and other aspects of the context into which a resource is to be delivered.

Mobile Web 2.0: The evolution of the Mobile Web in a direction that is driven by collective intelligence, realized by information technology, and characterized by user participation, openness, and network effects.

Mobile Web Engineering: A discipline concerned with the establishment and use of sound scientific, engineering, and management principles, and disciplined and systematic approaches to the successful development, deployment, and maintenance of 'high-quality' mobile applications.

Pattern: An empirically proven solution to a recurring problem in a given context.

Personalization: An individualization strategy that enables delivery that is customized to the user and user's environment.

Semiotics: The field of study of communication of signs and their representations.

User Profile: An information container describing user needs, goals, and preferences.

Chapter 14
Combinatorial Testing

Renée C. Bryce
Utah State University, USA

Yu Lei
University of Texas, Arlington, USA

D. Richard Kuhn
National Institute of Standards and Technology, USA

Raghu Kacker
National Institute of Standards and Technology, USA

ABSTRACT

Software systems today are complex and have many possible configurations. Products released with inadequate testing can cause bodily harm, result in large economic losses or security breaches, and affect the quality of day-to-day life. Software testers have limited time and budgets, frequently making it impossible to exhaustively test software. Testers often intuitively test for defects that they anticipate while less foreseen defects are overlooked. Combinatorial testing can complement their tests by systematically covering t-way interactions. Research in combinatorial testing includes two major areas (1) algorithms that generate combinatorial test suites and (2) applications of combinatorial testing. The authors review these two topics in this chapter.

I. INTRODUCTION

Software systems are complex and can incur exponential numbers of possible tests. Testing is expensive and trade-offs often exist to optimize the use of resources. Several systematic approaches to software testing have been proposed in the literature. Category partitioning is the base of all systematic approaches as finite values of parameters are identified for testing. Each of these finite parameter-values may be tested at least once, in specified combinations together, or in exhaustive combination. The simplest approach tests all values at least once. The most thorough approach exhaustively tests all parameter-value combinations. While testing only individual values may not be enough, exhaustive testing of all possible combinations is not always feasible. Combination strategies are a reasonable alternative that falls in between these two extremes.

DOI: 10.4018/978-1-60566-731-7.ch014

Table 1. Four parameters that have three possible settings each for an on-line store

Log-in Type	Member Status	Discount	Shipping
New member - not logged in	Guest	None	Standard (5-7 day)
New-member - logged in	Member	10% employee discount	Expedited (3-5 day)
Member - logged in	Employee	$5 off holiday discount	Overnight

Consider an on-line store that has four parameters of interest as shown in Table 1. There are three log-in types; three types of member status; three discount options; and three shipping options. Different end users may have different preferences and will likely use different combinations of these parameters. To exhaustively test all combinations of the four parameters that have 3 options each from Table 1 would require $3^4 = 81$ tests.

In this example, exhaustive testing requires 81 test cases, but pair-wise combinatorial testing uses only 9 test cases. Instead of testing every combination, all individual pairs of interactions are tested. The resulting test suite is shown in Table 2, and is contains only 9 tests. All pairs of combinations have been combined together at least once during the testing process. For instance, the first test from Table 2 covers the following pairs: (New member - not logged in, Guest), (New member - not logged in, $5 off holiday discount), (New member - not logged in, Standard (5-7 day)), (Guest, None), (Guest, Standard (5-7 day)), and (None, Standard (5-7 day)). The entire test suite covers every possible pairwise combination between components. This reduction in tests amplifies on larger systems - a system with 20 factors and 5 levels each would require $5^{20} = 95,367,431,640,625$ exhaustive tests! Pairwise combinatorial testing for 5^{20} can be achieved in as few as 45 tests.

II. BACKGROUND

Combinatorial testing is simple to apply. As a specification-based technique, combinatorial testing requires no knowledge about the implementation under test. Note that the specification required by some forms of combinatorial testing is lightweight, as it only needs to identify a set of parameters and their possible values. This is in contrast with other testing techniques that require a complex operational model of the system under test. Finally, assuming that the parameters and

Table 2. A pair-wise combinatorial test suite

Test No.	Log-in Type	Member Status	Discount	Shipping
1	New member - not logged in	Guest	None	Standard (5-7 day)
2	New member - not logged in	Member	10% employee discount	Expedited (3-5 day)
3	New member - not logged in	Employee	$5 off holiday discount	Overnight
4	New-member - logged in	Guest	$5 off holiday discount	Expedited (3-5 day)
5	New-member - logged in	Member	None	Overnight
6	New-member - logged in	Employee	10% employee discount	Standard (5-7 day)
7	Member - logged in	Guest	10% employee discount	Overnight
8	Member - logged in	Member	$5 off holiday discount	Standard (5-7 day)
9	Member - logged in	Employee	None	Expedited (3-5 day)

values are properly identified, the actual combination generation process can be fully automated, which is a key to industrial acceptance.

In this section, we review applications of combinatorial testing. Two major research themes exist on the empirical effectiveness of combinatorial testing:

1. *What measures of effectiveness exist for combinatorial testing?*
2. How much combinatorial testing is enough? (i.e.: what is largest number of variables which may be involved in failures)

Combinatorial testing is based on the premise that many errors in software can only arise from the interaction of two or more parameters. A number of studies have investigated the application of combinatorial methods to software testing (Burr 1998; Cohen 1997; Dunietz 1997; Kuhn 2002; Kuhn 2004; Wallace 2001; Williams 2001; Yilmaz 2006). Early research focused on pairwise testing, i.e., testing all 2-way combinations of parameter values, thus exercising all interactions between parameters or components at least once. Some of these were designed to determine the degree of test coverage obtained using combinatorial methods, e.g. (Dunietz 1997), (Cohen 1996). These studies use code coverage, rather than fault detection, to measure the effectiveness of combinatorial testing. They show that combinatorial methods can produce coverage results that are comparable or better than other test schemes. Code coverage is an important metric, but only an indirect one. Testers seek to detect faults in an application, so a direct measure of effectiveness for a test method is the fault detection rate.

Many studies demonstrated the effectiveness of pairwise testing in a variety of applications. But what if some failure is triggered only by a very unusual combination of more than two values? What degree of interaction occurs in real failures in real systems? Studies that investigated the distribution of t-way faults are summarized in Figure

1 and Table 3 (Kuhn 2002; Kuhn 2004). As can be seen from the data, across a variety of domains, all failures could be triggered by a maximum of 4-way to 6-way interactions. Figure 1 shows that the detection rate increases rapidly with interaction strength. With the server, for example, 42% of the failures were triggered by only a single parameter value, 70% by 2-way combinations, and 89% by 3-way combinations. The detection rate curves for the other applications are similar, reaching 100% detection with 4 to 6-way interactions. That is, six or fewer variables were involved in all failures for the applications studied, so 6-way testing could in practice detect nearly all of the failures. So far we have not seen a failure from combinatorial interaction involving more than six variables. While not conclusive, these results suggest that combinatorial testing which exercises high strength interaction combinations can be an effective approach to software assurance. Much more empirical work will be needed to understand the effectiveness of combinatorial testing in different domains. Note that the detection rate at different interaction strengths varies widely for the studies shown in Figure 1. Additional research will help determine the extent to which these limited results can be generalized to other types of software.

III. TOOLS THAT GENERATE COMBINATORIAL TEST SUITES

Three main types of algorithms construct combinatorial test suites: algebraic, greedy, or heuristic search algorithms. A high-level overview of the major advantages and disadvantages of the algorithms that construct combinatorial test suites include:

1. *Algebraic methods* offer efficient constructions in regards to time; however, it is difficult to produce accurate results on a broad and general variety of inputs with algebraic

Figure 1. Fault detection at interaction strengths 1 to 6 (Source: Kuhn 2004; Bell 2006)

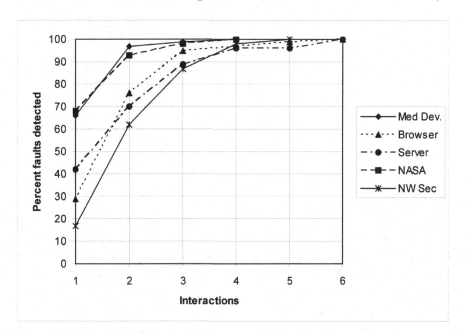

methods. (See Colbourn 2004 and references given therein.)

2. *Greedy algorithms* are a well-studied type of algorithm for the construction of covering arrays because they have been found to be relatively efficient in regards to time and accuracy (Bryce 2007; Bryce to appear; Cohen 1996; Cohen 1997; Lei 2008; Tai 2002; Tung 2000).

3. *Heuristic search*, particularly through the application of Simulated Annealing (SA) has provided the most accurate results in several instances to date. This local search method has provided many of the smallest test suites for different system configurations; however, at a cost in execution time to generate test suites (Cohen 2008).

We refer the reader to the papers above for more details of these algorithms and here we include an overview of a freely available research tool, called FireEye, to generate combinatorial test suites. The IPOG algorithm was first proposed for pairwise testing (Tai 2002), and was later extended

Table 3. Percent fault detection at interaction strengths 1 to 6 (Source: Kuhn 2004; Bell 2006)

Interaction strength	Med Devices	Browser	Server	NASA Database	Network Security
1	66%	29%	42%	68%	17%
2	97	76	70	93	62
3	99	95	89	98	87
4	100	97	96	100	98
5	100	99	96	100	100
6	100	100	100	100	100

Figure 2. Illustration of IPO

P1	P2
0	0
0	1
1	0
1	1

(a)

P1	P2	P3
0	0	0
0	1	1
1	0	2
1	1	0

(b)

P1	P2	P3
0	0	0
0	1	1
1	0	2
1	1	0
0	1	2
1	0	1

(c)

to general t-way combinatorial testing (Lei 2008). The FireEye tool implements the general version of the IPOG algorithm, called IPOG (Lei 2008). We provide both an overview of the algorithm and screenshots of the tool that uses the algorithm. Thus the readers have an example that helps them to build their own test suites.

Overview of IPOG

The general framework of the IPOG algorithm can be described as follows: For a system with at least t parameters, the IPOG strategy first builds a t-way test set for the first t parameters, it then extends the test set to a t-way test set for the first $t + 1$ parameters, and then continues to extend the test set until it builds a t-way test set for all the parameters. The extension of an existing t-way test set for an additional parameter begins with horizontal growth, which extends each existing test by adding one value for the new parameter. The t-way tuples covered by the addition of those new values are tracked and removed from the set of uncovered tuples. Note that horizontal growth does not add any new tests, but only extends the existing ones. After horizontal growth, if all the tuples have not yet been covered the test set is extended vertically, i.e., new tests are added to cover the remaining tuples. The IPOG algorithm utilizes local optimums to provide a bound of accuracy for worst case scenarios.

In the following we use an example system to illustrate the working of the IPO algorithm. This example system consists of three parameters P_1, P_2, and P_3, where P_1, and P_2 have two values 0 and 1, and P_3 has three values 0, 1, and 2. Figure 2 shows the construction of a 2-way test set for the example system using the IPO algorithm.

The IPO algorithm first builds a 2-way test set for the first two parameters P_1 and P_2, which is shown in Figure 2 (a). This test set simply contains 4 tests, each of which is one possible combination of values of P_1 and P_2. Next, this test set is extended to cover parameter P_3. In order to cover P_3, we only need to cover all the combinations involving P_3 and P_1 and those involving P_3 and P_2. This is because all the combinations involving P_1 and P_2 have already been covered. There are in total 12 combinations to cover: 6 combinations involve P_3 and P_1, and 6 combinations involve P_3 and P_2. Those combinations are covered in the following two steps:

- *Horizontal growth*: This step extends each of the four existing tests by adding a value for the P3, as shown in Figure 2 (b). These values are chosen in a greedy manner. That is, each value is chosen and added into a test such that it covers the most combinations that have not been covered yet. In Figure 2 (b), the four existing tests are extended with values 0, 1, 2, 0, respectively, each of which covers two new combinations. Note that since there are only three parameters, adding a value of P3 can cover at most two combinations. For example, the 1st test is extended with 0, which covers two new combinations $\{(P_1.0, P_3.0), (P_2.0, P_3.0)\}$. Note that adding value 1 or 2 into the 1st test also covers two new combinations. In this case, the tie is broken arbitrarily for value 0. As another example, the last test is extended with value 0, which covers two new combinations combinations $\{(P_1.1, P_3.0), (P_2.1, P_3.0)\}$. If the fourth test was extended with value 1 or 2, it would only cover one new combination. This is because $(P_2.1, P_3.1)$ (or $(P_1.1, P_3.2)$) has already been covered in the second test (or in the third test) when it is extended with value 1 (or value 2).

- *Vertical growth*: This step adds two new tests to cover the remaining uncovered combinations, as shown in Figure 2 (c). After horizontal growth, there are four combinations that have not been covered yet: $\{(P_1.0, P_3.2), (P_1.1, P_3.1), (P_2.0, P_3.1), (P_2.1, P_3.2)\}$. To cover $(P_1.0, P_3.2)$, we add a new test $(P_1.0, P_2.*, P_3.2)$, where P2.* indicates that the value of P2 is not determined yet. To cover $(P_1.1, P_3.1)$, we add a new test $(P_1.1, P_2.*, P_3.1)$. To cover $(P_2.0, P_3.1)$, we change the value of P2 from * to 0 in the last test. To cover $(P_2.1, P_3.2)$, we change the value of P2 from * to 1 in the 5th test. At this point, we have covered all the 2-way combinations, and thus have built a pairwise test set for the example system.

Due to space limitation, the readers are referred to (Lei 2008) for a detailed presentation of the IPO algorithm.

Generating a Combinatorial Test Suite with FireEye

The FireEye tool implements the IPOG algorithm to generate combinatorial test suites for users. Consider the input from Table 1 which has four parameters: *Log-in type, Member status, Discount, and Shipping*. Each of these parameters can take on one of three possible options. The FireEye tool can generate a combinatorial test suite for this input. Users enter the parameters and their possible values and FireEye then automatically generates a *t*-way test suite, where *t* is the strength of coverage that the user specifies. Figure 3 provides an example of the input from Table 1. The user entered the parameters and values on the left side of the window. The right side shows a summary of the parameters and values that have been entered. The user may additionally specify relations or constraints on other tabs from this window if there are combinations of parameters and values that can only occur together, or can not be combined together. The user may then choose to save the data that they enter on this screen and choose to generate a combinatorial test suite. In this example, we choose for FireEye to build a pairwise combinatorial test suite. The test suite is shown in Figure 4. (Note that the asterisks in the test cases are "don't care" values, meaning that a tester can use any option for a parameter and still cover all pairwise combinations.) The test suite can be saved in multiple formats for testing purposes. Figure 5 shows an subset of the test case from our example in XML format. The left side of the figure shows that the parameters and values are saved in a simple format and the right side shows a few tests in XML format.

IV. RESEARCH DIRECTIONS

In this section, we will discuss research directions of both algorithms and applications. We can

Figure 3. Example inputs to FireEye

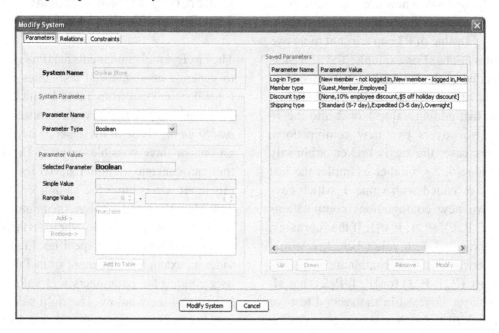

Figure 4. Example Combinatorial Test Suite created with FireEye

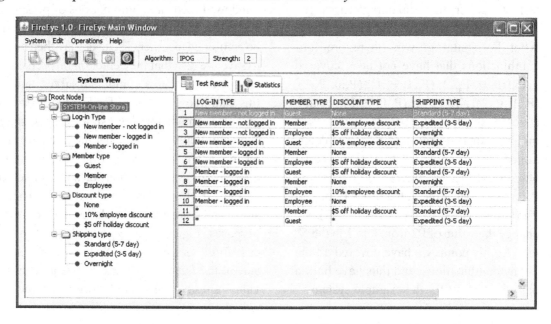

categorize these issues as algorithms for *t*-way combinatorial testing and approaches to the application of combinatorial testing.

Algorithms for *t*-way Combinatorial Testing

Combinatorial test suites can also provide higher strength *t*-way coverage. Generating covering

Figure 5. An abbreviated example of a test case in XML format

Sample of Abbreviated Output of the first two parameters and values from the test suite in Figure 4, using XML formatted output	Sample of Abbrevieted Output of the first three test cases from the test suite in Figure 4, using XML formatted output

`<?xml version="1.0" encoding="UTF-8" ?>`
`<System name="On-line Store">`
`<Parameters>`
`<Parameter id="1" name="Log-in Type" type="1">`
`<values>`
`<value>New member - not logged in</value>`
`<value>New member - logged in</value>`
`<value>Member - logged in</value>`
`</values>`
`</Parameter>`
`<Parameter id="2" name="Member type" type="1">`
`<values>`
`<value>Guest</value>`
`<value>Member</value>`
`<value>Employee</value>`
`</values>`
`</Parameter>`
`...`
	`<Testcase TCNo="0">`
	`<Value>1</Value>`
	`<Value>New member - not logged in</Value>`
	`<Value>Guest</Value>`
	`<Value>None</Value>`
	`<Value>Standard (5-7 day)</Value>`
	`</Testcase>`
	`<Testcase TCNo="1">`
	`<Value>2</Value>`
	`<Value>New member - not logged in</Value>`
	`<Value>Member</Value>`
	`<Value>10% employee discount</Value>`
	`<Value>Expedited (3-5 day)</Value>`
	`</Testcase>`
	`<Testcase TCNo="2">`
	`<Value>3</Value>`
	`<Value>New member - not logged in</Value>`
	`<Value>Employee</Value>`
	`<Value>$5 off holiday discount</Value>`
	`<Value>Overnight</Value>`
	`</Testcase>`

arrays of higher *t*-way coverage can consume significant computational resources and produce large results. For instance, Table 5 shows a sample of inputs and the combinatorial growth of tuples that occur as *t* increases. The input 3^{13} (read as 13 parameters have 3 possible values each) includes 702 pairs, 7,722 triples, and reaches over a million 6-tuples. As the size of the tuples and their number increase, the size of corresponding test suites increase. Managing this combinatorial growth with regard to both accuracy and execution time is still an open research issue.

The majority of algorithms for combinatorial testing focus on the special case of 2-way combinatorial testing. Two greedy algorithms recently appeared for *t*-way combinatorial testing (Bryce to appear; Lei 2008). However, the efficient generation of *t*-way combinatorial test suites remains an ongoing research topic.

Approaches for Combinatorial Testing

There are basically two approaches to combinatorial testing – use combinations of *configuration* parameter values, or combinations of *input* parameter values. In the first case, the covering array is used to select values of configurable parameters, possibly with the same tests run against all configuration combinations. For example, a

Table 5. A sample of the exponential growth of t-tuples as t increases

	10^4	3^{13}	11^{16}
$t=2$	600	702	14,520
$t=3$	4,000	7,722	745,360
$t=4$	10,000	57,915	26,646,620
$t=5$	10,000	312,741	703,470,768
$t=6$	10,000	1,250,954	1,301,758,600
$t=7$	10,000	1,594,323	45,949,729,863,572,200

server might be tested by setting up all 4-way combinations of configuration parameters such as number of simultaneous connections allowed, memory, OS, database size, etc., with the same test suite run against each configuration.

In the second approach, the covering array is used to select input data values, which then become part of complete test cases, creating a test suite for the application. Applying this form of combinatorial testing to real-world software presents a significant challenge: for higher degree interactions, a very large number of tests can be required. Thousands of tests may be needed to cover all 4-way to 6-way combinations for many typical applications, and for each test, the expected result from the application under test must be determined. Approaches to solving this "oracle problem" for combinatorial testing include:

Crash testing: the easiest and least expensive approach is to simply run tests against the system under test (SUT) to check whether any unusual combination of input values causes a crash or other easily detectable failure. This approach clearly produces limited information – a bookstore application that crashes is clearly faulty, but one that runs and produces incorrect results may cost the e-commerce firm its business. Crash testing using combinatorial methods can be an inexpensive yet thorough basic method of checking a system's reaction to rare input combinations that might take months or years to occur in normal operation.

Embedded assertions: An increasingly popular "light-weight formal methods" technique

is to embed assertions within code to ensure proper relationships between data, for example as preconditions, post-conditions, or input value checks. Tools such as the Java Modeling language (JML) (Leavens 1999) can be used to introduce very complex assertions, effectively embedding a formal specification within the code. The embedded assertions serve as an executable form of the specification, thus providing an oracle for the testing phase. With embedded assertions, exercising the application with all *t*-way combinations can provide reasonable assurance that the code works correctly across a very wide range of inputs. This approach has been used successfully for testing smart cards detecting 80% - 90% of application faults (du Bousquet 2004).

Model-checker based test generation uses a mathematical model of the SUT and a model checker to generated expected results for each input. Conceptually, the model checker can be viewed as exploring all states of a system model to determine if a property claimed in a specification statement is true. What makes a model checker particularly valuable is that if the claim is false, the model checker not only reports this, but also provides a "counterexample" showing how the claim can be shown false. If the claim is false, the model checker indicates this and provides a trace of parameter input values and states that will prove it is false. In effect this is a complete test case, i.e., a set of parameter values and expected result. It is then simple to map these values into complete test cases in the syntax needed for the

Figure 6. A process for model-checker based test generation with covering arrays

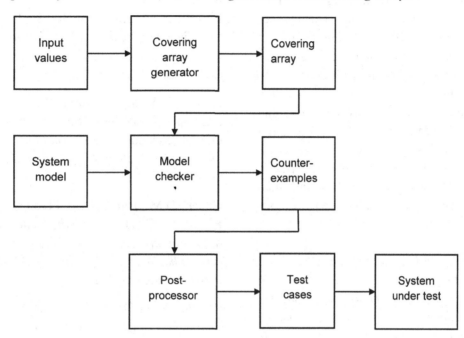

system under test (Ammann 1999). This process is illustrated in Figure 6.

V. FUTURE AND INTERNATIONAL IMPACT

Combinatorial testing has attracted a lot of attention from both academia and industry. Several studies have indicated that combinatorial testing could dramatically reduce the number of tests while remaining effective for detecting software faults. Moreover, combinatorial testing is relatively easy to apply. As a black-box technique, combinatorial testing does not require analysis of source code, which is often difficult for practical applications. To apply combinatorial testing, a set of parameters, as well as their possible values, need to be identified. This information is often much easier to obtain than an operational model as required by many other black-box techniques. After the parameters and their values are identified, the actual test generation process can be

fully automated, which is the key to industrial acceptance.

Combinatorial testing research has made significant progress in recent years, and continues to make progress every day, especially in the directions outlined in the previous section. With these progresses, combinatorial testing is expected to be fully integrated with the existing testing processes and become an important tool in the toolbox of software practitioners. The wide use of combinatorial testing will help to significantly reduce the cost of software testing while increasing software quality. It will also improve the productivity of software developers by reducing the time and effort they spend on testing.

VI. CONCLUSION

Software is growing in complexity. This poses a challenge to testers since there are often more combinations of system settings than there is time for testing. Combinatorial testing is an approach that can systematically examine system settings in a manageable number of tests. This chapter provides a summary of the different types of algorithms that exist to efficiently generate tests. This provides readers not only with one example of how test suites can be constructed, but they are also pointed to a publicly available tool that generates tests. Further, we provide a discussion of empirical studies that reveal the effectiveness of combinatorial testing for different types of applications. These studies show how and when to apply the techniques, but also open questions for future research.

Certain commercial equipment or materials are identified in this paper. Such identification is not intended to imply recommendation or endorsement by NIST, nor is it intended to imply that the equipment or materials identified are necessarily the best available for the purpose.

The FireEye tool has been renamed as ACTS (Advanced Combinatorial Test Suites); an executable version of ACTS tool can be obtained from kuhn@nist.gov

REFERENCES

Ammann, P., & Black, P. E. (1999). Abstracting Formal Specifications to Generate Software Tests via Model Checking. *IEEE 18th Digital Avionics Systems Conference, 2*(10), 1-10.

Bell, K. Z. (2006). *Optimizing Effectiveness and Efficiency of Software Testing: a Hybrid Approach.* PhD Dissertation, North Carolina State University.

Bryce, R., & Colbourn, C. J. (2007). The Density Algorithm for Pairwise Interaction Testing. *Journal of Software Testing. Verification and Reliability, 17*(3), 159–182. doi:10.1002/stvr.365

Bryce, R., & Colbourn, C. J. (2009). A Density-Based Greedy Algorithm for Higher Strength Covering Arrays. *Journal of Software Testing, Verification, and Reliability, 19*(1), 37-53. doi:10.1002/stvr.393

Burr, K., & Young, W. (1998). Combinatorial test techniques: Table-based automation, test generation, and code coverage. *International Conference on Software Testing Analysis and Review* (pp. 503-513).

Cohen, D.M., Dalal, S. R., Fredman, M. L., & Patton, G. C. (1996). *Method and system for automatically generating efficient test cases for systems having interacting elements* [United States Patent, Number 5, 542, 043].

Cohen, D. M., Dalal, S. R., Fredman, M. L., & Patton, G. C. (1997). The AETG system: an approach to testing based on combinatorial design. *IEEE Transactions on Software Engineering, 23*(7), 437–444. doi:10.1109/32.605761

Cohen, D. M., Dalal, S. R., Parelius, J., & Patton, G. C. (1996). The combinatorial design approach to automatic test generation. *IEEE Software, 13*(5), 83–88. doi:10.1109/52.536462

Cohen, M. B., Colbourn, C. J., Gibbons, P. B., & Mugridge, W. B. (2003). Constructing test suites for interaction testing. *International Conference on Software Engineering* (pp. 38-48).

Cohen, M. B., Colbourn, C. J., & Ling, A. C. H. (2008). Constructing Strength 3 Covering Arrays with Augmented Annealing. *Discrete Mathematics, 308,* 2709–2722. doi:10.1016/j.disc.2006.06.036

Colbourn, C. J. (2004). Combinatorial aspects of covering arrays. *Le Matematiche (Catania), 58,* 121–167.

Dalal, S. R., Jain, A., Karunanithi, N., Leaton, J. M., Lott, C. M., Patton, G. C., & Horowitz, B. M. (1999). Model-Based Testing in Practice. *International Conference on Software Engineering* (pp. 285-294).

du Bousquet, L., Ledru, Y., Maury, O., Oriat, C., & Lanet, J.-L. (2004). A case study in JML-based software validation. *IEEE International Conference on Automated Software Engineering* (pp. 294-297).

Dunietz, S. Ehrlich, W. K. Szablak, B. D. Mallows, C. L. & Iannino, A. (1997). Applying design of experiments to software testing. *International. Conference on Software Engineering* (pp. 205-215).

Fischer, R. A. (1926). The Arrangement of Field Experiments. *Journal of Ministry of Agriculture of Great Britain, 33*, 503–513.

Hartman, A., Klinger, T., & Raskin, L. (2008). *IBM Intelligent Test Case Handler*. Retrieved on August 30, 2008, from http://www.alphaworks.ibm.com/tech/whitch

Hartman, A., & Raskin, L. (2004). Problems and algorithms for covering arrays. *Discrete Mathematics, 284*, 149–156. doi:10.1016/j.disc.2003.11.029

Kuhn, D. R., & Reilly, M. (2002). An investigation of the applicability of design of experiments to software testing. *NASA Goddard/IEEE Software Engineering Workshop* (pp. 91-95).

Kuhn, D. R., Wallace, D., & Gallo, A. (2004). Software Fault Interactions and Implications for Software Testing. *IEEE Transactions on Software Engineering, 30*(6), 418–421. doi:10.1109/TSE.2004.24

Leavens, G. T., Baker, A. L., & Ruby, C. (1999). JML: A notation for detailed design. In H. Kilov, B. Rumpe, & I. Simmonds, (Ed.) *Behavioral Specifications of Businesses and Systems.*

Lei, Y. Kacker, R. Kuhn, D. R., Okun, V. & Lawrence J. (2008). IPOG/IPOD: Efficient Test Generation for Multi-Way Combinatorial Testing. *Journal of Software Testing, Verification, and Reliability, 18*(3), 125–148. doi:10.1002/stvr.381

Lei, Y., & Tai, K. C. (1998). In-parameter-order: a test generation strategy for pairwise testing. *International High-Assurance Systems Engineering Symposium* (pp. 254-261).

NIST. (2003). *The Economic Impacts of Inadequate Infrastructure for software testing.* Retrieved from http://www.nist.gov/director/prog-ofc/report02-3.pdf

Tai, K. C., & Lei, Y. (2002). A test generation strategy for pairwise testing. *IEEE Transactions on Software Engineering, 28*(1), 109–111. doi:10.1109/32.979992

Tung, Y. W., & Aldiwan, W. S. (2000). Automating test case generation for the new generation mission software system. *IEEE Aerospace Conference* (pp. 431-437).

Wallace, D. R., & Kuhn, D. R. (2001). Failure Modes in Medical Device Software: an Analysis of 15 Years of Recall Data. *International Journal of Reliability Quality and Safety Engineering, 8*(4). doi:10.1142/S021853930100058X

Williams, A., & Probert, R. L. (2001). A measure for component interaction test coverage. *ACS/IEEE International Conference on Computer Systems and Applications* (pp. 301-311).

Yilmaz, C., Cohen, M. B., & Porter, A. (2006). Covering arrays for efficient fault characterization in complex configuration spaces. *IEEE Transactions on Software Engineering, 32*(1), 20–34. doi:10.1109/TSE.2006.8

KEY TERMS AND DEFINITIONS

Covering Array: $CA_\lambda(N;t,k,v)$, is an N x k array. In every N x t subarray, each t-tuple occurs at least λ times. In combinatorial testing, t is the *strength* of the coverage of interactions, k is the number of components (degree), and v is the number of symbols for each component.

Covering Array Number (CAN): The size of a covering array, or a mixed-level covering array and is considered optimal when it is as small as possible.

Pairwise Combinatorial Testing: An interaction test in which the strength, t, is equal to two. Pair-wise permutations of factors are executed during testing.

Pseudo-Exhaustive Testing: The term used when interaction testing is considered effectively exhaustive. Interaction testing at levels of 4-way to 6-way coverage have been suggested to be pseudoexhaustive (Kuhn, Reilly 2002)

***n*-way Combinatorial Testing:** An interaction test in which the strength, t, is equal to a specified value n. Permutations of n-tuples of factors are executed during testing

Chapter 15
A Systematic Review of Distributed Software Development
Problems and Solutions

Miguel Jiménez
Alhambra-Eidos, Spain

Mario Piattini
University of Castilla-La Mancha, Spain

Aurora Vizcaíno
University of Castilla-La Mancha, Spain

ABSTRACT

In last years, software development activity tends to be decentralized, thus expanding greater development efforts towards more attractive zones for organizations. The type of development in which the team members are distributed in remote sites is called distributed software development (DSD). The main advantage of this practice is mainly that of having a greater availability of human resources in decentralized zones with less cost. On the other hand, organizations must face some disadvantages due to the distance that separates the development teams related to project organization, project control and product quality. Coordination becomes more difficult as the software components are sourced from different places, and new processes and tools are needed. This chapter presents a systematic review of the literature related to the problems of DSD with the purpose of obtaining a vision about the solutions proposed up to the present day.

1 INTRODUCTION

Nowadays, software industry tends to relocate their production units to decentralized zones with greater availability of skilled workforce, taking advantage of

politic and economic factors (Aspray, et al., 2006). The objective consists of optimizing resources in order to develop higher quality products at a lower cost than is in co-located developments. In this sense, Software Factories (Greenfield, et al., 2004)

DOI: 10.4018/978-1-60566-731-7.ch015

is an approach that, automate parts of software development by imitating industrial processes originally linked to more traditional sectors such as those of the automobile and aviation, decentralize production units, and promote the reusability of architectures, knowledge and components.

Distributed Software Development (DSD) allows the team members to be located in various remote sites during the software lifecycle, thus making up a network of distant sub-teams. In this context the traditional face-to-face meetings are no longer common and interaction between members requires the use of technology to facilitate communication and coordination.

The distance between the different teams can vary from a few meters (when the teams work in adjacent buildings) to different continents (Prikladnicki, et al., 2003). The situation in which the teams are distributed beyond the limits of a nation is called Global Software Development (GSD). This kind of scenario is interesting for several reasons (Herbsleb and Moitra, 2001), mainly because it enables organizations to abstract themselves from geographical distance, whilst having qualified human resources and minimizing cost (Werner, et al., 2001), increasing their market area by producing software for remote clients and obtaining a longer workday by taking advantage of time differences (Ebert & De Neve, 2001). On the other hand we must confront a number of problems (Layman, et al., 2006), caused mainly by distance and time and cultural differences (Krishna, et al., 2004), which depend largely on the specific characteristics of each organization.

In this context, "offshoring" refers to the transfer of an organizational function to another country, usually where human resources are cheaper. We speak about "nearshoring" when jobs are transferred to geographically closer countries, thus avoiding cultural and time differences between members and saving travel and communication costs. Outsourcing is a way to contract an external organization, independently of its location, instead of developing in-house (McConnell, 1996).

The aforementioned development practices have as a common factor the problems arising from distance that directly affect the processes of communication as well as coordination and control activities (Damian, et al., 2003). In these environments, communication is less fluid than in colocalized development groups, as a consequence, problems related to coordination, collaboration or group awareness appear which negatively affect productivity and, consequently, software quality. All these factors influence the way in which software is defined, built, tested and delivered to customers, thus affecting the corresponding stages of the software life cycle.

In order to mitigate these effects and with the aim of achieving higher levels of productivity, organizations require facilities to support collaboration, coordination and communication among developers through new technologies, processes and methods (Damian and Lanubile, 2004). Iterative approaches are commonly used in contrast to traditional waterfall or sequential methods, but they become more difficult to use consistently when teams are geographically distributed (Cusumano, 2008).

This work presents a systematic review of the literature dealing with efforts related to DSD and GSD with the purpose of discovering the aspects upon which researchers have focused until this moment. The objective is to identify, evaluate, interpret and synthesize most of the important studies on the subject, by conducting a rigorous and objective review of literature which will allow us to analyze the issues and the solutions contributed up to the present about de-located development with the aim of obtaining information with a high scientific and practical value through a rigorous systematic method.

Table 1. Basic search strings

	Basic search strings
1	(*"distributed software development"* OR *"global software development"*) AND ((*enterprise* OR *organization* OR *company* OR *team*) AND (*offshore* OR *offshoring* OR *outsource* OR *outsourcing* OR *nearshore* OR *nearshoring*))
2	(*"distributed software development"* OR *"global software development"*) AND (*model* OR *strategy* OR *technique*)

2 THE IMPORTANCE OF SYSTEMATIC REVIEWS

A systematic review of literature (Kitchenham, 2004) permits the identification, evaluation and interpretation of all the available relevant studies related to a particular research question, topic area or phenomenon, providing results with a high scientific value by classifying studies between primary studies and secondary or relevant studies, by means of synthesizing existing work according to a predefined strategy.

This systematic review has been carried out within the context of the FABRUM project, whose main objective is the development of a process with which to manage the relationships between a planning and design center and a software production factory, serving this work as starting point to focus future research to carry on

In order to carry out this study we have followed the systematic search procedure proposed by (Kitchenham, 2004), and the selection of primary studies method followed in (Pino, et al., 2007).

2.1 Question Formularization

The research question is: What are the initiatives carried out in relation to the improvement of DSD processes?

The keywords that guided the search to answer the research question were: *distributed, software, development, global, enterprise, organization, company, team, offshore, offshoring, outsource, outsourcing, nearshore, nearshoring, model, strategy* and *technique*.

During a first iteration, we also included the keywords CMM, CMMI, COBIT and ITIL in an attempt to obtain studies based on these standards, but due to the scarcity of good results these words were misestimated in subsequent iterations.

The ultimate goal of this systematic review consists of identifying the best procedures, models and strategies employed, and to determine the most important improvement factors for the main problems found. The population will be composed of publications found in the selected sources which apply procedures or strategies related to DSD.

2.2 Sources Selection

By combining the keyword list from the previous section through the logical connectors "AND" and "OR", we established the search strings shown in Table 1.

The studies were obtained from the search sources: *Science@Direct, Wiley Interscience, IEEE Digital Library and ACM Digital Library*. The quality of this sources, guarantee the quality of the studies. The basic search chains had to be adapted to the search engines of each source.

2.3 Studies Selection

The inclusion criteria for determining whether a study should be considered relevant (potential candidate to become a primary study) was based on analyzing the title, abstract and keywords from the studies retrieved by the search to determine whether they dealt with the DSD subject orientated towards process improvement, quality, coordination, collaboration, communication and related

Table 2. Distribution of studies found

Sources	Search date	Studies				
		Found	Not repeated	Relevant	Primaries	%
Science@Direct	30/04/2008	170	140	52	**19**	32,0
Wiley InterScience	30/04/2008	27	18	15	**12**	20,0
IEEE Digital Library	30/04/2008	7	7	5	**5**	8,0
ACM Digital Library	02/05/2008	408	302	63	**24**	40,0
	Total	612	467	135	**60**	100,0

issues that carry on any improvement about the subject.

Upon analyzing the results of the first iteration of the systematic review, we decided to exclude those studies which, despite addressing the issue of DSD, did not contribute to any significant improvement method, and we also dismissed those studies which focused solely upon social issues, cultural or time differences or focused solely upon free software, although we have taken into account other articles that address these topics in a secondary manner.

To obtain the primary studies we have followed the iterative and incremental model proposed by (Pino, et al., 2007). It is iterative because the search, retrieval and information visualization of results is carried out entirely through an initial search source and then repeats the same process on the rest. It is incremental because the document evolves incrementally, including new studies to complete the final version.

By applying the procedure to obtain the primary studies, 612 initial studies were found, of which 467 were not repeated. From these, we selected 135 as relevant and 60 as primary studies (the complete list of primary studies is shown in Appendix A). Table 2 shows the distribution of studies found according to the sources employed.

2.4 Information Extraction

The process of extracting information from the primary studies followed an inclusion criterion based on obtaining information about the key success factors, improvement strategies employed, processes improved and the most important ideas in each study, thus establishing a categorization between objective and subjective results. All articles were categorized by attending to the methodology study followed according to the models presented in (Zelkowitz & Wallace, 1998). We used the following categories: case studies, literature review, experiment, simulation and survey. The nonexperimental model for studies which makes a proposal without testing it or performing experiments was also applied.

3 TRENDS IN DISTRIBUTED SOFTWARE DEVELOPMENT RESEARCH

This section analyzes and discusses proposals and success factors in order to extract relevant information from the information provided by the primary studies. In (Prikladnicki, et al., 2008) is studied DSD attending to its evolution providing quantitative analysis. They indicate that distributed software development should be better contextualized. Their main conclusions were referred to the lack of studies related at the level of projects or focused on technical aspects.

Attending to our results, Figure 1 (*left*) shows that most of the primary studies analyzed are case studies and experimental articles. Surveys and nonexperimental studies also have a significant

Figure 1. Type of articles analyzed (left) and environments of study development (right)

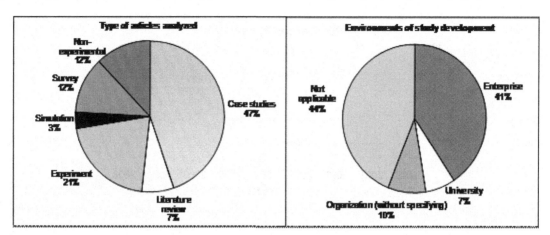

representation, in which members involved in the distributed development take part in outlining their difficulties.

On the other hand, as is shown in Figure 1 (*right*), the majority of primary studies are focused upon the enterprise field, but studies in the university environment also appear, in which groups of students carried out developments in different locations. Near 45% of the studies did not indicate their field of work or their characterization did not proceed, while 10% were from organizations which did not specify their corporate or university environment.

3.1 Publications Tendency

After attending to the number of relevant studies found through the systematic search carried out, it can be concluded that the subject of DSD is evidently an area which was not widely studied until a few years ago, and it is only recently that a greater number of publications have appeared; thus in Figure 2 we can see that 2006 is by far the year in which most studies were published, bearing in mind that the data shown for 2008 only reflects the studies found before May.

3.2 Improved or Analyzed Processes

Taking the primary studies analyzed as a reference, we carried out a classification in terms of processes in the software life cycle to which improvements were proposed or success factors or areas to be improved related to DSD were discussed. Primary studies were classified according to the improved or studied processes, in each case based on the ISO/IEC 12207 standard (2002), with the aim of obtaining a vision of the processes life cycle that requires special attention when working in a distributed environment and discovering the improvement efforts carried out until that moment.

The ISO 12207 standard establishes the activities that may be carried out during the software life cycle, which are grouped into main processes, support processes and general processes. The results are presented graphically in Figure 3 where for every process, its frequency in function of the number of studies that address it is indicated.

The results obtained indicate that greater efforts are focused on human resources, infrastructure, software construction and management and project organization processes. From these data we can infer that communication between team

Figure 2. Trends in publications about DSD

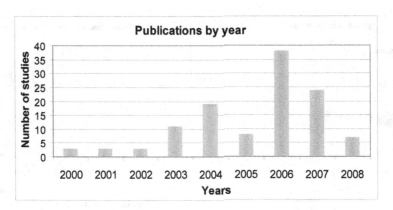

members is a critical factor. On the other hand, other processes, such as software installation or usability are not mentioned in any study. This information will be useful in the focusing of future research efforts.

3.3 Employed Standards

Attending to the standards followed by the organizations, we found that there is a need for more studies focused on capability models.

Figure 4 presents the standards that the analyzed articles address. Based on the available data, it may be inferred that few studies indicate the use of specific standards. In part, this is attributable to the fact that the great majority of studies deal with issues such as communication difficulties in which the standard used does not matter. The standards supported by most primary studies are CMM and ISO 9001, it being common to jointly apply both. All applications of CMM and CMMI studied employed a maturity level 2 with the exception of one which was certified at CMM level 5. No studies relative to ITIL or COBIT models were obtained.

3.4 Contents of the Studies

Table 3 shows in a schematic way the lines towards which the primary studies have focused. Most of

the works study tools or models designed specifically for DSD which attempt to improve certain aspects related to development and coordination. Another large part of the studies are related to communication processes and integration of collaborative tools, combining tools such as e-mail or instant messaging, and studying their application by means of different strategies. Most of the studies address the subject of communication difficulties in at least a secondary manner, presenting this aspect as being one of the most important in relation to the problematic nature of DSD.

On the other hand, 63% of the studies analyze or provide strategies, procedures or frameworks related to DSD. The remaining 37% study tools were designed specifically for distributed environments. As an example, tools such as FASTDash (Biehl, et al., 2007), Augur (Froehlich and Dourish, 2004) or MILOS (Goldmann, et al., 1999) may be of particular interest.

4 PROBLEMS AND SOLUTIONS

In this section, we synthesize the problems and solutions identified through the systematic review, discussing the main subjects.

Figure 3. Improved or analyzed processes by the primary studies adjusted to ISO 12207

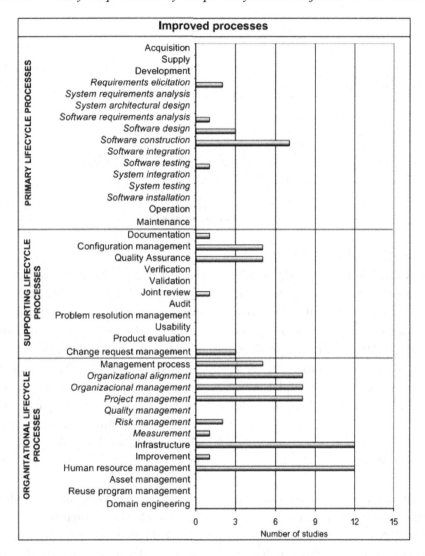

4.1 Communication

The software life cycle, especially in its early stages, requires a great deal of communication between members involved in the development who exchange a large number of messages through different tools and different formats without following communication standards and facing misunderstandings and high response times. These drawbacks, combined with the great size of personal networks which change over time, are summarized in a decrease in communication frequency and quality which directly affects productivity. To decrease these effects, both methodologies and processes must be supported by collaborative tools as a means of avoiding face-to-face meetings without comprising the quality of the results, as is proposed by M. A. Babar et al. (2007). K. Mohan and B. Ramesh (2007) discuss the need for user-friendly tools, integrating collaborative tools and agents to improve knowledge integration. M. R. Thissen et al. (2007) examine communication tools and describe collaboration processes, dealing with techniques such as conference calls and email.

Figure 4. Standards employed in the studies

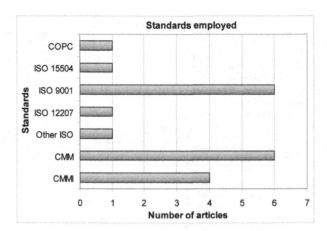

Cultural differences imply different terminologies which cause mistakes in messages and translation errors. Different levels of understanding the problem domain exist, as do different levels of knowledge, skills and training between teams. The use of translation processes, and codification guidelines is therefore useful (Carey, 1998; Prikladnicki, Audy, Damian, & de Oliveira, 2007).

4.2 Group Awareness

Members who are part of a virtual team tend to be less productive due to feelings of isolation and indifference. They have little informal conversation across sites, and their trust is reduced. Developers need to know the full status of the project and past history which will allow them to create realistic assumptions about how work is done on other sites. Frequent changes in processes, lack of continuity in communications and lack of collaborative tool integration cause the remote groups to be unaware of what is important because they do not know what other people are working on. As a consequence, they cannot find the right person and/or timely information which will enable them to work together efficiently, resulting in misalignment, rework and other coordination problems.

M.-A. D. Storey et al (2005) proposes a framework for comparing and understanding visualization tools that provide awareness of software development activities, giving a solid grounding in the existing theoretical foundation

Table 3. Thematic areas dealt with in the primary studies

Thematic areas	Studies (%)
Process control, task scheduling and project coordination	43,6
Collaborative tools, techniques and frameworks orientated towards communication and integration of existing tools	35,9
Configuration management	6,4
Multi-agent systems	5,1
Knowledgement management	5,1
Defects detection	2,6
Test management	1,3

of the field. In this way, it is described Augur, a visualization tool that supports DSD processes by creating visual representations of both software artifacts and software development activities, thus allowing developers to explore relationships between them.

J. D. Herbsleb et al. (2001) present a tool that provides a visualization of the change management system, making it easy to discover who has experience in working on which parts of the code, and to obtain contact information for that person.

4.3 Source Control

Distributed environments present problems derived from conflicts caused by editing files simultaneously. Coordination and synchronization become more complex as the degree of distribution of the team grows. Source control systems must support access through internet, confronting its unreliable and insecure nature and the higher response times.

To reduce these drawbacks, S. E. Dossick and G. E. Kaiser (1999) propose CHIME, an internet and intranet based application which allows users to be placed in a 3D virtual world representing the software system. Users interact with project artifacts by "walking around" the virtual world, in which they collaborate with other users through a feasible architecture. With the same purpose, J. T. Biehl et al. (2007) present FASTDash as a user-friendly tool that uses a spatial representation of the shared code base which highlights team members' current activities, allowing a developer to determine rapidly which team members have source files checked out, which files are being viewed, and what methods and classes are currently being changed, providing immediate awareness of potential conflict situations, such as two programmers editing the same source file.

A. Sarma et al. (2003) presents Palantír, which complements existing configuration management systems informing a developer of which other developers change and calculating a measure of severity of those changes.

4.4 Knowledge Flow Management

The team members' experiences, methods, decisions, and skills must be accumulated during the development process, so that each team member can use the experience of his/her predecessor and the experience of the team accumulated during development, saving cost and time by avoiding redundant work. For this purpose, documentation must always be updated to prevent assumptions and ambiguity, therefore facilitating the maintainability of the software developed. Distributed environments must facilitate knowledge sharing by maintaining a product/process repository focused on well understood functionality by linking content from sources such as e-mail and online discussions and sharing metadata information among several tools.

To solve the drawbacks caused by distribution, H. Zhuge (2002) presents an approach that works with a knowledge repository in which information related to every project is saved, using internet-based communication tools and thus enabling a new team member to become quickly experienced by learning the knowledge stored.

K. Mohan and B. Ramesh (2007) present an approach based on a traceability framework that identifies the key knowledge elements which are to be integrated, and a prototype system that supports the acquisition, integration, and use of knowledge elements, allowing knowledge fragments stored in diverse environments to be integrated and used by various stakeholders in order to facilitate a common understanding.

4.5 Coordination

Coordination can be interpreted as the management of the right information, the right people and the right time to develop an activity. Coordination in multi-site developments becomes more difficult in terms of articulation work, as problems derived from communication, lack of group awareness and the complexity of the organization appear which influence the way in which the work must be managed. In this sense, more progress reports, project reviews, conference calls and regular meetings to take corrective action are needed, thus minimizing task dependencies with other locations. Collaborative tools must support analysis, design and development, allowing monitoring activities and managing dependencies, notifications and implementation of corrective measures. We shall deal with many of these issues in the following sections.

P. Ovaska et al. (2003) study the coordination of interdependencies between activities including the figure of a chief architect to coordinate the work and maintain the conceptual integrity of the system.

S. Setamanit et al. (2007) describe a simulation model to study different ways in which to configure global software development processes. Such models based on empirical data, allow research into and calculation of the impact of coordination efficiency and its effects on productivity.

J. D. Herbsleb et al. (2001) suggest that multi-site communication and coordination requires more people to participate, which causes a delay. Large changes involve multiple sites and greater implementation times. Changes in multiple distributed sites involve a large number of people.

C. R. de Souza et al. (2007) presents the tool Ariadne which analyzes software projects for dependencies and help to find coordinations problems through a visual environment.

4.6 Collaboration

Concurrent edition of models and processes requires synchronous collaboration between architects and developers who cannot be physically present at a common location. Software modelling requires concurrency control in real time, enabling geographically dispersed developers to edit and discuss the same diagrams, and improving productivity by providing a means through which to easily capture and model difficult concepts through virtual workspaces and the collaborative edition of artifacts by means of tools which permit synchronized interactions.

A. De Lucia (2007) proposes STEVE, a collaborative tool that supports distributed modelling of software systems which, provides a communication infrastructure to enable concurrent edition of the same diagram at the same time by several distributed developers.

A further approach is presented by J. Suzuki and Y. Yamamoto (1996) with the SoftDock framework which solves the issues related to software component modelling and their relationships, describing and sharing component models information, and ensuring the integrity of these models. Developers can therefore work analyzing, designing, and developing software from component models and transfer them using an exchange format, thus enabling communication between team members. S. Sarkar et al. (2008) develop CollabDev, a human assisted collaborative knowledge tool to analyze applications in multiple languages and render various structural, architectural, and functional insights to the members involved in maintenance.

J. T. Biehl (2008) present IMPROMPTU, a framework for collaborating in multiple display environments which allows users to share task information across displays via off-the-shelf applications.

In another direction, W. Xiao et al. (2007) study Galaxy Wiki, an on-line collaborative tool based on the wiki concept which enables a collaborative authoring system for documentation and coordination purposes, allowing developers to compile, execute and debug programs in wiki pages.

4.7 Project and Process Management

Due to high organizational complexity, scheduling and task assignment becomes more problematic in distributed environments because of volatile requirements, changing specifications, and the lack of informal communication and synchronization. Managers must control the overall development process, improving it during the enactment and minimizing the factors that may decrease productivity, taking into account the possible impacts of diverse cultures and attitudes.

In this context, S. Goldmann et al. (1999) explains the main ideas of MILOS, a system orientated towards planning and scheduling which supports process modeling and enactment.

The maturity of the process becomes a key factor for success. In this sense, M. Passivaara and C. Lassenius (2003) propose incremental integration and frequent deliveries by following informing and monitoring practices. B. Berenbach (2006) describes different organizational structures that can overshadow technical problems caused by globalization, enumerating the problems introduced and the mitigation techniques that were effective.

R. J. Madachy (2008) deals economic issues presenting a set of cost models to estimate distributed teams work taking into account diffent environmental characteristics of the teams, localized labor categories, calendars, compensation rates, and currencies for costing.

4.8 Process Support

Processes should reflect the direct responsibilities and dependencies between tasks, notifying the people involved of the changes that concern them, thus avoiding information overload of team members. Process modeling and enactment should support inter-site coordination and cooperation of the working teams, offering automated support to distributed project management. Problems derived from process evolution, mobility and tool integration appear within this context. Process engines have to support changes during enactment. Furthermore, distributed environments usually involve a large network of heterogeneous, autonomous and distributed models and process engines, which requires the provision of a framework for process system interoperability.

In relation to these problems, A. Fernández et al. (2004) present the process modelling environment SPEARMINT, which supports extensive capabilities for multi-view modelling and analysis, and XCHIPS for web-based process support which allows enactment and simulation functionalities.

S. Setamanit et al. (2007) describe a hybrid computer simulation model of software development processes to study alternative ways to configure GSD projects in order to confront communication problems, control and coordination problems, process management and time and cultural differences.

N. Glasser and J.-C. Derniane (1998) analyse CoMoMAS, a multi-agent engineering approach that describes different viewpoints in a software process, permitting the transformation of conceptual models into executable programs. In this context, the agents will be able to cover with the high mobility of the members involved in the development process, taking charge of the management of information and permitting artifacts to communicate both with each other and with human users.

4.9 Quality and Measurement

Quality of products is highly influenced by the quality of the processes that support them. Organizations need to introduce new models and metrics to obtain information adapted to the distributed scenarios that could be useful in improving products and processes. With this aim, K. V. Siakas and B. Balstrup (2006) propose the capability model eSCM-SP, which has many similarities with other capability-assessment models such as CMMI, Bootstrap or SPICE and the SQM-CODE model, which considers the factors that influence software quality management systems from a cultural and organizational perspective.

J. D. Herbsleb et al. (2000) work with several interesting measures, such as the *interdependence measure* which allows the determination of the degree of dispersion of work among sites by looking up the locations of all the individuals. In this sense, F. Lanubile et al. (2003) propose metrics associated with products and processes orientated towards software defects such as: discovery effort, reported defects, defects density, fixed defects or unfixed defects.

Furthermore, software architecture evaluation usually involves a large number of stakeholders, who need face-to-face evaluation meetings, and for this reason adequate collaborative tools are needed, such as propose M. A. Babar et al. (2007).

4.10 Defects Detection

In distributed environments it is necessary to specify requisites with a higher level of detail. Software defects become more frequent due to the added complexity, and in most cases, this is related to communication problems and lack of group awareness. Defects control must be adapted by making a greater effort in relation to risk management activities.

To minimize these problems, F. Lanubile et al. (2003) define a process, specifying roles, guidelines, forms and templates, and describe a web-based tool that adopts a reengineered inspection process to minimize synchronous activities and coordination problems to support geographically dispersed teams.

An adequate model cycle must allow the localization and recognition of defect-sensitive areas in complex product development. In this line, J. van Moll et al. (2004) indicate that transitions between constituent sub-projects are particularly defect-sensitive. By means of an appropriate modelling of the overall project lifecycle and by applying adequate defect detection measures, the occurrence of defects can be reduced. The goal is to minimize the amount of defects that spread to the subsequent phases early in the software life cycle, and reuse existing components or the application of third-party components, thus minimizing product quality risks by using tested components.

5 SUCCESS FACTORS

From the experimental studies analyzed, we have extracted the following success factors of DSD, in which the primary studies referenced are listed in the Appendix A:

- Intervention of human resources by participating in surveys (Babar, Kitchenham, Zhu, Gorton, & Jeffery, 2007; Herbsleb, Mockus, Finholt, & Grinter, 2000). Their problems, experiences and suggestions can be very helpful.

- Carrying out the improvement based on the needs of the company, taking into account the technologies and methodologies used (Akmanligil & Palvia, 2004). The tools employed at the present must be adapted and integrated (Sarma, Noroozi, & van der Hoek, 2003).

- Training of human resources in the tools and processes introduced (Herbsleb, Mockus, Finholt, & Grinter, 2001). Their skills are an important factor for a successful application of both tools and processes.

- Registration of activities with information on pending issues, errors and people in charge (Biehl, Czerwinski, Smith, & Robertson, 2007) and provide awareness of software development activities (Storey, Čubranić, & German, 2005).

- Establishment of an efficient communication mechanism between the members of the organization, allowing a developer to discover the status and changes made within each project (Baentsch, Molter, & Sturm, 1995; Biehl, Czerwinski, Smith, & Robertson, 2007).

- Using a version control tool in order to control conflictive situations (Pilatti, Audy, & Prikladnicki, 2006).
- There must be a way to allow the planning and scheduling of distributed tasks, taking into account costs and dependencies between projects, application of corrective measures and notifications (Froehlich & Dourish, 2004; Madachy, 2008).
- Application of maturity models and agile methodologies (Lee, DeLone, Espinosa, 2006) based on incremental integration and frequent deliveries.
- Systematic use of metrics tailored to the characteristic of the organization attending to the different types of distribution (Herbsleb, Mockus, Finholt, & Grinter, 2001).

6 CONCLUSION

In this work we have applied a systematic review method in order to analyze the literature related to the topic of DSD within the FABRUM project context whose main objective is to create a new DSD model to manage the relationships between a planning and design center and a software production factory, this work serving as a starting point from which to establish the issues upon which subsequent research will be focused.

Results obtained from this systematic review have allowed us to obtain a global vision of a relatively new topic which should be investigated in detail. However, every organization has concrete needs which basically depend on its distribution characteristics, its activity and the tools it employs. These are the factors that make this such a wide subject, and lead to the necessity of adapting both the technical and organizational procedures, according to each organization's specific needs.

Generally, the proposals found in the analyzed studies were mainly concerned with improvements related to the use of collaborative tools, integration of existing tools, source code control or use of collaborative agents. Moreover, it should be considered that the evaluation of the results obtained from the proposed improvements are often based on studies in a single organization, and sometimes only takes into account the subjective perception of developers.

On the other hand, it should be noted that maturity models such as CMM, CMMI or ISO, which would be of particular relevance to the present investigation, represent only 17% of all analyzed works. The fact that almost all experimental studies that employed CMMI and CMM applied a maturity level 2 suggests that the cost of implementing higher maturity levels under distributed environments might be too high. The application of agile methodologies based on incremental integration and frequent deliveries, and frequent reviews of problems to adjust the process become important success factors.

Finally, we must emphasize that the search excluded studies which addressed the subject of DSD but did not contribute any significant method or improvement in this research context. However, since this is such a wide area, some of these works present interesting parallel subjects for the development of this investigation, which is why their study would be important in a future work.

ACKNOWLEDGMENT

We acknowledge the assistance of MELISA project (PAC08-0142-3315), financiered by the "Junta de Comunidades de Castilla-La Mancha" of Spain. This work is part of FABRUM project (PPT-430000-2008-63), financiered by "Ministerio de Ciencia e Innovación" of Spain and by Alhambra-Eidos (http://www.alhambra-eidos.es/).

REFERENCES

Akmanligil, M., & Palvia, P. C. (2004). Strategies for global information systems development. *Information & Management, 42*(1), 45–59.

Aspray, W., Mayadas, F., & Vardi, M. Y. (2006). *Globalization and offshoring of software. A report of the ACM job migration task force.* New York: ACM Press.

Babar, M. A., Kitchenham, B., Zhu, L., Gorton, I., & Jeffery, R. (2006). An empirical study of groupware support for distributed software architecture evaluation process. *Journal of Systems and Software, 79*(7), 912–925. doi:10.1016/j.jss.2005.06.043

Baentsch, M., Molter, G., & Sturm, P. (1995). WebMake: Integrating distributed software development in a structure-enhanced Web. *Computer Networks and ISDN Systems, 27*(6), 789–800. doi:10.1016/0169-7552(95)00019-4

Berenbach, B. (2006). Impact of organizational structure on distributed requirements engineering processes: Lessons learned. In *Proceedings of the 2006 International Workshop on Global Software Development for the Practitioner* (pp. 15-19).

Biehl, J. T., Baker, W. T., Bailey, B. P., Tan, D. S., Inkpen, K. M., & Czerwinski, M. (2008). In *Proceedings of the Twenty-Sixth Annual SIGCHI Conference on Human Factors in Computer Systems* (pp. 939-948).

Biehl, J. T., Czerwinski, M., Smith, G., & Robertson, G. G. (2007). FASTDash: A visual dashboard for fostering awareness in software teams. In *Proceedings of the SIGCHI conference on Human factors in computing systems* (pp. 1313-1322). San Jose, CA: ACM Press.

Carey, J. M. (1998). Creating global software: A conspectus and review. *Interacting with Computers, 9*(4), 449–465. doi:10.1016/S0953-5438(97)00028-3

Cusumano, M. A. (2008). Managing software development in globally distributed teams. *Communications of the ACM, 51,* 15–17. doi:10.1145/1314215.1340930

Damian, D., & Lanubile, F. (2004). The 3rd international workshop on global software development. In *Proceedings of the 26th International Conference on Software Engineering (ICSE)* (pp. 756-757).

Damian, D., Lanubile, F., & Oppenheimer, H. (2003). Addressing the challenges of software industry globalization: The workshop on global software development. In *Proceedings of the 25th International Conference on Software Engineering (ICSE)* (pp. 793-794).

De Lucia, A., Fasano, F., Scanniello, G., & Tortora, G. (2007). Enhancing collaborative synchronous UML modelling with fine-grained versioning of software artefacts. *Journal of Visual Languages and Computing, 18*(5), 492–503. doi:10.1016/j.jvlc.2007.08.005

de Souza, C. R., Quirk, S., Trainer, E., & Redmiles, D. F. (2007). Supporting collaborative software development through the visualization of socio-technical dependencies. In *Proceedings of the 2007 International ACM Conference on Supporting Group Work* (147-156).

Dossick, S. E., & Kaiser, G. K. (1999). CHIME: A metadata-based distributed software development environment. In *Proceedings of the 7th European Software Engineering Conference held jointly with the 7th ACM SIGSOFT International Symposium on Foundations of Software Engineering* (pp. 464-475).

Ebert, C., & De Neve, P. (2001). Surviving global software development. *IEEE Software, 18,* 62–69. doi:10.1109/52.914748

Fernández, A., Garzaldeen, B., Grützner, I., & Münch, J. (2004). Guided support for collaborative modeling, enactment and simulation of software development processes. *Software Process Improvement and Practice, 9*(2), 95–106. doi:10.1002/spip.199

Froehlich, J., & Dourish, P. (2004). Unifying artifacts and activities in a visual tool for distributed software development teams. In *Proceedings of the 26ᵗʰ International Conference on Software Engineering* (pp. 387-396). Washington, DC: IEEE Computer Society.

Glaser, N., & Derniame, J.-C. (1998). Software agents: Process models and user profiles in distributed software development. In *Proceedings of the 7ᵗʰ IEEE International Workshops on Enabling Technologies: Infrastructure or Collaborative Enterprises* (pp. 45-50).

Goldmann, S., Münch, J., & Holz, H. (1999). A meta-model for distributed software development. In *Proceedings of the IEEE 8ᵗʰ International Workshops on Enabling Technologies: Infrastructure for Collaborative Enterprises, 1999. (WET ICE '99)* (pp. 48-53). Stanford, CA, USA.

Gorton, I., & Motwani, S. (1996). Issues in co-operative software engineering using globally distributed teams. *Information and Software Technology, 38*(10), 647–655. doi:10.1016/0950-5849(96)01099-3

Greenfield, J., Short, K., Cook, S., Kent, S., & Crupi, J. (2004). *Software factories: Assembling applications with patterns, models, frameworks, and tools*. New York: John Wiley & Sons.

Herbsleb, J. D., Mockus, A., Finholt, T. A., & Grinter, R. E. (2000). Distance, dependencies, and delay in a global collaboration. In *Proceedings of the 2000 ACM Conference on Computer Supported Cooperative Work* (pp. 319-328).

Herbsleb, J. D., Mockus, A., Finholt, T. A., & Grinter, R. E. (2001). An empirical study of global software development: Distance and speed. In *Proceedings of the 23ʳᵈ International Conference on Software Engineering* (pp. 81-90).

Herbsleb, J. D., & Moitra, D. (2001). Global software development. *IEEE Software, 18*, 16–20. doi:10.1109/52.914732

ISO/IEC 12207:2002. (2002). *ISO/IEC 12207:2002. AMENDMENT 1: Information technology - software life cycle processes*. International Organization for Standardization.

Kitchenham, B. (2004). *Procedures for performing systematic reviews* (Joint Tech. Rep.). Software Engineering Group, Department of Computer Science, Keele University and Empirical Software Engineering National ICT Australia Ltd.

Krishna, S., Sundeep, S., & Geoff, W. (2004). Managing cross-cultural issues in global software outsourcing. *Communications of the ACM, 47*, 62–66. doi:10.1145/975817.975818

Lanubile, F., Mallardo, T., & Calefato, F. (2003). Tool support for geographically dispersed inspection teams. *Software Process Improvement and Practice, 8*(4), 217–231. doi:10.1002/spip.184

Layman, L., Williams, L., Damian, D., & Bures, H. (2006). Essential communication practices for extreme programming in a global software development team. *Information and Software Technology, 48*, 781–794. doi:10.1016/j.infsof.2006.01.004

Lee, G., DeLone, W., & Espinosa, J. A. (2006). Ambidextrous coping strategies in globally distributed software development projects. *Communications of the ACM, 49*(10), 35–40. doi:10.1145/1164394.1164417

Madachy, R. J. (2008). Cost modeling of distributed team processes for global development and software-intensive systems of systems. *Software Process Improvement and Practice, 13*(1), 51–61. doi:10.1002/spip.363

McConnell, S. (1996). *Rapid development: Taming wild software schedules,* Redmond, WA: Microsoft Press.

Mohan, K., & Ramesh, B. (2007). Traceability-based knowledge integration in group decision and negotiation activities. *Decision Support Systems, 43*(3), 968–989. doi:10.1016/j.dss.2005.05.026

Ovaska, P., Rossi, M., & Marttiin, P. (2003). Architecture as a coordination tool in multi-site software development. *Software Process Improvement and Practice, 8*(4), 233–247. doi:10.1002/spip.186

Paasivaara, M., & Lassenius, C. (2003). Collaboration practices in global inter-organizational software development projects. *Software Process Improvement and Practice, 8*(4), 183–199. doi:10.1002/spip.187

Pilatti, L., Audy, J. L. N., & Prikladnicki, R. (2006). Software configuration management over a global software development environment: Lessons learned from a case study. In *Proceedings of the 2006 International Workshop on Global Software Development for the Practitioner* (pp. 45-50).

Pino, F. J., García, F., & Piattini, M. (2007). Software process improvement in small and medium software enterprises: A systematic review. *Software Quality Journal, 16*(2), 237–261. doi:10.1007/s11219-007-9038-z

Prikladnicki, R., Audy, J. L. N., Damian, D., & de Oliveira, T. C. (2007). Distributed software development: Practices and challenges in different business strategies of offshoring and onshoring. In *Proceedings of the Second IEEE International Conference on Global Software Engineering* (pp. 262-274).

Prikladnicki, R., Audy, J. L. N., & Evaristo, J. R. (2003). Distributed software development: Toward an understanding of the relationship between project team, users and customers. In *Proceedings of the 5th International Conference on Enterprise Information Systems (ICEIS)* (pp. 417-423).

Prikladnicki, R., Damian, D., & Audy, J. L. N. (2008). Patterns of evolution in the practice of distributed software development: Quantitative results from a systematic review. In *Proceedings of the 12th International Conference on Evaluation and Assessment in Software Engineering (EASE)* University of Bari, Italy.

Sarkar, S., Sindhgatta, R., & Pooloth, K. (2008). A collaborative platform for application knowledge management in software maintenance projects. In *Proceedings of the 1st Bangalore Annual Compute Conference* (pp. 1-7).

Sarma, A., Noroozi, Z., & van der Hoek, A. (2003). Palantír: Raising awareness among configuration management workspaces. In *Proceedings of the 25th International Conference on Software Engineering* (pp. 444-454).

Setamanit, S.-o., Wakeland, W., & Raffo, D. (2007). Using simulation to evaluate global software development task allocation strategies. *Software Process Improvement and Practice, 12*(5), 491–503. doi:10.1002/spip.335

Siakas, K. V., & Balstrup, B. (2006). Software outsourcing quality achieved by global virtual collaboration. *Software Process Improvement and Practice, 11*(3), 319–328. doi:10.1002/spip.275

Storey, M.-A. D., Čubranić, D., & German, D. M. (2005). On the use of visualization to support awareness of human activities in software development: A survey and a framework. In *Proceedings of the 2005 ACM Symposium on Software Visualization* (pp. 193-202).

Thissen, M. R., Page, J. M., Bharathi, M. C., & Austin, T. L. (2007). Communication tools for distributed software development teams. In *Proceedings of the 2007 ACM SIGMIS CPR Conference on Computer Personnel Doctoral Consortium and Research Conference: The Global Information Technology Workforce* (pp. 28-35).

van Moll, J., Jacobs, J., Kusters, R., & Trienekens, J. (2004). Defect detection oriented lifecycle modelling in complex product development. *Information and Software Technology, 46*(10), 665–675. doi:10.1016/j.infsof.2003.12.001

Werner, K., Rombach, D., & Feldmann, R. (2001). Outsourcing in India. *IEEE Software, 18*, 78–86.

Xiao, W., Chi, C., & Yang, M. (2007). On-line collaborative software development via Wiki. In *Proceedings of the 2007 International Symposium on Wikis* (pp. 177-183).

Zelkowitz, M. V., & Wallace, D. R. (1998). Experimental models for validating technology. *Computer, 31*(5), 23–31. doi:10.1109/2.675630

Zhuge, H. (2002). Knowledge flow management for distributed team software development. *Knowledge-Based Systems, 15*(8), 465–471. doi:10.1016/S0950-7051(02)00031-X

KEY TERMS AND DEFINITIONS

Systematic Review: Literature review focused on a research question which tries to identify, evaluate and interpretate all high quality studies to answer the question following a well-defined method.

Software Factory: is an organizational structure that, automates parts of software development through an assembly process, decentralizing production units, and promoting the reusability of architectures, knowledge and components.

Relevant (or Secondary) Study: Studies related to a particular research question but which has a secondary interest.

Primary Study: Individual studies obtained by applying an inclusion and exclusion criteria whose information is extracted and synthesised to contribute to a systematic review.

Outsourcing: Is a way to contract a particular function to a third-party organization defining how the client and the supplier will work together.

Offshoring: Transference of an organizational function to another country, usually where human resources are cheaper.

Nearshoring: Transference of an organizational function to geographically closer countries, thus avoiding cultural and time differences between members and saving travel and communication costs.

Virtual Team: Group of individuals who work physically separated across time and space and who primarily interact through electronic media and may meet face-to-face occasionally to achieve a task.

Chapter 16
Tools and Techniques for Model Based Testing

Swapan Bhattacharya
National Institute of Technology, Durgapur, India

Ananya Kanjilal
B. P. Poddar Institute of Management & Technology, Kolkata, India

Sabnam Sengupta
B. P. Poddar Institute of Management & Technology, Kolkata, India

ABSTRACT

Software testing has gained immense importance in the present competitive world of developing software more quickly, more efficiently and more accurately. Testing activity is carried out throughout the lifecycle of software development and not only towards the end of development. Time and effort required to correct errors, detected later is much more compared to those, which are detected earlier. This has direct impact on costs and has led to a splurge of research activities in this domain. Model-based testing has recently gained attention with the popularization of modeling itself. It refers to testing and test case generation based on a model that describes the behavior of the system. The OMG initiative MDA has revolutionized the way models would be used for software development. There are a number of modeling techniques in use today- some have formal syntax like Z, VDM while some are semi-formal like UML. We have made a comprehensive summary of a considerable number of research works on Model Based testing. First, the issues, challenges and problems of model based testing have been discussed. Then the different methods developed for testing or test case generation based on the models are summarized. Finally a list of model based testing tools used for testing has been collectively presented.

TOOLS AND TECHNIQUES FOR MODEL BASED TESTING

Software development is a human intensive activity and over the years the need for a disciplined approach for development of better quality and reliable software has led to the evolving field of Software Engineering. The software community continually attempts to develop technologies and methodologies to enable easier, faster and cheaper ways to build high quality software. One of the principal elements of software quality assurance

DOI: 10.4018/978-1-60566-731-7.ch016

is software testing or verification as it represents the ultimate review of specification, design and code generation.

The importance of software testing cannot be overemphasized. The chances of errors creep in right from the very beginning and industries invest huge amount of effort and time to identify and remove them. Since exhaustive testing in most cases is an impractical solution, the need for effective testing strategies becomes important.

Along with traditional testing techniques, model based testing has emerged as a new domain of research and has recently gained attention with the popularization of models in software design and development. Models not only enhance understanding what a product is supposed to do and how its architecture is designed, but enable one to semi-automatically derive test scenarios at an early development stage where coding has not yet finished. There are a number of models in use today, a few of which make good models for testing. Model based testing focuses on verification or testing based on the models that depict the behavior of the system. It helps in assessing and measuring the degree to which a system faithfully implements a given model. Some models have formal syntax and semantics, yet others are semi formal in nature. The need for test automation for reduced costs and higher quality software provides challenging opportunities to researchers to innovate, develop and propose new methodologies for maximizing the efficiency of the testing techniques. Implementation of these methodologies for use as test automation tools is the area of interest of the software industries.

This chapter gives a comprehensive summary about Model based Testing. First, the concept and overview of MBT is described. The benefits offered by MBT are numerous but at the same time there are several issues that need to be handled for efficient use and implementation of MBT techniques. The previous section discusses the benefits and problems of MBT. Next the various methods for test generation developed so far are summarized based on models in one of the five categories – Formal models, State transition based models, Graphical models, UML diagrams and combinatorial models. All the research works are summarized in a tabular format with focus on the model used, testing strategy developed and tool implementation, if any. A comprehensive list of tools that are commercially available is discussed as well as some academic tools. The tools are described along with various other details like manufacturer details, information source and models used. Finally the chapter concludes with identification of possible areas of research in the domain of model based testing.

MODEL BASED TESTING: OVERVIEW

Model Based testing (MBT) is a new and evolving technique for generation of test suite from models that represent a system design or behavior. The paradigm of model-based testing shifts the focus of testing from writing individual test cases to developing a model from which a test suite can be generated automatically. It may be used for all cycles of testing – for unit testing of individual modules, integration testing of some of the modules to verify simple behaviors and overall system testing for verification of the total system behavior as represented by its model. MBT relies on three key technologies – the notation used for data model, test generation algorithm and tools that generate the supporting infrastructure for tests (DACS, 2003), MBT offers considerable promise in reducing the cost of test generation, increasing the effectiveness of the tests, and shortening the testing cycle. Test generation becomes especially effective for systems that are changed frequently, because testers are able to update the data model and then rapidly regenerate a test suite, avoiding tedious and error-prone editing of a suite of hand-crafted tests.

MBT: BENEFITS AND PROBLEMS

Model based testing is especially useful for automatic generation of test sequences from the defined model. Since models are abstractions of system behavior they are much easier and simpler to deal with and managing requirement changes and thereby growing test suites becomes easy. With a considerable number of MBT tools available, model based testing has become a promising domain for the future of software testing discipline. This section lists some of the significant benefits and several issues related to model based testing.

3.1 Benefits

1. Early error detection
2. Models need to be managed instead of test cases since they are auto generated.
3. Auto generation helps in having a larger number of significant test cases as compared to manual testing. This increases the efficiency of testing.
4. Leads to reduction of effort and costs in software testing.
5. Almost full coverage of software is ensured whereas tests designed manually only covers 70-80%
6. Test automation is cheaper and more effective.
7. Test suite grows with the product and managing changes becomes easier.
8. Model exposes ambiguities in specification and design of software.
9. Model consists of behavioral information, which may be re-used in future testing even when specifications change.

3.2 Issues and Challenges

1. Testing based on formal models ensures full coverage of specifications but requires testers or people in the software community to understand and be able to create complex models. This requires significant investment in learning and training.
2. As opposed to traditional testing where the requirements and testing were considered two separate domains, model based testing brings about a tight coupling between the two. Testing is based on specifications – both functional and design. Ensuring complete functional specifications for complete coverage of test generation requires that the testing team and requirements team work very closely and understand the requirements of each other.
3. Models are sometimes partial and unable to represent the complete system. Combination of different models may be required for completeness in specification and hence in testing.
4. Models are simplified abstractions and hence may not be able to represent all the features of a system. Some of the models are excellent in representing specifications but may not be very useful for testing. So effort must be employed to develop testable models
5. Model based testing also entails automatic code generation. Hence verification of the entire cycle starting from specification to the code developed to implement that is necessary. This leads to methodologies to be developed for conformance testing.
6. Formal models are advantageous for testing purposes as it has defined syntax and semantics. However the rigidity and complexity of formal methods make them unpopular for use.
7. Most other models are semi formal in nature and owing to that verification or testing based on such models becomes difficult.

MODEL BASED TESTING METHODS

Test Methods Based on Formal Models

Z Specification Language

The formal specification notation Z, useful for describing computer-based systems, is based on Zermelo-Fraenkel set theory and first order predicate logic and is now defined by an ISO standard. Z is a model-based formal specification language, which uses predicate logic to specify operations as a relation between the input and the output. Several works have used Z for modeling systems in a formal way.

In (Bussow, R. et. al, 1998), the authors describe how Z can be combined with dynamic modeling techniques such as Statecharts and temporal interval logic. The presented formalism exploits the advantages of Z's power to describe data and data-transformation, statecharts for dynamic modeling and temporal logic for expressing behavioral properties. These components are integrated within a component model which provides a uniform means for instantiation and reuse. The application of formal techniques is of utmost importance for safety-critical embedded systems which is however difficult to apply. This is addressed in (Grieskamp, W. et. al, 1998) by the concept of an *agenda*. Agendas are used to support the application of formal specification techniques to provide detailed guidance for specifiers, templates of the used specification language that only need to be instantiated, and application independent validation criteria. In (Buessow R. & Grieskamp, W., 1997), authors describe Dynamic Z, a moderate extension of Z by discrete temporal interval logics for formalization of behavior as well as properties of embedded systems. Dynamic Z adds few new syntactic constructs and statecharts are derived from these specifications as the authors aim for a tool environment centered around the Statemate tool.

We have used Z to model functional specifications of object oriented systems. In (Sengupta, S. & Bhattacharya, S., 2006) we have presented a formalization methodology to represent SRS and design artifacts using Z-notation. Z is a strongly typed mathematical specification language (Spivey J.M., 1992), (Woodcock, J., & Davis, J., 1996). As a step towards prototyping, in our earlier work in (Sengupta, S., 2007), we have presented an approach to automatically derive design components (UML component diagrams) from functional requirements specified in SRS.

Object-Z

Object-Z is an object-oriented extension of the formal specification language Z. In (Carrington, D. et. al, 2000), a method for specification-based class testing is described that incorporates test case generation, execution, and evaluation based on formal specifications. The initial step of the method is to generate test cases for individual operations from a specification written in the Object-Z specification language. These test cases are combined to produce a finite state machine that is used as the basis for test case execution with the ClassBench test execution framework. An oracle derived from the Object-Z specification is used to evaluate the outputs generated by the test cases. The work in (MacColl, I. et. al, 1998) contains a case study demonstrating a complete process for specification-based class testing. The process starts with an abstract specification written in Object-Z and concludes by exercising an implementation with test cases and evaluating the results. The test cases are derived using the Test Template Framework for each individual operation. They are analyzed to generate a finite state machine that can execute test sequences within the ClassBench framework. An oracle is also derived from the Object-Z specification. In (McDonald, J. et. al, 1997) the translation of Object-Z specifications of container classes to C++ test oracle classes is presented. It presents a three-stage translation process and describes how the derived test oracles are integrated into the ClassBench testing framework. In (Fletcher, R. & Sajeev, A. S. M., 1996) a formal model of Java concurrency using the Object-Z specification language is presented. This model captures the Java thread synchronization concepts of locking, blocking, waiting and notification. Object-Z inheritance is used to integrate the model with the classical producer-consumer system to create a specification directly incorporating the Java concurrency constructs.

Other Formal Models

An approach to derive test cases in the RAISE method is proposed in (Dan, L. & Aichernig, B. K., 2004) whose specification language RSL combines the model-based and algebraic style. The approach integrates the testing techniques of algebraic specifications and model-based specifications. In this testing strategy, first, every function definition is partitioned using Disjunctive Normal Form (DNF) and then test arguments are generated. Next, sequences of function calls are formed. Finally, the test cases are built by replacing the variables, on both sides of the axioms, with the sequences of functions calls. These kinds of test cases not only provide the data for testing, but also serve as test oracles. Based on this combined approach, a test case generation tool has been developed.

In (Meudec, C., 1998) a rationale is presented for using tests derived from high level formal specifications and then an efficient technique is proposed for the generation of adequate test sets from specifications in VDM-SL. Another strand of research, based on test generation from Z predicates, is examined and extended using the proposed formalism to include quantified expressions and other, more complex, constructs of formal specification languages. Then it is shown that this more refined technique complements the previous work and that their combination should

allow the generation of adequate test sets from formal specifications. It has been illustrated that to synthesize pragmatically the two techniques, one must find heuristics for the detection of redundant test cases, which is done based on the independence of some divisions of the input domain of the system under test, which allows the contraction of test sets without impairing their likelihood of revealing an error in the system under test. Finally, a technique for the efficient generation of adequate test cases is proposed.

(Aichernig, B. K., 1999) uses the formal method VDM to demonstrate that abstract requirements models can be used as test oracles for concrete software. The automation of the resulting testing framework is based on modern CASE-tools that support a light-weight approach to formal methods. The specification language used is VDM-SL, but the results are easily transferred into similar model oriented methods such as B, Z or RAISE. VDM-SL, the general purpose specification language of VDM, provides mathematical objects, like sets, sequences, maps etc., to model a system's state. An implicit operation defines what should happen by pre- and post-conditions. The pre-condition is a logical constraint on the input stating what must hold that the functionality is defined. The essential part is the post-condition, a relation between the input, the old state, the output and the new state. Modern tools like the VDM-SL Toolbox allow the interpretation or even code-generation of such pre- and post-conditions which leads to an automated test evaluation through post-condition oracles.

(Cheng B.H.C. & Wang E. Y., 2002) presents a well-defined formal model for the object and dynamic models and their integration. The formal model is described in terms of a well-known specification language, LOTOS. Formalization of the graphical notation enables numerous automated processing and analysis tasks, such as behavior simulation and consistency checks between levels of specifications.

In (Javed, F., et al, 2005) the authors present a grammar based approach for validating UML class diagrams. The approach involves the representation of UML class diagrams as a DSL. An XSLT transformation is used to convert an XML representation of a model to the representative DSL. The LISA compiler generator tool generates a parser for the DSL. Positive and negative use cases are provided to the generated parser in the form of strings in the DSL. A string similarity measure is employed in order to provide feedback to the user regarding validation criterion. It is also shown that the approach can deal with issues like cyclical relations and multiple inheritances in class diagrams.

The work in (Pretschner, A.& L¨otzbeyer, H. & Philipps, J., 2001) presents a method for model based test sequence generation for reactive systems on the grounds of Constraint Logic Programming and its implementation in the CASE tool Auto-Focus. AUTOFOCUS is a tool for developing graphical specifications of embedded systems based on a simple, formally defined semantics. It supports different views on the system model: structure, behavior, interaction, and data type view. Each view concentrates on certain aspects of the specified model.

STATE TRANSITION BASED MODELS

Markov Chains

Model based testing using Markov chain usage models provide a powerful way to address testing concerns. Unfortunately, the use of Markov chain usage models on systems which have multiple streams of control, or which have many modeless dialogs, has required approaches which limit automated testing (strong abstractions) or make models difficult to analyze (notations hiding a state explosion). In (Prowell, S. J., 2005) Prowell presents a new approach, which relies on applying concurrency operators to the test cases, generated from simple Markov chain usage models to create

sophisticated test cases. This approach leverages existing tools and notations. A statistical method for software testing based on a Markov chain model of usage is discussed in (Whittaker, J. A. & Thomason, M. G., 1994). The Markov chain first allows test input sequences to be generated from multiple probability distributions and secondly the test input sequences generated from the chain and applied to the software are a stochastic model and are used to create a second Markov chain to encapsulate the history of the test including failures. A stopping criterion is derived also based on the sequence generating properties of the two chains.

Software validation is an important activity in order to test whether or not the correct software has been developed. Several testing techniques have been developed, and one of these is statistical usage testing (SUT). The main purpose of SUT is to test a software product from a user's point of view. Hence, usage models are designed and then test cases are developed from the models. Another advantage of SUT is that the reliability of the software can be estimated. In (Guen, H. L., Marie, R. & Thelin, T., 2004), Markov chains are used to represent the usage models. Several approaches using Markov chains have been applied. This paper extends these approaches and presents a new approach to estimate the reliability from Markov chains. The reliability estimation is implemented in a new tool for statistical usage testing called MaTeLo. The purpose of the tool is to provide an estimate of the reliability and to automatically produce test cases based on usage models described as to Markov models.

The work described in (Hosain S. & Alam S., 2004), is also an investigation of applying Markov chain techniques to measure software reliability. An example is taken from database based application software to develop two stochastic models called usage model and testing model for the software. The log likelihood of two stochastic processes tells how similar these processes are. This information is used to determine reliability of the example software. The results prove the viability and effectiveness of the approach to measure software reliability for large and complicated systems.

In (Prowell, S., 2004), an overview of statistical testing using Markov chain usage models is presented. Statistical testing of software is an approach which treats software testing as a statistical experiment, in which a sample is drawn, and performance on the sample is used to make inferences about important quantities, such as reliability, time to failure, and the like. Markov chains provide such a model for such statistical analysis.

In the last few years, there have been many advances in the use of Markov chain usage models. These have included the introduction of standard notations and modeling languages specifically suited to describing Markov chain usage models, the use of mathematical programming techniques to determine transition probabilities, more powerful test case generation through the use of concurrency operators, stopping criteria based on cost-benefit analysis, and improved reliability models. Three generations of tools to support the use and analysis of Markov chain usage models have been developed, with the latest generation - the JUMBL toolkit (Prowell, S.J., 2003) providing support for a variety of notations and test case execution methods.

(Al-Ghafees, M.A., 2000) extends the concept of data flow testing to the case of black box testing where source code is unavailable. In such cases a behavioral model is constructed analogous to program flow graph which is a graph representation of externally visible states and input-induced state transitions. New data flow selection rules are proposed and test cases are generated from them. State transition coverage analogous to path coverage is done based on the Markov chain graphical model.

Coverage testing in the context of Markov chain usage models refers to coverage of a model of the specification and profile of intended use, rather than coverage of the code that implements the specification. A new measure of specification complexity based on the number of statistically typical paths through the model of the specification is derived in (Walton, G. H. & Poore, J. H., 2000). Formulae are presented to compute bounds on the expected number of test cases required to achieve state and arc coverage. Formulae are presented to compare different usage models with respect to the amount of testing required to achieve coverage of typical paths. Convexity properties are established for these formulae to facilitate their use in optimization calculations that are used to generate transition probabilities for the usage models.

ABSTRACT STATE MACHINE AND FINITE STATE MACHINE

A finite state machine (FSM) or finite automaton is a model of behaviour composed of states, transitions and actions. The Abstract State Machine (ASM) was started by Yuri Gurevich as an attempt to bridge the gap between formal models of computation and practical specification methods. The ASM thesis is that any algorithm can be modeled at its natural abstraction level by an appropriate ASM. The result is a simple methodology for describing simple abstract machines, which correspond to algorithms. In this section we discuss some model based testing approaches developed based on FSM and ASM.

In (Barnett, M. et al, FATES 2003) the authors' present work on a tool environment for model based testing with the Abstract State Machine Language (AsmL). The environment supports semi-automatic parameter generation, FSM generation, sequence generation for deriving test sequences from FSM and conformance testing. One important application we see for AsmL is automated testing. Given manually or automatically generated test scenarios, formal models can be used to automate the test oracle.

In (Grieskamp, W. et. al, 2002) an algorithm is proposed that derives a finite state machine (FSM) from a given abstract state machine (ASM) specification. This allows for integration of ASM specifications with the existing tools for test case generation from FSMs. ASM specs are executable but have typically too many, often infinitely many states. The ASM states are grouped into finitely many hyperstates, which are the nodes of the FSM. The links of the FSM are induced by the ASM state transitions. The purpose of the FSM extraction algorithm is to produce an FSM that can be used for test case generation.

The authors in (Barnett, M. et al, 2003) present work on a tool environment for model-based testing with the Abstract State Machine Language (AsmL). The environment supports semi-automatic parameter generation, FSM generation, sequence generation for deriving test sequences from FSM and conformance testing.

In (Barnett, M. et al, SCESM 2003) an approach is presented for modeling use cases and scenarios in the Abstract State Machine Language and how to use such models for validation and verification purposes is discussed. The most unique feature of AsmL is its foundation on Abstract State Machines (ASMs). An ASM is a state machine, which in each step computes a set of updates of the machines variables. Upon the completion of a step, all updates are "fired" (committed) simultaneously. The computation of an update set can be complex, and the numbers of updates calculated may depend on the current state. Control flow of the ASM is described in AsmL in a programmatic, textual way.

In (Grieskamp, W. et. al, 2003), the problem of algorithmic generation of an FSM from a given AsmL spec is studied. A major benefit of formal specifications is their use as a source for algorithmic generation of test suites, which is an integral part of the model-based testing approach to software testing. Typically, the models are required to be finite state machines (FSMs) mainly due to the existing tool support. FSM based tools are useful because they are supported by well-established automata theory and efficient graph algorithms. However FSM based modeling approach has its limitations in the sense that the FSM model may not be suited for testing. In (Grieskamp, W., Nachmanson, L., Tillmann, N., & Veanes, M., 2003), the problem is studied keeping in view that the desired FSM should reflect important functionalities of the spec, so that the test suites generated from the FSM are meaningful and target the testing problem at hand. The FSM also should be of manageable size. The basic algorithm that is described in detail in (Grieskamp, W., Nachmanson, L., Tillmann, N., & Veanes, M., 2003) has been extended in several ways in the tool to address these issues.

(Riccobene, E., Gargantini, A. & Asmundo, M. N., 2002), addresses both problems of components integration and specification-based testing of components using sequential Abstract State Machines (ASMs). ASMs have theoretical foundations, clear & precise semantics and hence this formal method is adopted to construct rigorous integration operations for partial specifications and to define methods for generating test suites from high-level specifications. A prototype tool has been developed that implements the proposed method.

In (Farchi, E., Hartman, A. & Pinter, S. S., 2002), authors show how certain complex aspects of software standards can be described using finite state machine (FSM) models. In this paper they have developed an FSM model to substitute for the natural language description. The test suite is automatically obtained from the model using an FSM model-based test generator named GOTCHA-TCBeans. In (Paradkar, A., 2003), a model-based approach to generate conformance tests for interactive applications is described. This method addresses generation of: (i) small yet effective set of test frames for testing individual operations, (ii) a Set up sequence that brings the system under test in an appropriate state for a test frame (self-priming) (iii) a Verification sequence for expected output and state changes (self-checking) and (iv) negative test cases in the presence of exceptions. This method exploits a novel scheme applied to operations modeled as relationships among parameters and state variables; a set of abstraction techniques resulting in a compact finite state automaton; and search techniques to automatically generate the set up and verification sequences.

In (Bŏrger, E., Cavarra, A. & Riccobene, E., 2004) a framework for defining the semantics of the dynamic UML diagrams has been presented here using ASMs. The method has been illustrated for state diagrams making semantic variation points of UML explicit as well as various ambiguities and omissions in official UML documents. In (Hong, H.S., Kwon, Y. R. & Cha, S.D., 1995), the authors discuss how FSMs can be effectively used for class testing. A major characteristic of classes is the interaction between data members and member functions. This interaction is represented as definitions and uses of data members in member functions and can be properly modeled with finite state machines (FSM). They demonstrate how to specify the behavior of classes using FSMs and present a test case generation technique based on FSMs. FSMs are transformed into a flow graph from which one can explicitly identify data flows of the FSM. Then test cases are generated using conventional data flow testing techniques upon the flow graph.

GRAPHICAL MODELS

Graphical models are yet another method of representing software behavior. Graph theory is an area of mathematics that helps us in using this model information to test applications in many different ways. In (Robinson, H., 1999), several graph theory techniques are discussed, where they came from, and how they can be used to improve software testing.

Petrinets

In (Van der Aalst, W.M.P., Van Hee, K.M., Houben, G.J., 1994), a Petri Net based framework is presented that facilitates specification of workflow applications, serves as tool for modeling the system at conceptual level, enable analysis, simulation and validation of the system. Workflow system is basically a heterogeneous and distributed information system where tasks are performed using autonomous systems and prerequisite to tasks are a set of constraints that reflect business rules and user requirements. This paper analyses the various structural properties of PNs to identify inconsistent dependency specification among tasks, test whether a workflow terminates at an acceptable state, test whether a workflow is feasible for execution within temporal constraints.

(Jiang, T., Klenke, R.H, Aylor, J.H. & Han, G., 2000) describes a technique that provides the designer with a feedback on testability of the specific architecture being modeled at an abstract level. The testability measure helps in identifying and reducing testing difficulties early in the design cycle. The testability is expressed as relative controllability and observability of signals in the system architecture. This is derived from reachability graph analysis of the corresponding Petri net representation of the system architecture. The authors claim that this method would help in designing systems with lower costs, higher performance and meeting testability requirements. (Lamch, D., 2002), presents an example of using petrinets for analyzing of the dynamic features of telecommunication systems and developed a software tool to verify and analyze the features in an algebraic way.

In (Berthomieu, B. & Diaz, M., 1991) a description and analysis of concurrent systems like communication systems whose behavior is dependent on explicit values of time is presented. An enumerative method is proposed in order to exhaustively validate the behavior of Merlin's time Petri net model (TPN). This method allows verification of time dependent systems. This is applied to the specification and verification for a communication system as an example. The focus of (Lee, J., Panb, J. I. & Kuoc, J. Y., 2001), is on the use of time Petri-nets (TPNs) to serve as the verification mechanism for the acquired scenarios. Scenarios are useful to elicit user requirements or to validate requirements specifications. As scenarios are useful for the lifecycle of requirements engineering, it is important to enable verification of these scenarios, to detect any wrong information and missing information that are hidden in scenarios. Use cases are used to elicit the user needs and to derive the scenarios. Each of the use cases is described from a user's perspective and depicts a specific flow of events in the system. After specifying all possible scenarios, each of them can be transformed into its correspondent time Petri-nets model. Through the analysis of these TPNs models, wrong information and missing information in scenarios can be detected.

The verification and validation of Petri nets are important in the development of concurrent and distributed systems. An approach to testing Petri nets is to develop test criteria so that test adequacy can be measured objectively and test cases can be generated efficiently. (Zhu, H. & He, X., 2002) presents four types of testing strategies – State-oriented, transition oriented, flow-oriented and specification-oriented testing.

Flow Graphs

ESML is a graphics-based language and is an extension of the data flow diagram notation for representing control logic in models of real-time systems. In (Richter, G. & Maffeo, B., 1993), analysis and summary is presented to provide a rigorous interpretation of ESML symbols and their combinations. Based on Petri Nets, formal foundations of ESML and its transformation schema notation have been proposed. The resulting Petri Nets are accurate models of the dynamics of real-time systems. The authors state that due to their

formal definition, the models may be executed for studying indeterminism and concurrency of events. (Muccini, H., Bertolino, A. & Inverardi, P., 2004), deals with the use of Software Architecture (SA) as a reference model for testing the conformance of an implemented system with respect to its architectural specification. The SA dynamics is modeled by Labeled Transition Systems (LTSs). The specification of SA dynamics is used to identify useful schemes of interactions between system components and to select test classes corresponding to relevant architectural behaviors. The approach consists of deriving suitable LTS abstractions called ALTSs and then deriving an adequate set of test classes by deriving a set of paths that appropriately cover the ALTS. In this paper authors also discuss the insights gained and highlight some issues, problems, and solutions of general interest in architecture-based testing.

In (Marré, M. & Bertolino, A., 2003) the notion of spanning sets of entities for coverage testing is introduced. A test coverage criterion defines a set of entities E_c of the program flowgraph and requires that every entity in this set is covered under some test case. Coverage criteria are also used to measure the adequacy of the executed test cases. A spanning set is a minimum subset of E_c, such that a test suite covering the entities in this subset is guaranteed to cover every entity in E_c. When the coverage of an entity always guarantees the coverage of another entity, the former is said to subsume the latter. Based on the subsumption relation between entities, a generic algorithm is developed to find spanning sets for control flow and data flow-based test coverage criteria. This approach helps in reducing and estimating the number of test cases needed to satisfy coverage criteria and is also shown how the use of spanning sets affects the fault detection effectiveness.

(Wooff, D.A., Goldstein, M. & Coolen, F.P.A., 2002), describes a new approach to the problem of software testing based on Bayesian graphical models and presents formal mechanisms for the logical structuring of the software testing problem, the probabilistic and statistical treatment of the uncertainties to be addressed, the test design and analysis process, and the incorporation and implication of test results. Once constructed, the models produced are dynamic representations of the software-testing problem. They may be used to drive test design and provide decision support to managers and testers. The models capture the knowledge of the software tester for further use.

(Bertolino, A., & Marre, M., 1994) presents a generalized algorithm that provides path cover for a given program flowgraph. Branch testing a program involves generating a set of paths that will cover every arc in the program flow and finding a set of test inputs that will execute every path. The analysis is conducted on a reduced graph and provides flexibility in executing all oaths and even infeasible paths. In (Kanjilal A., Kanjilal G. & Bhattacharya S., ICGSE 2008), the authors present a new hierarchical graph Distributed Scenario Graph (D-SG) to model the interleaving of sequence diagrams realizing a requirement. Analysis based on the based is able to identify test paths for a requirement in distributed development scenario.

In (Harrold, M. J. & Rothermel, G., 1994), a new approach to class testing is presented that supports dataflow testing for dataflow interactions in a class. For individual methods in a class, and methods that send messages to other methods in a the class, this technique is similar to existing dataflow testing techniques. This technique is also useful for determining which sequences of methods should be executed to test a class, even in the absence of a specification. Finally, as with other code-based testing techniques, a large portion of it can be automated.

We have proposed a new hierarchical graphical model named Extended Control Flow Graph (ECFG) for Object Oriented systems in (Kanjilal, A., Kanjilal, G. & Bhattacharya, S., 2003). Analogous to Control Flow graph, it identifies different kinds of method connections and derives Extended

cyclomatic complexity of the software. This work is extended in (Bhattacharya, S. & Kanjilal, A., TENCON 2004), where analysis of object oriented systems is done using ECFG. Further test paths are identified and automated generation of test paths from a set of OO programs is presented in (Kanjilal, A. & Bhattacharya, S., ADCOM 2004). An analysis of object oriented systems based on its extended flow graph developed based on code is presented in (Bhattacharya, S. & Kanjilal, A., 2006).

Unified Modeling Language (UML)

OMG's Model Driven Architecture (MDA) (OMG, 2003) initiative aims to separate business and application logic from underlying platform technology. It is based on UML and other associated OMG modeling standards and its acceptance has led to popularity of UML being widely used as an industry standard for modeling object oriented systems. However, UML lacks the rigor of formal syntax and semantics and hence lot of work is associated with formalization of UML diagrams for the purpose of verification and testing. This section lists some of them in the context of model based testing.

In (Traoré, I., & Demissie B. A., 2004) authors propose a development framework that supplements structured review with model-based verification. The proposed approach uses the Unified Modeling Language (UML) as a modeling notation. A set of correctness arguments is discussed that can be used in conjunction with formal verification and validation (V&V) in order to improve the quality and dependability of systems in a cost-effective way. The proposed framework is based on the integration of lightweight formal methods and structured reviews.

(Cavarra, A., Crichton, C. & Davies, J., 2004) shows how object-oriented specifications, written in UML can be translated into formal, behavioral descriptions and used as a basis for automatic test generation. The behavioral descriptions are written in a language of communicating state machines, the Intermediate Format (IF). The translation from UML to IF is based upon an earlier formal semantics, written in the Abstract State Machine (ASM) notation. Descriptions written in IF can be automatically explored, the results of these explorations are test trees, ready for input to a variety of testing packages.

Software artifacts like model descriptions, diagrammatic languages, abstract (formal) specifications, and source code—are highly interrelated where changes in some of them affect others. Trace dependencies characterize such relationships abstractly. (Egyed, A., 2003) presents an automated approach to generating and validating trace dependencies. It addresses the severe problem that the absence of trace information or the uncertainty of its correctness limits the usefulness of software models during software development.

(Bertolino, A., Marchetti, E., & Muccini, H., 2004) proposes as to how UML behavioral models, such as Sequence and State Diagrams, may be integrated together in order to provide a more informative base for software model-based testing in industrial projects. The information from Sequence and State diagrams and implied scenarios are taken to improve upon the model. (Engels, G., Hausmann, J. H., Heckel, R. & Sauer, S., 2002), proposes dynamic meta modeling rules DMM as a notation for the specification of UML consistency conditions and provide the concept for an automated testing environment using those rules. DMM is an operational semantics description that uses the idea of meta modeling to define abstract syntax of UML. This helps in capturing consistency conditions in a precise and formal way and presents them in a notation that closely relates to UML collaboration diagrams. (Andr´e, P., Romanczuk, A., Royer, J. C., 2000) introduces formal semantics for UML based on algebraic abstract data types. In this paper, only class and object diagrams have been considered. It suggests first-class association, it allows association constraints, it formalizes structural inheritance, it

gives useful and rigorous definitions to specialized association. It is also shown that tool like Larch Prover helps in the proof of properties and also can detect some ill-formed designs.

Formal verification Tools (FVTs) provide a mathematical background for formally verifying systems. With the popularity of visual modeling tools like UML, the need for formal verification of such models (before implementation) has gained importance. In (Mota, E., et. Al., 2004) work has been done in integrating the FVTs and the CASE tools (creating UML) by translation of diagrams to model checker's notations and also creates an interface for integrating the two technologies as a reliable solution to bridge the gap. In (Ramalho, F., Robin, J. & Schiel, U., 2004) a Concurrent Transaction Frame Logic (CTFL) is presented as a language to provide formal semantics to UML activity and Class diagrams. The application of state diagrams to class testing have been discussed in (Kim, Y.G., Hong, H.S., Cho, S.M, Bae, D.H. & Cha, S.D., 1999). A set of coverage criteria has been proposed based on control and data flow in state diagrams and generation of test cases from them are shown.

An alternative semantics for UML statechart diagrams is proposed in (Simons, A. J. H, 2000), The semantics designed around twelve rules ensures that under specified design rules the statecharts may be constructed to have true compositional properties. The notion of pseudostates were abandoned, independence of nested state machines examined, boundary-crossing transitions eliminated from composite states, all leading to independent analysis of state machines.

In (Toth, A. Varro, D. & Pataricza, A., 2003) Andras et al proposes a methodology for automatic test generation for UML statecharts. For automatic test generation they have used planner algorithms to deal with the complexity of UML models. The input to their framework is an UML statechart in a tool-independent XMI format (done by commercial UML tool), which is transformed to an output text file which forms the input to the planner tool (GraphPlan has been used). Finally planner tools automatically generate test cases for a given test criterion – typical test criterion include testing at each transition, each state, execution path at least once.

UML 2.0 testing profile (U2TP) initiated by OMG enables the specification of tests for structural and behavioural aspects of computational UML models, which is capable of inter-operating with existing technologies for black box testing. (Schieferdecker, I., Dai, Z.R., Grabowski, J. & Rennoch, A., 2003) discusses different approaches for testing with UML and mapping of UML 2.0 testing concepts to the standardized Testing and Test Control Notation (TTCN-3). Another paper (Schieferdecker, I. & Grabowski, J., 2003), discusses GFT, graphical format of TTCN-3, which also forms the basis for the definition of U2TP to test development with UML models. Like UML, Message sequence chart (MSC) is another graphical system design technique and this paper discusses GFT in relation to both MSC and U2TP.

An approach for verification of UML activity diagrams is proposed in (Eshuis, R. & Wieringa, R., 2004), It translates an activity diagram to an input format for a model checker and verifies the workflow against requirements. The formal semantics proposed has been substantiated with example verifications.

P. Krishnan in (Krishnan, P., 2000), presents an approach to defining UML diagrams in terms of state predicates and uses the theorem prover PVS (Prototype Verification System) to verify consistency between various diagrams. The dynamic aspects of the various diagrams have been considered.

In (Egyed, A., 2001), an approach for automated consistency checking named VIEWIN-TEGRA has been developed. It provides support for active (preventive) and passive (detective) consistency checking. An UML-based transformation framework is introduced and discusses how it aids comparison and improves consistency

checking. In (Wolf, M., Ivanov, E., Burkhardt, R. & Philippow, I., 2000) model examination defines strategies to ensure consistency in object-oriented models. It also makes it possible to recognize and minimize errors already on the level of the individual models. For both innovations, specific elements were integrated in the UML modeling tool Object Technology Workbench OTW(r). A UML based textual language UML-L for the formal description of static and dynamic object models is proposed in (Hamed, H., & Salem, A., 2001), UML-L is used to analyze the static object model and check consistency between the definitions of static and dynamic object models.

In (Zisman, A. & Kozlenkov, A., 2001), a knowledge base goal-driven approach for consistency management of UML specifications represented as axioms, which define goals, is presented. An inference procedure as a flexible pattern-based abduction used to build and morph paths based on the specifications is proposed. The approach involves a two-step interaction process between the specifications: observation and comparison. Prototypes of the knowledge base engine and of a tool to map UML specifications in XMI format to the knowledge base have been developed to demonstrate and evaluate the approach.

An approach to define an executable semantics for UML is presented in (Ober, I., 2000). Using the semantic a symbolic execution of an UML model was possible. Abstract State Machines (ASM) have been used as an underlying formalism for the semantics definition, which is composed of static semantics and dynamic semantics. A part of the static semantics was done by expressing in ASM the UML meta model and well-formedness rules defined in the UML standard. The dynamic semantics is based on a set of behavior primitives (time, communication, etc.). The ASM transition rules are defined corresponding to UML actions.

The work in (Kim, S. K. & Carrington, D., 2004), introduces a formal object-oriented meta-modeling approach to define integrity constraints between different UML models. Adopting a formal approach, constraints are formally defined using Object-Z. This work demonstrates how integrity consistency constraints for UML models can be precisely defined at the language-level. An algorithmic approach to a consistency check between UML Sequence and State diagrams is described in (Litvak, B., Tyszberowicz, S. & Yehudai, A., 2003). The algorithm provided handles complex State diagrams including forks, joins and concurrent composite states. A tool, BVUML is implemented that assists in automating the validation process. A consistency concept for sequence diagrams and state-chart diagrams is presented in (Küster, J. M., 2001), which focuses on the establishment of timing constraints. The consistency concept discussed in the paper distinguishes between syntactical, semantic and real-time consistency and takes into account the influence of processor allocation and scheduling.

Zhiming Liu in (Liu, Z., 2004), stresses on the problems of consistency in UML models and the need for a precise semantics. He presents a framework for formal analysis based on CBOOL and use only those models that are definable in CBOOL like – class diagrams, sequence, state machines, component diagrams and activity diagrams. In (Küster J. M. & Stehr, J., 2003), a declarative approach for consistency checking between sequence and statecharts has been presented. Different behavioral consistency has been stated and the models are translated into the semantic domain using process algebra CSP. On the other hand, in (Mens, T., Ragnhild, Van der Straeten & Simmonds, J., 2003), Description logic – a decidable fragment first order predicate logic is used to specify and detect inconsistencies between UML models. Using this formalism, UML models have been transformed to DL and they have validated their approach using two tools Loom and Racer.

In (Kanjilal A., Kanjilal G. & Bhattacharya S., INFOCOMP 2008), a novel approach is presented to quantitatively estimate the consistency among UML Sequence and Class diagrams based on a set of Design Consistency metrics, DCM and an XML based implementation approach is illustrated with an example.

In (Egyed, A., 2001), a new approach is introduced for consistency checking based on model transformations. Their approach can validate consistency of an abstract view (design model) that has been reverse engineered from concrete view (code) or vice versa. This paper discusses consistency check between abstract view (UML class diagrams) to concrete view (Classes in code). In (Xia, F., & Kane, G. S., 2003) a lightweight approach is proposed which uses only basic set notations and defines semantics of UML class and sequence diagrams based on certain innovative attributes reflecting semantics properties of programs. In (Tsiolakis, A. & Ehrig, H., 2000) consistency rules and analysis between UML class and sequence diagrams using attributed graph grammars have been discussed. The diagrams have been represented as attributed graphs and algorithms have been developed for analysis.

In (Traoré, I. & Aredo, D. B., 2004) a framework is proposed that extends structured review to incorporate model-based verification. The proposed approach uses UML as a modeling notation. The framework is based on integration of lightweight formal methods and structured reviews. The work in (Apvrille, L. Coutiat, J. P., Lohr, C & Saqui-Sannes, P. D., 2004), presents a UML 1.5 profile named TURTLE (Timed UML and RT-LOTOS Environment) represented as formal semantics given in terms of RT-LOTOS. TURTLE relies on UML's extensibility mechanism to extend class and activity diagrams. An end user is allowed to directly check the TURTLE model against logical errors and timing inconsistencies.

In (Kozlenkov, A. & Zisman, A.), a goal-driven knowledge based approach for checking and analyzing behavioral and structural inconsistencies in UML specifications is presented. UML metamodel is represented as axioms defining the goals within a knowledge base (KB) and is dynamically bound to concrete model instances at runtime. Querying and comparing paths through the specifications verify inconsistencies.

Test adequacy criteria require coverage of various parts of UML models such as Structural (Class) or behavioral (Sequence) views. (Pilskalns, O., Andrews, A., France, R. & Ghosh, S) proposes a new graph that encapsulates the many paths that exist between objects via their method calls as a directed acyclic graph (OMDAG). An Object method execution table (OMET) is introduced that captures both execution sequence and attribute values. Through an algorithm that merges the views, generates and executes tests.

In (Sengupta, S., Kanjilal, A., Bhattacharya, S., 2006), we have identified the dependencies between some of the commonly used UML diagrams, proposed a methodology for deriving a set of behavioral diagrams and for ensuring consistency among them. A set of rules has been developed which verifies existence of elements between two diagrams as well as certain metrics formulated within the diagrams. In (Sengupta, S., Kanjilal, A., & Bhattacharya, S., 2005), we have used OCL for proposing a methodology for derivation of statechart diagram from a set of sequence diagrams. An XML based approach has been followed for comparing and verifying different UML diagrams. In (Kanjilal, A., 2007), we have proposed a model based testing methodology to model sequence diagrams as Message sequence Graphs (MSG) and derive test paths based on MSG. An XML based approach to trace requirements to design models is also proposed and partly implemented in a prototype. As a step towards prototyping, we have presented in (Sengupta, S., 2007), an approach to automatically derive design components (UML component diagrams) for functional requirements from SRS.

Combinatorial Models

In this section we showcase some works that focus on SOFL and AETG, which uses combinatorial design processes and an integration of other mod-

eling techniques for model based testing. SOFL is a formal specification language and methodology which is a hierarchical condition data flow diagram (CDFD) consisting of data flows, data stores and condition processes.

(Offutt, A. J. & Liu, S., 1997) presents a new method for generating tests from formal specifications. This method is comprehensive in specification coverage and applies at several levels of abstraction and can be highly automated. The paper applies the method to SOFL specifications and describes the technique and demonstrates the application on a case study. SOFL, standing for Structured Object-Oriented Formal Language, integrates VDM-SL, Data Flow Diagrams, and Petri Nets to provide an intuitive, rigorous, and comprehensible formal notation for specifications at different levels

(Dalal, S. R., Jain, A., Patton, G., Rathi, M., & Seymour, P., 1998) presents AETGSM, a web based service developed by Bellcore researchers to enable model based testing. It employs a web based user interface to model the functional requirements of the system under test (SUT) and automatically generate test cases for the system using AETGSM automated test generation technology. (Cohen, D. M., Dalal, S. R., Fredman, M. I., & Patton, G. C., 1997), describes a new approach to testing that uses combinatorial designs to generate tests that cover the pairwise, triple, or n-way combinations of a system's test parameters. These are the parameters that determine the system's test scenarios like system configuration parameters, user inputs and other external events. In this new approach, the tester first identifies parameters that define the space of possible test scenarios. The tester then uses combinatorial designs to create a test plan that "covers" all pair-wise, triple, or n-way combinations of the test parameters. The AETG system uses new combinatorial algorithms to generate test sets that cover all valid n-way parameter combinations. The size of an AETG test set grows logarithmically with the number of test parameters. Hence it is possible to define test models that use dozens of parameters but a small number of test sets and increase in eth number of parameters does not lead to test set explosion.

The combinatorial design method substantially reduces testing costs. The authors in (Cohen, D. M., Dalal, S. R., Parelius, J. & Patton, G. C., 1996), describe an application in which the method reduced test plan development from one month to less than a week. In several experiments, the method demonstrated good code coverage and fault detection ability. The paradigm of model-based testing shifts the focus of testing from writing individual test cases to developing a model from which a test suite can be generated automatically. (Dalal, S. R., Jain, A., Karunanithi, N., Leaton, J. M., & Lott, C. M., 1998), discusses the approach used in U.S. Telephone network. The approach used automatic test-case generation technology to develop sets of self-checking test cases based on a machine-readable specification of the messages in the protocol under test. The AETGTM software system selected a minimal number of test-data tuples that covered pairwise combinations of tuple elements. It was found that the combinatorial approach of covering pairwise interactions between input fields was more effective than the traditional, manual approach and was able to uncover errors that would have not been otherwise possible. It also discusses four case studies to establish the usefulness and need for Model based testing. The combinatorial approach AETGTM has been used for the approach. AETG Spec, a simple notation has been used to capture the functional requirements of the system in such a way that test cases may be developed easily.

MODEL BASED TESTING TOOLS

Generically speaking, all software testing activity is model based, since any test case must be designed using some mental model of the application under test. In recent years the use of explicit models for software development like UML has increased and the OMG initiative of MDA also has revolutionized the way models are used for development. The use of these models for the generation of test cases is gaining importance as it leads to low testing costs due to early error detection and more reliable software. This section summarizes a list of Model based testing tools available and in use in the industry.

Table 1 shows a list of MBT tools along with the company and the model used.

CONCLUSION

Model based testing aims at automation of the software testing process resulting in low cost but efficient testing techniques and higher quality product. It deals with test case generation based on models rather than code unlike traditional testing techniques. Since models are abstract representations of system, ensuring error-free and higher quality product becomes viable with MBT as management of requirement changes in models are easy. However, models do have their limitations in expressing system behavior and functions. Some models are better suited for design but difficult for testing purposes. In this chapter we have attempted to give a summary of the various kinds of testing techniques being developed.

Formal models are useful for testing purposes as they are unambiguous representations of systems but are difficult to be applied because of their complex syntax and semantics. Training in formal languages and thereby its application in the software industry would be cumbersome in comparison to use of user friendly tools based on such formal models. Hence lot of scope remains for development of complete test frameworks and tools such that they may be applied in the software industry easily to gain the maximum benefit of MBT.

UML is a semi formal model and is widely used to describe static as well as behavioral aspects of Object oriented systems. However it lacks the

Table 1. MBT tools

Tool Name	Company	Model
AETG™ Web Service	Telcordia Technologies	Efficient Test case generation service model
ASML	Microsoft Corporation	Abstract State Machines
COW SUITE	PISATEL (Pisa Initiative on Software Architectures for Telecommunications), http://pacinotti.isti.cnr.it/ERI/	UML
CONFORMIQ Test generator	Conformiq Software Ltd	UML state diagrams
GOTCHA-TCBEANS	IBM Corporation	None
JUMBL	Stacy Prowell	Markov Chains
MULSAW	Research project in MIT	AAL(Alloy Annotation Language), Prioni (a tool)
PARASOFT JCONTRACT	Embedded Star™.	Simulink and Stateflow models
REACTIS	Reactis Systems Inc.	Simulink and Stateflow models
TAU TTCN Suite	Telelogic	TTCN-2
TAU UML Suite	TeleLogic	UML(Unified Modeling Language) and SDL (Specification Description Language)
TESTMASTER	Free software written by Alan Pearson	None
T-VEC	T-VEC Technologies	SCR models
UNITESK	UniTesK, http://www.unitesk.com	Sec and Java for C and Java.
TOSTER	DACS: The Data and Analysis Centre for Software	UML diagrams
TGV/CADP	IRISA and VERIMAG	LOTOS, SDL

rigor of formal languages. Hence the need for formalization of such models is extremely necessary. Lot of research work focuses on formalization of one or more UML diagrams and OMG has taken various initiatives, which focus on UML testing. A complete formal standard for all UML diagrams is yet to be developed and most of the research works in the domain of UML are now working towards achieving that.

Combinatorial models are yet another promising domain of research. In most practical cases a single model sometimes becomes insufficient to truly represent a software system. Hence combination of models, which embodies the best of each of its component models, may be very useful in development of efficient testing strategies leading to higher quality software products.

REFERENCES

Aichernig, B. K. (1999). Automatic Black-box testing with VDM oracles. *18th International Conference on Computer Safety, Reliability and Security, SAFECOMP '99,* (pp. 250-259).

Al-Ghafees, M. A. (2000). Markov Chain based test data adequacy criteria. *IRMA* '00. (pp. 141)

Andr´e, P., Romanczuk, A., Royer, J. C. (2000). Checking the Consistency of UML Class Diagrams Using Larch Prover. *Electronic Workshops in Computing eWiC, Rigorous Object-Oriented Methods 2000.*

Apvrille, L., Coutiat, J. P., Lohr, C., & Saqui-Sannes, P. D. (2004). TURTLE-A Real time UML profile supported by a Formal validation Toolkit. *IEEE Transactions on Software Engineering, 30*(7), 473–487. doi:10.1109/TSE.2004.34

Barnett, M., & Grieskamp, W. Nachmanson, Gurevich, Y., L. Schulte, W., Tillmann, N. & Veanes, M. (2003). Scenario oriented modeling in Asml and its instrumentation for testing. *2nd International Workshop on Scenarios and State Machines: Models, Algorithms and Tools (SCESM).*

Barnett, M., Grieskamp, W., & Nachmanson, L. Schulte, W., Tillmann, N. & Veanes, M. (2003), Model-Based Testing with AsmL. NET. *1st European Conference on Model-Driven Software Engineering.*

Barnett, M., Grieskamp, W., & Nachmanson, L. Schulte, W., Tillmann, N. & Veanes, M. (2003). Towards a tool environment for model based testing with AsmL. *3rd International Workshop on Formal Approaches to Testing of Software (FATES 2003),* (pp. 252-256).

Berthomieu, B., & Diaz, M. (1991). Modeling and Verification of Time Dependent Systems Using Time Petri Nets. *IEEE Transactions on Software Engineering, 17*(3), 259–273. doi:10.1109/32.75415

Bertolino, A., Marchetti, E., & Muccini, H. (2004). Introducing a Reasonably Complete and Coherent Approach for Model-based Testing. *10th International Conference on Tools and Algorithms for the Construction and Analysis of Systems, (TACAS'04).*

Bertolino, A., & Marre, M. (1994). Automatic Generation of path covers based on Control Flow analysis of Computer programs. *IEEE Transactions on Software Engineering,* 885–899. doi:10.1109/32.368137

Bhattacharya, S., & Kanjilal, A. (2004). Static Analysis of Object Oriented systems using Extended Control Flow graph. *IEEE TENCON, 2004,* B310–B313.

Bhattacharya, S., & Kanjilal, A. (2006). Code Based Analysis of Object Oriented Systems. *Journal of Computer Science & Technology JCST, 21*(6), 965–972. doi:10.1007/s11390-006-0965-0

Börger, E., Cavarra, A., & Riccobene, E. (2004). On Formalizing UML State Machines using ASMs. *Information and Software Technology, 46*(5), 287–292. doi:10.1016/j.infsof.2003.09.009

Buessow, R., & Grieskamp, W. (1997). Combining Z and Temporal Interval Logics for the Formalization of Properties and Behaviors of Embedded Systems. *3rd Asian Computing Science Conference on Advances in Computing Science, 1345,* 46-56.

Bussow, R., & Geisler, R. Grieskamp, W. & Klar, M. (1998). *Integrating Z with Dynamic Modeling Techniques for the Specification of Reactive Systems.*

Carrington, D., MacColl, I., McDonald, J., Murray, L., & Strooper, P. (2000). From Object-Z Specifications to ClassBench Test Suites, *Journal on Software Testing . Verification and Reliability, 10*(2), 111–137. doi:10.1002/1099-1689(200006)10:2<111::AID-STVR204>3.0.CO;2-P

Cavarra, A., Crichton, C., & Davies, J. (2004). A method for the automatic generation of test suites from object models . *Information and Software Technology, 46*(5), 309–314. doi:10.1016/j.infsof.2003.09.004

Cheng, B. H. C., & Wang, E. Y. (2002). Formalizing and integrating the dynamic model for object oriented modelling . *IEEE Transactions on Software Engineering,* 747–762. doi:10.1109/TSE.2002.1027798

Cohen, D. M., Dalal, S. R., Fredman, M. I., & Patton, G. C. (1997). The AETG system: An approach to testing based on Combinatorial design. *IEEE Transactions on Software Engineering, 23*, 437. doi:10.1109/32.605761

Cohen, D. M., Dalal, S. R., Parelius, J., & Patton, G. C. (1996). The combinatorial design approach to automatic test generation. *7th International Symposium on Software Reliability Engineering.* DACS Gold Practice™ Document Series (n.d.). *Model-Based Testing, GP-34 V 1.1.* Retrieved October 20, 2003 from http://www.goldpractices. com/dwnload/practice/pdf/Model_Based_Testing.pdf

Dalal, S. R., Jain, A., Karunanithi, N., Leaton, J. M., & Lott, C. M. (1998). Model-Based Testing of a Highly Programmable System. *9th International Symposium on Software Reliability Engineering, ISSRE'98 (IEEE Computer Society Press)*, (pp. 174–178).

Dalal, S. R., Jain, A., Patton, G., Rathi, M., & Seymour, P. (1998). AETG^SM Web: A Web based Service for Automatic Efficient Test Generation from Functional Requirements. *2nd IEEE Workshop on Industrial Strength Formal Specification Techniques.*

Dalal, S. R. A. Jain, N. Karunanithi, J. M. Leaton, C. M. Lott, G. C. Patton, B. M. Horowitz, (1999). Model Based Testing in Practice. *International Conference of Software Engineering ICSE'99*, (pp. 285-294).

Dan, L., & Aichernig, B. K. (2004) Combining Algebraic and Model Based Test Generation, Proceedings of ICTAC 2004. *1st International Colloquium on Theoretical Aspects of Computing*, (LNCS Vol. 3407, pp. 250-264). Berlin: Springer-Verlag.

Egyed, A. (2001). Automatically Validating Model Consistency during Refinement. *23rd International Conference on Software Engineering (ICSE 2001).*

Egyed, A. (2001). Scalable Consistency Checking Between Diagrams-The ViewIntegra Approach. *16th IEEE International Conference on Automated Software Engineering (ASE'01)*, (pp. 387-390).

Egyed, A. (2003). A Scenario-Driven Approach to Trace Dependency Analysis. *IEEE Transactions on Software Engineering, 29*(2), 116–132. doi:10.1109/TSE.2003.1178051

Engels, G., Hausmann, J. H., Heckel, R., & Sauer, S. (2002). Testing the Consistency of Dynamic UML Diagrams. *6th International Conference on Integrated Design and Process Technology.*

Eshuis, R., & Wieringa, R. (2004). Tool Support for Verifying UML Activity Diagrams. *IEEE Transactions on Software Engineering, 30*(7), 437–447. doi:10.1109/TSE.2004.33

Farchi, E., Hartman, A., & Pinter, S. S. (2002). Using a model-based test generator to test for standard conformance. *IBM Systems Journal, 41*(1), 89–110.

Fletcher, R., & Sajeev, A. S. M. (1996). A Framework for Testing Object Oriented Software Using Formal Specifications. *Reliable Software Technologies* (LNCS). Berlin: Springer-Verlag.

Grieskamp, W., Gurevich, Y., Schulte, W. & Margus Veanes (2002). Generating Finite state machines from abstract state machines. *ACM SIGSOFT 2002 International Symposium on Software Testing and Analysis, ISSTA'02.*

Grieskamp, W., Heisel, M., & Dorr, H. (1998). Specifying Embedded Systems with Statecharts and Z: An Agenda for Cyclic Software Components in Egidio Astesiano. *1st International Conference on Fundamental Approaches to Software Engineering - FASE'98*, (pp. 88-106).

Grieskamp, W., Nachmanson, L., Tillmann, N., & Veanes, M. (2003). Test Case generation from Asml specifications Tool overview. *10th International Workshop on. Abstract State Machines.*

Guen, H. L., Marie, R., & Thelin, T. (2004). Reliability Estimation for Statistical usage Testing using Markov chains. *15th International Symposium on Software Reliability Engineering (ISSRE'04)*.

Hamed, H., & Salem, A. (2001). UML-L: An UML Based Design Description Language. *ACS/IEEE International Conference on Computer Systems and Applications (AICCSA'01)*, (pp. 438-441).

Harrold, M. J., & Rothermel, G. (1994). Performing Data Flow testing on Classes. *2nd ACM SIGSOFT symposium on Foundations of Software Engineering (FSE '94)* (pp. 154-163).

Hong, H. S., Kwon, Y. R., & Cha, S. D. (1995). Testing of Object-Oriented Programs based on Finite State Machines. *2nd Asia-Pacific Software Engineering Conference (ASPEC'95)*, (p. 234).

Javed, F., Mernik, M., Bryant, B. R., & Gray, J. (2005). A Grammar based approach to Class Diagram Validation. *4th International Workshop on Scenarios and State Machines: Models, Algorithms and Tools (SCESM'05)*

Jiang, T., & Klenke, R. H. Aylor & J.H., Han, G. (2000), System level testability analysis using Petri nets. *IEEE International High-Level Design Validation and Test Workshop, 2000.* (pp. 112 – 117).

Kanjilal, A. (2007). *Analysis and Testing of Object-oriented Systems*. Ph.D. Thesis, Jadavpur University, India.

Kanjilal, A., & Bhattacharya, S. (2004). Test Path Identification for Object Oriented systems using Extended Control Flow Graph. *12th International Conference on Advanced Computing and Communication (ADCOM 2004)*.

Kanjilal, A., Kanjilal, G., & Bhattacharya, S. (2003). Extended Control Flow Graph: An Engineering Approach. *6th Intl. Conference on Information Technology, CIT'03,* (pp. 151-156).

Kanjilal, A., Kanjilal, G., & Bhattacharya, S. (2008). Integration of Design in Distributed Development using D-Scenario Graph. *IEEE Intl. Conference on Global Software Engineering, ICGSE'08,* (pp. 141-150).

Kanjilal, A., Kanjilal, G., & Bhattacharya, S. (2008). Metrics based Analysis of Requirements for Object-Oriented systems: An empirical approach. *INFOCOMP Journal of Computer Science, J7*(2), 26–36.

Kim, S. K., & Carrington, D. (2004). A Formal Object-Oriented Approach to defining Consistency Constraints for UML Models. *Australian Software Engineering Conference (ASWEC'04)*, (p. 87).

Kim, Y. G., Hong, H. S., Cho, S. M., Bae, D. H., & Cha, S. D. (1999). Test Cases generation from UML State diagrams. *IEEE Software, 146*(4), 187–192. doi:10.1049/ip-sen:19990602

Kozlenkov, A., & Zisman, A. (n.d.). *Checking Behavioral Inconsistencies in UML Specifications*. Retrieved from http://www.cs.tut.fi/tsystm/ICSE/papers/6.pdf, Krishnan, P. (2000). Consistency checks for UML. *7th Asia-Pacific Software Engineering Conference (APSEC'00)*, (p. 162).

Küster, J. M. (2001). Consistent Design of Embedded Real-Time Systems with UML-RT. *4th International Symposium on Object-Oriented Real-Time Distributed Computing*.

Küster, J. M., & Stehr, J. (2003). Towards Explicit Behavioral Consistency Concepts in the UML. *2nd International Workshop on Scenarios and State Machines: Models, Algorithms and Tools*.

Lamch, D. (2002). Verification and Analysis of Properties of Dynamic Systems Based on Petri Nets. *Proceedings of International Conference on Parallel Computing in Electrical Engineering (PARELEC'02)*, (pp. 92-94).

Lee, J., Panb, J. I., & Kuoc, J. Y. (2001). Verifying scenarios with time Petri-nets. *Information and Software Technology, 43*(13), 769–781. doi:10.1016/S0950-5849(01)00184-7

Litvak, B., Tyszberowicz, S., & Yehudai, A. (2003). Behavioral Consistency Validation of UML Diagrams. *1ˢᵗ International Conference on Software Engineering and Formal Methods (SEFM'03).*

Liu, Z. (2004). Consistency and refinement of UML models. *UML 2004 Workshop on Consistency Problems in UML-Based Software Development.*

MacColl, I., Murray, L., Strooper, P., & Carrington, D. (1998). Specification-based class testing – A case study. *2ⁿᵈ International Conference on Formal Engineering Methods (ICFEM'98). IEEE Computer Society*, (pp. 222-231).

Marré, M., & Bertolino, A. (2003). Using Spanning Sets for Coverage Testing. *Information and Software Technology, 29*(11), 974–984.

McDonald, J., Murray, L., & Strooper, P. (1997). Translating Object-Z Specifications to object-oriented Test Oracles. *4th Asia-Pacific Software Engineering and International Computer Science Conference (APSEC'97 / ICSC'97),* (p. 414).

Mens, T. Ragnhild, Van der Straeten & Simmonds, J. (2003). Maintaining Consistency between UML Models with Description Logic Tools. *4ᵗʰ International Workshop on Object-oriented Re-engineering (WOOR2003).*

Meudec, C. (1998). *Automatic Generation of Software Test Cases From Formal Specifications.* Ph. D. Thesis, The Queen's University of Belfast.

Mota, E., Clarke, E., Groce, A., Oliveira, W., Falcao, M., & Kanda, J. (2004). VeriAgent: An Approach to integrating UML and Formal Verification Tools. [ENTCS]. *Electronic Notes in Theoretical Computer Science, 95*, 111–129. doi:10.1016/j.entcs.2004.04.008

Muccini, H., Bertolino, A., & Inverardi, P. (2004). Using Software Architecture for Code Testing. *IEEE Transactions on Software Engineering, 30*(3), 160–171. doi:10.1109/TSE.2004.1271170

Ober, I. (2000) More Meaningful UML Models. *37ᵗʰ International Conference on Technology of Object-Oriented Languages and Systems (TOOLS-37'00),* (pp. 146-157).

Object Management Group. (n.d.). *MDA Guide Version 1.0.* Retrieved from http://www.omg.org, document no. - omg/2003-05-01

Offutt, A. J., & Liu, S. (1997). *Generating Test Data from SOFL Specifications.* (Tech. Rep.) ISSE-TR-97-02, Department of Information and Software Systems Engineering, George Mason University, VA, (pp. 1-24).

Paradkar, A. (2003). Towards model-based generation of self-priming and self-checking conformance tests for interactive systems Symposium on Applied Computing. *ACM symposium on Applied Computing*, (pp. 1110 – 1117). New York: ACM Press.

Pilskalns, O., Andrews, A., France, R., & Ghosh, S. (2003). Rigorous Testing by Merging Structural and Behavioral UML Representations. *6ᵗʰ International Conference on Unified Modeling Language.*

Pretschner, A. & L˜otzbeyer, H. & Philipps, J. (2001). Model Based Testing in Evolutionary Software Development. *12th IEEE Intl. Workshop on Rapid System Prototyping (RSP'01).*

Prowell, S. (2004). *State of the art Model based Testing with Markov chain usage models.* Dagstuhl Seminar No. 04371, September 5-10.

Prowell, S. J. (2003). JUMBL: A tool for model based testing using Markov chains. *36th Hawaii International Conference on System Sciences, HICSS 2003,* (p. 337).

Prowell, S. J. (2005). Using Markov chain usage models to test complex systems. *38th Annual Hawaii International Conference on System Sciences, HICSS'38.*

Ramalho, F., Robin, J., & Schiel, U. (2004). Concurrent Transaction Frame Logic Formal Semantics for UML activity and class diagrams. [ENTCS]. *Electronic Notes in Theoretical Computer Science, 95*, 83–109. doi:10.1016/j.entcs.2004.04.007

Riccobene, E., Gargantini, A., & Asmundo, M. N. (2002). Consistent Composition and Testing of Components using Abstract State Machines. *Workshop CoMeta – Computational Metamodels*, Richter, G. & Maffeo, B. (1993). Towards a rigorous interpretation of ESML – Extended Systems Modelling Language. *IEEE Transactions on Software Engineering, 19*(2), 165–180.

Robinson, H. (1999). Graph theory techniques in model based testing. *International Conference on Testing Computer Software.* Hosain S. & Alam S., (2004). Software reliability using markov chain usage model. *3rd International Conference on Electrical & Computer Engineering.*

Schieferdecker, I., Dai, Z. R., Grabowski, J., & Rennoch, A. (2003). *The UML 2.0 Testing profile and its Relation to TTCN-3*, (LNCS Vol. 2644, pp. 79-94). Berlin: Springer-Verlag.

Schieferdecker, I., & Grabowski, J. (2003). *The Graphical Format of TTCN-3 in the context of MSC and UML,* ([]. Springer-Verlag]. *LNCS, 2599*, 233–252.

Sengupta, S. (2007). *Functional Specifications of Object Oriented Systems: A Model Driven Framework.* Ph.D thesis, Jadavpur University, Kolkata, India.

Sengupta, S., & Bhattacharya, S. (2006). Formalization of Functional Requirements and Their Traceability in UML Diagrams- A Z Notation Based Approach. *11th Systems Engineering Test & Evaluation Conference (SETE'06).*

Sengupta, S., & Bhattacharya, S. (2006). Formalization of UML Use Case Diagram- A Z Notation Based Approach. *IEEE International Conference on Computing & Informatics (ICOCI'06),* (pp. 61-66).

Sengupta, S., & Bhattacharya, S. (2007). Functional Specification of Object Oriented Systems: A Model Driven Framework. *31st Annual IEEE International Computer Software and Applications Conference (COMPSAC'07).*

Sengupta, S., Bhattacharya, S., (2008). Formalization of Functional Requirements of Software Development Process. *Journal of Foundations of Computing and Decision Sciences (FCDS), Institute of Computing Science, Poznan University of Technology, Poland, 33*(1).

Sengupta, S., Kanjilal, A., & Bhattacharya, S. (2005). Automated Translation of Behavioral Models using OCL and XML. *IEEE TENCON, 05*, 86–91.

Sengupta, S., Kanjilal, A., & Bhattacharya, S. (2006). Behavioral Specification of Object Oriented Systems using OCL. *Conference on Recent Trends in Emerging Technologies (RTET06),* (pp. 31-35).

Sengupta, S., Sengupta, A., & Bhattacharya, S. (2007). Requirements to Components: A Model View Controller Architechture. *14th Monterey Workshop,* (pp. 167-184).

Simons, A. J. H. (2000). On the Compositional Properties of UML statechart diagrams. *Rigorous Object-Oriented Methods (ROOM'00).*

Spivey, J. M. (1992). *The Z Notation, A Reference Manual,* (2nd Ed.). Upper Saddle River, NJ: Prentice Hall International.

Toth, A. Varro, D. & Pataricza, A. (2003). Model-Level Automatic Test Generation for UML statecharts. *6th IEEE workshop on Design and Diagnostics of Electronic Circuits and System, (DDECS 2003).*

Traoré, I., & Aredo, D. B. (2004). Enhancing Structured Review with Model-based Verification. *IEEE Transactions on Software Engineering, 30*(11), 736–753. doi:10.1109/TSE.2004.86

Traoré, I., & Demissie, B. A. (2004). Enhancing Structured Review with Model-Based Verification. *IEEE Transactions on Software Engineering, 30*(11), 736–753. doi:10.1109/TSE.2004.86

Tsiolakis, A., & Ehrig, H. (2000). Consistency Analysis of UML Class and Sequence Diagrams using Attributed Graph Grammars. *Joint APPLIGRAPH and GETGRATS workshop on graph transformation systems,* (pp. 77-86).

Van der Aalst, W. M. P., Van Hee, K. M., & Houben, G. J. (1994). Modeling and Analysing Workflow using a Petri Net based approach. *2nd Workshop on Computer-Supported Cooperative Work, Petri nets and related Formalisms.*

Walton, G. H., & Poore, J. H. (2000). Measuring complexity and coverage of software specifications. *Information and Software Technology, 42*(12), 859–872. doi:10.1016/S0950-5849(00)00102-6

Whittaker, J. A., & Thomason, M. G. (1994). A Markov Chain Model for Statistical Software Testing. *IEEE Transactions on Software Engineering, 20*(10), 812–824. doi:10.1109/32.328991

Wolf, M., Ivanov, E., Burkhardt, R., & Philippow, I. (2000). UML Tool Support: Utilization of Object-Oriented Models. *Technology of Object-Oriented Languages and Systems (TOOLS 34 '00),* (p. 529).

Woodcock, J., & Davis, J. (1996). *Using Z Specification, Refinement and Proof.* Englewood Cliff, NJ: Prentice Hall.

Wooff, D. A., Goldstein, M., & Coolen, F. P. A. (2002). Bayesian Graphical Models for Software Testing. *IEEE Transactions on Software Engineering, 28*(5), 510–525. doi:10.1109/TSE.2002.1000453

Xia, F., & Kane, G. S. (2003). Defining the Semantics of UML Class and Sequence Diagrams for Ensuring the Consistency and Executability of OO Software Specification. *1st International Workshop on Automated Technology for Verification and Analysis (ATVA'2003).*

Zhu, H., & He, X. (2002). A methodology for testing high level Petri Nets. *Information and Software Technology, 44,* 473–489. doi:10.1016/S0950-5849(02)00048-4

Zisman, A., & Kozlenkov, A. (2001), Knowledge Base Approach to Consistency Management of UML Specifications. *16th IEEE International Conference on Automated Software Engineering (ASE'01),* (pp. 359-363).

KEY TERMS AND DEFINITIONS

Software Testing: Software testing is an empirical investigation conducted to provide stakeholders with information about the quality of the product or service under test, with respect to the context in which it is intended to operate. This includes, but is not limited to, the process of executing a program or application with the intent of finding software bugs. Software Testing is an activity carried out throughout the lifecycle of the software development process that ensures that a software product is built as per user specifications.

Model Driven Architecture (MDA): Model-driven architecture (MDA) is a software design approach for the development of software systems. It provides a set of guidelines for the structuring of specifications, which are expressed as models. Model-driven architecture is a kind of domain engineering, and supports model-driven engineering of software systems. It was launched by the Object Management Group (OMG) in 2001.

Model Based Testing (MBT): Model-Based Testing is the automatic generation of efficient test procedures/vectors using models of system requirements and specified functionality. Model-based testing is software testing in which test cases are derived in whole or in part from a model that describes some (usually functional) aspects of the system under test (SUT). As opposed to traditional testing techniques, MBT refers to development and use of testing techniques based on models that depict different aspect of a software system.

Formal Models: A formal model consists of a formal language together with a deductive system (also called a deductive apparatus), which consists of a set of inference rules and/or axioms. A formal system is used to derive one expression from one or more other expressions antecedently expressed in the system.

Graph Based Models: A graph-based model is a model based on graph theory. Testing an application can be viewed as traversing a path through the graph of the model. Graph theory techniques therefore allow us to use the behavioral information stored in models to generate new and useful tests.

Unified Modeling Language (UML): Unified Modeling Language (UML) is a standardized general-purpose modeling language in the field of software engineering. UML includes a set of graphical notation techniques to create abstract models of specific systems. It is used for visual modeling of object-oriented systems.

Testing Tools: The wide range of tools that is available for the purpose of automating the software testing activity.

Chapter 17
Matilda
A Generic and Customizable Framework for Direct Model Execution in Model-Driven Software Development

Hiroshi Wada
University of Massachusetts, USA

Junichi Suzuki
University of Massachusetts, USA

Adam Malinowski
Harvard University, USA

Katsuya Oba
OGIS International, Inc., USA

ABSTRACT

Traditional Model Driven Development (MDD) frameworks have three critical issues: (1) abstraction gap between modeling and programming layers, (2) a lack of traceability between models and programs, and (3) a lack of customizability to support various combinations of modeling technologies and implementation/deployment technologies. In order to address these issues, this chapter proposes a new MDD framework, called Matilda, which is a framework to build execution runtime engines (or virtual machines) for software models. It directly executes models defined with certain modeling technologies such as UML and BPMN by automatically transforming them to executable code. Matilda is designed based on the Pipes and Filters architectural pattern, which allows for configuring its structure and behavior flexibly by replacing one plugin with another one or changing the order of plugins. Also, plugins can be deployed on multiple network hosts and seamlessly connect them to form a pipeline. This facilitates distributed software development in which developers collaboratively work at physically dispersed places. This chapter overviews Matilda's architectural design, describes the implementations of Matilda-based virtual machines, and evaluates their performance.

DOI: 10.4018/978-1-60566-731-7.ch017

INTRODUCTION

Software modeling has advanced to the point where it can offer significant leverage to manage complexity and improve productivity in software development. A driving force in this advance is a series of mature modeling technologies. For example, the Unified Modeling Language (UML) provides a wide range of modeling notations and semantics used in various types of applications (UML Super Structure Specification 2.1.2, 2007). The Business Process Modeling Notation (BPMN) provides a set of well-defined notations and semantics for business process modeling (Business Process Modeling Notation (BPMN) 1.0, 2004). UML and BPMN allow developers to specify and communicate their application designs at a high level of abstraction. Using these modeling technologies, the notion of model-driven development (MDD) aims to graphically build application design models and transform them into running applications.

A key process in MDD is automated (or semi-automated) transformation of implementation independent models to lower-level models (or application code) specific to particular imple-mentation/deployment technologies such as programming languages, databases, middleware and business process engines (Booch, Brown, Iyengar, Rumbaugh, & Selic, 2004; Sendall & Kozaczynki, 2003). Traditional MDD frameworks allow developers to model their applications with modeling languages such as UML and BPMN, generate skeleton code in a programming language such as Java, and manually complete the generated skeleton code by, for example, adding method code (Figure 1). There exist three critical research issues in traditional MDD frameworks: (1) abstraction gap between modeling and programming layers, (2) a lack of traceability between models and programs, and (3) a lack of customizability to support various combinations of modeling technologies and implementation technologies.

The first issue is that, when programmers complete generated skeleton code to the final (compilable) code, they often suffer from abstraction gap between modeling and programming layers because the granularity of skeleton code is usually much finer than that of models. Skeleton code tends to be complicated to read and maintain. Thus, it is hard for programmers to obtain a broad view of an application design, and they have to repeatedly

Figure 1. Traditional MDD process

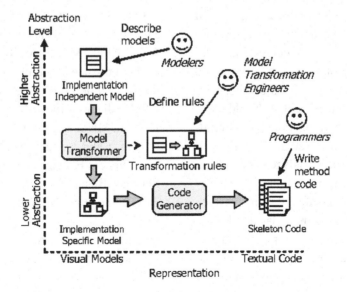

go up and down abstraction gap to identify where to implement what in skeleton code.

The second issue is that models tend to lose synchronization with programs through development process. For example, when programmers find bugs or design/implementation alternatives in the final (compilable) code, they often change the code directly rather than models. As a result, the program code becomes untraceable from models. Due to the above two issues, traditional MDD frameworks do not maximize the benefits of modeling application designs at a higher level of abstraction than programming layer.

The third issue in traditional MDD framework is that they often lack generality to support a variety of choices in modeling technologies and lack customizability to tailor model transformation and code generation according to the implementation/deployment technologies used in application development. This degrades reusability and longevity of application models; it is often hard to evolve application models for a long time by, for example, introducing new modeling technologies and changing implementation/deployment technologies.

This chapter describes and evaluates a new MDD framework, called Matilda, which addresses the three issues described above. Matilda is a generic framework to build execution runtime engines (or virtual machines) for various types of software models. Each virtual machine (VM) accepts and directory executes models defined with certain modeling technologies such as UML and BPMN through automatically transforming them to executable code (Figure 2). Matilda addresses the abstraction and synchronization issues by hiding the existence of source code from developers. Using Matilda, developers analyze, design, test, deploy and execute their applications consistently at the modeling layer, rather than shifting between the modeling and programming layers (Figure 2). Each Matilda-based VM accepts a model as an input, validates it against its metamodel, and transforms the input model to an implementation/deployment specific model by applying a given transformation rule (Figure 2). Matilda allows developers (model transformation engineers in Figure 2) to define arbitrary transformation rules, each of which specifies how to specialize an input model to a particular implementation/deployment technology. For example, a transformation rule may specialize an input model to a database, while another rule may specialize it to a remoting middleware.

Matilda addresses the customizability issue with its architectural design using a pipeline of plugins. Different plugins implement different functionalities in Matilda, such as visualizing, validating and transforming models. The pipeline architecture allows Matilda to flexibly customize its structure and behavior by replacing one plugin with another or changing the order of plugins. Also, Matilda's pipeline can be distributed over the network. Matilda can spread plugins to multiple network hosts and seamlessly connect them to form a pipeline. This enables distributed software development in which developers can collaboratively build, integrate and execute models at physically dispersed places.

Currently, Matilda provides two different VMs: UML-VM and SOA-VM. UML-VM accepts UML 2.0 class and sequence diagrams, validates them against the UML metamodel, transforms them to a JAST (Java Abstract Syntax Tree), generates Java bytecode and runs the generated code on a Java VM (JVM). SOA-VM accepts BPMN and UML sequence diagrams, validate them against the BPMN and UML metamodels, transforms a BPMN diagram to a UML class diagram, transforms UML diagrams to JAST, generates Java bytecode and a deployment descriptor in Business Process Execution Language (BPEL) (Web Services Business Process Execution Language, 2003), and runs the generated code on a BPEL engine.

This chapter overviews the design and implementation of Matilda, describes how UML-VM and SOA-VM are built on Matilda, evaluates their performance, and concludes with some discussion on related and future work.

DESIGN PRINCIPLES IN MATILDA

Matilda is designed based on the following principles.

1. Avoidance of Round-Tripping. In order to address the abstraction and synchronization issues, Matilda inherently avoids the round-trips between models and source code by hiding the existence of source code from developers. All bug fixes and design changes are directly made on models instead of source code (Figure 2).

2. Metamodel-Driven. Matilda performs all of its functionalities in a metamodel-driven manner. For example, UML model validation is performed against the UML metamodel, and JAST generation is performed with a metamodel of Java program elements. By following metamodels consistently, plugins in Matilda avoid to perform their functionalities ambiguously. Matilda represents UML, BPMN and Java metamodels as a set of objects (APIs), and aids its plugins to implement their functionalities on a metamodel basis.

3. Modularity and Loose Coupling. Matilda is designed to maximize the reusability of plugins by making them modular and loosely coupled. Matilda decomposes its functionalities into independent processing units and implements them as plugins. The functionality of each plugin does not depend on other plugins.

4. Configurability. Matilda is intended to be used in a variety of development projects; from in-house development, distributed open-source development to off-shore development. Different projects use different sets of plugins in different orders. For example, a project may require a plugin for generating Java bytecode, and another project may require a plugin for generating BPEL deployment descriptors as well as a Java bytecode generation plugin. Therefore, Matilda is designed to make pipelines configurable and extensible. It defines common APIs for pipelines and plugins so that each

Figure 2. Development process with Matilda

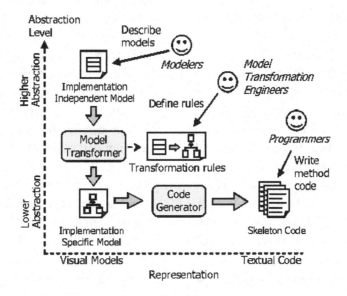

developer can choose plugins and configure a pipeline of the plugins. Matilda also allows developers to implement new plugins with its plugin API.

5. Transparent Distribution. Matilda supports distributed execution of plugins for distributed software development. Different plugins can run on different hosts in the network. For example, the plugins for model visualization and validation can run at a place, and the plugins for code generation can run at a different remote place. Plugins can be transparently distributed; each of them does not have to know whether others reside on the same host.

THE ARCHITECTURE OF MATILDA

There are four roles of users who involve in development process with Matilda. A modeler, or application developer, builds application design models (M1 models) and load them to Matilda (Figure 2). A metamodel engineer builds and/or registers metamodels (M2 models) including the UML metamodel, UML profiles and BPMN metamodel. A plugin engineer develops and registers plugins. A transformation engineer is a special type of plugin engineer, who defines transformation rules and implements them as plugins (Figure 2). A VM maintenance engineer is responsible for customizing a pipeline for a given VM.

The pipeline architecture of Matilda is designed based on the Pipes and Filters architectural pattern (Buschmann et al., 1996; Vermeulen, Beged-Dov, & Thompson, 1995). This pattern defines system architecture to process data streams. The task of a system is divided into several processing steps. These steps are connected along with a data flow in the system; an output data in a step becomes an input to a subsequent step. Each processing step is implemented as a filter, and filters are connected with pipes. The Pipes and Filters pattern is well applicable when a system can naturally decompose

its data processing task into independent steps and the task is likely to change over time. This pattern increases the reusability of filters, and allows a system to be flexible for exchanges and recombination of filters (Buschmann et al., 1996).

In Matilda, each plugin works as a filter and implements an individual step in an application development (Figure 3). For example, a model loader plugin accepts a UML model in the format of XML Metadata Interchange (XMI) (MOF 2.0 XMI Mapping Specification, 2007), a model validation plugin validates a UML model against the UML metamodel, and a JAST generation plugin transforms a validated UML model to a JAST. A pipeline contains one or more plugins on each network host, and multiple pipelines form a distributed, composite pipeline over multiple hosts (Figure 3). Each pipeline downloads required plugins form a plugin repository and connects them based on a configuration file that a VM maintenance engineer defines. The configuration file specifies plugins used in a pipeline and their execution order. Plugins can be executed sequentially or in parallel. Each plugin operates on the Matilda runtime, which operates on a JVM.

The Pipes and Filters pattern often lacks robust error handling because multiple asynchronous threads of execution do not share the global system state (Buschmann et al., 1996). In order to overcome this issue, Matilda implements a shared repository, called blackboard, based on the Blackboard architectural pattern (Figure 3) (Buschmann et al., 1996). This pattern is organized as a collection of independent processing units that work cooperatively on common data structures. Each processing unit specializes to process a particular part of the overall task. It fetches data from a blackboard, and stores a result of its data processing to the blackboard.

In Matilda, a blackboard stores data that each plugin generates (e.g., UML models and JASTs), and makes the data available to subsequent plugins (Figure 3). It also stores a processing log in each plugin (e.g., successful completion, errors, warn-

Figure 3. The behavioral architecture of Matilda

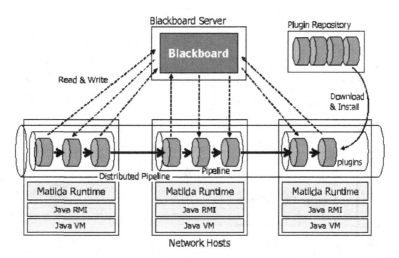

ings and time stamp) in order to trace the processing status in a pipeline. In Matilda, data flow between a blackboard and plugins, and processing control flows between pipelines (Figure 3).

Figure 4 shows the structural architecture of Matilda. Matilda consists of its kernel and plugins. The kernel is responsible for low-level house-keeping functionalities required to operate plugins. Matilda-based VMs are defined and deployed on Matilda by choosing particular plugins in particular configurations. Currently, Matilda's codebase contains 18,294 lines of Java code, which implements Matilda, UML-VM and SOA-VM.

Figure 4. The structural architecture of Matilda

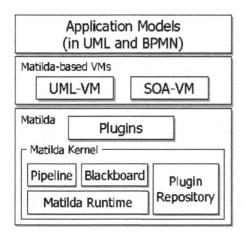

MATILDA KERNEL

Matilda's kernel consists of Matilda runtime, pipeline, blackboard and plugin repository. Figure 5 shows the class structure of Matilda's kernel. The class Runtime instantiates and configures Pipeline according to a given pipeline configuration file. The class Pipeline contains a set of plugins. They are defined as subclasses of the abstract class Plugin, which provides the methods to access a blackboard (readFromBB() and writeOnBB()). A Pipeline executes plugins by calling their execute() methods; each plugin implements its own functionality in execute(). The interface Blackboard defines the methods to read/write data from/on a blackboard.

The Matilda runtime (Runtime) configures a Pipeline by loading a pipeline configuration file with Config::LoadFile(). Config and PluginConfig maintain the configuration at runtime. Listing 1 shows an example pipeline configuration file that defines a sequential execution of four plugins. Each plugin's name and class file are specified with the plugin and class tags, respectively. For example, a plugin called ModelLoader is implemented by the class matilda.plugins.frontend. ModelLoader. The parameter tag defines a set of parameters passed to a plugin. The name attribute

255

Figure 5. A class structure of Matilda's Kernel

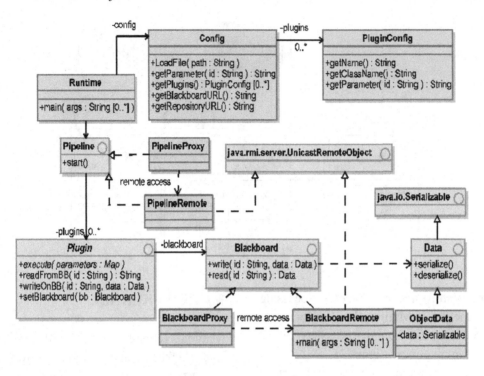

specifies the name of a parameter. The parameters in the pipeline tag are passed to all plugins, while the parameters in the plugin tag are passed only to a plugin that is designated by the plugin tag. For example, the parameter uml2resource can be referred by all plugins; however, the parameter modelpath can be referred only by ModelLoader. Once a Runtime configures a Pipeline, the Pipeline downloads required plugin class files from a plugin repository and executes them.Listing 1. A pipeline configuration file

```
<pipeline >
<parameter name="uml2resource">
jar:file:org.eclipse.uml2.uml.re-
sources_2 .0.2.jar!/
</parameter >
<plugin name="Model Loader">
<class >matilda.plugins.frontend.
ModelLoader </class >
<parameter name="modelpath">models/
model.uml2 </parameter >
```

```
</plugin >
<plugin name="Class to JAST Trans-
former">
<class >matilda.plugins.backend.
CD2JASTTransforder </class >
</plugin >
<plugin name="Sequence to JAST
Transformer">
<class >matilda.plugins.backend.
SD2JASTTransformer </class >
</plugin >
<plugin name="Java Executor">
<class >matilda.plugins.backend.
JavaExecutor </class >
<parameter name="args">-h</param-
eter >
</plugin >
</pipeline >
```

In Matilda, Pipeline and Blackboard are defined as interfaces with Java Remote Method Invocation (RMI) so that plugins can be distributed over the network. The two interfaces define remotely-accessible methods, and its implementation classes (PipelineRemote and BlackboardRemote) implement the interface methods. PipelineProxy and BlackboardProxy hide remoting details in Java RMI and provide location transparency for callers/clients for Pipeline and Blackboard, respectively. (These proxy classes are generated by Java RMI.)

Plugins are implemented as regular Java classes and contained in a pipeline. Then, the pipeline allows plugins to communicate with a blackboard. This design hides remoting details from plugins, and plugin developers do not need to know them. It makes it easy to develop and deploy plugins.

Figure 6 shows how kernel components interact with each other. A pipeline executes its contained plugins one by one by calling their execute() methods. When it calls execute() on a Plugin, it passes a set of configuration parameters as the method's argument. According to the parameters, the Plugin downloads necessary data from a blackboard, process the data and write processed data to the blackboard. When all plugins are executed in a pipeline, the pipeline calls start() on another pipeline running on another network host if multiple pipelines are connected over the network.

MATILDA UML VIRTUAL MACHINE (UML-VM)

This section describes a Matilda-based VM for UML models, called UML-VM. UML-VM accepts UML 2.0 class and sequence diagrams, validates them against the UML metamodel, transforms them to a JAST (Java Abstract Syntax Tree), generates Java bytecode and runs the generated code as a command-line application on a Java VM (JVM). UML-VM is built with a set of plugins as well as the Matilda UML VM profile.

Matilda UML VM Profile

The Matilda UML VM profile is a UML profile that provides modeling conventions to build input UML models and run them as Java bytecode. A UML profile is an extension to the standard UML metamodel. The UML metamodel specifies the syntax (or notation) and semantics of every standard (default) model element (e.g., class, interface and association) (UML Super Structure Specification 2.1.2, 2007). In addition to standard model elements, UML provides extension mechanisms (e.g., stereotypes and tagged-values) to specialize the standard model elements to precisely describe domain or application specific concepts (Fuentes & Vallecillo, 2004). A stereotype is applied to a standard model element, and specializes its semantics to a particular domain or application. Each stereotyped model element can have data fields, called tagged-values, specific to the stereotype. Each tagged-value consists of a name and value. A particular set of stereotypes and tagged-values is called a UML profile. The Matilda UML VM profile defines a set of stereotypes and tagged-values to precisely describe computationally-complete[1] UML models for Matilda.

In Matilda, a UML input model is defined as a set of UML 2.0 class diagrams and sequence diagrams. Class diagrams are used to define the structure of an application, and sequence diagrams are used to define its behavior. Each sequence diagram specifies the body of a method (operation). The model elements in a class diagram are mapped to structural elements in a Java program, such as Java types, generalization (inheritance) relationships, data fields and method declarations. The model elements in a sequence diagram are mapped to behavioral elements in a Java program, such as object instantiations, value assignments, method calls and control flows.

The Matilda UML VM profile defines two types of stereotypes: (1) stereotypes for application semantics and (2) stereotypes for Java mapping. Figure 7 shows the stereotypes for application

Figure 6. Interactions among pipeline, plugins and Blackboard

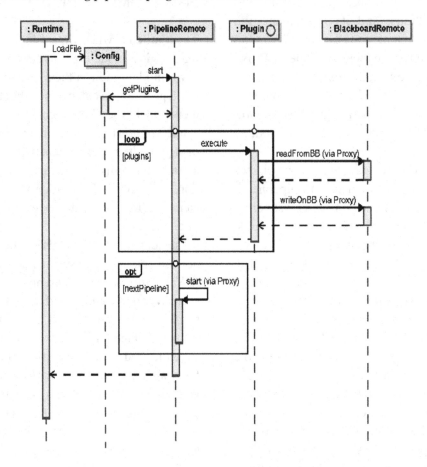

semantics. A message stereotyped with <<UM-LVMarrayelement>> represents an array access (i.e., data retrieval or insertion on an array). Its tagged-value index specifies the array index where data retrieval or insertion is performed (Table 1). The tagged-value element specifies a data element to be inserted to an array (Table 1). A message or comment stereotyped with <<UMLVMexpression>> has Java expressions or statements. A class stereotyped with <<UMLVMexecutable>> indicates an entry point at which a model execution starts. The class must contain a main method (public static void main (String[])). Each application has only one class stereotyped with <<UMLVMexecutable>>.

Figure 8 shows an example sequence diagram defined with the Matilda UML VM profile. abcInc

(an instance of Corporation) creates a new instance of Engineer, and inserts the new Engineer instance into the array engineers (an array of Engineers). A message stereotyped with <<create>> indicates that the message instantiates a class[2] . For data insertion on the array engineers, a message stereotyped with <<UMLVMarrayelement>> specifies that abcInc inserts an Engineer instance (contained in the variable emp) to the array at the index of currIndex. At the end, abcInc increments currIndex by using a comment stereotyped with <<UMLVMexpression>>.

The Matilda UML VM profile also defines a stereotype and five tagged-values to specify a mapping between UML models and Java programs (Table 2). A class stereotyped with <<JavaInterface>> represents a Java interface. JavaStrictfp

Figure 7. Stereotypes for application Semantics

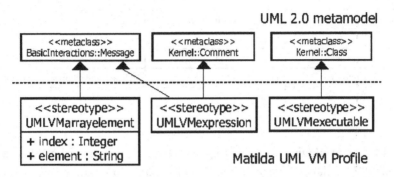

Table 1. Tagged-Values of <<UMLVMarrayelement>>

Name	Type	Description
index	Integer	Index of an array element to be accessed (retrieved or inserted). Must be between 0 and (array size − 1).
element	String	If null is assigned, array access is data retrieval. Otherwise, it is data insertion. Represents a variable that contains an element to be inserted.

indicates whether a Java class is FP-strict. If it is true, all float and double values in the class are used in the IEEE standard float/double size during floating point calculation. JavaStatic indicates whether a class/interface is static in Java. JavaDimensions specifies the number of array dimensions declared by corresponding field or parameter in Java. JavaFinal indicates whether a parameter is final in Java.

Plugins in Matilda UML Virtual Machine

UML-VM consists of 10 plugins: *model loader, UML metamodel validator, Matilda UML VM profile class diagram (CD) validator, Matilda UML VM profile sequence diagram (SD) validator, Integrated diagram validator, CD2JAST transformer, SD2JAST transformer, JAST validator, JAST2Bytecode transformer* and *Java executor.* Plugins are categorized into two groups: frontend and backend. Frontend plugins are used to validate

Figure 8. An example sequence diagram using the Matilda UML VM profile

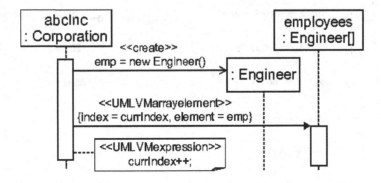

Table 2. Tagged-values in the Matilda UML VM profile

Name	Type	Applied To	Description
JavaStrictfp	Boolean	Class	Indicates a class is FP-strict
JavaStatic	Boolean	Class or Interface	Indicates a class/interface is static.
JavaDimensions	Integer	Property or Parameter	Indicates the number of array dimensions.
JavaFinal	Boolean	Parameter	Indicates a parameter is final.

UML models, and backend plugins are used to transform validated UML models to Java bytecode through JASTs. Figure 9 shows the class structure of plugins in UML-VM. All plugins implement the Plugin interface. UML-VM provides extra interfaces (ModelLoader, Validator and Transformer) to indicate common functionalities in plugins.

UML-VM accepts a UML model as an input in two ways: using UML-VM's modeling GUI or third-party modeling tools. UML-VM provides a modeling GUI, which allows developers to define UML class diagrams and sequence diagrams (Figures 10(a) and 10(b)). The modeling GUI serializes a UML model into XMI data and writes it to a blackboard (Figure 11). It is implemented with the Eclipse Rich Client Platform (RCP), and runs on the Eclipse platform. A *model loader* is a plugin used to read XMI data from third-party modeling tools and store the data in a blackboard (Figure 11).

Each input UML model is validated with four validators: *UML metamodel validator, Matilda UML VM profile CD validator, Matilda UML VM profile SD validator* and *Integrated diagram validator*. A UML metamodel validator validates an input UML model against the UML metamodel using the UML2Validator class provided by Eclipse UML2[3]. A *Matilda UML VM profile CD/SD validator* validates an input model against the Matilda UML VM profile. These validation steps are intended to determine whether an input model is ready to be transformed to a JAST. An *integrated diagram validator* examines the consistency between a class diagram and sequence

Figure 9. Class structure of plugins in Matilda UML VM

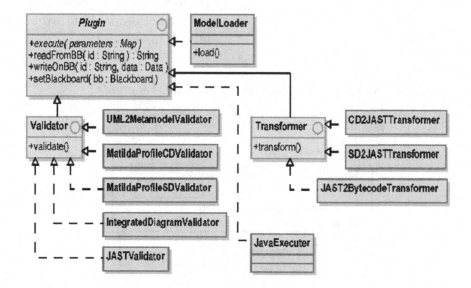

Figure 10. Matilda modeling GUI

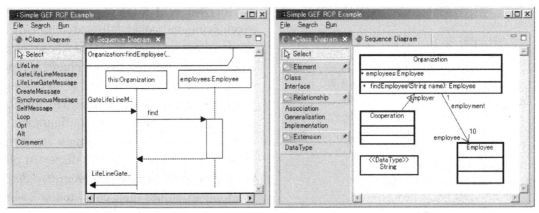

(a) Class Diagram   (a) Sequence Diagram

diagrams. Its major responsibility is to validate that sequence diagrams are defined for all methods of each class.

Listing 2 shows a code fragment of *Matilda UML VM profile CD validator*. The plugin reads an UML model from a blackboard and executes its validation process. It examines whether the model is compliant with the Matilda UML VM profile. For example, it validates that a model element stereotyped with <<UMLVMexecutable>> is a class that has a main method.Listing 2. A code fragment of UML profile CD Validator

```
class MatildaProfileCDValidator
implements Plugin {
  void execute(Map<String , String
> parameters) throws PluginExcep-
tion {
    // read a UML model from a
blackboard
    UMLData data = (UMLData)this.
```

Figure 11. A typical pipeline configuration for Matilda UML virtual machine

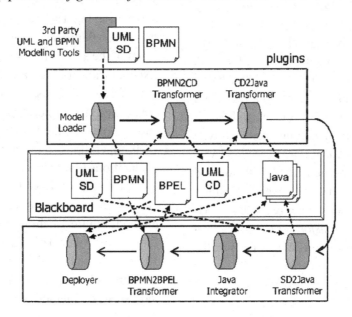

```
readFromBB(parameters.get("uml"));
   UMLModel model = data.getMod-
el();
   // validate the obtained model
   validate( model );
}
  void validate( UMLModel model ){
   foreach (element in model){
     // check if each model ele-
ment is stereotyped with <<UMLVMex-
ecutable >>
     if( element.stereotyped( "UM-
LVMexecutable" ) ){
       // checks whether
     // - the element is a class
       // - the class has a main
method
       // - the main method con-
forms a predefined signature (pub-
lic void main(...))
     } }
     // if validation fails , an ex-
ception is thrown.
     if( valid != true ) throw new
PluginException("An input UML model
is invalid");
} }
```

Once frontend plugins complete validating an input UML model, UML-VM transforms the model to a JAST with two backend plugins: *CD2JAST transformer* and *SD2JAST transformer*. They transform a class diagram and sequence diagrams to a JAST, respectively, using the data structures in the Eclipse Java Development Tooling (JDT). A *CD2JAST transformer* creates a new JAST based on the types (class and interface), data fields and method declarations in a UML model, and then it generates a JAST compilation unit for each type declaration. A *SD2JAST transformer* reads a JAST from a blackboard and updates it with method definitions mapped from each sequence diagram. A *JAST validator* validates the generated JAST, and a *JAST2Bytecode transformer* generates Java bytecode (i.e., class files) using Eclipse JDT. Finally, a *Java executor*, reads the generated class files, sets up a JVM, and executes the class files.

Figure 11 shows a typical pipeline configuration for UML-VM. In this configuration, a pipeline executes plugins sequentially and controls their execution. For example, when a blackboard receives an execution error log from a plugin, a pipeline stops executing plugins. Figure 12 shows another pipeline configuration customized for distributed software development. In this configuration, class diagrams and sequence diagrams are intended to be developed at physically dispersed places. Once they are validated, an *integrated diagram validator* examines their consistency. Then, the validated models are transformed to Java bytecode via JAST as shown in Figure 11.

An Example Application for Matilda UML Virtual Machine

This section shows an example application built with UML-VM. The example application is a command-line calculator that accepts an arithmetic expression in the Reverse Polish Notation and returns a calculation result. It supports summation, difference, division, multiplication and factorial operations. Figure 13 shows the class diagram for the calculator application. Calculator is the execution entry class, which is stereotyped with <<UMLVMexecutable>>; it has the main method to which an input arithmetic expression is passed. An input arithmetic expression can be passed as a part of the application's pipeline configuration. Except local variables, all variables and methods are defined in the class diagram. (Local variables are defined in sequence diagrams.) UML attributes and associations are mapped to Java data fields. UML operations are mapped to Java method declarations that have empty bodies.

Currently, UML-VM requires developers to define a sequence diagram for each operation/method. Figure 14 shows the sequence diagram for getNextToken() of Tokenizer (see also Figure 13). Each sequence diagram is described with the sd frame. The upper left corner of each sd frame indicates the method signature that the frame

Figure 12. A pipeline configuration for distributed software development with Matilda UML virtual machine

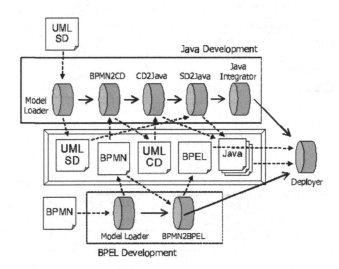

(sequence diagram) models. getNextToken() is used to obtain tokens of an input arithmetic expression one by one. The tokens are stored in exprArr (an array of string data)[4]. Tokenizer keeps track of the index of the next token to be obtained, using currIndex, and getNextToken() returns an instance of Operator or Operand depending on the type of the token being obtained. The entry and exit points to/from a sequence diagram are represented by an arrow (message) from/to the left most edge of the diagram. The arrow labeled with getNextToken() shows the entry point, and the arrow labeled with nextToken shows the exit point. (nextToken contains a value returned to a caller of getNextToken().)

The object this and its lifeline represent the execution flow of a method (or sequence diagram). Each sequence diagram can reference the data fields and methods declared in the class of this. For example, the diagram in Figure 14 can reference exprArr, operators and currIndex, which are the data fields of Tokenizer.

Matilda uses the opt, alt and loop fragments to specify control flows. Figure 14 uses the opt and alt frames to define *if* and *if-then* control flows, respectively. Guard conditions for the frames are represented with the expressions between [and].

The messages (arrows) between the objects in a sequence diagram are either synchronous, reply or <<create>> messages. A synchronous message indicates a method call and parameters associated with the call. For example, in Figure 14, calling get() on the instance operations of HashMap is expressed with a synchronous message. A reply message represents the return from a method call, and indicates the assignment of a return value to a variable. In Figure 14, the return value of calling get() on operations is casted to Operator[5], and the casted value is assigned to nextToken. A <<create>> message represents an instantiation of a class. It points a class being instantiated, passes parameters to the class's constructor, and specifies the assignment of a newly created instance to a variable. In Figure 14, an instance of Double is created, and the instance is assigned to variable.

Local variables are defined as the notes attached to sd frames or fragments (e.g., ExprToken nextToken in Figure 14), within a reply message (e.g., Token nextToken, or within a <<create>> message (e.g., Double valueST)). The scope of

Figure 13. Class diagram of an example calculator application

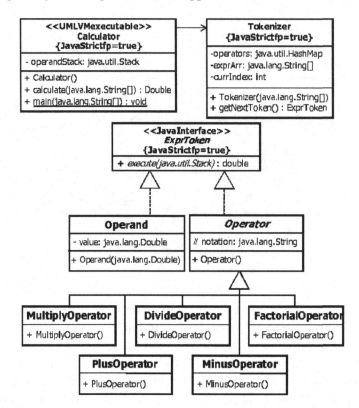

each local variable is limited to the innermost fragment or sd frame.

EMPIRICAL EVALUATION OF MATILDA UML VIRTUAL MACHINE

This section empirically evaluates the execution overhead and memory footprint of UMLVM. Its pipeline is sequentially configured with eight plugins in order to (1) load an input UML model with a *model loader (ML)*, (2) validate the input model with a *UML Metamodel Validator (MV)*, a *Matilda UML VM profile CD validator (CDV)* and a *Matilda UML VM profile SD validator (SDV)*, (3) transform the validated model to a JAST with a *CD2JAST transformer (CDJ)* and a *SD2JAST transformer (SDJ)*, (4) transform the generated JAST to Java bytecode with a *JAST2Bytecode transformer (JBC)*, and (5) execute the generated

bytecode with a *Java executor (JE)*. All measurements used a Sun J2SE 5.0.4 VM running on a Windows 2000 PC with an AMD Sempron 3.0 Ghz CPU and 512 MB memory space. Plugins are executed on the same process in the PC, and a blackboard run on a different process on the same PC.

Figure 15 shows the overhead to execute each plugin. The overhead includes the time for each plugin to process an input model, which contains varying numbers of classes (from 1 to 100 classes)[6] and read/write the input model from/to a blackboard. The proportion of each plugin's overhead to total overhead does not change significantly by varying the number of classes in an input model. The overhead of MV is extremely larger than those of other plugins. It occupies over 60% of total overhead. This result comes from the performance of UML2Validator in Eclipse UML2, which UML-VM uses to validate input

Figure 14. A sequence diagram of an example calculator application

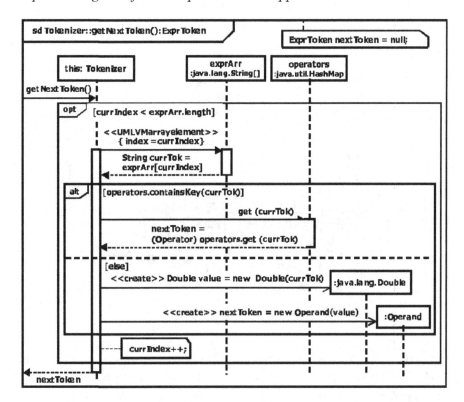

UML models. The execution of MV can be omitted to improve the total overhead by extending the Matilda modeling GUI (Figure 10) so that it validates an input model in background while developers draw the model.

Table 3 shows the overhead to execute frontend plugins (ML, MV, CDV and SDV) and backend plugins (ML, CDJ, SDJ and JBC) as well as the overhead of javac to compile Java code equivalent to input models. By comparing the backend overhead and javac overhead, because javac does not validate UML model elements, Table 3 shows that UML VM's performance is comparable with javac when the number of classes is less than 25 in an input model. (UML-VM's overhead is less than 10 times of the javac overhead.)

Figure 16 shows the breakdown of plugin execution overhead. Each plugin's overhead is divided to the time to process an input model containing 25 classes and the time to access a blackboard to write/read the model. Every plugin is efficient enough to process an input model except MV. Since it is relatively heavyweight to transform XMI data to an in-memory model representation[7], the time to access a blackboard is much longer than the time to process an input model (except the case of MV). For example, in CDV, blackboard access takes 23 times longer than processing an input model. Note that JBC reads a JAST from a blackboard; however, the blackboard access overhead is very small (less than 0.1 second) because JBC simply transforms the JAST to Java bytecode rather than transforming it to an in-memory model representation.

In order to eliminate the blackboard access overhead, UML-VM can deploy multiple plugins in a single process so that they can pass an in-memory model representation between them. Table 4 shows a variation of Table 3; it measures the frontend and backend overhead when all the

Figure 15. Execution overhead of plugins

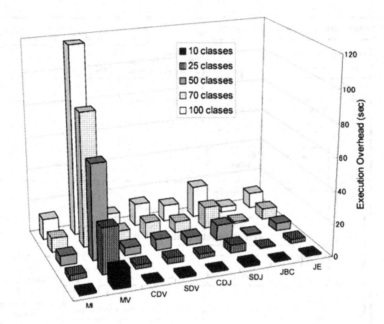

eight plugins run in the same process. As shown in this table, UML-VM's backend overhead is comparable with javac's overhead when the number of input classes is less than 70. Tables 3 and 4 show that UML-VM works efficiently in small to medium scale applications.

Figure 17 shows the cumulative memory consumption of each plugin to execute an input model containing 70 classes. In this measurement, Java VM's garbage collection is disabled. Therefore, the memory consumption includes the footprint of each plugin and the amount of data the plugin generates. Compared with the size of XMI data each plugin reads from a blackboard (11 MB in

the case of 70 classes in an input model), UML-VM's memory consumption is acceptable in small to medium scale applications. ML consumes memory space most because it loads an input model and the UML metamodel and Matilda UML VM profile, and validates the model against the UML metamodel definitions.

MATILDA SOA VIRTUAL MACHINE (SOA-VM)

This section describes another Matilda-based VM: SOA-VM. SOA is an emerging style of software

Table 3. Execution Overhead of UML-VM's Frontend and Backend

# of classes	Matilda (sec)			javac (sec)
	Frontend	Backend	Total	
10	15.2	4.4	18.4	1.0
25	37.3	11.0	45.2	1.2
50	76.7	21.6	92.1	1.4
70	108.2	30.4	129.9	1.5
100	153.9	45.9	187.2	1.7

Figure 16. Breakdown of UML VM plugin execution overhead

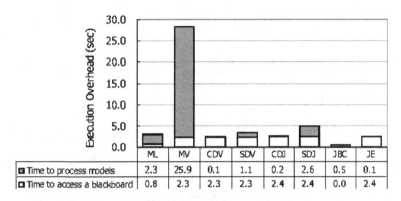

	ML	MV	CDV	SDV	CDJ	SDJ	JBC	JE
◼ Time to process models	2.3	25.9	0.1	1.1	0.2	2.6	0.5	0.1
◻ Time to access a blackboard	0.8	2.3	2.3	2.3	2.4	2.4	0.0	2.4

Table 4. Execution overhead of the frontend and backend

# of classes	Matilda (sec)			javac (sec)
	Frontend	Backend	Total	
10	12.2	2.4	13.7	1.0
25	29.7	5.7	33.1	1.2
50	61.8	11.2	68.2	1.4
70	87.3	15.6	96.2	1.5
100	123.8	24.7	138.8	1.7

architectures to build, integrate and maintain distributed applications (Bichler & Lin, 2006; Papazoglou & Heuvel, 2007). In SOA, each application is often designed with a set of *services* and a *business process*. Each service encapsulates the function of an application component, and each business process defines how services interact to accomplish a certain business goal. SOA-VM allows developers to model their service oriented applications in BPMN and UML and directly execute the models.

Plugins in Matilda SOA Virtual Machine

SOA-VM (1) accepts a BPMN model that defines a business process (i.e., control and data flows among services) and UML sequence diagrams that define behaviors of services, (2) transforms the input models to Java code implementing services and a BPEL script, (3) deploys the generated Java code as XML web services on an application server,

Figure 17. Memory consumption of UML VM plugins

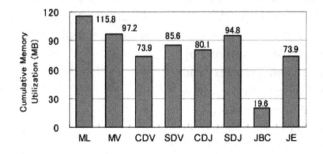

Figure 18. A typical pipeline configuration for Matilda SOA VM

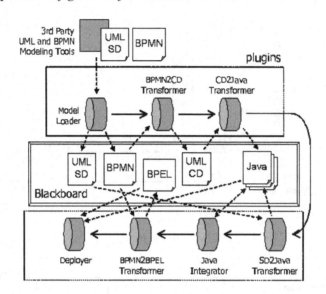

and (4) deploys the generated BPEL script on a BPEL engine to establish a workflow between the XML web services.

SOA-VM consists of 7 plugins: *model loader, BPMN2CD transformer, CD2Java transformer, SD2Java transformer, Java integrator, BPMN2B-PEL transfomer* and *deployer*. Figure 18 shows a typical pipeline configuration. First, a *model loader* loads a BPMN model and UML sequence diagrams into a blackboard.

A *BPMN2CD transformer* extracts the structural aspect of an input BPMN model and generates a UML class diagram that defines the structure of services. A BPMN model generally consists of *pools, tasks* and *sequence/message flows*. A pool, represented by a rectangle, denotes a participant in a business process; for example, Client and Server in Figure 19. A task, represented as a rounded-corner rectangle, denotes a task performed by a participant; for example, Send Query in Client. A sequence flow, represented as a solid arrow, denotes the order of tasks performed by a participant. For example, Client executes Send Query and Show Results in order. A message flow is represented as a dashed arrow between two participants. A participant starts its process from a message start event (a circle with an envelope icon), when it receives a message from other participants. Also, a participant returns a message to a caller when its process ends with a message end event (a bold circle with an envelope icon). Sequence/message flows also define parameters that they carry. (Their graphical representations are not available in BPMN.) In Figure 19, Send Query returns a String value that is delivered to Server. Show Results takes a String value as a parameter. Process Query takes and returns a String value. A *BPMN2CD transformer* transforms a BPMN pool to a UML class and transforms a BPMN task to a UML method. Listing 3 shows a code fragment of a *BPMN2BPEL transformer*. This transformer transforms a BPMN model in Figure 19 to a UML diagram in Figure 20. Method parameters in a UML class are generated according to the parameter definitions in a BPMN model. Listing 3. A code fragment of BPMN to class diagram transformer

```
class BPMN2CD implements Plugin {
  void execute(Map<String , String
> parameters)
    throws PluginException {
    // read a BPMN model from a
```

Figure 19. An example BPMN model

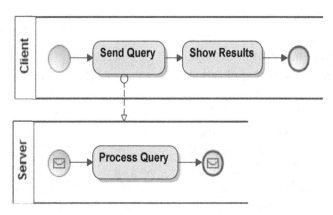

Figure 20. A generated UML class Diagram

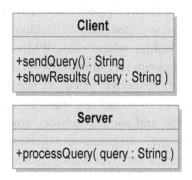

```
blackboard
    BPMNData bpmndat = (BPMN-
Data)this.readFromBB(parameters.
get("bpmn"));
    BPMNModel bpmnmodel = bpmndat.
getModel();
    // transform to BPMN
    UMLModel umlmodel =
toUML(bpmnmodel);
    UMLData umldat = new
UMLData(umlmodel);
    // write a UML model on a
blackboard
    this.writeOnBB(parameters.
get("umlclass"), umldat);
  }
  UMLModel toUML(BPMNModel bpmn-
model){
    UMLModel umlmodel = ... // cre-
ate a new UML model
```

```
// check each model element in a
BPMN model
    foreach (element in bpmnmodel){
      if( element instanceof Pool )
{ // if an element is Pool
        Class c = ... // create a
new UML class
        umlmodel.add(c); // add a
class to a UML model
        foreach (ce in element.
ownedElements){ // check all nested
elements
          if(ce instanceof Task){
// if a Pool contains a Task
          Method m = ... // cre-
ate a corresponding UML method
          c.add(m); // add a
method to a UML class
    } } } }
    return umlmodel;
} }
```

A *CD2Java transformer* transforms a generated UML class diagram into Java code. Methods are empty in the generated Java code because a BPMN model does not define behaviors of tasks. An *SD2Java transformer* transforms input UML sequence diagrams, which are defined with the Matilda UML VM profile, into Java code (method implementations). A *Java integrator* integrates Java code generated by a *CD2Java transformer* and an *SD2Java transformer* in order to complete

Java implementations of services.

A *BPMN2BPEL Transformer* transforms a BPMN model into a BPEL script. After a BPEL script is generated, a *deployer* deploys the BPEL script and services on an application server. SOA-VM currently uses Apache Axis[8] and Apache Orchestration Director Engine (ODE)[9] to operate XML Web services and a BPEL script, respectively. Listing 4 shows a code fragment of a deployer. First, it obtains a BPEL script from a blackboard and writes it as a file to be deployed on Apache ODE. Then, it obtains Java classes (i.e., services) from a blackboard and deploys them on Apache Axis. Finally, it downloads WSDL interfaces generated for deployed services, and copies the WSDL interfaces to a directory where a BPEL script is deployed. The BPEL script requires the WSDL interfaces to access services. Listing 4. A code fragment of BPMN to class diagram transformer

```
class Deployer implements Plugin {
  void execute(Map<String , String
> parameters)
    throws PluginException {
    // obtain a directory to deploy
a BPEL script.
    // For example , /tomcat/we-
bapps/ode/WEB-INF/processes/SOAVM/
    String bpelPath = this.
readFromBB(parameters.
get("bpelpath"));

    // obtain a BPEL script from a
blackboard and write it in bpelPath
    String bpelPath = this.
readFromBB(parameters.get("bpel"));
    FileWriter writer = ...

    // obtain a directory to deploy
services.
    // For example , /tomcat/we-
bapps/axis/services/
    String deployPath = this.
readFromBB(parameters.
get("deploypath"));
```

```
    // obtain Java classes from a
blackboard
    String[] classes = (String[])
this.readFromBB(parameters.
get("java"));
    // deploy each services
    foreach(class in classes){
      FileWriter j = ... // write a
Java class in deployPath
      String wsdl = ... // read a
WSDL file corresponding to a Java
class
      FileWriter w = ... // write a
WSDL file in bpelPath
    }
} }
```

Figure 21 shows a pipeline configuration customized for distributed software development with SOA-VM. In this configuration, BPMN and UML sequence diagrams are intended to be developed at physically dispersed places. A network host accepts a BPMN model and transforms it into a BPEL script, and another network host accepts UML sequence diagrams and generates Java classes. Then, a deployer deploys generated Java classes and a BPEL script.

An Example Application for Matilda SOA Virtual Machine

This section shows an example application build with SOA-VM: an electronic travel arrangement application. Figure 22 shows an international travel arrangement process in BPMN. This input BPMN model contains four participants: Travel Agent, Airline Reservation, Hotel Reservation and Currency Converter. Once a travel agent receives an itinerary from a customer with the Receive Itinerary task, the travel agent calls Airline Reservation and Hotel Reservation in parallel to search airline tickets and hotel rooms according to the itinerary. Each itinerary contains the departure date, return dates, travel destination and currency that a customer uses. Airline Reservation and Hotel Reservation start their processes with Message events.

Figure 21. A pipeline configuration for distributed software development with Matilda SOA virtual machine

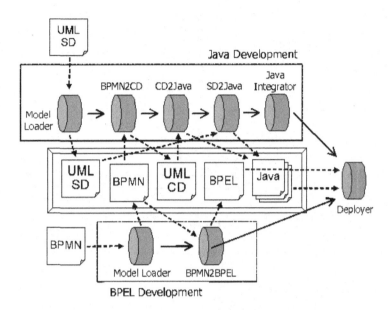

The Search task searches airline tickets or hotel rooms. The Convert Currency task converts airfare and room charge to the currency a customer uses by sending a message to Currency Converter. Once Currency Converter receives a message, it executes Convert and returns a result to a caller. Travel Agent returns search results of airline tickets and hotel rooms to a customer by executing Send Results.

Figure 23 shows a fragment of a UML class diagram that a *BPMN2CD Transformer* generates from a BPMN model in Figure 22.

Figure 24 shows one of input UML sequence diagrams, which defines the behavior of the Convert task in Currency Converter. This task takes two parameters, a set of search results (results) and the currency that a customer uses (currency), and converts the currency that each of results uses (from USD to EUR, or from EUR to USD).

EMPIRICAL EVALUATION OF MATILDA SOA VIRTUAL MACHINE

This section empirically evaluates the execution overhead and memory footprint of SOA-VM. Matilda's pipeline is sequentially configured with seven plugins in order to (1) load input models with a model loader (ML), (2) transform a BPMN model to a UML class diagram with a *BPMN2CD transformer (B2C)*, (3) transform a UML class diagram to Java code with a *CD2Java transformer (C2J)*, (4) validate UML sequence diagrams with a *Matilda UML VM profile SD validator (SDV)*, (5) transform UML sequence diagrams to Java code with a *SD2Java transformer (S2J)*, (6) integrate Java code with a *Java integrator (JI)*, (7) transform a BPMN model to a BPEL script with a *BPMN2BPEL transformer (B2B)*, and (8) deploy Java code and a BPEL script on Apache Axis and Apache ODE with a *deployer (DE)*.

Figure 25 shows the breakdown of plugin execution overhead of each plugin when SOAVM processes a BPMN model in Figure 22. Plugins and a blackboard are deployed on the same host.

Figure 22. A travel process in BPMN

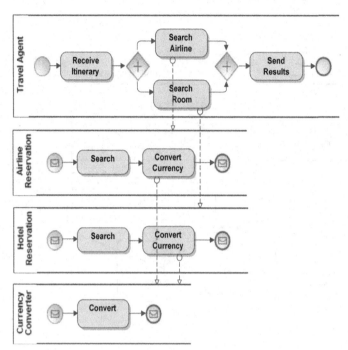

Each plugin's overhead is divided to the time to process a model and the time to access a blackboard to write/read the model. As Figure 25 illustrates, every plugin runs efficient enough; the total overhead is 9.9 second. Similar to UML-VM, a *model loader* has a relatively large overhead to transform XMI data to in-memory model representations.

Also, a *deployer*'s overhead is the largest because it involves in downloading and uploading Java classes and WSDL interfaces.

Since SOA-VM uses Apache Axis and Apache ODE to deploy applications, it requires a host where both software installed beforehand. Since plugins in Matilda-based virtual machine can be

Figure 23. Generated UML classes

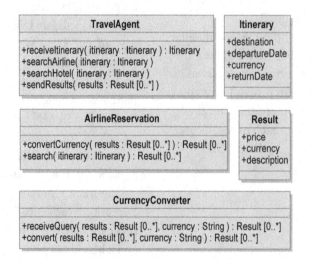

Figure 24. An input sequence diagrams

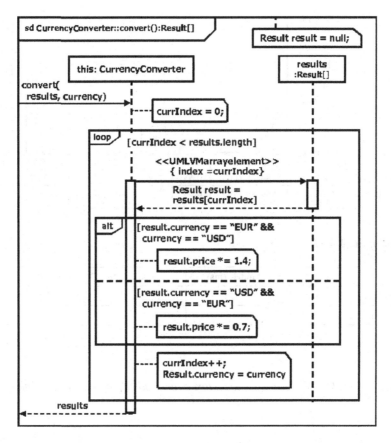

distributed over a network, SOA-VM can use a *deployer* on a remote host with Apache Axis and Apache ODE via a distributed pipeline. It allows multiple SOA-VMs to share a host for deploying the final applications and frees application developers to prepare a host themselves. Depending on requirements, a configuration of a distributed pipeline can be altered. For example, when a machine where application developers work is not powerful enough, all plugins except a *model loader* are deployed on a remote host and all processes are performed on a remote host.

Table 5 shows the overhead when plugins and a blackboard are deployed on different hosts. Figure 26 shows the breakdown of plugin execution overhead when plugins and a blackboard are distributed over a network. Plugins exchange data via a blackboard deployed on a remote host that

connected via 802.11g wireless router. Since an input model (i.e., a BPMN model and sequence diagrams) are same as in the previous measurement study, the overhead to process models are almost same. Although the overhead to access to a blackboard increases 250% when a blackboard is deployed on a remote host, the total overhead increases only 7% since the overhead to access to a remote blackboard is quite small compare to compared to the overhead to process models. It shows that Matilda works efficiently in distributed environment as well as in a non-distributed environment.

Figure 27 shows the cumulative memory consumption of each plugin. (Java VM's Garbage collection is disabled.) As well as in UML-VM, a *model loader* consumes memory space most because it loads a BPMN model and UML se-

Figure 25. Breakdown of SOA VM plugin execution overhead

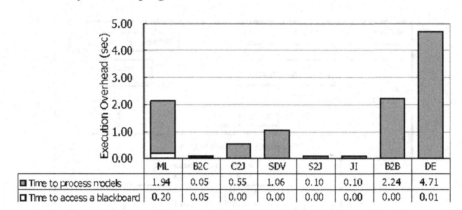

	ML	B2C	C2J	SDV	S2J	JI	B2B	DE
▣ Time to process models	1.94	0.05	0.55	1.06	0.10	0.10	2.24	4.71
☐ Time to access a blackboard	0.20	0.05	0.00	0.00	0.00	0.00	0.00	0.01

Table 5. Overhead of SOA-VM

	Process Models (ms)	Access to a Blackboard (ms)	Total (ms)
SOA-VM on a single host	10.78	0.28	11.02
SOA-VM on distributed hosts	10.82	0.98	11.80

Figure 26. Breakdown of SOA-VM plugin execution overhead (distributed pipeline)

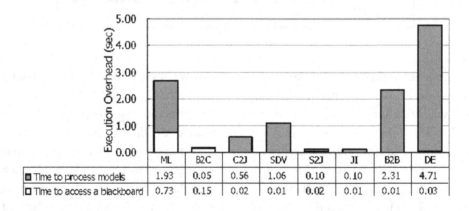

	ML	B2C	C2J	SDV	S2J	JI	B2B	DE
▣ Time to process models	1.93	0.05	0.56	1.06	0.10	0.10	2.31	4.71
☐ Time to access a blackboard	0.73	0.15	0.02	0.01	0.02	0.01	0.01	0.03

quence diagrams, however SOA-VM's memory consumption is small enough and acceptable.

Table 6 shows a set of artifacts consisting of the final deployed application. As the table shows, even a simple service-oriented application requires application developers to learn various technologies and tools. SOA-VM, however, hides the details of these implementation technologies and tools. This way, SOA-VM removes the existence of a programming layer and allows application developers to work on only a modeling layer.

RELATED WORK

This chapter describes a set of extensions to the authors' prior work (Wada, Babu, Malinowski, Suzuki, & Oba, 2006). One extension is to investi-

Table 6. Artifacts consisting of an application

Artifacts	LOCs
6 Java Classes	145
4 WSDL Interfaces	94
A BPEL Script	60

gate a new application of Matilda, i.e., SOA-VM, which (Wada et al., 2006) does not consider.

There are several work to investigate UML virtual machines. (Riehle, Fraleigh, BuckaLassen, & Omorogbe, 2001) addresses the issues of validating models and generating executable code. It maintains causal connections among four meta layers in UML (M0 to M3 layers), and uses the connections to validate models and propagate changes between models. For example, the connections can be used to validate the consistency between M1 and M2 models and reflect changes in an M2 model to M1 models. Although Matilda implements model validation, it does not explicitly maintains causal connections among different meta layers. (Riehle et al., 2001) does not support behavioral modeling, and it is not clear how to transform models to executable code. Matilda supports behavior modeling, and provides workable plugins to generate executable code.

ASM virtual machine (Shen, Compton, & Huggins, 2003) and USE (UML-based Specification Environment) (Gogolla, Bohling, & Richters, 2003) address the issue of validating models. They support Object Constraint Language (OCL) (UML Super Structure Specification 2.1.2, 2007) to validate the consistency and integrity of models. Matilda is similar to ASM VM and USE in that it also supports model validation; however, the model validation logic in Matilda is hard coded in model validator plugins rather than using OCL. Matilda currently puts a higher priority on model execution through operating plugins in distributed environments. Matilda validates the consistency and integrity of class diagrams and sequence diagrams, while ASM VM and USE checks those of class diagrams only. They do not focus on model execution.

Similar to Matilda, executable UML (xUML) focuses on directly executing models. In xUML, developers use class diagrams for structural modeling, and statechart diagrams and textural action languages for behavioral modeling (Mellor & Balcer, 2002; Raistrick, Francis, & Wright, 2004; Balcer, 2003). Action languages implement the UML action semantics, defined as a part of the UML specification (UML Super Structure Specification 2.1.2, 2007). However, the UML action semantics does not provide the standard language syntax; therefore, different action languages have different syntax with different (proprietary) extensions (e.g., BridgePoint[10] and iUML[11]). This means that developers need to learn action language syntax every time they use different xUML tools. Also,

Figure 27. Memory consumption of SOA-VM plugins

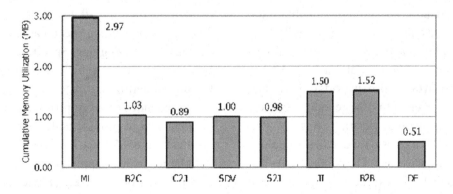

there is no interoperability of models between different xUML tools because different xUML tools assume different subsets of the UML metamodel. Thus, an xUML tool cannot correctly interpret a model that is defined with other xUML tools. On the other hand, Matilda uses the UML metamodel and its standard extensions (profiles) for both structural and behavioral modeling. (Matilda does not require developers to use non-standard mechanisms to build and execute models.) It is more open for future extensions and integration with third party tools such as code generators and optimizers. Furthermore, Matilda inherently supports the distributed execution of plugins. No xUML tools address this issue.

openArchitectureWare[12] is similar to Matilda in that it provides a set of plugins (e.g., model loader, validators and transformers) and allows developers to form a sequence of plugins using its workflow language. However, unlike Matilda, it does not support executing models and deploying plugins in a distributed manner.

The current common practice in MDD is to model application designs with modeling languages and transform them to skeleton source code. For example, OptimalJ[13], Rose XDE[14], Together[15], UMLX (Willink, 2002), KMF (Patrascoiu, 2004) and J3 (White, Schmidt, & Gokhale, 2005) support UML. Visual Paradigm[16], Intalio[17] and eClarus[18] support BPMN. (Gardner, 2003; Chowdhary et al., 2006) leverages UML for modeling business processes. Unlike them, Matilda focuses on direct execution of UML models so that no manual programming is necessary (see Figures 1 and 2).

Several research and products facilitate the simulation of business processes such as TIBCO Business Studio[19], activeBPEL[20] and (Jansen-Vullers & Netjes, 2006). Matilda SOA-VM is similar to them in that it also supports direct model execution; however, SOA-VM generates artifacts required for the final applications (e.g., WSDL interfaces and Java classes) and actually deploys on an application server. Therefore, SOA-VM verifies not only business process models but also

whole systems including artifacts and runtime environment. Verification through SOA-VM is more comprehensive and it reduces the cost and time for verifying and testing the final applications compared to business process simulators.

CONCLUSION

This chapter describes and empirically evaluates a new MDD framework, Matilda, which is a framework to build virtual machines for software models. Matilda allows developers to analyze, design and execute their applications consistently at the modeling layer by hiding the existence of programming layer. It also enables distributed software development in which developers can collaboratively build, integrate and transform software models at physically dispersed places. Empirical measurement results show that Matilda-based virtual machines work efficiently with small memory consumption in small to medium scale applications.

Several extensions to Matilda are planned as future work. One of them is to implement and evaluate additional plugins. They include a model debugging plugin. It is being designed to intercept transformation errors of input models and runtime errors of generated Java bytecode, and identify the sources of the errors in textual and graphical manners. For example, the error sources will be graphically displayed on input BPMN/UML diagrams so that developers can intuitively understand and fix the errors. The design of the model debugging plugin will follow the Model-level Testing and Debugging Specification (Model-level Testing and Debugging Specification, Revised Submission, 2006), which Object Management Group standardizes.

An extended set of empirical measurements is also planned to provide additional performance implications of Matilda. Matilda will be evaluated with larger scale of applications on larger size of network environments (e.g., PlanetLab (Bavier et al., 2004)) to identify the impacts of application/ network size on Matilda's performance.

REFERENCES

Balcer, M. (2003, June). An executable uml virtual machine. In *Omg workshop on uml for enterprise applications: Delivering the promise of mda.*

Bavier, A., Bowman, M., Chun, B., Culler, D., Karlin, S., Muir, S., et al. (2004, March). Operating system support for planetary-scale services. In *Symposium on network system design and implementation.*

Bichler, M., & Lin, K. (2006, June). Service-oriented computing. *IEEE Computer, 39*(6).

Booch, G., Brown, A., Iyengar, S., Rumbaugh, J., & Selic, B. (2004, December). An mda manifesto. In *The mda journal: Model driven architecture straight from the masters* (chap. 11). Meghan-Kier Press.

Buschmann, F., Meunier, R., Rohnert, H., Sommerlad, P., Stal, M., Sommerlad, P., et al. (1996). *Pattern-oriented software architecture,* (Vol. 1: *A system of patterns*). Chichester, UK: John Wiley & Sons.

Business process modeling notation (bpmn) 1.0. (2004). Business Process Modeling Initiative.

Chowdhary, P., Bhaskaran, K., Caswell, N. S., Chang, H., Chao, T., & Chen, S. K. (2006). Model driven development for business performance management. *BM SYSTEMS JOURNAL, 45*(3), 587–605.

Fuentes, L., & Vallecillo, A. (2004, April). An introduction to uml profiles. *The European journal for the Informatics Professional, 5*(2).

Gardner, T. (2003, July). Uml modeling of automated business processes with a mapping to bpel4ws. In *Ecoop workshop on object orientation and web services.*

Gogolla, M., Bohling, J., & Richters, M. (2003). Validation of uml and ocl models by automatic snapshot generation. In *International conference on unified modeling language.*

Jansen-Vullers, M., & Netjes, M. (2006, Oct). Business process simulation - a tool survey. In *Workshop and tutorial on practical use of coloured petri nets and the cpn tools.*

Mellor, S., & Balcer, M. (2002). *Executable uml: A foundation for model driven architecture.* Reading, MA: Addison-Wesley.

Model-level testing and debugging specification, revised submission. (2006). Object Management Group.

Mof 2.0 xmi mapping specification. (2007). Object Management Group.

Papazoglou, M., & Heuvel, W. (2007, July). Service oriented architectures: Approaches, technologies and research issues. *The International Journal on Very Large Data Bases, 16*(3), 389–415. doi:10.1007/s00778-007-0044-3

Patrascoiu, O. (2004, September). Mapping edoc to web services using yatl. In *International conference on enterprise distributed object computing.*

Raistrick, C., Francis, P., & Wright, J. (2004). *Model driven architecture with executable uml.* Cambridge, UK: Cambridge University Press.

Riehle, D., Fraleigh, S., Bucka-Lassen, D., & Omorogbe, N. (2001). The architecture of a uml virtual machine. In *Acm international conference on object-oriented programming, systems, languages and applications.*

Sendall, S., & Kozaczynki, W. (2003, September/October). Model transformation: The heart and soul of model-driven software development. *IEEE Software, 20*(5). doi:10.1109/MS.2003.1231150

Shen, W., Compton, K., & Huggins, J. (2003). A method of implementing uml virtual machines with some constraints based on abstract state machines. In *Ieee asia-pacific software engineering conference*.

Uml super structure specification 2.1.2. (2007). Object Management Group.

Vermeulen, A., Beged-Dov, G., & Thompson, P. (1995, October). The pipeline design pattern. In *Acm sigplan conference on object-oriented programming, systems, languages, and applications, workshop on design patterns for concurrent parallel and distributed object-oriented systems*.

Wada, H., Babu, E. M. M., Malinowski, A., Suzuki, J., & Oba, K. (2006, November). Design and implementation of the matilda distributed uml virtual machine. In *Iasted international conference on software engineering and applications*.

Web services business process execution language. (2003). OASIS.

White, J., Schmidt, D., & Gokhale, A. (2005, October). Simplifying autonomic enterprise java bean applications. In *Acm/ieee international conference on model driven engineering languages and systems*.

Willink, E. (2002, November). Umlx: A graphical transformation language for mda. In *Acm international conference on object-oriented programming, systems, languages and applications*.

KEY TERMS AND DEFINITIONS

Model-Driven Development: A development process aims to build application/process design models and transform them into running applications.

Unified Modeling Language: A standardized general-purpose modeling language in the field of software engineering

UML Profile: A generic extension mechanism for customizing UML models for particular domains and platforms

Business Process Modeling Language: A graphical representation for specifying business processes in a workflow

Metamodel: The construction of a collection of "concepts" (things, terms, etc.) within a certain domain

Virtual Machine: A software implementation of a machine (computer) that executes programs like a real machine

ENDNOTES

[1] "Computationally complete" means sufficiently expressive so that Matilda can interpret and execute models

[2] The stereotype _<<create>>_ is one of the standard stereotypes defined in the UML 2.0 specification. The UML notation of a message is an arrow in a sequence diagram.

[3] http://www.eclipse.org/uml2

[4] Calculator is designed to pass an input arithmetic expression to Tokenizer via its constructor. In the constructor, Tokenizer tokenizes the passed expression and stores tokens in exprArr.

[5] operations maintains pairs of a string and object representing an operator (e.g., a pair of "+" and an instance of PlusOperator)

[6] Each class has a method that contains message sequences corresponding to 100 lines of code (LOC) in Java. This LOC is obtained from the average per-class LOC (101.2) in major development environments such as J2SE 5.0 standard library, JBoss 4.0.4, Mule ESB 1.2, ArgoUML 0.20 and Teamwork 3.0.

[7] When a plugin reads XMI data from a blackboard, it compresses the data with the zip encoding to reduce the data transmission overhead between the plugin and blackboard.

For example, the XMI data containing 100 classes is compressed from 15.7 MB to 1.0 MB. This significantly reduces the data transmission overhead between plugins and a blackboard. However, it is still a heavy-weight process to transform XMI data to an in-memory model representation.

[8] ws.apache.org/axis/

[9] ode.apache.org

[10] www.mentor.com/products/sm/uml_suite/

[11] www.kc.com

[12] www.openarchitectureware.org

[13] www.compuware.com/products/optimalj/

[14] www.ibm.com/software/awdtools/developer/rosexde/

[15] www.borland.com/together/architect/

[16] www.visual-paradigm.com

[17] bpms.intalio.com

[18] www.eclarus.com

[19] www.tibco.com/devnet/business_studio/

[20] www.activevos.com

Chapter 18

A Software Tool and a Network Simulation for Improving Quality of Service Performance in Distributed Database Management Systems

Ismail Omar Hababeh
United Arab Emirates University, UAE

Muthu Ramachandran
Leeds Metropolitan University, UK

ABSTRACT

The efficiency and effectiveness of Quality of Service QoS performance methods in a Distributed Database Management System DDBMS environment are measured by their successfully simulation on the real world applications. To achieve the goals of the simulation modules and to analyze the behaviour of the distributed database network system and the QoS performance methods of fragmentation, clustering and allocation, an integrated software tool for a DDBMS supported by the OPNET is designed and presented. It is developed to wisely distribute the data among several sites on a database network system, effectively enhance the QoS performance at lower cost, successfully provide reliability to the DDBMS in case of site failure, and efficiently increase the data availability where multiple copies of the same data are allocated to different sites. The integrated software tool supply the database administrators with a software that is friendly use, easy to navigate, comprehensive, and expandable that simulate the techniques of database fragmentation, clustering network sites, and fragment allocation and replication in a DDBMS. The tool performs the database transactions operations efficiently and effectively through reliable forms that allow the database administrators to control over their operations and follow up the system improvements and QoS enhancements. The performance evaluation and simulation results indicate that the proposed methods significantly improves the QoS performance in the DDBMS even with manageable extra information, network sites, communication and processing cost functions.

DOI: 10.4018/978-1-60566-731-7.ch018

1. INTRODUCTION

During recent years, the interest in DDBMS applications has increased steadily. This interest is mainly due to the large communication costs between network sites and the huge number of transactions that need to be executed throughout database systems. From this point of view, simulation models are adequate tool for understanding and evaluating the QoS methods in DDBMS.

To achieve the goals of the simulation models and to analyze the behaviour of the techniques proposed by Hababeh, Ramachandran, and Bowring (2007A, 2008), a software integrated tool for a DDBMS is developed to wisely distribute the data among several sites on a database network system, effectively enhance the system performance at lower cost, successfully provide reliability to the DDBMS in case of site failure, and efficiently increase the data availability where multiple copies of the same data are allocated to different sites if possible.

The proposed tool presents integrated user-friendly application software used for database fragmentation, clustering network sites, and fragment allocation and replication in a DDBMS. It has been developed to support fragmentation of global relations into pair-wise disjoint fragments to accomplish the benefits of allocating each fragment independently at each site. Some fragments may be allocated to multiple sites in order to achieve some constraints such as availability, consistency, and integrity.

The software tool is tested on a heterogeneous database system that has several types of computers distributed at various network sites which have different processing and communication costs. Within such a tool, experiments can be set up to test the proposed techniques of database fragmentation, clustering network sites, and fragment allocation in a DDBMS environment and verify the comprehension degree in each method.

The following sections and subsections will discuss the importance of DDBMS applications, describe the tool architecture, address the tool network requirements, process global relations, define the transactions processing cost functions, and simulate the performances of the database network system.

2. THE DDBMS APPLICATIONS IN THE LITERATURE

The increasing success of relational database technology in data processing is due, in part, to the availability of nonprocedural languages, which can significantly improve application development and end-user productivity Ozsu and Valduriez (1999).

Apers (1988) addressed the necessity of supplying a Database Management System DBMS with tools to efficiently process queries and to determine allocations of the data such that the availability is increased, the access time is decreased, and/or the overall usage of resources is minimized.

Hoffer, Prescott, and McFadden (2004) have investigated a comparison between different types of database systems and described the results in terms of reliability, expandability, communications overhead, manageability, and data consistency. They conclude that there has been an increase in the demand for DDBMS tools that interconnect databases residing in a geographically distributed computer network.

Greene et. al (2008) noted that the National Virtual Observatory (NVO) Open SkyQuery portal allows users to query large, physically distributed databases of astronomical objects. Queries can be generated through a simple forms-based interface or through an advanced query page in which the user generates a SQL-type query. The portal provides both a simple form and advanced query interface for users to perform distributed queries to single or multiple SkyNodes. However, Open SkyQuery currently limits the number of matches to 5000, data duplication is still available between

Figure 1. Distributed fragmentation clustering and Allocation model

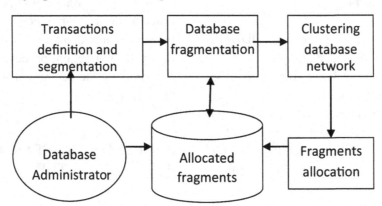

queries, and no disjoint database fragments are generated by this application.

Therefore, and to the best of our knowledge, this is the first work in the database context that integrates database fragmentation, clustering database network sites, and fragment allocation and replication techniques together in one application and depicts its efficiency and performance improvement on the distributed relational database system environment. The architecture of the proposed tool is novel in the sense that it supports the use of knowledge extraction to help achieve the effective use of the proposed techniques.

3. TOOL ARCHITECTURE

The **modeling technique** of this tool defined as DFCA (Distributed Fragmentation Clustering and Allocation) is novel in the sense that it supports the use of knowledge extraction technique to help achieve the effective use of fragmentation, clustering and fragment allocation methods. Figure 1 describes the architecture of the DFCA.

Initially, the transactions triggered from the distributed database system sites are defined by Microsoft SQL Server 2005 Express Edition (http://www.microsoft.com/sql/editions/express/default.mspx) and Microsoft Access (http://www.functionx.com/access/), and stored in the database as database segments that could be overlapped and contain repeated data. The Database fragmentation technique is then used to reduce the size of the data accessed between the network sites by filtering the segments, removing the redundant data, and produce fragments that are completely disjoint. Grouping database network sites into clusters will take place to minimize the communication costs required for transferring data between the network sites. Allocating database fragments to the sites where there is allocation benefit is considered in this tool to maximize the DDBMS throughput and to increase the network system reliability and data availability in case of a site failure.

The Fragment Life Cycle (FLC) development phases in DDBMS defined by Hababeh, Ramachandran, and Bowring (2006) are implemented by this tool in four main processes; data identification, data segmentation, data fragmentation, and data allocation. The Segments Creator and Fragments Generator (SCFG) methods developed by Hababeh, Ramachandran, and Bowring (2006) are implemented in this tool for the purpose of defining queries, creating segments, and extracting disjoint fragments.

To start up the tool, a set of requirements have to be defined for the DDBMS to control the transactions processing throughout the methods execution.

Figure 2. DDBMS network model

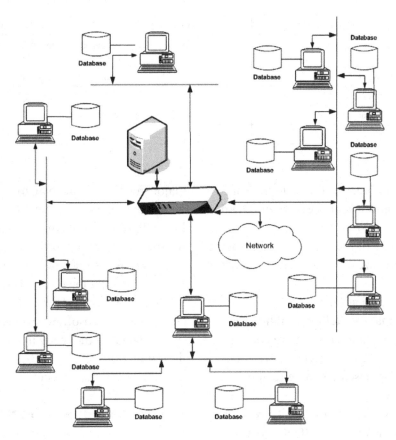

4. TOOL SET UP AND QUALITY OF SERVICE REQUIREMENTS

The software tool is identified and addressed in a DDBMS environment for the purpose of database fragmentation, network sites clustering, and database fragments allocation decision. The description of the parameters that determine the tool set up and QoS requirements will be identified and discussed in the following subsections.

4.1 Network Environment

Throughout N number of sites connected in a heterogeneous network system, some sites are used for executing database applications, and the others are used for developing database applications. For simplicity, twelve sites of a large enterprise

are proposed for the simulation of a DDBMS that execute and develop database applications. The distribution of proposed network system topology is described in figure 2.

The network sites represented by nodes; each node is linked with a center node. The **center nodes** (clusters) are connected with servers and each server is responsible for executing and developing the database applications and transactions of its sites.

4.2 Database Relations

The **database relations** are the primary containers of the data subject for segmentation, fragmentation and allocation at the sites of the DDBMS. Five global relations and forty five transactions triggered from the twelve different network sites

Table 1. Distributed database relations

Relation #	Relation Name	# of Records	Data Fields
1	Employee	20	Employee #, employee name, rank #, site #, major #
2	Salary	7	Rank #, basic salary, allowances, deductions
3	Sites	12	Site #, site name, location
4	Major	4	Major #, major name
5	Classes	7	Rank #, class name

are also assumed in order to illustrate the database relations and how it could be segmented and fragmented through the proposed methods. Table 1 shows the structure of each relation (table) assuming each record size (for simplicity) is equal to 1 kilobyte.

The database relations have specific fields in their structure that can help in building relationships between them to create more complex queries in the DDBMS environment. The relationship between the proposed database relations is described in figure 3.

The emp relation connected to the sites relation in one to many by the field site # (that is, one site can hold many employees), and connected to the salary relation in one to many by the rank # where one salary rank designed for many employees. In addition to this, emp relation is also connected to

majors relation in one to many by the field major #, as many employees have the same major. In line with this, classes' relation connected salary relation in one to one by the field rank # in which one salary is assigned to one class only.

Database relations are represented as tables in the database system. These tables are created and designed in Microsoft Access Database software. As the data become ready in the database tables, the transactions on the DDBMS network sites can be defined and then executed.

4.3 Transactions Definition

The transactions triggered from the network sites hold queries that require extracting information from different database relations (tables). To better understand the fragmentation approach, 45 trans-

Figure 3. Relationship between database relations

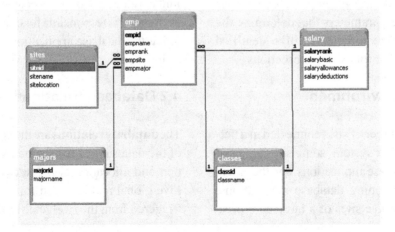

actions are proposed and described in table 2.

In this table some transactions require some data records from 1 table, other transactions require all data records from 1 table, and the other transactions require some data records from 2 or more tables. Different criteria are considered for transactions to show the efficiency and the applicability of this fragmentation method.

The described transactions are then defined by Structured Query Language SQL in order to extract the exact data which matches the transactions criteria from the database tables. The defined transactions statements used Select, Join, Semi join, Inner join, Where, And, Or, In, and other SQL operators to define its data records requirements over the DDBMS network sites. So, the transactions' definitions are ready for execution to get their records from the database tables in a form of database segments. The database transactions processing cost functions will be described in the following section.

4.4 Transactions Processing Costs

The computations of fragments allocation in a DDBMS require costs of communication between the network sites, costs of retrieval, update, and storage at each site, as well as transactions retrieval and update frequencies.

The costs of space, retrieval, and update of each cluster are required for the computation of the fragment allocation and computed as the average costs of space, retrieval, and update for all sites in the cluster. Cost of space is determined by the storage cost and the fragment size. The storage cost is a number that represents the cost of storing data occupied / byte. The fragment size represents the storage occupied by the fragment in bytes.

The cost of retrievals/updates represents the average cost of retrieval/update transactions that may occur on each fragment, and determined by the distributed database system administrators as a number of milliseconds / byte.

The numbers of retrieval and update frequen-

cies represent the average number of retrieval and update transactions that may occur on each fragment at each cluster and their respective sites in a time period (hour, day, week, month, or year). These frequencies are required for the computation of the fragment allocation status at each cluster.

The following section presents the software tool and describes the way in which the integrated methods of database fragmentation, network sites clustering, fragments allocation are simulated, validated, and tested on a real world DDBMS application. The performance evaluation of such methods is depicted in graphical representations.

5. DDBMS TOOL ARCHITECTURE

To simulate the integrated methods of database fragmentation, network sites clustering, and fragments allocation proposed by Hababeh, Ramachandran, and Bowring (2007A, 2008), a tool is designed and developed using Visual Basic .Net programming (Vick 2004) and Microsoft SQL Server 2005 Express Edition (http://www.microsoft.com/sql/editions/express/default.mspx), performed and tested on the network system, database relations, and transactions cost functions defined by Hababeh, Ramachandran, and Bowring (2005 and 2007B). The architecture of this tool will be illustrated throughout this chapter. Figure 4 shows the start up menu of the tool.

This figure displays the major QoS issues that have been simulated by this DDBMS tool; objectives of the tool, description of the tool method, database relations structure, creating database segments, generating database fragments, sites cost functions, grouping database sites into clusters, allocating database fragments to the clusters and their respective sites, and evaluating the DDBMS performance. The descriptions of such QoS issues are illustrated in the following subsections.

Table 2. Database transactions description

Site #	Transaction #	Transaction description
1	1	List of all employees
1	2	List of all classes
1	3	List of all salaries
1	4	List of all sites
1	5	List of all majors
2	6	List of all employees
2	7	Employees who have major # 3 at site # 2
2	8	Classes of employees at site # 2
2	9	Salaries of employees at site # 2
2	10	List of all sites
3	11	List of all salaries
3	12	Employees who have major # 2 at site # 3
3	13	Classes of employees at site # 3
3	14	List of all sites
4	15	List of all majors
4	16	Employees who have major # 4 at site # 4
4	17	Classes of employees at site # 4
4	18	List of all sites
5	19	List of all employees
5	20	Classes of employees at site # 5
5	21	Employees who have major # 4 at site # 5
6	22	List of all majors
6	23	List of all sites
6	24	Classes of employees at site # 6
7	25	List of all classes
7	26	Employees who have classes rank <= 4
7	27	Sites at locations between locations 1 and 5
8	28	List of all sites
8	29	List of all salaries
8	30	Employees who have basic salary > 3500
9	31	List of all salaries
9	32	List of all sites
9	33	Employees who have allowances >= 500
9	34	Employees who have rank >= 5
10	35	List of all majors
10	36	Employees at site # 10
10	37	List of all salaries
10	38	Classes who have allowances <= 450
10	39	Employees who have deductions >= 300

continued on following page

Table 2. continued

Site #	Transaction #	Transaction description
11	40	Employees who have major #1 at site # 11
11	41	List of all sites
11	42	List of all classes
12	43	Employees who have rank # 3 at site # 12
12	44	List of sites where site # <= 7
12	45	Employees at site # 4

Figure 4. The Software tool start up menu

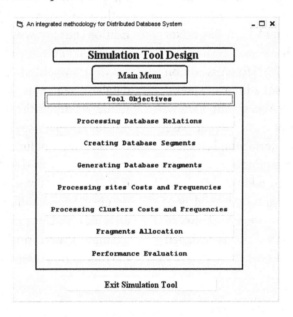

Figure 5. The Tool objectives

5.1 Tool Objectives

The tool introduces the objectives of the fragmentation, clustering, and allocation techniques. Figure 5 shows the objectives of this tool.

This tool presents an integrated method for DRDBMS design that efficiently and effectively achieves the objectives of data segmentation, data fragmentation, data allocation, and clustering mechanisms.

5.2 Processing Database Relations

The tool is developed by using Visual Basic .Net (http://en.wikipedia.org/wiki/Visual_Basic_. NET), Microsoft SQL Server 2005 Express Edition (http://www.microsoft.com/sql/editions/express/ default.mspx), and Microsoft Access (http://www. functionx.com/access/) to provide the database administrators with an easy interface and efficient forms for entering new data, editing existing data, and deleting unused data. In addition, the tool allows the database administrators to add new database relations and set the relationship between them. Figure 6 shows the form which is designed for processing database relations.

The database relations form allows view, add, edit, and delete records in the selected relation. The help menu assist to perform the processing operations on these relations.

5.3 Creating Database Segments

Segmentation is the process of extracting the database records that satisfy certain criterion/ criteria according to the requirement of each database transaction, this process is necessary for generating the database disjoint fragments. In this tool, Microsoft SQL Server 2005 Express Edition (http://www.microsoft.com/sql/editions/ express/default.mspx) is used to define the database transactions and extracts its records as database segments. The tool form illustrated in figure 7 extracts the transaction information and creates database segments accordingly.

This form includes a large number of defined transactions stored in the list, the database segments can be created simply by selecting the required transaction from the combo box then clicking on create transaction segment button. For example, to perform the segmentation process for the transaction (employees who have allowances

Figure 6. Processing database relations

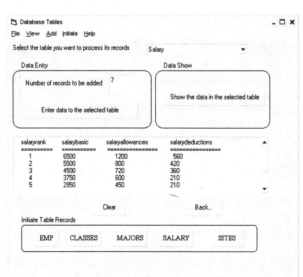

Figure 7. Extracting transactions segments

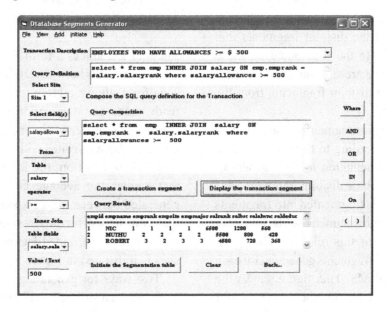

>= $500), select the desired transaction from the transaction description combo box, click on create transaction segment button, and then click display the transaction segment button to show the results of this transaction. The result of this transaction is constructed by inner-join from two tables emp and salary. In case the desired transaction is not listed in the transaction description combo box, then the transaction is simply created by the composition

buttons available on the form; i.e. the SQL buttons, table lists, field lists, and text boxes.

5.4 Generating Database Fragments

The database segments could be repeated or overlapped, this is considered as redundant data, and the tool is designed to eliminate data redundancy so that the communication costs that are

Figure 8. Generating database disjoint fragments

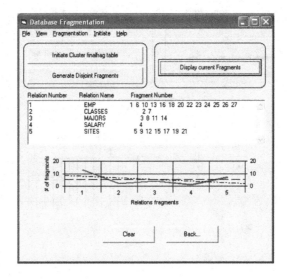

required in the further steps of data allocation are minimized. The database fragmentation technique is used to generate the disjoint fragments that would be allocated to the distributed database system sites. Figure 8 presents the form which is used for generating disjoint fragments from the database segments.

On the basis of the segments created for all transactions and according to the relations data entry, the tool fragmentation method generates and displays the database disjoint fragments. For example, relation 3 is fragmented into fragments 3, 8, 11, and 14; each fragment holds a number of disjoint records of this relation. The graph shows the number of fragments generated for each relation in the DDBMS. This figure shows the regression of the fragments numbers generated for each relation. It is noted from the regression that the relation number of fragments is increased as the number of different transactions on the same relation increased.

5.5 Processing Sites Costs and Transactions Frequencies

The tool introduces a form for processing communication costs between DDBMS network sites. This form allows adding, editing, and deleting ready made communication costs between the sites as well as generating random communication costs between sites within certain mean and variance. In addition, the form presents a chart that depicts the average communication costs generated between network sites. The tool form that is designed for processing communication costs between distributed database system network sites is illustrated in Figure 9.

Two ways for generating the communication costs between sites are available. If the cost is already known then the data entered through dialogue box, for example, the communication cost value 6 is entered 2 times; between site 1 and site 2 and between site 2 and site 1. On the other hand, the form allows generating random communication costs between distributed database network sites by determining the communication cost mean, number of sites, and the variance. In either way

Figure 9. Processing the DDBMS network sites communication costs

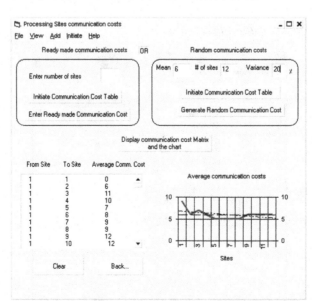

Figure 10. Processing retrieval's and update's transactions frequencies

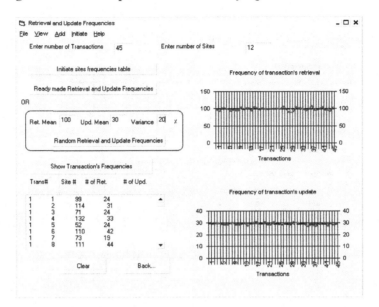

the tool presents a graph that shows the average communication cost for each site. This figure shows the average random communication costs between 12 sites with mean 6 and variance 20%.

In addition to this, the transactions retrievals and updates frequencies at each site are part of the cost functions required for the computations of the fragments allocation method. Figure 10 presents the form that is used for processing these frequencies.

The form allows entering or generating random numbers of transactions retrievals and updates frequencies. The form presents graphs that show the generated average random number of retrievals when retrievals mean equals to 100 and updates mean 30 with a variance for both frequencies equals to 20%.

Moreover, costs of storage space, retrieval, and update have major effect in determining the fragments allocation. Figure 11 shows the form that is used for processing these costs.

This form enables adding, editing, and deleting costs of space, retrieval, and update for each site, and generates a graph for each cost type. This form shows the generated random costs of space, retrieval, and update of means 0.1, 0.3, and 0.4 respectively and a variance of 20% for 12 network sites.

5.6 Clusters Processing Costs

The tool is used to group the DDBMS network sites into set of clusters according to the sites communication costs and the clustering range. Clusters are generated based on the least average communication cost. Figure 12 introduces the clustering technique processing form.

This form presents 4 generated clusters and their respective sites at clustering range 5, cluster 1 consists of sites number (4, 11, 12), cluster 2 consists of sites number (3, 9, 10), cluster 3 consists of sites number (2, 5, 6, 7, 8), and cluster 4 consists of site number (1). The graph shows the number of clusters and the number of sites grouped in each cluster.

The local and remote average retrieval and update frequencies are computed for each transaction at each cluster for the purpose of fragments allocation. Figure 13 shows the form that used to generate the average number of frequencies in all clusters.

Figure 11. Processing the sites costs of space, retrieval, and update

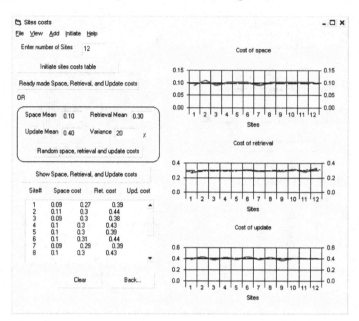

Figure 12. Clustering distributed database network sites

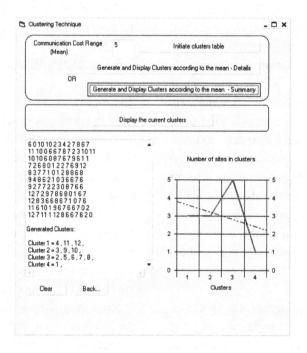

The average number of local retrieval frequencies for the 45 transactions is computed according to proposed local retrievals of the sites in each cluster. The charts show the average number of local retrievals is about 100 frequencies, the average number of local update frequencies is about 30 frequencies, and the remote average number of retrieval and update frequencies are about 35

Figure 13. Transactions average retrieval and update frequencies

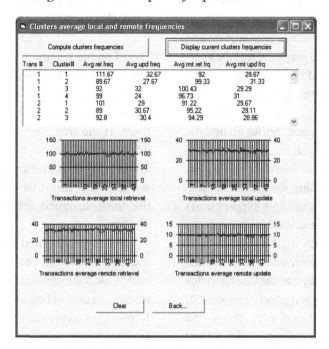

Figure 14. Clusters average communications costs

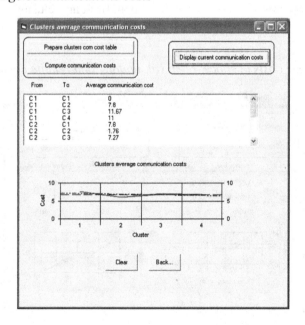

and 10 frequencies respectively.

The average communications cost for each cluster is required for processing allocation costs in the phase of fragment allocation. Figure 14

shows the form used for computing the clusters average communication cost.

This form computes the average communication costs between clusters according to the communication costs of their sites. As shown in this figure, the average communication costs in the clusters are less than average communication costs between clusters. The graph depicts the average communication costs for each cluster, where cluster 1 has the highest average because its sites are far away from the sites of other clusters.

The clusters costs of space, retrieval, update, and remote communications are computed according to the costs of their sites. Figure 15 presents the form designed for processing the clusters costs.

This form computes the clusters average costs of space, retrieval, update, and remote communication and the charts in this figure show that the cost of remote communication is much higher than other costs because the clusters sites are distributed far from each other. The cost of update is higher than retrieval cost; this is the case in the real world database applications. Cost of space is the least because of large and cheap storage devices that are set up on the servers of the distributed database systems.

5.7 Fragments Allocation and Replication

Based on the fragment allocation method developed by Hababeh, Ramachandran, and Bowring (2007A), the database fragments are initially allocated to all clusters having transactions using them. If the fragment shows positive allocation decision at a certain cluster, then the fragment is allocated to this cluster, otherwise the fragment is cancelled from this cluster. Figure 16 shows the form designed for fragments allocation at clusters.

This form designed for computations of fragments allocation at each cluster has transactions which used these fragments. Allocation cost represents the cost of fragments allocation at clusters. Remote cost represents the cost of processing the fragment remotely in other clusters. Decision represents the results of fragments allocation at clusters. If the fragment shows no allocation benefit in any cluster, then the tool allocate it at

Figure 15. Clusters average costs of space, retrieval, update, and remote communication

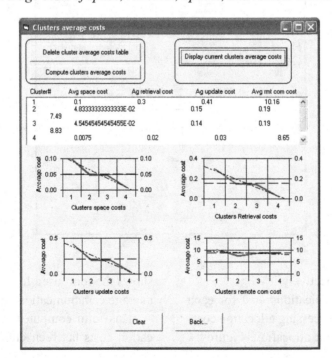

Figure 16. Fragments allocation to clusters

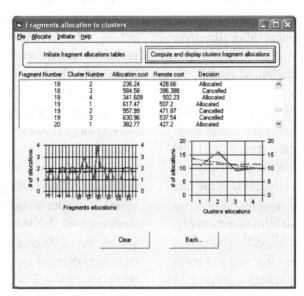

Figure 17. Fragments allocation at the DDBMS sites

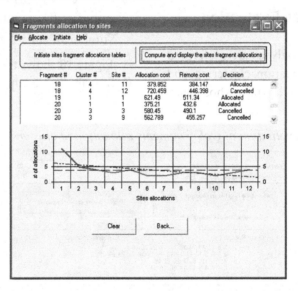

the cluster with the least communication cost for the purpose of data consistency and availability; for example, fragment 19 shows negative allocation benefit at all clusters and the tool allocated it at cluster 1 according to the allocation technique for the purpose of data consistency. On the other hand fragment 16 shows positive allocation benefit at all clusters, so the tool allocated this frag-

ment to all clusters for the purpose of increasing system reliability. The graphs show the number of clusters allocated for each fragment and the number of fragments allocated for each cluster respectively.

The fragments that show positive allocation benefit in any cluster are considered for allocation at the clusters sites to precisely and wisely allocate and distribute the fragments over the sites. Figure 17 presents the tool form prepared for the computations of fragments allocation over the DDBMS sites.

This form allows calculation of the allocation costs and remote costs of all fragments for all sites in each cluster initially allocated by the fragments, and results in deciding which fragments are eligible for allocation at each site. If the fragment shows no allocation benefit at any site in the cluster, then the tool allocate it at the site with the least communication cost for the purpose of data consistency and availability; for example, fragment 19 shows negative allocation benefit at all sites and the tool allocated it at site 1 according to the allocation technique for the purpose of data consistency. The chart shows the number of fragments allocated at each site.

5.8 Quality of Service Evaluation

Extensive experimental analyses are performed by this tool on the fragmentation, clustering, and allocation and replication techniques, whose char-acteristics are reported in Hababeh, Ramachandran, and Bowring (2008). The following are the details of the performance evaluations of the QoS results obtained and the improvements achieved by these methods.

The tool introduces a form for computing and displaying the performance evaluation of the fragment allocation and replication technique over the clusters.

The performance improvement of the DDBMS is defined as a percentage measure of data storage saved from allocating and replicating the disjoint fragments at DDBMS network sites. The data storage saved is equal to the number of fragments cancelled divided by the initial number of fragments allocation. The QoS performance improvement can be computed by the formula:

$$\text{QoS Performance Improvement} = \frac{\text{Number of fragments cancelled}}{\text{Number of initial fragments}}$$

Figure 18 shows the allocation results and the QoS performance improvement of the DDBMS.

Figure 18. Performance evaluation of QoS fragments allocation at clusters

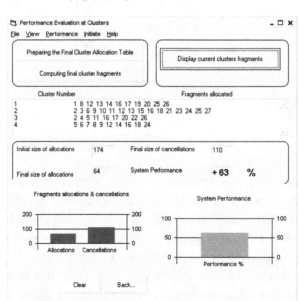

Figure 19. Performance evaluation of QoS fragments allocation at the sites

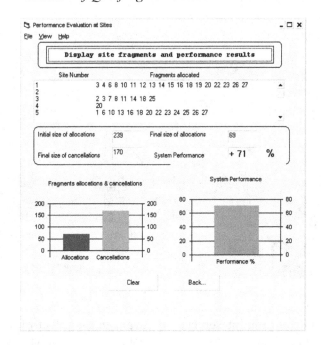

This form displays the distribution of fragments over the clusters, and computes the performance evaluation of the QoS fragments allocation. The charts depict the number of fragments allocation and the performance improvement achieved by applying the proposed techniques of the DDBMS.

The tool provides a form for computing and displaying the performance evaluation of the allocation and replication technique over the sites. Figure 19 shows the results of QoS allocation and the performance improvement achieved by applying the allocation and replication technique on the DDBMS network sites.

This form displays the fragments distribution over the sites, computes the performance evaluation of this QoS fragment allocation, and depicts the performance improvement on the DDBMS.

6. DDBMS NETWORK PERFORMANCE SIMULATION

The DDBMS network workload involves the queries from a number of database users who access the same database simultaneously. The amount of data needed per second and the time in which the queries should be processed depend on performance of the database applications running under DDBMS network. The DDBMS network system performance evaluation will be simulated by using the OPNET IT Guru Academic Edition 9.1 (2003) software for the proposed **network topology** discussed in figure 2. Figure 20 depicts the proposed network topology when grouping 12 sites into 1 cluster.

This figure depicts the simulation of initial DDBMS network topology which consists of 12 sites represented by nodes number (0,1,2,3,4,5,6,7,8,9,10,11). Each node has the following specifications: A stack of two 3Com SuperStack II 1100 and two Superstack II 3300 chassis (3C_SSII_1100_3300) with four slots (4s), 52 auto-sensing Ethernet ports (ae52), 48 Ethernet ports (e48), and 3 Gigabit Ethernet ports (ge3). The centre node number (12) has the following specifications: 3Com switch Opnet model and the periphery node model is internet workstation (Sm_Int_wkstn). The internet node

Figure 20. The network system topology for 12 network sites connected to 1 server

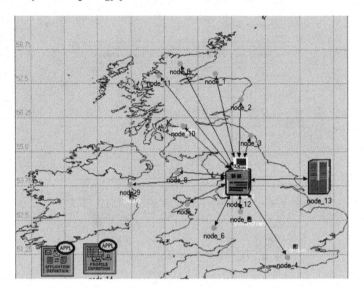

number (13) server is considered (Sm_Int_server) Opnet model, while the link model is 10BaseT model. Moreover, the centre node number (12) is connected with internet node number (13) server model (Sm_Int_server) by 10BaseT.

Two factors that affect the network performance; the server load and the network delay, have to be discussed. The following subsections

evaluate the effect of server load and network delay on the DDBMS QoS performance.

6.1 Network System Load

The server load determines the speed of the server in terms of (bits/sec). Figure 21 shows the network topology when 12 sites are distributed

Figure 21. The network system topology for 12 database sites distributed over 4 servers

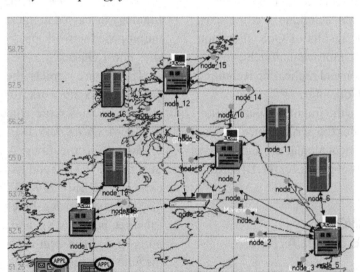

Figure 22. The load on a network server 1 (12 sites and 4 servers)

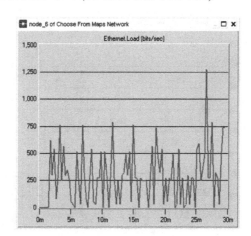

over 4 servers. The router Cisco 2514 (node 22) connects the 4 servers by 10BaseT.

The network server 1 load for 5 sites is depicted in figure 22.

This figure shows that at its **peak**, the load on server 1 is well below 1300 bits/sec. 3 sites are connected to each of server 2 and server 3, so the load of the network server 3 for example is depicted in figure 23.

This figure shows that at its peak, the load on server 3 is well below 750 bits/sec, and an average load less than 500 bits/sec. The network server 4 load for 1 site in a DDBMS is depicted in figure 24.

This figure shows that at its peak, the load on server 4 is well below 750 bits/sec, but with

an average load less than 300 bits/sec. Figure 25 shows servers load comparison on the network of the DDBMS of 4 servers.

This figure shows that increasing the number of servers clusters does not affect the overall network system load, thus the improvement of the DDBMS is achieved. Distinctly, it is noted that the servers load decrease as the number of servers increase; i.e. distributing 12 network sites over 4 servers will result in reducing the servers load rather than having them in 1 or 2 servers.

The network delay caused by the transactions traffic on the server of the DDBMS will be discussed in the following subsection.

Figure 23. The load on a network server 3 (12 sites and 4 servers)

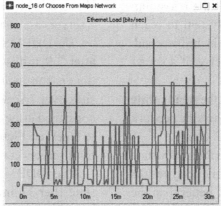

Figure 24. The load on a network server 4 (12 sites and 4 servers)

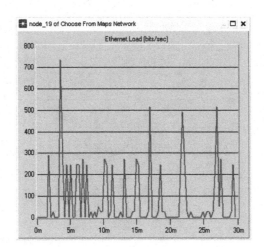

Figure 25. The load comparison on the DDBMS network of 4 servers

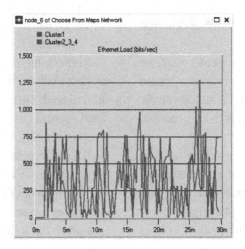

6.2 Network System Delay

The network delay is defined as the maximum time required for the network system to reach the steady state and measured in millisecond. Figure 26 shows the network delay of a server connecting 12 sites.

The DDBMS network reaches the **steady state** after 4 milliseconds. Figure 27 shows the network delay for 2 servers connecting 12 sites.

The DDBMS network reaches the steady state after 3.7 milliseconds. The network delay results generated by using 2 servers are better than the network delay results when using 1 server. Figure 28 shows a comparison of the system delay for the servers on the network of the DDBMS when 2 servers are considered.

The DDBMS network reaches the steady state after 3.9 milliseconds and less network delay time is consumed in the case of distributing the sites over 2 servers compared to the delay time consumed in the case of having all sites connected to 1 server. Figure 29 shows the network delay for 4 servers connect 12 sites.

The DDBMS network reaches the steady state after 3.4 milliseconds. So, the speed of the

Figure 26. The network delay for a server connects 12 sites

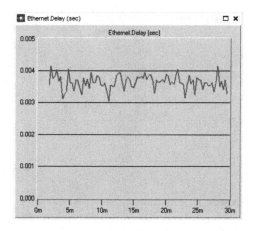

Figure 27. The network delay for 2 servers connect 12 sites

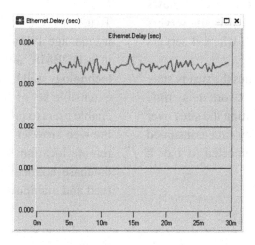

Figure 28. Network system delay comparison for 12 sites distributed over 2 servers

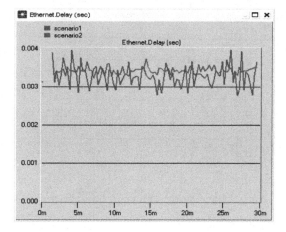

Figure 29. The network delay for 4 servers connect 12 sites

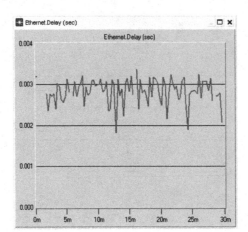

network system is not affected much by distributing the sites over the servers. Figure 30 shows a comparison of the system delay for the servers on the network of the DDBMS where 4 servers are considered.

The DDBMS network reaches the steady state after 3 milliseconds and less network delay time is consumed in case of distributing the sites over 4 servers compares to the delay time consumed in case of having all sites connected to 1 or 2 servers.

7. FUTURE TRENDS

To increase the QoS in terms of usability, flexibility, manageability, maintainability, and scalability in a DDBMS; an **Active Server Pages** (ASP) technology will be used to design interactive and extensible set of web pages (user services) that enable users to interact with the database through the web browser in a user friendly manner from remote location. It provides user to access the database application and optionally permits to feed and manipulate data.

Figure 30. Network system delay comparison for 12 sites distributed over 4 servers

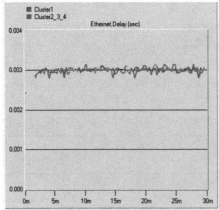

As this software tool designed for a dynamic distributed database management system environment where data records, relations, and queries are subject to change over the time, maintaining a high performance QoS at lower costs of transaction processing and communication is a major issue in a dynamic distributed database management system environment. Therefore, developing a feasibility study to compare the new iterative costs of transactions processing and communication against maintaining high level of performance within grid and cloud environments is useful to monitor and control the system's reliability and the network load.

8. CONCLUSION

The software tool supply the database administrators with application that is user friendly, easy to navigate, comprehensive, and expandable that simulates the techniques of database fragmentation, clustering network sites, and fragment allocation and replication in a DDBMS. The tool performs the database transactions operations efficiently and effectively through reliable forms that allow the database administrators to control over their operations and follow up the QoS improvements.

This tool is successfully used to define database transactions, create their segments, and generate their disjoint fragments. Grouping database network sites into clusters is performed to fit sites into suitable clusters according to their communication costs. Allocating fragments is computed precisely and distributed wisely over the clusters and their respective sites. The servers load on the network system and the network delay are analyzed and show significant performance improvements which increase the distributed database network system throughput.

The QoS evaluation results support the applicability of this tool and ensure that high system performance is achieved by using the proposed fragmentation, clustering, and allocation techniques even if the number of sites and cost parameters are large.

REFERENCES

Apers, P. (1988). Data Allocation in Distributed Database Systems. *ACM Transactions on Database Systems*, *13*(3), 263–304. doi:10.1145/44498.45063

Greene, G., Budavári, T., Li, N., Nieto-Santisteban, M., Szalay, A., & Thakar, A. (2008). Web-based Tools—Open SkyQuery: Distributed Database Queries and Crossmatching. In *The National Virtual Observatory: Tools and Techniques for Astronomical Research*, (Vol. 382). Provo, UT: ASP Conference Series.

Hababeh, I., Ramachandran, M., & Bowring, N. (2005). Developing Distributed Database Applications with Integrated Method for Data Fragmentation And Allocation. *Proceedings of the International Advanced Database Conference (IADC 2005), June 28-30, San Diego, California USA*. Washington, DC: National University & US Education.

Hababeh, I., Ramachandran, M., & Bowring, N. (2006). Dynamical Processing Technique for data fragmentation in Distributed Database Systems: Design and Tool Support. *Journal of Dynamical Systems and Geometric Theories*, *4*(2), 103–116.

Hababeh, I., Ramachandran, M., & Bowring, N. (2007a). A High-performance Computing Method for Data Allocation in Distributed Database Systems. *The Journal of Supercomputing*, *39*(1), 3–18. doi:10.1007/s11227-006-0001-8

Hababeh, I., Ramachandran, M., & Bowring, N. (2007b). *Application Design for Data Fragmentation and Allocation in Distributed Database Systems.* Research & Practice Conference 2007, 9-11 July, INN-School of Computing, Leeds Metropolitan University, Leeds, UK.

Hababeh, I., Ramachandran, M., & Bowring, N. (2008). Designing a High Performance Integrated Strategy for Secured Distributed Database Systems. [IJCR]. *International Journal of Computer Research, 16*(1), 1–52.

Hoffer, J., Prescott, M., & McFadden, F. (2004). *Modern Database Management,* (7th Ed). Englewood Cliffs, NJ: Prentice Hall.

Microsoft, S. Q. L. *Server 2005 Express Edition.* (2005). Retrieved January 29th, 2008 from http://www.microsoft.com/sql/editions/express/default.mspx

Microsoft Access, (n.d.). Retrieved January 18th, 2008 from http://www.functionx.com/access/

OPNET IT Guru Academic Edition 9.1, OPNET Technologies, Inc. (2003). Retrieved January 30th, 2008 from http://www.opnet.com/university_program/itguru_academic_edition/

Ozsu, M., & Valduriez, P. (1999). *Principles of Distributed Database Systems* (2nd Ed.). Englewood Cliffs NJ: Prentice-Hall.

Vick, P. (2004). *The Visual Basic. Net Programming Language.* Reading. MA: Addison-Wesley.

Visual Basic. *Net.* (n.d.). Retrieved February 9th, 2008 from http://en.wikipedia.org/wiki/Visual_Basic_.NET

KEY TERMS AND DEFINITIONS

DDBMS: Distributed Database management system is database software that manages and controls access to the database.

DFCA: Distributed Fragmentation Clustering and Allocation modelling technique

FLC: Fragment Life Cycle is a distributed database process which represents the architecture of the Segments Creator and Fragments Generator.

SCFG: Segment Creator and Fragment Generator is a distributed database method used for creating database segments and generating fragments.

SQL: Structural Query Language

QoS Performance Improvement: Quality of Service Performance Improvement

OPNET: Network simulation software

Network Simulation: Simulation the DDBMS network system performance

Server Load: Determines the speed of the server in terms of (bits/sec)

Network Delay: The maximum time required for the network system to reach the steady state and measured in millisecond

Chapter 19
Models Oriented Approach for Developing Railway Safety– Critical Systems with UML[1]

Jean-Louis Boulanger
CERTIFER, France

Alban Rasse
MIPS, France

Akram Idani
LIG / VASCO, France

ABSTRACT

This chapter presents an approach for certified design of railway critical systems. This approach, which realizes the software development cycle, relies on metamodeling architecture and model-transformations. It combines semi-formal UML models and formal models in order to check, proof and generate code by refinement; we use the process algebra FSP to check the dynamic behavior and B to generate proved code. Initially, the authors select an UML subset, which could be uses to model the key aspects of critical systems. Then, from this subset, the authors perform projections to obtain B and FSP models which are exploited by tools for checking, refinement and proof.

INTRODUCTION

The design of safety-critical software systems is a very difficult task, see Sanz Ricardo and Arzen,

Karl-Eric Arzen (2003). Moreover, the failures of these systems can produce tragic material, environmental or human consequences. In this context, it is necessary to propose an approach, which allows to produce reliable software applications. With this aim, standards were proposed. The references

DOI: 10.4018/978-1-60566-731-7.ch019

Figure 1. Link between CEI 61508 and specific norms

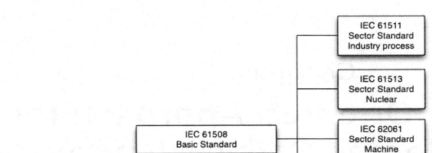

standard are most often European (CENELEC reference system: EN 50126 CENELEC (2000), EN50129 CENELEC (2001) and EN50128 CENELEC (2003)), indeed International (CEI 61508 IEC (2000)).

The later one (applicable to all type of electrical/electronic/programmable safety-related system) is furthermore the founding one: many aspects of EN50126, EN50128 and EN50129 are railway applications of CEI61508 prescriptions. Figure 1

presents the link between the general standard CEI 61508 and the domain specific standard such as railways standard or the next automotive standard called ISO 26262.

Figure 2 presents the scope and application areas of each of the CENELEC standards concerned with the development and certification of safety-critical application in railway sector. Facing the complexity of new systems, the RAMS (Reliability, Availability, Maintainability and Safety)

Figure 2. Scope and application areas of CENELEC Standards

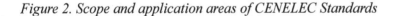

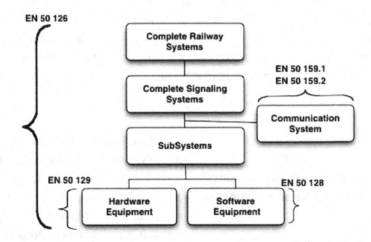

Table 1. Link between THR (tolerable hazard rate) and SIL (safety integrity level)

Probability of failure (by hour) THR	SIL
10-9 <= ... <10-8	4
10-8 <= ... < 10-7	3
10-7 <= ... <10-6	2
10-6 <= ... <10-5	1

requirements are an essential point in the project development of railway transportation systems.

As a particularly important example, systems known as safety critical are systems, which can in case of failure cause important damage to people and by extension to the goods or the environment. For this class of systems, it is necessary to perform analyses in order to demonstrate the absence of failures scenarios, whatever are the causes of elementary faults involved in these scenarios (physical, environment, development, interaction, ...), which could lead to this kind of consequences. Not all systems share the same criticality level; there are scales, which make it possible to define levels, which are associated to safety targets. In the field of the complex electronic and/or programmed systems, CEI standard 61508 (IEC (2000)) defines the concept of SIL (Safety Integrity Level).

The SIL makes it possible to quantify (See table 1) the safety level of a system and consequently to evaluate criticality. It can take the following values 0 (system without impact on the safety of people), 1 (system which can cause light wounds), 2 (system which can cause serious wounds), 3 (system which can cause the death of a person: individual accident) and 4 (system which can cause the death of a whole of people: collective accident). Design of SIL 3 or 4 systems (that one finds in many fields related for example to transport, energy production, as in many sectors of industrial production) is subjected to the respect of technical reference frames.

The assessment of such a product (whole system, subsystems, control/command equipments generally including software) consists of evaluating the product's conformity in relation to a reference system (generally a standard, a part of a standard or a set of standards), according to the method used. The assessment procedure consists of five main processes:

- Planning the Assessment;
- Specifying the Requirements of the Assessment;
- Assessing the Process used to develop the Product;
- Assessing the Product;
- Documenting the Findings in a Report.

The software integrated in railway systems consequently also undergoes RAMS constraints. There are several techniques making it possible, on one hand, to avoid or eliminate the development faults and, on the other hand, to make the execution of the software applications safe in case of occurrence of physical or environmental faults. These techniques include in particular tests, simulation, proofs, and design of safe and reliable architectures including the RAMS analyses (Failure Modes Effects and Criticality Analysis / Software Error Effects Analyses, Fault trees, ...).

The standard EN 50128 (CENELEC (2001)) is particularly dedicated to the software development for the railway field. The Safety Integrity Level (SIL), becomes SSIL (Software SIL) with levels from 0 (not critical) to 4 (critical), and for each SSIL, the specific development activities (including verification and validation: V&V) are prescribed. For of a component of a given SSIL, EN 50128 describes the processes, methods and tools to be implemented during the development. It is about an obligation of means, which is added to the obligations of quantitative and/or qualitative results.

Software certification demonstrates the reliability, or safety of software systems in such a way that an independent authority can check it with sufficient trust in the techniques and tools used in the certification process itself. It can be built on existing validation and verification techniques but introduces the notion of explicit software certificates, which contain all the information necessary for an independent assessment of the demonstrated properties. Software certificates support a product-oriented assurance approach, combining different techniques and forms of evidence (e.g., fault trees, safety cases, formal proofs, ...) and linking them to the details of the underlying software.

These standards aim to increase the quality of critical applications by controlling the process of development; they recommend a methodology, which is based on:

- Comprehensible notations in order to describe system requirements and reduce the efforts of specification and certification;
- Formal automated treatment in order to preserve the quality of the cycle development and increase the confidence towards the final application.

On the hand, semi-formal specification languages (such as UML (2007)) have been widely used for specifying, visualizing, documenting (in a comprehensible way) large and complex software systems. They make it possible to better organize the design of software in order to manage its complexity and to create applications more extensible and easier to maintain. Nowadays Unified Modeling Language (UML) is a "de facto" standard used as well complex dynamic systems as distributed systems or real times systems; it is a part of the culture of software engineers. However, UML suffers from the lack of precise semantics that can cause misinterpretations and limit their use on critical systems, which address safety challenges (Jean-Louis Boulanger (2007).).

On the over hand, formal methods are specifically used for safety-critical systems see Clarke Edmund.M, Grumberg Orna and Peled Doron (2000); they are based on mathematical notations (process algebra, B, temporal logics, finites states machines, ...) which allow to:

1) formally specify the needs, the properties and the functionalities of software systems and
2) rigorously check the correctness of critical systems by model-checking, proof or refinement (B method).

However formal methods lead to complex models that may difficult to read and understand that limits their use on a large scale of applications; traditional designers of software prefer used semi-formal notations more largely employed (such as the UML notation).

In this context, we propose to combine formal methods and the UML notation, in order to:

1) benefit from their complementarities (formal aspects for the first, flexibility and comprehensive aspects for the second) and
2) realizes all the software development cycle (from the specification until the generation of the code by refinement). To do that, we propose an approach, which is based on a tooled, coherent and recognized method: the Models Driven Engineering (or MDE) see Estublier Jacky, Vega German and Ionita Anca Daniela (2005).

SAFE UML: OUR APPROACH

The standards, described in the previous section, give a lot of methodological issues and advocate for two major trends:

(i) the use of automated formal reasoning's to increase confidence in such systems, and
(ii) the use of comprehensible and accessible notations (such as UML) to reduce certification effort for the design phase.

Figure 3. Proposed approach Idani Akram., Okasa Ossami D-D., and Boulanger Jean-Louis (2007)

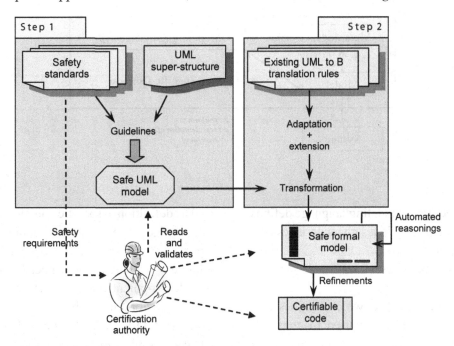

So, for applications that need to fulfill these safety standards, it seems inescapable to follow a development process based on both formal and graphical notations (e.g. UML and B). Figure 3 shows how our activities are integrated within a classical development process based on UML.

The left hand side of the figure shows our previous work: Idani Akram., Okasa Ossami D-D., and Boulanger Jean-Louis (2007), Okalas Ossami D.-D., Mota J.-M., and Boulanger J.-L. (2007), Jean-Louis Boulanger (2007) which is intended to determine a well-defined UML core accompanied by a set of safety commandments (inspired by the cited standards).

The interest of this first step is to guide stakeholders when using UML in a safety critical software development process with certification settings. On the right hand side of the figure, the current step of our work, which is investigated in this paper, builds formal models from the various UML documents produced during the previous step.

This second step improves the state of the art by:

- Exploiting the projection of the safety guidelines on the translation rules.
- Defining explicitly mappings between UML and B in terms of their meta-models.

As a result, certifiable code can be produced by refinements and assisted by proofs. Indeed, the B formal model produced from the said safe UML core is subject to automated formal reasoning's in order to check its correctness and to generate source code.

MODEL DRIVEN ENGINEERING

Model Driven Engineering provides an unified and homogeneous process covering all the software development cycle; it allows a coherent integration of various domains, various activities and various artifacts (tools, models, or methods) which are used in the software development. This coherent integration is only possible through a formally defined meta-modeling architecture (figure 4).

Figure 4. Meta-modeling architecture

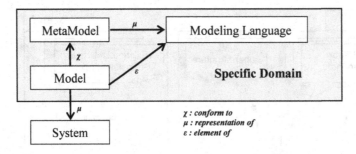

In this architecture, a modeling language defines a set of models that includes characteristics of a specific domain.

To do that, it provides:

- An abstract syntax which defines the concepts and the rules used to construct models;
- A concrete syntax which describes the notation (textual or graphical) used to represent models ;
- A semantic which defines the meaning of the concepts used in this specific domain.

A meta-model (figure 4) is a representation (a model) of a modeling language; it formalizes the aspects and the concepts used by a modeling language, and models the domain in question.

The definition of specific domains allows realizing bridges between various domains. Thus, it is possible to chose the domain which is the most suitable to realize a particular activity of the software development. Such bridges are realized with model-transformations; from the correspondence between meta-models, it is possible to deduce a set of transformation rules, which can be used to transform a model into another model. These transformation rules are applied to the elements of a source model in order to produce the elements of a target model (figure 5).

Thus, MDE makes it possible the realization of a global coherent software development, and the reduction of the efforts to bridge a domain to another domain.

Figure 5. Model transformations

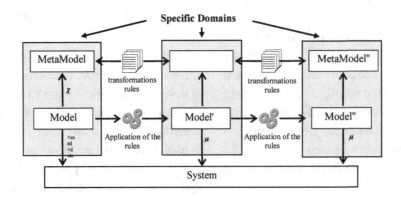

THE PROPOSED APPROACH

This article proposes an approach, which allows the certified design of critical software systems. This approach, which is applied here to railway applications (Jean-Louis Boulanger (2007)), realizes all the software development cycle; it integrates a phase of modeling, a phase of formal checking and a phase of refinement and proof (figure 6):

- The phase of modeling relies on object-oriented modeling and a subset of UML. This subset must be enough formalized to produce models which are usable in a MDE process; these models are transformed into formal models which are used during the phase of formal checking and the phase of refinement.
- The phase of formal checking aims to guarantee that the behavioral aspects of UML models are conform to safety and progress properties. This phase relies on model-checking and process algebras. For this approach, the process algebra FSP and the model-checker LTSA are used.
- The phase of refinement and proof relies on the B method; it realizes refinements and proof of static properties (invariable on the states, pre and post condition on the

operations…) in order to produce a proved code.

Thus, in the phase of modeling, the designer performs an UML model of the software under development. This model is transformed into a FSP model, which is checked by LTSA. Thus, it is possible to guarantee that behavioral aspects of UML model are conformed to requirements.

Then, the UML model is transformed into a B model in order to obtain a proved code, which is conform to the static aspects of the UML model. In this context, MDE makes it possible a coherent approach, which allows to:

- Define and formalize (through a meta-model architecture) specific domains (UML, FSP and B);
- Obtain from UML models (by models transformations) FSP and B models.

MODELING DOMAIN: UML

UML Overview and Subset of the Notation Selected

The Unified Modeling Language (UML) is proposed by the Object Management Group (OMG)

Figure 6. Conceptual representation of the proposed approach

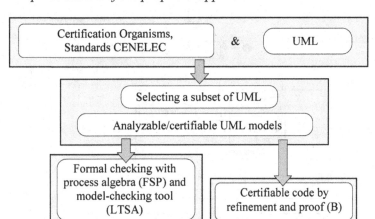

see OMG (2007) and is, de facto, used in most of software developments. More precisely, UML is a graphical notation to describe, to specify and to document object-oriented software systems. UML is defined by 13 diagrams to represent, or to model, static and dynamic aspects of the systems at various level of abstraction. For example, in the figure 6, we present 4 diagrams (use-case, sequence diagram, stat/transitions diagram and a class diagram) that are a potential part of an UML model for a railway application.

Although the UML notation is a model representation language, the model development process is not specified. The authors, of the UML notation, nevertheless recommend using an iterative and incremental approach, which is guided by the needs of users and centered, on the software architecture.

As the UML notation does not impose a specific working method, it can be integrated in a transparent manner within any process of software or system development. It should therefore be regarded as a toolbox, which provides a means of gradually improving working methods while retaining domain-specific modes of operation. The popularity of the UML notation has been increased by a large number of tools, such as computer-aided software engineering (case) tools with which the notation can be implemented graphically and which also assist the development process by permitting partial code generation, the generation of documentation and reverse engineering. In addition to being supported by all the information processing stakeholders, the UML notation is today used in every domain and has recently been introduced into the field of safety-critical applications.

Some difficulties appear during the used of UML:

- UML is a notation;
- UML is an oriented object approach: polymorphisme, inheritance and overloading provide dead code and instanciation/destruction provide dynamical memory allocation;

Figure 7. A part of UML model for train

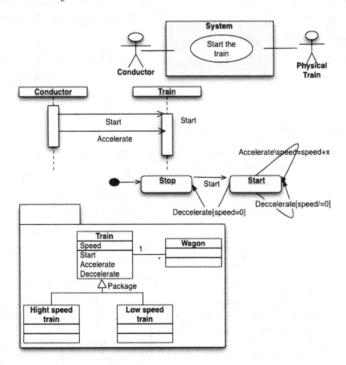

- UML is too big: In practice, UML size makes it impractical and causes analysis paralysis;
- UML have a partial semantic;
- UML provides construction that introduced non-determinism;
- …

However, these difficulties and the absence of a formal semantic (property that facilitates the use of the notation in various domains/applications) are a problem in critical software systems. Indeed, these systems, due to the standard CENELEC EN 50128, require precise and unambiguous specifications of the functionalities, of the operational scenarios, of the architecture and of the dynamic behaviors.

Thus, the first step of the approach proposed is to analyze the concepts in which UML is based on, to identify a subset of the notation that can be "safely" used in a development process. Such a subset has been proposed in previous works (Idani Akram., Okasa Ossami D-D., and Boulanger Jean-Louis (2007), Okasa Ossami D-D., Mota, J-M., Okalas Ossami D.-D., Mota J.-M., and Boulanger J.-L. (2007)) and is restricted to class diagrams; use case diagrams, sequence diagrams and state-transition diagrams:

- Class diagrams are used to describe the architecture and the organization of the components inside a system; the modeling concepts retained are classes (of objects/ components) and relations.
- Use case diagrams are used to represent the functionalities with actors link to use cases (i.e. the functionalities).
- Sequence diagrams are used to model interactions necessary to realize a use case; each interaction is modeled by messages exchanged between the objects inside the system.
- State-transition diagrams are used to describe the internal behaviors of each class (of objects).

UML in a MDE Process

In order to use the subset of UML in a MDE process (with tools proposed by MDE, for instance), it is necessary to define an abstract syntax and a concrete syntax for the elements retained. The visual representation, i.e. the concrete syntax, is given by the OMG (2007). The abstract syntax is (partially) represented by the meta-model of the figure 8.

MODEL-CHECKING DOMAIN

Model-Checking Overview

Model-checking aims to check that the behavioral model of a software system is conformed to safety and liveness properties (Clarke Edmund.M, Grumberg Orna and Peled Doron (2000)). These properties assert respectively that "nothing bad will never happens" and that "something good eventually happens".

A model-checking process is based on:

- A behavioral model of the software system that is described using formal specifications such as Labeled Transition Systems (LTS), finites states machines or processes algebras.
- A formal model of properties that is described using temporal logic or process algebras.
- An algorithm of checking which is integrated in a model-checking tool. This tool checks automatically that the behavioral model is conforming to the model of properties. If a violation of properties is detected, the tool provides the sequence of actions (traces) that leads to the undesirable situation. This trace can be used advantageously to identify and correct the errors of the behavioral model.

Figure 8. Abstract syntax of class diagrams a), state-transition diagrams b), sequence diagrams c) and use case diagrams

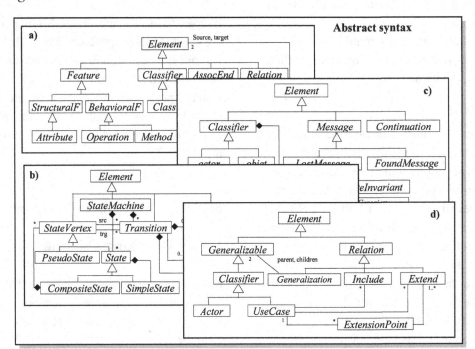

In our approach, properties and behavioral models are described using a process algebra notation called Finite State Processes (or FSP) see Magee Jeff and Kramer Jeff (2006). In FSP, models are realized using primitive processes, composite processes, actions and operators such as choice, parallel composition or relabeling (figure 8).

The checking is realized with the model-checking tool called LTSA, which is associated with FSP.

The main interests of FSP and LTSA consist in their ability to:

- Model, in a formal, concise and comprehensible way, the discrete behavior of software systems;
- Detect the design error as soon as possible in the software development cycle, at the design level, what facilitates their correction and reduces their costs;
- Realize, in addition to the formal checking, an interactive simulation of behavioral

aspects, what increases the effectiveness of the checking and makes it possible to produce more reliable software.

FSP in a MDE Process

In order to use FSP and LTSA in a MDE process, it is necessary to define an abstract syntax, a concrete syntax and a semantic of FSP. Abstract and concrete syntaxes are shown in figure 9 and the semantics considered is the semantics of the Labeled Transition Systems (or LTS).

B DOMAIN

Overview of the B Method

The B method seems to be the most appreciated formal method in industrial world for railway critical software development such as SAET-METEOR (Behm Patrick, Benoit Paul, Faivre

Figure 9. Abstract syntax (in a form of grammar) and concrete syntax of FSP

Abstract syntax

BProcessDef :
BProcessBody AlphabetExtension$_{opt}$ Relabel$_{opt}$ Hiding$_{opt}$
BProcessBody :ProcessIdent = BlocalProcess
BProcessBody , ProcessIdent = BLocalProcess
BLocalProcess:
STOP
ERROR
ProcessIdent (BChoice)
BChoice:
            ActionLabel -> BlocalProcess
            BChoice | ActionLabel -> BlocalProcess
BCompositeDef:|| ProcessIdent = BCompositeBody Priority$_{opt}$
Hiding$_{opt}$.

Concrete syntax

    PrimitiveProcess = LocalProcessA,
    LocalProcessA = ({actionA, actionB}-> LocalProcessN),
    …
    LocalProcessN = (actionN   -> LocalProcessA   ).

    || **CompositeProcessA** = (instanceA1 : PrimitiveProcessA
    || … || instanceN : PrimitiveProcessN)
    /{ actionA.insanceA / actionB.instanceN, … }.

Alain and Meynadier Jean-Marc (1999)) for example. In fact, B method allows building a gate between mathematical modeling and informatics realization. The B method due to J.R Abrial (Abrial Jean-Raymond (1996)) is a formal method for the incremental development of specifications and

Figure 10. Example of abstract machine

```
MACHINE
   STACK ( max_object )
CONSTRAINTS
   max_object ∈ NAT1
SEES
   OBJECT
VARIABLES
   stack
INVARIANT
   stack ∈ seq(Object) ∧
   size(stack) ≤ max_object
INITIALISATION
   stack := <>
OPERATIONS
   PUSH (XX) =
      PRE XX ∈ Object ∧ size(stack) < max_object
      THEN stack := stack ← XX END;
   XX ← POP = PRE size(stack) > 0
      THEN XX,stack := last(stack),front(stack) END
END
```

their refinements down to an implementation. It is a model-based approach similar to Z and VDM.

The abstract machine, see J. R. Abrial (1992), (figure 10) is the basic element of a B development. It encapsulates some state data and offers some operations. The description of an abstract machine is composed of three parts, the declarative part that describes the states and their properties, the execution part that introduces operations, and composition clauses. The Abstract Machine Notation (AMN) captures specification, refinement concepts and implementation in one notation.

An abstract Machine consists of several clauses allowing to specify the static and dynamic parts of a system; it is composed by data, operation, an invariant, a set of parameters and finally the initialization of variables. The static part correspond to the declarations of data precisely sets (clause SET), constants (clause CONSTANTS) and variables (clause VARIABLES). Note that in a B machine the characterization of these data is specified in terms of properties of the constants (clause PROPERTIES) and the invariants (clause

Table 2. A subset of generalized substitutions

Simple substitution	x:= E	[x:=E] R <=> replacing all free occurrences of x in R by E.
Empty substitution or no-op	skip	[skip] R <=> R
Parallel substitution	S ‖ T	[S ‖ T] R <=> [S] $R_s \wedge$ [T] R_t where $R=R_s \wedge R_t$; T and S modify distinct sets of variables V_s and V_t; Vs (resp. V_t) is not free in R_t (resp. R_s).
Preconditioning	P | S	[P | S] R <=> P ∧ [S] R
Bounded choice	S [] T	[S [] T] R <=> [S] R ∧ [T] R
Guarded choice	P => S	[P => S] R <=> P =>[S] R
Unbounded choice	@ x . S	[@ x . S] R <=> ∀x.[S] R where x is not free in R.

Note: x denotes a variable, E is a set theoretical expression, P and R denote predicates, S and T denote generalised substitutions.

INVARIANTS). The dynamic part corresponds to the declarations of the operations (clause OPERATIONS).

The execution part introduces some operations that are described under the form of a pre-condition and an action. These operations provide the interface for the outside world to the state variables encapsulated within the abstract machine. Operations are described by syntactic structures that are interpreted in the generalized substitution language (J. R. Abrial (1992)), an extension of earlier work by E.W Dijkstra (1976). The generalized substitutions (see table 2) are predicate transformers. [S] P denotes the result of applying substitution S to the predicate P.

To facilitate the development of abstract machines, syntactic sugar is introduced. For example, the preconditioning substitution is rewritten as PRE S THEN Q END. The multiple substitution x, y:= E,F or the well known IF Q THEN S ELSE T END are other examples of actions described in the body of an operation. They are interpreted in the generalized substitution language as the parallel substitution x:= E ‖ y:= F and as the guarded choice Q => S [] not(Q) => T.

The composition clause part introduces relationships between abstract machines (SEES, USES, INCLUDES, IMPORTS, EXTENDS) according to various visibility rules on the encapsulated states and operations.

An example of abstract machine is given in figure 2 where a fairly simple STACK is presented.

The declarative part defines one formal parameter with its constraint, and the stack variable with its typing invariant and its initialization. The type of stack is described as a finite sequence built on a set Object, this set being defined elsewhere, in a "seen" machine.

Two operations provide access to the encapsulated variable. Note, in the PUSH operation, the special operator "¬" which adds an element at the end of the sequence.

To illustrate the notion of predicate transformation, let us apply the initialization substitution to the invariant predicate:[stack:= <>] (stack ∈ seq(Object)∧size(stack)≤max_object)gives: *(<> ∈ seq(Object)∧size(<>)≤max_object)*which can be reduced to the true predicate. Likewise, each operation can be applied to the invariant.

Each abstract machine involves a development chain including the top level, its refinement(s) and its implementation, the latter being easily translated into a programming language. Although the AMN covers the whole chain, a few syntactic structures cannot be used at any level. For example, the non-deterministic choice ANY x WHERE P THEN S END cannot be found in an implementation while the loop structure WHILE B DO S END is not accepted at the abstract top level. At each step of the B development, a collection of proof obligations is introduced.

It is worth noting that the links established by the composition clauses provide access to the top level of the referred abstract machines: machines can be refined, implemented and proved separately, which introduces modularity in the B development.

In the B development, the proofs accompany the construction of software. Each time an abstract machine is defined or modified, there are proof obligations related to its mathematical consistency; if the machine is a refinement or an implementation, there are also proofs of its correctness with respect to the previous steps of the development chain. The B tools allow to generate automatically the POs for each abstract machine. Generally speaking, the POs will be all the more complex as concrete details are introduced. Then these proof obligations are discarded either automatically for the simple ones or in cooperation with the designer for the complex ones. So, at the last refinement called the implementation, we obtain a safe software which does not need

to be tested. At this low level stage, it may be easily translated automatically to a programming language (ADA, C, C++).

Drawbacks of Existing UML to B Approaches and Contributions

A significant effort has been devoted by the research community in order to combine UML (2007) and B2 (Jean-Raymond Abrial (1996)) but the transformation process is subject to the following drawbacks:

1. The model-to-model transformation rules present a lack of conceptual basis which prevents to assume or to prove that semantics of models are preserved during the transformation.

Figure 11. Abstract and concrete syntax of B

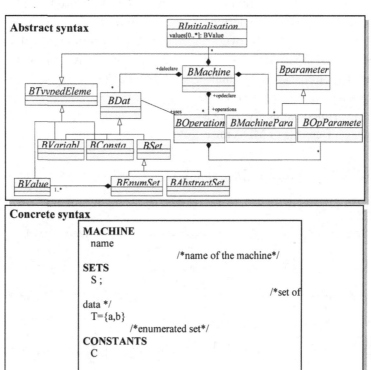

2. Transformations are not explicitly defined which makes it difficult to know on what semantic basis the transformation has taken place.

3. A variety of personalized UML-to-B tools exist (C. Snook and M. Butler (2004), R. Laleau and A. Mammar (2000), H. Ledang, J. Souquières, and S. Charles (2003), L. Hazem, N. Levy, and R. Marcano-Kamenoff (2004)), but they are not evolutive (because of the two previous reasons) and produce distinct B specifications from the same UML model.

In order to circumvent these shortcomings, we developed an MDA3 (Model Driven Architecture) framework intended to involve a generic and automated transformation process from UML to B. The MDA is a development process that aims to separate business logic from underlying platform technology. Otherwise, in MDA a Platform Independent Model (PIM) of a system is formalized and a Platform Specific Model (PSM) is derived from the PIM using transformations. The overall model transformation process in MDA is defined in terms of meta-model projections: given the meta-models of different modeling languages, a set of transformation rules is defined explicitly using a transformation language. Benefits of MDA raise

from the fact that meta-models and transformations are normalized by the meta-language standard of UML called MOF (Meta Object Facility). Indeed, this confers a homogeneous, evolutive and reusable framework to model integration.

We apply this technique in order to define a generic UML-to-B transformation process. Indeed, a generic transformation is a representation of a set of specialized transformations that can be used to manipulate an existing model. As integration of heterogeneous models (B and UML) is described by a sequence of high-level mappings, the transformation process is then defined independently of the kind of transformation and it can be applied to a wide range of translations from UML to B. In MDA the transformation process leans on a precise definition of links between models in a meta-level, and then effective transformation is done by instantiating these links. Such an approach allows not only to fill the previously cited gaps of existing UML-to-B transformation approaches, but also to be reused for all these techniques.

Figure 12 shows how we are inspired by the MDA transformation technique in order to put in practice derivation of B specifications from UML models.

Figure 12. Overview of the proposed UML to B process

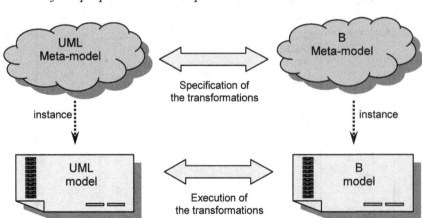

B in a MDE Process

In order to use B in a MDE process, it is necessary to define an abstract syntax, a concrete syntax and a semantic of B. Abstract and concrete syntaxes (Akram Idani, Jean-Louis Boulanger and Laurent Philippe (2007)) are shown in figure 9 and the semantics of B is the Hoare's axiomatic semantics.

MDE PROCESS

Last sections have described the three domains used in the proposed approach. In order to integrate theses domains in a coherent software development, we propose to realize a MDE process.

As explain in section 2, such process implies:

- The formalization (with meta-model) of the various domains;
- The construction of transformation rules.

The meta-models of UML, FSP and B have been shown figures 8, 9 and 11. Some examples of transformation rules are illustrated figure 13. As, the description of this rules are not the aims of this paper, we invite the reader to read the work of Akram Idani, Jean-Louis Boulanger and Laurent Philippe (2007), Meyer Eric, Souquières Jeanine (1999) and Rasse Alban, Perronne Jean-Marc, Muller Pierre-Alain and Thirion Bernard (2005).

The formalization of meta-models and transformation rules allows to use models transformations tools in order to generate specific target models automatically. Thus, the transformations of UML into FSP are realized automatically with MetaEdit (MetaCase (2007)). The transformations of UML into B (Akram Idani, Jean-Louis Boulanger and Laurent Philippe (2007)) are realized automatically with openArchitectureWare (M. Völter (2006)).

CASE STUDY: RAILWAY LEVEL CROSSING EXAMPLE

Presentation

For illustrating ideas developed in the chapter, we consider the simplified generalized railway crossing example. The general requirements are to produce a computerized system to control trains and a gate at a railroad crossing which lies in a region of interest R. Trains travel in one direction through R. Sensors indicate when a train enters or exits the region R. For space and clarity reasons, we restrict ourselves to elements that are relevant to illustrate our approach. More details can be found in (Jansen L., Schnieder Eckehard (2000)).

Model of the Level Crossing

Figure 14, shows the architecture of the level crossing (LC); it is composed of barriers, traffic lights, sensors and three control systems: Train-Borne Control System (Tcs), Level-Crossing Control System (Lccs) and Operation Center (Oc). The Tcs controls functionalities of the train. The Lccs controls barriers and traffic lights. The Oc supervises the level crossing and manage its failures.

In order to describe the behavioral aspects of the level crossing, we associate to each class of figure 14, a states-transitions diagram. As an example, the diagram of figure 15 represents the behavior of the Lccs; it is composed of a composite state Activated and two simple states Deactivated and Default. The Lccs is activated when the train is approaching the level Crossing. In the activated mode, the Lccs performs a sequence of action (at a specific time) in order to safety close (then safety open) the crossing. First, the yellow lights are switched on (yl.on), then after 3 seconds (named t1), yellow lights are switched off (yl. off) and red lights are switched on (rl.on). After 9 seconds (named t2), the barriers are started to be lowered. (b1.close, b2.close).

Figure 13. Examples of models transformations

UML model	B model	FSP model
Class & objects	**Abstract Machine**	**Primitive processus & instance of process**
$\begin{array}{c}2\\ \hline c1, c2\end{array}$ Class / attribut : Type	**MACHINE** Class **SET** CLASS **VARIABLES** class, attribut, c1, c2 **INVARIANT** class $\subseteq$ CLASS $\wedge$ c1 $\in$ class $\wedge$ c2 $\in$ class attribut $\in$ class $\rightarrow$ Type	Class = ... , ... = (...), ... = (...). {c1 , c2} : Class
Transitions & States S1 — ev → S2	**Operations** ... **OPERATION** ev (obj) = **PRE** obj $\in$ class $\wedge$ class_State(obj) = S1 **THEN** class_State(obj) := S$_2$ **END**	**Action prefix & local process** Class = S1, S1 = (ev $\rightarrow$ S2), S2 = (...

When the train has completely passed the crossing area (deactivate) the level crossing may be opened (b1.open, t2.open) for road traffic and the Lccs switches back to the Deactivated mode. The Lccs is in a Default mode, if the time of opening/closing of the barriers is higher than maximum times (named timeOut1 and timeOut2). This failure is forwarded to the Oc, which manage the maintenance of the system.

At this stage, the system is fully modeled; it can be translated into a FSP model then a B model.

Formal Checking of the Level Crossing

In the checking phase proposed here, attention will be given to safety properties, which assert that "trains and road traffic must not enter in the crossing area at the same time" in order to avoid collision. In agreement with the proposed ap-

Figure 14. Architecture of the Level Crossing

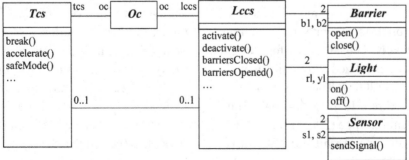

Figure 15. States-transitions diagram that described the behavior of the Lccs

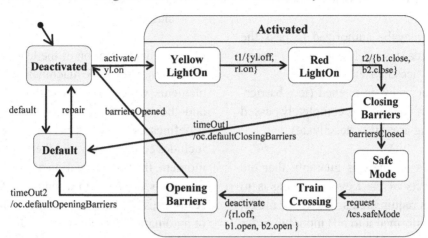

proach, this property will be checked by LTSA.

The used of LTSA implies (in the first time) to specify the primitive processes, which compose the system. These processes are defined as a Labeled Transition System (LTS) and are modeled using the process algebra notation FSP. Thus, the classes Light, Sensor, Barrier, Oc, Tcs, Lccs and their behaviors (states-transitions diagrams) are transformed into primitive processes. For example, figure 16 shows the primitive process Lccs which is obtained from the diagrams of the figures 14 and 15. In accordance with the models transformation shown figure 10, the states (Default, YellowLightOn, Deactivated, etc.) are transformed into local processes (Default, YellowLightOn, Deactivated, etc.) and the events (activate, deactivate, t1, etc.) into action prefix (activate, deactivate, t1, etc.).

In a second step, the FSP model of the Level Crossing (figure 16) is obtained from the instances of primitives processes. These instances are composed in a parallel way (||), then synchronized (/) thank to the event/action expression which are presents in the states-transitions diagrams of the UML model. This LC model is then checked using LTSA.

LTSA allows an interactive simulation of specific scenarios in order to ensure that the LC model satisfies the expected behavior. Simulation, which is a non-exhaustive validation, can be completed with a search for violation of liveness and safety properties.

Thus, the safety property mentioned earlier is

Figure 16. FSP model of the Lccs

```
Lccs= Deactivated,
Deactivated = (activate → YellowLightOn| default → Default),
YellowLightOn = ( t1 → RedLightOn),
RedLightOn = ( t2 → ClosingBarriers),
ClosingBarriers = (barriersClosed → SafeMode| timeOut1 → Default),
SafeModel = (request → TrainCrossing),
TrainCrossing = (deactivate ⊠ OpeningBarriers),
OpeningBarriers = (barriersOpened→ Deactivated | timeOut2→ Default),
Default = (repair → Deactivated).
```

Figure 17. FSP model of the Level Crossing

```
|| LC= (lccs : Lccs || tcs : Tcs || s1: Sensor || ... || rl: Light)
/{  lccs.activate / yl.on,
         lccs.t2 / {b1.close, b2.close},
         lccs.deactivate / {rl.off, b1.open, b2.open },
         ...
}.
```

Figure 18. FSP model of the safety properties

```
property SafeClosing
         = (lccs.barriersClosed -> tcs.safeMode -> SafeClosing).

property SafeOpening
         = (lccs.deactivate -> lccs. barriersOpened  -> SafeOpening).
```

shown in figure 18; it consists to check that:

- The train may be authorized to pass the crossing area (tcs.safeMode) if the barriers are closed (lccs.barriersClosed)
- The barriers may be opened (lccs.barriersOpened) if the train has completely passed the crossing area (lccs.deactivate)

These phases of analysis guaranty that the behavioral aspects of the Level Crossing is in accordance with requirements. The UML model can be now transformed into a B model in order to generate an executable code.

The B Model of the Level Crossing

The B model of the level crossing is obtained from the class diagrams and the states-transitions diagrams. Thus, the classes Light, Sensor, Barrier, Oc, Tcs, Lccs, and their behaviors are transformed into a B machine. For example, figure 19 represents the skeleton of the B machine that is obtained from the Lccs class (cf. figures 14 and 15).

This machine is composed of:

- A set LCCS (in the SETS clause) and a variable lccs, which represents respectively the set of possible and existing instances (here lccs) of the Lccs class.
- A set of operations which are obtained from methods (cf. figure 8) such as the activate() method for example. For each operation there is an additional parameter obj that represents the object of the class that executes the operation.
- A set of Pre and Post condition obtained from the transition of the states-transitions diagrams.
- An enumerated set (LCCS_STATE = {Deactivated, …, safeMode}) which represent the states of the states-transitions diagram associated with the Lccs class.
- A variable lccs_State, which represents the

courant state of each instance of the Lccs class.

The transformation of the UML model, leads to 7 B machines; 6 machines represent the 6 elements which composed the Level Crossing and the seventh represents the global system; it defines associations between the classes and includes consequently all other machines. At this moment, the transformation of UML models into B models (realized in a manual (Philippe Bon, Jean-Louis Boulanger et Georges Mariano (2003)) or automatically (Akram Idani, Jean-Louis Boulanger and Laurent Philippe (2007)) way) allows to produced machines and the implementations that allow to realize the functional links between machines. The refinement (C. Morgan (1990)) of the B models is a manual process, which is partially automated see Lilian Burdy, Jean-Marc. Meynadier (1999).

In this context, the following perspectives consist to:

- Perform the refinement automatically
- Introduce OCL constraints into the UML/B transformation. These OCL constraints will express the safety and liveness properties.

CONCLUSION

This chapter has proposed an original approach for certified design of safety-critical systems. This approach, which has been prototyped on a railway level crossing, proposes to use MDE, UML and formal methods (B and FSP) in order to cover all the software development cycle; it integrates (in a coherent way) a phase of modeling, a phase of formal checking and a phase of refinement. In a first step, the approach proposes to use a subset of UML in order to model software under development. In order to complete the lack of semantics of UML, we realize the transformation of UML models into B and FSP models. In this way, it is

Figure 19. Abstract B machine of the Lccs

```
MACHINE
  Lccs
SETS
  LCCS
  LCCS_STATE = {Deactivated, ..., SafeMode }
VARIABLES
  lccs, lccs_State
INVARIANT
  lccs ⊆ LCCS ∧
  lccs_State ∈ lccs → LCCS_STATE
OPERATION
  activate(obj) =
          PRE
          obj ∈ lccs ∧
          lccs_State(obj) = Deactivated

          THEN
          lccs_State (obj) := YellowLightOn
          END
  ...
END
```

possible to realize a formal checking of the UML models then the generation of certified code by refinement and proof.

The railway standard gives a lot of methodological issues and advocate for two major trends that are in phase with our process:

- The use of automated formal reasoning (such B method or FSP) to increase confidence in such systems;
- The use of comprehensible and accessible notations (such as UML) to reduce certification effort for the design phase.

This work will be continue by proposing to use other model-checking tools (such as Uppaal) in order to check the temporal aspects of critical applications and ensure a more effective checking of these applications. Thus, we hope that the approach described in this paper will contribute to integrate formal methods and UML in a realistic industrial context.

APPENDIX A: OUR MDA-BASED TOOL TO TRANSFORM UML INTO B

The main guideline we follow to realize the UML-to-B tool is the concept of transparency from the final user point of view. In other words, the tool must be "user-friendly". Moreover, we choose to realize it in a "modern" way, using quite innovator softwares and an object-oriented language (Java). Our UML-to-B tool is based on Eclipse IDE[4], which is an open-source development platform for building, deploying and managing softwares. It is an extensible and universal platform that allows tool developers to add functionalities via tool plug-ins. In our work, the plug-in we use is *oAW* (openArchitectureWare). This plug-in is composed by numerous tools that allow many MDA-based operations such as: code generation, model-to-model transformation, model verification using constraints, loading/storing models, etc. We use it as a transformation engine and a code generator.

Figure 20. Practical use of oAW

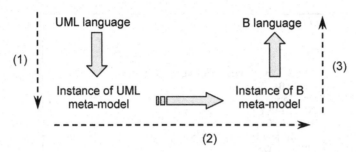

Overview

The UML and B meta-models are encoded in Eclipse IDE thanks to the Eclipse Modelling Framework (EMF) and more precisely thanks to eCore tool. Indeed, the eCore language used to create models in EMF is conform to the MOF. Furthermore, EMF allows Java code generation from meta-models. This makes it possible to create effective java objects that are up to the encoded meta-models. Translation rules are written in oAW (using xTend tool). On this basis, the overall development methodology we adopted to transform UML into B can be summarized in three steps:

- **Instantiation:** in this step the input file, which is an XMI serialization of the UML diagram, is parsed. This instantiates the UML meta-model and then produces an effective UML object up to the UML meta-model and ready to be transformed into a B object.
- **Transformation:** this step is managed by our transformation engine. It executes an instance of transformation rules on base of the previously produced UML object, and then it generates the corresponding B object.
- **Serialization:** this last step generates a B machine source code from the B object (produced by the transformation step). This code generation is performed by oAW

thanks to its modulexPand.

Transformation and Serialization Rules

Transformation

Figure 22 gives a part of the xTend module of oAW in which we have written rules used to produce machine Train_Wagon from the class diagram of figure 6. First of all, we will describe the xTend tool mechanism and then we will give a piece of our translator code as an example.

The xTend tool is quite easy to use, mainly thanks to the simplicity of its declarative language called Extend. It provides the possibility to define rich libraries of independent operations and no-invasive meta-model extensions based on either Java methods or oAW expressions. An Extend file may be composed by three different statements:

- Import statements: to import meta-models linked to the project,
- Extension import statements: to import other Extend files,
- Expression or Java extensions: to perform transformations.

The main part which interests us is the last one: encoding of translation expressions. The syntax of a simple expression extension is as follows: ReturnType extensionName(ParamType1 paramName1, ParamType2...): expression-using-

Figure 21. Fragment of UML meta-model

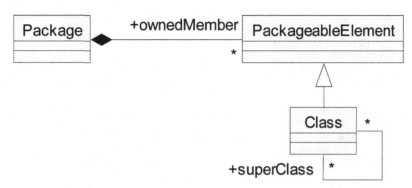

params;

Each expression can call another one, by recursion or not. Many other details could be added to this description but this seems enough to introduce an example from our transformation rules (figure 22). Our xTend file starts by importing UML and B meta-models. The portion of UML meta-model appointed here in figure 21.

In figure 22 three rules are presented:

(i) **translate**: creates a *BMachine* from an UML Package,

(ii) **setBSets**: generates a *BAbstractSet* for each class in the package,

(iii) **setBVar**: generates a *BVariable* from each UML subclass in the package.

We can note some details about the syntax:

- Use of the "create" primitive: kind of basic

polymorphism implementation is xTend (avoid problems with multiple references),

- Multiple calls by expression: use of the "->" representation,

- Use of compound operators, encapsulation, etc.

To conclude with generalities and implementation of this second step, we can note the mere aspect of the xTend tool in spite of its powerfulness. In the complete implementation of our tool, we never found any deadlock to translate a piece of UML meta-model into B meta-model.

Serialization

Application of the second step of figure 20 on the package Train_Wagon produces a Java object instance of the meta-class BMachine. This object is also linked to instances of meta-classes BAbstractSet and BVariable. The serialization step

Figure 22. Example of rules written in xTand module of oAW

```
1 importuml2; importb;
2 createBMachinebmtranslate(Packagep):
3     bm.setName(p.name)->
4     bm.setData(p.ownedMember.typeSelect(Class).setBSets())->
5     bm.setData(bm.data.addAll(p.ownedMember.typeSelect(Class).setBVar()).toList());
6 createBAbstractSetbassetBSets(Classc):
7     (c.superClass.isEmpty==true)?bas.setName(c.name):null;
8 createBVariablebvsetBVar(Classc):
9  (c.superClass.isEmpty==true)?null:bv.setName(c.name);
```

Figure 23. Serialization Rules written in xPand

```
≪ IMPORT b ≫
≪ DEFINE file FOR BMachine ≫
  ≪ FILE name + ''.mch'' ≫
  MACHINE ≪ name ≫
  SETS
  ≪ FOREACH data.typeSelect(BAbstractSet) AS dabs SEPARATOR ';'- ≫
    ≪ dabs.name- ≫
  ≪ ENDFOREACH ≫
  VARIABLES
  ≪ FOREACH data.typeSelect(BVariable) AS dvar SEPARATOR ';'- ≫
    ≪ dvar.name- ≫
  ≪ ENDFOREACH ≫
  INVARIANT
  OPERATIONS
  ≪ ENDFILE ≫

≪ ENDDEFINE ≫
```

aims at interpreting this Java object in order to produce the effective B machine source file. The xPand component of oAW allows writing serialization rules in terms of the B meta-model. The xPand tool is quite similar to xTend one. There are obviously some syntax differences but the basics remain the same: we have to import a meta-model and then to describe how to generate code from an instance matching the meta-model.

The advantage of this step is that the serialization rules are expressed once and for all and are applicable on every object instance of the output meta-model (B meta-model in our case). Serialization rules conform to the transformation approached are given in figure 23. We can also note some details about the syntax:

- *xPand* primitives or expressions are between << and >> markers, then code to be generated is not the code that appears in italic,
- Multiple files can be generated from only one *xPand* template, thanks to the **"DEFINE"** primitive.

So exactly like the second step, this third step uses a language quite easy to use and to understand but actually effective.

Java Integration

In order to develop an autonomous tool, we have to run the transformation and the serialization rules in an Eclipse Action, implemented in Java. As a result, the final user will just have to push a button (button UML2B in Fig. 22) to obtain the B model from a UML diagram.

Figure 24 shows the output of the tool after running rules of figures 22 and 23 on the Train_Wagon package. In the oAW plug-in, the Eclipse Action is developed thanks to the "Facades" mechanisms. They consist of particular classes that allow to manipulate xTend and xPand files with Java. Thus, in order to develop the UML2B Eclipse Action we used both XTendFacade and XpandFacade.

Advantages of the Tool and Future Directions

A crucial idea of Model Driven Engineering is that transformations between heterogeneous models can be described uniformly in terms of meta-model mappings. Based on the fact that meta-models define an abstract syntax from which one can describe model semantics, transformation rules that arise from MDA-based techniques are explicit and precise. In our contribution we applied such

Figure 24. Screenshot of UML-to-B tool after running rules of figures 22 and 23

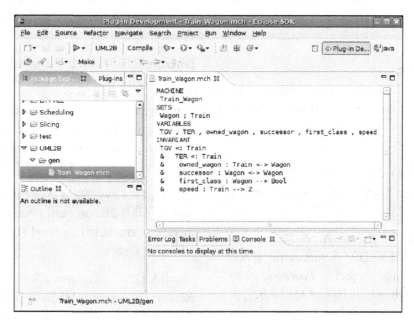

a technique in order to address the derivation of formal B specifications from UML diagrams.

Contrary to the existing translation tools from UML to B, our tool is based on a generic transformation process. Indeed, it can be easily adapted to any existing translation approach by simply implementing transformation and corresponding serialization rules. In this paper we considered a simple translation in which a class diagram is traduced by a unique B machine. However, more complex translations exist such as those proposed by R. Laleau and A. Mammar (2000) where a B machine is produced for each class in the class diagram. Such a translation will lead to as many B machines as UML classes and hence composition links between these B machines must be considered. Thus, in order to reuse our MDA-based framework for such an approach we will need to extend the B meta-model to B compositions. Currently, we are working on these extensions in order to encode, in oAW, the more complete B meta-model.

In our work (figure 3), we select the most pertinent UML to B translations and apply them in safety critical systems (railway applications). So our tool must allow to run every existing rule in order to evaluate whether the resulting B specification is useful or not for these particular systems. Experiments done by our tool showed that we are able to encode the most commonly used UML-to-B translation approaches (A. Idani (2007)) and hence remedy their lack of conceptual basis. However, as our intention is not to extend existing UML to B approaches by providing new rules, the completeness of the model conversion is the same that these approaches. Because of the semantic gap between B and UML languages we note that neither B nor UML are completely covered. The tool results are encouraging and showed that our tool reached its intended objective: to circumvent the limitations of existing approaches. Still, further experiments are needed to broaden the scope of our tool and address more efficiently this challenge. Indeed, actual version of the tool takes into account only UML structural features (i.e. class diagram). We plan in the future to also integrate transformations of UML behavioral features (i.e. state/transition diagrams, etc). Other future directions consist on proposing more UML to B rules in order to cover more B and UML constructs.

REFERENCES

Abrial, J. R. (1992). On constructing large software systems. *IFIP 12th World Computer Congress*, (Vol. A-12, pp. 103-112).

Abrial, J.-R. (1996). *The B-book: assigning programs to meanings*. Cambridge, UK: Cambridge University Press.

Behm, P., Benoit, P., Faivre, A., & Meynadier, J.-M. (1999). « METEOR: A successful application of B in a large project ». *Proceedings of FM'99: World Congress on formal Methods*, (pp. 369-387).

Bon, P., Boulanger, J-L. & Mariano, G. (2003). Semi formal modelling and formal specification: UML & B in simple railway application. *ICSSEA 2003, PARIS*, Novembre 2003.

Boulanger, J.-L. (2007). TUCS: How Build a certifiable railway application with UML. *ICSSEA 2007*, Paris, December 2007.

Burdy, L., Meynadier, J-M. (1999). *Automatic refinement FM'99 workshop -- Applying B in an industrial context: Tools, Lessons and Techniques - Toulouse – 1999*.

CENELEC. (2000). *EN 50126: Railway applications - The specification and demonstration of dependability, reliability, availability, maintainability and safety* (RAMS).

CENELEC (2001). EN 50128 CENELEC. *Railway applications – software for railway control and protection systems*.

CENELEC (2003). EN 50129 CENELEC. *Railway applications – Safety related electronic systems for signaling*.

Clarke, E. M., Grumberg, O., & Peled, D. (2000). *A. Model-Checking*. Cambridge, MA: MIT Press.

Dijkstra, E. W. (1976). *A Discipline of Programming*. Englewood Cliffs, UK: Prentice Hall.

Estublier, J., Vega, G. & Ionita, A. D. (2005). Composing Domain-Specific Languages for Wide-scope Software Engineering Applications. *MoDELS*, Jamaique, Octobre 2005.

Hazem, L., Levy, N., & Marcano-Kamenoff, R. (2004). UML2B: un outil pour la génération de modèles formels. In J. Julliand, (Ed.), *AFADL'2004 - Session Outils*.

Idani, A. (2007). *Computer Software Engineering Research, chapter UML2B vs B2UML: Bridging the gap between formal and graphical software modelling paradigms*. Hauppauge, NY: Nova Science Publishers.

Idani, A., Boulanger, J.-L., & Laurent, P. (2007). A generic process and its tool support towards combining UML and B for safety critical systems. *CAINE 2007*, November 7-9, 2007, San Francisco.

Idani, A., Okasa Ossami, D.-D., & Boulanger, J.-L. (2007). Commandments of UML for safety. In *2nd International Conference on Software Engineering Advances*, August 2007. Washington, DC: IEEE CS Press.

IEC. (2000). *IEC61508, Functional safety of electrical/electronic/programmable electronic safety-related systems*. Geneva, Switzerland: International Electrotechnical Commission.

Jansen, L., & Schnieder, E. (2000). *Traffic control system case study: Problem description and a note on domain-based software specification*. Tech. Rep., Colorado State University, USA.

Laleau, R., & Mammar, A. (2000). An Overview of a Method and Its Support Tool for Generating B Specifications from UML Notations. In *15th IEEE International Conference on Automated Software Engineering*, (pp. 269–272). Washington, DC: IEEE CS Press.

Ledang, H., Souquières, J., & Charles, S. (2003). Argo/UML+B: un outil de transformation systématique de spécifications UML en B. In *AFADL'2003*, (pp. 3–18).

Magee, J., & Kramer, J. (2006). *Concurrency: State Models & Java Programs,* (2nd Ed.). Hoboken, NJ: John Wiley & Sons.

MetaCase. (2007). *Domaine Specific Modeling with MetaEdit+*. Retrieved from http://www.metacase.com/

Meyer, E., & Souquières, J. (1999). A systematic approach to transform OMT diagrams to a B specification. *World Congress on Formal Methods in the Development of Computing System.*

Morgan, C. (1990). *Deriving programs from specifications*. Englewood Cliffs, NJ: Prentice Hall International.

Okalas Ossami, D.-D., Mota, J.-M., & Boulanger, J.-L. (2007). A model process towards modeling guidelines to build certifiable UML models in the railway sector. In *SPICE'2007: Software Process Improvement and Capability.*

Okasa Ossami, D.-D., & Mota, J.-M. Thierry, Laurent., Perronne, J-M. & Boulanger, J-L. (2007). A method to model guidelines for developing railway safety-critical systems with UML. In *proceedings of 7th International SPICE Conference (Software Process Improvement and Capability determination).*

OMG. (2007). *Unified Modeling Language Specification*. Retrieved from http://www.omg.org/docs/formal/05-07-04.pdf, Version 2.0.

Rasse, A., Perronne, J.-M., Muller, P.-A., & Thirion, B. (2005). Using process algebra to validate behavioral aspects of object-oriented models. In *Model design and Validation Workshop, MODEVA'05*, (LNCS). Berlin: Springer.

Sanz, R., & Arzen, K.-E. (2003). Trends in software and control. *IEEE Control Systems Magazine, 23*, 12–15. doi:10.1109/MCS.2003.1200238

Snook, C., & Butler, M. (2004). U2B – A tool for translating UML-B models into B. In J. Mermet, (Ed.), *UML-B Specification for Proven Embedded Systems Design.*

UML. (2007). *Unified Modeling Language, OMG Std. Final Adopted Specification.*

Völter, M. (2006). *openArchitectureWare 4 - The flexible open source tool platform for model-driven software development.*

KEY TERMS AND DEFINITIONS

Certification: Certification refers to the confirmation of certain characteristics of an object, person, or organization. This confirmation is often, but not always, provided by some form of external review or assessment.

Formal method: Formal methods are particular kind of mathematically-based techniques for the specification, development and verification of software and hardware systems.

MDA: Model Driven Architecture

Metamodel: A metamodel is a representation (a model) of a modeling language; it formalizes the aspects and the concepts used by a modeling language, and models the domain in question.

RAMS: Reliability, Availability, Maintainability and Safety

Safety: is the state of being "safe", the condition of being protected against physical, financial, environmental or other types or consequences of failure, damage, error, accidents, harm or any other event which could be considered non-desirable.

   SIL: Safety Integrated Level
   UML2: Unified Modeling Language

ENDNOTES

[1]   This work is supported by the French regional project RT3-TUCS dedicated to UML (2007) technology for complex systems certification and the French national project ANR-ACI-SAFECODE about safety components design.

[2]   A state of the art synthesizing existing approaches which studied the combination of B and UML notations can be found in A. Idani (2007).

[3]   http://www.omg.org/docs/ptc/03-08-02.pdf

[4]   http://www.eclipse.org/

Chapter 20

Commonality Analysis
Implications Over a Successful Product Line

Sathya Ganeshan
Leeds Metropolitan University, UK

Muthu Ramachandran
Leeds Metropolitan University, UK

ABSTRACT

The success of initiating a software product line based approach on an organization depends on a few critical factors. Among them is a thoroughly performed commonality analysis process. This can be imagined as a collecting the supplies and road map required to reach a particular destination. This chapter analyses this critical process and presents our own views and methods of conducting commonality analysis.

INTRODUCTION

Software Product Line engineering has emerged as a successful faction of producing quality products in a rapid pace. Underlying the success of software product lines is the concept of high level use applied in a structured fashion with constant stress on improvement and adaption. This is all based on the idea that all development process is reuse of existing artefacts (Hoey, 2006). Software Product lines are just a clever way of reusing existing assets, given that most organisations develop products in a single domain constantly releasing new products with new variations. The ultimate goal of software

product lines is to improve the productivity of product development and the quality of products. Over the years, a wide array of techniques and models (Eriksson, 2006) has been invented to systematically install this approach. We use the abbreviation SPL to denote Software Product Lines in this chapter.

The global agenda towards software development is taking a marked shift towards family based approaches which have proven to be more efficient and trustworthy. Many global players are already using SPL or family based approaches. Even concerns which are not fully involved into product line based techniques are using some of the SPL processes within their development approach and

DOI: 10.4018/978-1-60566-731-7.ch020

have come to understand the justification behind those approaches.

The success of any product line based approach depends on how accurately the product line engineers can predict the members of the family (Weiss, 1998). This crucial stage of predicting family members also falls within the boundary of Commonality Analysis process. Commonality analysis can be considered the one most important stage of any product line based approach along with architecture, cost analysis etc. We try to understand how crucial this stage is when it comes to product line, what is achieved and what more could be done to tune this process to deliver an efficient software product line family. We shall use the acronym CA to denote Commonality Analysis and SPL to denote Software Product Lines throughout this chapter.

FIRST STEP TOWARDS PRODUCT LINE: THE COMMONALITY ANALYSIS

Commonality analysis is a sort of confidence building measure to first and foremost find out if it is worth the trouble of building a family of products.

Figure 1 shows the list of outcomes which could be used to decide if venturing into SPL approach for a given product within the selected domain could be feasible or not. If all the intended family products share many things in common such as architecture, code, test cases, components etc as shown in figure 1, then it can be said with confidence that SPL approach is worth a try. Following are some of the questions for which a clear answer is required before beginning to apply SPL methods for the given project.

- Are there enough common characteristics present among the intended family of

Figure 1. Justification for applying SPL through commonality analysis

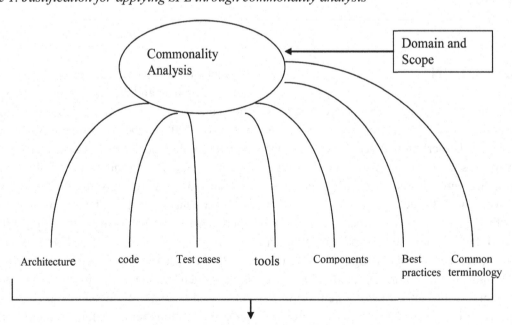

products so that its worthwhile employing SPL approach?

- Is it technically feasible to create a family of products given the constraints and requirements expected off the resulting family of products?
- Would the organisation be ready to bare the cost during the initial periods and accept the change in streamlining the organisation that SPL approach requires?
- Are the application engineers well versed with the technical knowledge about the domain and products which is a compulsory necessity required for such an endeavour?

If the answer to one of the above questions is a no, then its time to rethink applying SPL methods. After all, an organisation would be better off with whatever approach it is using at present. But if it is decided that confidence has been gained by answering yes to all the above questions, then its time to get ready for change and innovation. The core belief of SPL methods is to be as dynamic to changes as possible so as to deliver better products, faster.

THE COMMONALITY ANALYSIS PROCESS

Once the initial decision to shift towards SPL based approaches is made, its time to do the ground works. Commonality analysis is conducted in group meetings with a range of experts who are involved with the project. But for reasons of simplicity, only those directly involved with the development approach are gathered in these discussions. A typical commonality analysis group might contain

- Engineers
- Team leaders
- Project managers
- Developers

- Market analysts
- Moderator
- Writer

The audience of this group might vary depending on organisations and the kind of domain they are involved in. But it is essential that all concerns of developing products within this domain are expressed through these experts. The roles of the first five types of stake holders are quite obvious. Moderator is the person who is responsible for conducting the sessions. His role can be compared to that of a speaker in a parliament. He/she ensure that the meetings do not get out of hands and nothing regarding the process is left unturned. And writer holds the unimpressive job of recording all the decisions made. But this is crucial to the entire process.

At first glance, it appears as if an unbalanced amount of pressure is placed for the role of moderator since his job requires herding all the experts which could be quite a daunting task. But when it is understood that all these experts have been working in the same domain, developing the same products for years consensus might not be that hard to achieve since they are all in the same wave length. But then again, there might be issues which might not be resolved or left hanging, but generally once everyone is made to understand clearly what is required of the family of products, a common ground is reached for the general good of the product family.

THE OUTCOME: LIST OF ESSENTIALS

Exactly what is achieved through these group meetings? To be factual, everything that leads to developing a facility for developing a family of products. Here is the list of essential outputs achieved through commonality analysis process.

- Purpose and Introduction
- Scope and Products
- Library of terms
- Commonality
- Variability and parameters of variation
- Diary of unresolved issues
- Appendices

Purpose and Introduction

- All the ground work that is essential for a product lines starting from how the organisation's goals are about to be met by applying SPL approach.
- All legal and geographical constraints associated with countries and laws and how they would be adhered by this new product line.

Scope and Products

- Definition of all the products that are to be included into the family and their requirements
- Defining the scope within which these family of products should operate
- Deriving at a common architecture for all the family members

Library of Terms

- All terms used to describe various aspects of this SPL and definitions of those terms
- Publication of a clear dictionary of terms and their associated meanings

Commonality

- This is the central task of commonality analysis. Identifying assumptions that are true for all family members.
- List of assets that could be used for all products
- Architecture, components or any key asset

which is common for all family members and the economy, feasibility of reusing them is discussed, decided and recorded here.

Variability and Parameters of Variation

- Those features that make each product in the family different
- Variations and parameters of variations for each product
- Each variation is checked if it falls within the scope and does not over stretch it.
- For certain variations the time of the occurrence of the variation is also fixed (e.g. runtime, build time etc)

Diary of Unresolved Issues

- As this process involves a range of experts from different fields, it cannot be expected to run the whole process without difference in opinions and thoughts. All those issues where unanimity has not been reached are denoted here.

Appendices

- Contains useful information for observers, reviewers and other stake holders of the product family.
- Recommendations for tools

These are some of the expected common outcomes of any commonality analysis process. Perhaps different approaches may include a few extra points, but generally all methods cater all the above outputs. Once a decisive and exhaustive documentation for all the above tasks are gathered, the physical work of implementing a SPL can begin. The next stage to enter the scene would be to develop a production facility for creating the members of the family.

DOMAIN AND APPLICATION ENGINEERING

This stage does not fall within the boundary of commonality analysis, but it does implement whatever decisions taken in the CA process directly. It is important to understand this stage to learn the crucial part CA process plays while SPL is used. To put it simply, domain engineering is the process of creating a facility for rapid production of the family of products. Application engineering uses this facility to actually produce the family of products. So domain engineering can be compared to the task of setting up the assembly line in a factory. While application engineering involves using this assembly line and raw materials to actually make the products required.

It is also at this stage is the inclusion of variation occurs. Different products have different variation points. This can be compared to a car manufacturing plant where the same chassis is used for different cars. At this point we would recommend a sub team of application engineers whose sole purpose is to activate these variations at the pre decided variation points. The task of setting up the pre calculated variation points would also fall under this team. One would be right to imagine that the task of this team would be dynamic because it installs different variations for different products.

COMMONALITY ANALYSIS ROADMAP

The first few paragraphs of this chapter had given an over simplified view of CA process. The idea behind this was to make a reader understand that CA process is as much a management process as it is technical. The intended outcome expected of the group meetings is far more complicated. It should be obvious at this point that moderating these meetings would be a mammoth task.

Commonality Analysis: General Usage

Figure 2 shows the steps of CA analysis as a map. The process starts with the assembling of the CA group with various experts. And each phase, starting with purpose and introduction until the recording of unresolved issues. As can be seen, each phase delivers a hard document of what has been decided and agreed upon to avoid future disagreements. Those that have been recorded on unresolved issues could be left to a majority consensus decision.

MODERATION OF CA ANALYSIS MEETINGS

The criteria mentioned above can give the idea on how much is relied upon the CA group meetings. Below we present a structured way of conducting these meetings. The points are to be adhered by the moderator as well as other stake holders of the meeting.

For each identified issue the following rules apply

- Create right atmosphere for a group session
- Identify issue that is to be discussed currently
- Fix time frame for that issue
- Conduct discussion
- Record the outcome and collect consensus from all stake holders

It cannot be said that each task could be discussed in a particular period of time. For example critical issues such as architecture and identifying commonalities could take more time. So it is up to the moderator to fix a time table for each of these issues. As such the role of the moderator would be the following

Figure 2. Commonality analysis map

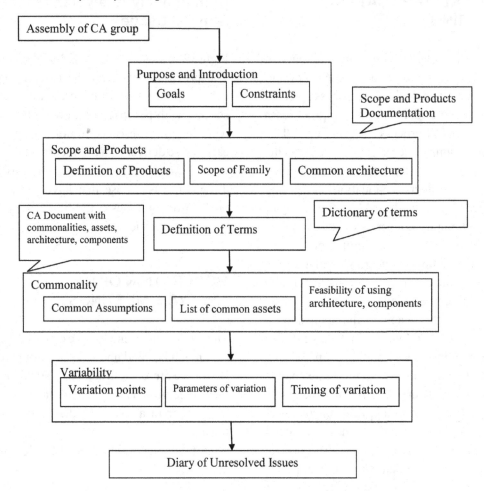

- Plan and Prepare each session
- Create a congenial atmosphere for discussions
- Allow meaningful objections
- Control the audience if a particular issue drags beyond timescale or add it to unresolved issues to be discussed later
- Make sure every stakeholder's concerns are heard
- Assemble the finished document of agreed upon decisions

Apparent from the above points, is the fact that CA stage needs support from all the stake holders involved in the meetings. The members must be willing to negotiate and give up certain aspects for the general good of the product family. There is nothing more confident inducing than a well conducted CA analysis. The finished document is a clear roadmap for building an efficient SPL family.

TOOL SUPPORT AND COMMONALITY ANALYSIS

There aren't many methods specifically designed to CA analysis except for approaches such as FAST (Weiss, 1998) which offers CA analysis as a part of a larger model for applying SPL to an organisation. There are methods to conduct CA analysis on software process (Ocampo, 2005), but is not suitable as an initiating approach for SPL since it deals with processes.

CA analysis from what we have seen above appears more like a team effort of people rather than automated software. But the reality is that tools can highly aid in the CA group meetings and can help the members reach a faster conclusion. We have developed our own named CARE or Commonality Analysis through Requirements Engineering. This tool focuses on mapping requirements with features and assets. Thereby when a new requirement is added, it is possible to trace this requirement to an existing feature or to a new one. Charts and reports from tools like these could help in quick decision making and also standardize the entire process of CA analysis. The CARE method is based on EFARE (Ramachandran and Allen, 2005) which is just a set of guidelines that are derived from domain Knowledge.

But it should be noted, that due to the enormity of this area, not all aspects of commonality analysis could be automated. But over time, methods have evolved that do automate some parts of this process that would have been too cumbersome to be conducted manually. Architecture design methods for product lines such as COPA, FAST, FORM, KobrA and QADA provide some form of commonality analysis but their main goal is to design architecture for the product family. Tools such as SPEARSIM (Ocampo et al, 2004) are capable of performing commonality analysis from a particular perspective.

REFINING CA

Careful engineering at appreciable rapidity can be a decisive solution for small organisations. If one questions why such structured practice methods are required to apply SPL to any organisation, one only has to look at the vast examples of successes. Market Maker is a family of software applications for computing stock market situation for over a period of time. This company invested two years in building, developing core assets, common architecture etc. At the end, this burden of work paid off. It is said; that Market maker (Verlage, 2004) now has the capability to deliver a new product according to customised requirements in as less as three days. This example alone reinforces the importance of deploying structured practice methods to start up with SPL. Moreover a well-planned approach gives flexibility in the future to adapt to change (Ocampo et al, 2004). The product would be able to manoeuvre swiftly to product support technology changes. Some of the new generation of SPL success stories employ methods that significantly reduce the barriers such as adoption and enable the SPL development approach to be more mainstream (Krueger, 2006).

Figure 3 shows the process of constant refinement that can enhance and make the CA process more dynamic. Once the initial CA is over and a development facility has been established, further adaption to changes in market can be done by just a few people by allowing a graceful evolution of the entire SPL. Generally market demands are converted into new requirements that are fed back to the CA process that does assimilation of these new requirements into the system.

While each aspect of this process is completed, it produces a by-product of hardcopy documents that serves as an ultimatum of standards that are to be adhered to or which would serve as a base for all assumptions and plans laid, further on.

SHIFT TOWARDS PRODUCT LINE

There has to be one more dimension that needs to be addressed. When SPL is mentioned, not all clients are comfortable with adapting to a massive change in process of building their products. And their fear is understandable especially when they have proved pretty successful with whatever methodology they are following at the present.

Figure 3. Feedback and refinement into commonality analysis process

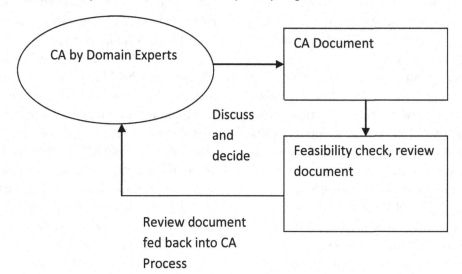

But a good understanding and maturity of what they are performing and the problems they face in regard to their current techniques might tempt them to change a particular part of their process and to adapt to reuse approach for these areas. Usually one area of concern might be commonality. Adoption is the process of switching from any method currently used within the organisation to a software product line based approach. Adoption does not have to be complete. An organisation does not need to be fully following all SPL based methods, but could adopt some parts of it and follow a more gradual shift towards software product line based software production.

For most organisations that are at the dilemma of whether to enter or exit with SPL, CA should be able to provide some decisive answers. Once confidence is gained, the actual process of adoption can take over starting with the domain engineering process. The change in management to accommodate SPL is a totally different area and needs a further look into the domain, scope and product. But for reasons of simplicity we shall understand that management of staff would be divided into domain engineers and application engineers.

COMMONALITY ANALYSIS: A SUCCESS STORY

One interesting aspect of reuse is that, even companies that impose partial SPL approach seem to be more successful than what they currently are. By the word 'partial', I mean those organisations that aren't into hard-core software product line approach, but are in the process of including it or borrowed some concepts from SPL in key areas wherever it suits them. One such company is UGS.

UGS offers technology solutions to high and middle level companies. It has developed its own product lifecycle management technology. One of its clients was Air International which caters technical solutions to Ford and General Motors. Air International provided innovations in design for components and spare for both these companies. Even though both the clients had similar needs, air international faced the following issues:

1) Lack of reuse, since air international designed components separately for GE and Ford.

2) Lack of common platform reduced chance of reuse.

3) Communication between different development teams was poor, since each team was specialised in their specific task and they cannot be shuffled.

The commonality analysis gave a clear picture of the problems associated with the above areas. It was deduced that it was a simple case of not exploiting the commonality already present. To resolve this, the following approach was adopted.

Air International received the aid of UGS with their new Product Lifecycle Management technology. UGS offered to solve the above issues with the following three-part change in their development process:

1) Introduction of common Unigraphix software platform for their CAD/CAM/CAE applications. This opened the gate for reuse and increases the opportunity for reusing components that are common for both Ford and GE since their requirements are similar.
2) Next was the installation of a better data transfer through a tool named Teamcenter. This tool gives access to product data for engineers rapidly.
3) Third the collaboration solution offered by teamcenter was used for better communication between teams separated by geographical constraints.

It is reported that Air International has experienced considerable reduction in production costs and development time after introducing the recommended change. There has been a marked increase in profits too.

Case studies such as these offer the bright side of using commonality analysis to the advantage. It also gives a belief that concerns on the way of achieving high-level reuse get paid in the process of transition itself. Now let's get into the mechanism of commonality analysis, what it is a part of and the general theme of applying CA.

CONCLUSION

As we have seen a brief tour into the process of Commonality Analysis, we hope the reader would have understood the importance that role plays within any SPL. We have not dealt with the management or technical area of SPL, which usually undergoes a lot of change. That is entirely a difference dimension and needs a lot of research. But to conclude the following can be accepted to be true for all CA process

- CA denotes the entire process of setting up the ground work for a successful software product line.
- CA can be a confidence building measure to understand if SPL approach would be suitable for a prospective organisation.
- CA is predominantly a manual process depending on group meetings but aspects of this decision making can rely on help of tools.
- Once the initial CA is over, the maintenance of the already unearthed assets, features, architecture could be managed by a combination of manual and tool based approaches.

REFERENCES

Eriksson, B., & Borg, K. (2006). Software Productline Modelling made practical: An example of Swedish Defence Industry. *Communications of the ACM*, (December): 2006.

Hoey, P. (2006). Software Product line Engineering. *Communications of the ACM, 49*(December).

Krueger, C (2006). New methods in Sotware Product Line Practice Examining the benefits of next-generation SPL methods. *Communications of ACM*.

Ocampo, A., Bella, F., & Münch, J. (2004). Software Process Commonality Analysis. Special Issue on ProSim. *The 5th International Workshop on Software Process Simulation and Modeling, August.*

Ocampo, A., Münch, J., & Bella, F. (2004). *Software Process Commonality Analysis.* Washington, DC: IEEE.

Ramachandran, M., & Allen, P. (2005). *Special Issue on Software Variability: Process and Management: Commonality and variability analysis in industrial practice for product line improvement.*

Ramachandran, M., & Ganeshan, S. (2008). *Domain Engineering Method for Product Line Development.* Published at software engineering research and practice, Las Vegas, NV.

Schmid, K., & Verlage, M. (2004). The Economic Impact of Product Line Adoption and Evolution. *IEEE Software . Special Issue on Software Product Lines*, *10*(4), 50–57.

Weiss, D. (1998). *Commonality Analysis: A systematic process for defining families* (ARES '98), (LNCS 1429). Berlin: Springer-Verlag.

Chapter 21

Rapid Productivity and Quality
Software Product Lines and Trends of the Future

Sathya Ganeshan
Leeds Metropolitan University, UK

Muthu Ramachandran
Leeds Metropolitan University, UK

ABSTRACT

The aim of this chapter is to introduce a reader to the world of software product lines, how it is used and what the future of this field might be. The authors present some of the success stories of organizations who have employed this approach, the benefits they have derived as opposed to conventional approaches. They also present their own views and innovations in touch with cutting edge developments in this field.

INTRODUCTION

By this time the word Software Product Lines or Family Oriented Engineering would need no introduction. A couple of decades ago, this was a promising new venture. Or a famous hot topic for project managers and team leaders alike in the dormitory. Gone are these days when product line based development used to be a favorite past time talk. It is now a reality and ready or not, it is everywhere. At this time, it is interesting to look back at what has been achieved throughout since this technology debuted into the software industry and what new promises are made in the form of new technologies and innovations for the future.

Software Product Lines attempt to reduce development time, cost and effort by taking advantage of the common characteristics among a group of products (Groher et al, 2008). The traditional definition for software product lines explains it as a set of software intensive systems sharing a common managed set of features that satisfy the specific needs of a particular market segment or a mission and that are developed from a common set of core assets in a prescribed way (Clements & Northrop, 2004). Generally speaking, software product lines allow developers to take advantage of common characteristics among a family of products they produce and as a result increase quality, reduce cost and save time. To establish this approach systematically is

DOI: 10.4018/978-1-60566-731-7.ch021

a challenge that involves cooperation between from wide ranging departments. The notion of this chapter is to introduce the reader to a brief introduction, history, and industrial usage and future prospects of software product lines.

DEFINING SOFTWARE PRODUCT LINES

There are many definitions for software product lines. One of the widely accepted ones, given by SEI is:

'..a set of software-intensive systems that share a common, managed set of features satisfying the specific needs of a particular market segment or mission and that are developed from a common set of core assets in a prescribed way.' (SEI, 2005).

In its most simplified form, Software Product Line aims at producing a family of software by taking advantage of the common aspects among them, as opposed to producing applications individually, in a rapid and cost effective manner and at the same time satisfying quality attributes. To be precise software product lines generate a family of products with many common properties and some variant properties so that it caters the individual needs for a wide variety of users. Henceforth throughout the chapter we will use the abbreviation SPL to denote Software Product Lines. The terms product line and product family are often used in the same meaning. But some European companies take a different synonym for product line. Through product line they mean a set of products which appears similar in functionality but has an entirely different technology inside. But product family often represents a set of products that have common functionality with some minor variations but built from the same technology (Linden, 2002).

Today's customer demands products that are tailored to their specific needs. Product family ap-proach facilitates producing bulk products with intended variants. SPL engineering has the potential to offer great cost savings and productivity gains to organizations that provide family of products. Rapid production of product that adapt quickly to market needs offers competitive advantage. It is also pivotal for applications where quality is critical. For Safety critical systems the approach has shown the way for potential reuse of analysis and test results (Thompson and Heindahl, 2001). Reuse allows tried and tested techniques to be reused and thereby reducing the risk of failure in safety critical systems. Thompson (2001) further states that even though there are difficulties in properly defining the boundaries of the product family the approach would work. Research in software reuse has observed that the most successful reuse attempts have been achieved through collections of components with well defined domain boundaries. If a domain is mature, solution to a problem can be deduced easily without complex systems. A potentially larger return on investment lies in support for problems that have not yet matured. Let's take a peek at how this approach came into being and how it is employed in various organizations.

PRODUCT LINES: BEGINNING

Re-write introduction to SPL. Starting from the humble burger shops to airliners, product lines are ever present. When it comes to the literature, product lines did not appear until 1969. Tracing back its history, Parnas introduced the idea of program families, which became the foundation for family based engineering. Later a model of domain engineering called Draco (Neighbors, 1989) emerged which paved the way for major research into the area of software reuse and family based engineering. Further SEI or Software Engineering Institute expanded the research in the domain engineering field and named this area as product line engineering (Clements & Northrop, 2002).

Figure 1. An example for a product family

A Family of Houses built using Lego Blocks

Figure 1 shows an example product family. A variety of different toy houses built using lego blocks. This would constitute a perfect product family since the raw materials, in this case plastic blocks are all similar. But by arranging them in different ways with differences in colors it is possible to generate quite a variety of outputs.

WHY SHOULD WE OPT FOR SPL?

To understand why one should use SPL approach, one should also understand the traditional issues involved in software engineering. Sommerville (2004) says that the following are the key challenges faced by software engineering,

1. The heterogeneity challenge: Problems associated with the process of operating software in different environments, with legacy systems etc.
2. The delivery challenge: The traditional processes of software engineering techniques are time consuming. Delivering the product on time is always a major challenge.
3. The trust challenge: the right functioning of software sometimes means the difference between life and death in case of safety critical applications. In any case, the trust challenge is to develop techniques to demonstrate that the software can be trusted.

SPL if applied effectively is known to satisfy all these issues. It performs above expectations in some areas, which makes it worthwhile to understand and enhance several aspects of SPL to tap the full potential this approach could offer. In fact some companies gained more than what they bargained for. Just as the original product lines made Ford the biggest automobile industry in the world, SPL are well in the way to make a similar effect in the software industry. The next big deciding factor would be the cost.

Cost factor underlies every issue and solution in software engineering. The best solution for the worst problem must sometimes be abandoned simply because the cost is more than what the benefits are worth. One of the main reasons why software product lines are said to thrive in the present software industry is because of its cost benefits.

Figure 2 shows that the initial cost of setting up a family production facility, adapting the organization to change to SPL approach is much higher than conventional methods. But the benefits of SPL are long termed. Over a period of time, more time and cost are spent for maintaining, modifying and adapting to new requirements. But this cost is surprisingly low for companies using SPL approach. It's well understood, that survival of software in this competitive industry depends on how well the software adapts to change and how readily it is able to accommodate new requirements.

Figure 2. Cost of applying SPL

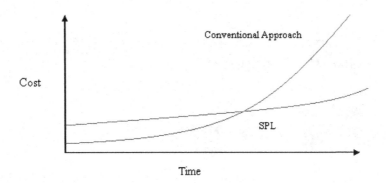

This cost comparison of cost between conventional approaches or one-off projects against SPL is shown in the simple graph above. It clearly shows a marked difference in cost. Even though the conventional projects start off at low budget, as the software matures, more time and money are spent maintaining and adapting the product to changes, while the curve of SPL almost remains constant for long duration.

TO START WITH: WHAT SHOULD WE KNOW?

To start with, Software Product Lines are ever growing, ever evolving and dynamic arena where there are several complex interactions between various interrelated dimensions. To view it as mainly a technical challenge is grossly underestimating the complexity which includes other dimensions such as management and process (Sugumaran et al, 2006). This point has been Hence Product Line engineering depends on the smooth functioning and co-operation of the following:

1) Management and Practices
2) Process
3) Technology

Figure 3 illustrates the various interrelated dimensions of product line based engineering. Each dimension has several aspects within them that need to be addressed. The above figure is just one view among others of approaching product lines. Some other views include:

1) Domain engineering and application engineering, supervised by management
2) Core asset development and product development orchestrated by a management function

Although there are several ways of looking at how product lines operate, upon closer observation they denote one and the same. The core understanding behind these views is that product line engineering involves several disciplines with a wide focus and ever increasing complexity. Several key areas of study within the above mentioned disciplines include but are not limited to:

1) Core asset development
2) Product development
3) Commonality and Variability Analysis
4) Domain Engineering and Application Engineering
5) Product Line Testing
6) Product line initiation and Adoption

Figure 3. The three dimensions of product line engineering

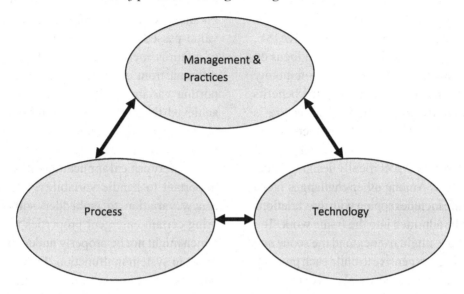

7) Domain analysis
8) Product line architecture
9) Product line process and maturity

Figure 4 illustrates the wide areas of interest within product line engineering. Each area is wide and extensively researched. The growing interest in product line engineering has triggered a sturdy increase in organizations venturing into family based production. There are a variety of tools and techniques available to support a prospective organization that aims to adapt to product line based development.

Figure 4. Core areas of interest in software product lines

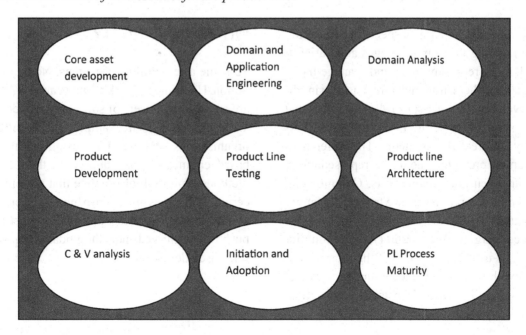

METHODS AND TECHNOLOGIES

Hugely funded projects such as ARES, PRAISE, ESAPS, CAFÉ, and FAMILIES, which focus on reuse, are testament that the software community is getting serious and wants to reap the benefits of product family engineering. Architecture is one key feature that affects all products made. Methods such as COPA, FAST, FORM, KobrA and QADA are used to specifically design product line architecture. Among other challenges faced by architecture includes coping with the variations that need to be admitted into the frame work. Too many variations might over extend the scope and thereby making it expensive to build each product. This again goes against the initial goal of products based on more common features than variability. This situation could be avoided if the commonality analysis process was performed in a systematic way. But it should be clear at this point that certain processes are more important than others within the SPL approach. Commonality and variability analysis is one among them.

COMMONALITY AND VARIABILITY ANALYSIS

One of the most important aspects of SPL would be maintaining the commonalities and variability's, how to represent them and manage them. Representing them in architecture sensibly simplifies development. Karlsson (1995) describes that different members of the family might address slightly different requirements. The differences that can be predicted should be represented by associated reusable components. Commonality is a set of assumptions that are true for all family members.

According to Weiss(2004), commonality analysis is used to design what the members of a family should be. This technique is a part of FAST or Family-oriented Abstraction Specifica-

tion and Translation. Weiss (2005) also specifies Parameters of Variation, where depending on a value passed to a parameter, the characteristic of a family member changes, thereby making it different from other family members, thus supporting variability. While commonality can be achieved through use of common architecture, variability could be added thorough abstractions in the common architecture.

In safety critical applications, it becomes more important to handle variability. Clearly adding a new variation to embedded software, might bring certain emergent properties to the system which might not be properly understood and thus result in system malfunction. In systems such as pacemakers it becomes more critical that these faults be detected by standard hazard analysis techniques. Formal methods can find errors which are difficult to detect using manual effort, but are complex, expensive and limited to a smaller scope (Jing Liu et al, 2002). The authors also describe a UML based modeling technique that allows the faults to be fed into the model and analyzed. This model is based on the background of hazard analysis for pacemaker product lines with effects brought by variations.

WHO ARE USING IT?

To name a few Phillips, Siemens, Nokia, DOD, Salion, Hp Printers, Market Maker and NXP GTV are some known users of software product lines. We shall try to present examples of how different organisations benefited from using product line based engineering as opposed to their former methods. You shall also notice that not only did certain companies managed to bypass the pressure of time-to-market, release and quality constraints, but how they thrived under the guidance of product line based development.

Engenio Information Technologies (Hetrick, 2005)

Engenio is a provider of future rich storage solutions to major vendors such as IBM, SGI, Teradata, Cray and StorageTek. With approximately 200 developers around the world, they provided firmware for around 82 products, with approximately 1 million lines of embedded code for each product. 80% of this code was common and the remaining variation was handled during run-time by downloading variables stored in non-volatile memory. To support the software for their new RAID storage, the development department struggled to maintain, evolve and create the firmware. Further the demand to release several products at the same time that operate at varying platforms demanded a need for an approach wherein these variations could be handled. Software product line was the obvious choice, and after the initial investment, the company found out that it was repaid within four months. The product line approach also allowed Engenio to allow it to support hardware of varying portfolio to be included into its family.

HP Printers (Toft, 2000)

HP is a known producer of printers with a wide range of features and caters different users. There was a need to develop a wide range of firmware. Many of these products have a lot in common. But sharing this commonality information among the developers in different projects might prove elusive. To overcome this difficulty HP came up with the concept of Firmware Cooperative following the principle of cooperative organizations. These were called owen cooperative. There were extensive collection of components and codes of all projects that were voluntarily united. Teams were encouraged to share, use and change assets from this cooperative. By providing such environment, HP made sure that knowledge and assets are reused among varying projects. The owen cooperative was a huge success. When compared

with developing firmware independently for each printer variant, the team reported: a 3X improvement in time to market, with a 4X reduction in overall team size, and a 25X reduction in typical defect densities. The cooperative approach yielded a 70% increase in the amount of code shared across participating printer product lines.

Market Maker (Verlage, 2004)

Market Maker is a leading German company that provides forecasts and predictions of market behavior using financial models. Initially market maker used to supply data to its software through external storage devices. Today market maker operates as a website that can answer to queries and brings up the result as HTML pages. To support its product line Market maker deployed a product line approach that supports a business model that is responsive and open to future markets. Creating new products relied on a repository of domain-specific assets, helping to reduce development time by more than 50% and reduce cost by roughly 70%.

DESIGN METHODS FOR SPL

Design methods for SPL vary diversely in approach and technique. Some of the popular ones currently used in the industry include methods such as COPA, FAST, KobrA, QADA etc.

COPA focuses mainly on software intensive devices or electronic systems. The aim of this multi layered approach is to derive a systematic scheme to manage the entire process of creating a family of product for embedded systems that are software intensive.

FAST uses a technique called PASTA or Process and Artefact State Transition Abstraction model to systematically implement the concept of FAST. FAST can be generally divided into three sub processes,

1. Identifying the feasibility of investing on the family of products.
2. Domain engineering for creation of production facility for the family of members.
3. Application engineering to use that facility for a creating family of members.

Besides these divisions into sub processes, FAST distinguishes between artefacts, roles and activities (Harsu, 2002). Besides these aspects, FAST uses certain assumptions on which the foundation of FAST concept relies on. The first step of this method is to use commonality analysis. This method is based on a series of discussions conducted by experts to decide on various factors about commonality and variability attributes. The output of this phase is a specification language.

Certain features that makes FAST desirable include the following,

1. Predicting changes for a family over a period of time.
2. Separation of concerns.
3. Creating an application modelling language.
4. Designing for change using abstraction and information hiding.

Besides FAST also uses an approach for formally specifying and modelling systems. Altogether FAST does provide very useful features as a development process for a family of products.

FODA or Family Oriented Domain Analysis is supported by the concept of abstraction and refinement. The idea here is that there exist several applications and designs in a domain. The concept of abstraction is used to generalise all the products in this domain, as a result creating a product which accommodates all the applications. It is done by abstracting away the properties/ features that make a product unique.

Refinement is the process of refining either the end product with applying those variations/ refinement that makes a product unique until the unique product is evolved. FODA was invented after analysing many domain analysis languages and hence it carries the properties of many domain analysis techniques. This approach underlies on the assumption that features that differentiate a class/ group of products from another. Hence by adding or chipping away features, a product can be generalised or refined.

The result of this approach is a set of abstractions and refinements with parameterisation.

Adding to these Kobra, FORM and Pulse are some other domain analysis and family oriented software production techniques that follow similar patterns. Below is a set of comparisons between the methods that are currently being used

TOOL SUPPORT

The growth of SPL in the industry as spawned an equally fast growth in the amount of tool support available to handle various aspects of SPL based software development. Some of the tools that already exist for SPL tool support include meta programming Text Processor EDGE, Odyssey, DARE-COTS, DADSE, DOMAIN, PuLSE-BEAT etc(Giancarlo Et al, 2001). They also specify their own tool called Holmes. Holmes supports all core activities of software product line analysis and development. These activities include defining the product line, identifying the market and characterizing users, analyzing the relationships among products in the line and competing or complementary products, analyzing and modeling the line, and designing and developing the line in an integrated way (Giancarlo Et al, 2001).

DARE-COTS is a domain analysis tool. The purpose of this tool is to identify the commonalities and variability within a family of software in a domain. It facilitates the extraction of domain knowledge from domain experts, documents and code in domain. This information is then stored in a domain-book that has all needed knowledge about that particular domain.

DADSE (Terry *et al.*, 1995) is a support environment for DICAM (Distributed Intelligent Control and Management) application development. It is also similar to other domain analysis tools that are used in product line engineering for commonality analysis. Similarly PuLSE-BEAT is a decision support system for scoping product lines.

It should be understood that there is no master tool to handle each and every area of product lines. But rather a wide range of tools that can help in specific areas like initiation, scoping, commonality analysis etc. We have developed our own tool for performing commonality analysis using guidelines called EFARE or Extended Family-Oriented Analysis and Reuse Engineering.

FUTURE OF SOFTWARE PRODUCT LINES

With the innovations introduced to this field on a daily basis, it would be hard to figure the place of this method into the future. But by guessing from some of the results we have already seen we can be sure that the following would hold true. Among other advancements achieved through this approach, the most important place that we believe this method would have been granted is the priority given in decision making processes. Managers, team leaders and designers would consider resolving any product development through the eyes of family based production and or especially product line based methods.

- Product Line engineering will be considered as a standard technique in software engineering.
- Priority would be given to assess if a group of products could be built through product line based methods.
- There will be a heavy tool support for all aspects of product line based software development.

- Stakeholders with have the expertise and knowledge required to help them make decisions in view of product line based methods.
- Product building will take much less time, cost and would enjoy more quality owing to software product lines.

CONCLUSION

This chapter brought a brief introduction to the world of software product lines, the inherent concepts associated with it, technologies used to apply this method, success stories of organizations using this method and the future prospects in store for this approach. There are wide range of literature and case studies available for software product lines in the internet and in the form of books.

REFERENCES

Clements, P., & Northrop, L. (2002). *Software product Lines*. Reading, MA: Addison Wesley Publications.

Clements, P., & Northrop, L. (2004). *Software product Lines: Practices and Patterns*. Reading, MA: Addison Wesley Publications.

Giancarlo, J., & Pedrycz, W. (2001). *Holmes: An Intelligent System to Support Software Product Line Development*. Washington, DC: IEEE.

Groher, K., & Charles, C. (2008 March 31 – April 4). A Tool based feature to manage Crosscutting Feature Implementations. *AOSD '08*, Brussels, Belgium.

Harsu, M. (2002). *FAST-Product Line Architecture Process*.

Hetrick, W., & Moore, C. (2005). Incremental Return on Incremental Investment. *Engenio's Transition to Software Product Line Practice*.

Karlsson, E. (1995). *Software Reuse: A Holistic Approach*. Sweden: Q-Labs.

Klaus, S., & Martin, V. (2004). The Economic Impact of Product Line Adoption and Evolution. *IEEE Software. Special Issue on Software Product Lines, 10*(4), 50–57.

Linden, D., & Van, F. (2002). Initiating Software Product Lines. *Software Product Families in Europe: the Esaps and Café projects*. Washington, DC: IEEE.

Liu, J., Lutz, R., & Dehlinger, J. (2003). *Safety Analysis of Variabilities Using State-Based Modeling*.

Neighbors, J. Draco. (1989). A method for engineering reusable software systems. In *Software Reusability*, (Vol. I: *Concepts and Models*, pp. 295–219). New York: ACM Frontier Series, Addison-Wesley.

Peter, T., Derek, C., & Joni, O. (2000). HP Product Generation Consulting, A Cooperative Model for Cross-Divisional Product Development for a Software Product Line. In P. Donohoe (Ed.), *Proceedings of the First Software Product Lines Conference (SPLC1)* (pp. 111-132). Boston: Kluwer Academic Publishers.

SEI. (2005). *Software Product Lines*. Retrieved from http://www.sei.cmu.edu/productlines/bibliography.html

Sommerville, (2004). *Software engineering*, (p. 13). Reading, MA: Addison Wesley.

Sugumaran, V., Park, S., & Kang, C. (2006). Software product line engineering. *Communications of ACM*, December.

Terry, A., Dabija, T., Barnes, X., & Teklemariam, A. (1995). *DADSE 2.3 User Manual*. Paolo Alto, CA: Teknowledge Federal Systems.

Thompsun, J., & Heimdahl, M. (2001). *Extending the Product Family Approach to support n-dimensional and Hierarchical products*. Washington, DC: IEEE.

Toft, P. (2004). *The HP Owen Firmware Cooperative: A Software Product Line Success Story*.

Weiss, D. (2004). *Defining Families: Commonality analysis*. Madison, WI: Lucent Technology, Bell Laboratories.

Chapter 22
Software Components

Adnan Bader
Monash University, Australia

Sita Ramakrishnan
Monash University, Australia

ABSTRACT

Component-based software engineering (CBSE) has rapidly gained currency over recent years. Software developed as components and as assemblies of components has realised the reuse slogan originally associated with object-oriented design. In this chapter we define what software components are along with their different characteristics and classifications. We also cover the widely debated definitions of software components to emphasise the fact that components possess different properties that can mean different things to different people. We discuss the impact of using components on the software development lifecycle and review a number of different approaches developed to procure and integrate components in software systems. Finally, the risks associated with using software components are discussed in detail with along with a trust model. Trends in CBSE research are discussed towards the end to explore some potential areas of future research.

INTRODUCTION

Today, software components are available to software developers from numerous different sources including off-the-shelf (physical), component marketplaces (virtual) and within organisations, where teams of software engineers produce components for other teams within the organisation. While components have played an important role in bringing maturity to the software industry, they have also added new risks to software construction and use. It is very important for software engineers to understand the risks associated with using components, particularly off-the-shelf components.

Some of the earliest component frameworks emerged in the GUI domain with the arrival of 4GLs and Rapid Application Development (RAD). The objective of those frameworks was to allow

DOI: 10.4018/978-1-60566-731-7.ch022

developers to reduce their development time by reusing frequently used prebuilt user interface components. These component frameworks were very tightly coupled with the underlying development environment and as a result provided very well-defined interfaces.

The idea of treating units of software as independent components has existed for some time in the computing world. With the arrival of object-oriented (OO) paradigm, components gained increased popularity. However, while objects in the OO paradigm were very clearly defined along with their properties, the definition of software components triggered a series of useful debates among different researchers proposing different meanings for the term *component*.

Szyperski, Gruntz and Murer (2002) define software components as units of independent deployment and third-party composition with no externally observable state. This definition emphasises that a component encapsulates its constituent features and is deployable as a complete unit even when only a subset of its features are actually used by the consumer.

Meyer (1999) defines components as pieces of software that can be used by other program elements (clients) while the clients and their authors remain unknown to the authors of the component. This definition is closer to the idea of off-the-shelf components than that of components developed within the same organisation (or project) by developers who can easily communicate with other component developers.

Fundamentally, components are purely client-oriented pieces of software that are developed with a very clear distinction between the provider and the consumer. This distinction exists even when the provider and the consumer is the same entity. Components are developed to be used by other software components, systems, and users. This is achieved by packaging and presenting the features of the component to the outside world as an independently deployable unit. Whether the developers of a component are known to its consumers or not does not affect the *component-hood* of a piece of software. It should be noted that while the knowledge about the developers of a component can have direct implications on a consumer's trust in the component, it is irrelevant in the context of defining what a component is. Therefore, while we agree with Meyer's view of components as client-oriented software, we mainly use Szyperski's definition when investigating properties of software components in this chapter.

The debate on the definition of components has attracted a lot of attention in recent years (e.g. Carney, 2000; Basili, 2001; Clark, 2004). This has resulted in new varieties of components being suggested by researchers including the following:

Commercial-Off-The-Shelf (COTS): The term COTS (commercial-off-the-shelf) originated in a non-software engineering context where US military referred to different off-the-shelf components for their weaponry as COTS components. COTS components range from the smallest ActiveX components to the largest commercially off-the-shelf available database systems (like Oracle, SQL Server).

Modifiable-Off-The-Shelf (MOTS): These refer to components that can be modified either through customisation or direct modification of source code (e.g. open source components).

Non-Developmental Item (NDI): These refer to software components that are obtained from outside the development team. Whether that component was purchased or obtained free of cost is irrelevant as long as no resources from within the development team were consumed on the development of these components.

This chapter describes in detail the characteristics of software components that differentiate these software entities from other forms of software artifacts with the aim to emphasise the role of trusted software components in the future of software engineering.

CHARACTERISTICS OF SOFTWARE COMPONENTS

From a consumer's perspective, software components are deployable, configurable, opaque, non-modifiable and resist transfer of ownership.

Components are Deployable

This is a fundamental requirement for a piece of software to qualify as a component. A component is required to be packaged with enough information and sufficient interface features to make it possible for the consumers to deploy it. Such deployment should ideally be independent of the vendor/developer of the component.

Components are Configurable

In a majority of situations, a software component is utilised by its consumers for only a subset of its features. In order for the component to function optimally, it needs to be configurable. In other words, configurability adds to the generic nature of the component. Making components configurable by the consumers is one of the key aims of component developers.

Components are Opaque

Access to a component's features should only be allowed through its public interface with no details about the internal working of the component visible to the consumer. This requirement of opacity is even more evident for COTS components.

As a consequence of the characteristics described above, some further characteristics of software components become evident.

Components are Non-Modifiable

While consumers need to be able to configure software components based on their needs, they should never be able to modify the existing behaviour of any of its features.

Components Resist Transfer of Ownership

Most often, the usage of software components is controlled through licensing agreements between the vendor and the consumer. Under such arrangements, the ownership of the component stays with the vendor both in terms of copyright and production. Consumers may ask the vendor for enhancements and/or modifications to the component based on their individual requirements but that does not affect the vendor's ownership of the component.

Components Cause Transfer of Risk

As a consequence of opaqueness and non-transfer of ownership, software components cause transfer of risk from the vendor to the consumer. Such transfer of risk becomes more evident when the consumers themselves are component vendors and use one component as part of another component. Such transfer of risk is one of the major causes of lack of trust in software components, particularly COTS components.

COMPONENT LIFECYCLES

The two processes of component production (by the vendor/developer) and consumption (by the consumer) are disjoint. Vendors of components follow their own processes to design and develop components based mostly on their own perceived set of requirements. Consumers, on the other hand, evaluate components against their requirements following their own processes. In some instances, component vendors use a pool of potential consumers to gather and validate requirements. Some vendors go a step further by using a group of potential consumers for beta testing the components

Figure 1. Component development lifecycle

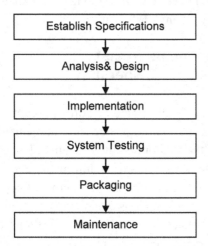

to ensure that the client expectations are met, both at functional and non-functional levels.

Component Development Lifecycle

Figure 1 lists the different phases involved in the production of software components. For the sake of simplicity, iterations and feedback loops have not been included in Figure-1. These phases are independent of the particular software engineering process followed by any particular vendors. Whether a vendor adopts the Extreme Programming or Cleanroom approach, they still need to go through these phases.

Establish Specifications

Component vendors aim to make their components as generic as possible while staying within a particular application domain (e.g. database, data communication, graphics etc.). Based on the application domain, vendors establish a set of specifications for developing the component. These specifications are technical, concrete and are, generally, independent of any particular consumer in order to keep the component as generic as possible. Due to this independence, it is crucial for vendors to have a realistic set of component

specifications that are established with a client-oriented approach. This can be achieved by having very well-defined interfaces to components that can be published to potential consumers in order to get feedback on the usefulness and understandability of the interface.

Analysis and Design

Based on the technical specifications established in the previous phase, vendors analyse those specifications in terms of feasibility and required resources. A design is then developed based on this analysis. This analysis and design phase is the same as for non-component oriented software development. Vendors may choose any approach for doing this, however, object-oriented analysis and design has been most widely used by component vendors.

Implementation

During this phase different parts of the component are coded using selected programming language(s). The most important element of this phase is to keep the implementation in-line with the pre-established interface. Unit testing is also usually performed as part of the implementation phase.

System Testing

Depending on the application domain of a component, vendors need to test it as a whole at different levels, perhaps under different possible host settings. This is achieved by test drivers that interact with the component only via its published interface. The ideal approach is to view the component as a consumer would view it for integration-level testing. Some vendors actually involve a group of potential consumers of the component to take part in a beta testing process before the component is released to the wider audience.

Packaging

Component packaging is synonymous with system deployment. However, since components are not directly deployed by their vendors, vendors need to make their components available to consumers in a form that facilitates integration. In addition to the component itself, a component package usually includes any other components that are used by the packaged component, licensing material, technical documentation for integrators/users and a help system (if required).

Maintenance

Vendors' maintenance activities can cover the entire iterative development cycle that may produce another completely new version of the component that can be packaged again. We have collapsed these activities under the maintenance phase in order to keep the focus on consumers' view of the component.

Component Usage Lifecycle

Figure 2 lists the different phases for consumers of software components. Once again, the iterations among the different phases have been abstracted out to keep the focus on the different phases

Figure 2. Component usage lifecycle

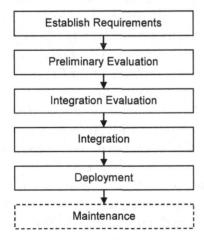

involved. The key difference, as can be seen in Figure-2, between component production and usage is the order in which testing is performed by the two parties. Consumers perform acceptance testing first, followed by integration testing and if required and if possible, unit testing.

Establish Requirements

Contrary to the specifications established by component vendors, consumer specifications are based on concrete requirements. Consumers always have a defined context in which they intend to use a component. This context includes the technical specifications of the host system along with the functional and non-functional requirements for the required component. As part of this phase, consumers need to classify their requirements as critical and non-critical requirements. This aids the consumers in finding more candidate components that can address the critical requirements since it is not likely that they will find a component that addresses the complete set of consumer requirements (critical and non-critical).

Preliminary Evaluation

Based on the requirements established in the previous phase, consumers search and evaluate candidate components. This evaluation process is mainly based on comparing the component specifications as published by the vendors against the component requirements as established by the consumer. It also involves acceptance testing and assessment of non-functional attributes of the component (e.g. efficiency, dependency, support level etc.).

Integration Evaluation

Once a candidate component has successfully gone through the evaluation and acceptance testing phase, consumers start to look at the possible ways the component can be integrated in their host setting. This is where integration testing is done to ensure that the functionality offered by the component combines with the rest of the system in an acceptable fashion. While focus of the preliminary evaluation phase is on the non-functional attributes of a component, integration evaluation focuses more on the functional aspects of the component.

Integration

Integration involves writing any glue code in addition to using the interfaces provided by the component as well as performing integration testing on the host system in the context of the component usage.

Deployment

Deployment is only in the context of the selected COTS component and not the entire system that the component is a part of. This phase may involve configuring the component, if required.

Maintenance

While exclusive maintenance of the component is usually not required by consumers, occasional configuration changes may take place. Additionally, any updates to the component from the vendor also require some re-testing effort that becomes part of the maintenance phase for the consumer.

IMPLICATIONS OF SOFTWARE COMPONENT USAGE

One of the key characteristics of software components is the transfer of risk from the vendor to the consumer. Vendors aim to maximise such transfer of risk through detailed licensing agreements that protect the vendor in cases of serious damage caused by failure of their product. Consumers, on the other hand, try to minimise this transfer of risk

by rigorously testing and evaluating a component before deciding to use it.

As mentioned earlier, such transfer of risk becomes more critical when the consumers of a component are using the component for developing a system for some other consumers, thereby acting as middle-men in some sense. Such system developers need to be extremely careful to properly manage the transfer of risk from the vendor of the component to the consumers of their software system. McGraw (1999) suggests that developers can achieve this by determining the robustness of the system if the component fails, demanding warranties from the vendor or by using wrappers on the component to gain better control on its behaviour. Fault injection can be used as a primary tool for determining the robustness of a system that uses components.

It should be noted that consumers (or developers) usually choose to use components for one or more of the following reasons: reduced time-to-market; reduced cost; and reduced risk of using a well-tested component instead of developing a new one that may not be as thoroughly tested. Trade offs are made on the basis of how well a component satisfies any of these criteria, e.g. high-risk components may be selected by developers in order to achieve quicker time-to-market but costs, in such cases, will have to be considered carefully to cover support for a high-risk product in the market.

The increased risk to software systems by component usage has attracted some research attention in recent years. Carney (2003) proposed a process for COTS Usage Risk Evaluation (CURE) based on the predicate that most of COTS associated risks to software systems can be predicted since such risks are common and can be identified by experience. The CURE process depends on collection of data based on interviews and questionnaires for both the consumer and the vendor. The down side of CURE is that it is applicable only to COTS usage in large-scale software systems and it relies heavily on lessons learnt from past usage of any COTS products instead of the nature and characteristics of the particular product that may be in question.

Nonetheless, consumers of components, particularly COTS components, always take a risk, small or large, in using a component developed by someone else. They have to trust what the vendors of those components say and, most of the time, also evaluate the worthiness of those vendors in the market. The amount of testing performed on such components directly affects the amount of trust the consumer is going to have in those components. All this is done in an attempt to reduce the amount of risk associated with deploying a particular component. Therefore, software components need to be as trustable as possible in their packaged form in order to speed up the evaluation and integration process. Unfortunately, this is not so due to the lack of product standards in the IT industry. In the IT industry, we have a healthy collection of process standards, but the fact remains that an excellent process does not guarantee an excellent product. With the availability of highly trustable software components the speed of building software systems increases and the cost goes down since there is no need for the integrators to repeatedly perform acceptance testing or cover the untested risks associated with the usage of any particular component.

The Trusted Components initiative of Meyer et al (1998) was focused on applying a mix of formal and informal approaches to produce more trustable components. These approaches include design-by-contract, formal validation, reuse techniques, global public scrutiny, extensive testing and applying a mix of metrics to software components in order to track component properties.

Managing Dependencies

Reusability in software development means that components are used to build new components, more often to perform new tasks that the constituent components could not perform individually. This results in production of components that are very tightly coupled with the constituent components and depends heavily on the functionality and quality of the constituents.

Software components are almost always dependent on other entities. These entities can be operating systems, virtual machines, language platforms, other software components or even human entities like vendors and suppliers. The dependency of a component on these entities can be weak or strong, and always contributes to the overall trust of the component. A component's dependency on other entities causes additional constraints in terms of the product usage in real life and can directly affect consumers' trust level. For instance, an email client component would depend on the Internet connection service that is most likely managed by the operating system. How the email client addresses this dependency and how it handles any problems that may arise from errors in the operating system service will dictate the level of consumers' trust in it.

Managing Trust

Consumers of software components always take a risk, small or large, in using a component developed by someone else. Components, therefore, need to be as trustable as possible. At the very outset, a component needs to be highly testable and have a low degree of risk for the consumers. Trust can be achieved either by thoroughly testing a component or by using the component over a period of time with an accepted degree of risk. When the opportunity and appropriate tools are given to consumers for monitoring the usage of components within their environment, it results in increased trust. Consumers, in these situations, can support themselves at the initial level and feel more secure about using such components.

Properties of a software component can be categorised as functional and non-functional. Functional properties refer to what a component does or can do. All the other properties are non-

Figure 3. Different perspectives on non-functional properties of software

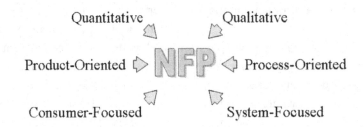

functional properties of the component. Some researchers have used the term extra-functional properties instead (e.g. Reussner and Schmidt, 2002). For example, displaying account balances, transferring money from one account to another and paying bills are all possible functional properties of an online personal banking system. Timely response to customer request for an account balance, secure access to a customer's bank account and a user-friendly interface to the online banking are all possible candidates for non-functional properties of the same system.

Various techniques have been developed to assess the functional aspects of software in general, including requirements engineering, software testing and formal proofs. Work has been done in applying these techniques to software components and component-based systems. Software testing is perhaps the most practical approach for assessing functional properties of any software. The history of software testing techniques is as old as that of software itself. Testing techniques have evolved with the evolution of different software engineering approaches from testing small programs written as sets of procedures to testing real-time distributed applications comprising of hundreds of heterogeneous components. A non-exhaustive list of different software testing approaches includes function-based testing, model-based testing, state-based testing, regression testing, mutation testing, conformance testing etc.

Contrary to functional properties, non-functional properties of software components are inherently more difficult to deal with. It is difficult to precisely specify and measure such properties. It is due to this natural characteristic of non-functional properties that a significant body of researchers have focused their work solely on identifying and assessing such properties (e.g. McCall (1979), Chung et al. (2000), Schmidt et al. (2001), Bertoa and Vallecillo (2002) etc.). Such research work ranges from identification of simple metrics to the development of comprehensive metric models involving inter-dependencies among different metrics.

In Figure 3 we summarise the different views held by researchers on non-functional properties of software. Different researchers have focused on a variety of combinations of these views. For example, the work by Chung et al. (2000) looks at non-functional properties from a qualitative, process-oriented and system-focused stand point.

In the context of trust, security is perhaps the most widely researched non-functional property of software components. Models and standards exist in the industry that are widely accepted and used to ensure security of software and its users e.g. Information Technology Security Evaluation Criteria (ITSEC). A number of ISO standards have been developed to ensure the quality of software products and software development processes. These include ISO-9126, ISO-14598 and ISO-14756 among others. However, it should be noted that most of this work has been focused on process-oriented approaches and there is a lack of product-oriented trust development methodologies for software components. Components are, by

Figure 4. Software component trust mode

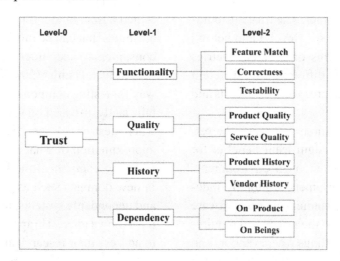

definition, products that are aimed at a consumer audience and from a consumer's stand point the quality of the component is entirely judged based on its properties that are observable in its packaged form.

Consumers of software components face uncertainty during the procurement process. In most cases, this uncertainty can extend to the integration process. Consumers, generally, address this uncertainty by searching for answers to the following four questions. Q1. Does the component correctly perform the job we want it to perform? Q2. How well does the component perform the job? Q3. How well has the component performed in the past for any users? Q4. What does the component depend on for performing its job?

Consumers' trust in components, therefore, depends on the answers to these questions. Satisfactory answers to these questions lead to better trust. However, getting these answers is not trivial even when we, as humans, do it sub-consciously so often. Our trust model is based on these questions and provides a useful means for assessing the trustability of software entities, especially COTS components.

Figure 4 presents the high-level trust model for software components based on the notions of trust, the characteristics of components and the four key trust questions listed above. Each level in the model provides a more detailed and concrete view of the level before it. Level-1 of this Trust Model corresponds to the four key trust questions. Items listed in Level-2 provide meanings of their corresponding item in Level-1. For instance, Product Quality and Service Quality help us determine the overall quality-based trust of a component. Based on the less abstract concepts at Level-2 of the trust model and their own usage context for a given component, consumers are able to explicate any of these concepts further before they meaningfully measure the trustability of their selected component. The final level of any of the four main branches (at level-1) of the trust model will, therefore, include metrics for a component that are directly measurable and can be mapped back to the trust requirements according to the model. This trust model provides us with a gradual evolution of trust from the abstract to the concrete, thus bridging the gap that has long existed between the philosophy of trust and quantitative metrics for software components (Bader et al., 2003; Bader, 2005).

In this Trust Model, Levels 1 and 2 are common to all software component usage and can be understood independently of the context of usage. Level-3 and any further levels are specific to any given context of component usage and need to be formulated by the consumer. The trust attributes at lower levels of the model (level-3 and below) can be measured in terms of different metrics and will be interpreted differently by different consumers based on their respective contexts and usage requirements.

Addressing trust requirements using the reference trust model has significant benefits for consumers, particularly in open environments where vendors and consumers are totally independent entities and consumers choose software components according to their need and requirements. Even in closed settings where vendors and consumers may already have established trusted relationships, following the approach of the trust model has positive implications by documenting and monitoring the component behavior in a more effective manner.

TRENDS IN CBSE RESEARCH

The number of software components is increasing rapidly and so is the number of software systems built from assembly of components. The behavioral dependencies of components in such systems need to be considered to ensure consistent composition. Ishikawa et al (2003) proposed an approach based on finite state machines to help address the issue of behavioral dependencies of components. Kotonya et al (2003) proposed a classification model for CBSE research, and aimed to provide a scheme for classifying CBSE research results. Hamlet et al (2001) looked at the theory of software reliability based on components, and tried to address the technical problems associated with certifying components to be used later in a different setting. They showed how component producers can design and test their components to produce metrics that can be used by software system developers to derive composite system reliability without the implementation and testing phase. Their measurements are independent of

operational profiles whereas Bader (2005) presented a trust model for components to concrete attributes that can be monitored and managed by consumers to keep track of their level of trust in the product. Hamlet (2007) has proposed a novel way for testing components and systems, and details analysis based on test-based specifications, where test-based specification is an empirical approximation of what a program actually does. Recently component models have been created in new domains such as safety-critical software and dependable systems, and these communities have shown interest in applying CBSE approaches to address their research and practical problems. CBSE is also being combined with model-based development, service-oriented architectures and aspect-oriented models (Grunbacher et al, 2008).

The Integration of Software-Intensive Systems (ISIS) initiative at SEI is addressing the interoperability issue for systems that result from composition of components and/or other systems (referred to as System of Systems). Fisher (2006) claims that new software and systems engineering methods are needed to address and manage the emergent behaviour of Systems of Systems that result from composition of autonomous constituent components. He believes that such methods need to focus on system-wide implications of local actions, minimising the number of constraints and managing trust, among other factors. This is needed for systems that exhibit emergent behaviour. These systems are composed of independent constituent components, exhibit emergent behaviour that cannot be translated to a simple combination of actions of the individual constituents and are expected to survive and function even under unanticipated events. This expectation from component-based systems is leading to increased focus on interoperability of components within a system. It is, therefore, evident that interoperability will remain an area of active research for some time as more and more components and component-based systems emerge.

Component frameworks have emerged to address the interoperability issue. Component frameworks are sets of well-defined interfaces that establish the protocols for component cooperation within the framework. These protocols are used by component developers to ensure the interoperability of their components within the scope of a given component framework. Examples of component frameworks include Sun Microsystems Java 2 Enterprise Edition (or J2EE), Microsoft .Net, Ajax etc.

Governments around the world are also taking the initiative to define and promote component based frameworks. The Services and Components Based Architecture (SCBA) claims to be one of the most widely accepted architectural approaches based on the focus on reuse of services and components (CIO, 2006). It identifies Service Components as entities that can be shared among multiple consumers, can be utilised by consumers on any platform and can be updated and improved without affecting consumers' processes and interfaces.

Interoperability among component frameworks is another area that needs further research. To date, this issue has largely been addressed with the use of data interchange technologies, like XML. The emergence of Web Services (also based on XML) has facilitated inter-framework interoperability. However, we believe that more work is needed to improve the quality of component-based systems and to make such systems more reliable under unpredictable circumstances. Techniques such as fault propagation and localisation, usage of constraints and development of trusted relationship among components are expected to play a key role in this context. Furthermore, capturing design decisions and making those available to consumers of components will have a direct and positive impact on their trust level.

The importance of the role that third parties can play in establishing and/or facilitating trust cannot be denied. This approach has been widely used in the computer security area through the us-

age of certification authorities (CAs). We strongly believe that involvement of third parties (like CAs) in the software component domain will drastically improve the trust process as well as encourage a wider use of off-the-shelf components.

Another area of growth in the software components domain is that of component marketplaces. To date, these marketplaces only provide descriptive specifications of components and consumers need to rely mainly on understanding and testing the component against these specifications. There is also a notion of ranking system in some component marketplaces that depends on feedback from existing consumers of a component. We anticipate component marketplaces to mature significantly in the future to provide extensive search and match facilities for consumers. Consumers should be able to specify and accurately match their requirements to candidate components in a marketplace. Formal specifications or requirements models are just some of the possible technique that can explored in this context.

CONCLUSION

Software components are packaged software artifacts that present a black-box view to their consumers. Consumers use components with the aim to reduce costs, reduce time-to-market and possibly increase the quality of their component-based system by employing high-quality, thoroughly tested and soundly trusted components. In this respect, software components have played a key role in the modern software engineering discipline. The disjoint processes of software components production and procurement pose a significant problem for all stakeholders in the software components marketplace. Further research needs to be carried out in this area in order to promote a more trusted and efficient procurement of software components by consumers.

REFERENCES

Bader, A. (2005). *Modelling Trust for Reusable Software Components*. PhD thesis, School of Computer Science & Software Engineering, Monash University, Australia.

Bader, A., Mingins, C., Bennett, D., & Ramakrishnan, S. (2003). Establishing Trust in COTS Components. In *Proceedings of the 2nd Int Conference on COTS-Based Software Systems*, (LNCS, Vol. 2580, pp. 15-24). Berlin: Springer-Verlag.

Basili, V., & Boehm, B. (2001). COTS-Based Systems Top 10 List. *IEEE Computer*, (pp. 91-93)

Bertoa, M., & Vallecillo, A. (2002). Quality Attributes for COTS Components. In *6th ECOOP Workshop on Quantitative Aproaches in OO Software Engineering*.

Carney, D., & Green, F. (2000). What Do You Mean by COTS? Finally, a Useful Answer. *IEEE Software*, *17*(2), 83–86. doi:10.1109/52.841700

Carney, D., Morris, E., & Place, P. (2003). *Identifying COTS Product Risks: The COTS Usage Risk Evaluation* (Tech. Rep. CMU/SEI-2003-TR-023). Pittsburgh, PA: Carnegie Mellon University, Software Engineering Institute.

Chung, L., Nixon, B., Yu, E., & Mylopoulos, J. (2000). *Non-Functional Requirements in Software Engineering*. Boston: Kluwer Academic Publisher

CIO. (2006), *Services and Components Based Architectures – A Strategic Guide for Implementing Distributed and Reusable Components and Services in the Federal Government*. Architecture and Infrastructure Committee, Federal Chief Information Officers Council.

Clark, B., & Torchiano, M. (2004). *Can We Reach a Consensus*. International Workshop on COTS Terminology and Categories.

Fisher, D. (2006). *An Emergent Perspective on Interoperation in Systems of Systems* (Tech. Rep. CMU/SEI-2006-TR-003, ESC-TR-2006-003). Pittsburgh, PA: Carnegie Mellon University, Software Engineering Institute.

Grunbacher, P., Crnkovic, I., & Muller, P. (2008)... *Journal of Systems Architecture*, 54.

Hamlet, D. (2007). Test-Based Specifications of Components and System. In *Proceedings of 7th International Conference Quality Software (QSIC '07)*, October 11-12 (pp. 388-395). Los Alamitos, CA: IEEE Computer Society.

Hamlet, D., Mason, D., & Woit, D. (2001). Theory of Software Reliability based on components. In *Proceedings of the 23rd International Conference on Software Engineering*, Toronto, Canada, (pp. 361-370).

Ishikawa, H., Ogata, Y., Adachi, K., & Nakajima, T. (2003). Requirements of a Component Framework for Future Ubiquitous Computing. In *Proceeding of the IEEE Workshop on Software Technologies and Future Embedded System*.

Kotonya, G., Sommerville, I., & Hall, S. (2003). Towards a Classification Model for Component-based Software Engineering Research. In *Proceedings 29th EuroMicro Conference "New Waves in System Architecture" (EuroMicro'03)*, Belek-Antalya, Turkey, (pp. 43-52).

McCall, J. A. (1979). Introduction to Software Quality Metrics. In J. Cooper, & M. Fisher, (Ed.) *Software Quality Management,* Petrocelli, (pp. 127 – 140).

McGraw, G., & Viega, J. (1999 May). Why COTS Software Increases Security Risks. In *1st International ICSE Workshop on Testing Distributed Component-based System*.

Meyer, B. (1999). *The Significance of Component*. Software Development.

Meyer, B. (2003). *The Grand Challenge of Trusted Components*. 25th International Conference on Software Engineering, Portland, Oregon.

Meyer, B., Mingins, C., & Schmidt, H. (1998). Providing Trusted Components to the Industry. *IEEE Computer, 31*(5), 104–105.

Reussner, R., & Schmidt, H. (2002). Using Parameterised Contracts to Predict Properties of Component Based Software Architectures. In I. Crnkovic, S. Larsson, & J. Stafford, (Ed.), *Workshop on Component-Based Software Engineering*.

Schmidt, H., Poernomo, I. & Reussner, R. (2001). Trust-By-Contract: Modelling, Analysing and Predicting Behaviour in Software Architecture. *Journal for Integrated Process and Development Science, September*, 25-51.

Szyperski, C., Gruntz, D., & Murer, S. (2002). *Component Software: Beyond Object-Oriented Programming (2nd Ed.)*. Reading, MA: Addison-Wesley.

KEY TERMS AND DEFINITIONS

Component Based Software Engineering (CBSE): Software Engineering discipline that deals with building software systems from independent functional and/or logical components. Components in such systems have well-defined interfaces and communicate with one another via message-passing.

Component Framework: Component frameworks are sets of well-defined interfaces that establish the protocols for component cooperation within the framework. These protocols are used by component developers to ensure the interoperability of their components within the scope of a given framework.

COTS Components: Commercial-off-the-shelf components. This term is used to refer to deployable units of software that offer a predefined set of services and are made available to consumers in a packaged form by vendors.

Emergent Behaviour: Behaviour of a system that emerges from the composition of its constituent parts and that is more than the sum of the behaviours of the independent constituent components.

Interoperability: The ability of systems and components to interact with other systems and components, which are generally implemented on or for heterogeneous platforms. The focus is usually kept on information exchange between interacting systems.

Non-Functional Requirements: Requirements of a system that deal with aspects other than its functionality. Usually, these requirements are focused on how well the system does what it is required to do. Examples of non-functional requirements include performance, reliability, availability, scalability, security etc.

Reusability: The property of a component or system to be used again and again, possibly in different scenarios. This term gained popularity with the arrival of object-oriented systems but can equally be applied to other types of software systems.

Service Components: Software entities that can be shared among multiple consumers, can be utilised by consumers on any platform and can be updated and improved by the provider without affecting consumers' processes and interfaces.

Chapter 23
The Role of Information Technology Managers in the Significant Company in Case of Natural Disasters in Qatar

Salem Al-Marri
Leeds Metropolitan University, UK

Muthu Ramachandran
Leeds Metropolitan University, UK

ABSTRACT

Natural disasters are increasingly frequent in recent years taking peoples' lives and destructions to our economy, for example, Hurricane Katrina (US 2006), Tsunami (Asia 2004), and other IT related failures. The major aims of this study were to outline the disaster management steps, actions and procedures in the computer environment. The study focused on the role of Information Technology manager (IT) in case of any disaster events. IT manager job to perform a pre-disaster preparedness, mitigation and prevention necessary steps to protect the organisation Information Technology manager resources. Than proposes a model for Disaster Recovery management. This model will support contingencies and will provide a continuous planning management and monitor its activities along with a clear description of the hierarchical roles and activities. Also proposes a model for contingency and continuity planning management and its activities. This model consists of hierarchical roles and activities.

INTRODUCTION

Global technology has been recently affecting different fields in our life as it has been effectively employed to many domains such as e-commerce, control systems, information gathering and management. World economy faced destruction and people lives were taking by many natural disasters and other events happened in the last recent years such as Hurricane Katrina .US 2006, Tsunami .Asia 2004, September 11 attacks and other Information Technology related failures. Such incidents showed that people lives and both technical and constructed infrastructure can be easily damaged especially

DOI: 10.4018/978-1-60566-731-7.ch023

that the increasing use of technology put more stress and uncertainties when disasters happen. According to a report by the secretariat of the International Strategy for Disaster Reduction (ISDR, 2004), over than 478,100 people were killed, more than 2.5 billion people were affected and about $ 690 billion losses in economy caused by natural and man-made disasters. Disasters triggered by hydro-meteorological hazards amounted for 97% of the total people affected by disasters, and 60% of the total economic losses (Shaw 2006). Also According to the International Federation of Red Cross and Red Crescent Societies (IFRCRCS), world disasters report 2004; the number of natural and technological disasters in the last decade has increased by 67 percent reaching 707 disasters each year (IFRCRCS, 2004). Therefore, as Lavell (1999) said the risks and disasters are dynamic and changing rapidly. This risk differs from one person in the same organisation to another and from one organisation to another.

On the other hand, sometimes a expected natural disaster or a man-made incident occurs like for example last Asia tsunami earthquake (2004), which killed around three hundred thousand people in eleven countries and destroyed a whole area and infrastructure in the disaster (Aljazeera, 2005). Also the World Trade Centre attack in September 11th 2001 which destroyed one of the most important trading centres in the world and the area around it (www.Reopen911. org, 2005). Therefore, the Information Technology manager should be ready all times for such kind of disaster by taking on this consideration the provisions by pre-disaster planning which guarantee the business continuity and less damage (Christoplos et al. 2001). It is evident that each type of a disaster has a different impact and each country and government has a different way to deal with such incidents. Therefore, it is essential to design an appropriate policy and apply successful strategy that can minimize the threat of disasters. Developing a global emergency management in-

formation network that provides electronic access to emergency management knowledge would be crucial. However, the emergency management coordination processes did not act effectively and broke down in the wake of the aforementioned disasters (Shaw 2006).

Moreover, Environmental problems exacerbated by natural or human-made events can contribute to area instability and convict. Such environmental security related disasters hinder economic development; displace populations, and the increase of weapons of mass destruction, the growth of undesirable elements. Qatar faces environmental challenges unlike any other region in the world. The regional environmental challenges include: water shortages, hazardous materials and waste, oil spills in the Gulf, shipping incidents, and transmission of new diseases. Therefore, the main aims of this research are to integrate information systems models with project management strategies:

- A model for Disaster Recovery Management System and its detailed activities, contingency and continuity planning model for recovery actions.
- A model for Natural Disasters (ND) and Risks Management System to help us to identify common pattern of events
- Clear guidelines on information flow and person responsibilities as this can be very difficult in large organisations that are linked as in government departments.
- Clear identification of contingency planning guidelines, information flow, timing, and specific roles

The following sections of the paper propose and discusses, in detail, information system model for disaster recovery planning along with the implications of different Disaster Management Models to be implemented in case of generating an effective and efficient Response System.

Figure 1. Disaster risk management cycle diagram

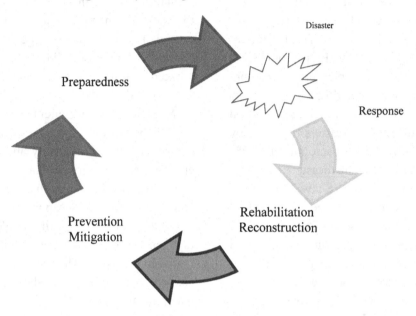

A MODEL FOR RECOVERY MANAGEMENT INFORMATION SYSTEM

Many researchers in the same boundaries recommended disaster preparation without providing sufficient documentation of their validity and effectiveness. Few describe a limited disaster recovery or business plans, or advice what should happen rather than what really does happen (Hosseini, and Izadkhah, 2006). The disaster risk management cycle, shown in Figure 1, consists of four phases: Prevention/Mitigation and Preparedness in the pre-disaster stage, and Response and Rehabilitation/Reconstruction in post-disaster stage. In the "Prevention/Mitigation" phase, efforts are made to prevent or mitigate damage (e.g. constructing appropriate dams or dikes to prevent flooding and building breakwaters in ports and low-lying coastal areas) in case of a natural hazard. Activities and measures for ensuring an effective response to the impact of hazards are classified as "Preparedness" (e.g. emergency drills and public awareness, equipping and training specialized personnel) and are not aimed at averting the occurrence of a disaster. "Response" includes such activities as rescue efforts, first aid, fire fighting and evacuation. In the "Rehabilitation/Reconstruction" phase, considerations of disaster risk reduction should form the foundations for all activities.

Very few countries and organizations commit sufficient resources to disaster management, regardless of past experience or future potential. Disaster management becomes a pressing concern only after the disaster has struck—a concern that may be short-lived, as other needs quickly resurface. While this is obviously true for poorer developing nations, it is also often the case in richer developed countries; there are always higher-priority projects that need funding, and investment in disaster preparedness remains low around the world (Currion.2007). Despite these challenges, the Tsunami Evaluation Commission (TEC) in its evaluation of the international response to the Indian Ocean tsunami stated that "the information technology revolution, the primary driving force in changes to disaster response, was well reflected in the overall response to the tsunami" (Tsunami 2006). One can justify this as a slightly optimistic view by focusing on the more visible

Figure 2. Disaster recovery management activity model

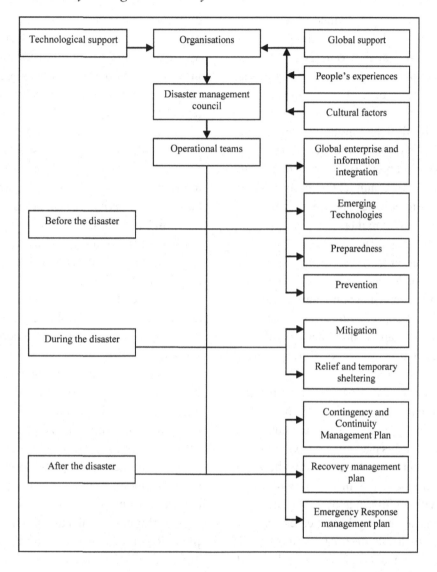

aspects of this revolution such as remote sensing, yet there are still substantial gaps in the information systems for large-scale disaster response. One of the recommendations that was made by the Commission was "significant effort and funding should be dedicated to organizing open source, easily shareable software and training tools to prepare for all stages of disaster response" (Currion. 2007)

Figure 2 in the following page shows an activity model for disaster recovery management system. This model consists of hierarchical roles and activities. It is critical that organization must support and provide infrastructure for managing and preventing disasters and its aftermath to a full recovery. As depicted the different operational teams should be assigned to work in coordination with each other in different phases of before, during and after a disaster with assigned roles and responsible. The various activities are explained in details as below:

Technological support: The rapid change in IT (both hardware and software) has increased the demand of the IT managers in meeting up their dynamic information requirements. The relevant support areas must be highly trained and equipped enough so that up-to-date and real time information is present and available to users.

Global support: There has be an increasing awareness of other modes of communication in case of a disaster in the global information network so that the flow and mode of transferring the information is ensured to the right person at a right time and in an orderly format in order to make a decision. For example: the importance of the existence of telephones and fax machines as communication tools should not be eliminated as they are the only modes of transferring information in case of an internet access problem.

People's experiences: Different people face disaster in a different manner and the experiences are totally unique People handle disasters according to their cultural and ethnic backgrounds. As such experiences from all walks of people must be taken into account.

Global enterprise and information integration management: There should be a contingency plan available in the time of a disaster and such a rigorous testing of this plan must be executed for a successful execution. A strategy should be setup for faster communications in times of business crisis along with an impact analysis of Business Continuity and Emergency Management plan.

Emerging technologies: As technology is changing, the knowledge and the use of different emerging technologies must be updated in order to leverage the significant computing power on demand with the ability to manage massive sets of distributed data.

Preparedness: A continuing development of Community Emergency Response Plan along with exercises to test them; training in evacuation procedures should be conducted. The activities and measures for ensuring an effective response to the impact of hazards should be classified (e.g. emergency drills and train citizens and government personnel to respond to local emergencies, equip) accordingly.

Prevention and mitigation: In this phase, efforts are to be made to prevent or mitigate damage (e.g. having a detailed back up plan, setting up a data centre offshore, restore databases and information as quickly as possible). A detailed plan to eliminate a hazard, or to reduce the potential for damage should a disaster emergency occur should also be presented. Similar back up plans should be present in case a natural disaster occur e.g., constructing appropriate dams or dikes to prevent flooding and building breakwaters in ports and low-lying coastal areas.

Relief and temporary sheltering: This group consists of the relief, temporary and emergency shelters team for disaster time. Some of their activities are as follows:

Listing of the patients and classifying them according to their health conditions so that emergency patients can be attended at the first instance.

Emergency welfare including water supply and distribution of food and medicines among patients and injured; or establishing shelters (emergency tents, immediate buildings repair) and temporary settlement for the patients in safe and appropriate places. Emergency Response management plan should include search and rescue, fire suppression, evacuation, emergency feeding and sheltering.

Contingency and continuity management plan: Resources recovery and data availability, Security, safety, insurance of the workforce

Emergency response management plan: Communication is maintained between different emergency services and between the emergency services and control centres before and after the occurrence of a disaster.

Recovery management plan: This includes those processes required to return the jurisdiction to normal following an emergency. Recovery could include reconstruction of roads and public facilities, securing financial aid for disaster victims, offering community counseling and psychological support services, and reviewing and critiquing of response activities.

Figure 3. Contingency and continuity plan management activities

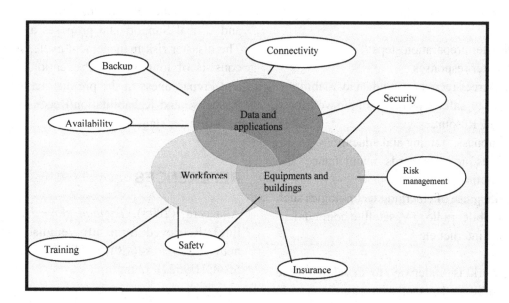

Occurrence of natural disasters challenges the power of the whole system of any society. They can be categorized as:

- Sudden disasters such as earthquakes, oil overflow, floods, hurricanes, land slide, tsunamis, volcanic eruptions and accidents
- Slowly developing disasters such as epidemics, famine, droughts.

Both kinds have a destructive impact on human being. This paper will concentrate on communication facilities, which help providing countermeasures against catastrophic failure of power system and the impact of natural disasters on different kinds of conflict.

Contingency and continuity management plan: Development Planning must ensure support risk reduction or elimination. Compilation of reactive departmental disaster management plans to ensure service continuation during emergency/disaster situations. Establishing and maintaining a resources database for the disaster management and facilitating feedback regarding disaster management initiatives (cf. Figure 3).

The main fact that the information technology manager needs to take into consideration is the technical and functional legacy data, equipments, IT places and finally the technical workforce. All significant issues around these considerations such as the safety, security, data availability, insurance, training and education, and contingency and DRPs should be clearly addressed as shown in Figure 2.

One of the major factors that make the role of Information Technology Manager important is that the major organisation functions are computerised and the data electronically stored. Consequently, this makes threats and management risk incredibly high and a greater need to be stored, protected and made available all the time (24 hours/ 7 days) to the users by reducing the downtime of the systems and applications (Mountain, 2004). It can be seen therefore, that the importance of reviewing the literature on roles of the Information Technology Manager in case of any kind of disaster is to increase the efficiency and effectiveness of the organisation IT resources to build secure, scaleable, reliable, maintainable, robust, and highly available applications and data. To accomplish this goal, these issues must be explained:

- Disaster preparation steps
- Disaster responses
- Resources recovery and data availability
- Security, safety, insurance of the workforce and IT Resources
- Awareness, training and education
- Polices and standards maintenance and promotions
- Making use of emerging technologies such as mobile, radio, TV, satellite communications, internet etc

The work is underway to develop online questionnaire to be sent to various levels in the government, managers, and organisations in Qatar to assess their readiness, risk and cost management.

CONCLUSION

Many issues about disaster preparedness and response will be discussed. Advices and solutions to reduce the damage and injuries will be explored too. This paper proposes a model for Disaster Recovery management activity model. Disaster Recovery management activity modal as shown in this model consists of hierarchical roles and activities. It is critical that organization must support and provide infrastructure for managing and preventing disasters and its aftermath to a full recovery. Various operational teams should be assigned to work in coordination with each other in different phases of before, during and after a disaster with assigned roles and responsible. Some teams can be more functional before the disaster happens, whereas some of team should be coordinating in all three phases. Finally, the study will suggest a solution for data availability and online backup. This paper proposes a triangular model for disaster recovery management

system which constitutes of the use of emerging technology, the role of people and their culture, and Global Support and proposes a model for The disaster risk management cycle, shown the consists of four phases: Prevention/Mitigation and Preparedness in the pre-disaster stage, and Response and Rehabilitation/Reconstruction in post-disaster stage.

REFERENCES

Aljazeera, (2005). *Tsunami slowed time* [Online]. Retrieved from http://english.aljazeera. net/NR/exeres/A46E0B05-1DC7-4852-83A1-5B6C1D9521E3.htm

Christoplos, I., Mitchell, J., & Liljelund, A. (2001). Re-framing Risk: The Changing Context of Disaster Mitigation and Preparedness. *Disasters Journal, 25*(3), 185. doi:10.1111/1467-7717.00171

Currion, P., Chamindra, S., & Bartel, V. W. (2007, March). Open source software for disaster management evaluating how the Sahana disaster information system coordinates disparate institutional and technical resources in the wake of the Indian Ocean tsunami. *Communications of the ACM, 50*(3). doi:10.1145/1226736.1226768

Hosseini, M., & Izadkhah, Y. O. (2006). Earthquake disaster risk, management planning in schools. *Disaster Prevention and Management, 15*(4), 649–661. doi:10.1108/09653560610686595

IFRCRCS. (2004). *International Federation of Red Cross and Red Crescent Societies*. World Disasters Report [Online]. Retrieved from http://www.ifrc.org/publicat/wdr2004/chapter8.asp

Iron Mountain. (2004). *The Business Case for Disaster Recovery Planning: Calculating the Cost of Downtime* [white paper]. London: Iron Mountain.

Lavell, A. (1999). *Natural and Technological Disasters, Capacity Building and Human Resource Development for Disaster Management* [Online]. Retrieved from http://www.desenredando.org/public/articulos/1999/ntd/ntd1999_mar-1-2002.pdf

Reopen911.org. (2005). Retrieved April 2007 from http://www.reopen911.org/?src=overture&OVRAW=world%20trade%20center%20attack&OVKEY=world%20trade%20center%20attack&OVMTC=standard

Shaw, R. (2006). Indian Ocean tsunami and aftermath Need for environment-disaster synergy. *Disaster Prevention and Management, 15*(1), 5–20. doi:10.1108/09653560610654202

Tsunami Evaluation Coalition. (2006). *Joint Evaluation of the International Response to the Indian Ocean Tsunami*. Tsunami Evaluation Coalition.

Section 3
Enterprise Systems and Globalisation

Chapter 24

Enterprise Resource Planning Systems for Small and Medium–Sized Enterprises

Rogério Atem de Carvalho
Fluminense Federal Institute, Brazil

Björn Johansson
Center for Applied ICT, Copenhagen Business School, Denmark

ABSTRACT

After the implementation peak of ERPs that occurred during the pre- and post-Y2K periods, the high-end ERP market started to saturate and major ERP vendors started to seek for new business opportunities, in special towards Small and Medium-sized Enterprises (SMEs). On the buyer side, demands for becoming more competitive in a globalized market, have been pushing SMEs to adopt ERP too. Additionally, influenced by the free/open source movement, new types of ERP licensing appeared by the beginning of the decade, creating a classification according to the basic licensing model: free/open source ERP (FOS-ERP) and proprietary ERP (P-ERP). Therefore, this paper aims at exploring the merge between SMEs, P-ERP, and FOS-ERP, by analyzing the differences between the two proposals and offering guidance for prospective adopters.

INTRODUCTION

For the last fifteen years the biggest software category in terms of investment has been Enterprise Resource Planning (ERP) systems and nowadays most of the bigger companies, including practically all global-players, have implemented ERP systems in the search for achieving competitive edge in their business areas (Church, 2008; Hendricks, Singhal and Stratman, 2007). After the implementation peak that occurred during the pre- and post-Y2K periods, the high-end ERP market started to saturate and, according to Kim and Boldyreff (2005), major ERP vendors started to seek for new business opportunities, in special towards small and medium-sized enterprises (SMEs).

On the buyer side, demands for becoming more competitive in a globalized market, have been pushing SMEs to adopt ERP too. However, the

DOI: 10.4018/978-1-60566-731-7.ch024

Figure 1. GERAM lifecycle phases

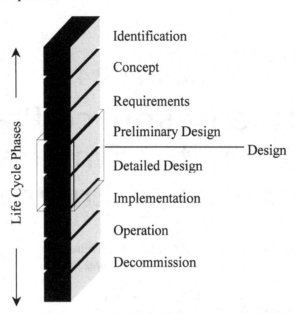

ERP strategic nature (Caulliraux, Proença and Prado, 2000), and the fact that it cannot be used instantaneously (Dreiling, Klaus, Rosemann and Wyssusek, 2005), makes ERP a different kind of software which implementation requires high quantities of resources and entails high risks. These factors have been raising the interest on ERP versions for SMEs on both the demand and supply side of the market, making a recent market movement towards simplified versions of proprietary ERP (P-ERP) and bringing more attention to free/open source ERP (FOS-ERP). Therefore, it is clear that the merge of P-ERP, FOS-ERPs and SMEs is a topic with many facets and yet to be more explored in both theory and practice.

This chapter aims to explore this merge, firstly by briefly introducing Generalized Enterprise Reference Architecture and Methodology conceptual framework, which in the following section is used to guide the description of the adoption process by SMEs, followed by an detailed analysis of the differences of each proposal, and finally by a basic guidance for prospective adopters.

A FRAMEWORK TO GUIDE ERP ADOPTION

Selecting an ERP for adoption is a complex process, because, besides the size of the task, it is an important enterprise component that impacts the adopter organization in financial and self-knowledge terms. In that aspect, the Generalized Enterprise Reference Architecture and Methodology (GERAM) is a well-known standard that can be used to identify the main phases of an ERP adoption project, helping guiding the comparison of free and proprietary alternatives.

The GERAM framework provides a description of all elements recommended in enterprise engineering and a collection of tools and methods to perform enterprise design and change with success (IFIP – IFAC, 1999), providing a template lifecycle to analyze ERP selection, deployment, and evolution. GERAM defines seven lifecycle phases for any enterprise entity that are pertinent during its life. These phases, presented in Figure 1, can be summarized as follows:

Identification: identifies the particular enterprise entity in terms of its domain and environment.

a) **Concept:** conceptualizes an entity's mission, vision, values, strategies, and objectives. During this phase, high-level objectives are established, such as the acquisition strategy, preliminary time and cost baselines, and the expected impact of ERP adoption.

b) **Requirements:** comprise a set of activities needed to develop descriptions of operational requirements of the enterprise entity, its relevant processes and the collection of all their functional, behavioral, informational, and capability needs. The requirements phase deals with ERP's functional and non-functional requirements. The adopter may model some main business processes – part of the Preliminary Design – as a way to check how the alternatives fit to them.

c) **Design:** activities that support the specification of the entity with all of its components that satisfy the entity requirements. The scope of design activities includes the design of all human tasks, and all machine tasks concerned with the entity's customer services and products and the related management and control functions. The design of the operational processes includes the identification of the necessary information and resources. This phase is divided into Preliminary Design, which deals with overall enterprise specifications - sufficient to obtain approximate costs and management approval of the ongoing project, and Detailed Design, which is the work necessary for guiding the creation of the final physical system. The detailed design phase focus on refining models, and is associated to business process modeling and parameter identification and value definition.

d) **Implementation:** transforms the design into real components. Comprises implementation in the broadest sense, covering a) commissioning, purchasing, (re)configuring or developing all resources needed; b) hiring and training personnel, and developing or changing the human organization; c) component testing and validation, system integration, validation and testing, and releasing into operation.

e) **Operation:** is the actual use of the system, and includes user feedback that can drive to a new entity lifecycle. The resources of the entity are managed and controlled so as to carry out the processes necessary for the entity to fulfill its mission. During the operation phase the resources of the entity are managed and controlled so as to carry out the processes necessary for the entity to fulfill its mission. Deviations from goals and objectives or feedbacks from the environment may lead to requests for change; therefore during this phase system maintenance and evolution occur.

f) **Decommission:** represents the disposal of parts of the whole entity, after its successful use.

Taking as a principle that most software development (and customization) today is done through interactive and incremental lifecycles, it can be considered that there is no clear borderline between the Requirements and Preliminary Design phases and between the detailed design and implementation phases, thus they are considered together in this approach.

Except for *identification* and *decommission*, which are not influenced by licensing models, the GERAM phases can be used to better understand the differences between FOS-ERP and P-ERP, providing key aspects for evaluating alternatives and successively refining objectives, requirements and models, as the next section addresses.

ANALYZING FOS-ERP AND P-ERP ADOPTION

Concept

In the case of FOS-ERP, the level of involvement of the adopter in development can be established from the beginning of the adoption process. In other words, at this point the adopter can already start considering the possibility of actively contributing to an open source project, or at least making by itself the necessary customization. Of course, the final decision will only be possible during the more advanced phases, when the adopter better knows the solution requisites and the decision alternatives.

The level of involvement in development of P-ERP is something that an adopter could also consider. However, involvement comes in another shape since P-ERPs often are delivered under a partnership model. This means that adopters are not directly involved in the development, but they are involved indirectly by cooperation with the specific partner hired to deploy the system. This also means that adopters in a way choose the level of involvement by selecting between different P-ERPs, since the way adopters engage in the development differ. Examples of different engagement could be understood if comparing the "old" partnership model (such as SAP/R3) and the "new" way of delivering P-ERPs as software as a service (SaaS, such as –Workday). In the SaaS model the adopter engagement in development of the P-ERP is lower than in the partnership model, since the partnership model to a higher extent builds on engagement through cooperation between adopters and partners when adjusting the specific ERP.

Requirements and Preliminary Design

During this phase evaluation takes place. At this point FOS-ERP starts to differ more from P-ERP.

Evaluating P-ERP involves comparing alternatives under the light of functionality, Total Cost of Ownership (TCO), and technological criteria. For FOS-ERP these criteria and others related specifically to FOSS, such as the maturity level of the project, its survivability, and its partner network strength (Carvalho, 2006), must be also taken into account – remembering that even if the implementation represents a smaller financial impact, in terms of a company's self-knowledge it can assume a much bigger importance, since it holds not only a inventory of records and procedures, but also how those records and procedures are realized in technological form – through source code.

At this point the core matter of the so-called "best practices" becomes more visible. A best practice can be defined as the most efficient and effective way of accomplishing a given business process, based on repeatable procedures that have proven themselves over time for large numbers of organizations. However, since organizations differ from each other, the adopters first need to find the solution that fits their business, and after doing that they have to either reconfigure existing business processes or reconfigure the software so that the software and the business processes fits each other. In the case of P-ERP, best practices are built on top of many years of experience of the global players, making these practices well tested and experimented, allowing a safer implementation on the adopter side. On the other hand, if FOS-ERP, being younger software projects, offer less experimented practices, an adopter can use the ones based on standardized procedures - such as accounting - *as is* and for free; and then expend its resources on adapting solutions related to more strategic procedures. This adaptation can be done by the adopter – demanding more knowledge on the solution, or by someone from the FOS-ERP partner network, like in P-ERP.

From this standpoint, the strategic positioning of an adopter in relation to a FOS-ERP seems to be of greatest importance, given the possibility of deriving competitive advantage from the source code. Therefore, the adopter must decide to behave as a simple *consumer*, only getting the solution from the vendor, or become a *prosumer*, by mixing passively purchasing commodity parts of the system with actively developing strategic ones by itself. Thus it is clear that when an adopter considers FOS-ERP as an alternative, it should also consider developing parts of it to fit its requirements – taking into account that, as said before, this kind of positioning involves allocating managerial and technical resources for development tasks in a FOSS environment.

In other words, a FOS-ERP can have a smaller financial impact but a much bigger knowledge and innovation impact. Although P-ERP are also highly parameterized, and adaptable through APIs and/or dedicated programming languages, the access to the source code in FOS-ERP can drive much better exploration of the ERP's capabilities, thus allowing a better implementation of differentiated solutions. But, as stated above, this demands a high level of knowledge about the ERP's platform, and if the adopters do not have this they have to trust on other sources for having that knowledge, and since in some countries there is a reduced number of FOS-ERP experts, costs for hiring them can be higher than it is for P-ERP consultants in these cases.

Detailed Design and Implementation

This phase is the one where the two kinds of ERP differ more. In the case of FOS-ERP, if the adopter decided to participate actively in the project, deeper design decisions are involved, such as creating entire new modules or extending the basic system's framework. A consequence of assuming a more active role is to invest more human and financial resources for learning the FOS-ERP platform and framework, developing and maintaining parts of it, and managing the relationship with the project community. In that case, customization and maintenance contracts must define responsibilities of each part on the deployment process. For instance, what should the vendor do if the adopter finds a bug in the original code, written by the first, which is being adapted by the second? What is the priority that the vendor must follow for correcting this bug? Actually, is the vendor responsible for correcting this bug, since for this part the adopter decided to take advantage of the solution's free license, therefore exempting the vendor of responsibility for the bug?

Still on FOS-ERP, the adopter has the option of assuming different grades of involvement for each part of the system. For ordinary modules, such as payroll, the adopter can let the vendor do the work. However, for strategic modules, where the adopter believes that it holds competitive advantage in the related business processes, it can take an active role, to be sure that the business knowledge, or at least the more precious details that keep the competitive advantage, will be kept in the adopter environment. In that situation the vendor is limited to act as a kind of advisor to the adopter. One can think that it is possible to keep secrecy on parts of the system by properly contracting a P-ERP vendor, which is true, but the adopter will become dependent of the vendor in a strategic part of the system. Becoming dependent means to wait for other vendor's priorities or pay a high price to become the priority when changes are needed.

In P-ERP new features development takes a different way, usually in the form of add-ons. A solution partner often develops these add-ons for a specific vendor's product, which can be customer specific, but most often can be used by several adopters. If the adopter decides to develop add-ons, it has to consider that it could be problematic in the future when new versions of the core product are released. In some cases software vendors do not take responsibility for that the new version is interoperable with the customers developed and implemented add-ons.

Operation

When it comes to operation, giving the licensing differences, it can be suggested that there are also major differences between FOS-ERP and P-ERP. In the first case, during operation the adopter can decide at any moment, unless specific contractual clauses hinders, to shift to another vendor or to assume the system's maintenance by itself. Minor changes can also be conducted by the own adopter or even by community individuals that may help on specific matters.

In the P-ERP case the adopter are to some extent dependent on the software vendor, but, it can be claimed that they also have a high grade of support from the vendor. This support depends on if the adopters chose to sign a service contract or not. The service agreement is nothing that are forced on the adopter but if the adopter chose that they have access to a service organization that helps them out if they have problems with the software. In the case of FOS-ERP, prospective adopters must be aware of the type of FOSS project the ERP is, since in sponsoring terms there are two kinds of free/open source projects, which are the community and the commercially sponsored projects (West and O'Mahony, 2005). In the first case, the adopter will become more or less dependent on voluntarism or in others words, uncertain schedules and priorities. Only the commercially sponsored FOS-ERP normally offers a partner network in a similar mode of P-ERP.

FOS-ERP AND P-ERP DIFFERENCES

ERP for SMEs is a relative new market; however a series of conclusions, from different categories, can be drawn from the comparison of the proprietary and the free/open source solutions.

On the economic side, the most obvious, and a motivator for this work, is that lower costs in both FOS-ERP and P-ERP open new opportunities for SME to become ERP adopters. Moreover, some P-ERP and FOS-ERP are offering basic modules for free, such as Microsoft's small ERP system Office Accounting (in US and UK), and the Accounting module of ERP5 on its SaaS version. However, lower costs can also mean that adopters have to deal with lower service levels, then stressing the necessity of carefully evaluating ERP options regarding service levels and pricing. In the case of FOS-ERP, consulting certification is yet on the early stages, thus quality of service must be carefully addressed during contract negotiation. On the other hand, although SMEs can change their business processes faster than bigger companies, cheaper but restrictive P-ERP support contracts can make the software change slower than the real business.

Also on the economic side, following the common reasoning about FOSS pricing, FOS-ERP vendors can take advantage from open source software because, according to Riehle (2007), open source systems "increase profits through direct costs savings and the ability to reach more customers through improved pricing flexibility", allowing partners and free-lance vendors switch from more expensive proprietary software to less expensive open source software, since, as a general rule, FOS-ERP relies on other open technologies. For instance, while most P-ERP systems export and import data to and from MS-Office, FOS-ERP in general interacts with the also free Open Office. The same can be affirmed for databases and operational systems – thus reducing costs on ERP supportive software too.

Another economic factor is that P-ERP vendors generally impose high costs and a rigid set of rules for companies that desire to enter their partner network, raising the difficulties for smaller firms to become players in this market. In contrast, smaller consulting firms can enter the FOS-ERP market in an incremental way, increasing their commitment to a project as new business opportunities appear and bring more financial income. In other words, firms can start contributing with small improvements to the project as a way of gaining knowledge on the system platform and framework, and, as customers to the solution appears, more money can be invested on a growing commitment to the project. With more partners entering the market, consulting costs can be reduced, help shifting the market perspective from vendor to adopter. On the other hand, the P-ERP partner networks rely on more mature consulting processes and experiences of global ERP players. In that sense, FOS-ERP must learn on how to create certification and consulting processes that are at the same time high quality products, like the P-ERP ones, and cheaper than those, to survive on the market.

Regarding the access to the source code, the experience has shown that most of the times the adopter will not get involved on customization or even maintenance tasks. Still, FOS-ERP can be a good choice, since it reduces vendor dependency. Moreover, its code openness also makes adapting it to specific needs easier, thus reducing costs in customization and further evolution of the software.

Yet on the development and customization arena, another interesting remark is the fact that FOS-ERP and P-ERP development becomes more and more similar. The similarities are that P-ERP developers work more and more with open source in their products and they also to a higher degree starts to make the source code available. It can also be claimed that more and more open source development is carried by developers that are paid by software vendors – the so-called Sponsored Open Source (West et al., 2005).

However, when thinking on customizing the ERP by itself, a critical question for an organization adopting ERPs is if they have the resources needed for implementing ERPs. In both FOS-ERP and P-ERP cases it is very unlikely that a small company will have the resources and the knowledge for making the necessary modifications by itself. This situation is allowing a shift to the SaaS business model, which indicates that in the future SaaS as delivery model could solve this problem

for adoption of ERPs regardless their type (open or proprietary). As examples on the evolution of SaaS delivered ERPs there are ERP5 Express[1] on the FOS-ERP side and Fortnox on the P-ERP side. For the Medium Enterprise, which has more IT resources, it could be easier to adopt a FOS-ERP and take part on its customization, as occurred with some adopters.

The question is then what the new delivery models of P-ERP means when it comes to differences between support in the FOS-ERP case and the P-ERP case. One possible outcome of this is that it will only be the solutions that have a high level of relevant services connected to the specific ERP solution delivered that will survive. It also means that FOS-ERPs and P-ERPs will become closer to each other and this movement maybe, to some extent, makes it harder for the adopting organization to decide on which kind of ERP to select.

Following this reasoning, it can be stated that FOS-ERPs, when evaluated as products and not as services in a SaaS mode, can be harder to evaluate than P-ERPs. When evaluating FOS-ERPs the adopting organization is supposed to also carefully evaluate the maturity of the FOSS project, its survivability, and its partner network – having special attention on the risks associated with adopting a community founded ERP project.

Independent if it is FOS-ERPs or P-ERPs that are discussed, another interesting observation is the fact that empirical evidence (Hendricks et al., 2007) shows that it is not the software as such that provides an organization with competitive advantage, instead it can be claimed that it is the usage of the software, in the form of internal capabilities (Mata, Fuerst and Barney, 1995), that influences whether an organization is competitive or not. This then implies that even if two organizations working in the same industry adopts the same ERP they could have different performance. The question is then if this depends on that the inherited business process in the software are so generic that its supports only the very basic needs. It could be the fact that to be able to gain competitive advantage from adoption of ERPs, the system needs to be highly adjustable, but, also that the adopters could adjust the software by itself in a convenient way.

FINAL CONSIDERATIONS: GUIDANCE FOR ADOPTERS AND FUTURE RESEARCH

From the previous conclusions, some guidance for SME adopters can be provided, and it can be concluded that specific size of the company makes a difference. For small enterprises, the SaaS model seems to be the solution, and the adopter must evaluate, besides the necessary functionalities, service levels and pricing, regardless the licensing model.

In the case of medium enterprises, it can be suggested that if the company have enough development and supporting resources and already uses other open source applications in its organization it could consider an FOS-ERP solution, analyzing carefully the maturity of the project. A medium enterprise could also consider FOS-ERP if it needs to develop a solution that is very different from others, given innovative business processes. On the other hand, if the company does not have the resources or do not want to invest on customization by itself, and if it already uses – and is satisfied with - a partner helping with other software applications, it should definitely consider to stick to P-ERP, considering, again, whether a SaaS model should be adopted.

Future research subjects are to obtain experimental data on both kinds of ERP adoption by SMEs, investigate which changes FOS-ERP caused on the ERP market, and also investigate the differences on adoption of both kinds of ERP by SMEs in different regions of the world.

REFERENCES

Carvalho, R. A. (2006). Issues on evaluating Free/open source ERP sysyems. In Research and Practical Issues of Enterprise Informations Systems (pp. 667-676). New York: Springer Verlag, Inc.

Caulliraux, H. M., Proença, A., & Prado, C. A. S. (2000). *ERP Systems from a Strategic Perspective*. Sixth International Conference on Industrial Engineering and Operations Management, Niteroi, Brazil.

Church, Z. (2008). *SAP ERP on-demand challenge lofty, but not impossible.*

Dreiling, A., Klaus, H., Rosemann, M., & Wyssusek, B. (2005). *Open Source Enterprise Systems: Towards a Viable Alternative*. 38th Annual Hawaii International Conference on System Sciences, Hawaii.

Hendricks, K. B., Singhal, V. R., & Stratman, J. K. (2007). The impact of enterprise systems on corporate performance: A study of ERP, SCM, and CRM system implementations. *Journal of Operations Management, 25*(1), 65–82. doi:10.1016/j.jom.2006.02.002

IFIP – IFAC. (1999). *GERAM: Generalized Enterprise Reference Architecture and Methodology*, (p. 31). Task Force on Architectures for Enterprise Integration.

Kim, H., & Boldyreff, C. (2005). *Open Source ERP for SMEs*. Third International Conference on Manufacturing Research, Cranfield, UK.

Mata, F. J., Fuerst, W. L., & Barney, J. B. (1995). Information technology and sustained competitive advantage: A resource-based analysis. *MIS Quarterly, 19*(4), 487–505. doi:10.2307/249630

Riehle, D. (2007). The Economic Motivation of Open Source: Stakeholders Perspectives. *Computer IEE Computer Society,* 25-32.

West, J., & O'Mahony, S. (2005). *Contrasting Community Building in Sponsored and Community Founded Open Source Projects*. 38th Annual Hawaii International Conference on System Sciences, Hawaii.

KEY TERMS AND DEFINITIONS

Enterprise Resources Planning (ERP): A kind of software which main goal is to integrate all data and processes of an organization into a unified system.

Free Software: According to the Free Software Foundation, is a Software that gives to the user the freedom to run the program for any purpose, study how the program works and adapt it to his/her needs, redistribute copies, improve the program, and release his/her improvements to the public, so that the whole community benefits.

Open Source Software: According to the Open Source Initiative, licenses must meet ten conditions in order to be considered open source licenses: 1) The software can be freely given away or sold; 2) The source code must either be included or freely obtainable; 3) Redistribution of modifications must be allowed; 4) Licenses may require that modifications be redistributed only as patches; 5) No discrimination against persons or groups; 6) No discrimination against fields of endeavor; 7) The rights attached to the program must apply to all to whom the program is redistributed without the need for execution of an additional license by those parties; 8) The program cannot be licensed only as part of a larger distribution; 9) The license cannot insist that any other software it is distributed with must also be open source; 10) License must be technology-neutral. The official definition of Open Source Software is very close to the definition of Free Software; however, it allows in practice more restrictive licenses, creating a category of "semi-free" software.

Free/Open Source ERP: ERP systems that are released as Free Software or Open Source Software.

Proprietary Software: According to Wikipedia proprietary software is a term for computer software with restrictions on use or private modification, or with restrictions judged to be excessive on copying or publishing of modified or unmodified versions. The term is coined by the free software community and means that these restrictions are placed on it by one of its proprietors. Similarly, closed source is a term for software whose license does not meet the Open Source Definition.

Small and Medium-sized Enterprises (SMEs): In the chapter the definition of SMEs follows the definition presented by the European Commission in 1996 which state that: a small enterprise is an enterprise with fewer than 50 employees and a medium-sized enterprise is an enterprise with more than 49 and fewer than 250 employees.

Software as a Service (SaaS): According to the Software and Information Industry Association, in this model, the application, or service, is deployed from a centralized data center across a network providing access and use on a recurring fee basis. In other words, users "rent," "subscribe to," "are assigned", or "are granted access to" the applications from a central provider.

ENDNOTE

[1] In the specific case of ERP5 Express, an innovative business model allows the adopter to, at any moment, download all code and data and adopt it as a local version of the system, regardless the level of customization that was applied to the adopter's instance.

Chapter 25
Directed Basic Research in Enterprise Resource Planning (ERP) Systems

S. Parthasarathy
Thiagarajar College of Engineering, India

ABSTRACT

Enterprise Resource Planning (ERP) covers the techniques and concepts employed for the integrated management of businesses as a whole, from the viewpoint of the effective use of management resources, to improve the efficiency of an enterprise. One way of looking at ERP is as a combination of business processes and information technology. The objective of this chapter is to highlight the research challenges in ERP projects from the viewpoint of software engineering and draw round the solutions in hand. This chapter on the directed basic research in ERP systems gives us two outputs: (1) A comprehensive framework presenting the current research problems in the ERP systems from the viewpoint of software engineering and (2) The channel to solve these problems. The outcome is a high quality, reliable and complete ERP software solution.

INTRODUCTION

The practice of the implementation of ERP systems is flooded with stories of devastating implementation. It seems to be an accepted fact that ERP implementations never are on time, within the budget and never meet the desired business outcome. A number of surveys support this fact, and at the same time, we see an increasing attention to the extended implementation process, the so-called "second wave". Going live is not the end of the ERP journey and most companies actually report a decline from baseline performance during the initial stage after going live. Enterprise Resource Planning Software or ERP does not live up to its acronym. Forget about planning—it does not do much of that—and forget about resource, a throwaway term. But remember the enterprise part. This is ERP's true ambition. It attempts to integrate all departments and functions across a company onto

DOI: 10.4018/978-1-60566-731-7.ch025

a single computer system that can serve all those different departments' particular needs. That is a tall order, building a single software program that serves the needs of people in finance as well as answers the needs of the people in human resources and in the warehouse. Each of those departments typically has its own computer system optimized for the particular ways that the department does its work. But ERP combines them all together into a single, integrated software program that runs off a single database so that the various departments can more easily share information and communicate with one another. That integrated approach can have a tremendous payback if companies install the correct software. Enterprise Resource Planning (ERP) covers the techniques and concepts employed for the integrated management of businesses as a whole, from the viewpoint of the effective use of management resources, to improve the efficiency of an enterprise. ERP packages are integrated software packages that support these ERP concepts. In the beginning, they were targeted at the manufacturing industry, and consisted mainly of functions for planning and managing core businesses such as sales management, production management, accounting and financial affairs, etc. However, in recent years, adaptation not only to the manufacturing industry, but also to diverse types of industry, has become possible and the expansion of implementation and use has been progressing on a global level.

ERP software standardizes an enterprise's business processes and data. The software converts transactional data into useful information and collates the data so that they can be analyzed. In this way, all of the collected transactional data become information that companies can use to support business decisions. The perspective that ERP software is simply a means of cutting cost is still prevalent. As a result, organizational resistance to ERP implementation has often been high, and not all ERP implementation programs delivered the promised enterprise improvements.

BACKGROUND

Software Engineering is a discipline that integrates the process, methods and tools that are required for the development of the software. An Enterprise Resource Planning (ERP) system is an integrated software system reflecting the business processes of an enterprise. ERP is often referred to as the packaged software. This is different from the traditional software in the sense the ERP software adapts the best practices in the industry as the base for the customer's requirements. An ERP system can be regarded as one of the most innovative developments in the information technology of the 1990s. The motivations for the enterprises to implement ERP systems are the integration, standardization capabilities, flexibility to customize the software and their abilities to drive the effective business process re-engineering and the management of core and support processes.

According to the AMR Research Report (www.amrresearch.com), the ERP market had a spectacular year, with total revenue growing by 14% and license revenue up an amazing 18% from 2005. While sales of traditional ERP applications were very healthy in 2006, many vendors also saw substantial revenue growth from the acquisition of other software companies. Large organizations continue to roll out SAP or Oracle, while many SMEs or smaller divisions of the large organizations are still in the ERP selection process, searching for the right point product or upgrading applications. As per the AMR Research report on ERP called "Enterprise Resource Planning Spending Report, 2006-2007," U.S. companies increased their ERP budgets by 11.3% in 2007. It also states that the enterprise resource planning (ERP) applications market grew to $25.4B in 2005, reached $29B in 2006 and over the next five years, the market will grow at an average of 10%.

The growth in ERP spending is fueled by several factors. As midsize organizations fight for market share against increasingly diverse global competition, increased profitability, revenue growth, and customer satisfaction become priorities. In addition, with globalization, the pool of potential customers is widening, creating a need for streamlined processes to help meet demand. "We found that midsize companies, whether divisions of large enterprises or stand-alone small businesses, are prepared to make the necessary investments to support profitable growth in today's global economy," said Simon Jacobson, senior research analyst at AMR Research. In addition, by 2010, 43% of companies would like to employ a single, global financial and shared services ERP system.

The difficulties and high failure rate in implementing ERP systems have been widely cited in the literature (Davenport, 1998), but research on critical success factors in ERP implementation is rare and fragmented. Among the managerial factors and technical factors leading to the ERP's success, the latter contributes much to the success of ERP systems. Since ERP is packaged software, it is very much appropriate to address it from the viewpoint of software engineering. To date, little has been done to theorize the important factors for initial and ongoing ERP implementation success (Brown et al., 1999). Enterprise Resource Planning (ERP) systems (Fiona Fui-Hoom Nah et al., 2001) have emerged as the core of successful information management and the enterprise backbone of organizations. An enterprise resource planning (ERP) system is a packaged business software system that enables a company to manage the efficient and effective use of resources by providing a total, integrated solution for the organization's information-processing needs. It supports a process-oriented view of the business as well as business processes standardizes across the enterprise (Fiona Fui-Hoom Nah et al., 2001).

However, research in ERP from the viewpoint of software engineering is still lacking and the gap in the ERP literature is huge. Based on a comprehensive review of much of what has been done so far about ERP, a new research agenda to advance the research on the ERP phenomenon

with software engineering as the base is proposed and an outlet to derive solutions to the research problems is indicated. This research agenda should be of great value to researchers and practitioners to catch the current research problems in ERP systems from the row of software engineering and to define solutions using the outlets briefed in this chapter. This will pay the way for the development of a high quality, reliable and complete ERP software solution.

RESEARCH FRAMEWORK FOR ERP SYSTEM

Figure 1 shows the proposed research framework for ERP system. This framework will explore the current research issues found in the literature as well as those faced by the consultants involved in the ERP implementation for the past few years. The critical success factors for the ERP implementation are depicted in the research framework. Each of these factors is discussed briefly and the possible solutions in hand to manage these issues are hinted to enable the researchers and the practitioners to carry out the ERP implementation successfully. A deeper research into each one of these research issues highlighted in the framework will enable us to provide a complete ERP software solution to the customers leading to successful ERP implementation.

Customization

Customizations that must be carried over from one version of enterprise software to the next are the biggest technology headache (Beatty et al., 2006). An enterprise resource planning (ERP) system is a packaged business software system that enables a company to manage the efficient and effective use of resources (materials, human resources, finance, etc.) by providing a total, integrated solution for the organization's information-processing needs. It supports a process-oriented view of the business

Figure 1. Research framework for ERP system

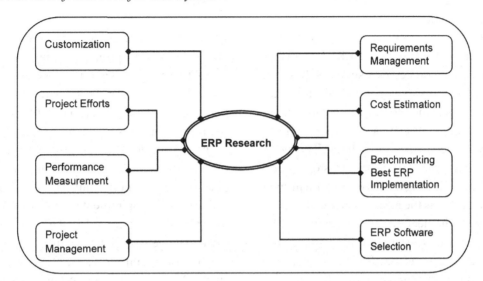

as well as the business processes standardized across the enterprise. Among the most important attributes of ERP are its abilities to: automate and integrate an organization's business processes; share common data and practices across the entire enterprise; to produce and access information in a real-time environment. Usually businesses have their own existing proven competitive advantage processes set in place. Businesses will have to change their proven processes to fit the software in order to take advantage of future releases, to benefit from the improved processes, and avoid costly irreparable errors.

Several studies have demonstrated that the implementation of ERP systems requires the examination of many business processes and it is vital for the company's processes to be accurately aligned with those of the ERP system if the full benefits are to be realized (Redouane et al., 2006). Customization is believed to be the critical success factor for ERP implementation (Hong and Kim, 2002). From the viewpoint of system adaptation, Davenport (1998) says that ERP systems need to be changed to fit existing or reengineered business processes. From the viewpoint of organization adaptation, Robey (2002) says that organizations

need to be changed to fit the ERP system. This clearly indicates the need for carefully carrying out customization during ERP implementation.

Customization is an integral part of ERP implementation. The rate of customization is directly proportional to ERP success. Customization tends to pose a challenge to time and the funds allocated. The challenge of successful management lies in balancing them and making both ends meet. It is a difficult task but the success speaks for the process. The major issues that require attention in the process of customizing ERP are a good knowledge of the current system and the likelihood of innovations in ERP.

The prime goal of customization in ERP implementation is to ensure that the company's requirements match with the ERP solution. This can be achieved by either changing our existing business processes to those of the ERP system, as ERP provides the best practices in the industry, or, on the other hand, changing the system according to the business processes. The former process is called Process Customization and the latter process is called System Customization. The decision on the degree of customization and the method of doing it in ERP implementation is really a challenging task for the management and the ERP consultants.

The success of an ERP system is assured when there is a perfect fit between the ERP system and the organizational processes it supports. In short, when the ERP software is perfectly customized, then the success of the ERP implementation is assured. It is vital for the company's processes to be accurately aligned with those of the ERP system if the full benefits are to be realized. Customization is the process of tuning the ERP software in such a way that it reflects the business processes of the organization. The need for customization of the ERP software arises because of the mismatch between the requirements specified by the customer and the requirements for which the ERP software is developed. The requirements collected from the customer to develop the software can be broadly classified as application requirements, process requirements and design requirements. Applications requirements are prepared from the basic requirements collected from the customer. From application requirements, process requirements are prepared. From process requirements, design requirements are prepared. All these requirements account for the development of a software.

An ERP vendor who could provide ERP implementation with minimum customization is always preferred by the customer as over customization will prevent the customer from reaping the full benefits of the ERP software. Hence, when the customer is provided with n number of ERP vendors with their estimated degree of customization for each type of requirements discussed above, he is left with the complex problem of deciding the best ERP vendor based on the degree of customization. The question of optimality does not arise here, as the estimation of the degree of customization is done only to ensure that the ERP software meets the requirements of the customer completely. We deem that the rank correlation in the statistics is the suitable technique to select the best ERP vendor who could provide a better ERP solution to the customer.

Project Efforts

Effort estimation is the most important and the first step in the software project planning process which gives the effort calculation for the development of the software to satisfy the given requirements and the time to complete the project. To estimate cost the primary need is to estimate effort that would be needed to develop the project. The estimate of the cost enables the client or the developer to perform a cost benefit analysis. Effort in a project is due to staff requirement for software, hardware and staff activities needed for the product development. The general practices of effort estimation in software organizations are algorithmic models like COCOMO and most often by expert judgments. Existing models like the one proposed by Shepperd (Shepperd, 1997) for effort estimation has to be enhanced in terms of number of project attributes and considering the attrition rate in the Information Technology (IT) industry.

Each of the software projects must estimate the efforts required to complete software development. The most appropriate unit of effort is Person-Months (PM), meaning thereby the number of persons involved for specified months. The ERP software projects require a careful estimation of efforts. The size of the software is initially determined using the function points. Based on the function points, the efforts require to develop the software can be estimated. In the case of ERP Projects, the degree of customization required for the ERP software has to be taken into account while calculating the project efforts for ERP implementation. A solution to this problem could be the creation of an ERP project database which will have the details of successfully completed ERP projects such as the size of the software, the project efforts used, the duration of the project, the platform, the technology used, the cost of the project, the degree of customization and other similar relevant details. Using the ERP project database, the ERP implementation team can very well predict (or estimate) the efforts required for the new ERP projects by applying statistical techniques such as regression analysis. This estimated result can be taken as a guideline for planning the resources and efforts required for the ERP implementation.

Performance Measurement

Learning from high performance projects is crucial for software process improvement. Last, but not least, by determining the crucial factors of a successful ERP system, we create incentives that likely will yield higher performance. Weinberg (Weinberg, 1971) demonstrated many years ago that the proverb "You get what you measure" also is highly valid in the software engineering field. ERP projects are a subclass of software projects (Stensrud et al., 2003). ERP implementation is a lengthy and complex process and there have been many cases of unsuccessful implementation, which have had major impacts on business performance (Parr and Shanks, 2000). As a growing number of companies adopt ERP systems, the performance of ERP systems is identified as one of the top five IT priorities among global CIOs according to independent surveys conducted by the Morgan Stanley (Togur et al., 2003) and the Deloitte & Touche/IDG Research Services Groups (Deloitte and Touche, 2002).

Measuring the performance of an ERP system remains an open issue even today. The critical success factors of successful ERP projects have to be identified to improve the performance of the ERP system. Before the ERP implementation, the consultants should consider the following: (i) Defining what the ERP is to achieve. (ii) Checking whether all the business processes are well defined and understood. (iii) Identifying the performance metrics for the ERP project. (iv) The need to do BPR and (v) The Feasibility of executing data and system integration. Current practice in the IT industry is to provide a questionnaire to the end-users and evaluate their satisfaction. This will not however help the ERP consultants to quanti-

tatively evaluate the ERP system and indicate the processes in which the customer has improved substantially. In addition, we could not map the performance of the company before and after the ERP implementation. A solution to achieve this objective is that the ERP consultants come out with a set of performance metrics of the ERP system for each of their customers separately.

Performance indicators need not be unique in the case of ERP software, which is a packaged software made out of Business Process Reengineering. The basic question to be addressed here is to question ourselves on what we think as the performance of the ERP system for a company. From the view point of software engineering, the performance can be measured in terms of software productivity, whereas from the managerial point, the performance of the ERP system is maximum utilization of available resources, improved customer satisfaction, increased customer base and cost reduction. The performance metrics of the ERP system should address both these perspectives to yield high performance.

A couple of exploratory case studies on the ERP projects have to be conducted to identify the managerial factors such as top management involvement, end-user training, change management etc and the technical factors such as project efforts estimation, technical customization, process customization etc. that influences the performance of the ERP software. The outcome of these case studies is the identification of critical success factors for the ERP projects. To manage these critical success factors, a suitable methodology such as Analytical Hierarchy Process (AHP), Nominal Group Technique (NGT), Data Envelopment Analysis (DEA), Vienna Development Method (VDM), and PLanguage could be studied. Using these methodologies, a model or a framework, algorithms can be developed to manage these critical success factors. Then, as said earlier, the performance metrics defined to measure the performance of the ERP software has to be used to analyse the results yielded by these methodologies, frameworks, algorithms to improve the performance of the ERP software. Based on these results, the newly defined models and algorithms can be refined and improved in a better way with additional features to manage the critical success factors of ERP projects.

Project Management

Managing the ERP projects is considered quite complex when compared to the traditional software projects. There are a couple of software quality models in hand to help the software team to prepare the software project planning effectively. Still the buzzword in ERP implementation is "Project Schedule Slippage" and "Poor Software Maintenance". Software maintenance is as important as software project planning. In fact, the actual software development takes place only after implementation in the case of ERP projects. The consultants, too, admit that the problems encountered during the software development are simply transferred to the customer during the implementation thereby pushing a higher burden to the software maintenance team. The successful management of the software process is necessary in order to satisfy the final quality, cost and time of the marketing of the software products (Holland et al., 2001).

Key issues in ERP projects are the larger project duration due to schedule slippage and less support for maintenance from the ERP vendor (Robey et al., 2002; Kitchenham et al., 2001). A solution for effective ERP project management is to define our own software metrics to fix the slippage in the project duration. Specifically, in using the metrics we need to identify the exact phase in the ERP implementation accounting for schedule slippage, the root cause for the slippage and so on. Similarly, the number of problems reported by the customer during the software maintenance phase, the age of the open problems and the age of the closed problems in the software maintenance phase have to be estimated using the metrics which

will enable us to allocate the necessary resources for the software maintenance phase and ensure the implementation of a complete ERP software solution to the customer in the right time.

Low user productivity and reduced performance of ERP software lead the top management team to intervene directly and push the functional managers to rectify their positions, notably by insisting on the cross-functional aspects of the process that they had not wanted to resolve previously (Redouane et al., 2006). The importance of formal software process management practices as a mechanism for enhancing software development performance is well recognized in Information Systems Development (ISD) literature (Fitzgerald, 1996). ERP is not a panacea for all performance problems, but rather an enabler for business process integration (Grant et al., 2005). ERP software's incompatibility can also impede performance of the enterprise leading to lessening the performance of ERP projects (Girish et al., 2005).

Software processes that cannot be measured cannot be managed. The best way for effective project management during the ERP implementation is to identify the key process areas cited here, monitor and manage those processes with the help of software metrics defined exclusively for this purpose. This will ensure that the ERP project is on the track and produces the right deliverables in the right period.

Requirements Management

In systems engineering and software engineering, requirements analysis encompasses those tasks that go into determining the needs or conditions to be met for a new or altered product, taking account of the possibly conflicting requirements of the various stakeholders, such as beneficiaries or users. Requirements analysis is critical to the success of a development project. Requirements must be actionable, measurable, testable, related to identified business needs or opportunities, and defined to a level of detail sufficient for system design. Systematic requirements analysis is also known as Requirements Engineering. It is sometimes referred to loosely by names such as requirements gathering, requirements capture, or requirements specification. Requirements engineering is an important component of ERP projects. A Requirements Engineering (RE) method for ERP system requirements (ERPRE) is essential to capture the requirements from different types of users of an ERP system, verifying and validating them. ERP projects integrate three major areas of Information Technology (IT) projects--such as knowledge management (KM), customer relationship management (CRM), and supply chain management systems (SCM)--as predicted by Holland and Light (Holland and Light, 2001). Among the keys to success of the ERP projects are applying a Requirements Engineering (RE) Model in the client's context and installing processes to support key RE activities (Daneva, 2004). A requirements dialog meta-model is currently available to manage inconsistencies in a requirements document during software development (Robinson et al., 1999). Workflow and process modeling provide some solutions for the management of requirements development. Software requirement analysis and specification is an important activity in software development and maintenance. Without explicitly specifying the customer's requirements, software engineers do not know what to build and how to validate the software (Frank Liu, 1998). How to align the ERP application components and business requirements for coordination and cooperation is hardly known (Daneva et al., 2006). It is still a difficult process to find a match between the flexibility often required by the business processes and the rigidity usually imposed by the ERP system. This difficulty is recognized as the central problem of ERP implementation. It is a fact that the software is difficult to understand, change and maintain. Several software engineering techniques have been suggested to ameliorate this situation (Heninger,

1980): (a) Modularity and Information Hiding (b) Formal Specifications (c) Abstract Interfaces (d) Resource Monitors and (e) Process Synchronization Routines. It is also clear from the literature that the mismatch between the ERP software and the customer's requirements is a long standing problem. The work of software correction caused by the changes in requirements is one of the most significant and difficult areas in software development and maintenance processes. However, a requirements-driven COTS project ensures that the final product possesses the required functionality and quality (Lawlis et al., 2001). Thus we find that the requirements of the customer that are on hand in the ERP software and those not offered by it should be prepared in the form of a catalog. There are no methods available to do this process. This can be done by quantitatively estimating the customization required for the ERP software to meet the requirements of the enterprise. The Requirements Engineering (RE) method for ERP has a more multi-user perspective than the usual software projects, and it integrates the requirements from the ERP end users, the supply chain systems users, the CRM users, and the KM users. This gives us an indication that we have to define a Requirements Engineering (RE) method for ERP system requirements (ERPRE) to capture the requirements from the different types of users of an ERP system, verifying and validating them. Unlike the RE done for traditional software projects, the RE method for ERP projects must have provision to collect requirements from different types of ERP users discussed earlier, utilize the customers' requirements recorded in the project database created from the successfully completed ERP projects and accordingly draft a software requirements specification (SRS) for the new ERP project. This SRS will have to be verified and validated in order to ensure that the SRS is consistent and complete. It must be noticed that such an exclusive RE method for ERP projects will help the ERP consultants to minize the customization during the ERP implementation.

Cost Estimation

Estimating the work effort and the schedule to develop and/or to maintain a software system are the most critical activities in managing software projects. This task is known as Software Cost Estimation. During the development process, the cost and time estimates are useful for initial rough validation and monitoring of the project's progress; after completion, these estimates may be useful for project productivity assessment for example. Several cost estimation techniques are used within an organization; these techniques may be grouped into two major categories: Algorithmic models and Non-Algorithmic Models. Popular software cost estimation models (Pressman, 2005) like COCOMO, PUTNAM-SLIM, Expert Judgement, Delphi Method, Work Breakdown Structure are used for software cost estimation with its own limitations.

Boehm and Papaccio (1988) suggests seven techniques of software cost estimation namely algorithmic cost modelling, expert judgment, estimation by Analogy, Parkinson's Law, pricing to win, Top-Down estimation and Bottom-Up estimation. Unlike the traditional software projects, in the case of ERP implementation, there are two costs to be determined: One is the fixed cost for developing the ERP software and the other is the on-going cost for the customization of the ERP software and its maintenance during the ERP implementation. The cost estimation models described earlier consider the project efforts required, function points, etc as the parameters to estimate the software costs. In ERP projects, the customization process has to be taken into account during the software cost estimation and the model should estimate the two types of costs as mentioned earlier. Hence, it would be appropriate to design an exclusive software cost estimation model for ERP projects, of course retaining the basic principles of the existing software cost estimation models/techniques.

Benchmarking Best ERP Implementation

An Enterprise Resource Planning (ERP) system is a critical investment that can significantly affect future competitiveness and performance of a company. The first and foremost expectation of the customer from the ERP system is its ability to support the business goals and strategies of his enterprise. Secondly, the optimal usage of resources by the ERP system. Apart from these, the ERP system should reduce the costs incurred in carrying out the various processes in the enterprise, achieving 100% customer satisfaction and increased profit through improved performance in a continuous manner. These are some managerial parameters to assess an ERP system. From the viewpoint of software engineering, the ability to handle the process of customization, the technology used, the reduced project duration, the reduced software cost and the software productivity are considered the performance measures for the ERP system. Thus it is the need of the hour to critically examine the performance indicators of the Enterprise Resource Planning (ERP) projects both from the managerial point and from the technical point and make it available to the ERP consultants to enable them to prepare themselves to produce a high performance ERP software to the customer.

The growing number of horror stories about failed or out-of-control projects should certainly give managers the pause (Davenport, 1998). ERPs are information systems that manage the data for a company's main business processes, from customer orders to accountability. Their functions include data capture, processing and customized distribution to any customer (Serrano et al., 2006). Demands from the customers are increasing day by day. It's time for the consultants to create benchmarks from the past performance of successful ERP implementation. Learning from high performance projects is crucial for software process improvement. Therefore, we need to identify outstanding projects that may serve as role models. A minimum prerequisite for identifying these best practice projects is the ability to measure the performance. If you cannot measure it, you cannot possibly know which projects are best and whether you have improved or not. Also, if you are able to find the best projects, they may serve as role models guiding you on how to improve. For practitioners, identifying and studying the best practice projects is an invaluable source of learning. Last, but not least, by measuring project performance, you create incentives that likely will yield higher performance.

ERP Software Selection

ERP software selection has become a buzz word in the IT industry. Earlier there were only a few ERP vendors. But nowadays there are so many, providing solutions to the companies at less cost. Hence the question of selecting a right ERP vendor is becoming complex. Selecting the right vendor will solve most of the problems and will also help the customer to get through the various phases of ERP implementation very easily. There are customers doing different business and using different ERP products for each one of them. This shows the competition that exists among the various ERP vendors. The customers are of the opinion that it is difficult to have a single vendor to provide solutions to all their businesses and hence the selection of ERP vendor gains significance.

An important phase in ERP implementation is selecting the right ERP software from the right ERP vendor. The customer can choose either a module of the ERP software or a complete ERP software solution where all the modules are integrated with one another. In practice, the customer prefers the ERP vendor who comes forward to satisfy all their requirements by customizing the software suitably. However, the customer has to remember that the ERP implements the "best practices" in the industry and hence the higher the degree of customization, the lower the benefits a customer

can reap from the ERP. The customer finds it difficult to choose the right vendor among the ERP vendors offering the ERP software solution.

In literature, a couple of ERP software selection models are available which makes use of some questionnaire to collect the requirements of the customers and enable them to choose a ERP vendor. The ERP software selection process is divided into four phases (Alexis Leon, 2003): Phase 1: Initial requirements, Phase 2: Developing the short list of candidate solutions and Phase 3: Final selection. The Information Technology (IT) industry will appreciate us very much if we could design the ERP software selection process as an optimization problem with the necessary constraints as desired by the customer and evaluate each of the ERP vendors accordingly and select the right ERP vendor who could deliver a complete ERP software solution at a lower cost, without changing the basic structure of the ERP integrated software system.

The ERP software selection process could be carried out successfully only if the enterprise could see the readiness of the ERP software to fit into their enterprise. To get this process done, one must estimate the degree of customization required for the ERP software to meet the requirements of the enterprise completely. This can be done by means of an algorithm using the software engineering concepts such as requirements traceability and requirements engineering. This algorithm could also be used to reduce the gap between the enterprise and the ERP software. This phase is called "Gap Analysis" and considered more critical during the ERP implementation lifecycle.

CONCLUSION AND FUTURE RESEARCH SCOPE

Organizations must broaden their perspective in order to put their ERP efforts on a successful path. Too many overlook a critical stage: new business processes must be established, thought through, and implemented before the selection, purchase and deployment of a software solution. As more and more organizations worldwide choose to build their corporate knowledge base around complex infrastructure solutions, the need to understand how to successfully implement an ERP system and enhance its performance has become increasingly important. While ERP implementation horror stories highlight serious business consequences and criticize leading ERP vendors for botched deployments, often the software giants are not to blame. Companies must realize that ERP systems are not a stand-alone solution, but instead an enabling technology to support a broad corporate change and the key to a successful deployment is in the process. Organizations too often ignore the need to define an optimal process and then use the technology as an enabler for the process. In too many instances, organizations either try to adopt a process that is inherent in the ERP solution, even if it does not fit their business requirements, or they try to shoehorn their legacy processes into a software package that is not designed to support their processes. In both cases, they sub-optimize the capabilities in the technology and don't take advantage of the opportunity to streamline their business process—the entire point of technology implementations. The successful implementation of an ERP system is a significant challenge for the software engineering community. The growing number of horror stories about failed ERP implementation is the basis for this research study. Because ERP covers so much of what a business does, a failure in the software can bring a company to a halt, literally. An ERP system is an enterprise-wide integrated software package designed to uphold the highest quality standards of business process. As it is very complex, maintaining the system by trial and error is very costly. At its simplest level, ERP is a set of best practices for performing different job in a company, including finance, manufacturing and the warehouse. To get the most from the software, we have to get people inside our company to adopt the work methods outlined in the software. If the people in the different departments which will be using ERP don't agree that the work methods embedded in the software are better than the ones they currently use, they will resist using the software or will want IT to change the software to match the ways they currently do things. This is where the ERP projects break down. Customizations make the software more unstable and harder to maintain when it finally does come to life. The horror stories we hear every day about ERP can usually be traced to the changes the company made in the core ERP software to fit its own work methods. Because ERP covers so much of what a business does, a failure in the software can bring a company to a halt, literally. We have discussed the research issues in the ERP implementation and the possible solution to fix the problems are hinted out. This discussion briefly outlines a range of current issues in the ERP implementation and the research work done on these issues in the past and the current opportunities to explore these research issues further to provide a better ERP software solution to the customers by the ERP vendors. A survey of research relating to some major issues in ERP implementation has been presented. A research framework is designed and each one of the parameters in the framework represents the current research issue in the ERP projects. Each of these parameters has been briefly discussed and guidelines are provided to do research on these parameters to enhance the performance of the ERP system. Much research is still needed to better understand the ERP phenomenon from a balanced perspective. The data set of various ERP projects could be captured from the International Software Benchmarking Standards Group (ISBSG) and the small-to-medium enterprises (SMEs) involved in ERP implementation. Using the research framework for the ERP system in this study, a performance enhancement model for ERP Projects can be developed and validated using the data sets of the ERP projects from the ISBSG and the SMEs. This research study to enhance the performance of ERP projects will gain greater momentum if the ERP implementation team addresses the performance indicators of ERP projects discussed here appropriately with the required inputs to the models and the algorithms to manage these indicators leading to successful ERP implementation. A future research on the ERP projects could be in the directions such as mobile ERP system, ERP system capable of working platform independent, CRM and SCM enabled ERP solution, DSS enabled ERP system and Migration of the ERP system from one operating system to another. It is anticipated that the current and the future work will collectively provide the researchers and practitioners with a fine reference to research and practice in this emerging field.

REFERENCES

Alexis, L. (2003). *Enterprise Resource Planning*. New Delhi: Tata McGraw-Hill.

Amrani, EI, R., Rowe, F. & Geffroy-Maronnat, B. (2006). The effects of enterprise resource planning implementation strategy on cross-functionality. *Information Systems Journal*, (1): 79–104. doi:10.1111/j.1365-2575.2006.00206.x

Beatty, R. C., & Williams, C. D. (2006, March). ERP II: Best Practices for Successfully Implementing an ERP upgrade. *Communications of the ACM, 49*(3). doi:10.1145/1118178.1118184

Boehm, B. W., & Papaccio, P. N. (1988). Understanding and controlling software costs. *IEEE Transactions on Computers*, 1462–1467.

Brown, C., & Vessey, I. (1999). ERP implementation approaches: toward a contingency framework. *Proceedings of the International Conference on Information Systems*, (pp. 411-416).

Daneva, M. (2004). ERP Requirements Engineering Practice: Lessons Learned. *IEEE Software*, 26–33. doi:10.1109/MS.2004.1270758

Daneva, M., & Wieringa, R. J. (2006). A requirements engineering framework for cross-organizational ERP systems. *Requirements Engineering, 11*, 194–204. doi:10.1007/s00766-006-0034-9

Davenport, T. H. (1998, July/August). Putting the enterprise into the enterprise system. *Harvard Business Review, 76*(4), 121–131.

Deloitte & Touche (2002). *Achieving, measuring and communicating IT value*. An IDG Research Services Group report.

Fitzgerald, B. (1996). Formalized systems development methodologies: A critical perspective. *Information Systems Journal, 6*(1), 3–23. doi:10.1111/j.1365-2575.1996.tb00002.x

Frank Liu, X. (1998). Fuzzy Requirements. *IEEE POTENTIALS*, 24-26.

Fui-Hoom Nah, F., & Lee-Shang Lau, J. (2001). Critical factors for successful implementation of enterprise systems. *Business Process Management Journal, 7*(3), 285–296. doi:10.1108/14637150110392782

Girish, H. S., & Christopher, S. H. (2005). An Exploratory Case Study of Enterprise Resource Planning Implementation. *International Journal of Enterprise Information Systems, 1*(1), 23–38.

Grant, D., & Qiang, T. (2005). Levels of Enterprise Integration: Study using Case Analysis. *International Journal of Enterprise Information Systems, 1*(1), 1–22.

Heninger, K. L. (1980). Specifying software requirements for complex systems: New techniques and their application. *IEEE Transactions on Software Engineering, 6*(1), 2–13. doi:10.1109/TSE.1980.230208

Holland, C. P., & Light, B. (2001). A stage for maturity model for enterprise resource planning systems use. *The Data Base for Advances in Information Systems, 32*(2).

Hong, K., & Kim, Y. (2002). The Critical success factors for ERP implementation: An organizational fit perspective. *Information & Management, 40*(1), 25–40. doi:10.1016/S0378-7206(01)00134-3

Kitchenham, B. A., Huges, R. T., & Linkman, S. G. (2001). Modeling software measurement data. *IEEE Transactions on Software Engineering, 27*(9), 788–804. doi:10.1109/32.950316

Lawlis, K. P., & Mark, E. K. (2001). A formal process for evaluating COTS software products. *Computer, 34*, 58–63. doi:10.1109/2.920613

Parr, A., & Shanks, G. (2000). A Model of ERP Project Implementation. *Journal of Information Technology*, 289–303. doi:10.1080/02683960010009051

Pressman, R. S. (2005). *Software Engineering – A Practitioner's Approach* (6th Edition). New Delhi, India: McGraw-Hill International Edition.

Robey, D., Ross, J. W., & Boudreau, M. C. (2002). Learning to implement enterprise systems: An exploratory study of the dialectics of change. *Journal of Management Information Systems, 19*(1).

Robinson, W. N., Suzanne, D., & Pawlowski, S. (1999). Managing Requirements Inconsistency with Development Goal Monitors. *IEEE Transactions on Software Engineering, 25*(6), 816–835. doi:10.1109/32.824411

Serrano, N., & Sarriegi, J. M. (2006). Open source software ERPs: A new alternative for an old need. *IEEE Software*, 94–96. doi:10.1109/MS.2006.78

Shepperd, M. & Schofiled, C. (1997, February). Estimating Software Project Effort Using Analogies. *IEEECS Log No. 104091*.

Stensrud, E., & Myrtveit, I. (2003, May). Identifying High Performance ERP Projects. *IEEE Transactions on Software Engineering, 29*(5). doi:10.1109/TSE.2003.1199070

Togur, D. M., Bloomberg, E. & Morgan Stanley (2003). *CIO Survey Series: Release 4.5*. Morgan Stanley Research Report.

Weinberg, G. (1971). *The Psychology of Computer Programming*. New York: van Nostrand Reinhold Co.

KEY TERMS AND DEFINITIONS

Business Process Reengineering (BPR): Business Process Reengineering is defined as the fundamental rethinking and radical redesign of business processes to achieve dramatic improvements in critical, contemporary measures of performance, such as cost, quality, service, and speed.

Customer Relationship Management (CRM): The fundamental theory behind CRM is to identify profitable customers, attract and retain them, and maximize their useful life span and the profits from them by establishing and fostering good relationships with them.

Customization: Customization is the core process for adjusting the software to fit the organization.

Decision Support System (DSS): Decision support system is the information and planning system that provides the ability to interrogate computers on an ad–hoc basis, analyze information and predict the impact of decisions before they are made.

Enterprise Resource Planning (ERP): The ERP package aims at integrating all key business activities through improved relationships at all levels to achieve a competitive advantage. ERP systems can be considered an IT infrastructure able to facilitate the flow of information between all business processes in an organization.

Knowledge Management (KM): Knowledge is a derivative of symbols, data, and information. Knowledge management is defined as the management of information and knowledge and their usage in organizational routines/processes within organizations.

Requirements Engineering (RE): Systematic requirements analysis is also known as requirements engineering. It is a software engineering task that bridges the gap between system level requirements engineering and software design.

Supply Chain Management (SCM): Supply chain management is the practice of coordinating the flow of goods, services, information and finances as they move from raw materials to parts supplier to manufacturer to wholesaler to retailer to consumer.

Software Engineering: A discipline that integrates process, methods and tools for the development of computer software.

Software Metric: It refers to a broad range of measurements for computer software. Measurements can be applied to the software process with the intent of improving it on a continuous basis. Software metrics are analyzed and assessed by software managers. Measures are often collected by software engineers.

Chapter 26
Trends in Improving Performances in Distributed Database Management Systems

Ismail Omar Hababeh
United Arab Emirates University, UAE

Muthu Ramachandran
Leeds Metropolitan University, UK

ABSTRACT

Database technology has been a significant field to work in for developing real life applications in network information systems. An enterprise's reliance on its network and database applications in Distributed Database Management systems (DDBMS) environment is likely to continue growing exponentially. In such a system the estimation and prediction of Quality of Service (QoS) performance improvements are crucial since it increases understanding the issues that affect the distributed database networking system behaviour; like database fragmentation, clustering database network sites, and data allocation and replication that would reduce the amount of irrelevant data and speed up the transactions response time. This chapter introduces the trends of database management systems DBMS and presents an integrated method for designing Distributed Relational networking Database Management System DRDBMS that efficiently and effectively achieves the objectives of database fragmentation, clustering database network sites, and fragments allocation and replication. It is based on high speed partitioning, clustering, and data allocation techniques that minimize the data fragments accessed and data transferred through the network sites, maximize the overall system throughput by increasing the degree of concurrent transactions processing of multiple fragments located in different sites, and result in better QoS design and decision support.

1. INTRODUCTION

The database management systems (DBMS) are now such an integral part of the organizations daily life that have major roles in designing, analysing and developing real world applications, and have major effects in data control to achieve best system performance.

This chapter aims to introduce the literature review in the design issues of the distributed database

DOI: 10.4018/978-1-60566-731-7.ch026

management systems (DDBMS) that were seen to be relevant to particular areas of database fragmentation, sites clustering, data allocation, query processing, metrics and QoS. New methods in this context are proposed and investigated against the available methods in the literature.

There have been a lot of models, programs, and tools in the literature used to describe, execute, and implement the operations in the databases. Therefore, setting up the definition for each field may help to distinguish between different types of DBMS and to categorize them accordingly.

In this context, the database, database management system (DBMS), database application, and database system are defined by Connolly (2004):

- *Database:* collection of related data
- *Database Management System (DBMS):* software that manages and controls access to the database.
- *Database Application:* program that interacts with the database at some point in its execution.
- *Database System:* collection of application programs that interact with the database along with the DBMS and database itself.

Too many enterprises consider the distributed databases as a best platform for their services that spread over a wide geographical area. Most recent database researches have focused on DDBMS because of the high cost of the network connectivity and impracticality of the centralized database systems.

In addition, Ozsu and Valduriez (1991) have defined the distributed database as a collection of multiple, logically interrelated databases distributed over a computer network. On the other hand, Hoffer, Prescott, and McFadden (2004) define the distributed database as single **logical database** that is spread physically across computers in multiple locations that are connected by a data communications link, where it is different from decentralized databases which are defined as a collection of independent databases on non-networked computers.

Traditionally, DBMS have been classified according to the database environment, data model, and user-computer systems basis. Hoffer, Prescott, and McFadden (2004) have distinguished two main types of DBMS in a distributed database environment:

- *Homogeneous:* The same DBMS is used at each node. This type is easy to manage but difficult to enforce. It can be divided into two subtypes; **Autonomous** in which independent DBMS are used and **Non-autonomous** where central and coordinating DBMS are considered together.
- *Heterogeneous:* The different database management systems are used at different nodes. This type is difficult to manage and preferred by independent organizations. Two subtypes can be distinguished in this database environment; Systems which can be divided into full DBMS functionality or **partial-multidatabase** and Gateways where simple paths are created to other databases without the benefits of one logical database. Partial-multidatabase consists of **federated** type which is categorized by loose and tight integrations, and **unfederated** type that allows remote access.

Alternatively, (Graham 2005) has categorized DBMS based on their data model into the following groups:

- *Hierarchical:* In this model data are stored as a series of records (e.g. IBM's IMS). Although the hierarchical model is no longer used as the basis for current commercially produced systems, there are still legacy systems in existence based on this model.

- *Network:* This model represents data as a network of records and sets which are related to each other, forming a network of links (e.g. IDMS). A few network models still exist, but very few new network model applications are developed.

- *Relational:* This is the dominant model in use today, with the vast majority of new applications based on it (e.g. Oracle, Sybase, DB2, and Access). Relational model is based on relational algebra, which gives it a firm mathematical foundation. In this model, data is stored in a table-like format.

- *Object Relational:* The databases of this model are essentially relational databases with object oriented front end (e.g. Illustra and O2). However, they do not support inheritance, have limited support for complex relationships and typically do not allow users to define their own types.

- **Object Oriented:** This model of database stores objects and permits their retrieval and manipulation (e.g. Objectstore, and Gemstone). The major goal of this database is to maintain a direct correspondence between real world objects and database objects.

In relation to this clarification, Ozsu and Valduriez (1999) have observed that the object oriented database management systems (OODBMS) lack from theoretical foundation. Contrary to relational model, there is no object based model commonly accepted by database professionals. This makes it hard to define or compare OODBMS, which tend to be application specific. The incorporation of the functions like long lived transactions, dynamic schema evolution, and versions of objects required by new applications in distributed object oriented database management systems (DOODBMS) will affect the performance.

Elmasri and Navathe (2004) have categorized the DBMS based on the users and computer sys-tems as single user (typically used with micro computers), multi user (most database management systems), centralized (uses a single computer with one database), or distributed (uses multiple computers, multiple databases).

Graham (2005) has noted that the DDBMS have been developed to meet the needs of businesses for enterprises that have many sites located around the world. The separation of sites suggests that communication delays will be a major problem and therefore the placement of data is crucial.

Chen (2007) has declared that DDBMS can split the data into fragments that can be stored on different computers and perhaps replicated. The system is expected to make the distribution transparent to the user and the objective of the transparency is to make the DDBMS to appear like a centralized system. However, it is not necessary for every site in the system to have its own local database as shown in figure 1.

2. CENTRALIZED VERSUS DISTRIBUTED DBMS

A centralized database management system (CDBMS) is a database where all the data is stored on a single computer Hoffer, Prescott, and McFadden (2004). In this type of DBMS, as the number of transactions increases, the system performance significantly decreases and creates a bottleneck which slows down performance of both the computer and its running programs. However, well distributed data methods that can satisfy geographically dispersed data processing demands are considered an appropriate solution that resolves the CDBMS tradeoffs and increase the system performance.

Despite the complexity and security constraints of the DDBMS, Ozsu and Valduriez (1999) outlined the following advantages of distributed over CDBMS:

Figure 1. DDBMS with partial local databases

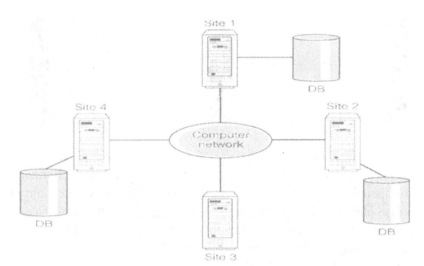

- *Reflects organizational structure:* Database fragments are located in the departments they relate to.
- *Local autonomy:* A department can control the data about them (as they are the ones familiar with it).
- *Improved reliability/availability:* A fault in one DBMS will only affect one fragment, instead of the entire database.
- *Improved performance:* Data is located near the site of greatest demand, and the DBMS themselves are parallelized, allowing load on the databases to be balanced among servers. A high load on one module of the database will not affect other modules.
- *Economics:* It costs less to create a network of smaller computers with the power of a single large computer.
- *Modularity:* Systems can be modified, added and removed from the DDBMS without affecting other systems.
- *Expandability:* In a distributed environment, it is much easier to accommodate increasing database sizes.
- *Shareability:* A DDBMS makes feasible data sharing between sites.

Moreover, Hoffer, Prescott, and McFadden (2004) have pointed that the DDBMS increase system reliability and data availability, provide more local control over data, allow system growth, decrease communication costs, and achieve faster transactions processing response time.

Khalil, Eid and Khair (1999) have noted that the DDBMS concept evolved from the CDBMS to achieve also goals such as availability, data independence and ease of expendability. Therefore, the DDBMS design is processed similarly to the CDBMS for the requirement analysis and the conceptual design phases. However, it is a complex optimization task that requires solutions to several interrelated sub-problems including data fragmentation, data allocation data replication.

As the major purposes of the DDBMS are to improve the system performance and increase system reliability, Ma, Schewe, and Wang (2007) have noticed that the distribution design for databases usually addresses the problems of fragmentation, allocation and replication.

Klein, Kamvar and Manning (2002) have defined the data clustering as a process of gathering a large amount of unlabeled data. Clustering is cheap, easy, and it helps to get a small amount of

Figure 2. Vertical database fragmentation

prior knowledge, indicating whether particular items are similar or dissimilar.

Clustering has also played an important role in DDBMS, in other disciplines such as biology, geology, geography, marketing, and in many other related areas Jain, Murty, and Flynn (1999). The construction of a cluster representation is an important step in decision making. However, it has not been examined closely by researchers.

In the background discussion that follows in this chapter, three main areas are considered; database fragmentation, clustering database network sites, and allocating and replicating database fragments among different sites. The discussion attempts to highlight these key areas and study its effect on improving the performance of the DDBMS.

3. DATABASE FRAGMENTATION

The transactions on the applications are usually subsets of relations (fragments), so using these fragments and distributing them over the network sites increases the system throughput by means of parallel execution. Khalil, Eid, and Khair (1999) have defined database fragmentation as the process of subdividing global relations into subsets to be distributed over sites. In particular, they have proposed three types of fragmentation; vertical, horizontal and mixed.

Various strategies have already partitioned data across distributed systems. Ozsu and Valduriez (1999) have also determined three main partition-

ing categories; vertical, horizontal, and hybrid.

The following sub-sections discuss in details the benefits and the drawbacks of some vertical, horizontal, and mixed fragmentation schemes in the related research.

3.1 Vertical Fragmentation

The **vertical fragmentation** improves the performance of transactions execution by minimizing the access cost of required fragments, and enhances the system throughput by reducing the number of fragments transferred between transactions. Figure 2 shows how data is fragmented vertically.

Chakaravarthy, Muthuraj and Varadarajian (1994) have defined the vertical fragmentation is the process of projecting a global relation over subsets of attributes called vertical fragments. On the other hand, (Son and Kim 2004) define the vertical fragmentation as a process of generating the fragments, each of which is composed of attributes with high affinity.

Son and Kim (2004) have introduced two different vertical fragmentation mechanisms according to the restriction on the number of fragments finally generated; best-fit vertical fragmentation that minimizes the processing cost of queries without restriction on the number of fragments generated, and n-way vertical fragmentation that generates the specific number of fragments required by the user. However, most vertical fragmentation approaches proposed so far support only best-fit vertical fragmentation (generating an optimal partitioning without regard to the number of fragments finally generated) and consider this problem under a single site environment; there are some limitations to extend them to DDBMS.

Vertical fragmentation method may be more effective and useful if it can support n-way (a certain number of fragments are required to be generated by vertical partitioning) as well as best-fit vertical fragmentation since there are some cases where a certain number of fragments are required to be generated by n-way vertical fragmentation. An adaptable vertical fragmentation method called AVP is proposed that can support both best-fit and n-way vertical fragmentation in a single algorithm. AVP is based on a cost model which can reflect the objective of vertical fragmentation in the DDBMS and composed of two consecutive phases: constructing a partition tree and then selecting a set of fragments as the output of the vertical fragmentation.

On the other hand, Lim and Ng (1997) have proposed different approach for vertical fragmentation of relations that are referenced by rules and allocation method for rules and fragments in a distributed deductive database systems. The advantages of such approach are the maximal locality of query evaluation and minimization of communication cost in DDBMS. However, they confess that their vertical fragmentation approach is inherently more complicated than horizontal fragmentation due to the total number of alternatives that are available in the vertical case. Moreover, there is no information regarding access pattern in horizontal fragmentation is needed as it required by conventional vertical fragmentation methods.

Tamhankar and Ram (1998) have declared that the vertical partitioning comes generally with side effects and requires a detailed analysis for establishing its benefits. It normally requires much more detailed application specific information and usually comes with negative side effects. For example, the record key should be stored with each database fragment to identify each data field in each relation.

Agrawal, Narasayya and Yang (2004) have proposed a vertical fragmentation approach and noted that vertical fragmentation can reduce the amount of data that needs to be accessed to answer the query since many queries access only a small subset of the columns in a table. In this approach, the vertical fragmentation algorithm allows a table to be partitioned into disjoint sets of columns that can reduce the data required for transactions processing and then significantly impact the performance of the distributed relational networking database management systems (DRDBMS).

However, simulating a vertical fragmentation to the query optimizer requires creating regular tables, one for each sub-table in the vertical fragment. Unlike indexes or materialized views, in most of today's commercial DBMS there is no native Data Definition Language (DDL) support for defining vertical fragments of a table.

Besides vertical fragmentation, Agrawal, Narasayya, and Yang (2004) have addressed the necessity of horizontal fragmentation to make database servers easier to manage, and performing the backup and restore processes become much easier. Hence, the database administrators have a confidence to use horizontal fragmentation.

3.2 Horizontal Fragmentation

Horizontal fragmentation improves the system performance by means of processing response time and data availability. Ceri, Navathe, and Wiederhold (1983) have defined the horizontal fragmentation as the process of selecting from global relation subsets of records called horizontal fragments, each of which is identified by a unique predicate. Figure 3 depicts the way that data is fragmented horizontally.

In this context, Tamhankar and Ram (1998) have pointed out that horizontal fragmentation involves forming a subset of the global relation by selecting records based on the value of one or more attributes (known as scan attributes).

Figure 3. Horizontal database fragmentations

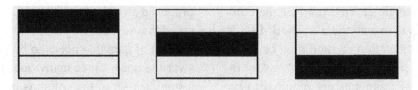

Zhang (1993) believed that the horizontal fragmentation is carried out on each relation based on the predicate affinity and the bond energy algorithm. This approach considers only primary horizontal fragmentation and it is an extendable work of Navathe and Ceri (1984) method which is considered as a divide tool in order to adapt the vertical partition algorithm for horizontal partitioning. Even though the results of this technique may be effective in DDBMS, the derived horizontal fragmentation (multi-level fragmentation) is not considered which might produce more reasonable solutions by eliminating the repeated records in the distributed database fragments.

Alternatively, Borzemski (1996) has presented a generic optimal partitioning algorithm and focus on the partitioning of relational databases for multistage decision making support systems. Although the optimal database partitioning that generates the minimum number of partitions was considered, more irrelevant data was still stored in the selected data blocks.

Tamhankar and Ram (1998) have declared that the benefits of horizontal fragmentation are substantial when fragments can be formed such that queries or update transactions for a relation at a site are largely localized to the fragment at that site. They observed that the existing studies that deal with fragmentation and allocation as separate issues often end up with the optimal solution for either allocation or fragmentation. Instead, a proposed approach is presented where the fragmentation process through the distribution design decision is considered and the horizontal fragmentation takes place at every stage. However, it is very difficult to reach an optimal solution because the problem is very complex.

Khalil, Eid and Khair (1999) have developed horizontal fragmentation algorithm using the vertical partitioning algorithm. The optimal binary horizontal partitioning algorithm can be implemented exactly in the same manner with the vertical partitioning by substituting the predicate usage matrix by the attribute usage matrix. The optimal binary horizontal partitioning produces two fragments. The same algorithm is implemented recursively on each two sub-fragments separately to obtain the desired fragments. However, in case there are a large number of fragments, the optimal binary partitioning can be implemented on each group of the reasonable cuts with a large complexity $O(2^n)$ where n is the number of transactions.

Costa and Lifschitz (2003) have proposed a new type of database fragmentation in a biocomputing context that leads to fragments that have approximately the same number of sequences. This method involves clustering the small sequences in the first fragment, the following smaller sequences in the second fragment and so on, such that sequences of about the same length will be in the same fragment. If an analogy makes for relational model, then the entire database is considered to contain only one relation and the records of this relation are the sequences. The horizontal fragmentation is used to create fragments containing a subset of sequences of the database. These fragments would satisfy entirely the completeness, reconstruction and disjointness rules that ensure correct fragmentation. However, the fragments which do not contain entire sequences cannot be created because this would affect the correctness of algorithm executions.

In their database fragmentation study, Ma, Schewe, and Wang (2007) considered each record in each database relation as a disjoint fragment that is subject for allocation in a distributed database sites. However, large number of database fragments is generated in this method, thus more communication costs are required to transmit and process the fragments. In contrast to this approach, Huang and Chen (2001) considered the whole relation as a fragment, not all the records of the fragment have to be retrieved or updated, and a selectivity matrix that indicates the percentage of accessing a fragment by a transaction is proposed. However, more redundant data are available, and the generated fragments are overlapped.

Therefore, Hababeh, Ramachandran, and Bowring (2008) introduce an efficient horizontal fragmentation method, through which the Fragment Life Cycle (FLC) and the two phase partitioning algorithms; segmentation algorithm and a non-overlapping fragmentation algorithm are proposed. The segmentation algorithm extracts the exact number of segments that match the transactions requirements, while the fragmentation algorithm eliminates the redundant data records in the database segments and generate the minimum number of disjoint fragments that would be allocated to the distributed network sites.

The following proposed algorithm defines the process of creating database segments.

Segmentation Algorithm

Input: $N_{transactions}$: Number of Transactions in the distributed database system
Database relations' records
Output: The set of database segments
Step 1: Set 1 to i
Step 2: Do steps (3 - 5) until i > $N_{transactions}$
Step 3: Segment (i) = Set of records that satisfy transaction(i) definition
Step 4: Add 1 to i
Step 5: Loop
Step 6: Stop.

Each transaction creates a segment and the resulted segments could be full intersected, partial intersected, or not intersected.

The Fragment Life Cycle (FLC) in DDBMS is identified by Hababeh, Ramachandran, and Bowring (2006) in four main processes; data identification, data segmentation, data fragmentation, and data allocation. So, generating data fragments can be accomplished by performing these processes respectively; defining queries, creating segments, and extracting disjoint fragments.

Figure 4 describes the FLC which represents the architecture of the Segments Creator and Fragments Generator (SCFG) methods that will be used for creating database segments, generating fragments, supporting the use of knowledge extraction, and helping to achieve the effective use of small fragments.

As shown in this Figure, The data request is initiated from the distributed database system sites (S1, S2, S3). The requested data defined as queries (Q1, Q2, Q3) which are extracted from the database a set of segments (Sg1, Sg2, Sg3, Sg4). These segments are then processed and disjoint fragments (F1, F2, F3) are generated. The final fragments then are allocated at the sites which request the data. The database query could be associated with more than one relation, in this case the query is divided into number of sub-queries equal to the number of database relations used that query.

The fragmentation technique that can generate database disjoint fragments is based on the following proposed horizontal fragmentation algorithm by which the global database is partitioned into disjoint fragments.

Fragmentation Algorithm

Input: K: Number of the last fragment in the DDBMS
Rmax: Number of database relations in the DDBMS

Figure 4. The fragment life cycle

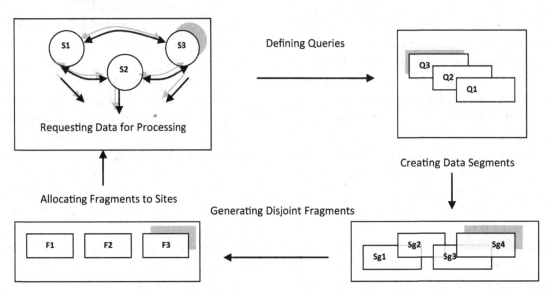

Nmax: Number of segments in each relation of the DDBMS

Output: F: The set of disjoint fragments for each relation in DDBMS

Step 1: Set 0 to K

Step 2: Set 1 to R

Step 3: Do steps (4-28) until R > Rmax

Step 4: Set 1 to I

Step 5: Do steps (6-26) until I > Nmax

Step 6: Set 1 to J

Step 7: Do steps (8-24) until J > Nmax

Step 8: If I ≠ J and ∃ S_i, S_j Є S_R go to step (9) Else Add 1 to J, go to step (18)

Step 9: If S_i ∩ S_j ≠ Ø do steps (10) – (17) Else, Add 1 to J and go to step (17)

Step 10: Add 1 to K

Step 11: Create new fragment F_k = S_i ∩ S_j and add it to F

Step 12: Create new fragment F_{k+1} = S_i - F_k and add it to F

Step 13: Create new fragment F_{k+2} = S_j - F_k and add it to F

Step 14: Delete S_i

Step 15: Delete S_j

Step 16: Set Nmax + 1 to J

Step 17: End IF

Step 18: End IF

Step 19: Loop

Step 20: Add 1 to I

Step 21: Loop

Step 22: Set 1 to I

Step 23 Do steps (24-35) until I > Nmax

Step 24: Set 1 to J

Step 25: Do steps (26-33) until J > Nmax

Step 26: If I ≠ J and ∃ S_i, S_j Є S_R go to step (27) Else Add 1 to J, go to step (33)

Step 27: If S_i ∩ S_j = Ø do steps (28) – (33)

Step 28: Add 1 to K

Step 29: Create new fragment F_k = R_j - U F

Step 30: End IF

Step 31: If F_k ≠ Ø Add F_k to the set of F

Step 32: End IF

Step 33: Loop

Step 34: Add 1 to I

Step 35: Loop

Step 36: Set 1 to I

Step 37: Do steps (38-53) until I > F

Step 38: Set 1 to J

Figure 5. Hybrid database fragmentations

Step 39: Do steps (40-51) until J > F

Step 40: If I ≠ J and ∃ F$_j$, F$_j$ ∈ F$_R$ go to step (41)

Else, Add 1 to J and go to step (50)

Step 41: If F$_i$ ∩ F$_j$ ≠ Ø do steps (42) – (49)

Else, Add 1 to J and go to step (49)

Step 42: Add 1 to K

Step 43: Create new fragment F$_k$ = F$_i$ ∩ F$_j$ and add it to F

Step 44: Create new fragment F$_{k+1}$ = F$_i$ - F$_k$ and add it to F

Step 45: Create new fragment F$_{k+2}$ = F$_j$ - F$_k$ and add it to F

Step 46: Delete F$_i$

Step 47: Delete F$_j$

Step 48: Set F + 1 to J

Step 49: End IF

Step 50: End IF

Step 51: Loop

Step 52: Add 1 to I

Step 53: Loop

Step 54: Add 1 to R

Step 55: Loop

Step 56: Stop

In this fragmentation algorithm, steps 1–21 create new fragments from the intersection between the database segments in each relation. Three new distinguished fragments are recognized; the common records between the intersected pair of segments F$_k$ = S$_i$ ∩ S$_j$, the records in the first segment but not in the common records F$_{k+1}$ = S$_i$ - F$_k$, and the records in the second segment but not in the common records F$_{k+2}$ = S$_j$ - F$_k$. The intersected segments are then deleted and the new fragments are added to the initial list of relation fragments.

In case no more intersected segments in the relation are available and the relation still has non

used (free) records, steps 22-35 illustrates that the fragmentation algorithm creates new fragments for the free records; F$_k$ = R$_j$ - U F, and adds it to the initial list of relation fragments.

Steps 36-53 in this algorithm describe the process of generating the final disjoint fragments for the current relation. In this process, new fragments are created from the intersection between the database initial fragments in each relation. Three new distinguished fragments are recognized; the common records between the intersected pair of fragments F$_k$ = F$_i$ ∩ F$_j$, the records in the first fragment but not in the common records F$_{k+1}$ = F$_i$ - F$_k$, and the records in the second fragment but not in the common records F$_{k+2}$ = F$_j$ - F$_k$. The intersected fragments are then deleted and the new disjoint fragments are added to the final list of relation disjoint fragments. The procedures of this fragmentation algorithm are then repeated for each database relation as described in steps 54 – 56.

In the fragmentation algorithm, all transactions are processed, redundant data records are eliminated, and disjoint fragments are achieved. Thus, the applications speed and efficiency are improved by getting the minimum number of fragments to be accessed, processed, and allocated at the DDBMS network sites.

3.3 Hybrid Fragmentation

In real world applications, horizontal or vertical fragmentation of a database will not be sufficient to satisfy the requirements of the user applications that access groups of data which are fragmented in both horizontally and vertically. In this case, a type of vertical fragmentation may be followed by a horizontal one, or vice versa, this alternative is called **hybrid** or "mixed" fragmentation which would be possible solution to solve the problem (Ozsu and Valduriez 1991). Figure 5 illustrates the way data is fragmented vertically and horizontally (hybrid).

Navathe, Karlapalem and Ra (1995) have presented an algorithm for generating a mixed fragmentation scheme (horizontal and vertical) for the initial DDBMS design phase. They form a grid on a relation, which suggests all possible ways that the global relation may be partitioned in a DDBMS. A set of grid cells are generated when applying horizontal and vertical fragmentation, each grid cell belongs to exactly one horizontal and exactly one vertical fragment. Merging these grid cells to form mixed fragments helps to reduce the number of transactions through data allocation phase. However, this algorithm can generate an overlapping set of fragments, that is, a set of mixed fragments wherein each grid cell may belong to one or more mixed fragments. In this step the non-overlapping fragments are generated by selecting the alternative that requires the least number of disk I/O accesses to process all the transactions. Thus, as the algorithm is a greedy, its optimality cannot be guaranteed due to the intractability behaviour. Moreover, this algorithm needs to incorporate performance evaluation methods for merging grid cells, and to articulate the architecture and functions that a database server should have.

In contrast, Agrawal, Narasayya, and Yang (2004) have introduced an integrated vertical and horizontal partitioning method for physical database design. They focus on the problem of how to merge a pair of physical design structures in the presence of vertical and horizontal partitioning which would be useful in any scheme that generates a set of merged structures, each of which satisfies the following criteria. First, the merged structure should be usable in answering all queries where each parent structure was used. Second, the cost of answering queries using the merged structures

should not be much higher than the cost of answering queries using the parent structures. However, the problem of merging becomes more complex when vertical and horizontal partitioning is considered. Moreover, their work focuses on database fragmentation over a single network site.

Due to the intractable nature of this type of fragmentation in DRDBMS, few researches have covered the problem of mixed fragmentation.

4. CLUSTERING SITES

Clustering is the process of grouping sites on the basis of similar measurements. It is a useful and challenging problem in the field of distributed database; machine learning, pattern recognition, and knowledge discovery applications like object image segmentation and information retrieval Kumar, et. al (2007).

Grid and cluster technologies have become part of mainstream computing. While the availability of grid and cluster technologies has brought considerable capabilities to users, the increased administration efforts and programming complexity required by these technologies have significantly reduced their ease of use. Today's scientists, engineers and industry experts rely on the ability to rapidly process complex data sets, and compute intensive problems. For most organizations, the challenge is to make the powerful computational resources and capacity of grid and cluster computing available to their users.

Jain, Murty and Flynn (1999) have categorized clustering algorithms using a set of different criteria, these admissibility criteria are based on:

- The manner in which clusters are formed.
- The structure of the data.
- Sensitivity of the clustering technique to changes that do not affect the structure of the data.

Kumar, et al (2007) have distinguished two main clustering categories; hierarchical and partitional. Hierarchical techniques create hierarchical decomposition of the database and can be either agglomerative or divisitive. The agglomerative technique starts with each element as a separate cluster and merges them into large clusters according to the distance between them until having all the elements in one cluster or certain termination criteria is satisfied. However, Jain, Murty, and Flynn (1999) noted that finding an efficient termination condition for the merging or division process is still an open research problem. The divisitive technique starts with one cluster having all elements together and splits them into small clusters based on the distance between them.

Kumar, et al (2007) added that the partitional techniques on contrast generate a partition of a database with a certain number of elements into a specific number of clusters and require some domain knowledge to specify the number of clusters, which is not available for many applications. Generally, partitional techniques are either parametric (reconstructive and generative) or non-parametric, parametric techniques try to solve an optimization problem so as to satisfy the optimality criterion imposed by the model, which often means minimizing the cost function.

However, Fraley and Raftery (1998) articulated that the reconstructive partition techniques attempt to decompose data set into a set of non-overlapping clusters as well as determine an integer number of partitions that optimize a certain criterion function. The criterion function may emphasize data structure and its optimization which is an iterative procedure that generates data clusters.

Lingras and West (2004) have different style for classifying clusters according to their nature; clusters are considered to be hard or soft. In conventional clustering, objects that are similar are allocated to the same cluster while objects that differ significantly are put in different clusters. These clusters are disjoint and are called hard clusters. In soft clustering an object may be a member of two or more clusters. On the other hand, Lingras and Yao (2002) noted that the traditional clustering methods such as k-means approach generate groups describing the members of each cluster whereas clustering techniques based on rough set theory generate clusters describing the main characteristics of each cluster. These concepts provide interpretations of different web page visit sessions and used to describe potentially new groups of web users.

Kumar, et al (2007) have proposed a hierarchical clustering algorithm that uses similarity upper approximation derived from a tolerance (similarity) relation and based on rough set theory that does not require any prior information about the data. The presented approach results in rough clusters wherein an object is a member of more than one cluster. Rough clustering can help researchers to discover multiple needs and interests in a session by looking at the multiple clusters which a session belongs to. However, in order to carry out rough clustering, two additional requirements, namely, an ordered value set of each attribute and a distance measure for clustering need to be specified Voges, Pope, and Brown (2002).

Quantifying the structural network properties can be measured by clustering coefficients. Fronczak, et al (2002) have proposed higher order clustering coefficients defined as probabilities that determines the shortest distance between any two nearest neighbours of a certain node when neglecting all paths crossing this node. The outcomes of this method declare that the average shortest distance in the node's neighbourhood is smaller than the whole network distances and the remainder depends only on the network parameter m. However, independent constant values as well as natural logarithm function are used in the shortest distance approximation function to determine the clustering mechanism which results in generating small number of clusters.

Measuring distances between data points is considered a major role for many clustering approaches. Halkidi, Batistakis, and Vazirgiannis (2001) have declared that many clustering techniques use distance measure to compute distance between the data points and cluster centres. Domain Knowledge is used to guide the formulation of a suitable distance measure of each particular application. If the components of the data points are all in the same physical devices, then Euclidean distance metric function for example, could be successfully sufficient to group similar data points.

There are many researches in the literature which use distance measure functions in their clustering techniques; Bradley, Managasarian, and Street (1997), and Chen, Xi, and Zhang (1998) have introduced the K-Means technique as an initial and efficient process to build an easy clustering approaches and implement image processing applications. However, K-Means uses a fixed number of clusters less than the number of data points to achieve reasonable convergence, there is no general solution to find the optimal number of clusters for any given dataset. In the meanwhile a simple approach is used to compare the number of clusters generated from different runs and the best result is chosen according to a certain criterion. Moreover, in case the number of data points are equal to the number of clusters where the number of clusters goes to N and each data point forms its own cluster, then the performance index would go to zero, so it would not be a realistic solution Bhatia and Deogun (1998).

Semeczko (1997) has introduced clustering technique based on the search diameter and increment factor. In this research, the clustering method starts with search diameter 1 and multiplies it by increment factor of 2 in iteration process. In this case, the number of clusters that could be generated is 2, 4, 8, 16, …, or $(2)^n$, so it is increasing in an exponential trend. However, this will generate large number of clusters when the number of sites becomes very large, and lead to unbalance distribution of sites into clusters when some clusters have very few sites and others have many.

A majority of the approaches and algorithms proposed in the literature cannot handle large data sets. Implementations of conceptual clustering optimize some criterion functions and are typically computationally expensive Jain, Murty, and Flynn (1999).

Unlike other current clustering methods that have a predefined number of clusters, Hababeh, Ramachandran, and Bowring (2008) introduce an efficient clustering method that distributes the sites over the clusters, determines, and generates the least number of clusters required for the distributed database network system. This clustering method applies the procedures of the clustering algorithm which assigns all sites on the DDBMS network to a small number of generated clusters that would be used for database fragments allocation in further steps. The clustering algorithm categorizes the distributed database network sites according to a Clustering Decision Value CDV that determines whether or not a site can be grouped in a specific cluster. Basically, the clustering decision value CDV is based on two factors; the communication cost between the sites of the DDBMS CC(Si,Sj), and the communication cost range CCR (ms/byte) that the site should match to be grouped in a specific cluster. In order to set up an efficient clustering method, the following assumptions have to be considered:

- Each site should be included in only one cluster
- The final distribution of the network sites will be represented by the cluster that satisfies the least average communication cost between the sites.

Based on the assumptions and parameters described above, the following clustering algorithm is defined to group the distributed database network sites into set of clusters.

Clustering Algorithm

Input:
$CC(S_i,S_j)$: Matrix of communication cost between sites
CCR: Communication Cost Range
NS: Number of sites in the DDBMS network
Output:CSM: Clusters Set Matrix
Step 1: Set 1 to i
Step 2: Do steps (3-12) until i > NS
Step 3: Set 1 to j
Set 0 to k
Set 0 to Sum
Set 0 to Average
Set 0 to clusters matrix CM
Step 4: Do steps (5-10) until j > NS
Step 5: If $i \neq j$ AND $CC(S_i,S_j)$ <= CCR, go to step (6)
Else, go to step (7)
Step 6: Set 1 to the $CM(S_i,S_j)$ and $CM(S_j,S_i)$ in the clusters matrix
Add $CC(S_i,S_j)$ to sum
Add 1 to k
Go to step 8
Step 7: Set 0 to the $CM(S_i,S_j)$ and $CM(S_j,S_i)$ in the clusters matrix
Step 8: End IF
Step 9: Add 1 to j
Step 10: Loop
Step 11: Average = Sum / k
Average(i) = Average
Add 1 to i
Step 12: Loop
Step 13: Set 1 to m
Step 14: Do steps (15-36) until m > NS
Step 15: Set 1 to q
Set 0 to Minaverage
Set 0 to Minrow
Step 16: Do steps (17-20) until q > NS or Minaverage > 0
Step 17: If Average(q) > 0 Then
Minaverage = Average(q)
Else
Go to Step 18

Step 18: End If
Step 19: Add 1 to q
Step 20: Loop
Step 21: If Minaverage = 0 Then
Set site number to a new cluster
Else
Go to Step 22
Step 22: End If
Step 23: Set 1 to p
Step 24: Do steps (25-28) until p > NS
Step 25: If Average(p) > 0 AND Average(p) < Minaverage Then
Minaverage = Average(p)
Minrow = p
Step 26: End IF
Step 27: Add 1 to p
Step 28: Loop
Step 29: Set 1 to a
Step 30: Do steps (31-34) until a > NS
Step 31: If $CM(S_{minrow},S_a)$ = 1 Then
Set 1 to $CSM(S_{minrow},S_a)$
$CM(S_{minrow},S_a)$ = 0
Step 32: End IF
Step 33: Add 1 to a
Step 34: Loop
Step 35: Add 1 to m
Step 36: Loop
Step 37: Stop

In this clustering algorithm, steps 1–12 determine the sites that match the CCR in order to group them initially in one separate cluster and an average communication cost is computed for each group.

Steps 13-28 in this algorithm describe the process of computing the minimum value of the generated average communication costs computed in steps 1-12 so as to determine the sites that should be grouped in each cluster according to the least average communication costs.

The rest of the algorithm; steps 29-37, create the cluster set matrix that decide which site(s) should be grouped in which cluster according to the computations done in the further steps of this algorithm.

The clusters average communication costs for each cluster can be used to represent the communication cost value for all sites in each cluster that is required for fragments allocation and replication in further processing phase.

5. DATA ALLOCATION AND REPLICATION

In the DDBMS environment, the programs are executed where the data resides, thus data placement is a critical performance issue and must be done to maximize system performance Ozsu and Valduriez (1991).

Data allocation is the way for distributing database fragments over different network sites so as to minimize the cost of data accessed and transferred for executing a set of transactions Park and Baik (1997).

Another point of view regarding the definition of data allocation; Wiesmann, et. al (2000) defined the database replication as a collection of databases that store copies of the same data items. As the replication in database systems is done mainly for performance reasons, the objective is to access data locally in order to improve response times and eliminate the overhead of communicating with remote sites. This is usually possible when an operation only reads the data, while write operations require some form of coordination among the replicas.

Khalil, Eid and Khair (1999) have declared that data allocation becomes a necessity to improve data availability and system reliability during site failure and network partitioning. Allocation could be achieved in a way that the cost transfer function is minimized with a general reduction of the execution time. This essential improvement brings with it its own problems, mainly inconsistency among replicas of the same objects (fragments).

Apers (1988) has compared between centralized data allocation and decentralized (distributed) data allocation models. In the centralized

data allocation, one advantage is considered that the overall cost of the allocation might be lower compared to the decentralized approach. The reason is that the whole processing schedules graph is considered. However, the disadvantages of centralized model are figured out; the allocation of all the data is considered at the same time and either one database administrator or one central database management system is allowed to change the existing allocation, and determining and actually implementing a new allocation is expensive because the allocation of all fragments have to be reconsidered again, and because of interaction between fragments many more of them may have to be reallocated then accessed by the new queries.

On the other hand, the distributed data allocation model is distinguished by the following advantages over the centralized data allocation:

- The data is owned by different database administrators or the distributed database is a collection of databases owned by different parties.
- The DBMS of the sites should, in cooperation with each other, try to determine an optimal allocation of the data required by the users of their own sites.
- The partition of the general data allocation problem into a number of smaller problems probably can be solved more easily.
- The data allocation can change more or less continuously through time. If a group of users starts using the database or changes its access pattern, their database administrator simply determines a new allocation for them without changing other user's allocations.

However, in this model, the overall cost of the allocation might be higher compared to the centralized approach. The reason is that a collection of smaller processing schedules graphs are considered.

Various investigations of the data allocation problem have been proposed for DDBMS. The objective in the data allocation problem is to find the number of database copies and their location in a way that minimizes the total operational cost. However, finding an optimal fragment allocation is a NP-complete problem because given n fragments and m sites, there will be $(2^m - 1)^n$ different combinations Huang and Chen (2001).

Therefore, near-optimal heuristic allocation algorithms in the context of file allocation, document allocation, and fragment allocation have been introduced Semeczko (1997). Moreover, in solving these optimization problems there has always been a trade-off between the optimality of the solution and the complexity of the problem being solved.

Ishfaq et al (2002) have argued that the optimal data allocation problem is intractable because of the mutual interdependence between data allocation and query optimization techniques, and thus requires developing efficient heuristic data allocation algorithms that are fast and capable of generating high speed near optimal solutions.

Chu (1969) was probably the first pioneer work on the file allocation problem. In this work and in the following work Chu (1973), the optimization goal is to minimize total transmission cost according to available secondary storage at each site and to maximize the expected retrieval time. The result is a zero one programming problem with nonlinear constraints, which can be solved in standard linear integer programming techniques. However, the proposed approaches are simple methods that allow only non redundant file allocation.

The model proposed by Ceri, Navathe, and Wiederhold (1983) considered the file allocation problem for distributed database applications with a simple model for query execution taking into account the interdependencies access between multiple fragments. This work is applied on simple local area network where all sites are linked with the same communication cost, and can be shown to result in optimal solutions. However, a constant ratio has been used to have updates being more expensive than queries. This method generates optimal solution for simple networks where the communication costs between the sites are the same, but for complex networks, the method fails to be optimal because the communication costs become another factor in the optimization cost function.

The solutions for the file allocation problem do not characterize solutions to the allocation problem in a DDBMS for the following reasons as defined by Apers (1988):

- The objects to be allocated are not known prior to allocation.
- The relations that describe logical relationships between data are not suited as units of allocation because users at different sites might be interested in different fragments of a relation.
- The way the data are accessed is far more complex.
- In the file allocation problem the only transmissions required to combine data from different files are transmissions from sites containing files to the result site, where the result is computed.
- In current research on distributed query processing we observe that to process a query, data transmissions between sites where fragments are allocated are also needed. This means that the fragments cannot be allocated independently.

Still in the allocation context, the work of Semeczko (1997) argue that using file allocation approach is inadequate for DDBMS due to the simple processing strategies not being realistic and not matching the complexity of the use of database operations. That is, as database transactions use more than one fragment at a time, allocation of a fragment cannot be handled in isolation of other fragment allocations.

In their multiprocessor document allocation problem (MDAP), Frieder and Siegelmann (1997) suggested an allocation algorithm that allocates a number of distinct documents agglomerated into multiple clusters to a number of homogeneous processors. They proposed a simple genetic algorithm to reduce the MDAP which is NP-complete problem to the binary quadratic assignment problem and solve it heuristically. However, Ishfaq et al (2002) noted that the drawback of the document allocation problems do not take into consideration the query structures of accessing the documents which play a vital role in DDBMS allocation schemes.

On the other hand, Semeczko (1997) extends the work in Ceri, Navathe, and Wiederhold (1983) and presents a redundant fragment allocation method that uses the concept of benefit functions in complex networks. The relationship between the weighted variance and the variation in total costs was explored a correlation found. The weighted variance is used as an indicator of the optimality of the solution. However, in this work it is assumed that the costs of transactions retrieval and update are to be the same. In the worst case the number of clusters, including the single-site clusters, is equal to $2n - 1$ where n is the number of initial sites. This method assumes that at least one site within each cluster will have a copy of the fragment.

Mukkamala and Bruell (1990) have evaluated two performance issues in partially replicated DDBMS, the average number of nodes accessed and the average number of data items accessed per node by a transaction. They figure out three performance measures of interest to the distributed database designers; the average transaction response time, the transaction reliability, and the system cost (communication, storage, etc.). The transaction response time may be expressed in terms of the number of messages exchanged between the coordinating and participating nodes and the number of data items accessed at each of the participating nodes. When a high speed networks are considered, where local processing costs dominate the communication, estimating the

average number of data items accessed per node is beneficial for transaction cost estimations and to make early design decisions. A database designer may like to determine the impact of the number of copies of data items on transaction performance. However, they consider an arbitrary grouping of data items, and also an arbitrary distribution of groups, so it is not necessary for all nodes to have the same number of data items, thus the average statistics derived for transactions at one node may not be valid at other nodes. Accordingly, the analysis for transactions may need to be repeated at every node in the database.

On the other hand, Apers (1988) introduces a model to compute the cost of a completely or partially specified allocation for various cost functions. A method for determining the unit of allocation by means of splitting a relation in the conceptual schema based on the queries and updates is presented. A framework was discussed for managing allocations in a DDBMS consisting of one database or a collection of already existing databases. In addition, threshold values are assumed regarding the minimum and maximum number of records per fragment and given as system parameters. So the fragments obtained for minimizing total transmission cost are horizontally split further based on the threshold values. The total transmission cost of an allocation by total data allocation algorithm using dynamic schedules is not necessarily less than when using static schedules, the reason is that virtual sites are united based on transmissions that also depend on the rest of the allocation. The integration of query processing and data allocation is also considered in Apers (1980, 1981, 1982). However, the total data allocation algorithm is greedy and does not necessarily obtain a completely specified allocation with the absolute minimum total transmission cost because the data fragmentation and data allocation techniques are addressed together, and then the algorithms computations become too complex.

Tamhankar and Ram (1998) have developed a comprehensive method for fragmentation and distribution of data across multiple sites such that design objectives in terms of response time and availability for transactions, and constraints on storage space are adequately addressed. However, data fragmentation and data allocation are considered in the same algorithm, where the horizontal fragmentation takes place at every stage of the distribution model. Since the fragmentation and allocation mechanisms are addressed together, and the fragmentation mechanism is considered to be an output of the allocation mechanism, the algorithm computations become more complex, the solution become non-optimal, and the applicability of these mechanisms become more limited especially when allocation is generated for ready fragments.

Data fragmentation and data allocation are considered as a single problem as in Apers (1988) and Tamhankar and Ram (1998), but in other works dealt as two separate issues. Khalil, Eid, and Khair (1999) have presented an approach where a horizontal fragmentation algorithm and a replication protocol are proposed to increase the availability and reliability for a DDBMS. They present an enhancement over the Replica Control Protocol, which is a conjunction of three parts; setting the work space area and quorums, applying the adaptive algorithm and replicating a matrix log. However, all fragments needed by the transaction Ti issued from a site (e.g. S1) must be located for example, in group of 8 sites. This group of sites represents the view of S1, in a manner that the most frequently used object is located at the view initiator (e.g. S1) to minimize the access, transfer and communication cost. Moreover, the criteria of grouping sites as views do not assure that the communication cost is minimized.

Some other interesting results are proposed by Huang and Chen (2001) where a comprehensive model is presented that reflects transaction behaviour in DDBMS. They developed two heuristic algorithms to find a near-optimal allocation such that the total communication cost is minimized. However, the fragment is considered to represent

the whole relation records and a constant fragment selectivity percentage is assumed for transactions retrieval and update processing. Thus, much data redundancy occurs through allocation process, more time processing is consumed. An Ethernet-based local area network (LAN) is used to simulate transaction behaviour on a WAN.

The literature contains other works that evaluate allocation algorithms in terms of response time. Ishfaq et. al (2002) developed a uniform framework for modelling data allocation problem, and facilitates generic solution to this problem. They present four different algorithms; each is based on different heuristics, and they evaluate their results by comparing them against the optimal solution. In this approach, no single algorithm outperforms all others in terms query response time and algorithm running time, instead, a diverse range of solutions are available for the problem of data allocation. However, in this approach they consider only non-redundant data allocation (i.e., each fragment is allocated to exactly one site), but neither full nor partial fragment replication over the network sites is considered, and thus, the data availability will be reduced, the system reliability will be decreased, and the risk of fault tolerant in case of system failure will be increased.

Data replication of course enlarges the cost of data storing, but owing to this way of data organization one can obtain more rapid and effective access to data and greater data safety than in the case when data are stored on one server only. Danilowicz and Nguyen (2003) addressed the important of redundant (replicated) data in DDBMS and presents methods for solving problems concerns maintenance of data semantic consistency, it means that the data should be semantically identical on all servers at any time. However, determining consensus of inconsistent data does not warrant faithful reproduction of correct data. The authors assume that the basis for consensus determining are versions (some of them may differ from each other) of replicated data, where it is not possible to recreate the data by returning neither to their resources nor to renewing the last performed operations on them.

Costa and Lifschitz (2003) have proposed a replicated allocation approach where the database file is fully copied to all participating nodes through the master node. This approach distributes the sequences through fragments with a round-robin method for sequence input set already ordered by size, where the number of sequences is about the same and number of characters at each fragment is similar. However, for this replicated schema there is no performance gain when moving up the number of nodes because of the implicit characteristics of this approach. When a non-previously determined number of input sequences are present, the replication model may not be the best solution and the other fragmentation strategies have to be considered.

Wiesmann, et al (2000) categorised database replication protocols using two parameters; one is when update propagation takes place, and the second is who can perform updates. Eager and lazy update schemes for the first parameter and update everywhere scheme for the second parameter are discussed. In eager, the user does not receive the commit notification until sufficient copies in the system have been updated, and this approach provides consistency in a straight forward way. Lazy schemes, on the other hand, update a local copy commit and only some time after the commit, the propagation of the changes takes place, this allows a wide variety of optimisations. In the second parameter, the primary copy approach requires all updates to be performed first at one copy (the primary or master copy) and then at the other copies, this will simplify replica control. The update everywhere approach allows any copy to be updated, thereby speeding up access. However, Eager scheme is expensive in terms of message overhead and response time, and since copies are allowed to diverge in Lazy scheme, inconsistencies might occur. The update everywhere scheme leads to a potential bottleneck and makes coordination more complex.

Few researchers have investigated the effect of partial replication in data allocation on DDBMS performance. Chen (2001) presents an incremental growth framework to address incremental expansion of DDBMS. This framework introduces two heuristic algorithms for data reallocation; partial reallocation and full reallocation. The incremental growth framework is invoked when system performance is below an acceptable threshold. To return to an acceptable state, new servers are introduced incrementally, one at a time, into the DDBMS. With the introduction of each new server, a new data reallocation for the system is computed. This process is iteratively executed until an acceptable performance is achieved or the number of servers equals the number of relations in the DDBMS. The partial and full reallocation algorithms have been used to reduce the problem of search space, hence, the cost of testing relation server combinations. Both algorithms require as input: the current data allocation, the relations, and the queries in the DDBMS. The relational data model is used to describe the data and query processing on the data. Only simple queries are considered and assumed to be independent and solved independently. However, the partial reallocation algorithm in this approach does not guarantee the optimum solution and in some cases it is more cost effective than either full reallocation or exhaustive search. On the other hand, the full reallocation algorithm does not reiterate with two servers, it works for more than two servers.

More recently researches addressed the fragment allocation problem in DDBMS. Menon (2005) presented an integer programming formulations for the non-redundant version of the fragment allocation problem. This formulation is extended to address problems which have both storage and processing capacity constraints. In this method, the constraints essentially state that there has been exactly one copy of a fragment across all sites which increase the risk of data inconsistency and unavailability in case of any site failure. However, the fragment size is not addressed while the storage capacity constraint is one of the major objectives of this approach. In addition to this, the transactions retrieval and update frequencies are not considered in the computations of fragments allocation which affects the distribution of fragments over the sites. Moreover, this research is limited by the fact that none of the approaches presented have been implemented and tested on a real DDBMS.

On the other hand, Ma, Schewe, and Wang (2007) distinguished between fragment allocation and fragment replication. Fragment allocation addresses the assignment of network node(s) to each fragment, while fragment replication deals with the decision whether a fragment is allocated to exactly one node or several ones and the corresponding implications for read and write operations. They present a heuristic algorithm in a DOODBMS for allocating fragments according to the needs of the fragments at each site. Each of the fragments should be allocated to the sites that need them the most, in which way the total query costs are minimal. However, the complexity of this allocation algorithm is intractable since it compares costs for all possible allocations of these fragments.

Therefore, a recent method by Hababeh, Ramachandran, and Bowring (2007) is proposed for fragment allocation and replication over the clusters and their sites in the DDBMS. The allocation and replication processes take place for each fragment at each cluster/site which has transactions using this fragment and can be summarized in the following allocation qualitative and quantitative procedures that performed for each fragment at both clusters and sites levels. Initially, all fragments are subject for allocating to all clusters having transactions using these fragments at their sites. If the fragment shows positive allocation decision value (i.e. allocation benefit greater than or equal to zero is achieved) for a specific cluster, then the fragment is subject for allocating at each site in this cluster, otherwise the fragment is not allocated (cancelled) from

this cluster. This step is repeated for each cluster in the DDBMS. As a result of the previous step, the fragment that shows positive allocation decision value at any cluster is a candidate for allocating at all sites of this cluster. If the fragment shows positive allocation decision value at a site of cluster that already shows positive allocation decision value, then the fragment is allocated at this site, otherwise, the fragment is not allocated to this site. This step is repeated for each site at this cluster.

To ensure the data consistency and availability in the DDBMS, each fragment should be allocated to at least one cluster and one site. In case a fragment shows negative allocation decision value at all clusters, then the fragment is allocated to the cluster that holds the least average communication cost and then to the site that has the least communication cost in this cluster.

To better understand the fragment allocation procedures that determine the fragment allocation status at each cluster in the DDBMS, Figure 6 describes the conceptual structure of the fragment allocation and replication method.

The descriptions of the processes in the previous figure are listed below:

1. Start
2. Next Fragment
3. Required by any transaction?
4. Cancel allocation
5. Considered for allocation at clusters
6. Positive allocation status?
7. Cancel allocation from the cluster
8. Last cluster?
9. Compute allocation for next cluster
10. Positive allocation status?
11. Allocate to this cluster
12. Allocate to cluster of the least average communication cost
13. Consider for allocation at first site of this cluster
14. Positive allocation status?
15. Allocate to this site

Figure 6. The fragment allocation and replication conceptual structure

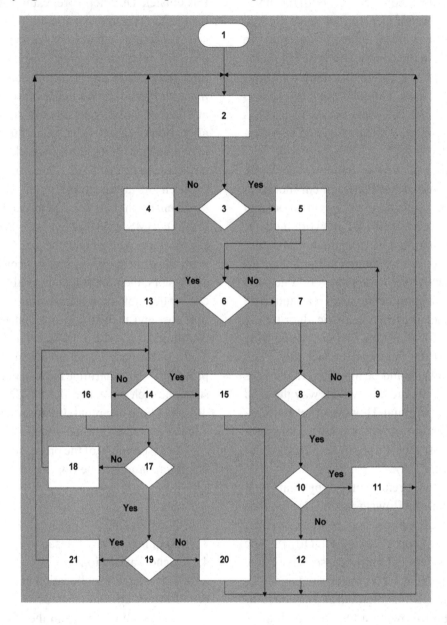

16. Cancel allocation from the site
17. Last site in the cluster?
18. Compute allocation for the next site in the cluster
19. Positive allocation status?
20. Allocate to the site of the least communication cost
21. Allocate to this site

In this figure, the fragment is checked against query processing, if any transaction requests this fragment at any cluster, then the fragment is considered for allocation at this cluster. The fragment is allocated at the cluster if the allocation computations generate positive allocation decision value, then the fragment is considered for allocation at all sites in this cluster and allocated to those who show positive allocation decision value. The frag-

Figure 7. The quality of service evaluation metrics

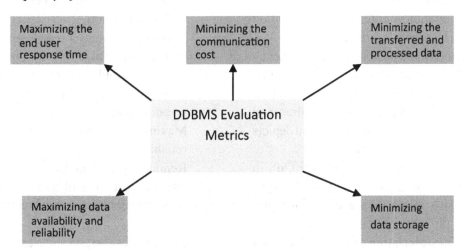

ment allocation procedures are also repeated for all clusters in the DDBMS.

6. QUERY PROCESSING

The query processing (**optimization**) is defined by Desai (1990) as the procedure of selecting the best plan or methodology to be used in responding to a database request. The plan is then executed to generate a response. The component of the DBMS responsible for generating this methodology is called a query processor.

Query processing is a critical performance issue and has received considerable attention in the context of both centralized and DDBMS Ozsu and Valduriez (1999). However, the query processing problem is much more difficult in distributed environments than in centralized one, because a larger number of parameters affect the performance of distributed queries.

On the other hand, Ishfaq et. al (2002) have pointed that the optimal data allocation is highly dependent on the query execution method used by a DDBMS. In addition, Apers (1988) has noted that without knowing anything about the final allocation of the fragments, the processing schedule of the query and its cost cannot be computed.

In addition, Ishfaq, et al (2002) have declared that the query execution cost is determined by the query location and the amount of data required. The more data required the more execution cost, and the more data locality the less execution time.

Because query processing is out of scope of this chapter, more details about this topic can be found in Freytag, Maier and Vossen (1994).

7. DDBMS METRICS AND QUALITY OF SERVICE

Significant efforts have been made in the last few years in improving the quality of service QoS in DDBMS which is considered to be an important component in almost all applications solutions and plays a key role in the DDBMS ability to provide comprehensive data distribution capability.

In this context, QoS procedures for selecting, deploying, and evaluating methods of database fragmentation, clustering network sites, and fragment allocation, are getting more necessary. Moreover, the database network system load has to be considered since it affects the overall DDBMS performance.

To meet this need, a software tool has been developed by Hababeh, Ramachandran, and

Bowring (2005) to evaluate the QoS of the proposed fragmentation, clustering and allocation techniques in DDBMS described in sections 3, 4, and 5 respectively and demonstrate its efficiency by means of tabular and graphical representation. Besides, a database network simulation model has been developed by Hababeh, Ramachandran, and Bowring (2007B) to evaluate the QoS and depicts the network system workload.

The optimality metrics adopted for QoS in DDBMS are maximizing the system throughput at each site on the database network, and minimizing the cost of data transferred and processed. The description of the software tool which is designed to test the proposed techniques of fragmentation, clustering, and allocation will be discussed throughout next chapter to show the applicability and usefulness of these techniques that might help in upgrading the system QoS.

8. EVALUATING DDBMS QUALITY OF SERVICE

The evaluation of the DDBMS QoS can be expressed by the following proposed metrics that might maximize the system throughput. Figure 7 depicts the set of metrics that affects the performance of DDBMS Quality of Service.

The metrics that will be used to evaluate the QoS of DDBMS tool are described as follows:

- Minimizing the transferred and processed data:
  This can be accomplished by database fragmentation.
- Minimizing data storage:
  Data allocation technique determines the data location where it is most used in the DDBMS.
- Minimizing the communication cost:
  Grouping DDBMS network sites into clusters helps to reduce the communication costs

between sites and then speeds up the process of data allocation.
- Maximizing the user response time:
  Placing data where it is most beneficial for the DDBMS aids to increase parallel transactions processing and thus increase the user response time.
- Maximizing data availability and reliability:
  Replicating data at the DDBMS network sites where it is useful assists to increase the system fault tolerant and data recovery.

Under such evaluation metrics, and to study the behaviour of the DDBMS over the network according to the proposed methods of fragmentation, clustering, and allocation described in sections 3, 4, and 5 respectively, a software tool and a simulation model will be discussed in following chapter to figure out the QoS effect on the performance of the database network system.

9. FUTURE TRENDS

In the future, an adaptive method to incorporate security constraints during the transmission of database fragments and processing of transactions retrieval and update operations will have to be considered in designing and developing distributed database management systems.

Investigating the effect of using wireless network topology on the user's response time in the distributed database management system in order to exceed the wire network limitations and increase the system reliability will be considered in the future studies of this research.

10. CONCLUSION

The developments in database systems are not over, where the applications that will have to be handled in the future are much more complex.

There are many researches available in the literature concerned generally with DBMS, or more specifically with DDBMS. Some approaches are in DRDBMS context and emphases specific problems like fragmentation, clustering or allocation. Few methods considered both problems of fragmentation and allocation or clustering and allocation together. It is still an open problem in the distributed database research area, to determine the optimal solution for these issues.

However, integrating database fragmentation, sites clustering and fragment allocation issues together and depicts their performance of the DRDBMS has not yet been studied carefully by the current approaches in the literature.

Therefore, contributions to this research field can be done in designing an integrated tool that introduces a near optimal solution to the open problems in DRDBMS through efficient techniques in the areas of database fragmentation, clustering sites and fragment allocation, as well as developing a simulation test bed which encompasses the details of these techniques and presents the performance improvements that can be achieved by the proposed QoS parameters.

REFERENCES

Agrawal, S., Narasayya, V., & Yang, B. (2004). Integrating Vertical and Horizontal Partitioning into Automated Physical Database Design. *SIG-MOD 2004,* Paris, France (pp. 359-370). New York: ACM.

Apers, P. (1988). Data Allocation in Distributed Database Systems. *ACM Transactions on Database Systems, 13*(3), 263–304. doi:10.1145/44498.45063

Bhatia, S., & Deogun, J. (1998). Conceptual Clustering in Information Retrieval. *IEEE Transactions on System, Man, Cybernetics, part B . Cybernetics., 28*(3), 427–436.

Borzemski, L. (1996). Optimal Partitioning of a Distributed Relational Database for Multistage Decision-Making Support systems. *Cybernetics and Systems Research, 2*(13), 809–814.

Bradley, P., Managasarian, O., & Street, W. (1997). Clustering via Concave Minimization. *Advances in Neural Information Processing Systems, 9,* 368–374.

Ceri, S., Navathe, S., & Wiederhold, G. (1983). Distribution Design of Logical Database Schemas. *IEEE Transactions on Software Engineering, 9*(4), 487–504. doi:10.1109/TSE.1983.234957

Chakravarthy, S., Muthuraj, J., Varadarajian, R., & Navathe, S. (1994). An Objective Function for Vertically Partitioned Relations in Distributed Database and Its Analysis. *Distributed and Parallel Databases, 2,* 183–207. doi:10.1007/BF01267326

Chen, A. (2001). Incremental Data Allocation and Reallocation in Distributed Database Systems. *Journal of Database Management, 12*(1), 35–45.

Chen, E. (n.d.). *Distributed DBMS Concepts and Design.* Retrieved November 9th, 2007 from: http://www.cs.sjsu.edu/~lee/cs157b/fall2003/Edward_Chen_Chapter%2022.ppt

Chen, J., Xi, Y., & Zhang, Z. (1998). A Clustering Algorithm for Fuzzy Model Identification. *Fuzzy Sets and Systems, 98,* 319–329. doi:10.1016/S0165-0114(96)00384-3

Chu, W. (1969). Optimal file allocation in a multiple-computer information system. *IEEE Transactions on Computers, 18,* 885–889. doi:10.1109/T-C.1969.222542

Chu, W. (1973). Optimal file allocation in a computer network. In N. Abramson & F. F. Kuo, (Eds.), *Computer Communication Networks* (pp. 83-94). Englewood Cliffs, NJ: Prentice-Hall.

Connolly, T., & Begg, C. (2004). *Database Systems:A Practical Approach to Design, Implementation and Management* (4th ed.). Reading, MA: Addison-Wesley.

Costa, R., & Lifschitz, S. (2003). Database Allocation Strategies for Parallel BLAST Evaluation on Clusters. *Distributed and Parallel Databases, 13*, 99–127. doi:10.1023/A:1021569823663

Danilowicz, C., & Nguyen, N. (2003). Consensus Methods for Solving Inconsistency of Replicated Data in Distributed Systems. *Distributed and Parallel Databases, 14*, 53–69. doi:10.1023/A:1022835811280

Desai, B. (1990). *An Introduction to Database Systems*. Eagan, MN: West Publishing Company.

Elmasri, R., & Navathe, S. (2004). *Fundamentals of Database Systems*, (4th Ed.). Upper Saddle River, NJ: Pearson Education, Inc.

Fraley, C., & Raftely, E. (1998). *How many clusters? Which Clustering Method? Answers via Model-based Cluster Analysis*. Tech. Rep. 329, Dept. of Statistics, University of Washington, Seattle, WA.

Freytag, J., Maier, D., & Vossen, G. (1994). *Query Processing for advanced Database Systems*. San Francisco: Morgan-Kaufmann.

Frieder, O., & Siegelmann, H. (1997). Multiprocessor document allocation: A genetic algorithm approach. *IEEE Transactions on Knowledge and Data Engineering, 9*(4), 640–642. doi:10.1109/69.617055

Fronczak, A., Holyst, J., Jedyank, M. & Sienkiewicz, J. (2002). Higher Order Clustering Coefficients: Barabasi-Albert Networks. *Physica A: Statistical Mechanics and its Applications, 316*(1-4), 688-694.

Graham, J. (2005). *Efficient Allocation in Distributed Object Oriented Databases with Capacity and Security Constraints*. Ph.D. Dissertation, University of Idaho.

Hababeh, I., Ramachandran, M., & Bowring, N. (2005). Developing Distributed Database Applications with Integrated Method for Data Fragmentation And Allocation. *Proceedings of the International Advanced Database Conference (IADC 2005)*, June 28-30, San Diego, CA. National University & US Education.

Hababeh, I., Ramachandran, M., & Bowring, N. (2006). Dynamical Processing Technique for data fragmentation in Distributed Database Systems: Design and Tool Support. *Journal of Dynamical Systems and Geometric Theories., 4*(2), 103–116.

Hababeh, I., Ramachandran, M., & Bowring, N. (2007). A High-performance Computing Method for Data Allocation in Distributed Database Systems. *The Journal of Supercomputing, 39*(1), 3–18. doi:10.1007/s11227-006-0001-8

Hababeh, I., Ramachandran, M., & Bowring, N. (2007B). Application Design for Data Fragmentation and Allocation in Distributed Database Systems. *Research & Practice Conference 2007*, July 9-11, INN-School of Computing, Leeds Metropolitan University, Leeds, UK.

Hababeh, I., Ramachandran, M., & Bowring, N. (2008). Designing a High Performance Integrated Strategy for Secured Distributed Database Systems. [IJCR]. *International Journal of Computer Research, 16*(1), 1–52.

Halkidi, M., Batistakis, Y., & Vazirgiannis, M. (2001). Clustering algorithms and Validity Measures. *Proceedings of the SSDBM Conference*.

Hoffer, J., Prescott, M., & McFadden, F. (2004). *Modern Database Management*, (7th Ed.). Upper Saddle River, NJ: Prentice Hall.

Huang, Y., & Chen, J. (2001). Fragment Allocation in Distributed Database Design. *Journal of Information Science and Engineering, 17*, 491–506.

Ishfaq, A., Karlapalem, K., & Kaiso, Y. (2002). Evolutionary Algorithms for Allocating Data in Distributed Database Systems. *Distributed and Parallel Databases*, *11*, 5–32. doi:10.1023/A:1013324605452

Jain, A., Murty, M., & Flynn, P. (1999). Data Clustering: A Review. *ACM Computing Surveys*, *31*(3), 264–323. doi:10.1145/331499.331504

Khalil, N., Eid, D., & Khair, M. (1999). Availability and Reliability Issues in Distributed Databases Using Optimal Horizontal Fragmentation. In T. J. M. Bench-Capon, G. Soda & A. Min Tjoa, (ed.), *'DEXA'99* (LNCS Vol. 1677, pp. 771-780). Berlin: Springer.

Klein, D., Kamvar, S., & Manning, C. (2002). From Instance-level Constraints to Space-Level Constraints: Making the Most of Prior Knowledge in Data Clustering. *Proceedings of the Nineteenth International Conference on Machine Learning*, July, (pp.307-314).

Kumar, P., Krishna, P., Bapi, R., & Kumar, S. (2007). Rough Clustering of Sequential Data. *Data & Knowledge Engineering*, *63*, 183–199. doi:10.1016/j.datak.2007.01.003

Lim, S., & Ng, Y. (1997). Vertical Fragmentation and Allocation in Distributed Deductive Database Systems. *The Journal of Information Systems*, *22*(1), 1–24. doi:10.1016/S0306-4379(97)00001-X

Lingras, P., & West, C. (2004). Interval set clustering of web users with rough k-means. *Journal of Intelligent Information Systems*, *23*(1), 5–16. doi:10.1023/B:JIIS.0000029668.88665.1a

Lingras, P., & Yao, Y. (2002). Time complexity of rough clustering: gas versus k-means. *Third International Conference on Rough Sets and Current Trends in Computing*, (LNCS, pp. 263-270). London: Springer-Verlag.

Ma, H., Scchewe, K., & Wang, Q. (2007). Distribution design for higher-order data models. *Data & Knowledge Engineering*, *60*, 400–434. doi:10.1016/j.datak.2006.03.006

Menon, S. (2005). Allocating Fragments in Distributed Databases. *IEEE Transactions on Parallel and Distributed Systems*, *16*(7), 577–585. doi:10.1109/TPDS.2005.77

Mukkamala, R., & Bruell, S. (1990). Efficient Schemes to Evaluate Transaction Performance in Distributed Database Systems. *The Computer Journal*, *33*(1), 79–89. doi:10.1093/comjnl/33.1.79

Navathe, S., & Ceri, S. (1984). A vertical Partitioning algorithms for database design. *ACM Transactions on Database Systems*, 9.

Navathe, S., Karlapalem, K., & Minyoung, R. (1995). A mixed fragmentation methodology for initial distributed database design. *Journal of Computer and Software Engineering*, *3*(4), 395–425.

Ozsu, M., & Valduriez, P. (1991). Principles of Distributed Database Systems. 1st ed. Englewood Cliffs NJ, Prentice-Hall.

Ozsu, M., & Valduriez, P. (1999). *Principles of Distributed Database Systems* (2nd Ed.). Englewood Cliffs NJ: Prentice-Hall.

Park, S., & Baik, D. (1997). A Data Allocation Considering Data Availability in Distributed Database Systems. *Proceedings of the 1997 International Conference on Parallel and Distributed Systems* (ICPADS '97) (pp. 708 – 713). Washington, DC: IEEE.

Semeczko, G. (1997). *Using a Double Weighted Clustering Technique for Fragment Allocation in Wide Area Networks,* (Tech. Rep. No. FIT-TR-97-11). School of Computing Science, Queensland University of Technology.

Son, J., & Kim, M. (2004). An Adaptable Vertical Partitioning Method in Distributed Systems. *Journal of Systems and Software*, 73(3), 551–561. doi:10.1016/j.jss.2003.04.002

Tamhankar, A., & Ram, S. (1998). Database Fragmentation and Allocation: An Integrated Methodology and Case Study. *IEEE Transactions on Systems, Man, and Cybernetics. Part A, Systems and Humans*, 28(3), 288–305. doi:10.1109/3468.668961

Voges, K., Pope, N., & Brown, M. (2002). Cluster analysis of marketing data examining online shopping orientation: a comparison of k-means and rough clustering approaches. In H.A. Abbass, R.A. Sarker, C.S. Newton (Eds.), *Heuristics and Optimization for Knowledge Discovery* (pp. 207 – 224). Hershey, PA: Idea Group Publishing.

Wiesmann, M., Pedone, F., Schiper, A., Kemme, B., & Alonso, G. (2000). Understanding Replication in Databases and Distributed Systems. *Proceedings of 20th IEEE International Conference on Distributed Computing Systems* (ICDCS'2000).

Zhang, Y. (1993). On Horizontal Fragmentation of Distributed Database Design. *Australian Database Conference*, (pp. 121-130).

KEY TERMS AND DEFINITIONS

DBMS: Database management system is software that manages and controls access to the database.

CDBMS: Centralized Database management system is database software that manages and controls access to the database centrally.

DDBMS: Distributed Database management system is database software that manages and controls access to the database.

DRDBMS: Distributed Relational Database Management System

QoS: Quality of Service

SCFG: Segment Creator and Fragment Generator is a distributed database method used for creating database segments and generating fragments.

FLC: Fragment Life Cycle is a distributed database process which represents the architecture of the Segments Creator and Fragments Generator.

CDV: Clustering Decision Value is the logical value that describes the sites clustering status; it determines whether the site included or excluded in a certain cluster.

Chapter 27

ERP System Implementation from the Ground Up
The ERP5 Development Process and Tools

Rogério Atem de Carvalho
Fluminense Federal Institute, Brazil

Renato de Campos
State University of São Paulo, Brazil

Rafael Manhães Monnerat
Nexedi SA, France

ABSTRACT

The design and implementation of an ERP system involves capturing the information necessary for implementing a system that supports enterprise management. This process should go down through different abstraction layers, starting on enterprise modeling and finishing at coding. For the case of Free/Open Source ERP, the lack of proper modeling methods and tools jeopardizes the advantages of source code availability. Moreover, the distributed, decentralized decision-making, and source-code driven development culture of open source communities, generally does not rely on methods for modeling the higher abstraction levels necessary for an ERP solution. The aim of this paper is to present a development process and supportive tools for the open source enterprise system ERP5, which covers the different abstraction levels involved, taking into account well established standards and practices, as well as new approaches, by supplying Enterprise, Requirements, Analysis, Design, and Implementation workflows and tools to support them.

1. INTRODUCTION

Enterprise Resource Planning (ERP) software is, by definition, integrated business software. Therefore, modeling ERP means dealing with the aspects related to the different abstraction layers that must be taken into account on integrated management. The ultimate goal of developing an ERP system should be going from the highest abstraction level considered - enterprise modeling, down to code generation, without losing modeling information. In other words, it is the ideal situation of guaranteeing

DOI: 10.4018/978-1-60566-731-7.ch027

that the software is in complete conformity with business requirements. To accomplish this, it is necessary to define methods that can improve quality and provide persistence for modeling information throughout each abstraction level considered.

For the specific case of Free/Open Source ERP Systems (FOS-ERP), modeling methods have their importance increased, given that they can empower the availability of source code. Modeling is many times devaluated in the normally distributed, decentralized decision-making, and source-code driven development environment of open source projects. This matter becomes important since FOS-ERP are increasingly gaining acceptance for many reasons. One reason is direct cost, since they impose no licensing costs in general. Other reason is the perception that if customization is inevitable, why not adopt a solution that exposes its code to the adopting organization, which can freely adapt the system to its needs[1] (Carvalho, 2006)?

Experience has shown that the analysis and documentation of business and software requirements by means of models are essential for the enterprise systems development, making necessary the use of proper techniques and tools (Odeh, Kamm, 2003). In this sense, a modeling architecture that properly contemplates business processes aspects can facilitate reuse and promote better functionality, performance, and system understanding, avoiding waste of efforts and resources (Campos, Carvalho, Rodrigues, 2007). Moreover, in the case of FOS-ERP systems, the advantage of free access to code can be jeopardized by the lack of references from where specializations of this code can be derived. Thus, for a FOS-ERP, the use of modeling methods and tools can lower risks and enhance competitive advantage through the access of every aspect that forms the development of ERP software. In other words, from enterprise models to source code, everything is opened for the adopter, that can freely adapt them to its needs (Carvalho, 2006).

This work presents a development process for the FOS-ERP ERP5, composed by set of activities and tools applied to each abstraction level considered: enterprise and business modeling, analysis, design, and code generation. The following sections will briefly present ERP5 framework, basic GERAM (Generalized Enterprise Reference Architecture and Methodology) concepts and their relation to ERP5, the process workflows and their specific tools, the tools that support the process as a whole, and finally conclusions and future directions.

2. ERP5

The ERP5 project (Smets-Solanes, Carvalho, 2002; Smets-Solanes, Carvalho, 2003) is a FOS-ERP that aims at offering an integrated management solution based on the open source Zope platform, written in the Python scripting language. This platform delivers an object database (ZODB), a workflow engine (DCWorkflow), and rapid GUI scripting based on XML. Additionally, ERP5 incorporates data synchronization among different object databases and a object-relational mapping scheme that stores indexing attributes of each object in a relational database, allowing much faster object search and retrieval, in comparison to ZODB, and also analytical processing and reporting. This project was initiated in 2001 by two French companies, Nexedi – its main developer, and Coramy – its first user, and since then is in development and use by a growing community from France, Brazil, Germany, Poland, Senegal, Japan, and India, among others. ERP5 is named after the five core business entities that define its Unified Business Model (UBM, Figure 1):

Resource: describes an abstract resource in a given business process (such as individual skills, products, machines etc). Material lists, as well as prototypes are defined by the relationship between nodes.

Figure 1. ERP5 unified business model

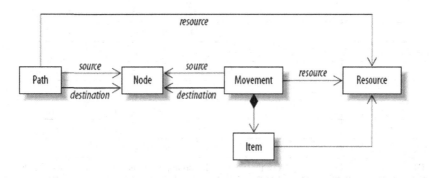

Node: a business entity that receives and sends resources. They can be related to physical entities (such as industrial facilities) or abstract ones (such as a bank account). Metanodes are nodes containing other nodes, such as companies.

Path: describes how a node accesses needful resources.

Movement: describes a movement of resources among nodes, in a given moment and for a given period of time. For example, such movement can be the shipping of raw material from the warehouse to the factory.

Item: a physical instance of a resource.

The structure of ERP5 instances is defined through mappings of the particular instance concepts to the five core concepts and supportive classes or, in very rare cases, through the extension of the UBM. This mapping is documented by a proper instance's lexicon. For example, debit and credit values can be mapped to the Quantity property of the Item class. Its behavior is implemented through workflows, which implement the business processes, and consider the concept of Causalities (chains of related events). Very flexible and extensible modules, called Business Templates, are also provided for Accounting, Production Planning, Payroll, Finance, MRP, CRM, Trading, Electronic Commerce, Reporting, and others.

3. GERAM AND THE ERP5 DEVELOPMENT PROCESS

GERAM provides a description of all elements recommended in enterprise engineering and a collection of tools and methods to perform enterprise design with success (IFIP, 1999). It also considers enterprise models as an essential approach to support enterprise engineering and integration (Kosanke, Vernadat, Zelm, 1999; Vernadat, 2002).GERAM defines enterprise engineering methodologies (EEM) and their enterprise modeling languages (EML), used to describe aspects of the enterprise, like the structure, content, and behavior of the entities to be modeled. Based on these elements, the proposed process defines a development architecture for the ERP5 system. Following these terms, the development process here presented is itself an EEM and the EML considered is the Unified Modeling Language (UML), because it is a *de facto* standard for modeling object oriented information systems, and it is extensible. According to GERAM, the modeling language semantics may be defined by ontologies, metamodels and glossaries that are collectively called Generic Enterprise Modeling Concepts (GEMC). For the ERP5 project, its Unified Business Model, and other concepts like Lexicons and Causalities compose the GEMC.

The modeling process results in enterprise models (EM) that represent all or part of the enter-

Table 1. GERAM concepts and respective development process elements

GERAM Element	Development Process Element (s)
EEM	Development Process Activities
EML	UML
GEMC	Universal Business Model, Lexicons, Causalities
EM	Business Processes Models
EOS	ERP5 Instance
PEM	Business Templates, Reference Models
EMO	Instance Modules
EET	CASE tools, ERP5 development, project management and collaboration tools

prise operations, its organization and management, and its control and information systems. These models can be transformed into an enterprise operational system (EOS), or used to promote changes in the enterprise. To facilitate the modeling process, partial models (PEM), which are reusable models of human roles, processes and technologies, are used.

In ERP5, the development process will generate EM, and the EOS is the ERP5 particular implementation itself. An EOS is a set of enterprise modules (EMO) that support the operational use of enterprise models. EMO provide prefabricated products like human skills, common business procedures or IT infrastructure services, used as components in the implementation of the EOS. Enterprise engineering tools (EET) support the methodologies and languages used for enterprise modeling. For the proposed process, CASE tools and ERP5 development support tools – described later in this article - act as EET. Table 1 summarizes the mappings between GERAM and the development process elements.

GERAM also defines seven life-cycle phases (Figure 2) for any enterprise or any of its entities that are pertinent during the life of the entity. These phases, which can be subdivided further into several lower level activities, can be summarized as follows:

1. **Identification:** identifies the particular enterprise entity in terms of its domain and environment.

2. **Concept:** conceptualizes an entity's mission, vision, values, strategies, and objectives.

3. **Requirements:** comprise a set of human, process, and technology oriented aspects and activities needed to describe the operational requirements of the enterprise.

4. **Design:** models the enterprise entity and helps to understand the system functionalities.

5. **Implementation:** the design is transformed into real components. After tested and approved the system is released into operation.

6. **Operation:** is the actual use of the system, and includes user feedback that can drive to a new entity life cycle.

7. **Decommission:** represents the disposal of parts of the whole entity, after its successful use.

The development process here presented focuses on Requirements, Design, and Implementation phases. Since it is also based on an iterative and incremental life cycle, it is considered that there are no clear borderlines between the phases; furthermore, in some situations, other phases, like Concept and Operation can be touched, as will be shown afterwards.

Figure 2. GERAM life cycle phases

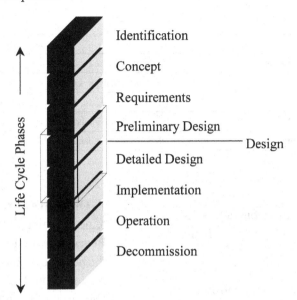

One of the GERAM components is the methodology to engineer the entity considered. For this proposal, it is used a variation of the Unified Process (UP) (Arlow, Neustadt, 2002) to describe an ERP5 instance development project lifecycle. The adopted UP's concepts are: (i) the four phases – Inception, Elaboration, Construction, and Transition, and (ii) the basic axioms – use case and risk driven, architecture centric, and iterative and incremental. However, the use of the Unified Business Model and specific modeling workflows makes the process here presented add, extend, and substitute some UP activities. Also, it is important to note that the phases from Requirements to Implementation of GERAM Life Cycle, must be interpreted not as a waterfall one, but as an iterative and incremental cycle, thus, looping among the referred phases until the system is complete.

To accomplish this, workflows are defined for the life cycle phases defined in GERAM that are directly related to software development: Enterprise workflow for the Conception phase, Requirements Workflow in Requirements phase, Analysis and Design Workflows in Design phase,

Implementation Workflow in Implementation phase, and Deployment activities as the initial part of the Operation phase. As a result, a new kind of development process can be defined for the ERP5 project, built on top of a composition of UP, GERAM, and new concepts. ERP5 development process extends the concept of Domain Specific Modeling Languages (DSML), which represent system elements and their relationships as well as their transformations to platform-specific artifacts (Balasubramanian et al, 2006), to the concept of a Domain Specific Development Environment (DSDE), since it uses a design environment to construct a software system that will involve extending the environment's framework, creating new cases and the cycle repeats itself, as envisioned by Henninger (2003).

Table 2 shows the Enterprise Engineering Tools that compose ERP5's DSDE, these tools can be classified into two categories: product and process related. The first set gives support for creating, configuring and changing code – and is directly related to the Requirements, Analysis, Design, and Implementations workflows; while the second set supports project management and team collabo-

*Table 2. ERP5 tools for system development and customization. Tools marked with a * are generic, out-of-the-shelf ones.*

Category	Task	Tools
Product Related	Requirements	Requirement, Use Case, Glossary
	Analysis & Design	Document Analysis, Lexicon, CASE*
	Implementation	Generator, Test Case, Subversion, Bug, Update, Zelenium*
Process Related	Project Management	Project, CRM, Simulation, Query
	Collaboration	DMS, Web, Calendar, PIM

ration. ERP5 Requirement, Use Case, Glossary, Document Analysis, and Lexicon compose a module called Consulting and are typically used together. Process related tools are in fact generic ERP modules that can be used in many other situations, like production planning and control. Tools marked with an asterisk are other open source tools adopted without modification. For the sake of avoiding confusion, the process related tools will be directly referred here by project management and collaboration tools. A detailed description of these tools and how they are integrated is given by Carvalho e Monnerat (2008).

4. ENTERPRISE MODELING

It is vital to include in the enterprise information systems development methodology, enterprise modeling concepts and methods to better capture organizational aspects and requirements, such as its processes, manufacturing resources and structure (Vernadat, 2002; Shen et al, 2004). Therefore, a specific Enterprise Modeling workflow is used to concentrate on the modeling of function, information, resources, and organization views, according to the GERAM modeling framework. This workflow stands between UP's Concept and Requirements phases.

The activities that compose the Enterprise Modeling workflow are shown in Figure 3 and summarized as follows:

1. **Objectives Modeling:** define the strategic planning of the organization.
2. **Process and Activities Modeling:** define the behavioral and functional aspects of the organization. These activities are directly related to the Business Modeling discipline.
3. **Resources Modeling:** describes the human, informational and technological resources.
4. **Information Modeling:** describe, in high level of abstraction, the information handled by the organization.
5. **Organization Modeling:** describe the structure, in departments for instance, of the organization.

These activities can be implemented according to CIMOSA (Kosanke, Vernadat, Zelm, 1999) or Eriksson & Penker (Eriksson, Penker, 2000) approaches, depending on the enterprise type and the modelers' preferences. The general goal of this phase is to discover the main resource flows and the structural organization of the enterprise being modeled.

5. REQUIREMENTS

The Requirements Workflow, shown on Figure 4, details and consolidates, as requirements for the ERP5 instance, the information captured by the Enterprise Modeling workflow. Its activities are the following:

Figure 3. Enterprise modeling workflow

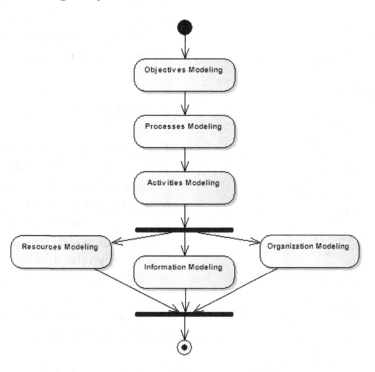

1. **System Requirements Definition:** provides a document with basic requirements for the ERP5 instance. These requirements are a composition of features identified by the Process and Activities Modeling phases of the Enterprise Modeling workflow with some more detailed system's functionalities that can be identified at this point and are necessary to the consolidation of the business process information needs.

2. **Use Case Identification:** Use Cases are identified from the activities of the Activity Diagrams that represent the business process, complementing the requirements definition through the definition of the basic system's architecture.

3. **Basic Iteration Planning:** although the detailed aspects of the system will be known only afterwards, it is necessary to define a basic iteration execution plan. This plan establishes priorities to use cases according to their criticality, defined by the aggregation

of the following criteria: being central to the system architecture, or representing primary business process, high risk functions, high complexity, high aggregated value for the client, and non-dominated or developed technology. Then use case activities (such as testing and programming and modeling) are allocated into iterations, in accordance to the defined iteration time(for instance weekly).

ERP5 Requirement is a tool that helps registering, controlling and managing system requirements. It keeps requirements' metadata, such as id and title, and, through an appropriate workflow, manages versioning, lists of sub-requirements, definition of team members responsible for the requirement, detailing, and change control. This tool is integrated with ERP5 Use Case and ERP5 Project, creating a chain that associates a functional requirement to one or more use cases, and then the use case to project tasks. Non-functional

Figure 4. Requirements workflow

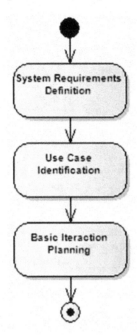

requirements are directly associated to tasks. In that way, it is possible to keep track of all requirements' implementation and associated resources and costs, in every development phase (Figure 5). Checking the status of individual or groups of requirements is facilitated, making management

and customer inquiries on implementation status easily answered. Additionally, this traceability also helps on change management, for both the product and the process.

6. ANALISYS

After the enterprise modeling stage it is necessary to define a set of activities that will take care of the issues needed to transform structural and behavioral models into source code that reflects business requirements. In other words, a method to transform models into source code, which is conceptually related to the Preliminary Design phase in GERAM. The workflow for this phase is presented in Figure 6. This workflow is characterized by the parallel execution of its iterative activities, as follows:

- **Use Case Detail – Actions:** two-column Use Cases are used, one for describing actors' actions and another for describing system's reactions (responsibilities) (Wirfs-Brock, 1993). For this incremental process, during the Analysis activities only

Figure 5. Requirements chain

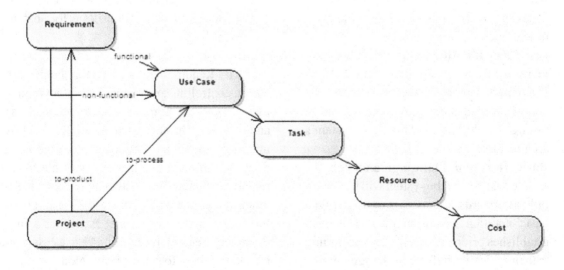

Figure 6. Analysis workflow

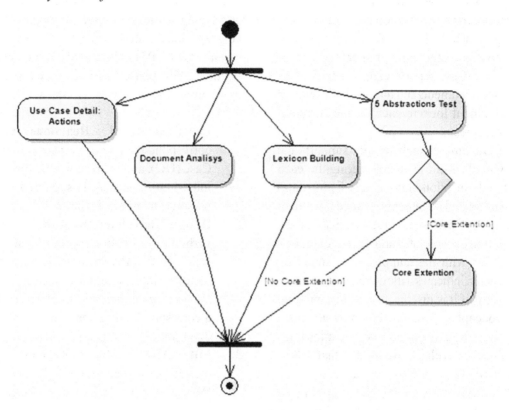

the actions and some basic reactions are listed, since detailed reactions are identified only during the Design activities. Security issues can also be addressed in this activity. Also, a first draft of a State Diagram, representing the basic Use Case process, can be done.

- **Documents Analysis:** ERP5 is a document oriented ERP based on document workflows, because documents are considered a common language understood by all employees in any organization. Therefore, a Use Case related to a functional requirement has at least one document associated to it. This activity consists of identifying the documents that support a given Use Case, starting by ERP5 template documents that provide a basis for customization.
- **The 5 Abstractions' Test:** this is one of the most important activities in ERP5

modeling, its goal is to find out if the UBM can support the use cases, or in other words, if the resources flows described in a given business process can be represented by the core model. If not, Core Extensions are implemented. When these extensions are needed, it is interesting to provide a Collaboration Diagram to help understanding the Use Case.

- **Lexicon Building:** maps concepts from the business world of the client to ERP5 core concepts, supporting reuse. A lexicon is necessary because ERP5 names are quite general.

This phase is supported by ERP5 Use Case Module, which allows the definition of actors and scenarios for every Use Case. Actors are classified into specific access levels (Assignor, Assignee, Author, Editor, Associate), for security modeling. Each scenario consists of a list of steps with their description. The condition of application of a scenario is defined for every scenario, and its steps may refer to requirements whenever relevant. Use Case reports can be exported as Open Office documents and included in a detailed design document for reference for the customer or the project team.

ERP5 Document Analysis tool supports the activity with the same name registering, for each use case, a description of document items (data) and a list of related documents – called document families in ERP5 parlance. This tool register all the customization on templates and generates reports that, together with the mappings registered by ERP5 Lexicon, indicates if the developer can either code directly, if it is just the case of instantiating existing concepts or, for more complex situations that involve sub-classing and new relationships among objects, develop UML models that will be used by ERP5 Generator to generate code.

ERP5 Lexicon supports the mapping of concepts from the client environment, listed on a Glossary, to the framework. This is necessary because, to support reuse, ERP5 names are quite general, and would be meaningless for the final user most of times. For example, a Movement's property named quantity is used to store both debit and credit values in the Accounting module. The main purpose of lexicons is to force the project team to identify all business terms that must be manipulated by the system and to accelerate the mapping of such terms into ERP5 concepts – creating dictionaries maintained by Localizer, an internationalization product. If all business concepts can be mapped to current UBM elements, this means that no modifications on structure will be needed, probably only in behavior.

7. DESIGN

The Design workflow is based on the Workflow, Object Oriented Method (WOOM) (Carvalho,

2005). This method takes into account that the underlying platform supplies an object-oriented language and a state-based workflow engine, fitting into the ERP5 environment, with some modifications. This phase's activities are represented by Figure 7 and described as follows:

1. **Use Case Detail – Reactions:** reactions correspond to the second column of the Use Case (UC), and are responsible for describing what the system is supposed to do in response to an actor's action.
2. **Design Statechart Diagram:** in an UC, verbs in the Actions column identify state transitions; verbs in the Reactions column identify states' internal activities. Figure 7 shows an example of a single UC row with a correspondingly transition in a statechart diagram.
3. **Fill WARC Table:** WOOM uses a new modeling artifact, named WARC Table (Workflow–Action/Reaction–Responsible

Figure 7. Design workflow

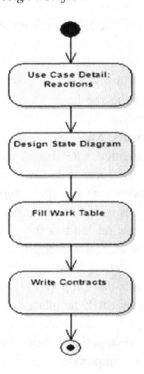

Figure 8. Example transformation from a Use Case row to a statechart diagram's transition and state in WOOM

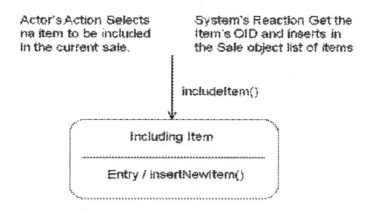

– Collaborators), which is used to associate structure to behavior, guaranteeing encapsulation. For the process here presented, a different use of the WARC table is considered: a state transition is associated for each action, and a state internal action to each reaction – forming the Responsible column of the table. Objects manipulated by transitions and internal actions are listed in the Collaborators column. Table 3 shows the rows that represent in the WARC Table the UC step exemplified on Figure 8.

4. **Write Contracts:** takes care of writing a contract (Meyer, 1992) for each action and reaction. Contracts will determine what each transition/internal activity must do to collaborate to the workflow correct realization. For describing operation's responsibilities, pseudo-code, proto-code, plain text, UML's Object Constraint Language (OCL) or Activity Diagrams can be used. Even more complex approaches can be used, like

extending the Python interpreter to directly support the Design By Contracts method (Plösch, 1997).

Given the growing tendency of UML users to describe workflows through Activity Diagrams (OMG, 2005; France et al., 2006), it is interesting to discuss about the use of state machines to model and implement workflows. Activity diagrams evolved from statechart specializations to Petri Nets derivations, a tendency identified by researchers even before the launching of UML 2.0 specifications (Delatour, Lamotte, 2003). However, the proposed process must use state machines to define workflows because the underlying development platform does so. This is not a problem since it is, most of times, straightforward to make translations between Statechart Diagrams and Petri Nets (Aalst, Hee), 2004, and it is reasonable to use Activity Diagrams to model business process in the Enterprise Modeling phase, and then Statechart Diagrams to model workflows during the Design phase. From this viewpoint, it is legitimate to consider that the correct use of states and states activities can represent most workflow patterns. Besides that, there are plenty of tools and methods for mathematically validating state based workflows (Knapp, Merz, 2002; Latella, Majzik, Massink, 1999; Henninger, 2003),

Table 3. Example WARC table row

Action/Reaction	Responsible	Collaborators
Select item	includeItem()	Product
Insert item on list	InsertNewItem()	Purchase, Item

Figure 9. Implementation workflow

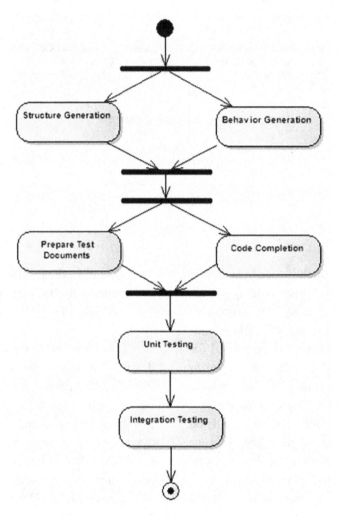

reducing time and cost. Last but not least, there is no real standard, and both academia and industry are still discussing the best approaches, including artifacts, for managing business processes (Moller, Maarck, Tan, 2007).

8. IMPLEMENTATION

Implementation is the final step of every development process, and by definition is the one that is more influenced by platform specific matters. In this process, the workflow activities defined in the Design phase implement the behavior of the process, and a portal type implements its structure. Portal types, a core Zope concept, are an assembly of ERP5 core classes' implementations, associated formularies (GUI) and a proper workflow. If the business process manipulates internal variables, the workflow can store these values as it own attributes. The Implementation workflow in Figure 9 can be described as follows:

1.   Structure and Behavior Generation: using a code generation tool – ERP5 Generator, the portal type and related workflow are automatically generated from a XMI file.

2. Prepare Test Documents: these documents are instances of each scenario of each Use Case with specific values. These documents can be written in any language that can be understood by programmers.

3. Code Completion: represents the implementation in source code of the workflow's transactions and internal activities.

4. Unit Testing: is run by a testing script, which automates the steps described in the Test Documents. This activity is supported by the ERP5 testing framework.

5. Integration Testing: Use Cases are tested altogether to check consistency among functionalities that must work integrated by definition.

ERP5 Generator is used when UML modeling applies. It is a tool that parses XMI files generated by any compatible UML CASE tool, and generates structural, behavioral, and GUI elements from specific artifacts. From Class Diagrams it generates Python classes, their relational mapping, and basic operations and their GUI (relationships, create, destroy, getters and setters). Workflows are generated from Statechart Diagrams, including states, transitions, local properties and conditions. In that way, through the use of a library of ERP5 UML models, Generator supports pattern use automation (Bulka, 2006), allowing the creation of almost the entire ERP5 instance automatically, except for specific algorithms, like calculations. It is important to note that most of times ERP5 framework generates the necessary customization code, including GUI and relationships, through configuration. Therefore, Generator is used in those situations where configuration does not supply all customization necessary.

For both Class and Statechart Diagrams, Generator takes care of UML constructions that are not used by the platform, logging warnings that indicate incompatibilities generated by non-supported UML features. As for now, Generator already generates code for structure, behavior,

GUI, and WARC integration. ERP5 Subversion encapsulates version control into the framework's development environment, with the extra feature of allowing the linkage and navigation from use cases to source code and XMI files.

ERP5 Test Case provides template testing scripts that automate most of Unit and Integration tests. For Unit Testing, initially every use case is instantiated into a collection of Test Documents, one for each possible scenario. Then testing scripts are created, automating the steps described in the Test Document. This phase is achieved in Python language using the ERP5 Unit Testing Framework. Integration Testing is based on the Business Templates, which hold information on module dependencies and how they interface with each other. For GUI testing it is used the open source Zelenium framework, a tool that checks adherence with project's and W3C's standards.

ERP5 Bug stores bug metadata such as id, description, type (documentation, code, GUI etc), priority, difficulty level, and related files (source code, models, articles, how-to's, etc). It also manages bug life cycle through workflows that keep control of status (open, closed, draft, canceled), and Follow Up, which is a kind of knowledge base about the bug, like causes, solutions, and consequences.

9. CONCLUSION

The main goal of the process here presented is to supply ERP5 adopters with an option of a model-driven development method, which, due to its simplified workflows, its set of highly integrated and framework-adherent tools, and the high level of reuse offered by this framework, reduces not only the programming effort, but also the number and complexity of modeling tasks. Hence, the contribution of this chapter is to show how a development process together with a set of highly integrated tools can augment developer and management productivity and help keeping modeling information during the transitions between abstraction layers, even for an software development area where problems are bigger than the average. Moreover, tools like Document Analysis and Lexicon, which are driven to the specific ERP5 framework, help the intensive use of the classical Prototype pattern in a highly automated and well-documented way.

The tools here presented are all product related, however ERP5 also offers a series of project management tools that can enhance the process, such as Project, Simulation, CRM and collaboration tools (Carvalho, Monnerat, 2008). These tools and the intensive use of design patterns makes the system very flexible, as validated by the implementation of instances in very different business segments, such as banking, aerospace, government, hospital, apparel and others, with relative small teams, even for big deployment projects. ERP5 development teams around the Globe customize it for specific needs in a faster and cheaper way. As a prove of that, customization for small businesses is achieved only by configuring the system – in fact, ERP5 Express is an Software as a Service (SaaS) variant of the system, aimed at small organizations, which can be customized by business experts without programming knowledge. Medium and big-sized instances of the system were developed by teams of three to ten programmers, and maintained by even smaller groups – showing that, providing that a well-done business analysis was done, it is possible to develop whole new instances of the system with much less people and in much less time than other ERP systems.

ACKNOWLEDGMENT

The authors thank Jean-Paul Smets-Solanes, Nexedi CEO and ERP5 main developer for supporting this work.

10. REFERENCES

Arlow, J., & Neustadt, I. (2002). *UML and the Unified Process – Practical Object-Oriented Analysis & Design.* London: Addison Wesley

Bulka, A. (2006, September). *Design Pattern Automation* [Online]. Retrieved from http://www.atug.com/andypatterns/

de Campos, R. de Carvalho, R. A. Rodrigues, J. S. (2007). Enterprise Modeling for Development Processes of Open Source ERP. In *Proc. 18th Production and Operation Management Society Conference*, Dallas, TX.

De Carvalho, R. A., & Monnerat, R. M. (2008, September). Development Support Tools for Enterprise Resource Planning. *IEEE IT Professional, 10*, 31–37. doi:10.1109/MITP.2008.36

Delatour, J., & De Lamotte, F. (2003). ArgoPN: A CASE Tool Merging UML and Petri Nets. In *Proc. 1st International Workshop on Validation and Verification of Software for Enterprise Information Systems*, Angers, France, (pp. 94-102).

Eriksson, H. E., & Penker, M. (2000). *Business Modeling with UML.* New York: John Wiley & Sons.

France, R. B., Ghosh, S., Ding-Trong, T., & Solberg, A. (2006, February). Model Driven Development and UML 2.0: Promises and Pitfalls. *IEEE Computer, 39*, 59–66.

Henninger, S. (2003). Tool Support for Experience-Based Software Development Methodologies. *Advances In Computers*, (59), 29-82.

IFIP – IFAC. (1999). *GERAM: Generalized Enterprise Reference Architecture and Methodology.* IFIP – IFAC Task Force on Architectures for Enterprise Integration.

Knapp, A. Merz, S. (2002). Model Checking and Code Generation for UML State Machines and Collaborations. In *Proc. 5th Workshop on Tools for System Design and Verification*, Augsburg, Germany.

Kosanke, K., Vernadat, F., & Zelm, M. (1999). CIMOSA: Enterprise Engineering and Integration. *Computers in Industry, 40*(2), 83–97. doi:10.1016/S0166-3615(99)00016-0

Latella, D., Majzik, I., & Massink, M. (1999). Automatic Verification of a Behavioral Subset of UML Statechart Diagrams Using the SPIN Model-Checker. *Formal Aspects in Computing, 11*(6), 637–664. doi:10.1007/s001659970003

Lilius, J., & Paltor, I. P. (1999). Formalizing UML State Machines for Model Checking. In *Proc. 2nd Int. Conf. in UML*, Berlin.

Meyer, B. (1992). Applying Design by Contracts. *IEEE Computer, 25*(10).

Moller, C., Maarck, C. J., & Tan, R. D. (2007). What is Business Process Management: A Two Stage Literature Review of a Emerging Field. *Research and Practical Issues of Enterprise Information Systems II*, (Vol. 1, pp. 19-32). Berlin: Springer-Verlag.

Odeh, M., & Kamm, R. (2003). Bridging the Gap Between Business Models and System Models. *Information and Software Technology, 45*, 1053–1060. doi:10.1016/S0950-5849(03)00133-2

OMG. (2005). *UML 2.0 Superstructure Specification* [OMG Standard]. De Carvalho, R. A. (2005, June 09). *Device and Method for Information Systems Modeling*. Brazilian Patent PI0501998-2. de Carvalho, R. A. (2006). Issues on Evaluating Free/Open Source ERP Systems. In *Research and Practical Issues of Enterprise Information Systems* (IFIP Series) (pp. 667-676). New York: Springer-Verlag.

Plösch, R. (1997). Design by Contract for Python. In *Proc. of IEEE Joint Asia Pacific Software Engineering Conference*, Hong Kong.

Shen, H., Wall, B., Zaremba, M., Chen, Y., & Browne, J. (2004). Integration of Business Modeling Methods for Enterprise Information System Analysis and User Requirements Gathering. *Computers in Industry, 54*(3), 307–323. doi:10.1016/j.compind.2003.07.009

Smets-Solanes, J.-P., & De Carvalho, R. A. (2002). An Abstract Model for An Open Source ERP System: The ERP5 Proposal. In *Proc. 8th International Conference on Industrial Engineering and Operations Management*, Curitiba, Brazil

Smets-Solanes, J.-P., & De Carvalho, R. A. (2003). ERP5: A Next-Generation, Open-Source ERP Architecture. *IEEE IT Professional, 5*(July), 38-44. Balasubramanian, K., Gokhale, A., Karsai, G. & Sztipanovits, J., Neema, S., (2006). Developing Applications Using Model-Driven Design Environments. *IEEE Computer, 39*(February), 33–40.

van der Aalst, W., & van Hee, K. (2004). *Workflow Management*. Cambridge: MIT Press.

Vernadat, F. B. (2002). Enterprise Modeling and Integration (EMI): Current Status and Research Perspectives. *Annual Reviews in Control, 26*, 15–25. doi:10.1016/S1367-5788(02)80006-2

Wirfs-Brock, R. (1993). *Designing Scenarios: Making the Case for a Use Case Framework*. Smalltalk Report Nov-Dec. New York: SIGS Publications.

KEY TERMS AND DEFINITIONS

ERP: Enterprise Resources Planning, a category of software focused on integrating all business processes of an organization into a unified information system, forming a unified database.

Free/Open Source ERP: ERP systems that are released as Free or Open Source Software.

ERP Customization: Customization represents the adaptation of an ERP system to the business environment of a given organization, involving both modification and extension of the system.

Enterprise Engineering: According to the CIO Council, it is a multidisciplinary approach to defining and developing a system design and architecture for an organization

Entity Life Cycle: An entity life cycle describes the tasks executed to change the status of a product during the phases that comprise its life, from conception, to design, implementation, operation and finally decommission.

Enterprise Modeling: Enterprise modeling is the process of understanding and modeling an enterprise business aiming to improve its performance. This includes the modeling of the relevant business domain, business processes, and business information.

Business Process Modeling (BPM): BPM is the activity of representing processes of an organization, so that they may be analyzed and improved for efficiency and quality. Generally these improvements require Information Technology involvement.

ENDNOTE

[1] In fact, these are two important issues related to maintenance and support continuity, which are addressed on the chapter "Enterprise Resource Planning Systems for Small and Medium-sized Enterprises" of this handbook.

Chapter 28

Open–Source Software Systems
Understanding Bug Prediction
and Software Developer Roles

R. B. Lenin
University of Arkansas at Little Rock, USA

S. Ramaswamy
University of Arkansas at Little Rock, USA

Liguo Yu
Indiana University South Bend, USA

R. B. Govindan
University of Arkansas Medical Sciences, USA

ABSTRACT

Complex software systems and the huge amounts of data they produce are becoming an integral part of our organizations. We are also becoming increasingly dependent on high quality software products in our everyday lives. These systems 'evolve' as we identify and correct existing defects, provide new functionalities, or increase their nonfunctional qualities - such as security, maintainability, performance, etc. Simultaneously, more software development projects are distributed over multiple locations (often globally) and are often several millions of dollars in development costs. Consequently, as the Internet continually eliminates geographic boundaries, the concept of doing business within a single country has given way to companies focusing on competing in an international marketplace. The digitalization of work and the reorganization of work processes across many organizations have resulted in routine and/or commodity components being outsourced.

INTRODUCTION

Currently there is an increase in the total worldwide investment in research and a wider worldwide distribution of research and development activities. It is predicted that government action and economic factors will result in more global competition in both lower-end software skills and higher-end endeavors such as research. Critical drivers include lower costs and increase quality, member flexibility and

DOI: 10.4018/978-1-60566-731-7.ch028

unorthodox round-the-clock approaches to project execution, enhanced creativity in the development environment, the interdependency between economic and software development and much more. It has been argued that standardized jobs are more easily moved from developed to developing countries than are higher-skill jobs. Employees in this global environment need to comfortable with the theory, blend it with necessary practice by understanding the business and cultural issues involved; while being able to effectively share, communicate, articulate and advance their ideas for an innovative product &/or solution.

From a project management perspective, it is imperative that project managers be able to deal with such geographically separated diverse groups in an effective manner. This implies that they need to address two critical issues: *(i)* Resource planning / forecasting based upon the need for software maintenance, which is influenced by the number of *bugs* occurring in the various software components, and *(ii)* understanding the interaction patterns among the various software developers. In this chapter, we concentrate on these two specific issues, both relating to issues of staffing / resource allocation, that impact cost and influence effective project management, using data produced from open-source software (OSS) repositories:

1. **Prediction of future bugs:** Given the globalized nature of such software development projects and the associated costs; even a slight improvement in predicting the expected bugs can lead to immense improvements in effective project planning and management, and,
2. **Understanding the dynamics of distributed OSS developer groups:** Development personnel in groups who are also team builders, are critical to sustain a long-term geographically dispersed project development. Understanding the interaction dynamics between team members in a distributed software development team can be critical

for issues relating to personnel and merit decisions.

1. CASE STUDY

1.1. Predicting Bugs in Open Source Software Systems

In this section, we discuss how software bugs can be predicted for open source software repositories, which are beginning to accumulate a large stash of usable data. This data can be effectively harnessed for significant productivity and efficiency gains in both software product development and software project management. Open source software bug repositories have been recognized as reliable data assets that can provide useful information to assist in software development and software project management. These repositories enable end-users to automatically submit bug information, as and when they are encountered. Moreover, these repositories help researchers mine the data to predict the occurrence of future bugs which helps in the optimization of available (limited) resources. Additionally in a competitive and rapidly changing world of software services delivery, it allows delivering quality products on time and within budget.

Open source software bug repositories have been recognized as reliable data assets that can provide useful information to assist in software development and software project management. Considerable attention has been paid in collecting such bug repositories in the recent past (Anvik, Hiew & Murphy, 2005; Bug reports for Eclipse projects, 2009; Mining Open Source Software Engineering Data 2008). These repositories enable end-users, who need not technically savvy in software development, to submit bug information, as and when they are encountered, in an automated manner. Moreover, these repositories can help researchers mine the data to predict future bugs which helps in the optimization of available (limited) resources. Additionally in a competitive and rapidly changing world of software services delivery, it allows delivering quality products on time and within budget (Hassan & Holt, 2005; Kagdi, Collard & Maletic, 2007; Lucr´edio, Prado & de Almeida, 2004).

Recently, a considerable amount of research has been done in **modeling** *bug* occurrence patterns. The data from open source repositories, including defect tracking systems are analyzed using probabilistic models to predict the files with *bug*s (Askari & Holt, 2006). A statistical model based on historical fault information and file characteristics was proposed to predict the files that contain the largest numbers of faults (Ostrand & Weyuker, 2002, 2004; Ostrand, Weyuker, and Bell 2004, 2005). Such information can be used to prioritize the testing components to make the testing process more efficient and the resulting software more dependable. In (Livshits & Zimmermann, 2005), the authors worked on the discovery of common method usage patterns that are likely to encounter violations in Java applications by mining software repositories. Their approach is more dynamic in the sense that it finds violation patterns from method pairs. Also bug prediction schemes utilizing association rules have been proposed to predict multi-component bugs (Song, Shepperd, Cartwright & Mair, 2006). In (Graves, Karr, Marron & Siy, 2000; Mockus & Weiss 2000; Nagappan & Ball, 2005), the authors predicted the bug density on a module base by using software change history.

In this case study, we use bug repositories of the Eclipse software to predict the number of component-level bugs. Originally created by IBM in November 2001, today the Eclipse software development platform is widely used by developers all over the world (Eclipse, 2009). This tightly interwoven platform of Java software products is constantly being extended with new features and capabilities by a global set of developers. All development plans and revision activities are governed by the decisions of the *Eclipse Founda-*

tion, founded in January 2004 (About the Eclipse Foundation, 2008). One important aspect that invites user participation in development is the fact that it is an "open source" software product. This means that not only the Eclipse software and its source code are freely available to anyone, but so are its bug report information, revision history, and developmental plans (Bug reports for Eclipse projects, 2009). While there are plenty of needs for the governing body of the *Eclipse Foundation,* a specific need exists for predicting the impacts from internal product changes.

We apply two mathematical **models** to predict Eclipse's bug reports. The first model is based on the Power-Law (PL) (Newman, 2005) and second one is based on *Detrended Fluctuation Analysis (DFA)* (Kantelhardt, Koscielny-Bunde, H.A. Rego, Havlin & Bunde, 2001). Researchers have demonstrated the existence of PL using fractal theory (Mandelbrot, 1983), self-organized criticality (Bak, Tang & Wiesenfeld, 1987) edge of chaos (Langton, 1990; Kauffman, 1993), and preferential attachment (Barab´asi, Alberta, Jeong & Bianconi, 2000). In (Carlson & Doyle, 1999, 2002; Csete & Doyle, 2002), the authors developed a theory known as *Highly Optimized Tolerance* to explain the genesis of **power laws** in many phenomena. Researchers have showed several interesting phenomenon that follow PLs. These include: the distributions of size of web file transfer (Barab´asi et al., 2000), forest fires (Malamud, Morein & Turcotte, 1998), city populations (Gabaix, 1999), degrees of software call graphs (Myers, 2003), internet topologies (Faloutsos, Faloutsos & Faloutsos, 1999), software architecture graphs (Jenkins & Kirk, 2007), software development (Cook, Harrison & Wernick, 2005; Van Belle, 2004; Yu 2008) and population growth (Parthasarathy, Lenin & Matis, 1999).

Many physical and physiological signals exhibit long range correlations. The knowledge of this correlation has led to data classification (Peng et al., 1994) and also to understand the underlying dynamics of the system (Bunde et al.,

Table 1. 31 Eclipse components analyzed

Equinox.Bundles	JDT.Text	Platform.Debug	Platform.SWT
Equinox.Framework	JDT.UI	Platform.Doc	Platform.Team
Equinox.Incubator	PDE.Build	Platform.IDE	Platform.Text
Equinox.Website	PDE.Doc	Platform.Releng	Platform.UI
JDT.APT	PDE.UI	Platform.Resources	Platform.Update
JDT.Core	Platform.Ant	Platform.Runtime	Platform.WebDAV
JDT.Debug	Platform.Compare	Platform.Scripting	Platform.Website
JDT.Doc	Platform.CVS	Platform.Search	

1998). One of the commonly used approaches for characterizing the long range correlations in the data is DFA. **DFA** was introduced by (Peng et al., 1992,) to understand the correlations in the coding and non-coding regions of the DNA sequence. DFA is the most reliable method to quantify the correlations in non-stationary data. It has been applied to wide variety of datasets ranging from heart-beat time series (Bunde et al., 2000; Govindan et al., 2007; Kantelhardt et al., 2002; Peng, Havlin, Stanley & Goldberger, 1995), atmospheric temperature data (Bunde et al., 1998), and wind speed data (Govindan & Kantz, 2004). Further DFA has been used to assess the performance of the global climate models (GCM) which simulate the atmospheric variables and thereby predict the global warming. It has been shown using DFA that the data simulated by GCMs do not preserve the scaling behavior which are found in the real data (Govindan et al., 2002). In this work, for the first time, we have used DFA for software system bug prediction analysis and show that it returns highly effective prediction results.

In section 2.1.1, we discuss the Eclipse bug repositories and Eclipse components for which we will carry out the prediction analysis. In section 2.1.2, we describe the **mathematical models** which will be used for the bug prediction. In section 2.1.3, we present some predicted results and show their efficiency by comparing our results with the available bug counts.

1.1.1. Eclipse Bugs

Eclipse, an open source community software project, is focused on building an open development platform comprised of extensible frameworks, tools and runtimes for building, deploying and managing the software development lifecycle (Eclipse – an open development platform, 2008). A large and vibrant ecosystem of major technology vendors, innovative startups, universities, research institutions and individuals extend, complement and support the Eclipse platform. The Eclipse bug repository is well-organized, contains enough bug data available from the year 2001 onwards, the repository is very active, and bug counts reports available on daily, weekly (assuming a span of 52 weeks per year) and monthly basis. Over 207,310 bugs associated with the Eclipse project over the past 7 years were reported. However for the purpose of this paper, we used 31 components (about 118,699 bugs) of Eclipse (Table 1), in part due to its adoption in the mining software repositories (MSR) challenge task (Mining Challenge 2007, 2007).

1.1.2. Model Description

In a typical software development project, the number of *bugs* in the software is expected to reduce with time (i.e. as the software system stabilizes). Moreover, future bugs tend to strongly depend on bugs from the recent past. We refer to this type of dependency as *recency*. In this work, we hypothesize that the reporting of bugs would be further influenced by seasonal factors (holidays, vacations, etc.). This is based on observations that bug reports may be usually less during holiday periods. We refer this kind of trend in the bug count as a *local* trend. We refer to the fluctuational trend of the bug counts collected over the period starting from year 2001 as the *global* trend.

Given the above, we propose a **mathematical model** which will use recency dependency, local trend and global trend of the collected data to predict the future data. We first introduce the notations which will be used in the model. Let N denote the total number of collected data on bug counts. Let B_i, $i = 1,2,...,N$, denote the bug count collected for the time period i. Then B_i may denote the bug count collected on day i, week i or month i, depending on which period we use to predict future bug counts. Hence, B_i can further be denoted by any of the following three notations depending on whether it is collected daily, weekly or monthly:

$$B_i = \begin{cases} B_{d_i}, & \text{for daily bug count,} \\ B_{w_i}, & \text{for weekly bug count,} \\ B_{m_i}, & \text{for monthly bug count.} \end{cases} \quad (1)$$

Let the (bug count) difference between B_i and B_{i-1} be denoted by d_i, that is, $d_i = B_i - B_{i-1}$, $i = 2,...N$ with $d_1 = 0$. We note that d_i denotes the slope of the graph connecting the two consecutive bug counts B_{i-1} and B_i. We define the weights of the slopes as

$$w_i^{(N)} = f(N - i), \quad i = 1, 2, ..., N, \quad (2)$$

where $f(x)$ is a function defined suitably to account for the *recency dependency* property of the collected data. In order to capture the *global trend*, we define the function Gt as follows:

$$Gt = \frac{\sum_{i=1}^{N} d_i w_i^{(N)}}{\sum_{i=1}^{N} w_i^{(N)}}. \quad (3)$$

To capture the *local trend*, we define functions depending on the time intervals (daily, weekly or monthly) the bug counts are collected. If daily bug counts are used, then the function to capture the local trend (annual trend based on calendar days) is defined as follows:

$$Lt_k^{(d)} = \frac{\sum_{i \in D_k} d_i w_i^{(|D_k|)}}{\sum_{i \in D_k} w_i^{(|D_k|)}}, \quad k = 1, 2, ..., 365, \quad (4)$$

where

$$D_k = \left\{ d_i^k \,\middle|\, d_i^k = \text{ day } k \text{ in year } i, i = 1, 2, ..., \left\lfloor \frac{N}{365} \right\rfloor \right\}, \quad (5)$$

where $\lfloor \cdot \rfloor$, denotes the floor function. Similarly, the local trends $Lt_k^{(w)}$ and $Lt_k^{(m)}$ for weekly and monthly bugs counts are defined as follows

$$Lt_k^{(w)} = \frac{\sum_{i \in W_k} d_i w_i^{(|W_k|)}}{\sum_{i \in W_k} w_i^{(|W_k|)}}, \quad k = 1, 2, ..., 52 \quad (6)$$

where

$$W_k = \left\{ w_i^k \,\middle|\, w_i^k = \text{ week } k \text{ in year } i, i = 1, 2, ..., \left\lfloor \frac{N}{52} \right\rfloor \right\}, \quad (7)$$

and

$$Lt_k^{(m)} = \frac{\sum_{i \in M_k} d_i w_i^{(|M_k|)}}{\sum_{i \in M_k} w_i^{(|M_k|)}}, \quad k = 1, 2, ..., 12 \qquad (8)$$

where

$$M_k = \left\{ m_i^k \, \middle| \, m_i^k = \text{ month } k \text{ in year } i, i = 1, 2, ..., \left\lfloor \frac{N}{12} \right\rfloor \right\}. \qquad (9)$$

The *bug* predictions for daily, weekly and monthly, are then computed using the following equations respectively, for $k = N+1, N+2, ...,$

$$B_{d_k} = Gt + Lt_k^{(d)} + \frac{1}{i-K} \sum_{j=K}^{i-1} B_{d_{j-1}}, \qquad (10)$$

$$B_{w_k} = Gt + Lt_k^{(w)} + \frac{1}{i-K} \sum_{j=K}^{i-1} B_{w_{j-1}}, \qquad (11)$$

and

$$B_{m_k} = Gt + Lt_k^{(m)} + \frac{1}{i-K} \sum_{j=K}^{i-1} B_{m_{j-1}}, \qquad (12)$$

Here $K (< i)$ is a parameter whose value will be chosen suitably based on the data. With these basic definitions, we have adopted two different approaches to compute. These are elaborated below:

(i) **PL-based Recency Approach:** Assuming that the trend d_i would decrease monotonically in a **power law** manner, in the first approach we model $f(x)$ using the power law function:

$$f(x) = \frac{1}{2^x}. \qquad (13)$$

Equations (2) and (13) have been defined in

such a way that the weighting functions will place more weight for recent bug counts and relatively lesser weights for bug counts from the distant past. Hence we refer these weights as *recency weights*.

(ii) **DFA Approach:** In the second approach, we attempt to exploit the autocorrelations in the bug count to predict the same. In this approach we quantify the correlations in the bug counts using **DFA**. DFA involves the following four steps:

(a) For the data B_i, $i = 1,...,N$, we remove the mean and compute the profile function as follows:

$$Y_n = \sum_{i=1}^{n} B_i - \langle B \rangle, \qquad (14)$$

where $\langle B \rangle$ denotes the mean of the data.

(b) The profile is divided into M disjoint time windows of size s indexed v, where $M = [N/s]$. If the length of the data is not integer multiple of the scale a small portion of the data towards the end of the record will be left unanalyzed. In order not to discard this part, we also divided the profile into disjoint time windows starting from other direction.

(c) Profile in $v-th$ window is fitted by a polynomial p_v^q of order q. To this end we compute the fluctuation function $F_v(s)$ in the $v-th$ window as follows:

$$F_v(s) = \sqrt{\frac{1}{s} \sum_{i=(v-1)s+1}^{v \cdot s} [Y_i - p^q(i)]^2} \qquad (15)$$

Finally, $F_v(s)$ is averaged over all the windows to get the Fluctuation function $F(s)$ as follows:

$$F(s) = \frac{1}{2M} \sum_{v=1}^{2M} F_v(s). \qquad (16)$$

(d) Steps (b)-(c) are repeated for different values of as to establish a relation between $F(s)$ and s. For power law correlated data, $F(s)$ follows a power law: $F(s) \sim s^{\alpha}$, where α is called scaling exponent or fluctuation exponent. If α <0.5, the data are anti-correlated; if α = 0.5, the data are uncorrelated and if α > 0.5, the data are long rage correlated.

In DFA analysis the profile is fitted by starting with a first order polynomial (straight line) in which case $q = 1$. The $F(s)$ obtained is called DFA1 fluctuation function. Thus the order of the polynomial determines the order of the DFA. As the nature of the trend in the data in unknown *a priori*, the order of polynomial is increased until a convergence in α is reached. Thus in DFA, the trends in the data (that may appear like correlations and remain blind to most of the conventionally used methods like autocorrelation function and power spectral analyses) are systematically eliminated by employing higher order polynomials and the correlations are quantified correctly. The fluctuation exponent α dictates the magnitude of correlation between the current value of B_i with its past value B_j, where $j < i$. This forms the basis of our idea to use α in the bug prediction. Based on the above arguments we define $f(x)$ based on the autocorrelations in the data as follows:

$$f(x) = \frac{1}{x^{\alpha}}. \tag{17}$$

We justify the above formalism by considering the following two scenarios: (i) $\alpha = 0.5$. This scenario indicates that there is no correlation in the data and hence to make a reasonable prediction, this approach also takes into account the bug counts located far away in the data to contribute for the prediction. (ii) $\alpha = 1$. This scenario indicates that the data are highly correlated and hence to make a reasonable prediction, the approach uses heavily the last few bug counts, that is, the approach

gives more weights to recent bug counts and lesser weights for bug counts from further in the past. Thus in the autocorrelation based approach the weights for the bug counts get adjusted themselves depending on the nature of the correlation in the data which is not the case with the power law weights of the first approach (recency). In the next section we discuss and compare the results obtained for the daily, weekly and monthly bug predictions obtained by the two approaches.

1.1.3. Results

In our analysis, to validate the **models**, we first used the above methods to predict the errors for the same time period as needed for (Mining Challenge 2008, 2008) and compared it against the actual bugs reported. These errors are plotted in Table 2. We used both Pearson's and Spearman's measures to verify that an effective prediction can be made. Since the time frame was not for prediction by exact number of months, to predict for the given time frame (Feb 7th – May 8th 2008) we use both monthly and weekly predictions. To predict the exact number of errors for this timeframe, we subtracted the weekly prediction of first week of February from the total (monthly) bugs for Feb-April, and added the prediction for the first week of May. From Table 2 it can be seen that compared to the final results of the challenge (the best prediction reported was off by 794.2 bugs), both measures have predicted a lower number of total bugs for the same set of components considered. Also our analysis using the Pearson and Spearman's methods indicate a highly positive correlation for the *DFA* method, better than the best method reported in the MSR challenge.

We also predicted the weekly *bug* counts of year 2007 using **PL** and DFA and relative errors of the predicted results with the actual ones are shown in Figure 2. In Figures 2(a) and 2(b), the relative errors of the data predicted by DFA and by PL are plotted, respectively. The mean relative errors of DFA and PL are 0.8355 and 0.8498, respectively. The maximum relative errors of DFA and PL are 18 and 19.5, respectively.

After validating the models using results available thus far, we have further analyzed some factors that influence our ability to make such predictions more accurately (Hurst, 2008). We have noticed that issues such as bug severity do not adversely affect prediction accuracy. We have noticed that even for the 31 components chosen here, the accuracy of the predictions depended upon the different window sizes (bug totals in weeks) used for the predictions (the last column in Figure 3). It can be seen that while for some of the components predictions are best made using a 3-week analysis window, others exhibit significantly different patterns.

Finally, we used our **models** to estimate and predict bugs (without considering best prediction window sizes) for the July 2008-June 2009 timeframe. The results are shown in Figure 2. The dotted and solid lines correspond to DFA and PL based predictions, respectively. We note that results from these two methods synchronized well for all components except for component 3, the Equinox.Incubator. This is a relatively new addition to Eclipse designed for use with OSGi (Open Services Gateway initiative) and is to enable experimentation with techniques that extend and broaden the range of Eclipse runtime configuration in more constrained environments such as hand-held devices, servers, etc. Being a relatively new component in the Eclipse model, there are no significant cyclic patterns in the reported bug reports for the two methods to utilize.

1.2. Linux Kernel Mailing List[1]

The Linux-kernel mailing list (*linux-kernel@vger. kernel.org*) is maintained by vger.kernel.org to provide email list services for the Linux kernel developers. Although there are several other mailing lists on specific subjects, such as *linux-net@ vger.kernel.org* for networking users and *netdev@ vger.kernel.org* for networking developers, the Linux-kernel mailing list (LKML) is the official and most heavily used communication platform. The earliest archived LKML message we found is in June 1995. Until now (February 2007), LKML has been used to provide the glue that holds the kernel development community together. Some features of LKML are listed below.

- The LKML is for discussion of the development of the Linux kernel itself. Other topics, such as applications on a Linux system, are not appropriate.

Figure 1. Relative error of predicted 2007 bug counts with the actual bug counts

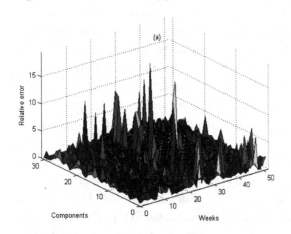
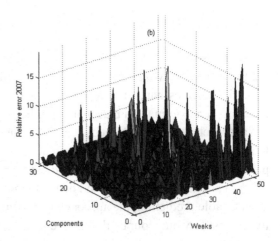

Figure 2. Results of prediction using DFA and Recency Approach for the 31 components for July 2008 – June 2009. Predictions for components 4, 23, and 30 have not been included as their bug counts are not more than 1 and hence lead to low predicted errors

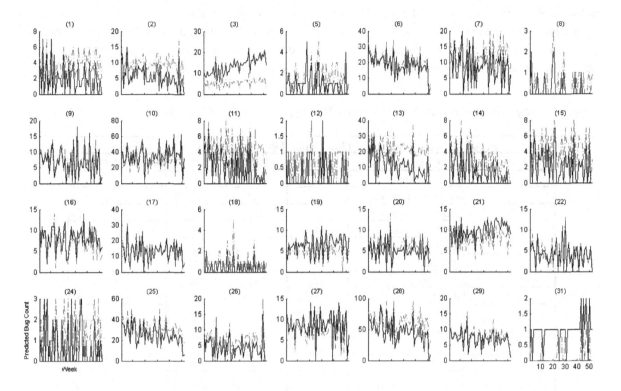

- Subscribing and unsubscribing are public and open to everyone at anytime.
- There is no effective rule to prevent subscribers from posting to the list. A weak regulation is that any message posted should contain new information about kernel development.

1.2.1. General Terminologies and Metrics

In this section, we introduce some terminologies to represent mailing lists and some metrics to measure mailing lists.

A *message* is the smallest unit of information posted by one person at a time. A message can be either an *initiating message* that starts a new topic or a *replied message* that responds to other messages

(either a new message or a replied message).

A *thread* is defined as a collection of messages that discuss the same topic. A thread contains one initiating messages and zero or more replied messages.

Thread replied-rate is the ratio of the number of threads with one or more replied messages over the total number of threads. In contrast, *thread unreplied-rate* is the ratio of the number of threads with zero replied messages over the total number of threads.

Message replied-rate is the ratio of the number of messages (both *initiating messages* and *replied messages*) with one or more replied messages over the total number of messages. In contrast, *message unreplied-rate* is the ratio of the number of messages with zero replied messages over the total number of messages.

A *poster* is a person posting a message on the list, who is either an initiator or a replier. An *initiator* is one who posts an initiating message on the mailing list. A *replier* is one who posts a replied message on the mailing list.

The traffic of a mailing list is measured by the message load and the thread load. The *mes-* *sage load* is the number of messages posted to the mailing list per day; the *thread load* is the number of initializing messages posted to the mailing list per day.

A mailing list is a forum for project managers, developers, bug-reporters, and users to exchange ideas, report problems, and find solutions. Any

Figure 3. Comparison of actual bug counts to DFA and PL based predictions

ID	Components	Actual	DFA	PL	Best Pred. Cycle
\multicolumn{6}{c}{**Predictions for MSR 2008 Timeframe (Feb 7th 2008 - May 8th 2008)**}
1	Equinox.Bundles	59	51	28	13
2	Equinox.Framework	74	117	55	26
3	Equinox.Incubator	61	187	308	26
4	Equinox.Website	2	0	0	too few reported
5	JDT.APT	13	26	23	14
6	JDT.Core	250	287	204	5
7	JDT.Debug	105	148	107	8
8	JDT.Doc	3	7	0	13
9	JDT.Text	193	110	54	13
10	JDT.UI	242	391	236	4
11	PDE.Build	38	57	50	28
12	PDE.Doc	8	5	1	3
13	PDE.UI	299	332	214	4
14	Platform.Ant	35	50	40	28
15	Platform.Compare	56	51	33	6
16	Platform.CVS	60	95	46	52
17	Platform.Debug	104	198	176	28
18	Platform.Doc	8	14	3	3
19	Platform.IDE	85	76	65	8
20	Platform.Releng	95	66	45	13
21	Platform.Resources	49	42	11	6
22	Platform.Runtime	41	57	63	4
23	Platform.Scripting	2	0	0	too few reported
24	Platform.Search	20	23	18	4
25	Platform.SWT	497	453	283	6
26	Platform.Team	69	75	32	6
27	Platform.Text	107	112	97	28
28	Platform.UI	659	829	653	6
29	Platform.Update	52	93	38	5
30	Platform.WebDAV	3	1	1	too few reported
31	Platform.Website	0	0	0	13
\multicolumn{2}{c}{Total Actual / Predicted Bugs:}	3289	3953	2884	
\multicolumn{2}{c}{Absolute Error difference in estimation:}		664	405	794.2*
\multicolumn{2}{c}{Pearson Correlation:}		0.961	0.8851	0.951*
\multicolumn{2}{c}{Spearman's Rank Correlation:}		0.9505	0.8953	0.9437*

*: Best Reported Result in 2008 MSR Challenge

posted messages will be delivered to all the sub-scribers. This broadcasting mechanism is shown in Figure 4(a). Although messages are delivered to all the subscribers, most of the topics are not interested to regular subscribers. Instead, a message thread might only be interested to those subscribes who participate in the discussion in this thread. Therefore, it is more accurate to represent the communication mechanism in a mailing list as channels shown in Figure 4(b).

In the channel representation of a mailing list, communication between two posters who posted the message and who replied to the message forms a *channel*. A channel could be either one way or two ways. A *one-way channel* exists between two posters P1 and P2, in which P1 replies to the message from P2. A *two-way channel* exists between two posters P1 and P2, in which both P1 and P2 replied to the messages posted by each other.

The *bandwidth* of a channel can be used to measure the communication frequency between two posters. The bandwidth of a one-way channel P1→P2 is the number of messages posted by P1 that reply the message from P2. The bandwidth of a two-way channel P1↔ P2 is the number of messages posted by P2 to reply the message from P1 plus the number of messages posted by P1 to reply the message from P2.

A one-way channel (say P1→P2) represents the *service relationship* between P1 and P2, i.e, P1 answers or comments on P2's message. The more bandwidth a one-way channel is, the more services P1 provides to P2. A two-way channel, especially the one with large bandwidth (say P1↔P2), represents the collaboration/coordination relationship between P1 and P2, i.e, P1 and P2 discuss on some common interesting topics. The more bandwidth a two-way channel is, the more discussions are between P1 and P2.

The *social network* (Wasserman, & Faust, 1994) representation has been widely used in the analysis of software developer community (Crowston, & Howison, 2005; Lopez, Gonzalez-Barahona, & Robles, 2004). In this study, we use two-way channels in mailing lists to construct the social networks. The study contains three steps, interaction representation, clustering, and analysis, each of which is described below in turn.

The bandwidth of the two-way channel is used to represent the degree of interactions between two posters. For a mailing list that contains n posters, the degree of interactions between these n posters is represented as an n×n matrix, in which the value at position (i, j) is the two-way bandwidth between poster i and poster j. It is worthwhile to note that (1) the value at position (i, i) in the matrix represents

Figure 4. (a) The broadcasting representation, and (b) the channel representation of the communication mechanism of a mailing list

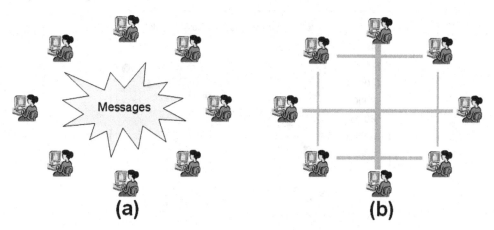

the degree of interactions within one poster, it is set to a maximum value, say ∞; (2) the matrix is symmetric because the bandwidths of two-way channels are used to construct the matrix.

The single-linkage hierarchical clustering (Johnson, 1967) is used to group distributed posters according to the interaction frequencies among them, in which the interaction frequency between one cluster and another cluster is considered to be equal to the largest interaction frequency from any member of one cluster to any member of the other cluster. In the clustering process, the single-linkage hierarchical clustering ensures that the two-way channel with a larger bandwidth is always clustered before the one with a smaller bandwidth.

Activities of a member in the *social network* can be measured by the bandwidth and the interaction degree. The *bandwidth* is used to represent the number of messages communicated between two posters. The *interaction degree* is the number of two-way channels between one particular member and all other members in the group. Generally speaking, a poster with a larger interaction degree plays a more central role in the community (Bird, Gourley, Devanbu, Gertz, & Swaminathan, 2006a, 2006b).

1.2.2. Results

We mined LKML archive (Linux-Kernel Mailing List, 2009) and extracted related data from 1996 to 2006, which contains over 769K messages. Figure 5 shows the total number of messages and total number of threads posted to LKML in different years. We can see from the figure that the total number of threads has a lower growth rate than that of messages. This indicates that, from 1996 to 2006, the average number of replied messages to a thread is increasing.

Figure 6 shows the number of messages with no reply and the number of threads with no reply. It can be seen that they follow the similar pattern as that of the total messages and the total threads: the number of threads with no reply grows slowly than the number of messages with no reply. However, Figure 7 shows that, from 2001 to 2006, the *message unreplied-rate* is about 70% and the *thread unreplied-rate* is about 50%. This indicates that no matter how many messages and threads are posted to the mailing list, the percentages that get replied are roughly same for every year since 2001.

Figure 8 shows that the number of unique posters and the number of unique initiators follow the similar evolution pattern during the time period of

Figure 5. The total number of messages and total number of threads posted to LKML in different years

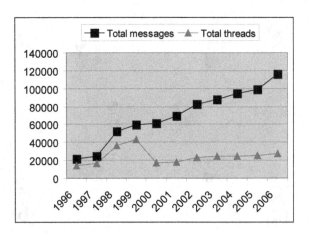

Figure 6. The number of messages and threads that received no reply

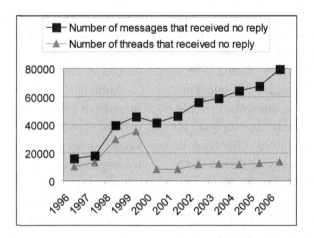

Figure 7. The thread unreplied-rate and the message unreplied-rate

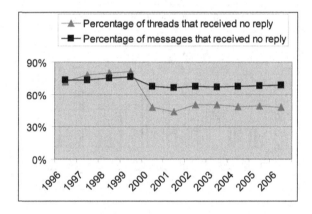

Figure 8. The number of unique posters and initiators

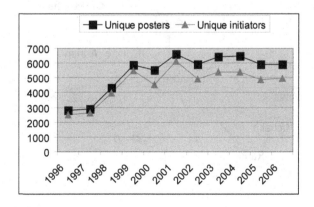

our investigation. The unique number means that multiple messages posted by the same poster are considered as one message. It also reveals that the difference between the number of unique posters and the number of unique initiators during 1996 ~ 2001 is smaller than that during 2002 ~ 2006. This means that roughly the same amount of people participate in posting new topics and replying to existing topics in early years (1996 to 2001) while more people participate in replying than posting new topics in later years (2002 to 2006).

Figure 9 shows the evolution of the message load and thread load of LKML. Generally speaking, an interested subscriber will read the initializing message of every thread to see if the topic is interesting. He or she will ignore all the replied messages if the initializing message is not interesting. Therefore, a core developer might need to read at least 60-70 messages every day.

Although the message load increases about five times from 1996 to 2006, the thread load increases just about two times. For a manager of the Linux kernel project, currently, reading 76 initializing messages is easier to be done than reading 318 all messages.

Figure 10 shows the social network of a core developer group (21 members) in 2006, in which each link represents a two-way bandwidth of at

Figure 9. The evolution of the average message load and thread load

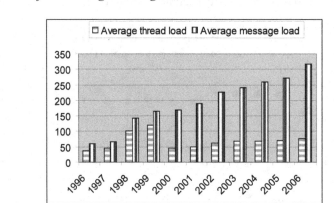

Figure 10. The social network of a core developer group (21 members) in 2006

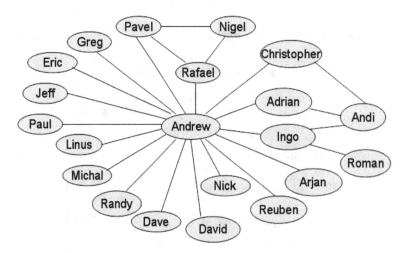

least 82. It shows that a few members, such as Andrew, have higher degrees of interaction and most others have lower interaction degrees. This agrees with what (Reis, & Fortes, 2002; Wagstrom, Herbsleb, & Carley, 2005) have found that a few members account for the bulk activities of the network. This property is further illustrated in Figure 11, which shows the composition of the whole 2006 core group (100 members) with different interaction degrees. In the figure, "ID: x, y" means that there are y members in the group that have interaction degree x. In the studied group, 7 members have interaction degrees greater than 6 while 93 members have interaction degree less than or equal to 6.

We studied the evolution of the average interaction degree and the average channel bandwidth of two clusters with size 20 and 100. They are shown in Figure 12 and Figure 13, respectively. The figures show that, from 1996 to 2006, the average interaction degree of core members are roughly in the range of 2 to 4. However, the average channel bandwidth has increased about 10 times. The average interaction degree and the average bandwidth have other meanings in the social network: the former can represent the network structure and the later can represent the amount of activities in the network. This indicates that, from 1996 to 2006, the basic social network structure has not changed too much. Instead, what has changed is

Figure 11. The composition of the whole 2006 core group (100 members) with different interaction degrees (ID)

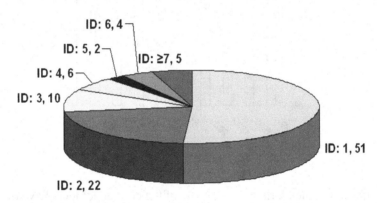

Figure 12. The evolution of the average interaction degree of core (20) group and core (100) group

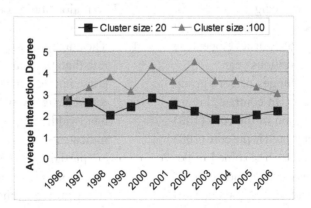

Figure 13. The evolution of the average channel bandwidth of core (20) group and core (100) group

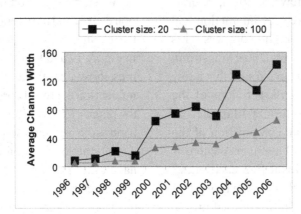

Figure 14. Percentage unchanged and changed core (100) developers from 1997 to 2006 comparing to their corresponding previous years

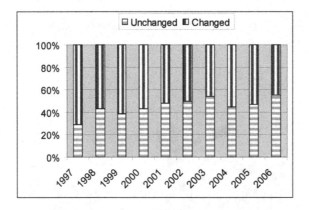

the amount of activities in this network.

Figure 14 and Figure 15 illustrate the evolution of the core (100) group. For example, Figure 14 shows that compared with 1996, 28%/72% of the core developers are unchanged/changed in 1997. Figure 14 indicates that in Linux core (100) group, every year, about 40-60% of developers are changed compared to the previous year.

Figure 14 shows the changes of core group in short term (year to year). In contrast, Figure 15 shows long term evolution of the core (100) developers. If a developer joined in the core (100) group in 2006, he has age 1; if he joined in the core group in 2005, he has age 2; and so on. It can be seen that by the end of 2006, about 50%

of the core developers have over 3 years' experiences as core members. This smooth evolution of core group is important for the steady evolution of the product.

Two major findings of this case study are:

1. The number of messages has a faster growth rate than the number of threads and the average interaction degree of core developers remains steady while the average channel bandwidth increases over 10 times. This indicates that more and more developers are participating in the discussion;

2. The core development group evolves smoothly with a changing rate of about 50%

Figure 15. The composition of different ages of core (100) developers in 2006

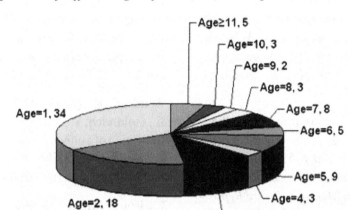

per year and about 50% of the core members have three or more years' experience in the core group communication. This evolution pattern is important for Linux project to grow steadily.

3. CONCLUSION

Significant, and to some extent ubiquitous, proliferation of computing to every aspect of an organization's business, and its increasing importance to not just business sustenance, but to provide unmatched competitive business value for businesses, has created constantly increasing demand for new software systems that are growing increasingly complex with time. In spite of tool support, OSS development still remains a craft, vastly dependent on the experience and expertise of the individual software developer. Consequently, this has led to search for, and the leveraging of, talent from across the world. Irrespective of localized labor dislocations, the global demand for software professionals has been increasing at a rapid pace during the past two decades. Thus globalization, both in terms of the economics and staffing of software development projects, has increasingly become a necessity and the two have become highly entwined and mutually dependent. The massive volume of electronically driven mercantile commerce would be unthink-

able without the support of globalized software applications. In this chapter, we have presented a brief outline of two specific methods that can be used for planning and management of global OSS development projects and teams.

ACKNOWLEDGMENT

This work is based in part, upon research supported by the National Science Foundation (under Grant Nos. CNS-0619069, EPS-0701890 and OISE 0729792), NASA EPSCoR Arkansas Space Grant Consortium (#UALR 16804) and Acxiom Corporation (#281539). Any opinions, findings, and conclusions or recommendations expressed in this material are those of the author(s) and do not necessarily reflect the views of the funding agencies. The authors would like to thank Dr. Dr. Hemant Joshi, Acxiom Corporation, Arkansas, for his insightful suggestions and engaging discussions on this subject.

REFERENCES

About the Eclipse Foundation (2009). Eclipse Software. Retrieved January 10, 2009, from http://www.eclipse.org/org

Anvik, J., Hiew, L., & Murphy, G. C. (2005). Coping with an open bug repository. In *OOPSLA workshop on Eclipse technology eXchange: Proceedings of the 2005 OOPSLA Workshop on Eclipse Technology eXchange (U.S.A.), San Diego, California* (pp. 35 - 39).

Askari, M., & Holt, R. (2006). Information theoretic evaluation of change prediction models for large-scale software. In *3rd ICSE workshop on mining software repositories: Proceedings of the 3rd ICSE Workshop on Mining Software Repositories (China), Shanghai* (pp. 126-132).

Bak, P., Tang, C., & Wiesenfeld, K. (1987). Self-organized criticality - An explanation of 1/f noise. *Physical Review Letters, 59*, 381–384. doi:10.1103/PhysRevLett.59.381

Barab'asi, A., Alberta, R., Jeong, H., & Bianconi, G. (2000). Power-law distribution of the world wide web. *Science, 287*, 1–2. doi:10.1126/science.287.5462.1

Bird, C., Gourley, A., Devanbu, P., Gertz, M., & Swaminathan, A. (2006a). Mining email social networks. In *Third international workshop on mining software repositories: Proceedings of Third International Workshop on Mining Software Repositories(China), Shanghai* (pp. 137-143).

Bird, C., Gourley, A., Devanbu, P., Gertz, M., & Swaminathan, A. (2006b). Mining email social networks in postgres. In *Third international workshop on mining software repositories: Proceedings of Third International Workshop on Mining Software Repositories (China), Shanghai* (pp. 185-186).

Bug reports for Eclipse projects (2009). Eclipse Software. Retrieved January 10, 2009, from https://bugs.eclipse.org/bugs/

Bunde, A., Havlin, S., Kantelhardt, J. W., Penzel, T., Peter, J.-H., & Voigt, K. (2000). Correlated and uncorrelated regions in heart-rate fluctuations during sleep. *Physical Review Letters, 85*, 3736–3739. doi:10.1103/PhysRevLett.85.3736

Bunde, E. K., Bunde, A., Havlin, S., Roman, H. E., Goldreich, Y., & Schellenhuber, H.-J. (1998). Indication of a universal persistence law governing atmospheric variability. *Physical Review Letters, 81*, 729–732. doi:10.1103/PhysRevLett.81.729

Carlson, J. M., & Doyle, J. (1999). Highly optimized tolerance: A mechanism for power laws in designed systems. *Physical Review E: Statistical Physics, Plasmas, Fluids, and Related Interdisciplinary Topics, 60*, 1414–1427.

Carlson, J. M., & Doyle, J. (2002). Complexity of robustness. *Proceedings of the National Academy of Sciences of the United States of America, 99*, 2538–2545. doi:10.1073/pnas.012582499

Challenge, M. *2007* (2007). Mining Software Repositories. Retrieved January, 10 2009, from http://msr.uwaterloo.ca/msr2007/challenge/

Challenge, M. *2008* (2008). Mining Software Repositories. Retrieved January 10, 2009, from http://msr.uwaterloo.ca/msr2008/challenge/index.html

Cook, S., Harrison, R., & Wernick, P. (2005). A simulation model of self-organising evolvability in software systems. In *1st IEEE international workshop on software evolvability: Proceedings of 1st IEEE International Workshop on Software Evolvability (Hungary)* (pp. 17-22).

Crowston, K., & Howison, J. (2005). The social structure of free and open source software development. *First Monday, 10*(2).

Csete, M. E., & Doyle, J. C. (2002). Reverse engineering of biological complexity. *Science, 295*, 1664–1669. doi:10.1126/science.1069981

Eclipse (2009). Eclipse Software. Retrieved January 10, 2009, from http://www.eclipse.org

Faloutsos, M., Faloutsos, P., & Faloutsos, C. (1999). On power-law relationships of the internet topology. In *Applications, Technologies, Architectures, and Protocols for Computer Communication:Proceedings of the Conference on Applications, Technologies, Architectures, and Protocols for Computer Communication, Cambridge, MA* (pp. 251-262).

Gabaix, X. (1999). Zipf's law for cities: An explanation. *The Quarterly Journal of Economics, 114*, 739–767. doi:10.1162/003355399556133

Govindan, R. B., & Kantz, H. (2004). Long-term correlations and multifractality in surface wind speed. *Europhysics Letters, 68*, 184–190. doi:10.1209/epl/i2004-10188-3

Govindan, R. B., Vjushin, D., Bunde, A., Brenner, S., Havlin, S., & Schellnhuber, H.-J. (2002). Global climate models violate scaling of the observed atmospheric variability. *Physical Review Letters, 89*, 028501. doi:10.1103/PhysRevLett.89.028501

Govindan, R. B., Wilson, J. D., Preissl, H., Eswaran, H., Campbell, J. Q., & Lowery, C. L. (2007). Detrended fluctuation analysis of short datasets: An application to fetal cardiac data. *Physica D. Nonlinear Phenomena, 226*, 23–31. doi:10.1016/j.physd.2006.10.019

Graves, T. L., Karr, A. F., Marron, J. S., & Siy, H. (2000). Predicting Fault Incidence Using Software Change History. *IEEE Transactions on Software Engineering, 26*, 653–661. doi:10.1109/32.859533

Hassan, A. E., & Holt, R. C. (2005). The top ten list dynamic fault prediction. In *21st International conference on software maintenance: Proceedings of the 21st International Conference on Software Maintenance (Hungary), Budapest* (pp. 263-272).

Hurst, W. B. (2008). *Eclipse bug count cycle analysis.* Unpublished M.S. Computer Science thesis, University of Arkansas at Little Rock, Little Rock, AR.

Jenkins, S., & Kirk, S. R. (2007). Software architecture graphs as complex networks: A novel partitioning scheme to measure stability and evolution. *Information Sciences: an International Journal, 177*, 2587–2601.

Johnson, S. C. (1967). Hierarchical Clustering Schemes. *Psychometrika, 32*, 241–254. doi:10.1007/BF02289588

Kagdi, H., Collard, M. L., & Maletic, J. I. (2007). A survey and taxonomy of approaches for mining software repositories in the context of software evolution. *Journal of Software Maintenance and Evolution: Research and Practice, 19*, 77–131. doi:10.1002/smr.344

Kantelhardt, J.W., Ashkenazy, Y., Ivanov, P.Ch., Bunde, A., Havlin, S., Penzel, T. et al. (2002). Characterization of sleep stages by correlations in the magnitude and sign of heartbeat increments. *Physics Review E, 65*, 051908-1-6.

Kantelhardt, J. W., Koscielny-Bunde, E., Rego, H. A., Havlin, S., & Bunde, A. (2001). Detecting Long-range Correlations with Detrended Flunction Analysis. *Physica A, 295*, 441–454. doi:10.1016/S0378-4371(01)00144-3

Kauffman, S. A. (1993). *The origins of order: self-organization and selection in evolution.* New York: Oxford University Press.

Langton, C. G. (1990). Computation at the edge of chaos. *Physica D. Nonlinear Phenomena, 42*, 12–37. doi:10.1016/0167-2789(90)90064-V

Livshits, B., & Zimmermann, T. (2005). DynaMine: Finding common error patterns by mining software revision histories. In *2005 European software engineering conference and 2005 foundations of software engineering: Proceedings of the 2005 European Software Engineering Conference and 2005 Foundations of Software Engineering (Portugal), Lisbon* (pp. 296-305).

Lopez, L., Gonzalez-Barahona, J. M., & Robles, G. (2004). Applying social network analysis to the information in CVS repositories. In *International workshop on mining software repositories:Proceedings of the Mining Software Repositories Workshop (U.K.), Edinburgh* (pp. 101-105).

Lucr'edio, D., Prado, A. F., & de Almeida, E. S. (2004). A survey on software components search and retrieval. In *30th EUROMICRO conference:Proceedings of the 30ᵗʰ EUROMICRO Conference (France), Rennes* (pp. 152-159).

Malamud, B., Morein, G., & Turcotte, D. (1998). Forest fires: an example of self-organized critical behaviour. *Science, 281,* 1840–1842. doi:10.1126/science.281.5384.1840

Mandelbrot, B. (1983). *The fractal geometry of nature.* New York: Freeman.

Mining Open Source Software Engineering Data (2008). Center for Open Software Engineering. Retrieved January 10, 2009, from http://ase.csc.ncsu.edu/projects/mose/

Mockus, A., & Weiss, D. M. (2000). Predicting Risk of Software Changes. *Bell Labs Technical Journal, 5,* 169–180. doi:10.1002/bltj.2229

Myers, C. R. (2003). Software systems as complex networks: structure, function, and evolvability of software collaboration graphs. *Physical Review E: Statistical, Nonlinear, and Soft Matter Physics, 68,* 046116. doi:10.1103/PhysRevE.68.046116

Nagappan, N., & Ball, T. (2005). Use of Relative Code Churn Measures to Predict System Defect Density. In *27th International conference on software engineering: Proceedings of 27th International Conference on Software Engineering (U.S.A.), Saint Louis, Missouri* (pp. 284-292).

Newman, M. (2005). Power laws, Pareto distributions and Zipf's law. *Contemporary Physics, 46,* 323–351. doi:10.1080/00107510500052444

Ostrand, T., & Weyuker, E. J. (2002). The distribution of faults in a large industrial software system. In *2002 ACM international symposium on software testing and analysis: Proceedings of 2002 ACM International Symposium on Software Testing and Analysis (Italy), Rome* (pp. 55-64).

Ostrand, T., Weyuker, E. J., & Bell, R. M. (2004). Where the bugs are? In *2004 ACM international symposium on software testing and analysis. Proceedings of 2004 ACM International Symposium on Software Testing and Analysis (U.S.A.), Boston, MA* (pp. 86-96).

Ostrand, T. J., & Weyuker, E. J. (2004). A tool for mining defect-tracking systems to predict fault-prone files. In *1st ICSE workshop on mining software repositories: Proceedings of the 1st ICSE Workshop on Mining Software Repositories (Scotland), Edinburgh,* (pp. 85-89).

Ostrand, T. J., Weyuker, E. J., & Bell, R. M. (2005). Predicting the location and number of faults in large software systems. *IEEE Transactions on Software Engineering, 31,* 340–355. doi:10.1109/TSE.2005.49

Parthasarathy, P. R., Lenin, R. B., & Matis, J. H. (1999). On the numerical solution of transient probabilities of the stochastic power law logistic model. *Nonlinear Analysis, 37,* 677–688. doi:10.1016/S0362-546X(98)00065-0

Peng, C.-K., Buldyrev, S. C., Havlin, S., Simons, M., Stanley, H. E., & Goldberger, A. L. (1994). Mosaic organization of DNA nucleotides. *Physical Review E: Statistical Physics, Plasmas, Fluids, and Related Interdisciplinary Topics, 49*, 1685–1689. doi:10.1103/PhysRevE.49.1685

Peng, C.-K., Buldyrev, S.V., Goldberger, A.L., Havlin, S., & Sciortino, F., Simon, M.et al. (1992). Long-range correlations in nucleotide sequences. *Nature, 356*, 168–170. doi:10.1038/356168a0

Peng, C.-K., Havlin, S., Stanley, H. E., & Goldberger, A. L. (1995). Quantification of scaling exponents and cross over phenomena in nonstationary heartbeat time series. *Chaos (Woodbury, N.Y.), 5*, 82–87. doi:10.1063/1.166141

Reis, C., & Fortes, R. (2002, February). An overview of the software engineering process and tools in the Mozilla project. In *Workshop on open source software development: Proceedings of Workshop on Open Source Software Development (U.K.), Newcastle* (pp. 155-175).

Song, Q., Shepperd, M., Cartwright, M., & Mair, C. (2006). Software Defect Association Mining and Defect Correction Effort Prediction. *IEEE Transactions on Software Engineering, 32*, 69–82. doi:10.1109/TSE.2006.1599417

Van Belle, T. B. (2004). *Modularity and the evolution of software evolvability*. Unpublished Ph.D. Computer Science thesis, The University of New Mexico, Albuquerque, NM.

Wagstrom, P. A., Herbsleb, J. D., & Carley, K. (2005). A social network approach to free/open source software simulation. In *First International Conference on Open Source Systems: Proceedings of the First International Conference on Open source Systems (Italy), Genova* (pp. 16-23).

Wasserman, S., & Faust, K. (1994). *Social network analysis: Methods and applications*. New York: Cambridge.

Yu, L. (2008). Self-organization process in open-source software: An empirical study. *Information and Software Technology, 50*, 361–374. doi:10.1016/j.infsof.2007.02.018

Yu, L., Ramaswamy, S., & Zhang, C. (2008). Mining email archives and simulating the dynamics of open-source project developer networks. In *Fourth international workshop on enterprise and organizational modeling and simulation: Proceedings of the Fourth International Workshop on Enterprise and Organizational Modeling and Simulation (France), Montpellier,* (pp. 17-31).

ENDNOTE

[1] Part of the work in this section has been published in The Fourth International Workshop on Enterprise & Organizational Modeling and Simulation (Yu, Ramaswamy & Zhang, 2008).

Chapter 29

Information System Model for Global Emergency–Response System in the Context of Natural Disaster Recovery Management System

Salem Al-Marri
Leeds Metropolitan University, UK

Muthu Ramachandran
Leeds Metropolitan University, UK

ABSTRACT

Emergency needs occurs anywhere anytime by naturally, manually and accidentally in addition to worldwide death by hunger and poverty. As such, the need of response system should be there to tackle this emergency. Natural disasters are increasingly frequent in recent years taking peoples lives and destructions, for example, Hurricane Katrina US 2006 and Tsunami Asia 2004. This study proposes a model for Classification of Natural Disasters and Catastrophic Failures activity model. This model consists of hierarchical roles and activities. It is critical that organization must support and provide infrastructure for managing and preventing disasters and its aftermath to a full recovery. Furthermore, this chapter also proposes a triangular model for global emergency response systems, which can be used as a preventive measure, as well as post-recovery management system for managing and tackling emergencies. This model also proposes the use of emerging technologies such as ubiquitous computing and wireless communications systems. Now-a-days people use these wireless technologies to communicate in case of a disaster. Lastly, the study proposes another two models namely the Disaster Risks categorization model, which help identify and to assess the threat levels.

DOI: 10.4018/978-1-60566-731-7.ch029

INTRODUCTION

The term "disaster" has been defined by different scholars in different ways (Van et al. 2007) have identified a set of characteristics, in addition to the list identified by Hiatt (2000) for the definition of a disaster: Surprise, Insufficient information, Escalating flow of information, Loss of control, Intense scrutiny from outside, Siege mentality, Panic, Short-term focus, Physical injury, Loss of business operations, Loss of employee morale and motivation, Loss of team co-operation, Non-integrity of enterprise information and data control, Inefficient information technology systems, Inadequate security in place, Lack of safety procedures and training – has been used to define the term. However, if we analyse the different terminologies we can see that they refer to the same situation but in different ways. Global technology has been recently affecting different fields in our life as it has been effectively employed to many domains such as e-commerce, control systems, information gathering and management and other areas of similar interest. The natural disasters in USA and Asia in 1994, the 9/11 attack revealed that people lives and both technical and constructed infrastructure can be easily damaged. The increasing use of technology put more stress and uncertainties when disasters happen. According to a report by the secretariat of the International Strategy for Disaster Reduction (IFRCRCS, 2004), over than 478,100 people were killed, more than 2.5 billion people were affected and about $ 690 billion losses in economy caused by natural and man-made disasters. Disasters triggered by hydro-meteorological hazards amounted for 97% of the total people affected by disasters, and 60% of the total economic losses (Shaw 2006).

It is evident that each type of a disaster has a different impact and each country and government has a different way to deal with such incidents. Therefore, it is essential to design an appropriate policy and apply successful strategy that can minimize the threat of disasters. Developing a global emergency management information network that provides electronic access to emergency management knowledge would be crucial. However, the emergency management coordination processes did not act effectively and broke down in the wake of the aforementioned disasters (Shaw 2006).

Moreover, the most advanced information systems and technologies did even contribute to relief the affected populations. When hurricane Katrina and Tsunami happened, the affected people relied to basic web sites to search for their friends or families instead of using information resources provided by government and professional relief organizations. In the wake of Tsunami, software engineers had to create other alternatives that they had created voluntarily to build a basic emergency response system (Aljazeera, 2005). This disaster made researchers and practitioners in emergency management to reconsider the function of information system in case of an emergency response. The system design, development, use, and evaluation of emergency response information systems obviously needs to take a far more prominent place on the agenda of researchers, emergency managers and policy makers worldwide.

Existing information system models have enormous challenges that have been identified over many years. However, current studies on information system models for large-scale projects are limited. Therefore, the main aims of this research are to integrate information systems models with project management strategies:

- Identified specific management roles to tackle large scale natural disaster recover planning and prevention techniques
- Clear guidelines on information flow and person responsibilities as this can be very difficult in large organisations that are linked as in government departments.
- Clear identification of contingency planning guidelines, information flow, timing, and specific roles.

- Integrating risk management strategies to help manage disaster recovery and contingency planning
- A model for disaster categorisation to help us to identify common pattern of events
- A globally integrated model that helps integrate people, technology, and disasters

The following sections of the paper propose and discusses, in detail, information system model for disaster recovery planning along with the implications of different Disaster Management Models to be implemented in case of generating an effective and efficient Response System.

NATURAL DISASTERS AND CATASTROPHIC FAILURES CLASSIFICATION

Natural disasters which may happen in the world are various including: earthquakes, oil overflow, famine, floods, hurricanes, land slide, tsunamis, volcanic eruptions, accidents, flight missing, etc. They have a significant impact on different resources like the natural, ecological and cultural resources. It has been known that some parts of the world are more likely to be affected by certain types of disasters such as earthquakes in southern California, Hurricane Hugo, Andrew, and Katrina in southern USA and floods in the southern coast of Asia. Moreover, world also faces disasters which are man-made such as the bombing of Oklahoma City Government and 9/11 terrorist attacks. Furthermore, computer systems are prone to hackers, security violations and viruses which can corrupt valuable information and data.

Due to the damage caused by disasters it is now the right time to have a deep understanding of the "complex emergencies" and the interconnections between man, environment, technology, social system and conflict. Catastrophic failure

of power system is a phenomenon which can happen all over the world. It cannot be totally prevented even with the use of new technologies in power engineering, communication systems and computer engineering. However, it is possible to reduce its frequency and hence its impact on the society. It can be defined as a complete, sudden, often unexpected breakdown in a machine, electronic system, computer or network resulted from hardware event such as a disk drive crash, memory chip failure of surge on the power line.

This model consists of hierarchical roles and activities. Organizations and governments must have a vital role in supporting and providing infrastructure for dealing with disasters and their aftermath. In addition, operational teams should be employed to work and cooperate between each others throughout the different phases of the disaster. Each team should be assigned for a specific phase and should perform its role and responsibilities effectively. We propose the Figure1 given below, to explain the Classification of Natural Disasters and Catastrophic Failures, as shown the Disaster Classification System:

The occurrence of natural disasters challenges the power of the whole system of any society. They can be categorized as:

- Sudden disasters such as earthquakes, oil overflow, floods, hurricanes, land slide, tsunamis, volcanic eruptions and accidents
- Slowly developing disasters such as epidemics, famine, droughts.

Both kinds have a destructive impact on human being.

This paper will concentrate on communication facilities which help providing countermeasures against catastrophic failure of power system and the impact of natural disasters on different kinds of conflict.

Figure 1. Classification of natural disasters and catastrophic failures

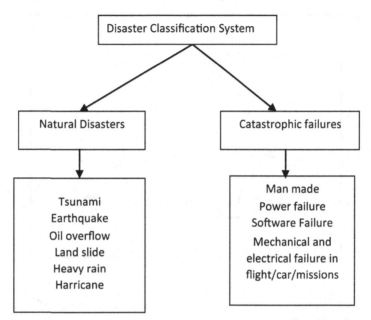

TRIANGULAR MODEL FOR GLOBAL EMERGENCY RESPONSE SYSTEM (GERS)

It has been stated by both practitioners and academic communities that emergency response system should be backed up with accurate information. Accurate and timely information is as crucial as the rapid reactions and the coherent coordination among the responding organizations (Semer, 1998). It is vital to have an effective information system that provides fast access to comprehensive, relevant, and reliable information. When emergency responders have the ability to collect, analyze, and act on the base of the given information, they will be able to respond quickly and meet the needs of the afflicted populations.

This section proposes a triangular model for Global Emergency Response System. It explains the use of communications, the use of emerging technology (e.g. the ability to leverage the significant computing power on demand and the ability to manage massive sets of distributed data) and people's experiences and predictions. It

is very important to view the experiences of the people who faced disasters and how they managed to deal with the disaster (e.g. the victims of the 2004 tsunami) especially that those people experienced multiple intense stresses. Additionally, this model examines global support whose role during the disaster is essential (presenting the right information in the right format, to the right person, in time to make the right decision). Figure 2 presents triangular model for Global Emergency Response System, which consists of the use of emerging technology, the role of the people and their culture, and global support.

The purpose of examining the triangular model for Global Emergency Response System is to know how Global Emergency Response System can function in a community. In addition to that, the paper describes the aspects of local community emergency system (collaborative efforts, geographic information, local area details, local culture, and emergency plans). It examines the role of the people involved in the system, the problems they might face and their approaches to emergency management.

Figure 2. Triangular model for global emergency response system

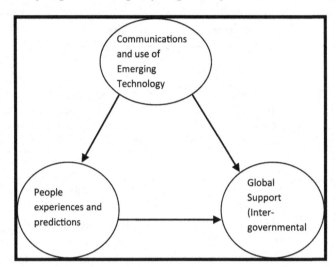

DISASTER RISKS LEVEL CATEGORISATION MODEL

It is well-known that each type of disaster has different impact and results. Additionally, the method used by each government or organization when dealing with disaster differs from one country to another. However, the basic important thing that every country should do is to design an appropriate policy with a strategic approach which can effectively help in determining the source and the degree of uncertainty which characterizes the potential threat. Disaster recovery is considered one of the phases of the emergency management cycle. It starts with the stabilization of the incident and finishes at the time when community recovers from the damages resulted from the disaster. The outcome information resulted from the disaster can be useful for four reason. First, this information can be useful to identify the pre-impact conditions which made communities vulnerable to disasters. Second, this information can be used to identify each country's specific segments that can be affected excessively (e.g. damage to properties and facilities, physical damages, or specific types of business). Third, this information can be utilized to know the event-specific conditions which

determine the level of disaster impact. Finally, examining this information gives planners the chance to identify suitable emergency management interventions. (Lavell, 1999)

In the wake of any disaster, it is essential to categorize risk level. This categorization can help in arranging and identifying the most priority work. Moreover, the purpose of this categorization is to divide disaster risk into levels. Those levels are: level 1 (Low Risk) such as minimal physical damage, minimal distress to employees, etc, level 2 (Moderate Risk) such as significant number of minor injuries, minor damage to properties and facilities, minor disruption of critical business operations, etc and level 3 (High Risk) such as major human casualties, major physical damage, significant impact on the economy and business activities. Figure 3 shows disaster risk levels and explains the three levels of disaster risk, as shown the three levels:

This model gives us a closer insight on the importance of categorising risks as this categorization gives us the chance to understand the risks, identify the gaps between risks and get more manageable risk-document with greater possibility to overview risks.

Figure 3. Disaster risk levels

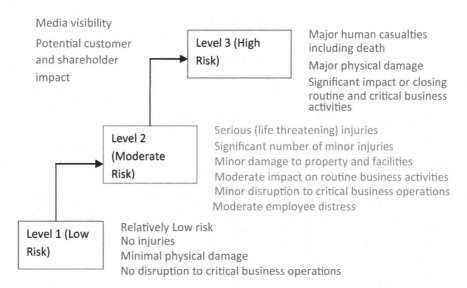

DISASTER RECOVERY IMPROVEMENT MODEL

Throughout the past years, the world faced many natural and man-made disasters. These disasters significantly affected economy causing huge amount of losses. Some businesses have managed to survive, whereas some did not have the ability to survive. The question here is that if those businesses had a disaster recovery system before the occurrence of the disaster, would they be still able to operate

It is well-known that disaster recovery system must be part of any business's information technology department. It must be accessible to all current and potential users and be approved by everyone especially upper management as a standard corporate policy that deals with impacts of disasters (Fledrich, & Burghardt, 2007). This system presents essential planning principles, practices, and enables personnel develop and reserve valuable information technology contingency plans. The principles of the system should meet the needs of most organizations such as Improve (e.g. measures collected, analysed and refined to increase maturity, continuously improve new technology which optimises performance and increases efficiency as well as speed, establish a global enterprise resource management system) Monitor (e.g. user training, security measurements and monitoring, protocol improvement and monitoring, established network maintenance management, network performance monitoring) Design (e.g. established key areas, wireless networking infrastructure management) Establish (e.g. fault management, accounting management, configuration management, performance, management, security management, help desk management system building infrastructure and safety requirements) Initial (e.g. identified need for disaster recovery plan, management authorisation and commitment). The Figure 4 illustrates Disaster Recovery Improvement Model.

Emergency services depend heavily on accurate timing and well-organized distribution of the tasks. It is stated that the future emergency response communication system should be more intelligent, robust, scalable and responsive. It is a must that the communication be maintained between different emergency services and between the emergency services and control centres before and after the occurrence of a disaster. Moreover,

Figure 4. Disaster recovery improvement model

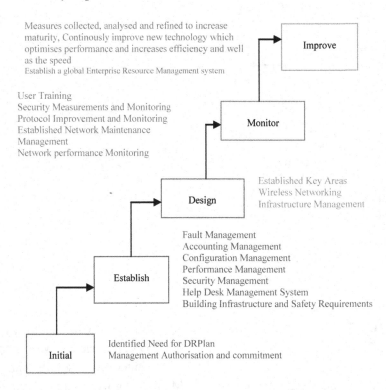

Measures collected, analysed and refined to increase
maturity, Continously improve new technology which
optimises performance and increases efficiency and well
as the speed
Establish a global Enterprise Resource Management system

User Training
Security Measurements and Monitoring
Protocol Improvement and Monitoring
Established Network Maintenance
Management
Network performance Monitoring

Improve

Monitor

Established Key Areas
Wireless Networking
Infrastructure Management

Design

Fault Management
Accounting Management
Configuration Management
Performance Management
Security Management
Help Desk Management System
Building Infrastructure and Safety Requirements

Establish

Identified Need for DRPlan
Management Authorisation and commitment

Initial

sensitive applications should be provided with information system that maintain high level of security yet are instantaneously accessible for authorized user.

CONCLUSION

Organizations and governments all over the world are facing a challenge of anticipating and managing risks. This is can be attributed to the ongoing changes that are happening in the human society, the increase of the number of population and the increase of both natural and man-made disaster. This paper discussed different aspects of disasters like threat, risk, and the management of risk. It has been discovered that the lack of preparedness in facing emergency events either natural or technological is the major threat that faces human society. It is essential to establish a policy and a system that can maintain all the informa-

tion needed and all the data. This is because one of the major threats of disasters lay in the loss of data and information.

REFERENCES

Aljazeera, (2005). *Tsunami slowed time [Online]*. Retrieved from http://english.aljazeera.net/NR/exeres/A46E0B05-1DC7-4852-83A1-5B6C1D9521E3.htm

Fledrich, F., & Burghardt, P. (2007). Agent–based systems for disaster management. *Communications of the ACM, 50*(3).

Hiatt, C. J. (2000). *A primer for disaster recovery planning in an IT environment*. Hershey, PA: Idea Group Publishing.

IFRCRCS. (2004). *International Federation of Red Cross and Red Crescent Societies World Disasters Report* [Online]. Retrieved from http://www.ifrc.org/publicat/wdr2004/chapter8.asp

Lavell, A. (1999). *Natural and Technological Disasters, Capacity Building and Human Resource Development for Disaster Management* [Online]. Retrieved from http://www.desenredando.org/public/articulos/1999/ntd/ntd1999_mar-1-2002.pdf

Semer, L. J. (1998). Disaster recovery planning for the distributed environment. *Internal Auditor, 55*(6), 41–47.

Shaw, R. (2006). Indian Ocean tsunami and aftermath need for environment-disaster synergy. *Disaster Prevention and Management, 15*(1), 5–20. doi:10.1108/09653560610654202

Tsunami Evaluation Coalition. (2006). *Joint Evaluation of the International Response to the Indian Ocean Tsunami, Tsunami Evaluation Coalition.*

Van, D. W., Bartel., & Turoff, M. (2007). Emergency-Response Systems: Emerging Trends and Technologies. *Communications of the ACM, 50*(3).

Compilation of References

Aaen, I. (2003). Software process improvement: Blueprints versus recipes. *IEEE Software*, *20*(5), 86–93. doi:10.1109/MS.2003.1231159

About the Eclipse Foundation (2009). Eclipse Software. Retrieved January 10, 2009, from http://www.eclipse.org/org

Abrahamsson, P., Hanhineva, A., Hulkko, H., Ihme, T., Jäälinoja, J., Korkala, M., et al. (2004, October 24-28). *Mobile-D: An Agile Approach for Mobile Application Development.* ACM SIGPLAN Conference on Object-Oriented Programming, Systems, Languages, and Applications (OOPSLA 2004), Vancouver, Canada, 2004.

Abrahamsson, P., Salo, O., Ronkainen, J., & Warsta, J. (2002). Agile Software Development Methods: Review and Analysis. *VVT Publications*, *478*, 7–94.

Abramson, N. (1963). *Information Theory and Coding.* New York: McGraw-Hill.

Abrial, J. R. (1992). On constructing large software systems. *IFIP 12th World Computer Congress*, (Vol. A-12, pp. 103-112).

Abrial, J.-R. (1996). *The B-book: assigning programs to meanings.* Cambridge, UK: Cambridge University Press.

Accenture, A. Inc., Commerce One, Inc., Fujitsu Limited, et al. (2000). UDDI Technical White Paper.

Accenture, A. Inc., Commerce One, Inc., Fujitsu Limited, et al. (2000). UDDI Technical White Paper.

Aczél, J., & Daróczy, Z. (1963). *On Measures of Information and their Characterization.* New York: Academic Press.

Agile Alliance. (2001). *Manifesto for Agile Software Development.* Retrieved May 02 2008 from http://www.agilemanifesto.org.

Agile Manifesto. (2006). *Manifesto for Agile Software Development.* Retrieved March 1, 2006 from http://agilemanifesto.org

Agrawal, S., Narasayya, V., & Yang, B. (2004). Integrating Vertical and Horizontal Partitioning into Automated Physical Database Design. *SIGMOD 2004,* Paris, France (pp. 359-370). New York: ACM.

Ahern, D. M., Clouse, A., & Turner, R. (2003). *CMMI Distilled: A Practical Introduction to integrated Process Improvement* (2nd ed.). London: Addison Wesley.

Ahern, D., Clouse, A., & Turner, R. (2008). *A Practical Introduction to Integrated Process Improvement,* (3rd Edition). Reading, MA: Addison-Wesley Professional.

Ahlgren, R., & Markkula, J. (2005, June 13-15). *Design Patterns and Organisational Memory in Mobile Application Development.* The Sixth International Conference on Product Focused Software Process Improvement (PROFES 2005), Oulu, Finland, 2005.

Ahluwalia, K. S., & Jain, A. (2006, October 21-23). *High Availability Design Patterns.* The Thirteenth Conference on Pattern Languages of Programs (PLoP 2006), Portland, USA, 2006.

Aichernig, B. K. (1999). Automatic Black-box testing with VDM oracles. *18th International Conference on Computer Safety, Reliability and Security, SAFECOMP'99,* (pp. 250-259).

Akmanligil, M., & Palvia, P. C. (2004). Strategies for global information systems development. *Information & Management, 42*(1), 45–59.

Albinet, A., Begoc, S., Boulanger, J.-L., et al. (2008). The MeMVaTEx methodology: from requirements to models in automotive application design. In *Proc. Embedded Real-Time Software*, January 2008.

Albinet, A., Boulanger, J.-L., Dubois, H., et al. (2007). Model-based methodology for requirements traceability in embedded systems. In *Proc. ECMDA*, June 2007.

Alexander Romanovsky, J. K. (2003, June). *Action-Oriented Exception Handling in Cooperative and Competitive Concurrent Object-Oriented Systems*. Paper presented at the Advances in Exception Handling Techniques, Darmstadt, Germany.

Alexander, I. F., & Stevens, R. (2002). *Writing Better Requirements*. Reading, MA: Addison-Wesley.

Alexis, L. (2003). *Enterprise Resource Planning*. New Delhi: Tata McGraw-Hill.

Al-Ghafees, M. A. (2000). Markov Chain based test data adequacy criteria. *IRMA '00*. (pp. 141)

Aljazeera, (2005). *Tsunami slowed time* [Online]. Retrieved from http://english.aljazeera.net/NR/exeres/A46E0B05-1DC7-4852-83A1-5B6C1D9521E3.htm

Aljazeera, (2005). *Tsunami slowed time [Online]*. Retrieved from http://english.aljazeera.net/NR/exeres/A46E0B05-1DC7-4852-83A1-5B6C1D9521E3.htm

Ammann, P., & Black, P. E. (1999). Abstracting Formal Specifications to Generate Software Tests via Model Checking. *IEEE 18th Digital Avionics Systems Conference, 2*(10), 1-10.

Amrani, EI, R., Rowe, F. & Geffroy-Maronnat, B. (2006). The effects of enterprise resource planning implementation strategy on cross-functionality. *Information Systems Journal*, (1): 79–104. doi:10.1111/j.1365-2575.2006.00206.x

Anderson, T., Feng, M., Riddle, S., & Romanovsky, A. (2003). Error Recovery for a Boiler System with OTS PID Controller. *Exception Handling in Object-Oriented Systems Workshop at ECOOP 2003*.

Andr'e, P., Romanczuk, A., Royer, J. C. (2000). Checking the Consistency of UML Class Diagrams Using Larch Prover. *Electronic Workshops in Computing eWiC, Rigorous Object-Oriented Methods 2000*.

André, C., Malet, F., & Peraldi-Frati, M.-A. (2007). A multiform time approach to real-time system modeling: Application to an automotive system. In *Proc. IEEE Industrial Embedded Systems, July 2007*.

Anvik, J., Hiew, L., & Murphy, G. C. (2005). Coping with an open bug repository. In *OOPSLA workshop on Eclipse technology eXchange: Proceedings of the 2005 OOPSLA Workshop on Eclipse Technology eXchange (U.S.A.), San Diego, California* (pp. 35 - 39).

Apache Ant (2008). Retrieved from http://ant.apache.org

Apache Jakarta Project - Tapestry. (2006). *Tapestry*. Retrieved June 2005, from http://tapestry.apache.org/

apd-El-Hafiz, S.K (2001). Entropies as measure of software information. *Software maintenance, Proceedings IEEE International conference* (pp. 110 -117).

Apers, P. (1988). Data Allocation in Distributed Database Systems. *ACM Transactions on Database Systems, 13*(3), 263–304. doi:10.1145/44498.45063

Apvrille, L., Coutiat, J. P., Lohr, C., & Saqui-Sannes, P. D. (2004). TURTLE-A Real time UML profile supported by a Formal validation Toolkit. *IEEE Transactions on Software Engineering, 30*(7), 473–487. doi:10.1109/TSE.2004.34

Arlow, J., & Neustadt, I. (2002). *UML and the Unified Process – Practical Object-Oriented Analysis & Design*. London: Addison Wesley

Arnold, K., Gosling, J., & Homes, D. (2000). *The Java Programming Language* (3rd ed.). Reading, MA: Addison-Wesley.

Askari, M., & Holt, R. (2006). Information theoretic evaluation of change prediction models for large-scale software. In *3rd ICSE workshop on mining software repositories: Proceedings of the 3rd ICSE Workshop on Mining Software Repositories (China), Shanghai* (pp. 126-132).

Aspray, W., Mayadas, F., & Vardi, M. Y. (2006). *Globalization and offshoring of software. A report of the ACM job migration task force*. New York: ACM Press.

ATESST. (2008). *Advancing traffic efficiency and safety through software technology.* European Commission [Online]. Retrieved from www.atesst.org

ATGSE. (2008). Workshop on Accountability and Traceability in Global Software Engineering (ATGSE2008). Technical Report ISCAS-SKLCS-08-07, State Key Laboratory of Computer Science, Institute of Software, Chinese Academy of Science.

Babar, M. A., Kitchenham, B., Zhu, L., Gorton, I., & Jeffery, R. (2006). An empirical study of groupware support for distributed software architecture evaluation process. *Journal of Systems and Software, 79*(7), 912–925. doi:10.1016/j.jss.2005.06.043

Baclawski, K., Kokar, M. M., & Waldinger, R. J. (2002). *Consistency Checking of Semantic Web Ontologies. the First International Semantic Web Conference on the Semantic Web* (pp. 454-459). London: Springer-Verlag.

Bader, A. (2005). *Modelling Trust for Reusable Software Components*. PhD thesis, School of Computer Science & Software Engineering, Monash University, Australia.

Bader, A., Mingins, C., Bennett, D., & Ramakrishnan, S. (2003). Establishing Trust in COTS Components. In *Proceedings of the 2nd Int Conference on COTS-Based Software Systems*, (LNCS, Vol. 2580, pp. 15-24). Berlin: Springer-Verlag.

Baentsch, M., Molter, G., & Sturm, P. (1995). WebMake: Integrating distributed software development in a structure-enhanced Web. *Computer Networks and ISDN Systems, 27*(6), 789–800. doi:10.1016/0169-7552(95)00019-4

Bak, P., Tang, C., & Wiesenfeld, K. (1987). Self-organized criticality - An explanation of 1/f noise. *Physical Review Letters, 59*, 381–384. doi:10.1103/PhysRevLett.59.381

Balcer, M. (2003, June). An executable uml virtual machine. In *Omg workshop on uml for enterprise applications: Delivering the promise of mda.*

Ballard, B. (2007). *Designing the Mobile User Experience*. Hoboken, NJ: John Wiley and Sons.

Balmelli, L. (2006). *An overview of the systems modeling language for products and systems development*. Tech. Rep., IBM, February 2006.

Bandinelli, S. C., Fuggetta, A., & Ghezzi, C. (1993). Software process model evolution in the SPADE Environment. *IEEE Transactions on Software Engineering, 19*(12), 1128–1144. doi:10.1109/32.249659

Banker, R.D., Datar, S.M., Kemerer, C.F. & Zweig, D. (1993). Software Complexity and Software Maintenance Costs. *Comm. ACM, 36.*

Bansiya, J., Davis, C., & Etzkon, L. (1999). An Entropy-Based Complexity Measure for Object-Oriented Designs. *Journal of Theory and Practice for Object Systems, 5*(2).

Barab'asi, A., Alberta, R., Jeong, H., & Bianconi, G. (2000). Power-law distribution of the world wide web. *Science, 287*, 1–2. doi:10.1126/science.287.5462.1

Barnett, M., & Grieskamp, W. Nachmanson, Gurevich, Y., L. Schulte, W., Tillmann, N. & Veanes, M. (2003). Scenario oriented modeling in Asml and its instrumentation for testing. *2nd International Workshop on Scenarios and State Machines: Models, Algorithms and Tools (SCESM).*

Barnett, M., Grieskamp, W., & Nachmanson, L. Schulte, W., Tillmann, N. & Veanes, M. (2003), Model-Based Testing with AsmL. NET. *1st European Conference on Model-Driven Software Engineering.*

Barnett, M., Grieskamp, W., & Nachmanson, L. Schulte, W., Tillmann, N. & Veanes, M. (2003). Towards a tool environment for model based testing with AsmL. *3rd International Workshop on Formal Approaches to Testing of Software (FATES 2003)*, (pp. 252-256).

Basili, V. R., Bomarius, F., & Feldmann, R. L. (2007). Get Your Experience Factory Ready for the Next Decade

-- Ten Years After "How to Build and Run One". *29th International Conference on Software Engineering, 2007, ICSE 2007 Companion,* 167-168.

Basili, V. R., Briand, L. C., & Melo, W. L. (1996). A Validation of Object-Oriented Design Metrics as Quality Indicators. *IEEE Transactions on Software Engineering, 22,* 751–761. doi:10.1109/32.544352

Basili, V., & Boehm, B. (2001). COTS-Based Systems Top 10 List. *IEEE Computer,* (pp. 91-93)

Bavier, A., Bowman, M., Chun, B., Culler, D., Karlin, S., Muir, S., et al. (2004, March). Operating system support for planetary-scale services. In *Symposium on network system design and implementation.*

Beatty, R. C., & Williams, C. D. (2006, March). ERP II: Best Practices for Successfully Implementing an ERP upgrade. *Communications of the ACM, 49*(3). doi:10.1145/1118178.1118184

Beck, K. (1999). *Extreme Programming Explained: Embrace Change* (pp. 10-70). Reading MA: Addison-Wesley.

Beck, K. (2000). *Extreme programming Explained Embraced Change.* Reading, MA: Addison-Wesley.

Beck, K., & Andres, C. (2004). *Extreme Programming Explained: Embrace Change.* Reading, MA: Addison-Wesley Professional.

Beck, K., & Andres, C. (2005). *Extreme Programming Explained: Embrace Change* (2nd Edition). Reading, MA: Addison-Wesley.

Beck, K., & Fowler, M. (2000). *Planning Extreme Programming.* Reading MA: Addison-Wesley Press.

Beecham, S., Hall, T., & Rainer, A. (2003, September). Defining a Requirements Process Improvement Model. *Software Quality Journal, 13*(13), 247–279.

Behm, P., Benoit, P., Faivre, A., & Meynadier, J.-M. (1999). « METEOR: A successful application of B in a large project ». *Proceedings of FM'99: World Congress on formal Methods,* (pp. 369-387).

Bell, K. Z. (2006). *Optimizing Effectiveness and Efficiency of Software Testing: a Hybrid Approach.* PhD Dissertation, North Carolina State University.

Berenbach, B. (2006). Impact of organizational structure on distributed requirements engineering processes: Lessons learned. In *Proceedings of the 2006 International Workshop on Global Software Development for the Practitioner* (pp. 15-19).

Berners-Lee, T., Hendler, J., & Lassila, O. (2001). The Semantic Web. *Scientific American, 5,* 29–37.

Berthomieu, B., & Diaz, M. (1991). Modeling and Verification of Time Dependent Systems Using Time Petri Nets. *IEEE Transactions on Software Engineering, 17*(3), 259–273. doi:10.1109/32.75415

Bertoa, M., & Vallecillo, A. (2002). Quality Attributes for COTS Components. In *6th ECOOP Workshop on Quantitative Aproaches in OO Software Engineering.*

Bertolino, A., & Marre, M. (1994). Automatic Generation of path covers based on Control Flow analysis of Computer programs. *IEEE Transactions on Software Engineering,* 885–899. doi:10.1109/32.368137

Bertolino, A., Marchetti, E., & Muccini, H. (2004). Introducing a Reasonably Complete and Coherent Approach for Model-based Testing. *10th International Conference on Tools and Algorithms for the Construction and Analysis of Systems, (TACAS'04).*

Bhatia, S., & Deogun, J. (1998). Conceptual Clustering in Information Retrieval. *IEEE Transactions on System, Man, Cybernetics, part B . Cybernetics., 28*(3), 427–436.

Bhattacharya, S., & Kanjilal, A. (2004). Static Analysis of Object Oriented systems using Extended Control Flow graph. *IEEE TENCON, 2004,* B310–B313.

Bhattacharya, S., & Kanjilal, A. (2006). Code Based Analysis of Object Oriented Systems. *Journal of Computer Science & Technology JCST, 21*(6), 965–972. doi:10.1007/s11390-006-0965-0

Bhuta, J., Sudeep, M., & Subrahmanya, S. V. (2007). A Survey of Enterprise Software Development Risks In a

Flat World. *First International Symposium on Empirical Software Engineering and Measurement, 2007, ESEM 2007,* 476-478.

Bichler, M., & Lin, K. (2006, June). Service-oriented computing. *IEEE Computer, 39*(6).

Biehl, J. T., Baker, W. T., Bailey, B. P., Tan, D. S., Inkpen, K. M., & Czerwinski, M. (2008). In *Proceedings of the Twenty-Sixth Annual SIGCHI Conference on Human Factors in Computer Systems* (pp. 939-948).

Biehl, J. T., Czerwinski, M., Smith, G., & Robertson, G. G. (2007). FASTDash: A visual dashboard for fostering awareness in software teams. In *Proceedings of the SIGCHI conference on Human factors in computing systems* (pp. 1313-1322). San Jose, CA: ACM Press.

Biffl, S., Aurum, A., Boehm, B., Erdogmus, H., & Grünbacher, P. (2006). *Value-Based Software Engineering.* Berlin: Springer-Verlag.

Bird, C., Gourley, A., Devanbu, P., Gertz, M., & Swaminathan, A. (2006a). Mining email social networks. In *Third international workshop on mining software repositories: Proceedings of Third International Workshop on Mining Software Repositories(China), Shanghai* (pp. 137-143).

Bird, C., Gourley, A., Devanbu, P., Gertz, M., & Swaminathan, A. (2006b). Mining email social networks in postgres. In *Third international workshop on mining software repositories: Proceedings of Third International Workshop on Mining Software Repositories (China), Shanghai* (pp. 185-186).

Boehm, B. (1981). *Software Engineering Economics.* Englewood Cliffs, NJ: Prentice Hall.

Boehm, B. (2000). Unifying software engineering and systems engineering. *Computer, 33*(3), 114–116. doi:10.1109/2.825714

Boehm, B. (2003). Value-Based Software Engineering. *ACM SIGSOFT Software Engineering Notes, 28*(2), 3–15. doi:10.1145/638750.638775

Boehm, B. (2006). Some future trends and implications for systems and software engineering processes. *Systems Engineering, 9*(1), 1–19. doi:10.1002/sys.20044

Boehm, B. W., & Papaccio, P. N. (1988). Understanding and controlling software costs. *IEEE Transactions on Computers,* 1462–1467.

Boehm, B., & Basili, V. (2001). *Software Defect Reduction Top 10 List.*

Boehm, B., & Turner, R. (2004). *Balancing Agility and Discipline: A guide for the perplexed* (1st ed. pp. 165-194). Reading, MA: Addison-Wesley.

Boehm, B., Port, D., Jain, A., & Basili, V. (2002). Achieving CMMI Level 5 Improvements with MBASE and the CeBASE Method. *Cross Talk Journal.* Retrieved October 11, 2007 from http://www.stsc.hill.af.mil/CrossTalk/2002/may/boehm.asp

Bohem, B. (1981). *Software Engineering Economics.* Englewood Cliffs, NJ: Prentice Hall.

Bon, P., Boulanger, J-L. & Mariano, G. (2003). Semi formal modelling and formal specification: UML & B in simple railway application. *ICSSEA 2003, PARIS,* Novembre 2003.

Booch, G. (1994). *Object Oriented Analysis and Design with Applications.* New York: The Benjamin/Cummings Publishing Company, Inc.

Booch, G., Brown, A., Iyengar, S., Rumbaugh, J., & Selic, B. (2004, December). An mda manifesto. In *The mda journal: Model driven architecture straight from the masters* (chap. 11). Meghan-Kier Press.

Borgatti, S. (2008). *Introduction to Grounded Theory.* Retrieved from http:// www.analytictech.com /mb870 / introtoGT.htm

Börger, E., Cavarra, A., & Riccobene, E. (2004). On Formalizing UML State Machines using ASMs. *Information and Software Technology, 46*(5), 287–292. doi:10.1016/j.infsof.2003.09.009

Borst, W. N. (1997). *Construction of Engineering Ontologies for Knowledge Sharing and Reuse.* PhD thesis, University of Twente, Enschede.

Borst, W. N. (1997). *Construction of Engineering Ontologies for Knowledge Sharing and Reuse.* PhD thesis, University of Twente, Enschede.

Bortolazzi, J. (2004). *Challenges in automotive software engineering.* Presented at International ICSE workshop on Software Engineering for Automotive Systems.

Borzemski, L. (1996). Optimal Partitioning of a Distributed Relational Database for Multistage Decision-Making Support systems. *Cybernetics and Systems Research, 2*(13), 809–814.

Bosch, J. (2000). *Design and Use of Software Architectures.* Reading, MA: Addison-Wesley Professional.

Bosse, T., Sharpanskykh, A., & Treur, J. (n.d.). *On the Complexity Monotonocity.* Thesis for Dept. of Artificial Intelligence, De Boelelaan 1081a, 1081 HV, the Netherlands.

Boulanger, J.-L. (2007). TUCS: How Build a certifiable railway application with UML. *ICSSEA 2007*, Paris, December 2007.

Boulanger, J.-L., & Van, Q.-D. (2007). A requirement-based methodology for automotive software development. In *Proc. MCSE,* July 2007.

Boulanger, J.-L., & Van, Q.-D. (2008). Experiences from a model-based methodology for developing embedded electronic software in automobile. In *Proc. ICTTA, April 2008.*

Boy, G. A. (2007). Perceived complexity and Cognitive Stability in Human-Centered Design. *Proceedings of the HCI International Conference, Beijing, China.*

Bradley, P., Managasarian, O., & Street, W. (1997). Clustering via Concave Minimization. *Advances in Neural Information Processing Systems, 9*, 368–374.

Brandt, I. (1983). A Comparative Study of Information Systems Development Methodologies: Proceedings of the IFIP WG8.1 Working Conference on Feature Analysis of Information Systems Design Methodologies. In T.W. Olle, H.G. Sol, & C.J. Tully, (eds.) *Information Systems Design Methodologies: A Feature Analysis* (pp. 9-36). Amsterdam: Elsevier.

Brockmans, S., & Haase, P. (2006). *A Metamodel and UML Profile for Rule-extended OWL DL Ontologies -A Complete Reference.* Tech. Rep. University Karlsruhe (TH), Karlsruhe, Germany.

Brockmans, S., & Haase, P. (2006). *A Metamodel and UML Profile for Rule-extended OWL DL Ontologies -A Complete Reference.* Tech. Rep. University Karlsruhe (TH), Karlsruhe, Germany.

Brodman, J., & Johnson, D. (1997, May 19th). A Software Process Improvement Approach for small organisation and small projects. In *Proceedings of the 19th International Conference in Software Engineering,* Boston (pp. 661-662). New York: ACM Press.

Brooks, F. P. (1987). No Silver Bullet: Essence and Accidents of Software Engineering. *Computer, 20*(4), 10–19. doi:10.1109/MC.1987.1663532

Brooks, F. P. (1995). *The Mythical Man-Month.* Reading, MA: Addison Wesley Longman Inc.

Brown, C., & Vessey, I. (1999). ERP implementation approaches: toward a contingency framework. *Proceedings of the International Conference on Information Systems,* (pp. 411-416).

Bryce, R., & Colbourn, C. J. (2007). The Density Algorithm for Pairwise Interaction Testing. *Journal of Software Testing . Verification and Reliability, 17*(3), 159–182. doi:10.1002/stvr.365

Bryce, R., & Colbourn, C. J. (2009). A Density-Based Greedy Algorithm for Higher Strength Covering Arrays. *Journal of Software Testing, Verification, and Reliability, 19*(1), 37-53. doi: 10.1002/stvr.393

Brynjolfsson, E. (1993). The Productivity Paradox of Information Technology. *Communications of the ACM, 36*(12), 66–77. doi:10.1145/163298.163309

Buchanan, G., Farrant, S., Jones, M., Thimbleby, H., Marsden, G., & Pazzani, M. (2001). Improving Mobile Internet Usability. *The Tenth International World Wide Web Conference* (WWW10), Hong Kong, China, May 1-5, 2001.

Buessow, R., & Grieskamp, W. (1997). Combining Z and Temporal Interval Logics for the Formalization of Properties and Behaviors of Embedded Systems. *3rd Asian Computing Science Conference on Advances in Computing Science, 1345*, 46-56.

Bug reports for Eclipse projects (2009). Eclipse Software. Retrieved January 10, 2009, from https://bugs.eclipse.org/bugs/

Bulka, A. (2006, September). *Design Pattern Automation* [Online]. Retrieved from http://www.atug.com/andypatterns/

Bunde, A., Havlin, S., Kantelhardt, J. W., Penzel, T., Peter, J.-H., & Voigt, K. (2000). Correlated and uncorrelated regions in heart-rate fluctuations during sleep. *Physical Review Letters, 85,* 3736–3739. doi:10.1103/PhysRevLett.85.3736

Bunde, E. K., Bunde, A., Havlin, S., Roman, H. E., Goldreich, Y., & Schellnhuber, H.-J. (1998). Indication of a universal persistence law governing atmospheric variability. *Physical Review Letters, 81,* 729–732. doi:10.1103/PhysRevLett.81.729

Burdy, L., Meynadier, J-M. (1999). *Automatic refinement FM'99 workshop -- Applying B in an industrial context: Tools, Lessons and Techniques - Toulouse – 1999.*

Burr, K., & Young, W. (1998). Combinatorial test techniques: Table-based automation, test generation, and code coverage. *International Conference on Software Testing Analysis and Review* (pp. 503-513).

Buschmann, F., Henney, K., & Schmidt, D. C. (2007a). *Pattern-Oriented Software Architecture, Volume 4: A Pattern Language for Distributed Computing.* Hoboken, NJ: John Wiley and Sons.

Buschmann, F., Henney, K., & Schmidt, D. C. (2007b). *Pattern-Oriented Software Architecture, Volume 5: On Patterns and Pattern Languages.* Hoboken, NJ: John Wiley and Sons.

Buschmann, F., Meunier, R., Rohnert, H., Sommerlad, P., & Stal, M. (1996). *Pattern Oriented Software Architecture, Volume 1: A System of Patterns.* Hoboken, NJ: John Wiley and Sons.

Buschmann, F., Meunier, R., Rohnert, H., Sommerlad, P., Stal, M., Sommerlad, P., et al. (1996). *Pattern-oriented software architecture,* (Vol. 1: *A system of patterns*). Chichester, UK: John Wiley & Sons.

Business process modeling notation (bpmn) 1.0. (2004). Business Process Modeling Initiative.

Busse, D. (2002, April 21,). *Usable Web Design Patterns for World-Ready E-Commerce Sites.* CHI Workshop on Patterns in Practice: A Workshop for UI Designers, Minneapolis, USA.

Bussow, R., & Geisler, R. Grieskamp, W. & Klar, M. (1998). *Integrating Z with Dynamic Modeling Techniques for the Specification of Reactive Systems.*

Cao, Y., Zhao, J., Han, Y., & Dai, G. (2002). A Paradigm of Software development for Mass Customization. *Journal of Computer Research and Development, 39*(5), 593–598.

Cao, Y., Zhao, J., Han, Y., & Dai, G. (2002). A Paradigm of Software development for Mass Customization. *Journal of Computer Research and Development, 39*(5), 593–598.

Capozucca, A., Gallina, B., Guelfi, N., Pelliccione, P., & Romanovsky, A. (2006). CORRECT Developing Fault-Tolerant Distributed Systems. *European Research Consortium for Informatics and Mathematics, 64.*

Cardoso, J. (2006). *Approaches to Compute Workflow Complexity.* "Dagstuhl Seminar," The Role of Business Process in Service Oriented Architectures, Dagstuhl, Germany.

Carey, J. M. (1998). Creating global software: A conspectus and review. *Interacting with Computers, 9*(4), 449–465. doi:10.1016/S0953-5438(97)00028-3

Carlson, J. M., & Doyle, J. (1999). Highly optimized tolerance: A mechanism for power laws in designed systems. *Physical Review E: Statistical Physics, Plasmas, Fluids, and Related Interdisciplinary Topics, 60,* 1414–1427.

Carlson, J. M., & Doyle, J. (2002). Complexity of robustness. *Proceedings of the National Academy of Sciences of the United States of America, 99,* 2538–2545. doi:10.1073/pnas.012582499

Carney, D., & Green, F. (2000). What Do You Mean by COTS? Finally, a Useful Answer. *IEEE Software, 17*(2), 83–86. doi:10.1109/52.841700

Carney, D., Morris, E., & Place, P. (2003). *Identifying COTS Product Risks: The COTS Usage Risk Evaluation* (Tech. Rep. CMU/SEI-2003-TR-023). Pittsburgh, PA: Carnegie Mellon University, Software Engineering Institute.

Carrington, D., MacColl, I., McDonald, J., Murray, L., & Strooper, P. (2000). From Object-Z Specifications to ClassBench Test Suites, *Journal on Software Testing. Verification and Reliability, 10*(2), 111–137. doi:10.1002/1099-1689(200006)10:2<111::AID-STVR204>3.0.CO;2-P

Cartwright, M., & Shepperd, M. (1996). *An Empirical Investigation of Object-Oriented Software in Industry.* Technical Report TR 96/ 01, Dept. of Computing, Talbot Campus, Bournemouth University.

Carvalho, R. A. (2006). Issues on evaluating Free/open source ERP sysyems. In Research and Practical Issues of Enterprise Informations Systems (pp. 667-676). New York: Springer Verlag, Inc.

Casey, V., & Richardson, I. (2002). *A Practical Application of Ideal Model.* Product Focused Software Process Improvement, 4th International Conference (PROFES), December 9-11, Rovaniemi – Finland (pp.172-184). Berlin: Springer.

Caulliraux, H. M., Proença, A., & Prado, C. A. S. (2000). *ERP Systems from a Strategic Perspective.* Sixth International Conference on Industrial Engineering and Operations Management, Niteroi, Brazil.

Cavarra, A., Crichton, C., & Davies, J. (2004). A method for the automatic generation of test suites from object models . *Information and Software Technology, 46*(5), 309–314. doi:10.1016/j.infsof.2003.09.004

CENELEC (2001). EN 50128 CENELEC. *Railway applications – software for railway control and protection systems.*

CENELEC (2003). EN 50129 CENELEC. *Railway applications – Safety related electronic systems for signaling.*

CENELEC. (2000). *EN 50126: Railway applications - The specification and demonstration of dependability, reliability, availability, maintainability and safety* (RAMS).

Ceri, S., Navathe, S., & Wiederhold, G. (1983). Distribution Design of Logical Database Schemas. *IEEE Transactions on Software Engineering, 9*(4), 487–504. doi:10.1109/TSE.1983.234957

Chakravarthy, S., Muthuraj, J., Varadarajian, R., & Navathe, S. (1994). An Objective Function for Vertically Partitioned Relations in Distributed Database and Its Analysis. *Distributed and Parallel Databases, 2*, 183–207. doi:10.1007/BF01267326

Challenge, M. (2007). Mining Software Repositories. Retrieved January, 10 2009, from http://msr.uwaterloo.ca/msr2007/challenge/

Challenge, M. (2008). Mining Software Repositories. Retrieved January 10, 2009, from http://msr.uwaterloo.ca/msr2008/challenge/index.html

Chan, S. S., Fang, X., Brzezinski, J., Zhou, Y., Shuang, X., & Lam, J. (2002). Usability for Mobile Commerce across Multiple Form Factors. *Journal of Electronic Commerce Research, 3*(3), 187–199.

Chan, S., & Fang, X. (2001). *Usability Issues in Mobile Commerce.* The Seventh Americas Conference in Information Systems (AMCIS 2001), Boston, USA, August 5-8, 2001.

Chandrasekaran, B., Josephson, J. R., & Benjamins, V. R. (1999). What are ontologies, and why do we need them? *IEEE Intelligent Systems, 14*(1), 20–26. doi:10.1109/5254.747902

Chandrasekaran, B., Josephson, J. R., & Benjamins, V. R. (1999). What are ontologies, and why do we need them? *IEEE Intelligent Systems, 14*(1), 20–26. doi:10.1109/5254.747902

Chen, A. (2001). Incremental Data Allocation and Reallocation in Distributed Database Systems. *Journal of Database Management, 12*(1), 35–45.

Chen, E. (n.d.). *Distributed DBMS Concepts and Design.* Retrieved November 9th, 2007 from: http://www.cs.sjsu.edu/~lee/cs157b/fall2003/Edward_Chen_Chapter%2022.ppt

Chen, J., Xi, Y., & Zhang, Z. (1998). A Clustering Algorithm for Fuzzy Model Identification. *Fuzzy Sets and Systems, 98*, 319–329. doi:10.1016/S0165-0114(96)00384-3

Cheng, B. H. C., & Wang, E. Y. (2002). Formalizing and integrating the dynamic model for object oriented modelling. *IEEE Transactions on Software Engineering*, 747–762. doi:10.1109/TSE.2002.1027798

Chidamber, S., & Kemerer, C. (1994). A Metrics Suite for Object-Oriented Design. *IEEE Transactions on Software Engineering*, 476–492. doi:10.1109/32.295895

Chowdhary, P., Bhaskaran, K., Caswell, N. S., Chang, H., Chao, T., & Chen, S. K. (2006). Model driven development for business performance management. *BM SYSTEMS JOURNAL, 45*(3), 587–605.

Chris M., & Lewis, G. A. (2006). *Model Problems in Technologies for Interoperability: OWL Web Ontology Language for Services (OWL-s)*. CMU/SEI Technical Notes (CMU/SEI-2006-TN-018).

Chrissis, M. B., Konrad, M., & Shrum, S. (2003). CMMI(R): Guidelines for Process. Integration and Product Improvement (2nd Ed.). Reading, MA: Addison-Wesley.

Chrissis, M. B., Konrad, M., & Shrun, S. (2003). *CMMI: Guidelines for Process Integration and Product Improvement*. London: Addison Wesley.

Chrissis, M. B., Wemyss, G., Goldenson, D., Konrad, M., Smith, K., & Svolou, A. (2003). CMMI Interpretive Guidance Project: Preliminary Report [Internet]. Software Engineering Institute. Retrieved June 6th, 2004 from http://www.sei.cmu.edu/pub/documents/03.reports/pdf/03sr007-body-revised.pdf

Christie, A. M. (1999). Simulation in support of CMM-based process improvement. *Journal of Systems and Software, 46*, 107–112. doi:10.1016/S0164-1212(99)00004-7

Christoplos, I., Mitchell, J., & Liljelund, A. (2001). Re-framing Risk: The Changing Context of Disaster Mitigation and Preparedness. *Disasters Journal, 25*(3), 185. doi:10.1111/1467-7717.00171

Christopoulou, E. (2008). Context as a Necessity in Mobile Applications. In J. Lumsden (Ed.), *Handbook of Research on User Interface Design and Evaluation for Mobile Technology* (Vol. I, pp. 187-204). Hershey, PA: IGI Global.

Chu, W. (1969). Optimal file allocation in a multiple-computer information system. *IEEE Transactions on Computers, 18*, 885–889. doi:10.1109/T-C.1969.222542

Chu, W. (1973). Optimal file allocation in a computer network. In N. Abramson & F. F. Kuo, (Eds.), *Computer Communication Networks* (pp. 83-94). Englewood Cliffs, NJ: Prentice-Hall.

Chung, L., Nixon, B., Yu, E., & Mylopoulos, J. (2000). *Non-Functional Requirements in Software Engineering*. Boston: Kluwer Academic Publisher

Church, Z. (2008). *SAP ERP on-demand challenge lofty, but not impossible.*

CIO. (2006). *Services and Components Based Architectures – A Strategic Guide for Implementing Distributed and Reusable Components and Services in the Federal Government*. Architecture and Infrastructure Committee, Federal Chief Information Officers Council.

Clark, B., & Torchiano, M. (2004). *Can We Reach a Consensus.* International Workshop on COTS Terminology and Categories.

Clarke, E. M., Grumberg, O., & Peled, D. (2000). *A. Model-Checking*. Cambridge, MA: MIT Press.

Clause, J., & Orso, A. (2007). A Technique for Enabling and Supporting Debugging of Field Failures. *29th International Conference on Software Engineering, 2007, ICSE 2007*. 261-270.

Clements, P., & Northrop, L. (2001). *Software Product Lines Practices and Patterns* (3rd ed.). Reading, MA: Addison-Wesley Professional.

Clements, P., & Northrop, L. (2002). *Software product Lines*. Reading, MA: Addison Wesley Publications.

Clements, P., & Northrop, L. (2004). *Software Product Lines: Practices and Patterns. SEI series in Software*

Engineering. Reading, MA: Addison-Wesley Publications.

Clements, P., & Northrop, L. (2004). *Software product Lines: Practices and Patterns.* Reading, MA: Addison Wesley Publications.

Clements, P., Kazman, R., & Klein, M. (2002). *Evaluating Software Architecture. Methods and Case Studies.* Reading, MA: Addison-Wesley Professional.

Cockburn, A. (2000). Selecting a Project's Methodology. In *IEEE Software*, (pp. 64-71).

Cockburn, A. (2004). *Crystal Clear A Human-Powered Methodology for Small Teams, and it.* Reading, MA: Addison- Wesley Press.

Cohen, D. M., Dalal, S. R., Fredman, M. I., & Patton, G. C. (1997). The AETG system: An approach to testing based on Combinatorial design. *IEEE Transactions on Software Engineering, 23*, 437. doi:10.1109/32.605761

Cohen, D. M., Dalal, S. R., Fredman, M. L., & Patton, G. C. (1997). The AETG system: an approach to testing based on combinatorial design. *IEEE Transactions on Software Engineering, 23*(7), 437–444. doi:10.1109/32.605761

Cohen, D. M., Dalal, S. R., Parelius, J., & Patton, G. C. (1996). The combinatorial design approach to automatic test generation. *IEEE Software, 13*(5), 83–88. doi:10.1109/52.536462

Cohen, D. M., Dalal, S. R., Parelius, J., & Patton, G. C. (1996). The combinatorial design approach to automatic test generation. *7th International Symposium on Software Reliability Engineering.* DACS Gold Practice™ Document Series (n.d.). *Model-Based Testing, GP-34 V 1.1.* Retrieved October 20, 2003 from http://www.goldpractices.com/dwnload/practice/pdf/Model_Based_Testing.pdf

Cohen, D.M., Dalal, S. R., Fredman, M. L., & Patton, G. C. (1996). *Method and system for automatically generating efficient test cases for systems having interacting elements* [United States Patent, Number 5, 542, 043].

Cohen, M. B., Colbourn, C. J., & Ling, A. C. H. (2008). Constructing Strength 3 Covering Arrays with Augmented Annealing. *Discrete Mathematics, 308*, 2709–2722. doi:10.1016/j.disc.2006.06.036

Cohen, M. B., Colbourn, C. J., Gibbons, P. B., & Mugridge, W. B. (2003). Constructing test suites for interaction testing. *International Conference on Software Engineering* (pp. 38-48).

Cohn, M. (2003). *User stories applied for Agile Software Development.* Reading, MA: Addison-Wesley.

Colbourn, C. J. (2004). Combinatorial aspects of covering arrays. *Le Matematiche (Catania), 58*, 121–167.

Collins-Cope, M. (2002). *Planning to be Agile? A discussion of how to plan agile, iterative and incremental developments* [white paper]. Ratio Technical Library. Retrieved July 20, 2008 from http://www.ratio.co.uk/whitepaper_12.pdf

Compiere. (2006). *Compiere.* Retrieved May 2006, from http://www.compiere.com/

Computer Associates. (2007). *The ROI of Developing Applications With CA Gen* (Tech. Rep.).

Connolly, T., & Begg, C. (2004). *Database Systems: A Practical Approach to Design, Implementation and Management* (4th ed.). Reading, MA: Addison-Wesley.

Cook, S., Harrison, R., & Wernick, P. (2005). A simulation model of self-organising evolvability in software systems. In *1st IEEE international workshop on software evolvability: Proceedings of 1st IEEE International Workshop on Software Evolvability (Hungary)* (pp. 17-22).

Coplien, J. O. (1998). *Multi-Paradigm Design for C++* (1st Ed.). Reading, MA: Addison-Wesley Professional.

Costa, R., & Lifschitz, S. (2003). Database Allocation Strategies for Parallel BLAST Evaluation on Clusters. *Distributed and Parallel Databases, 13*, 99–127. doi:10.1023/A:1021569823663

Coyle, F. (2001). Wireless Web: A Manager's Guide. Reading, MA: Addison-Wesley.

Crispin, L. House, T. & Wade, C. (2001). The Need for Speed: Automating Acceptance Testing in an Extreme Programming Environment. In *Proc. Second Int'l Conf. eXtreme Programming and Flexible Processes in Software Eng.,* (pp. 96-104).

Crnkovic, I. (2008). *Component Based Software Engineering–New challenges in Software Development*. Malardalen University, Department of computer engineering, Sweden.

Crowston, K., & Howison, J. (2005). The social structure of free and open source software development. *First Monday, 10*(2).

Cruise Control (2003). Retrieved from http://cruisecontrol.sourceforge.net/

Csete, M. E., & Doyle, J. C. (2002). Reverse engineering of biological complexity. *Science, 295*, 1664–1669. doi:10.1126/science.1069981

Cuenot, P., Chen, D., Gérard, S., et al. (2007). *Towards Improving Dependability of Automotive System by Using the EAST-ADL Architecture Description Language* (LNCS, vol. 4615, no. 200). Berlin: Springer.

Curbera, F., Nagy, W. A., & Weerawarana, S. (2001). *Web Services: Why and How*. Workshop on object oriented web services, OOPSLA, Florida.

Curbera, F., Nagy, W. A., & Weerawarana, S. (2001). *Web Services: Why and How*. Workshop on object oriented web services, OOPSLA, Florida.

Currion, P., Chamindra, S., & Bartel, V. W. (2007, March). Open source software for disaster management evaluating how the Sahana disaster information system coordinates disparate institutional and technical resources in the wake of the Indian Ocean tsunami. *Communications of the ACM, 50*(3). doi:10.1145/1226736.1226768

Cusumano, M. A. (2008). Managing software development in globally distributed teams. *Communications of the ACM, 51*, 15–17. doi:10.1145/1314215.1340930

Czarnecki, K., Eisenecker, U. W., Gluck, R., Vandevoorde, D., & Veldhuizen, T. L. (2000). Generative Programming and Active Libraries. In *Selected Papers from the International Seminar on Generic Programming* (pp. 25-39). Berlin: Springer-Verlag.

Daconta, M. C., Obrst, L. J., & Smith, K. T. (2003). *The Semantic Web: A Guide to the Future of XML, Web Services, and Knowledge Management*. Indianapolis, IN: Wiley Publishing.

Daconta, M. C., Obrst, L. J., & Smith, K. T. (2003). *The Semantic Web: A Guide to the Future of XML, Web Services, and Knowledge Management*. Indianapolis, IN: Wiley Publishing.

Dalal, S. R. A. Jain, N. Karunanithi, J. M. Leaton, C. M. Lott, G. C. Patton, B. M. Horowitz, (1999). Model Based Testing in Practice. *International Conference of Software Engineering ICSE'99*, (pp. 285-294).

Dalal, S. R., Jain, A., Karunanithi, N., Leaton, J. M., & Lott, C. M. (1998). Model-Based Testing of a Highly Programmable System. *9th International Symposium on Software Reliability Engineering, ISSRE'98 (IEEE Computer Society Press)*, (pp. 174–178).

Dalal, S. R., Jain, A., Karunanithi, N., Leaton, J. M., Lott, C. M., Patton, G. C., & Horowitz, B. M. (1999). Model-Based Testing in Practice. *International Conference on Software Engineering* (pp. 285-294).

Dalal, S. R., Jain, A., Patton, G., Rathi, M., & Seymour, P. (1998). AETG^SM Web: A Web based Service for Automatic Efficient Test Generation from Functional Requirements. *2nd IEEE Workshop on Industrial Strength Formal Specification Techniques*.

Damian, D., & Lanubile, F. (2004). The 3rd international workshop on global software development. In *Proceedings of the 26th International Conference on Software Engineering (ICSE)* (pp. 756-757).

Damian, D., Lanubile, F., & Oppenheimer, H. (2003). Addressing the challenges of software industry globalization: The workshop on global software development. In *Proceedings of the 25th International Conference on Software Engineering (ICSE)* (pp. 793-794).

Dan, L., & Aichernig, B. K. (2004) Combining Algebraic and Model Based Test Generation, Proceedings of ICTAC 2004. *1st International Colloquium on Theoretical Aspects of Computing*, (LNCS Vol. 3407, pp. 250-264). Berlin: Springer-Verlag.

Daneva, M. (2004). ERP Requirements Engineering Practice: Lessons Learned. *IEEE Software*, 26–33. doi:10.1109/MS.2004.1270758

Daneva, M., & Wieringa, R. J. (2006). A requirements engineering framework for cross-organizational ERP systems. *Requirements Engineering, 11*, 194–204. doi:10.1007/s00766-006-0034-9

Dangle, K., Larsen, P., & Shaw, M. (2005). Software process improvement in small organisation: A case study. *IEEE Software, 22*(6), 68–75. doi:10.1109/MS.2005.162

Danilowicz, C., & Nguyen, N. (2003). Consensus Methods for Solving Inconsistency of Replicated Data in Distributed Systems. *Distributed and Parallel Databases, 14*, 53–69. doi:10.1023/A:1022835811280

Davenport, T. H. (1998, July/August). Putting the enterprise into the enterprise system. *Harvard Business Review, 76*(4), 121–131.

de Campos, R. de Carvalho, R. A. Rodrigues, J. S. (2007). Enterprise Modeling for Development Processes of Open Source ERP. In *Proc. 18th Production and Operation Management Society Conference*, Dallas, TX.

De Carvalho, R. A., & Monnerat, R. M. (2008, September). Development Support Tools for Enterprise Resource Planning. *IEEE IT Professional, 10*, 31–37. doi:10.1109/MITP.2008.36

De Lucia, A., Fasano, F., Scanniello, G., & Tortora, G. (2007). Enhancing collaborative synchronous UML modelling with fine-grained versioning of software artefacts. *Journal of Visual Languages and Computing, 18*(5), 492–503. doi:10.1016/j.jvlc.2007.08.005

de Souza, C. R., Quirk, S., Trainer, E., & Redmiles, D. F. (2007). Supporting collaborative software development through the visualization of socio-technical dependencies. In *Proceedings of the 2007 International ACM Conference on Supporting Group Work* (147-156).

Dearle, A. (2007). Software Deployment, Past, Present And Future. *Future of Software Engineering, 2007 . FOSE, 07*, 269–284.

Delatour, J., & De Lamotte, F. (2003). ArgoPN: A CASE Tool Merging UML and Petri Nets. In *Proc. 1st International Workshop on Validation and Verification of Software for Enterprise Information Systems*, Angers, France, (pp. 94-102).

Deloitte & Touche (2002). *Achieving, measuring and communicating IT value*. An IDG Research Services Group report.

Desai, B. (1990). *An Introduction to Database Systems*. Eagan, MN: West Publishing Company.

Dey, A. K., & Häkkilä, J. (2008). Context-Awareness and Mobile Devices. In J. Lumsden (Ed.), *Handbook of Research on User Interface Design and Evaluation for Mobile Technology* (Vol. I, pp. 205-217). Hershey, PA: IGI Global.

Dijkstra, E. W. (1976). *A Discipline of Programming*. Englewood Cliffs, UK: Prentice Hall.

Dossick, S. E., & Kaiser, G. K. (1999). CHIME: A metadata-based distributed software development environment. In *Proceedings of the 7th European Software Engineering Conference held jointly with the 7th ACM SIGSOFT International Symposium on Foundations of Software Engineering* (pp. 464-475).

Dreiling, A., Klaus, H., Rosemann, M., & Wyssusek, B. (2005). *Open Source Enterprise Systems: Towards a Viable Alternative*. 38th Annual Hawaii International Conference on System Sciences, Hawaii.

Dromey, R. G. (2003). Software Quality - Prevention Versus Cure? *Software Quality Journal, 11*(3), 197–210. doi:10.1023/A:1025162610079

dSPACE (2007). *ECU testing with hardware-in-the-loop simulation*.

du Bousquet, L., Ledru, Y., Maury, O., Oriat, C., & Lanet, J.-L. (2004). A case study in JML-based software validation. *IEEE International Conference on Automated Software Engineering* (pp. 294-297).

Dunietz, S. Ehrlich, W. K. Szablak, B. D. Mallows, C. L. & Iannino, A. (1997). Applying design of experiments to software testing. *International. Conference on Software Engineering* (pp. 205-215).

Dutta, S., Lee, M., & Wassenhove, L. K. (1999). Software Engineering in Europe: A study of best practices. *IEEE Software, 16*(3). doi:10.1109/52.765792

Dyba, T. (2003). Factoes of Software Process Improvement Success in Small and Large Organizations: An Empirical Study in the Scandinavian Context. In *Proceedings of the 9th European Software Engineering Conference held jointly with 10th ACM ACM SIGSOFT International symposium on foundations of software Engineering,* September 2003, Helsinki – Finland (pp.148-157). New York: ACM Press.

EAST-ADL (2004). Electronic Architecture and Software Tools - Architecture Description Language. *Embedded Electronic Architecture Std. 1.02,* June.

Ebert, C., & De Neve, P. (2001). Surviving global software development. *IEEE Software, 18,* 62–69. doi:10.1109/52.914748

Ebert, Christ of Akins & Anthony, (2007). Bookshelf. *Software 24*(3), 110-112.

Eckes, G. (2003). *Six Sigma for Everyone.* New York: John Wiley & Sons Inc.

Egyed, A. (2001). Automatically Validating Model Consistency during Refinement. *23rd International Conference on Software Engineering (ICSE 2001).*

Egyed, A. (2001). Scalable Consistency Checking Between Diagrams-The ViewIntegra Approach. *16th IEEE International Conference on Automated Software Engineering (ASE'01),* (pp. 387-390).

Egyed, A. (2003). A Scenario-Driven Approach to Trace Dependency Analysis. *IEEE Transactions on Software Engineering, 29*(2), 116–132. doi:10.1109/TSE.2003.1178051

Egyed, A., Muller, H. A., & Perry, D. E. (2005, July-August). Guest Editors' Introduction: Integrating COTS into the Development Process. *Software IEEE, 22*(4), 16–18. doi:10.1109/MS.2005.93

Eisenecker, U., & Czarnecki, K. (2000). *Generative Programming: Methods, Tools, and Applications* (1st Ed.). Reading, MA: Addison-Wesley Professional.

Elmasri, R., & Navathe, S. (2004). *Fundamentals of Database Systems,* (4th Ed.). Upper Saddle River, NJ: Pearson Education, Inc.

Engels, G., Hausmann, J. H., Heckel, R., & Sauer, S. (2002). Testing the Consistency of Dynamic UML Diagrams. *6th International Conference on Integrated Design and Process Technology.*

Entwisle, S. (Oct 2007). *Model Driven Exception Management Framework.* PhD Thesis, Monash University, Melbourne, Australia.

Entwisle, S., & Kendall, E. (2007). A Model Driven Exception Management Framework. In P. Pelliccione, H. Muccini, N. Guelfi & A. Romanovsky (Eds.), *Software Engineering of Fault Tolerant Systems* (Vol. 19). Singapore: World Scientific Publishing.

Entwisle, S., Ramakrishnan, S., & Kendall, E. (2008, July 2008). *Domain Analysis of Exception Management.* Paper presented at the IADIS International Conference Informatics 2008, Amsterdam, The Netherlands.

Entwisle, S., Ramakrishnan, S., Peake, I., & Kendall, E. (2007). *RELIANT Domain Engineering Method for Exception Management* (Tech. Rep. No. 2007/218). Melbourne, Australia: Monash University.

Entwisle, S., Schmidt, H., Peake, I., & Kendall, E. (2006, October 2006). *A Model Driven Exception Management Framework for Developing Reliable Software Systems.* Paper presented at the Proceedings of the 10th IEEE International Enterprise Distributed Object Computing Conference (EDOC'06), Hong Kong.

Eriksson, B., & Borg, K. (2006). Software Productline Modelling made practical: An example of Swedish Defence Industry. *Communications of the ACM,* (December): 2006.

Eriksson, H. E., & Penker, M. (2000). *Business Modeling with UML.* New York: John Wiley & Sons.

Eshuis, R., & Wieringa, R. (2004). Tool Support for Verifying UML Activity Diagrams. *IEEE Transactions on Software Engineering, 30*(7), 437–447. doi:10.1109/TSE.2004.33

Estublier, J., Vega, G. & Ionita, A. D. (2005). Composing Domain-Specific Languages for Wide-scope Software Engineering Applications. *MoDELS,* Jamaique, Octobre 2005.

Etxeberria, L., & Sagardui, G. (2005, September). *Product-line Architecture: New Issues for Evaluation.* Paper presented at the in Proceeding of 9th International Conference on Software Product Lines (SPLC2005), Rennes, France.

Faloutsos, M., Faloutsos, P., & Faloutsos, C. (1999). On power-law relationships of the internet topology. In *Applications, Technologies, Architectures, and Protocols for Computer Communication: Proceedings of the Conference on Applications, Technologies, Architectures, and Protocols for Computer Communication, Cambridge, MA* (pp. 251-262).

Farchi, E., Hartman, A., & Pinter, S. S. (2002). Using a model-based test generator to test for standard conformance. *IBM Systems Journal, 41*(1), 89–110.

FAST C++ Compilation—IcrediBuild by Xoreax Software, (2003). Retrieved from http://www.xoreax.com/main.htm.

Faulk, S. (1996). Software Requirements: A Tutorial. In M. Dorfman & R. H. Thayer (Eds.) *Software Engineering* (pp 82-103).

Faulk, S. (1996). Software Requirements: A Tutorial. In M. Dorfman & R. H. Thayer (Eds.) *Software Engineering,* (pp. 82-103). Washington, DC: IEEE Computer Society Press.

Feldman, S. (2000). Mobile Commerce for the Masses. *IEEE Internet Computing, 4*(6), 74–75.

Fensel, D. (2001). *Ontologies: Silver Bullet for Knowledge Management and Electronic Commerce.* Berlin: Springer.

Fensel, D. (2001). *Ontologies: Silver Bullet for Knowledge Management and Electronic Commerce.* Berlin: Springer.

Fenton, N. E., & Pfleeger, S. L. (1997). *Software Metrics: A Rigorous & Practical Approach.* New York: International Thomson Computer Press.

Fernández, A., Garzaldeen, B., Grützner, I., & Münch, J. (2004). Guided support for collaborative modeling, enactment and simulation of software development processes. *Software Process Improvement and Practice, 9*(2), 95–106. doi:10.1002/spip.199

Fernandez, E. B., Larrondo-Petrie, M. M., Sorgente, T., & Vanhilst, M. (2007). A Methodology to Develop Secure Systems Using Patterns. In H. Mouratidis & P. Giorgini (Eds.), *Integrating Security and Software Engineering: Advances and Future Vision,* (pp. 107-126). Hershey, PA: Idea Group.

Filman, R. E., Barrett, S., Lee, D., & Linden, T. (2002). Inserting Ilities by Controlling Communications. *Communications of the ACM, 45*(1), 116–122. doi:10.1145/502269.502274

Finkelstein, A., & Savigni, A. (2001, May 14). *A Framework for Requirements Engineering for Context-Aware Services.* The First International Workshop from Software Requirements to Architectures (STRAW 2001), Toronto, Canada, 2001.

Fischer, R. A. (1926). The Arrangement of Field Experiments. *Journal of Ministry of Agriculture of Great Britain, 33*, 503–513.

Fisher, D. (2006). *An Emergent Perspective on Interoperation in Systems of Systems* (Tech. Rep. CMU/SEI-2006-TR-003, ESC-TR-2006-003). Pittsburgh, PA: Carnegie Mellon University, Software Engineering Institute.

Fitzgerald, B. (1996). Formalized systems development methodologies: A critical perspective. *Information Systems Journal, 6*(1), 3–23. doi:10.1111/j.1365-2575.1996.tb00002.x

Fledrich, F., & Burghardt, P. (2007). Agent – based systems for disaster management. *Communications of the ACM, 50*(3).

Fletcher, R., & Sajeev, A. S. M. (1996). A Framework for Testing Object Oriented Software Using Formal Specifications. *Reliable Software Technologies* (LNCS). Berlin: Springer-Verlag.

Fowler, M. (2000). Put Your Process on a Diet. *Software Development, 8*(12), 32–36.

Fowler, M. (2002). The Agile Manifesto: where it came from and where it may go. *Martin Fowler articles.*

Retrieved May 26 2008 from http://martinfowler.com/articles/agileStory.html.

Fowler, M. (2006). *Continuous Integration*. Retrieved from http://www.martinfowler.com/.

Fowler, M. (2007). *Cannot Measure Productivity*. Retrieved 1st August 2007, from http://www.martinfowler.com/bliki/CannotMeasureProductivity.html

Frakes, W. B., Fox, C. J., & Nejmeh, B. A. (1991). *Software Engineering in the UNIX/C Environment.* Englewood, Cliffs, NJ: Prentice Hall.

Fraley, C., & Raftely, E. (1998). *How many clusters? Which Clustering Method? Answers via Model-based Cluster Analysis.* Tech. Rep. 329, Dept. of Statistics, University of Washington, Seattle, WA.

France, R. B., Ghosh, S., Ding-Trong, T., & Solberg, A. (2006, February). Model Driven Development and UML 2.0: Promises and Pitfalls. *IEEE Computer, 39,* 59–66.

Frank Liu, X. (1998). Fuzzy Requirements. *IEEE POTENTIALS,* 24-26.

Freytag, J., Maier, D., & Vossen, G. (1994). *Query Processing for advanced Database Systems.* San Francisco: Morgan-Kaufmann.

Frieder, O., & Siegelmann, H. (1997). Multiprocessor document allocation: A genetic algorithm approach. *IEEE Transactions on Knowledge and Data Engineering, 9*(4), 640–642. doi:10.1109/69.617055

Froehlich, J., & Dourish, P. (2004). Unifying artifacts and activities in a visual tool for distributed software development teams. In *Proceedings of the 26th International Conference on Software Engineering* (pp. 387-396). Washington, DC: IEEE Computer Society.

Fronczak, A., Holyst, J., Jedyank, M. & Sienkiewicz, J. (2002). Higher Order Clustering Coefficients: Barabasi-Albert Networks. *Physica A: Statistical Mechanics and its Applications, 316*(1-4), 688-694.

Fuentes, L., & Vallecillo, A. (2004, April). An introduction to uml profiles. *The European journal for the Informatics Professional, 5*(2).

Fui-Hoom Nah, F., & Lee-Shang Lau, J. (2001). Critical factors for successful implementation of enterprise systems. *Business Process Management Journal, 7*(3), 285–296. doi:10.1108/14637150110392782

Gabaix, X. (1999). Zipf's law for cities: An explanation. *The Quarterly Journal of Economics, 114,* 739–767. doi:10.1162/003355399556133

Gamma, E., Helm, R., Johnson, R., & Vlissides, J. (1995). *Design Patterns: Elements of Reusable Object-Oriented Software.* Reading, MA: Addison-Wesley.

Garcia, A. F., & Rubira, C. M. F. (2000). An Exception Handling Software Architecture for Developing Robust Software. *Exception Handling in Object-Oriented Systems Workshop at ECOOP 2000.*

Garcia, A. F., & Rubira, F., C. M., Romanovsky, A., & Xu, J. (2001). A Comparative Study of Exception Handling Mechanisms for Building Dependable Object-Oriented Software. *Journal of Systems and Software, 59*(2), 197–222. doi:10.1016/S0164-1212(01)00062-0

Garcia, S., & Turner, R. (2006). *CMMI (R) Survival Guide: Just Enough Process Improvement.* Reading, MA: Addison-Wesley Professional.

Gardner, T. (2003, July). Uml modeling of automated business processes with a mapping to bpel4ws. In *Ecoop workshop on object orientation and web services.*

Ghosh, A. K., & Swaminatha, T. M. (2001). Software Security and Privacy Risks in Mobile E-Commerce. *Communications of the ACM, 44*(2), 51–57. doi:10.1145/359205.359227

Gi, H., & Dong, S. (2006). *A Technique to Represent Product Line Core Assets in MDA/PIM for Automation* (LNCS). Berlin: Springer.

Giancarlo, J., & Pedrycz, W. (2001). *Holmes: An Intelligent System to Support Software Product Line Development.* Washington, DC: IEEE.

Girish, H. S., & Christopher, S. H. (2005). An Exploratory Case Study of Enterprise Resource Planning Implementation. *International Journal of Enterprise Information Systems, 1*(1), 23–38.

Glaser, N., & Derniame, J.-C. (1998). Software agents: Process models and user profiles in distributed software development. In *Proceedings of the 7ᵗʰ IEEE International Workshops on Enabling Technologies: Infrastructure or Collaborative Enterprises* (pp. 45-50).

Glib, T. (2003). Software Project Management Adding Stakeholder Metrics to Agile Projects. *The European Journal for the Informatics Professional, IV*(4), 5–9.

Gogolla, M., Bohling, J., & Richters, M. (2003). Validation of uml and ocl models by automatic snapshot generation. In *International conference on unified modeling language*.

Goldmann, S., Münch, J., & Holz, H. (1999). A meta-model for distributed software development. In *Proceedings of the IEEE 8ᵗʰ International Workshops on Enabling Technologies: Infrastructure for Collaborative Enterprises, 1999. (WET ICE '99)* (pp. 48-53). Stanford, CA, USA.

Gong, J., & Tarasewich, P. (2004). *Guidelines for Handheld Mobile Device Interface Design*. The Thirty Fifth Annual Meeting of the Decision Sciences Institute (DSI 2004), Boston, USA, November 20-23, 2004.

Gorlenko, L., & Merrick, R. (2003). No Wires Attached: Usability Challenges in the Connected Mobile World. *IBM Systems Journal, 42*(4), 639–651.

Gorschek, T., & Tejle, K. (2002). *A Method For Assessing Requirements Engineering Process Maturity in Software Projects*. Master Thesis, Blekinge Institute of Technology.

Gorton, I., & Motwani, S. (1996). Issues in co-operative software engineering using globally distributed teams. *Information and Software Technology, 38*(10), 647–655. doi:10.1016/0950-5849(96)01099-3

Govindan, R. B., & Kantz, H. (2004). Long-term correlations and multifractality in surface wind speed. *Europhysics Letters, 68*, 184–190. doi:10.1209/epl/i2004-10188-3

Govindan, R. B., Vjushin, D., Bunde, A., Brenner, S., Havlin, S., & Schellnhuber, H.-J. (2002). Global climate models violate scaling of the observed atmospheric variability. *Physical Review Letters, 89*, 028501. doi:10.1103/PhysRevLett.89.028501

Govindan, R. B., Wilson, J. D., Preissl, H., Eswaran, H., Campbell, J. Q., & Lowery, C. L. (2007). Detrended fluctuation analysis of short datasets: An application to fetal cardiac data. *Physica D. Nonlinear Phenomena, 226*, 23–31. doi:10.1016/j.physd.2006.10.019

Graham, J. (2005). *Efficient Allocation in Distributed Object Oriented Databases with Capacity and Security Constraints*. Ph.D. Dissertation, University of Idaho.

Grant, D., & Qiang, T. (2005). Levels of Enterprise Integration: Study using Case Analysis. *International Journal of Enterprise Information Systems, 1*(1), 1–22.

Graves, T. L., Karr, A. F., Marron, J. S., & Siy, H. (2000). Predicting Fault Incidence Using Software Change History. *IEEE Transactions on Software Engineering, 26*, 653–661. doi:10.1109/32.859533

Gray, J., Bapty, T., Neema, S., & Tuck, J. (2001). Handling Crosscutting Constraints in Domain-Specific Modeling. *Communications of the ACM, 44*(10), 87–93. doi:10.1145/383845.383864

Greene, G., Budavári, T., Li, N., Nieto-Santisteban, M., Szalay, A., & Thakar, A. (2008). Web-based Tools—Open SkyQuery: Distributed Database Queries and Crossmatching. In *The National Virtual Observatory: Tools and Techniques for Astronomical Research*, (Vol. 382). Provo, UT: ASP Conference Series.

Greenfield, J., Short, K., Cook, S., & Kent, S. (2004). *Software Factories: Assembling Applications with Patterns, Models, Frameworks, and Tools*. New York: Wiley.

Greenfield, J., Short, K., Cook, S., Kent, S., & Crupi, J. (2004). *Software factories: Assembling applications with patterns, models, frameworks, and tools*. New York: John Wiley & Sons.

Grieskamp, W., Gurevich, Y., Schulte, W. & Margus Veanes (2002). Generating Finite state machines from abstract state machines. *ACM SIGSOFT 2002 International Symposium on Software Testing and Analysis, ISSTA'*02.

Grieskamp, W., Heisel, M., & Dorr, H. (1998). Specifying Embedded Systems with Statecharts and Z: An Agenda for Cyclic Software Components in Egidio Astesiano. *1st International Conference on Fundamental Approaches to Software Engineering - FASE'98*, (pp. 88-106).

Grieskamp, W., Nachmanson, L., Tillmann, N., & Veanes, M. (2003). Test Case generation from Asml specifications Tool overview. *10th International Workshop on. Abstract State Machines*.

Grimán, A., Pérez, M., Mendoza, L., & Losavio, F. (2006). Feature Analysis for Architectural Evaluation Methods. *Journal of Systems and Software, 79*(6), 871–888. doi:10.1016/j.jss.2005.12.015

Groher, K., & Charles, C. (2008 March 31 – April 4). A Tool based feature to manage Crosscutting Feature Implementations. *AOSD '08*, Brussels, Belgium.

Gruber, T. (1993). A Translation Approach to Portable Ontology Specifications. *Knowledge Acquisition, 5*, 199–220. doi:10.1006/knac.1993.1008

Gruber, T. (1993). A Translation Approach to Portable Ontology Specifications. *Knowledge Acquisition, 5*, 199–220. doi:10.1006/knac.1993.1008

Grunbacher, P., Crnkovic, I., & Muller, P. (2008). *Journal of Systems Architecture, 54*.

Guelfi, N., Razavi, R., Romanovsky, A., & Vandenbergh, S. (2004, October 2004). *DRIP Catalyst: An MDE/MDA Method for Fault-tolerant Distributed Software Families Development.* Paper presented at the 19th Annual ACM Conference on Object-Oriented Programming, Systems, Languages, and Applications, Vancouver, Canada.

Guen, H. L., Marie, R., & Thelin, T. (2004). Reliability Estimation for Statistical usage Testing using Markov chains. *15th International Symposium on Software Reliability Engineering (ISSRE'04)*.

Gumbrich, S. (2004). Embedded systems overhaul: It's time to tune up for the future of the automotive industry. *IBM Business Consulting Services,* (December).

Haase, P., Sure, Y., & Vrandecic, D. (2004). *Ontology Management and Evolution - Survey, Methods and Prototypes.* Technical Report.

Haase, P., Sure, Y., & Vrandecic, D. (2004). *Ontology Management and Evolution - Survey, Methods and Prototypes.* Technical Report.

Hababeh, I., Ramachandran, M., & Bowring, N. (2005). Developing Distributed Database Applications with Integrated Method for Data Fragmentation And Allocation. *Proceedings of the International Advanced Database Conference (IADC 2005), June 28-30, San Diego, California USA*. Washington, DC: National University & US Education.

Hababeh, I., Ramachandran, M., & Bowring, N. (2005). Developing Distributed Database Applications with Integrated Method for Data Fragmentation And Allocation. *Proceedings of the International Advanced Database Conference (IADC 2005)*, June 28-30, San Diego, CA. National University & US Education.

Hababeh, I., Ramachandran, M., & Bowring, N. (2006). Dynamical Processing Technique for data fragmentation in Distributed Database Systems: Design and Tool Support. *Journal of Dynamical Systems and Geometric Theories, 4*(2), 103–116.

Hababeh, I., Ramachandran, M., & Bowring, N. (2007). A High-performance Computing Method for Data Allocation in Distributed Database Systems. *The Journal of Supercomputing, 39*(1), 3–18. doi:10.1007/s11227-006-0001-8

Hababeh, I., Ramachandran, M., & Bowring, N. (2007a). A High-performance Computing Method for Data Allocation in Distributed Database Systems. *The Journal of Supercomputing, 39*(1), 3–18. doi:10.1007/s11227-006-0001-8

Hababeh, I., Ramachandran, M., & Bowring, N. (2007b). *Application Design for Data Fragmentation and Allocation in Distributed Database Systems.* Research & Practice Conference 2007, 9-11 July, INN-School of Computing, Leeds Metropolitan University, Leeds, UK.

Hababeh, I., Ramachandran, M., & Bowring, N. (2007B). Application Design for Data Fragmentation and Allocation in Distributed Database Systems. *Research & Practice Conference 2007*, July 9-11, INN-School of Computing, Leeds Metropolitan University, Leeds, UK.

Hababeh, I., Ramachandran, M., & Bowring, N. (2008). Designing a High Performance Integrated Strategy for Secured Distributed Database Systems. [IJCR]. *International Journal of Computer Research, 16*(1), 1–52.

Halkidi, M., Batistakis, Y., & Vazirgiannis, M. (2001). Clustering algorithms and Validity Measures. *Proceedings of the SSDBM Conference.*

Halloran, T. J., & Scherlis, W. L. (2002). High Quality and Open Source Software Practices. In *Meeting Challenges and Surviving Success: Second Workshop Open Source Software Eng., May.*

Hamed, H., & Salem, A. (2001). UML-L: An UML Based Design Description Language. *ACS/IEEE International Conference on Computer Systems and Applications (AICCSA'01),* (pp. 438-441).

Hamlet, D. (2007). Test-Based Specifications of Components and System. In *Proceedings of 7th International Conference Quality Software (QSIC '07),* October 11-12 (pp. 388-395). Los Alamitos, CA: IEEE Computer Society.

Hamlet, D., Mason, D., & Woit, D. (2001). Theory of Software Reliability based on components. In *Proceedings of the 23rd International Conference on Software Engineering,* Toronto, Canada, (pp. 361-370).

Hamming, R. (1980). *Coding and Information Theory.* Englewood Cliffs, NJ: Prentice-Hall.

Harper, S., & Yesilada, Y. (2008). Web Accessibility: A Foundation for Research. Berlin: Springer-Verlag.

Harrison, W. (1992). An entropy based measure of software complexity. *IEEE Transactions on Software Engineering, 18*(11), 1025–1029. doi:10.1109/32.177371

Harrold, M. J., & Rothermel, G. (1994). Performing Data Flow testing on Classes. *2nd ACM SIGSOFT symposium on Foundations of Software Engineering (FSE '94)* (pp. 154-163).

Harsu, M. (2002). *FAST-Product Line Architecture Process.*

Hartman, A., & Raskin, L. (2004). Problems and algorithms for covering arrays. *Discrete Mathematics, 284,* 149–156. doi:10.1016/j.disc.2003.11.029

Hartman, A., Klinger, T., & Raskin, L. (2008). *IBM Intelligent Test Case Handler.* Retrieved on August 30, 2008, from http://www.alphaworks.ibm.com/tech/whitch

Hassan, A. E., & Holt, R. C. (2005). The top ten list dynamic fault prediction. In *21st International conference on software maintenance: Proceedings of the 21st International Conference on Software Maintenance (Hungary), Budapest* (pp. 263-272).

Hazem, L., Levy, N., & Marcano-Kamenoff, R. (2004). UML2B: un outil pour la génération de modèles formels. In J. Julliand, (Ed.), *AFADL'2004 - Session Outils.*

He, K., He, F., & Li, B. (2005a). Research on Service-Oriented Ontology &Meta-Modeling Theory and Methodology. *Chinese Journal of Computers, 28*(4), 524–533.

He, K., He, F., & Li, B. (2005a). Research on Service-Oriented Ontology &Meta-Modeling Theory and Methodology. *Chinese Journal of Computers, 28*(4), 524–533.

He, Y. (2007a). *Research on ontology management metamodels for semantic interoperability.* Ph.D Thesis, Wuhan University, China.

He, Y. (2007a). *Research on ontology management metamodels for semantic interoperability.* Ph.D Thesis, Wuhan University, China.

He, Y., & He, K. (2007). Ontology Evolution Management Framework for Reliable Semantic Interoperation. *Computer Engineering, 33*(18), 26-27, 30.

He, Y., He, K., & Wang, C. (2005). Metamodel Framework for Ontology Registration (MMF4Ontology Registration) for Semantic Interoperation. *1st International Conference on Semantics, Knowledge and Grid (SKG 2005),* (p. 84). Beijing: IEEE Press.

He, Y., He, K., & Wang, C. (2005). Research on Semantic Web Service-Oriented MMFI for Complex Information

Registration. *IEEE International Workshop on Service-Oriented System Engineering (SOSE 2005)*, (pp. 237-243). Beijing: IEEE Press.

He, Y., He, K., & Wang, C. (2006). Ontology Registration Based Approach for Trustable Semantic Interoperation. *Computer Engineering and Applications, 34*(pp. 8-9, 25).

He, Y., He, K., & Wang, C. (2006). Ontology Registration Based Approach for Trustable Semantic Interoperation. *Computer Engineering and Applications, 34*(pp. 8-9, 25).

Hendricks, K. B., Singhal, V. R., & Stratman, J. K. (2007). The impact of enterprise systems on corporate performance: A study of ERP, SCM, and CRM system implementations. *Journal of Operations Management, 25*(1), 65–82. doi:10.1016/j.jom.2006.02.002

Heninger, K. L. (1980). Specifying software requirements for complex systems: New techniques and their application. *IEEE Transactions on Software Engineering, 6*(1), 2–13. doi:10.1109/TSE.1980.230208

Henninger, S. (2003). Tool Support for Experience-Based Software Development Methodologies. *Advances In Computers*, (59), 29-82.

Henry, S., & Li, W. (1992). Metrics for Object-Oriented Systems. *Proc. OOPSLA'92 Workshop: Metrics for Object-Oriented Software Development*, Vancouver, Canada.

Herbsleb, J. (2007). Global Software Engineering: The Future of Socio-technical Coordination. *Future of Software Engineering, 2007 . FOSE, 07*, 188–198.

Herbsleb, J. D., & Goldenson, D. R. (1996). A Systematic Survey of CMM experience and results. In *Proceedings of the 18th international conference on Software Engineering*, May 1996, Berlin, Germany(pp.323-330). Washington, DC: IEEE Computer Society.

Herbsleb, J. D., & Moitra, D. (2001). Global software development. *IEEE Software, 18*, 16–20. doi:10.1109/52.914732

Herbsleb, J. D., Mockus, A., Finholt, T. A., & Grinter, R. E. (2000). Distance, dependencies, and delay in a global collaboration. In *Proceedings of the 2000 ACM Conference on Computer Supported Cooperative Work* (pp. 319-328).

Herbsleb, J. D., Mockus, A., Finholt, T. A., & Grinter, R. E. (2001). An empirical study of global software development: Distance and speed. In *Proceedings of the 23rd International Conference on Software Engineering* (pp. 81-90).

Hetrick, W., & Moore, C. (2005). Incremental Return on Incremental Investment. *Engenio's Transition to Software Product Line Practice.*

Heyes, I. S. (2002). *Just Enough Wireless Computing.* Reading, MA: Prentice-Hall.

Hiatt, C. J. (2000). *A primer for disaster recovery planning in an IT environment.* Hershey, PA: Idea Group Publishing.

Highsmith, J. (2001). The Great Methodologies Debate: Part 1: Today, a new debate rages: agile software development versus rigorous software development. *Cutter IT Journal, 14*(12), 2–4.

Highsmith, J. (2002). Agile Software Development: why it is hot! *Cutter Consortium white paper, Information Architects, Inc*, (pp. 1-22).

Highsmith, J. (2002). *Agile Software Development Ecosystems* (pp. 1-50). Reading, MA: Addison-Wesley.

Highsmith, J. (2004). *Agile Project Management, Creating innovative products.* Reading, MA: Addison-Wesley.

Hinkle, M. M. (2007). Software Quality, Metrics, Process Improvement, and CMMI: An Interview with Dick Fairley. *IT Professional, 9*(3), 47–51. doi:10.1109/MITP.2007.57

Hjelm, J. (2000). *Designing Wireless Information Services.* New York: John Wiley and Sons.

Hoey, P. (2006). Software Product line Engineering. *Communications of the ACM, 49*(December).

Hoffer, J., Prescott, M., & McFadden, F. (2004). *Modern Database Management,* (7th Ed). Englewood Cliffs, NJ: Prentice Hall.

Hoffer, J., Prescott, M., & McFadden, F. (2004). *Modern Database Management,* (7th Ed.). Upper Saddle River, NJ: Prentice Hall.

Hofmann, H. F., Yedlin, D. K., Mishler, J. W., & Kushner, S. (2007). *CMMI for Out sourcing Guidelines for software, systems, and IT Acquisition.* Reading, MA: Addison Wesley Professional.

Holland, C. P., & Light, B. (2001). A stage for maturity model for enterprise resource planning systems use. *The Data Base for Advances in Information Systems, 32*(2).

Hong, H. S., Kwon, Y. R., & Cha, S. D. (1995). Testing of Object-Oriented Programs based on Finite State Machines. *2nd Asia-Pacific Software Engineering Conference (ASPEC'95),* (p. 234).

Hong, K., & Kim, Y. (2002). The Critical success factors for ERP implementation: An organizational fit perspective. *Information & Management, 40*(1), 25–40. doi:10.1016/S0378-7206(01)00134-3

Hosseini, M., & Izadkhah, Y. O. (2006). Earthquake disaster risk, management planning in schools. *Disaster Prevention and Management, 15*(4), 649–661. doi:10.1108/09653560610686595

Howell, C., & Vecellio, G. (2000). Experiences with Error Handling in Critical Systems. *Advances in Exception Handling Techniques in Object-Oriented Systems Workshop at ECOOP 2000.*

http://www.sei.cmu.edu/productlines/frame_report/config.man.htm (n.d.). Pittsburgh, PA: Software Engineering Institute, Carnegie Mellon University.

Huang, Y., & Chen, J. (2001). Fragment Allocation in Distributed Database Design. *Journal of Information Science and Engineering, 17,* 491–506.

Hudli, R., Hoskins, C., & Hudli, A. (1994). *Software Metrics for Object Oriented Designs.* Washington, DC: IEEE.

Humphrey, W. S. (1995, September 1995). *A Personal Commitment to Software Quality.* Paper presented at the Proceedings of the 5th European Software Engineering Conference, Lisbon, Portugal.

Hurst, W. B. (2008). *Eclipse bug count cycle analysis.* Unpublished M.S. Computer Science thesis, University of Arkansas at Little Rock, Little Rock, AR.

Idani, A. (2007). *Computer Software Engineering Research, chapter UML2B vs B2UML: Bridging the gap between formal and graphical software modelling paradigms.* Hauppauge, NY: Nova Science Publishers.

Idani, A., Boulanger, J.-L., & Laurent, P. (2007). A generic process and its tool support towards combining UML and B for safety critical systems. *CAINE 2007,* November 7-9, 2007, San Francisco.

Idani, A., Okasa Ossami, D.-D., & Boulanger, J.-L. (2007). Commandments of UML for safety. In *2nd International Conference on Software Engineering Advances,* August 2007. Washington, DC: IEEE CS Press.

IEC 61508 (2000). Functional safety of electrical/electronic/programmable electronic safety-related systems. *International Electrotechnical Commission Std. 61508.*

IEC. (2000). *IEC61508, Functional safety of electrical/electronic/programmable electronic safety-related systems.* Geneva, Switzerland: International Electrotechnical Commission.

IEEE Standard for Software Productivity Metrics. (1993). *IEEE Std 1045-1992.*

IFIP – IFAC. (1999). *GERAM: Generalized Enterprise Reference Architecture and Methodology,* (p. 31). Task Force on Architectures for Enterprise Integration.

IFIP – IFAC. (1999). *GERAM: Generalized Enterprise Reference Architecture and Methodology.* IFIP – IFAC Task Force on Architectures for Enterprise Integration.

IFRCRCS. (2004). *International Federation of Red Cross and Red Crescent Societies.* World Disasters Report [Online]. Retrieved from http://www.ifrc.org/publicat/wdr2004/chapter8.asp

IFRCRCS. (2004). *International Federation of Red Cross and Red Crescent Societies World Disasters Report* [Online]. Retrieved from http://www.ifrc.org/publicat/wdr2004/chapter8.asp

Ihme, T., & Abrahamsson, P. (2005). The Use of Architechural Patterns in the Agile Software Development of Mobile Applications. *International Journal of Agile Manufacturing, 8*(2), 97–112.

Ihme, T., & Abrahamsson, P. (2005). *The Use of Architectural Patterns in the Agile Software Development of Mobile Applications.* The 2005 International Conference on Agility (ICAM 2005), Otaniemi, Finland, July 27-28, 2005.

Institute for Experimental Software Engineering (IESE). (2008) Retrieved December 1, 2008, from http://www.iese.fhg.de/

Institute of Electrical and Electronics Engineers (IEEE). (1990). *IEEE Standard Computer Dictionary: A Compilation of IEEE Standard Computer Glossaries.* New York, IEEE Press.

International Organization for Standardization (ISO) (1993). *ISO/IEC 2382: Information Technology-Vocabulary.*

International Organization for Standardization (ISO) (2004). *ISO/IEC 11179: Information technology – Metadata Registries.*

International Organization for Standardization (ISO) (2006). *ISO/IEC 19763-3: Information technology – Framework for metamodel interoperability –Part 3(2nd Edition): Metamodel for ontology evolution.* Working Draft.

International Organization for Standardization (ISO) (2006). *ISO/IEC 19763-3: Information technology – Framework for metamodel interoperability –Part 3(2nd Edition): Metamodel for ontology evolution.* Working Draft.

International Organization for Standardization (ISO) (2007). *ISO/IEC 19763-3: Information technology – Framework for metamodel interoperability –Part 3: Metamodel for ontology registration.*

International Organization for Standardization (ISO). (2007). *ISO/IEC 19763-2: Information technology – Framework for metamodel interoperability –Part 2: Core Model.* Final Committee Draft.

International Organization for Standardization (ISO). (2007). *ISO/IEC 19763-4: Information technology – Framework for metamodel interoperability –Part 4: Metamodel for Model Mapping.* Committee Draft.

International Organization for Standardization (ISO). (2007). *ISO/IEC 19763-5: Information technology – Framework for metamodel interoperability –Part 5: Metamodel for Process Model Registration.* Working Draft.

Iron Mountain. (2004). *The Business Case for Disaster Recovery Planning: Calculating the Cost of Downtime* [white paper]. London: Iron Mountain.

Ishfaq, A., Karlapalem, K., & Kaiso, Y. (2002). Evolutionary Algorithms for Allocating Data in Distributed Database Systems. *Distributed and Parallel Databases, 11*, 5–32. doi:10.1023/A:1013324605452

Ishikawa, H., Ogata, Y., Adachi, K., & Nakajima, T. (2003). Requirements of a Component Framework for Future Ubiquitous Computing. In *Proceeding of the IEEE Workshop on Software Technologies and Future Embedded System.*

ISO/IEC 12207:2002. (2002). *ISO/IEC 12207:2002. AMENDMENT 1: Information technology - software life cycle processes.* International Organization for Standardization.

Jacobson, I. (1993). *Object Oriented Software Engineering: A Use Case Driven Approach.* Reading, MA: Addison-Wesley Publishing Company.

Jacobson, I., Booch, G., & Rumbaugh, J. (1999). *The Unified Software Development Process.* Reading, MA: Addison-Wesley.

Jain, A., Murty, M., & Flynn, P. (1999). Data Clustering: A Review. *ACM Computing Surveys, 31*(3), 264–323. doi:10.1145/331499.331504

Jansen, L., & Schnieder, E. (2000). *Traffic control system case study: Problem description and a note on domain-based software specification.* Tech. Rep., Colorado State University, USA.

Jansen-Vullers, M., & Netjes, M. (2006, Oct). Business process simulation - a tool survey. In *Workshop and tutorial on practical use of coloured petri nets and the cpn tools.*

Jaokar, A. (2006). *Mobile Web 2.0: The Innovator's Guide to Developing and Marketing Next Generation Wireless/ Mobile Applications.* London: Futuretext.

Javahery, H. (2006). *Pattern-Oriented UI Design based on User Experiences: A Method Supported by Empirical Evidence.* Ph.D. Thesis, Concordia University, Canada.

Javed, F., Mernik, M., Bryant, B. R., & Gray, J. (2005). A Grammar based approach to Class Diagram Validation. *4th International Workshop on Scenarios and State Machines: Models, Algorithms and Tools (SCESM'05)*

Jenkins, S., & Kirk, S. R. (2007). Software architecture graphs as complex networks: A novel partitioning scheme to measure stability and evolution. *Information Sciences: an International Journal, 177,* 2587–2601.

Jiang, T., & Klenke, R. H. Aylor & J.H., Han, G. (2000), System level testability analysis using Petri nets. *IEEE International High-Level Design Validation and Test Workshop, 2000.* (pp. 112 – 117).

Johnson, J., Boucher, K. D., Connors, K., & Robinson, J. (2001). Collaborating on Project Success. *Software Magazine.* Retrieved January 20th 2008, from http:// www.softwaremag.com/l.cfm?Doc=archive/2001feb/ collaborativeMgt.html

Johnson, P. (2008). Retrieved December 5, 2008, from http://code.google.com/p/hackystat/

Johnson, S. C. (1967). Hierarchical Clustering Schemes. *Psychometrika, 32,* 241–254. doi:10.1007/BF02289588

Jones, C. (1996). The economics of software process improvement. *Computer, 29*(1), 95–97. doi:10.1109/2.481498

Jones, M., & Marsden, G. (2006). *Mobile Interaction Design.* Hoboken, NJ: John Wiley and Sons.

Kagdi, H., Collard, M. L., & Maletic, J. I. (2007). A survey and taxonomy of approaches for mining software repositories in the context of software evolution. *Journal of Software Maintenance and Evolution: Research and Practice, 19,* 77–131. doi:10.1002/smr.344

Kamthan, P. (2007). Accessibility of Mobile Applications. In D. Taniar (Ed.), *Encyclopedia of Mobile Computing and Commerce,* (Vol. 2). Hershey, PA: Idea Group Publishing.

Kamthan, P. (2007). Addressing the Credibility of Mobile Applications. In D. Taniar (Ed.), *Encyclopedia of Mobile Computing and Commerce,* (Vol. 2). Hershey, PA: Idea Group Publishing.

Kamthan, P. (2008). A Situational Methodology for Addressing the Pragmatic Quality of Web Applications by Integration of Patterns. *Journal of Web Engineering, 7*(1), 70–92.

Kamthan, P. (2008). Towards High-Quality Mobile Applications by a Systematic Integration of Patterns. *Journal of Mobile Multimedia, 4*(3/4), 165–184.

Kan, S. H. (2002). *Metrics and Models in Software Quality Engineering.* Boston: Addison –Wesley Longman Publishing Co., Inc.

Kanjilal, A. (2007). *Analysis and Testing of Object-oriented Systems.* Ph.D. Thesis, Jadavpur University, India.

Kanjilal, A., & Bhattacharya, S. (2004). Test Path Identification for Object Oriented systems using Extended Control Flow Graph. *12th International Conference on Advanced Computing and Communication (ADCOM 2004).*

Kanjilal, A., Kanjilal, G., & Bhattacharya, S. (2003). Extended Control Flow Graph: An Engineering Approach. *6th Intl. Conference on Information Technology, CIT'03,* (pp. 151-156).

Kanjilal, A., Kanjilal, G., & Bhattacharya, S. (2008). Integration of Design in Distributed Development using

D-Scenario Graph. *IEEE Intl. Conference on Global Software Engineering, ICGSE'08,* (pp. 141-150).

Kanjilal, A., Kanjilal, G., & Bhattacharya, S. (2008). Metrics based Analysis of Requirements for Object-Oriented systems: An empirical approach. *INFOCOMP Journal of Computer Science, J7*(2), 26–36.

Kantelhardt, J. W., Koscielny-Bunde, E., Rego, H. A., Havlin, S., & Bunde, A. (2001). Detecting Long-range Correlations with Detrended Flunction Analysis. *Physica A, 295,* 441–454. doi:10.1016/S0378-4371(01)00144-3

Kantelhardt, J.W., Ashkenazy, Y., Ivanov, P.Ch., Bunde, A., Havlin, S., Penzel, T.et al. (2002). Characterization of sleep stages by correlations in the magnitude and sign of heartbeat increments. *Physics Review E, 65,* 051908-1-6.

Kappel, G., Pröll, B., Reich, S., & Retschitzegger, W. (2006). *Web Engineering.* Hoboken, NJ: John Wiley and Sons.

Karlsson, E. (1995). *Software Reuse: A Holistic Approach.* Sweden: Q-Labs.

Karlsson, E.-A. Andersson, L.-G. & Leion, P. (2000). Daily Build and Feature Development in Large Distributed Projects. In *Proc. 22ⁿᵈ Int'l Conf. Software Eng.,* (pp. 649-658).

Karlsson, J. (1996). Software Requirements Prioritizing. *IEEE Proceeding of ICRE'96.*

Karlsson, J., & Ryan, K. (1997). A cost-Value Approach for Prioritizing Requirements. *IEEE Software.*

Kastro, Y. (2004). *The Defect Prediction Method for software Versioning.* Bogazici University.

Kauffman, S. A. (1993). *The origins of order: self-organization and selection in evolution.* New York: Oxford University Press.

Khalil, N., Eid, D., & Khair, M. (1999). Availability and Reliability Issues in Distributed Databases Using Optimal Horizontal Fragmentation. In T. J. M. Bench-Capon, G. Soda & A. Min Tjoa, (ed.), *'DEXA' 99* (LNCS Vol. 1677, pp. 771-780). Berlin: Springer.

Kim, H., & Boldyreff, C. (2005). *Open Source ERP for SMEs.* Third International Conference on Manufacturing Research, Cranfield, UK.

Kim, K., Shine, Y., & Wu, C. (1995). Complexity measures for object oriented programming based on entropy. *Proceedings of the Asian pacific Conference on Software Engineering* (pp. 127-136).

Kim, S. K., & Carrington, D. (2004). A Formal Object-Oriented Approach to defining Consistency Constraints for UML Models. *Australian Software Engineering Conference (ASWEC'04),* (p. 87).

Kim, Y. G., Hong, H. S., Cho, S. M., Bae, D. H., & Cha, S. D. (1999). Test Cases generation from UML State diagrams. *IEEE Software, 146*(4), 187–192. doi:10.1049/ip-sen:19990602

Kinook Software—Automate Software Builds with Visual Build Pro, (2003). Retrieved from http://www.visualbuild.com/.

Kitchenham, B. (2004). *Procedures for performing systematic reviews* (Joint Tech. Rep.). Software Engineering Group, Department of Computer Science, Keele University and Empirical Software Engineering National ICT Australia Ltd.

Kitchenham, B. A., Huges, R. T., & Linkman, S. G. (2001). Modeling software measurement data. *IEEE Transactions on Software Engineering, 27*(9), 788–804. doi:10.1109/32.950316

Kitchenham, B., Jeffery, D. R., & Connaughton, C. (2007). Misleading Metrics and Unsound Analyses. *IEEE Software, 24*(2), 73–78. doi:10.1109/MS.2007.49

Kitchenham, B., Linkman, S., & Law, D. (1997). DESMET: A Method for Evaluating Software Engineering Methods and Tools. *Computing and Control Engineering, 8*(3), 120–126. doi:10.1049/cce:19970304

Klaus, S., & Martin, V. (2004). The Economic Impact of Product Line Adoption and Evolution. *IEEE Software . Special Issue on Software Product Lines, 10*(4), 50–57.

Klein, D., Kamvar, S., & Manning, C. (2002). From Instance-level Constraints to Space-Level Constraints:

Making the Most of Prior Knowledge in Data Clustering. *Proceedings of the Nineteenth International Conference on Machine Learning*, July, (pp.307-314).

Klein, M., & Dellarocas, C. (2000). *Domain-Independent Exception Handling Services That Increase Robustness in Open Multi-Agent Systems.* Working Paper CCS-WP-211, Massachusetts Institute of Technology, Cambridge, MA. Retrieved from http://ccs.mit.edu/papers/pdf/wp211.pdf

Knapp, A. Merz, S. (2002). Model Checking and Code Generation for UML State Machines and Collaborations. In *Proc. 5th Workshop on Tools for System Design and Verification*, Augsburg, Germany.

Kosanke, K., Vernadat, F., & Zelm, M. (1999). CIMOSA: Enterprise Engineering and Integration. *Computers in Industry, 40*(2), 83–97. doi:10.1016/S0166-3615(99)00016-0

Kotonya, G., & Somerville, I. (1998). *Requirements Engineering – Processes and Techniques.* Chichester, UK: John Wiley & Sons.

Kotonya, G., Sommerville, I., & Hall, S. (2003). Towards a Classification Model for Component-based Software Engineering Research. In *Proceedings 29th EuroMicro Conference "New Waves in System Architecture" (EuroMicro'03)*, Belek-Antalya, Turkey, (pp.43-52).

Kotyana, G., & Sommerville, I. (1997). *Requirements Engineering Processes and Techniques.* Hoboken, NJ: John Wiley and Sons Ltd.

Kozlenkov, A., & Zisman, A. (n.d.). *Checking Behavioral Inconsistencies in UML Specifications.* Retrieved from http://www.cs.tut.fi/tsystm/ICSE/papers/6.pdf, Krishnan, P. (2000). Consistency checks for UML. *7th Asia-Pacific Software Engineering Conference (APSEC'00)*, (p. 162).

Krishna, S., Sundeep, S., & Geoff, W. (2004). Managing cross-cultural issues in global software outsourcing. *Communications of the ACM, 47*, 62–66. doi:10.1145/975817.975818

Krueger, C (2006). New methods in Sotware Product Line Practice Examining the benefits of next-generation SPL methods. *Communications of ACM.*

Kuhn, D. R., & Reilly, M. (2002). An investigation of the applicability of design of experiments to software testing. *NASA Goddard/IEEE Software Engineering Workshop* (pp. 91-95).

Kuhn, D. R., Wallace, D., & Gallo, A. (2004). Software Fault Interactions and Implications for Software Testing. *IEEE Transactions on Software Engineering, 30*(6), 418–421. doi:10.1109/TSE.2004.24

Kumar, P., Krishna, P., Bapi, R., & Kumar, S. (2007). Rough Clustering of Sequential Data. *Data & Knowledge Engineering, 63*, 183–199. doi:10.1016/j.datak.2007.01.003

Küster, J. M. (2001). Consistent Design of Embedded Real-Time Systems with UML-RT. *4th International Symposium on Object-Oriented Real-Time Distributed Computing.*

Küster, J. M., & Stehr, J. (2003). Towards Explicit Behavioral Consistency Concepts in the UML. *2nd International Workshop on Scenarios and State Machines: Models, Algorithms and Tools.*

Laleau, R., & Mammar, A. (2000). An Overview of a Method and Its Support Tool for Generating B Specifications from UML Notations. In *15th IEEE International Conference on Automated Software Engineering*, (pp. 269–272). Washington, DC: IEEE CS Press.

Lamch, D. (2002). Verification and Analysis of Properties of Dynamic Systems Based on Petri Nets. *Proceedings of International Conference on Parallel Computing in Electrical Engineering (PARELEC'02)*, (pp. 92-94).

Langton, C. G. (1990). Computation at the edge of chaos. *Physica D. Nonlinear Phenomena, 42*, 12–37. doi:10.1016/0167-2789(90)90064-V

Lanowitz, T. (2005). *Now Is the Time for Security at the Application Level* (Tech. Rep.). Stamford, CT: Gartner.

Lanubile, F., Mallardo, T., & Calefato, F. (2003). Tool support for geographically dispersed inspection teams.

Software Process Improvement and Practice, *8*(4), 217–231. doi:10.1002/spip.184

Latella, D., Majzik, I., & Massink, M. (1999). Automatic Verification of a Behavioral Subset of UML Statechart Diagrams Using the SPIN Model-Checker. *Formal Aspects in Computing*, *11*(6), 637–664. doi:10.1007/s001659970003

Lavell, A. (1999). *Natural and Technological Disasters, Capacity Building and Human Resource Development for Disaster Management* [Online]. Retrieved from http://www.desenredando.org/public/articulos/1999/ntd/ntd1999_mar-1-2002.pdf

Lavenda, B. H., & Dunning-Davies, J. (2003). Arxiv: physics/0310117v1[physics.class-ph].

Lawlis, K. P., & Mark, E. K. (2001). A formal process for evaluating COTS software products. *Computer*, *34*, 58–63. doi:10.1109/2.920613

Layman, L., Williams, L., Damian, D., & Bures, H. (2006). Essential communication practices for extreme programming in a global software development team. *Information and Software Technology*, *48*, 781–794. doi:10.1016/j.infsof.2006.01.004

Leavens, G. T., Baker, A. L., & Ruby, C. (1999). JML: A notation for detailed design. In H. Kilov, B. Rumpe, & I. Simmonds, (Ed.) *Behavioral Specifications of Businesses and Systems*.

Ledang, H., Souquières, J., & Charles, S. (2003). Argo/UML+B: un outil de transformation systématique de spécifications UML en B. In *AFADL'2003*, (pp. 3–18).

Lee, G., DeLone, W., & Espinosa, J. A. (2006). Ambidextrous coping strategies in globally distributed software development projects. *Communications of the ACM*, *49*(10), 35–40. doi:10.1145/1164394.1164417

Lee, J., Panb, J. I., & Kuoc, J. Y. (2001). Verifying scenarios with time Petri-nets. *Information and Software Technology*, *43*(13), 769–781. doi:10.1016/S0950-5849(01)00184-7

Lei, Y. Kacker, R. Kuhn, D. R., Okun, V. & Lawrence J. (2008). IPOG/IPOD: Efficient Test Generation for Multi-Way Combinatorial Testing. *Journal of Software Testing, Verification, and Reliability*, *18*(3), 125–148. doi:10.1002/stvr.381

Lei, Y., & Tai, K. C. (1998). In-parameter-order: a test generation strategy for pairwise testing. *International High-Assurance Systems Engineering Symposium* (pp. 254-261).

Lhotka, R. (2006). *Expert C# 2005 Business Obejcts*. Berkeley, CA: Apress.

Li, E., Chen, H., & Lee, T. (2002). Software Process Improvement of Top Companies in Taiwan:a comparative study. *Total Quality Management*, *13*(5), 701–703. doi:10.1080/0954412022000002081

Li, W., & Henry, S. (1993). Object-Oriented Metrics that Predict Maintainability. *Journal of Systems and Software*, *23*, 111–122. doi:10.1016/0164-1212(93)90077-B

Lilius, J., & Paltor, I. P. (1999). Formalizing UML State Machines for Model Checking. In *Proc. 2nd Int. Conf. in UML*, Berlin.

Lim, S., & Ng, Y. (1997). Vertical Fragmentation and Allocation in Distributed Deductive Database Systems. *The Journal of Information Systems*, *22*(1), 1–24. doi:10.1016/S0306-4379(97)00001-X

Linden, D., & Van, F. (2002). Initiating Software Product Lines. *Software Product Families in Europe: the Esaps and Café projects*. Washington, DC: IEEE.

Linden, F. d., Bosch, J., Kamsties, E., Kansala, K., & Obbink, H. (2004, August). *Software Product Family Evaluation*. Paper presented at the Proceedings of the 3rd International Conference on Software Product Lines (SPLC '04), Boston, MA, USA.

Lindvall, M., Basili, V. R., Boehm, B., Costa, P., Dangle, K., Shull, F., et al. (2002). Empirical Findings in agile Methods. *Proceedings of Extreme Programming and agile Methods - XP/agile Universe*, (pp. 197-207).

Lingras, P., & West, C. (2004). Interval set clustering of web users with rough k-means. *Journal of Intelligent Information Systems*, *23*(1), 5–16. doi:10.1023/B:JIIS.0000029668.88665.1a

Lingras, P., & Yao, Y. (2002). Time complexity of rough clustering: gas versus k-means. *Third International Conference on Rough Sets and Current Trends in Computing*, (LNCS, pp. 263-270). London: Springer-Verlag.

Lisa, L. Brownsword, D. J. Carney, D. Fisher, et al (2004). *Current perspectives on interoperability.* Pittsburgh, PA: Software Engineering Institute, Carnegie Mellon University, CMU/SEI-2004-TR-009.

Litvak, B., Tyszberowicz, S., & Yehudai, A. (2003). Behavioral Consistency Validation of UML Diagrams. *1st International Conference on Software Engineering and Formal Methods (SEFM'03).*

Liu, J., Lutz, R., & Dehlinger, J. (2003). *Safety Analysis of Variabilities Using State-Based Modeling.*

Liu, Z. (2004). Consistency and refinement of UML models. *UML 2004 Workshop on Consistency Problems in UML-Based Software Development.*

Livshits, B., & Zimmermann, T. (2005). DynaMine: Finding common error patterns by mining software revision histories. In *2005 European software engineering conference and 2005 foundations of software engineering: Proceedings of the 2005 European Software Engineering Conference and 2005 Foundations of Software Engineering (Portugal), Lisbon* (pp. 296-305).

Lopez, L., Gonzalez-Barahona, J. M., & Robles, G. (2004). Applying social network analysis to the information in CVS repositories. In *International workshop on mining software repositories: Proceedings of the Mining Software Repositories Workshop (U.K.), Edinburgh* (pp. 101-105).

Lorenz, M., & Kidd, J. (1994). *Object Oriented Software Metrics.* Upper Saddle River, NJ: Prentice Hall Publishing.

Losavio, F., Chirinos, L., Matteo, A., Levy, N., & Ramdane-Cherif, A. (2004). ISO Quality Standards for Measuring Architectures. *Journal of Systems and Software, 72*(2), 209–223. doi:10.1016/S0164-1212(03)00114-6

Lucr'edio, D., Prado, A. F., & de Almeida, E. S. (2004). A survey on software components search and retrieval.

In *30th EUROMICRO conference: Proceedings of the 30th EUROMICRO Conference (France), Rennes* (pp. 152-159).

Lyard, A., & Orci, T. (2000). Dynamic CMM for Small organisations. *Proceedings ASSE 2000, the first Argentine Symposium on Software Engineering*, September 2000, Tandil- Argentina, (pp.133-149).

Lyardet, F., Rossi, G., & Schwabe, D. (1999). *Patterns for Adding Search Capabilities to Web Information Systems.* The Fourth European Conference on Pattern Languages of Programming and Computing (EuroPLoP 1999), Irsee, Germany, July 8-10, 1999.

Ma, H., Scchewe, K., & Wang, Q. (2007). Distribution design for higher-order data models. *Data & Knowledge Engineering, 60,* 400–434. doi:10.1016/j.datak.2006.03.006

MacColl, I., Murray, L., Strooper, P., & Carrington, D. (1998). Specification-based class testing – A case study. *2nd International Conference on Formal Engineering Methods (ICFEM'98). IEEE Computer Society,* (pp. 222-231).

MacCormack, A., Kemerer, C. F., Cusumano, M., & Crandall, B. A. (2003). Trade-Offs between Productivity and Quality in Selecting Software Development Practices. *IEEE Software, 20*(5), 78–85. doi:10.1109/MS.2003.1231158

Madachy, R. J. (2008). Cost modeling of distributed team processes for global development and software-intensive systems of systems. *Software Process Improvement and Practice, 13*(1), 51–61. doi:10.1002/spip.363

Magee, J., & Kramer, J. (2006). *Concurrency: State Models & Java Programs,* (2nd Ed.). Hoboken, NJ: John Wiley & Sons.

Mahmoud, Q. H., & Maamar, Z. (2006). Engineering Wireless Mobile Applications. *International Journal of Information Technology and Web Engineering, 1*(1), 59–75.

Malamud, B., Morein, G., & Turcotte, D. (1998). Forest fires: an example of self-organized critical behaviour. *Science, 281,* 1840–1842. doi:10.1126/science.281.5384.1840

Mallick, M. (2003). *Mobile and Wireless Design Essentials.* Hoboken, NJ: John Wiley and Sons.

Mandelbrot, B. (1983). *The fractal geometry of nature.* New York: Freeman.

Manolescu, D., & Kunzle, A. (2001, September 11-15). *Several Patterns for eBusiness Applications.* The Eighth Conference on Pattern Languages of Programs (PLoP 2001), Monticello, VA.

Marick, B. (1998). When Should a Test Be Automated? *Proc. 11th Int'l Software/Internet Quality Week,* May.

Marré, M., & Bertolino, A. (2003). Using Spanning Sets for Coverage Testing. *Information and Software Technology, 29*(11), 974–984.

Marte (2007). Modeling and Analysis of Real-time and Embedded systems. *OMG Std. Final Adopted Specification, August.*

Martinez Carod, N., Martin, A., & Aranda, G. N. (2004). *A Cognitive Approach to Improve Software Engineering Processes.* International Conference on Cognitive Informatics, ICCI'4 Canada.

Mata, F. J., Fuerst, W. L., & Barney, J. B. (1995). Information technology and sustained competitive advantage: A resource-based analysis. *MIS Quarterly, 19*(4), 487–505. doi:10.2307/249630

Matinlassi, M. (2004, May 2004). *Comparison of Software Product Line Architecture Design Methods: COPA, FAST, FORM, KobrA and QADA.* Paper presented at the Proceedings of 26th International Conference on Software Engineering.

Mauney, D. W., & Masterton, C. (2008). Small-Screen Interfaces. In P. Kortum (Ed.), *HCI Beyond the GUI Design for Haptic, Speech, Olfactory, and Other Nontraditional Interfaces,* (pp. 307-358). San Francisco: Morgan Kaufmann.

Mazhelis, O., Markkula, J., & Jakobsson, M. (2005, June 13-15). *Specifying Patterns for Mobile Applica-*

tion Domain Using General Architectural Components. The Sixth International Conference on Product Focused Software Process Improvement (PROFES 2005), Oulu, Finland.

McCall, J. A. (1979). Introduction to Software Quality Metrics. In J. Cooper, & M. Fisher, (Ed.) *Software Quality Management,* Petrocelli, (pp. 127 – 140).

McConnell, S. (1996). *Rapid development: Taming wild software schedules,* Redmond, WA: Microsoft Press.

McConnell, S. (1996). Best Practices: Daily Build and Smoke Test. *IEEE Software, 13*(4), 143–144.

McConnell, S. (1996). Software Quality at Top Speed. *Software Development, August.*

McDonald, J., Murray, L., & Strooper, P. (1997). Translating Object-Z Specifications to object-oriented Test Oracles. *4th Asia-Pacific Software Engineering and International Computer Science Conference (APSEC'97 / ICSC'97),* (p. 414).

McGraw, G., & Viega, J. (1999 May). Why COTS Software Increases Security Risks. In *1st International ICSE Workshop on Testing Distributed Component-based System.*

Mellor, S. J., Scott, K., Uhl, A., & Weise, D. (2004). *MDA Distilled.* Reading, MA: Addison-Wesley Professional.

Mellor, S., & Balcer, M. (2002). *Executable uml: A foundation for model driven architecture.* Reading, MA: Addison-Wesley.

MeMVaTEx. (2008). Méthode de modélisation pour la validation et la traçabilité des exigences. *Continental AG and ANR.* [Online]. Retrieved from www.memvatex.org.

Mendes, E., & Mosley, N. (2006). *Web Engineering.* Berlin: Springer-Verlag.

Menkhaus, G., & Andrich, B. (2005). Metric Suite for Directing the Failure mode Analysis of Embedded Software Systems. *In Proc. of the 7th International Conference on Enterprise Information Systems (ICEIS'05).*

Menkhaus, G., Frei, U., & Wuthrich, J. (2006). *Analysis and Verification of the Interaction Model in Software Design*. Retrieved from http://www.sei.cmu.edu/cmmi

Mennecke, B. E., & Strader, T. J. (2003). *Mobile Commerce: Technology, Theory, and Applications*. Hershey, PA: Idea Group Publishing.

Menon, S. (2005). Allocating Fragments in Distributed Databases. *IEEE Transactions on Parallel and Distributed Systems, 16*(7), 577–585. doi:10.1109/TPDS.2005.77

Mens, T. Ragnhild, Van der Straeten & Simmonds, J. (2003). Maintaining Consistency between UML Models with Description Logic Tools. *4th International Workshop on Object-oriented Reengineering (WOOR2003)*.

Meszaros, G., & Doble, J. (1998). A Pattern Language for Pattern Writing. In R. C. Martin, D. Riehle, & F. Buschmann (Eds.), *Pattern Languages of Program Design 3*, (pp. 529-574). Reading, MA: Addison-Wesley.

MetaCase. (2007). *Domaine Specific Modeling with MetaEdit+*. Retrieved from http://www.metacase.com/

Meudec, C. (1998). *Automatic Generation of Software Test Cases From Formal Specifications*. Ph. D. Thesis, The Queen's University of Belfast.

Meyer, B. (1992). Applying Design by Contracts. *IEEE Computer, 25*(10).

Meyer, B. (1999). *The Significance of Component*. Software Development.

Meyer, B. (2000). *Object-Oriented Software Construction* (2nd Ed.). New York: Prentice-Hall.

Meyer, B. (2003). *The Grand Challenge of Trusted Components*. 25th International Conference on Software Engineering, Portland, Oregon.

Meyer, B., Mingins, C., & Schmidt, H. (1998). Providing Trusted Components to the Industry. *IEEE Computer, 31*(5), 104–105.

Meyer, E., & Souquières, J. (1999). A systematic approach to transform OMT diagrams to a B specification. *World Congress on Formal Methods in the Development of Computing System*.

Microsoft Access, (n.d.). Retrieved January 18th, 2008 from http://www.functionx.com/access/

Microsoft, S. Q. L. *Server 2005 Express Edition*. (2005). Retrieved January 29th, 2008 from http://www.microsoft.com/sql/editions/express/default.mspx

Microsoft. (2006). *Pet Shop*. Retrieved April 2006, from http://msdn2.microsoft.com/en-us/library/ms978487.aspx

Mining Open Source Software Engineering Data (2008). Center for Open Software Engineering. Retrieved January 10, 2009, from http://ase.csc.ncsu.edu/projects/mose/

Mitani, Y., Matsumura, T., Barker, M., Tsuruho, S., Inoue, K., & Matsumoto, K. (2007). Proposal of a Complete Life Cycle In-Process Measurement Model Based on Evaluation Of an In-Process Measurement Experiment Using a Standardized Requirement Definition Process. *First International Symposium on Empirical Software Engineering and Measurement, 2007, ESEM 2007,* 11-20.

Mnkandla, E. (2008). *A Selection Framework for Agile Methodology Practices: A Family of Methodologies Approach*. Doctoral Thesis, University of the Witwatersrand, Johannesburg, South Africa.

Mnkandla, E., & Dwolatzky, B. (2004). Balancing the Human and the Engineering Factors in Software Development. *Proceedings of the IEEE AFRICON 2004 Conference*, (pp. 1207-1210).

Mnkandla, E., & Dwolatzky, B. (2004). A Survey of agile Methodologies. *Transactions of the South Africa Institute of Electrical Engineers, 95*(4), 236–247.

Mnkandla, E., & Dwolatzky, B. (2007). Agile Software Methods: State-Of-The-Art. In I. Stamelos, and P. Sfetsos, (Ed.) *Agile Software Development Quality Assurance* (pp. 1-22). Hershey, PA: Information Science Publishing.

Mockus, A., & Weiss, D. M. (2000). Predicting Risk of Software Changes. *Bell Labs Technical Journal, 5*, 169–180. doi:10.1002/bltj.2229

Model-level testing and debugging specification, revised submission. (2006). Object Management Group.

Mof 2.0 xmi mapping specification. (2007). Object Management Group.

Mohan, K., & Ramesh, B. (2007). Traceability-based knowledge integration in group decision and negotiation activities. *Decision Support Systems, 43*(3), 968–989. doi:10.1016/j.dss.2005.05.026

Moller, C., Maarck, C. J., & Tan, R. D. (2007). What is Business Process Management: A Two Stage Literature Review of a Emerging Field. *Research and Practical Issues of Enterprise Information Systems II,* (Vol. 1, pp. 19-32). Berlin: Springer-Verlag.

MonoDevelop Project. (2007). *MonoDevelop.* Retrieved June 2007, from http://www.monodevelop.com/

Morgan, C. (1990). *Deriving programs from specifications.* Englewood Cliffs, NJ: Prentice Hall International.

Morgan, P., (n.d.). *Process Improvement-Is it a lottery?* Marting and Associates-Software Process Improvement Resources and Assessments Results.

Morville, P., & Rosenfeld, L. (2006). *Information Architecture for the World Wide Web,* (3rd Ed.). Sebastopol, CA: O'Reilly Media.

Mota, E., Clarke, E., Groce, A., Oliveira, W., Falcao, M., & Kanda, J. (2004). VeriAgent: An Approach to integrating UML and Formal Verification Tools. [ENTCS]. *Electronic Notes in Theoretical Computer Science, 95,* 111–129. doi:10.1016/j.entcs.2004.04.008

Mozilla, (2003). Retrieved from http://ftp.mozilla.org/

Muccini, H., Bertolino, A., & Inverardi, P. (2004). Using Software Architecture for Code Testing. *IEEE Transactions on Software Engineering, 30*(3), 160–171. doi:10.1109/TSE.2004.1271170

Mukkamala, R., & Bruell, S. (1990). Efficient Schemes to Evaluate Transaction Performance in Distributed Database Systems. *The Computer Journal, 33*(1), 79–89. doi:10.1093/comjnl/33.1.79

Myers, C. R. (2003). Software systems as complex networks: structure, function, and evolvability of software collaboration graphs. *Physical Review E: Statistical, Nonlinear, and Soft Matter Physics, 68,* 046116. doi:10.1103/PhysRevE.68.046116

Nagappan, N., & Ball, T. (2005). Use of Relative Code Churn Measures to Predict System Defect Density. In *27th International conference on software engineering: Proceedings of 27th International Conference on Software Engineering (U.S.A.), Saint Louis, Missouri* (pp. 284-292).

National Information and Communication Technology Australia (NICTA). (2008). Retrieved November 25, 2008, from http://nicta.com.au/

Navathe, S., & Ceri, S. (1984). A vertical Partitioning algorithms for database design. *ACM Transactions on Database Systems, 9.*

Navathe, S., Karlapalem, K., & Minyoung, R. (1995). A mixed fragmentation methodology for initial distributed database design. *Journal of Computer and Software Engineering, 3*(4), 395–425.

Nawrocki, J., Walter, B., & Wojciechowski, A. (2001). Towards the maturity model for extreme programming. *27th Euromicro Proceedings,* September 4-6, (pp.233-239).

Neighbors, J. Draco. (1989). A method for engineering reusable software systems. In *Software Reusability,* (Vol. I: *Concepts and Models,* pp. 295–219). New York: ACM Frontier Series, Addison-Wesley.

Nelson, H. J., & Monarchi, D. E. (2007). Ensuring the Quality of Conceptual Representations. *Software Quality Journal, 15*(2), 213–233. doi:10.1007/s11219-006-9011-2

Newcomer, E. (2002). *Understanding Web Services.* Boston: Addison-Wesley.

Newcomer, E., & Lomow, G. (2005). *Understanding SOA with web services.* Boston: Addison-Wesley.

Newman, M. (2005). Power laws, Pareto distributions and Zipf's law. *Contemporary Physics, 46,* 323–351. doi:10.1080/00107510500052444

Nguyen, H. Q., Johnson, R., & Hackett, M. (2003). *Testing Applications on the Web: Test Planning for Mobile and Internet-Based Systems* (2nd Ed.). Hoboken, NJ: John Wiley and Sons.

Nielsen, S. (1996). Personal communication.

NIST. (2003). *The Economic Impacts of Inadequate Infrastructure for software testing.* Retrieved from http://www.nist.gov/director/prog-ofc/report02-3.pdf

Niu, N., Easterbrook, S. (2007). So You Think you know other's goal? A Repertory Grid Study. *IEEE Software, March/April.*

Noble, J., & Weir, C. (2001). *A Window in Your Pocket: Some Small Patterns for User Interfaces.* The Sixth European Conference on Pattern Languages of Programs (EuroPLoP 2001), Irsee, Germany, July 4-8, 2001.

NSF Center for Empirically Based Software Engineering (CeBASE). (2004). Retrieved December 4, 2008, from http://www.cebase.org/.

O'Reilly, T. (2005, September 30). *What Is Web 2.0: Design Patterns and Business Models for the Next Generation of Software.* Sebastopol, CA: O'Reilly Network.

OASIS/ebXML Registry Technical Committee. (2002). *OASIS/ebXML Registry Information Model.*

Ober, I. (2000) More Meaningful UML Models. *37th International Conference on Technology of Object-Oriented Languages and Systems (TOOLS-37'00),* (pp. 146-157).

Object Manage Group(OMG). (2006). *Meta Object Facility (MOF) Core Specification.* Retrieved from http://www.omg.org/docs/formal/06-01-01.pdf

Object Management Group(OMG). (2000). *OMG XML Metadata Interchange (XMI) Specification.*

Object Management Group. (2005). *UML Profile for Quality of Service and Fault Tolerance.* Retrieved 3rd August 2005, from http://www.omg.org/docs/ptc/05-05-02.pdf

Object Management Group. (n.d.). *MDA Guide Version 1.0.* Retrieved from http://www.omg.org, document no. - omg/2003-05-01

Ocampo, A., Bella, F., & Münch, J. (2004). Software Process Commonality Analysis. Special Issue on ProSim. *The 5th International Workshop on Software Process Simulation and Modeling, August.*

Ocampo, A., Boggio, D., Münch, J., & Palladino, G. (2003). Towards a Reference Process for Developing Wireless Internet Services. *IEEE Transactions on Software Engineering, 29*(12), 1122–1134. doi:10.1109/TSE.2003.1265526

Ocampo, A., Münch, J., & Bella, F. (2004). *Software Process Commonality Analysis.* Washington, DC: IEEE.

Odeh, M., & Kamm, R. (2003). Bridging the Gap Between Business Models and System Models. *Information and Software Technology, 45,* 1053–1060. doi:10.1016/S0950-5849(03)00133-2

Offutt, A. J., & Liu, S. (1997). *Generating Test Data from SOFL Specifications.* (Tech. Rep.) ISSE-TR-97-02, Department of Information and Software Systems Engineering, George Mason University, VA, (pp. 1-24).

Okalas Ossami, D.-D., Mota, J.-M., & Boulanger, J.-L. (2007). A model process towards modeling guidelines to build certifiable UML models in the railway sector. In *SPICE'2007: Software Process Improvement and Capability.*

Okasa Ossami, D.-D., & Mota, J.-M. Thierry, Laurent., Perronne, J-M. & Boulanger, J-L. (2007). A method to model guidelines for developing railway safety-critical systems with UML. In *proceedings of 7th International SPICE Conference (Software Process Improvement and Capability determination).*

Olsson, K. (1999). *Daily Build—The Best of Both Worlds: Rapid Development and Control.* Tech. Rep., Swedish Eng. Industries.

Olumofin, F. G., & Mišic, V. B. (2007). A Holistic Architecture Assessment Method for Software Product Lines. *Information and Software Technology, 49*(4), 309–323. doi:10.1016/j.infsof.2006.05.003

OMG. (2005). *UML 2.0 Superstructure Specification* [OMG Standard]. De Carvalho, R. A. (2005, June 09).

Device and Method for Information Systems Modeling. Brazilian Patent PI0501998-2. de Carvalho, R. A. (2006). Issues on Evaluating Free/Open Source ERP Systems. In *Research and Practical Issues of Enterprise Information Systems* (IFIP Series) (pp. 667-676). New York: Springer-Verlag.

OMG. (2007). *Unified Modeling Language Specification.* Retrieved from http://www.omg.org/docs/formal/05-07-04.pdf, Version 2.0.

Open WebMail (2003). Retrieved from http://openwebmail.org/.

OpenTaps. (2006). *OpenTaps.* Retrieved May 2006, from http://www.opentaps.org/

OPNET IT Guru Academic Edition 9.1, OPNET Technologies, Inc. (2003). Retrieved January 30th, 2008 from http://www.opnet.com/university_program/itguru_academic_edition/

Ostrand, T. J., & Weyuker, E. J. (2004). A tool for mining defect-tracking systems to predict fault-prone files. In *1st ICSE workshop on mining software repositories: Proceedings of the 1st ICSE Workshop on Mining Software Repositories (Scotland), Edinburgh,* (pp. 85-89).

Ostrand, T. J., Weyuker, E. J., & Bell, R. M. (2005). Predicting the location and number of faults in large software systems. *IEEE Transactions on Software Engineering, 31,* 340–355. doi:10.1109/TSE.2005.49

Ostrand, T., & Weyuker, E. J. (2002). The distribution of faults in a large industrial software system. In *2002 ACM international symposium on software testing and analysis: Proceedings of 2002 ACM International Symposium on Software Testing and Analysis (Italy), Rome* (pp. 55-64).

Ostrand, T., Weyuker, E. J., & Bell, R. M. (2004). Where the bugs are? In *2004 ACM international symposium on software testing and analysis. Proceedings of 2004 ACM International Symposium on Software Testing and Analysis (U.S.A.), Boston, MA* (pp. 86-96).

Ovaska, P., Rossi, M., & Marttiin, P. (2003). Architecture as a coordination tool in multi-site software development. *Software Process Improvement and Practice, 8*(4), 233–247. doi:10.1002/spip.186

Ozsu, M., & Valduriez, P. (1991). Principles of Distributed Database Systems. 1st ed. Englewood Cliffs NJ, Prentice-Hall.

Ozsu, M., & Valduriez, P. (1999). *Principles of Distributed Database Systems* (2nd Ed.). Englewood Cliffs NJ: Prentice-Hall.

Paasivaara, M., & Lassenius, C. (2003). Collaboration practices in global inter-organizational software development projects. *Software Process Improvement and Practice, 8*(4), 183–199. doi:10.1002/spip.187

Paavilainen, J. (2002). *Mobile Business Strategies: Understanding the Technologies and Opportunities.* Reading, MA: Addison-Wesley.

Paetsch, F., Eberlein, A., & Maure, F. (2003). Requirements Engineering and Agile Software Development. In *Proceedings of the Twelfth IEEE International Workshops on Enabling Technologies: Infrastructure for Collaborative Enterprises* 2003 (WETICE'03).

Papazoglou, M., & Heuvel, W. (2007, July). Service oriented architectures: Approaches, technologies and research issues. *The International Journal on Very Large Data Bases, 16*(3), 389–415. doi:10.1007/s00778-007-0044-3

Paradkar, A. (2003). Towards model-based generation of self-priming and self-checking conformance tests for interactive systems Symposium on Applied Computing. *ACM symposium on Applied Computing,* (pp. 1110–1117). New York: ACM Press.

Park, S., & Baik, D. (1997). A Data Allocation Considering Data Availability in Distributed Database Systems. *Proceedings of the 1997 International Conference on Parallel and Distributed Systems* (ICPADS '97) (pp. 708 – 713). Washington, DC: IEEE.

Parr, A., & Shanks, G. (2000). A Model of ERP Project Implementation. *Journal of Information Technology,* 289–303. doi:10.1080/02683960010009051

Parthasarathy, P. R., Lenin, R. B., & Matis, J. H. (1999). On the numerical solution of transient probabilities of the stochastic power law logistic model. *Nonlinear Analysis, 37*, 677–688. doi:10.1016/S0362-546X(98)00065-0

Patrascoiu, O. (2004, September). Mapping edoc to web services using yatl. In *International conference on enterprise distributed object computing.*

Patterson, D. A., Brown, A., Broadwell, P., Candea, G., Chen, M., Cutler, J., et al. (2002). *Recovery-Oriented Computing (ROC): Motivation, Definition, Techniques, and Case Studies.* UC Berkeley Computer Science Technical Report UCB/CSD-02-1175, Berkley, CA.

Paulk, M. C. (1998). Using the Software CMM in Small Organisations. *The Joint 1998 Proceedings of the Pacific Northwest Software Quality Conference and the Eighth International Conference on Software Quality*, 13-14 October 1998, Portland, OR, Software Engineering Institute, (pp.350-361).

Paulk, M. C. (2001). Extreme Programming from a CMM Perspective. *IEEE Software, 18*(6), 19–26. doi:10.1109/52.965798

Paulk, M. C., Weber, C. V., Curtis, B., & Chrissis, M. B. (1995). *The Capability Maturity Model for Software: Guidelines for Improving the Software Process (SEI).* Reading, MA: Addison Wesley.

Paulk, M., Curtis, M., & Weber, C. (1993). *Software Process Maturity Questionnaire: Capability Model version 1.1.* Carnegie Mellon-Software Engineering Institute. Retrieved January 1, 2007 from http://www.sei.cmu.edu/publications/documents/93.reports/93.tr.024.html

Paulk, M., Weber, C., & Curtis, M. (1999). The Capability Maturity Model for Software. In K. Emam & N. Madhavji (Eds.), *Elements of software process Assessment and Improvement* (pp. 3-22). Washington, DC: IEEE Computer Society Press.

Peng, C.-K., Buldyrev, S. C., Havlin, S., Simons, M., Stanley, H. E., & Goldberger, A. L. (1994). Mosaic organization of DNA nucleotides. *Physical Review E: Statistical Physics, Plasmas, Fluids, and Related Interdisciplinary Topics, 49*, 1685–1689. doi:10.1103/PhysRevE.49.1685

Peng, C.-K., Buldyrev, S.V., Goldberger, A.L., Havlin, S., & Sciortino, F., Simon, M. et al. (1992). Long-range correlations in nucleotide sequences. *Nature, 356*, 168–170. doi:10.1038/356168a0

Peng, C.-K., Havlin, S., Stanley, H. E., & Goldberger, A. L. (1995). Quantification of scaling exponents and cross over phenomena in nonstationary heartbeat time series. *Chaos (Woodbury, N.Y.), 5*, 82–87. doi:10.1063/1.166141

Perry, D. E., Romanovsky, A., & Tripathi, A. (2000). Current Trends in Exception Handling. *IEEE Transactions on Software Engineering, 26*(10), 921–922. doi:10.1109/TSE.2000.879816

Persse, J. (2007). *Project Management Success with CMMI: Seven CMMI Process Areas.* Upper Saddle River, NJ: Prentice Hall PTR.

Persse, J. R. (2001). *Implementing the Capability Maturity Model.* Hoboken, NJ: John Wiley & Sons Inc.

Peter, T., Derek, C., & Joni, O. (2000). HP Product Generation Consulting, A Cooperative Model for Cross-Divisional Product Development for a Software Product Line. In P. Donohoe (Ed.), *Proceedings of the First Software Product Lines Conference (SPLCI)* (pp. 111-132). Boston: Kluwer Academic Publishers.

Pikkarainen, M., & Mantyniemi, A. (2006). *An Approach for Using CMMI in Agile Software Development Assessments: Experiences from Three Case Studies, SPICE 2006 conference*, Luxemburg.

Pilatti, L., Audy, J. L. N., & Prikladnicki, R. (2006). Software configuration management over a global software development environment: Lessons learned from a case study. In *Proceedings of the 2006 International Workshop on Global Software Development for the Practitioner* (pp. 45-50).

Pilskalns, O., Andrews, A., France, R., & Ghosh, S. (2003). Rigorous Testing by Merging Structural and Behavioral UML Representations. *6th International Conference on Unified Modeling Language.*

Pino, F. J., García, F., & Piattini, M. (2007). Software process improvement in small and medium software enterprises: A systematic review. *Software Quality Journal, 16*(2), 237–261. doi:10.1007/s11219-007-9038-z

Pirolli, P. (2007). *Information Foraging Theory: Adaptive Interaction with Information*. Oxford, UK: Oxford University Press.

Plösch, R. (1997). Design by Contract for Python. In *Proc. of IEEE Joint Asia Pacific Software Engineering Conference*, Hong Kong.

Poppendeick, M., & Poppendeick, T. (2003). *Lean Software Development: An Agile Toolkit for Software Development Managers* (pp. xxi –xxviii). Reading MA: Addison Wesley.

Porter, A., Yilmaz, C., Memon, A. M., Schmidt, D. C., & Natarajan, B. (2007). Skoll: A Process and Infrastructure for Distributed Continuous Quality Assurance. *IEEE Transactions on Software Engineering, 33*(8), 510–525. doi:10.1109/TSE.2007.70719

Positive-g-Daily Build Product Information—Mozilla, (2003). Retrieved from http://positive-g.com/daily-build/.

Pressman, R. S. (2001). *Software Engineering a Practitioner's Approach*. New York: Mcgraw-Hill.

Pressman, R. S. (2005). *Software Engineering – A Practitioner's Approach* (6th Edition). New Delhi, India: McGraw-Hill International Edition.

Pretschner, A. & L"otzbeyer, H. & Philipps, J. (2001). Model Based Testing in Evolutionary Software Development. *12th IEEE Intl. Workshop on Rapid System Prototyping (RSP'01)*.

Pretschner, A., Broy, M., Kruger, I. H., & Stauner, T. (2007). Software Engineering for Automotive Systems: A Roadmap. *Future of Software Engineering, 2007 . FOSE, 07*, 55–71.

Prikladnicki, R., Audy, J. L. N., & Evaristo, J. R. (2003). Distributed software development: Toward an understanding of the relationship between project team, users and customers. In *Proceedings of the 5th International Conference on Enterprise Information Systems (ICEIS)* (pp. 417-423).

Prikladnicki, R., Audy, J. L. N., Damian, D., & de Oliveira, T. C. (2007). Distributed software development: Practices and challenges in different business strategies of offshoring and onshoring. In *Proceedings of the Second IEEE International Conference on Global Software Engineering* (pp. 262-274).

Prikladnicki, R., Damian, D., & Audy, J. L. N. (2008). Patterns of evolution in the practice of distributed software development: Quantitative results from a systematic review. In *Proceedings of the 12th International Conference on Evaluation and Assessment in Software Engineering (EASE)* University of Bari, Italy.

Prowell, S. (2004). *State of the art Model based Testing with Markov chain usage models*. Dagstuhl Seminar No. 04371, September 5-10.

Prowell, S. J. (2003). JUMBL: A tool for model based testing using Markov chains. *36th Hawaii International Conference on System Sciences, HICSS 2003*, (p. 337).

Prowell, S. J. (2005). Using Markov chain usage models to test complex systems. *38th Annual Hawaii International Conference on System Sciences, HICSS'38*.

Raistrick, C., Francis, P., & Wright, J. (2004). *Model driven architecture with executable uml*. Cambridge, UK: Cambridge University Press.

Ramachandran, M. (2005). *A Process Improvement Framework for XP based SMEs*. Paper presented at 6th International Conference on Extreme Programming and Agile Processes in Software Engineering, Sheffield, UK, June 2005.

Ramachandran, M., & Allen, P. (2005). *Special Issue on Software Variability: Process and Management: Commonality and variability analysis in industrial practice for product line improvement.*

Ramachandran, M., & Ganeshan, S. (2008). *Domain Engineering Method for Product Line Development*. Published at software engineering research and practice, Las Vegas, NV.

Ramalho, F., Robin, J., & Schiel, U. (2004). Concurrent Transaction Frame Logic Formal Semantics for UML activity and class diagrams. [ENTCS]. *Electronic Notes in Theoretical Computer Science, 95*, 83–109. doi:10.1016/j. entcs.2004.04.007

Rankins, R., Bertucci, P., Gallelli, C., & Silverstein, A. T. (2007). *Microsoft SQL Server 2005 Unleashed*. Sams.

Rasse, A., Perronne, J.-M., Muller, P.-A., & Thirion, B. (2005). Using process algebra to validate behavioral aspects of object-oriented models. In *Model design and Validation Workshop, MODEVA'05*, (LNCS). Berlin: Springer.

Rational Unified Process, I. B. M. (2008). Retrieved from http://www-306.ibm.com/software/awdtools/rup/

Rauterberg, M. (1996). *How to measure Cognitive Complexity in Human – Computer Interaction*. ED-MEDIA 96, Charlottesville, NC, AACE.

Rauterberg, M., & Aeppli, R. (1996). *How to measure the behavioural and Cognitive Complexity of learning process in Man-Machine Systems*, (pp.581- 586). Educational Multimedia and Hypermedia-ED- MEDIA'96, Charlottesville, NC, AACE.

Rauterberg, M., Schluep, S., & Fjuld, M. (1997). *How to model behavioural and cognitive complexity in Human -computer interaction with Petri nets*. IEEE Workshop on Robot and human communication.

Raynus, J. (1999). *Software process improvement with CMM*. London: Artech House.

Reimer, D., & Srinivasan, H. (2003). Analyzing Exception Usage in Large Java Applications. *Exception Handling in Object-Oriented Systems Workshop at ECOOP 2003*.

Reis, C., & Fortes, R. (2002, February). An overview of the software engineering process and tools in the Mozilla project. In *Workshop on open source software development: Proceedings of Workshop on Open Source Software Development (U.K.), Newcastle* (pp. 155-175).

Reopen911.org. (2005). Retrieved April 2007 from http://www.reopen911. org/?src=overture&OVRAW=world%20trade%20center%20attack&OVKEY=world%20trade%20center%20attack&OVMTC=standard

Reussner, R., & Schmidt, H. (2002). Using Parameterised Contracts to Predict Properties of Component Based Software Architectures. In I. Crnkovic, S. Larsson, & J. Stafford, (Ed.), *Workshop on Component-Based Software Engineering.*

Riccobene, E., Gargantini, A., & Asmundo, M. N. (2002). Consistent Composition and Testing of Components using Abstract State Machines. *Workshop CoMeta – Computational Metamodels*, Richter, G. & Maffeo, B. (1993). Towards a rigorous interpretation of ESML – Extended Systems Modelling Language. *IEEE Transactions on Software Engineering, 19*(2), 165–180.

Riehle, D. (2007). The Economic Motivation of Open Source: Stakeholders Perspectives. *Computer IEE Computer Society,* 25-32.

Riehle, D., Fraleigh, S., Bucka-Lassen, D., & Omorogbe, N. (2001). The architecture of a uml virtual machine. In *Acm international conference on object-oriented programming, systems, languages and applications.*

Risi, W. A., & Rossi, G. (2004). An Architectural Pattern Catalog for Mobile Web Information Systems. *International Journal of Mobile Communications, 2*(3), 235–247.

Robbins, J. (2000). *Debugging Applications*. Redmond, CA: Microsoft Press

Robey, D., Ross, J. W., & Boudreau, M. C. (2002). Learning to implement enterprise systems: An exploratory study of the dialectics of change. *Journal of Management Information Systems, 19*(1).

Robillard, P. N., & Detienne, F. (1998). *Measuring cognitive Activities in Software Engineering*. ICSE98, 20th International conference on Software Engineering, Kyoto, Japan.

Robinson, H. (1999). Graph theory techniques in model based testing. *International Conference on Testing Computer Software.* Hosain S. & Alam S., (2004). Software reliability using markov chain usage model. *3rd International Conference on Electrical & Computer Engineering.*

Robinson, W. N., Suzanne, D., & Pawlowski, S. (1999). Managing Requirements Inconsistency with Development Goal Monitors. *IEEE Transactions on Software Engineering, 25*(6), 816–835. doi:10.1109/32.824411

Rosenberg, L. H. (1998). *Applying and Interpreting Object Oriented Metrics.*

Rosenberg, L. H. (n.d.). *Software Quality Metrics for Object-Oriented Environments.* Unisys Government Systems Lawrence E. Hyatt, Software Assurance Technology Center. Fenton, N.E. & Pfleeger, S.L. (1996). Software Metrics: A Rigorous and Practical Approach (2nd Ed.) London: Int'l Thompson Computer press.

Rossi, G., Pastor, O., Schwabe, D., & Olsina, L. (2008). *Web Engineering: Modelling and Implementing Web Applications.* Berlin: Springer-Verlag.

Roth, J. (2001, September 10). *Patterns of Mobile Interaction.* Third International Workshop on Human Computer Interaction with Mobile Devices (Mobile HCI 2001), Lille, France.

Roth, J. (2002). Patterns of Mobile Interaction. *Personal and Ubiquitous Computing, 6*(4), 282–289. doi:10.1007/s007790200029

Rubin, J., Tracy, L. & Guevara, J. K. (2005). *Worldwide IT Benchmark Report 2006: Volume 4: Current Software Engineering Performance Results: Defect Rates* (Tech. Rep. No. G00133966).

Salmre, I. (2005). *Writing Mobile Code: Essential Software Engineering for Building Mobile Applications.* Reading, MA: Addison-Wesley.

Sandberg, J. (2006). *AUTOSAR today: A roadmap to an autosar implementation.* Master's thesis, Chalmers University of Technology, Sweden.

Sanz, R., & Arzen, K.-E. (2003). Trends in software and control. *IEEE Control Systems Magazine, 23*, 12–15. doi:10.1109/MCS.2003.1200238

Sarkar, S., Sindhgatta, R., & Pooloth, K. (2008). A collaborative platform for application knowledge management in software maintenance projects. In *Proceedings of the 1ˢᵗ Bangalore Annual Compute Conference* (pp. 1-7).

Sarma, A., Noroozi, Z., & van der Hoek, A. (2003). Palantír: Raising awareness among configuration management workspaces. In *Proceedings of the 25ᵗʰ International Conference on Software Engineering* (pp. 444-454).

Scacchi, W. (1995). Understanding and Improving Software Productivity. In D. Hurley (ed.), *Advances in Software Engineering and Knowledge Engineering,* (Vol. 4, pp. 37-70).

Schach, S. R. (2007). *Object oriented and classical software engineering,* (6ᵗʰ Ed., pp.64-75). New York: McGraw-Hill.

Schach, S. R., (1996). Testing: principles and practice. *ACM Computing Surveys (CSUR) March, 28* (1).

Schieferdecker, I., & Grabowski, J. (2003). *The Graphical Format of TTCN-3 in the context of MSC and UML,* ([]. Springer-Verlag]. *LNCS, 2599,* 233–252.

Schieferdecker, I., Dai, Z. R., Grabowski, J., & Rennoch, A. (2003). *The UML 2.0 Testing profile and its Relation to TTCN-3,* (LNCS Vol. 2644, pp. 79-94). Berlin: Springer-Verlag.

Schmettow, M. (2005, September 13). *Towards a Pattern Based Usability Inspection Method for Industrial Practitioners.* The INTERACT 2005 Workshop on Integrating Software Engineering and Usability Engineering, Rome, Italy.

Schmid, K., & Verlage, M. (2004). The Economic Impact of Product Line Adoption and Evolution. *IEEE Software. Special Issue on Software Product Lines, 10*(4), 50–57.

Schmidt, D. C., Stal, M., Rohnert, H., & Buschmann, F. (2000). *Pattern-Oriented Software Architecture, Volume 2: Patterns for Concurrent and Networked Objects.* Hoboken, NJ: John Wiley and Sons.

Schmidt, H., Poernomo, I. & Reussner, R. (2001). Trust-By-Contract: Modelling, Analysing and Predicting Behaviour in Software Architecture. *Journal for Integrated Process and Development Science, September,* 25-51.

Schuh, P. (2004). *Integrating Agile Development in the Real World,* (pp. 1-6). Boston: Charles River Media.

Schümmer, T., & Lukosch, S. (2007). *Patterns for Computer-Mediated Interaction.* Chichester, UK: John Wiley and Sons.

Schwaber, K. (2004). *Agile project management with Scrum.* Redmond, CA: Microsoft Press.

Schwaber, K., & Beedle, M. (2002). *Agile Software Development with SCRUM* (pp. 23-30). Upper Saddle River, NJ: Prentice-Hall.

Schwaber, S., & Beedle, M. (2002). *Agile Software Development With Scrum.* Englewood Cliffs NJ: Prentice Hall.

SEC. (2008) Retrieved December 5, 2008, from http://www.ipa.go.jp/english/sec/index.html.

SEI. (2005). *Software Product Lines.* Retrieved from http://www.sei.cmu.edu/productlines/bibliography.html

Semeczko, G. (1997). *Using a Double Weighted Clustering Technique for Fragment Allocation in Wide Area Networks,* (Tech. Rep. No. FIT-TR-97-11). School of Computing Science, Queensland University of Technology.

Semer, L. J. (1998). Disaster recovery planning for the distributed environment. *Internal Auditor, 55*(6), 41–47.

Sendall, S., & Kozaczynki, W. (2003, September/October). Model transformation: The heart and soul of model-driven software development. *IEEE Software, 20*(5). doi:10.1109/MS.2003.1231150

Sengupta, S. (2007). *Functional Specifications of Object Oriented Systems: A Model Driven Framework.* Ph.D thesis, Jadavpur University, Kolkata, India.

Sengupta, S., & Bhattacharya, S. (2006). Formalization of Functional Requirements and Their Traceability in UML Diagrams- A Z Notation Based Approach. *11th Systems Engineering Test & Evaluation Conference (SETE'06).*

Sengupta, S., & Bhattacharya, S. (2007). Functional Specification of Object Oriented Systems: A Model Driven Framework. *31st Annual IEEE International Computer Software and Applications Conference (COMPSAC'07).*

Sengupta, S., Bhattacharya, S., (2008). Formalization of Functional Requirements of Software Development Process. *Journal of Foundations of Computing and Decision Sciences (FCDS), Institute of Computing Science, Poznan University of Technology, Poland, 33*(1).

Sengupta, S., Kanjilal, A., & Bhattacharya, S. (2005). Automated Translation of Behavioral Models using OCL and XML. *IEEE TENCON, 05*, 86–91.

Sengupta, S., Kanjilal, A., & Bhattacharya, S. (2006). Behavioral Specification of Object Oriented Systems using OCL. *Conference on Recent Trends in Emerging Technologies (RTET06),* (pp. 31-35).

Sengupta, S., Sengupta, A., & Bhattacharya, S. (2007). Requirements to Components: A Model View Controller Architechture. *14th Monterey Workshop,* (pp. 167-184).

Serrano, N., & Sarriegi, J. M. (2006). Open source software ERPs: A new alternative for an old need. *IEEE Software,* 94–96. doi:10.1109/MS.2006.78

Setamanit, S.-o., Wakeland, W., & Raffo, D. (2007). Using simulation to evaluate global software development task allocation strategies. *Software Process Improvement and Practice, 12*(5), 491–503. doi:10.1002/spip.335

Shanks, G. (1999, September 29). *Semiotic Approach to Understanding Representation in Information Systems. Information Systems Foundations Workshop,* Sydney, Australia.

Sharble, R. C., & Cohen, S. S. (1993). The Object-Oriented Brewery: A Comparison of Two Object-Oriented Development Methods. *Software Eng. Notes, 18*, 60–73. doi:10.1145/159420.155839

Sharp, H., Galal, G. H., & Finkelstein, A. (1999, August 30-September 3). *Stakeholder Identification in the Requirements Engineering Process.* The Tenth International Conference and Workshop on Database and Expert Systems Applications (DEXA 1999), Florence, Italy.

SharpDevelop Project. (2006). *SharpDevelop.* Retrieved May 2006, from http://wiki.sharpdevelop.net/

SharpForge Project. (2007). *SharpForge*. Retrieved June, from http://sharpforge.org/

Shaw, R. (2006). Indian Ocean tsunami and aftermath Need for environment-disaster synergy. *Disaster Prevention and Management, 15*(1), 5–20. doi:10.1108/09653560610654202

Shaw, R. (2006). Indian Ocean tsunami and aftermath need for environment-disaster synergy. *Disaster Prevention and Management, 15*(1), 5–20. doi:10.1108/09653560610654202

Shen, H., Wall, B., Zaremba, M., Chen, Y., & Browne, J. (2004). Integration of Business Modeling Methods for Enterprise Information System Analysis and User Requirements Gathering. *Computers in Industry, 54*(3), 307–323. doi:10.1016/j.compind.2003.07.009

Shen, W., Compton, K., & Huggins, J. (2003). A method of implementing uml virtual machines with some constraints based on abstract state machines. In *Ieee asia-pacific software engineering conference.*

Shepperd, M. & Schofiled, C. (1997, February). Estimating Software Project Effort Using Analogies. *IEEECS Log No. 104091.*

Siakas, K. V., & Balstrup, B. (2006). Software outsourcing quality achieved by global virtual collaboration. *Software Process Improvement and Practice, 11*(3), 319–328. doi:10.1002/spip.275

Siemens (2006). *Introduction to future ISO 26262.* Siemens VDO internal presentation.

Simon, H. (1996). *The Sciences of the Artificial* (Third Edition). Cambridge, MA: The MIT Press.

Simons, A. J. H. (2000). On the Compositional Properties of UML statechart diagrams. *Rigorous Object-Oriented Methods (ROOM'00).*

Siviy, J. M., Penn, M. L., & Robert, W. (2007). *Standard CMMI (R) and Six Sigma: Partners in Process Improvement.* Reading MA: Addison Wesley Professional.

Sjoberg, D. I. K., Dyba, T., & Jorgensen, M. (2007). The Future of Empirical Methods in Software Engineering Research. *Future of Software Engineering, 2007. FOSE, 07,* 358–378.

Smets-Solanes, J.-P., & De Carvalho, R. A. (2002). An Abstract Model for An Open Source ERP System: The ERP5 Proposal. In *Proc. 8th International Conference on Industrial Engineering and Operations Management,* Curitiba, Brazil

Smets-Solanes, J.-P., & De Carvalho, R. A. (2003). ERP5: A Next-Generation, Open-Source ERP Architecture. *IEEE IT Professional, 5*(July), 38-44. Balasubramanian, K., Gokhale, A., Karsai, G. & Sztipanovits, J., Neema, S., (2006). Developing Applications Using Model-Driven Design Environments. *IEEE Computer, 39*(February), 33–40.

Snook, C., & Butler, M. (2004). U2B – A tool for translating UML-B models into B. In J. Mermet, (Ed.), *UML-B Specification for Proven Embedded Systems Design.*

Sommerville, I., & Sawyer, P. (2000). *Requirements Engineering – A Good Practice Guide.* Chichester, UK: John Wiley & Sons.

Sommerville (2004). *Software Engineering, (7ᵗʰ, Ed.).* Reading, MA: Addison Wesley.

Sommerville, I. (1992). *Software Engineering.* Reading, MA: Addison-Wesley Publishing Company.

Sommerville, I. Sawyer & P.Viller (1999). Managing process inconsistency using viewpoints. *IEEE Transactions on Software Engineering, 25*(6), 784 – 799.

Son, J., & Kim, M. (2004). An Adaptable Vertical Partitioning Method in Distributed Systems. *Journal of Systems and Software, 73*(3), 551–561. doi:10.1016/j.jss.2003.04.002

Song, Q., Shepperd, M., Cartwright, M., & Mair, C. (2006). Software Defect Association Mining and Defect Correction Effort Prediction. *IEEE Transactions on Software Engineering, 32,* 69–82. doi:10.1109/TSE.2006.1599417

Spinellis, Diomidis, Mariam, Naseem, Pepa & Caroline, (2007). Bookshelf - Software engineering for the rest of us. *Software IEEE, 24*(4), 107-109.

Spivey, J. M. (1992). *The Z Notation, A Reference Manual,* (2nd Ed.). Upper Saddle River, NJ: Prentice Hall International.

Spriestersbach, A., & Springer, T. (2004). Quality Attributes in Mobile Web Application Development. In F. Bomarius & H. Iida (Eds.) *Product Focused Software Process Improvement* (pp. 120-130). Berlin: Springer-Verlag.

Spring. (2007). *Spring Framework*. Retrieved January 2007, from http://www.springframework.org/

Stanoevska-Slabeva, K. (2003, June 16-21). Towards a Reference Model for M-Commerce Applications. *The Eleventh European Conference on Information Systems (ECIS 2003)*, Naples, Italy.

Staron, M. (2006, October 2006). *Adopting Model Driven Software Development in Industry - A Case Study at Two Companies.* Paper presented at the 9th International Conference Model Driven Engineering Languages and Systems (MODELS 2006), Genova, Italy.

Stensrud, E., & Myrtveit, I. (2003, May). Identifying High Performance ERP Projects. *IEEE Transactions on Software Engineering, 29*(5). doi:10.1109/TSE.2003.1199070

Stojanovic, L. (2004). *Methods and Tools for Ontology Evolution.* Ph.D Thesis, University of Karlsruhe, Karlsruhe, Germany.

Stojanovic, L. (2004). *Methods and Tools for Ontology Evolution.* Ph.D Thesis, University of Karlsruhe, Karlsruhe, Germany.

Storey, M.-A. D., Čubranić, D., & German, D. M. (2005). On the use of visualization to support awareness of human activities in software development: A survey and a framework. In *Proceedings of the 2005 ACM Symposium on Software Visualization* (pp. 193-202).

Subramanyam, R. & Krishnan, M. S. (2003). Empirical analysis of CK metrics for object-oriented design complexity: implications for software defects. *IEEE Trans. on SE, 29*(4).

Sugumaran,V., Park, S., & Kang, C. (2006). Software product line engineering. *Communications of ACM,* December.

Sun Microsystems. (2007). *Pet Store*. Retrieved January 2007, from https://blueprints.dev.java.net/petstore/

Sun, J., Hyeok, K., Ji, H., Oh, S., Yul, S., & Dong, S. (2007). *A framework for evaluating reusability of core asset in product line engineering.* Information and Software Technology archive.

SysML (2006). The Systems Modeling Language}. *OMG Std. Final Adopted Specification, May.*

Szyperski, C., Gruntz, D., & Murer, S. (2002). *Component Software: Beyond Object-Oriented Programming (2nd Ed.).* Reading, MA: Addison-Wesley.

Tai, K. C., & Lei, Y. (2002). A test generation strategy for pairwise testing. *IEEE Transactions on Software Engineering, 28*(1), 109–111. doi:10.1109/32.979992

Tamhankar, A., & Ram, S. (1998). Database Fragmentation and Allocation: An Integrated Methodology and Case Study. *IEEE Transactions on Systems, Man, and Cybernetics. Part A, Systems and Humans, 28*(3), 288–305. doi:10.1109/3468.668961

Tarasewich, P. (2003). Designing Mobile Commerce Applications. *Communications of the ACM, 46*(12), 57–60. doi:10.1145/953460.953489

Terry, A., Dabija, T., Barnes, X., & Teklemariam, A. (1995). *DADSE 2.3 User Manual.* Paolo Alto, CA: Teknowledge Federal Systems.

The Middleware Company. (2003). *Model Driven Development for J2EE Utilizing a Model Driven Architecture (MDA) Approach: Productivity Analysis.*

Thissen, M. R., Page, J. M., Bharathi, M. C., & Austin, T. L. (2007). Communication tools for distributed software development teams. In *Proceedings of the 2007 ACM SIGMIS CPR Conference on Computer Personnel Doctoral Consortium and Research Conference: The Global Information Technology Workforce* (pp. 28-35).

Thomas, E. (2004). *Service-oriented architecture: A Field Guide to Integrating XML and Web Services*. Upper Saddle River, NJ: Prentice Hall.

Thomas, E. (2004). *Service-oriented architecture: A Field Guide to Integrating XML and Web Services*. Upper Saddle River, NJ: Prentice Hall.

Thompsun, J., & Heimdahl, M. (2001). *Extending the Product Family Approach to support n-dimensional and Hierarchical products*. Washington, DC: IEEE.

Tidwell, J. (2006). *Designing Interfaces: Patterns for Effective Interaction Design*. Sebastopol, CA: O'Reilly Media.

Tim, K. (2004). *Practical insight into the CMMI*. New York: Artech house.

Toft, P. (2004).*The HP Owen Firmware Cooperative: A Software Product Line Success Story*.

Togur, D. M., Bloomberg, E. & Morgan Stanley (2003). *CIO Survey Series: Release 4.5*. Morgan Stanley Research Report.

Tolvanen, J.-P., Sprinkle, J., & Gray, J. (2006). *The 6th OOPSLA Workshop on Domain-Specific Modeling*. Paper presented at the Object-Oriented Programming, Systems, Languages, and Applications (OOPSLA).

Tomaszewski Farias, S., Mungas, D., & Reed, B. R. (2008). The measurement of Everyday Cognition (ECog) Scale Development and Psychometric Properties. *Neuropsychology, 22*(45), 31–544.

Toth, A. Varro, D. & Pataricza, A. (2003). Model-Level Automatic Test Generation for UML statecharts. *6th IEEE workshop on Design and Diagnostics of Electronic Circuits and System, (DDECS 2003)*.

Traoré, I., & Aredo, D. B. (2004). Enhancing Structured Review with Model-based Verification. *IEEE Transactions on Software Engineering, 30*(11), 736–753. doi:10.1109/TSE.2004.86

Traoré, I., & Demissie, B. A. (2004). Enhancing Structured Review with Model-Based Verification. *IEEE Transactions on Software Engineering, 30*(11), 736–753. doi:10.1109/TSE.2004.86

Trewin, S. (2006, May 22). *Physical Usability and the Mobile Web*. The 2006 International Cross-Disciplinary Workshop on Web Accessibility 2006 (W4A 2006), Edinburgh, Scotland.

Tsiolakis, A., & Ehrig, H. (2000). Consistency Analysis of UML Class and Sequence Diagrams using Attributed Graph Grammars. *Joint APPLIGRAPH and GETGRATS workshop on graph transformation systems*, (pp. 77-86).

Tsunami Evaluation Coalition. (2006). *Joint Evaluation of the International Response to the Indian Ocean Tsunami*. Tsunami Evaluation Coalition.

Tung, Y. W., & Aldiwan, W. S. (2000). Automating test case generation for the new generation mission software system. *IEEE Aerospace Conference* (pp. 431-437).

Turk, D., France, R., & Rumpe, B. (2002). Limitations of Agile Software Processes. In *Proceedings of the Third International Conference on eXtreme Programming and Agile Processes in Software Engineering*, (pp. 43-46).

Turner, R., & Jain, A. (2002). *Agile meets CMMI: Culture clash or common cause XP/Agile universe 2002*. (LNCS Vol. 2418 pp. 60-69). Berlin: Springer.

Tusena. (2006). *Tusena*. Retrieved 2nd December 2006, from http://sourceforge.net/projects/tustena/

UML (2007). Unified Modeling Language. *OMG Std. Final Adopted Specification, February*.

Uml super structure specification 2.1.2. (2007). Object Management Group.

Van Belle, T. B. (2004). *Modularity and the evolution of software evolvability*. Unpublished Ph.D. Computer Science thesis, The University of New Mexico, Albuquerque, NM.

Van der Aalst, W. M. P., Van Hee, K. M., & Houben, G. J. (1994). Modeling and Analysing Workflow using a Petri Net based approach. *2nd Workshop on Computer-Supported Cooperative Work, Petri nets and related Formalisms*.

van der Aalst, W., & van Hee, K. (2004). *Workflow Management*. Cambridge: MIT Press.

van der Linden, F. (2002). Software Product Families in Europe: The ESAPS & CAFE Project. *IEEE Software*, *19*(4), 41–49. doi:10.1109/MS.2002.1020286

Van Duyne, D. K., Landay, J., & Hong, J. I. (2003). *The Design of Sites: Patterns, Principles, and Processes for Crafting a Customer-Centered Web Experience*. Reading, MA: Addison-Wesley.

van Moll, J., Jacobs, J., Kusters, R., & Trienekens, J. (2004). Defect detection oriented lifecycle modelling in complex product development. *Information and Software Technology*, *46*(10), 665–675. doi:10.1016/j.infsof.2003.12.001

Van, D. W., Bartel., & Turoff, M. (2007). Emergency-Response Systems: Emerging Trends and Technologies. *Communications of the ACM*, *50*(3).

Van, P. (2003). *Wrekly non local irreversible thermodynamics*. arxiv:condmat / 0112214 v3 [cond-mat.mtrl-sci].

Vanderdonckt, J. (1999). Development Milestones towards a Tool for Working with Guidelines . *Interacting with Computers*, *12*(2), 81–118. doi:10.1016/S0953-5438(99)00019-3

Varshney, U., & Vetter, R. (2002). Mobile Commerce: Framework, Applications and Networking Support. *Mobile Networks and Applications*, *7*(3), 185–198. doi:10.1023/A:1014570512129

Vermeulen, A., Beged-Dov, G., & Thompson, P. (1995, October). The pipeline design pattern. In *Acm sigplan conference on object-oriented programming, systems, languages, and applications, workshop on design patterns for concurrent parallel and distributed object-oriented systems*.

Vernadat, F. B. (2002). Enterprise Modeling and Integration (EMI): Current Status and Research Perspectives. *Annual Reviews in Control*, *26*, 15–25. doi:10.1016/S1367-5788(02)80006-2

Vick, P. (2004). *The Visual Basic. Net Programming Language*. Reading. MA: Addison-Wesley.

Visual Basic. *Net*. (n.d.). Retrieved February 9th, 2008 from http://en.wikipedia.org/wiki/Visual_Basic_.NET

Voges, K., Pope, N., & Brown, M. (2002). Cluster analysis of marketing data examining online shopping orientation: a comparison of k-means and rough clustering approaches. In H.A. Abbass, R.A. Sarker, C.S. Newton (Eds.), *Heuristics and Optimization for Knowledge Discovery* (pp. 207 – 224). Hershey, PA: Idea Group Publishing.

Völter, M. (2006). *openArchitectureWare 4 - The flexible open source tool platform for model-driven software development*.

Von Wangenheim, C.G., Anacleto & Alviano, A. (2006). Helping small companies assess software Processes. *Software*, *23*(1), 91–98. doi:10.1109/MS.2006.13

Wada, H., Babu, E. M. M., Malinowski, A., Suzuki, J., & Oba, K. (2006, November). Design and implementation of the matilda distributed uml virtual machine. In *Iasted international conference on software engineering and applications*.

Wagstrom, P. A., Herbsleb, J. D., & Carley, K. (2005). A social network approach to free/open source software simulation. In *First International Conference on Open Source Systems: Proceedings of the First International Conference on Open source Systems (Italy), Genova* (pp. 16-23).

Wallace, D. R., & Kuhn, D. R. (1999). Failure Modes in Medical Device Software. An Analysis of 15 Years of Recall Data. *Journal, Information Technology Laboratory, NIST Gaithersburg . MD*, 20899.

Wallace, D. R., & Kuhn, D. R. (2001). Failure Modes in Medical Device Software: an Analysis of 15 Years of Recall Data. *International Journal of Reliability Quality and Safety Engineering*, *8*(4). doi:10.1142/S021853930100058X

Walton, G. H., & Poore, J. H. (2000). Measuring complexity and coverage of software specifications. *Information and Software Technology*, *42*(12), 859–872. doi:10.1016/S0950-5849(00)00102-6

Wang, C. (2005). *Research on Framework of MetaModel Interoperability for Ontology Registration.* Master Thesis, Wuhan University, China.

Wang, C. (2008). *Research on Process Model Management Framework for Mass Customization.* Ph.D Thesis, Wuhan University, China.

Wang, C., & He, K. (2007). Extending Metamodel Framework for Interoperability (MFI) to Register Networked Process Models. *Dynamics of Continuous Discrete and Impulsive Systems- Series B- Applications & Algorithms, 14*(S6), 72–78.

Wang, C., & He, K. (2007). Extending Metamodel Framework for Interoperability (MFI) to Register Networked Process Models. *Dynamics of Continuous Discrete and Impulsive Systems- Series B- Applications & Algorithms, 14*(S6), 72–78.

Wang, C., He, K., & He, Y. (2006). MFI4Onto: Towards Ontology Registration on the Semantic Web. *6th International Conference on Computer and Information Technology (CIT 2006)* (p. 40). Seoul: IEEE Press.

Wang, Y. (2006). *Cognitive Complexity of Software and its Measurement.* 5th IEEE International on Cognitive Informatics (ICCI'06).

Wasserman, S., & Faust, K. (1994). *Social network analysis: Methods and applications.* New York: Cambridge.

Web services business process execution language. (2003). OASIS.

Weinberg, G. (1971). *The Psychology of Computer Programming.* New York: van Nostrand Reinhold Co.

Weis, T. (2004). *Model Driven Development of QoS-Enabled Distributed Applications.* PhD, Technical University of Berlin, Berlin.

Weiss, D. (1998). *Commonality Analysis: A systematic process for defining families* (ARES '98), (LNCS 1429). Berlin: Springer-Verlag.

Weiss, D. (2004). *Defining Families: Commonality analysis.* Madison, WI: Lucent Technology, Bell Laboratories.

Weiss, D. M., & Lai, C. T. R. (1999). *Software Product-Line Engineering: A Family Based Software Development Process.* Reading, MA: Addison-Wesley Professional.

Weiss, S. (2002). *Handheld Usability.* Chichester, UK: John Wiley and Sons.

Werner, K., Rombach, D., & Feldmann, R. (2001). Outsourcing in India. *IEEE Software, 18,* 78–86.

West, J., & O'Mahony, S. (2005). *Contrasting Community Building in Sponsored and Community Founded Open Source Projects.* 38th Annual Hawaii International Conference on System Sciences, Hawaii.

Weyuker, E. (1988). Evaluating Software Complexity Measures. *IEEE Transactions on Software Engineering, 14*(9), 1357–1365. doi:10.1109/32.6178

White, J., Schmidt, D., & Gokhale, A. (2005, October). Simplifying autonomic enterprise java bean applications. In *Acm/ieee international conference on model driven engineering languages and systems.*

Whittaker, J. A., & Thomason, M. G. (1994). A Markov Chain Model for Statistical Software Testing. *IEEE Transactions on Software Engineering, 20*(10), 812–824. doi:10.1109/32.328991

Wiegers, K. (1999). First Things First: Prioritizing requirements. *Software Development, 7*(9) September. Retrieved from http://www.processimpact.com/pubs.shtml#requirements

Wiegers, K. (1999, September). First Things First: Prioritizing requirements. *Software Development, 7*(9). Retrieved from www.processimpact.com/pubs.shtml#requirements

Wiesmann, M., Pedone, F., Schiper, A., Kemme, B., & Alonso, G. (2000). Understanding Replication in Databases and Distributed Systems. *Proceedings of 20th IEEE International Conference on Distributed Computing Systems* (ICDCS'2000).

Williams, A., & Probert, R. L. (2001). A measure for component interaction test coverage. *ACS/IEEE International Conference on Computer Systems and Applications* (pp. 301-311).

Williams, M. (2002). *Microsoft Visual C#. NET*. Redmond, CA: MS Press.

Willink, E. (2002, November). Umlx: A graphical transformation language for mda. In *Acm international conference on object-oriented programming, systems, languages and applications.*

WINEDaily Builds, (2003). Retrieved from http://wine.dataparty.no/

Wirfs-Brock, R. (1993). *Designing Scenarios: Making the Case for a Use Case Framework*. Smalltalk Report Nov-Dec. New York: SIGS Publications.

Wolf, M., Ivanov, E., Burkhardt, R., & Philippow, I. (2000). UML Tool Support: Utilization of Object-Oriented Models. *Technology of Object-Oriented Languages and Systems (TOOLS 34'00)*, (p. 529).

Woodcock, J., & Davis, J. (1996). *Using Z Specification, Refinement and Proof*. Englewood Cliff, NJ: Prentice Hall.

Wooff, D. A., Goldstein, M., & Coolen, F. P. A. (2002). Bayesian Graphical Models for Software Testing. *IEEE Transactions on Software Engineering*, 28(5), 510–525. doi:10.1109/TSE.2002.1000453

World Wide Web Consortium. (W3C) (2006). *Extensible Markup Language (XML)* 1.0 (Fourth Edition). Retrieved from http://www.w3.org/TR/REC-xml/

World Wide Web Consortium. (W3C) (2006). *Extensible Markup Language (XML)* 1.0 (Fourth Edition). Retrieved from http://www.w3.org/TR/REC-xml/

World Wide Web Consortium. (W3C). (2003). *Simple Object Access Protocol (SOAP) Specification*. Retrieved from http://www.w3.org/TR/soap12/

World Wide Web Consortium. (W3C). (2004). *Resource Description Framework (RDF)*. Retrieved from http://www.w3.org/RDF/

EASE Project. (2007) Retrieved September 11, 2008, from http://www.empirical.jp/e_index.html

Eclipse (2009). Eclipse Software. Retrieved January 10, 2009, from http://www.eclipse.org

StagE Project. (2008) Retrieved December 8, 2008, from http://www.stage-project.jp/.

UML. (2007). *Unified Modeling Language, OMG Std. Final Adopted Specification.*

Xia, F., & Kane, G. S. (2003). Defining the Semantics of UML Class and Sequence Diagrams for Ensuring the Consistency and Executability of OO Software Specification. *1st International Workshop on Automated Technology for Verification and Analysis (ATVA'2003).*

Xiao, W., Chi, C., & Yang, M. (2007). On-line collaborative software development via Wiki. In *Proceedings of the 2007 International Symposium on Wikis* (pp. 177-183).

Yacoub, S. M., & Ammar, H. H. (2003). Pattern-Oriented Analysis and Design: Composing Patterns to Design Software Systems. Chichester, UK: Addison-Wesley.

Yilmaz, C., Cohen, M. B., & Porter, A. (2006). Covering arrays for efficient fault characterization in complex configuration spaces. *IEEE Transactions on Software Engineering*, 32(1), 20–34. doi:10.1109/TSE.2006.8

Yoder, J., & Barcalow, J. (1997, September 3-5). *Architectural Patterns for Enabling Application Security. The Fourth Conference on Pattern Languages of Programs (PLoP 1997)*, Monticello, VA.

Yu, L. (2008). Self-organization process in open-source software: An empirical study. *Information and Software Technology*, 50, 361–374. doi:10.1016/j.infsof.2007.02.018

Yu, L., Ramaswamy, S., & Zhang, C. (2008). Mining email archives and simulating the dynamics of open-source project developer networks. In *Fourth international workshop on enterprise and organizational modeling and simulation: Proceedings of the Fourth International Workshop on Enterprise and Organizational Modeling and Simulation (France), Montpellier*, (pp. 17-31).

Zadnik, M., Vincent, F., Vingerhoeds, R., et al. (2007). SI engine knock detection method robust to resonance frequency changes. In *International Conference on Engines for Automobiles*, September 2007.

Zaharan, S. (1998). *Software Process Improvement: Practical Guidelines for Business Success,* (1st Ed.). Reading, MA: Addision-Wesley.

Zajicek, M. (2007, May 7-8). *Web 2.0: Hype or Happiness? The 2007 International Cross-Disciplinary Workshop on Web Accessibility (W4A 2007)*, Banff, Canada.

Zelkowitz, M. V., & Wallace, D. R. (1998). Experimental models for validating technology. *Computer, 31*(5), 23–31. doi:10.1109/2.675630

Zhang, Y. (1993). On Horizontal Fragmentation of Distributed Database Design. *Australian Database Conference,* (pp. 121-130).

Zhong, X., Madhavji, N. H., & El Emam, K. (2000). Critical factors affecting personal software Processes. *Software, 17*(6), 76–83. doi:10.1109/52.895172

Zhu, H., & He, X. (2002). A methodology for testing high level Petri Nets. *Information and Software Technology, 44*, 473–489. doi:10.1016/S0950-5849(02)00048-4

Zhuge, H. (2002). Knowledge flow management for distributed team software development. *Knowledge-Based Systems, 15*(8), 465–471. doi:10.1016/S0950-7051(02)00031-X

Zisman, A., & Kozlenkov, A. (2001), Knowledge Base Approach to Consistency Management of UML Specifications. *16th IEEE International Conference on Automated Software Engineering (ASE'01)*, (pp. 359-363).

Zorzo, A. F., & Stroud, R. J. (1999). A distributed object-oriented framework for dependable multiparty interactions. In *OOPSLA '99: Proceedings of the 14th ACM SIGPLAN conference on Object-oriented programming, systems, languages, and applications* (pp. 435-446). New York: ACM Press.

About the Contributors

Muthu Ramachandran is currently a principal lecturer in the Faculty of Innovation North: Information and Technology, Leeds Metropolitan University, Leeds, UK. Previously he spent nearly eight years in industrial research (Philips Research Labs and Volantis Systems Ltd, Surrey, UK) where he worked on software architecture, reuse, and testing. Prior to that he was teaching at Liverpool John Moores University and received his PhD was from Lancaster University. His first career started as a research scientist from India Space Research Labs where he worked on real time systems development projects. Muthu has widely published articles on journals, chapters, and conferences on various advanced topics on software engineering and education. He did his masters degrees from Indian Institute of Technology, Madras and from Madurai Kamaraj University, Madurai, India. Muthu is also a member of various professional organisations and computer societies: IEEE, ACM, BCS, HEA.

Rogério Atem de Carvalho is a teacher, researcher, and innovation coordinator with the Instituto Federal Fluminense (IFF), Brazil, and a Brazilian representative at both IFIP Working Group and IEEE SMC Society Technical Committee on Enterprise Information Systems. He holds a B.Sc. in Computer Science and a D.Sc. in Industrial Engineering, his technical interests and publishing areas are Free Software, ERP, ECM, Project Management, and Decision Support Systems.

* * *

Salem Al-Marri is currently a PhD researcher at Leeds Metropolitan University. He graduated in MSc information system from University of Hertfordshire 2004. Al-Marri has widely published articles on chapters, and conferences on various advanced topics on Information Technology and disaster management. Al-Marri working for eight years Director, H.E. Minister of Education Office in Qatar

Adnan Bader has nearly 15 years of experience in IT industry and research. His areas of interest include Software Engineering, Component-Based Systems, Trust in Software Systems and Data Warehouse Techniques. He holds PhD and Masters Degrees in Computing from Monash University. Adnan has worked in the industry under various commercial and research settings before taking his current role of Senior Consultant. He is a member of IEEE.

Mike Barker's career has been in software development and project management, with over a decade spent in higher education at MIT and Nara Institute of Science and Technology (NAIST). He began his career in software development in 1977 with nine years work at a small systems house, a large systems integrator, and Bolt, Beranek, and Newman (BBN). Next was eight years in Japan, first as the technical half of BBN's two-person Japanese sales office, then in a Japanese company. After that, he spent nine years at MIT, first leading the Athena project and then setting up the Educational Media Creation Center to provide an enterprise-wide web-based support system for education. Since 2003, he has been a professor at NAIST, where his research interests include empirical methods in software engineering, project management, and elearning, or how to apply technology in support of education.

Wahida Banu is currently head of the department of Electronics & Communication Engineering in Government College of Engineering, Salem affiliated to Anna University, Chennai, Tamil Nadu, India. Her research interest areas are Software design & systems, Computer networks, Sensor Networks, Artificial Intelligence and Data Mining.

Swapan Bhattacharya is presently Director of National Institute of Technology, Durgapur, India and a faculty member in the Department of Computer Science & Engineering, Jadavpur University, Kolkata, India. He did his Ph.D in Computer Science in 1991 from University of Calcutta, India. His areas of research interests are distributed computing and software engineering. He had received Young Scientist Award from UNESCO in 1989. As a Sr. Research Associate of National Research Council, USA he had also served as the coordinator of Ph.D program in Software Engineering in Naval Postgraduate School, Monterey, CA during 1999-2001. He has published about 100 research papers in various international platforms. He is also actively involved in organizing international conferences on software engineering and distributed computing. He may be reached at swapan.bhattacharya@nitdgp.ac.in

Jean-Louis Boulanger is a specialist in the software engineering domain (requirement engineering, semi-formal and formal method, proof and model-checking). During 15 years, he worked at the RATP (authority that manage the subway at PARIS) such a validation responsible. After he worked 6 years at the University of Technology of Compiegne in the laboratory HEUDIASYC such a researcher/teacher. Actually, he is as an expert for the french notified body called CERTIFER in the field of certification of safety critical railway application based on software (ERTMS, SCADA, automatic subway, ..).

Renee Bryce is an Assistant Professor at Utah State University. She completed her PhD in Computer Science at Arizona State University in 2006. She received her B.S. and M.S. in Computer Science from Rensselaer Polytechnic Institute in 1999 and 2000. Her research interests include software engineering and software testing.

Renato de Campos holds Doctoral, Master and Bachelor degrees in Mechanical Engineering. He is a founder member of the Brazilian Chapter of the IFIP Working Group on Enterprise Information Systems, and author of scientific papers for international journals and conferences on production management, enterprise modeling, information systems and FOS-ERP.

Dr. Susan Entwisle has over 12 years experience in academia and industry. Susan has substantial experience in system architecture, software design and implementation using Microsoft and Java technologies on large projects. She has a PhD from Monash University. She is presently a System Architect in EDS, an HP company Asia Pacific Architect Practice. She is a member of IEEE and ACM.

Sathya Ganeshan is a part time researcher at the School of Computing, Leeds Metropolitan University, Leeds, UK. His topic of research is 'Investigation into Commonality Analysis Techniques for Software Product Lines'. Mr. Ganeshan started his career as a programmer and a data base administrator before initiating his research into software product lines. His other areas of interest include software product line process maturity and domain engineering for software product lines. His current research provides methods and tools to conduct commonality analysis systematically. He has also presented methods to conduct survey based methods to conduct SPL initiation within an organization.

Elias Canhadas Genvigir is a professor of Software Engineering at Federal University of Technology – Paraná (UTFPR), Brazil, where he acted as coordinator of Information System graduate course and worked in several projects. He graduated in Data Processing Technology from Londrina Center of Higher Education, Brazil, and he has a diploma in Management of Technology and Innovation from Federal Center of Technology (CEFET-PR), Brazil. He received his MS degree in Applied Computing from National Institute for Space Research (INPE), Brazil, where he is finishing his PhD in the same area. His research interests include software process, requirements engineering, requirements traceability, software modeling and software engineering experimentation.

Ismail Omar Hababeh research interests cut across data and service integration with an emphasis of enabling knowledge discovery and innovation in science and engineering. He is a worldwide recognized expert in Distributed Database Systems, Networks Simulation, and Applied Artificial Intelligence. Also, his expertise area covers the topics of software development and engineering methods for service-aware query processing, introducing high performance quality of service over the Web, and building an efficient large scale infrastructure for sciences and engineering based on service oriented architecture. He has an impressive publication record in his research field and has been heavily involved in several multi-disciplinary projects for building systems to support simulating networks experiments, data acquisition, analysis workflows for high throughput, building integrated access to large sets of data sources based on web services, and providing technical database support for both public and private surveillance enterprises.

Keqing He is a full professor in the State Key Lab of Software Engineering (SKLSE) and head of the SEFG (Software Engineering Fundamental Group) of SKLSE at the Wuhan University. His research interests include software engineering infrastructure, software engineering based on complex system, requirements engineering, and software engineering technical standards. He received his PhD in computer science from the Hokkaido University. He is a senior member of the IEEE and CCF (China Computer Federation). Contact him at hekeqing@sklse.org.

Yangfan He is a lecturer of State Key Lab of Software Engineering (SKLSE) at Wuhan University. She received the PhD degree from SKLSE in 2007, and her BA degree from Wuhan University in 2001, both in computer science. Her current research interests include ontology management, ontology dynamics, semantic web based software engineering and software engineering technical standards. In the past five years, she has published 1 domestic book (Science Press 2008) and over 10 peer-reviewed papers in English and Chinese. Contact her at heyangfan927@163.com

Katsuro Inoue received his B.S. and Ph.D. from Osaka University in 1979 and 1984, respectively. He was an associate professor at the University of Hawaii at Manoa from 1984 to 1986. After becoming an assistant professor in 1989 and an associate professor in 1991, he has been a professor in Osaka University since 1995. He holds a Ph. D. in engineering. He is engaged in the study of software engineering, especially in empirical approaches, program analysis, and software maintenance.

Miguel Jiménez is an engineer in computer science from the University of Castilla-La Mancha (UCLM). He is a PhD student at UCLM and works at Alhambra-Eidos S.L.U. as a team member of the FABRUM project, whose main objective is the development of a process to manage relationships between distributed production factories. His research interests include Global Software Development and Software Processes.

Björn Johansson holds a Doctoral and a Licentiate degree in Information Systems Development and a Bachelor degree in Business Informatics. Currently he works at the Center for Applied ICT at Copenhagen Business School, within the 3gERP project (http://www.3gERP.org). He is a member of the IFIP Working Group on Diffusion, Adoption and Implementation of Information and Communication Technologies and the research networks: VITS Work practice development, IT usage, Coordination and Cooperation and KiO Knowledge in Organizations.

Raghu Kacker is a mathematical statistician at the National Institute of Standards and Technology (NIST). He received his Ph.D. in statistics from the Iowa State University in 1979. After one year on the faculty of Virginia Tech, he worked for seven years in the former AT&T Bell Laboratories in New Jersey. He joined NIST in 1987. His current interests include evaluation of uncertainty in physical and virtual measurements, quantification of uncertainty from bias, combining information from interlaboratory evaluations and multiple methods of measurement, meta-analysis of clinical trials, measurement equations, Bayesian uncertainty, linear models and variance components, industrial statistics, quality engineering, and Taguchi methods. He is a Fellow of the American Statistical Association and a Fellow of the American Society for Quality. He was elected member of the International Statistical Institute. He has received Bronze medal from the U.S. Department of Commerce and Distinguished Technical Staff Award from the AT&T Bell Laboratories.

Pankaj Kamthan has been teaching in academia and industry for several years. He has also been a technical editor, participated in standards development, served on program committees of international conferences and editorial boards of international journals. His professional interests and experience include Knowledge Representation, Requirements Engineering, and Software Quality.

Ananya Kanjilal is presently an Assistant Professor in the Department of Information Technology, B. P. Poddar Institute of Management and Technology, under West Bengal University of Technology, Kolkata, India. She has done her Ph.D in Computer Science and engineering under the supervision of Professor Swapan Bhattacharya from Jadavpur University, India in 2008. Her areas of research interests are Analysis of Object Oriented Systems, software verification and testing, software architectures and software metrics. Her total number of publications in various international platforms is 11. She may be reached at ag_k@rediffmail.com

Elizabeth A. Kendall has over 25 years of experience in academia, including public and private universities in the USA, Australia, New Zealand, and China. She spent 10 years in the aerospace and defence industry in the USA as a Senior Research Scientist, and she was a Senior Research Fellow at BT Labs in the UK. She has a PhD and a Masters from the California Institute of Technology, and a Bachelors degree from the Massachusetts Institute of Technology. She is presently the Director of Information Technology Programs at the Melbourne Institute of Technology. She has over 100 refereed publications.

Amir Khan is a senior software engineering professional. He works as a senior engineering manager for a leading defense contractor. He has a master's degree in business administration from The Institute of Business Administration (IBA), Karachi; and a bachelor's degree in computer science from FAST - Institute of Computer Science, Karachi. Amir has more than 13 years of software engineering experience. He has led a number large scale software engineering projects including mission critical real-time software projects. He takes keen interest in process-based approaches to software engineering and loves imparting process knowledge to other professionals. He is a member of the ACM. He also leads a network of software engineering professionals with the goal of improving their software engineering capabilities.

Rick Kuhn is a computer scientist in the Computer Security Division of the National Institute of Standards and Technology . His primary technical interests are in information security, software assurance, and empirical studies of software failure, currently focusing on research in combinatorial testing. He co-developed (with David Ferraiolo) the role based access control model (RBAC) used throughout industry and led the effort to establish RBAC as an ANSI standard. From 1994 to 1995, he served as Program Manager for the Committee on Applications and Technology of the President's Information Infrastructure Task Force and from 1996 to 1999 as manager of the Software Quality Group at NIST. Before joining NIST in 1984, he worked as a systems analyst with NCR Corporation and the Johns Hopkins University Applied Physics Laboratory. He received an MS in computer science from the University of Maryland College Park.

Jeff Lei is an Associate Professor in Department of Computer Science and Engineering at the University of Texas, Arlington. He received his Bachelor's degree from Wuhan University (*Special Class for Gifted Young*) in 1993, his Master's degree from Institute of Software, Chinese Academy of Sciences in 1996, and his Ph.D. degree from North Carolina State University in 2002. He was a member of technical staff in Fujitsu Network Communications, Inc. from 1998 to 2001. His research is in the area of automated software analysis, testing and verification, with a special interest in software security assurance at the implementation level.

Peng Liang is an associate professor in the State Key Lab of Software Engineering (SKLSE) at the Wuhan University. His research interests include software engineering and software interoperability, with an emphasis on software architecture, requirements engineering, semantic interoperability, and ontology application on semantic web. He received his PhD in computer science from the Wuhan University. He is a member of the IEEE and CCF (China Computer Federation). Contact him at liangp@sklse.org.

Yutao Ma is a lecturer of State Key Lab of Software Engineering (SKLSE) at Wuhan University. He received the PhD degree from SKLSE in 2007, and his MS and BA degree from Wuhan University of Science and Technology in 2004 and 2001, all in computer science. His current research interests include software metrics, software evolution, and interdisciplinary research between software engineering and complex networks. In the last five years, he has published 2 domestic books (Science Press 2008 and South China University of Technology Press 2007) and over 20 peer-reviewed papers in English and Chinese. His honors and awards include the First Prize for Scientific and Technological Progress of Hubei Province (2008) and the Best Paper Award of IEEE International Conference on Computer and Information Technology (2006). He is a professional member of ACM, ACM SIGSOFT, and China Computer Federation (CCF). Contact him at ytma@mail.whu.edu.cn.

Adam Malinowski received his M.S. degree in Computer Science from University of Massachusetts, Boston in 2005. He followed with work as a software engineer for Motorola, Inc., where he specialized in development of a carrier-grade platform and embedded systems. Since 2008 he is a software engineer for Life Sciences at Harvard University. Adam's software experience and interest include operating systems, high availability networks, distributed systems and model-driven development.

Ken-ichi Matsumoto received the BE, ME, and PhD degrees in Information and Computer Sciences from Osaka University, Japan, in 1985, 1987, 1990, respectively. He is currently a professor in the Graduate School of Information Science at Nara Institute of Science and Technology, Japan. His research interests include software measurement and software user process. He is a senior member of the IEEE, and a member of the ACM, IEICE, IPSJ and JSSST.

Atif M. Memon is an Associate Professor at the Department of Computer Science, University of Maryland. He received his BS in Computer Science in 1991 from the University of Karachi, his MS in Computer Science in 1995 from the King Fahd University of Petroleum and Minerals, and his PhD in Computer Science from the University of Pittsburgh. He was awarded a Gold Medal during his undergraduate education, and received fellowships from the Andrew Mellon Foundation for his Ph.D. research. In 1995, he received the NSF CAREER award, which is providing five years of support for his research aimed at enhancing testing techniques for event-driven software. His research interests include program testing, software engineering, artificial intelligence, plan generation, reverse engineering, and program structures. He is a member of the ACM and the IEEE Computer Society and serves on the editorial boards of the Journal of Software Testing, Verification, and Reliability (STVR), The Open Software Engineering Journal, and the Canadian Journal of Pure and Applied Sciences. He has served on numerous National Science Foundation panels. He is currently serving on a National Academy of Sciences panel as an expert in the area of Computer Science and Information Technology, for the Pakistan-U.S. Science and Technology Cooperative Program, sponsored by United States Agency for International Development (USAID).

Ernest Mnkandla is a senior lecturer and a Deputy Head of Department in the Department of Business Information Technology in the Faculty of Management at the University of Johannesburg, South Africa. He has lectured in IT Project Management and Software Engineering and agile methodologies, and has presented several papers on agile methodologies and project management within Africa, Europe and the Pacific Islands. Doctor Ernest Mnkandla completed a Btech(honours) in Electrical Engineering at the University of Zimbabwe in 1992, completed an Msc(Comp. Sc) at the National University Science and Technology in Zimbabwe in 1997, and a PhD in Software Engineering obtained from the School of Electrical & Information Engineering at the University of the Witwatersrand, Johannesburg, South Africa. His current research is in the relationship between agile project management and the Project Management Institute's PMBoK approach, the adoption of agile methodologies, and Project Management Maturity Models.

Rafael Manhães Monnerat holds a Bachelor degree in Software Development at the Instituto Federal Fluminense (IFF). He is a Brazil based offshore consultant for Nexedi SA, maintaining various ERP5 modules and taking care of Brazilian customers.

T.R. Gopalakrishnan Nair is currently the Director of the DS Institutions in Bangalore, India.. He is a senior member of IEEE. He holds the degree M.Tech. (I.I.Sc., Bangalore) and Ph.D. in Computer Science. He was given the National technology award PARAM for developing the parallel computing flight simulation systems for Indian launch vehicles.His current interest areas are Software Engineering, Nanotechnology,Artificial Intelligence & Robotics, High speed computing and launch vehicle Simulations.

Katsuya Oba received the Bachelor of Arts degree from Osaka University, Osaka, Japan in 1989. He joined Osaka Gas Information System Research Institute Co., Ltd. (OGIS-RI) as a systems engineer. From 2000 to 2005, he worked for OGIS International, Inc. in Palo Alto, California as General Manager and leaded several software product development and R&D projects. He returned to OGIS-RI in 2006, and is leading R&D and business development relating to Service Oriented Architecture (SOA). His research interests include software architecture, business and systems modeling and software development processes. He is a member of Information Processing Society of Japan.

S. Parthasarathy is a Senior Grade Lecturer in the Department of Computer Applications, Thiagarajar College of Engineering, Madurai, India. He is a B.Sc., (Mathematics), M.C.A. (Master of Computer Applications), M.Phil., (Computer Science), P.G.D.B.A. (Business Administration), P.G.D.P.M. (Planning and Project Management) professional. A habitual rank holder, he has been teaching at the post-graduate level since 2002. He has published five articles in peer reviewed international journals and ten articles in the proceedings of national and international conferences. He has written two text books in his area of specialization and they were published by The New Age International Publishers (P), Ltd., India, in 2007. One of his research papers published in an international journal has been selected for publication in the Edited Book "Global Implications of Modern Enterprise Information Systems: Technologies and Applications" published by the Idea Group Inc. this year. He is the Principal Investigator for the research project "Requirements Management in COTS Software Projects" funded by the University Grants Commission, India. His current research interests include enterprise information systems, enterprise resource planning and software engineering.

Chetankumar Patel is a researcher at the School of Computing at Leeds Metropolitan University, Leeds, UK. His topic of research is 'Investigation into Story Cards Based Agile Software Development'. Mr. Patel started his career as a programmer before initiating his research into Agile software development and agile Requirements Engineering. His other areas of interest include Agile software process improvement and agile requirements process information and maturity model for agile methods. His current research provides methods and tools for Story cards (Agile requirements) based agile software development, Best practices guidelines for agile requirements engineering, adaptability and suitability framework for agile methods and process improvement framework for story cards.

Mario Piattini has an MSc. and PhD in Computer Science from the Technical University of Madrid and is a Certified Information System Auditor and Certified Information Security Manager by ISACA (Information System Audit and Control Association). He is a professor in the Department of Computer Science at the University of Castilla-La Mancha, in Ciudad Real, Spain. Author of several books and papers on software engineering, databases and information systems, he leads the ALARCOS research group of the Department of Information Systems and Technologies at the University of Castilla-La Mancha, in Ciudad Real, Spain. His research interests are: software process improvement, global software development, database quality, software metrics, software maintenance and security in information systems.

Kamakshi Prasad acquired his doctorate from Indian Institute of Technology, Chennai, India. Currently he is the professor in Jawaharlal Nehru Technological University, Hyderabad, India. His research interest areas are Computer Networks, Software Engineering and Image Processing, Data Mining & System software.

Sita Ramakrishnan has over 30 years of experience in academia and industry in Australia. She has PhD and Masters Degrees in Software Engineering from Monash University. She has held visiting academic appointments at Clemson University and in Technical University of Vienna. She has won several competitive grants, and has supervised a number of postgraduate Masters and PhD students. She has been the Director of the Undergraduate Software Engineering Program at Monash University since its inception in 1998. She has over 70 refereed publications. She is a member of IEEE.

R. Selvarani MI.Tech is a research professor in Research and Industry incubation Center DayanandaSagar Institutions, Bangalore, India. Currently pursuing Doctoral programme from Jawaharlal Nehru Technological University, Hyderabad, India. Her research interest includes novel approaches to systems and software modeling methods and techniques, analysis of algorithm and programming languages, development paradigms, cognitive approaches to software development, graphical notation and formal methods, domain engineering for reuse with knowledge based approaches.

Sabnam Sengupta is presently an Assistant Professor in the Department of Information Technology, B. P. Poddar Institute of Management and Technology; under West Bengal University of Technology, Kolkata, India. She has done her Ph.D under the supervision of Professor Swapan Bhattacharya from Jadavpur University, India in 2008. Her areas of research interests are Functional Specification of Object Oriented Systems, Formalization of requirements and design, software architectures and design patterns. Her total number of publications in various international platforms is 12. She may be reached at sabnam_sg@yahoo.com

Junichi Suzuki received a Ph.D. in computer science from Keio University, Japan, in 2001. He joined the University of Massachusetts, Boston in 2004, where he is currently an Assistant Professor of computer science. From 2001 to 2004, he was with the School of Information and Computer Science, the University of California, Irvine (UCI), as a postdoctoral research fellow. Before joining UCI, he was with Object Management Group Japan, Inc., as Technical Director. His research interests include model-driven software and performance engineering, autonomous adaptive distributed systems, biologically-inspired adaptive software and sensor networks. In these areas, he has authored two books and published over 90 refereed papers including five award papers. He has chaired or co-chaired four conferences including ICSOC'09, and served on technical program committees for over 50 conferences including ICCCN'09, SECON'09, CEC'09, BIOSIGNALS'09, AINA'08 and BIONETICS'08. He is an active participant and contributor in ISO SC7/WG19 and Object Management Group, Super Distributed Objects SIG. He is a member of IEEE and ACM.

Nandamudi L. Vijaykumar graduated in Computing Technology from the Technological Institute of Aeronautics (ITA), Brazil in 1978. He received the MS degree in Applied Computing from the National Institute for Space Research (INPE), Brazil in 1984, and the PhD in Electronic and Computing Engineering from the Technological Institute of Aeronautics (ITA), Brazil in 1999. He is currently a technologist at the National Institute for Space Research. His areas of interest include performance modeling, software test modeling, time series analysis and computational modeling of coastal climate.

Aurora Vizcaíno is an associate professor at the Escuela Superior de Informática of the University of Castilla-La Mancha, Spain. She is an MSc and has a European PhD in Computer Science from the University of Castilla-La Mancha. Her PhD work was based on the use of a Simulated Student in collaborative environments. Her research interests include Global Software Development, Collaborative Learning, Agents, Simulated Students and Knowledge Management. She is a member of the ALARCOS research group.

Hiroshi Wada received his M.S. degree in computer science from Keio University, Japan in 2002. He started the Ph.D. program in the University of Massachusetts, Boston in 2005. His research interests include model-driven software development, and service oriented architecture. Before enrolling in the Ph.D. program, he worked for Object Technology Institute, Inc., and engaged in consulting and educational services in the field of object oriented technologies, distributed systems and software modeling.

Chong Wang is a lecturer of State Key Lab of Software Engineering (SKLSE) at Wuhan University. She received the PhD degree from SKLSE in 2008, and her MS and BA degree from Wuhan University in 2005 and 2002, both in computer science. Her current research interests include ontology management, process model management, semantic web based software engineering and software engineering technical standards. In the past five years, she has published 1 domestic book (Science Press 2008) and over 10 peer-reviewed papers in English and Chinese. Her honors and awards include the First Prize for Scientific and Technological Progress of Hubei Province (2008), IBM Chinese Student Scholarship Award (2007) and the Second Prize for Scientific and Technological Progress of Wuhan (2006). Contact her at cwang@sklser.org.

Index